Believe and Destroy

For Guido Fanti

This work has been published under the
direction of Anthony Rowley.

Believe and Destroy

Intellectuals in the SS War Machine

By Christian Ingrao

Translated by Andrew Brown

polity

First published in French as *Croire et détruire* © Editions Fayard, 2010

First English edition © Polity Press, 2013
This English edition © Polity Press, 2015

Polity Press
65 Bridge Street
Cambridge CB2 1UR, UK

Polity Press
350 Main Street
Malden, MA 02148, USA

ISBN-13: 978-0-7456-6027-1

A catalogue record for this book is available from the British Library.

Typeset in 10 on 11.5pt Palatino
by Servis Filmsetting Ltd, Stockport, Cheshire
Printed and bound in the USA by Edwards Brothers Inc.

The publisher has used its best endeavours to ensure that the URLs for external websites referred to in this book are correct and active at the time of going to press. However, the publisher has no responsibility for the websites and can make no guarantee that a site will remain live or that the content is or will remain appropriate.

Every effort has been made to trace all copyright holders, but if any have been inadvertently overlooked the publisher will be pleased to include any necessary credits in any subsequent reprint or edition.

For further information on Polity, visit our website: www.politybooks.com

Contents

Preface

They were handsome, brilliant, clever and cultivated. They were responsible for the deaths of hundreds of thousands of human beings. This book tells their story. It is based on my doctoral thesis, written between 1997 and 2001, called 'Les intellectuels du service de renseignement de la SS, 1900–1945' ('Intellectuals in the SS intelligence service, 1900–1945').[1] This studied a group of eighty university graduates, economists, lawyers, linguists, philosophers, historians and geographers, some of whom pursued academic careers while simultaneously devising doctrines, carrying out political surveillance, or gathering intelligence on German or foreign affairs within the repressive organizations of the Third Reich, especially the Security Service (SD) of the SS. Most of them were, from June 1941, involved in the Nazi attempt to exterminate the Jews of East Europe, as members of the mobile commando units known as *Einsatzgruppen* and dedicated to slaughter. In this book, I have kept to the same basic methodologies as in the thesis.[2]

Being a French historian of Nazism, trained in historical studies by the proponents of a cultural history of belief and violence, has played a major role in my choice of analytical tools. Ever since the mid-1980s, a group of historians has addressed itself to reinterpreting the history of the great and decisive conflagration that broke out at the beginning of the twentieth century. This group is international, interdisciplinary and interested in the most varied sources, especially the world of material objects produced by European societies during the Great War, held in the collections of the Historial de la Grande Guerre (Museum of the Great War) in Péronne. The group includes historians such as Jean-Jacques and Annette Becker, Gerd Krumeich, John Horne and Jay Winter, who, with their colleagues, have played a considerable role in the shaping of the conceptual tools that have guided the present work.[3]

The key role was played by Stéphane Audoin-Rouzeau. Through his work on cultures of violence, on the world of children at war,[4] on mourning[5] and on the forms assumed by the *imaginaire* – the realm of images and representations – of war, he guided my studies, insisting that certain major factors be foregrounded while leaving the young researcher I then was at complete liberty to follow my own sometimes uncertain paths. I thus realized how great *this* war, the First World War, had been, and how central its apocalyptic dimensions – in two distinct ways. On the one hand, it had been a revelation for the historian, and on the other, it had indeed assumed a millenarian, seminal and crucial dimension for SS intellectuals.[6]

I also explored other horizons. The history of the great religious struggles of the medieval and modern periods, and my reading of Alphonse Dupront and, especially, Denis Crouzet, seemed to suggest that there was another way of approaching the question of belief, as well as violence, and that the utterances of the actors in these movements, far from being empty chatter, a mere by-product of sociological mechanisms inaccessible to the actors themselves, comprised a way of getting *into* their representations.[7] My starting point lay in grasping Nazism as a system of beliefs shaped into specific discourses and practices, one that of course emerged *also* from a machinery of public policies produced by people's impulses and decisions, but on a deeper level was infused by emotions of a different order from those grasped by the political sciences or sociology – disciplines which, governed for twenty years by the functionalist paradigm, had formed the basic conceptual resources of German historiography. These tools, after all, had not been able to tackle fervour or anxiety, suicide or cruelty, utopia, despair or hatred, or kindred emotions.

There was perhaps no great originality in these methodological choices: other French specialists in the human sciences also opted for alternative approaches and produced interesting work in the mid-1990s. Édouard Conte and Cornelia Essner published *La Quête de la race. Une anthropologie du nazisme* (*The Quest for Race. An Anthropology of Nazism*),[8] which invited us to pick up tools from structuralist social anthropology and apply them to studies of Nazism. Working on images and representations of lineage, on marriage, racial beliefs, funerary rituals and practices of colonization, Conte and Essner showed the benefits of a study that brought together ideological discourses, political decisions and concrete behaviour. And, between the lines, they also worked out a critique of the exaggerated functionalism of German historians.

But the essential interest of the men studied here is that they simultaneously produced a doctrinal discourse that made it possible for me to analyse their system of beliefs in detail, *and* carried out to their conclusion, at ground level, the practical consequences of this system of beliefs once they assumed command of the *Einsatzgruppen* that exterminated the Jews of Russia in the occupied territories – Crimea, Ukraine, Belorussia, Russia and the former Baltic States. Thanks to the work of Denis Crouzet, I have been able to sketch out a decisive reinterpretation of Nazi practices of violence. In *Les Guerriers de Dieu* (*God's Warriors*), he postulated that a system of gestures (*gestuelle*) of violence was itself a language reflecting the cultural system that had made it possible, and that it thus comprised an object in itself that could be grasped by tools taken from anthropology. Françoise Héritier was helpful in this regard,[9] as were Véronique Nahoum-Grappe,[10] Noëlie Vialles,[11] Élisabeth Claverie[12] and Catherine Rémy.[13] Their work questioned the relationship between violence and human beings or animals, and its link with bodiliness, lineage and belief.[14] Hence my decision to take modes of investigation from social anthropology and apply them to the history of Nazism. It is under these auspices, and equipped with these tools, that the present work has been written, following three main guidelines.

My initial ambition was to retrace what the German historian Gerd Krumeich called an *Erfahrungsgeschichte*, a history of the actual experience of these men,[15] so as to understand how the framework of their lives might have shaped their system of representations. This is where I was able to profit most fully from the heritage of the historians of the Great War: I tried to study children's wartime lives as a crucial experience, scarred by a collective narcissistic wound that was interpreted in apocalyptic and eschatological terms.

Secondly, I wanted to grasp Nazi activism as a cultural reaction to this first experience, and study it in the light of the anthropology of belief. In other words, I tried to analyse Nazism as a consoling, soothing system of beliefs: the coherence of its discourses and practices is underlined by the analytical tools I use, and embodied in the life stories and careers that I narrate.

This left the experience of the terrors wrought during the journey to the east: the genocidal practices of the *Einsatzgruppen* and their participation in Germanization and population displacement – policies that were fraught with utopian and murderous tensions. Finally, I sought to conclude my study by investigating how these men faced up to defeat, and their judicial fate after the war.

In short, I have tried to understand how these men came to *believe*, and how their beliefs led them to *destroy*.

Acknowledgements

To Laetitia.
Unspoken words are the flowers of silence.

As far as I know, no academic has ever confessed to reading the acknowledgements to a thesis before the rest. And yet, what part of academic work is more instructive about the world in which the historian has worked during the years of preparation leading to his or her first published work? It is a crucial moment of scholarly socialization: it crystallizes the places in which he or she has worked and demarcates at least part of his or her emotional world.

My thesis has been all of this. Work on it began in Angoulême, and was continued in Berlin, Warsaw and Ludwigsburg: it was completed in France, between the Canal Saint-Martin in Paris, Aix-en-Provence, Clermont-Ferrand, Poitiers, Lyon and Barjac. In all these places I found a family and friends without whom this work could not have achieved its final shape. Parents, sisters and more distant family have also, from time to time, given this work something of its subterranean rhythm. May they here find evidence of the ties that bind us.

I must also thank all those who have enabled me to pursue the archival and bibliographical explorations that this work required. The team of archivists in Berlin Lichterfelde, Mme Namsler in Dahlwitz-Hoppegarten, Michelina Wysocka in Warsaw, at the archives of the Commission of Inquiry into Nazi Crimes in Poland, Heinz-Lutger Borgert at the *Zentrale Stelle der Landesjustizverwaltungen* of Ludwigsburg, and also Anne-Marie Pathé, in Cachan, the archivists of the CDJC and the BDIC of Nanterre gave me free rein to follow my explorations. My thanks to them, as well as to Jean Astruc, the 'Venerable Jorge' of the library of the IHTP, who was happy to include German-themed books in his lists of purchases, despite being aware that there was every chance they would find but a single reader. Finally, Gabrièle Muc initiated me into the construction of the index and the table of contents.

A thesis, however, is not made solely from archives, books and computers. This thesis was constructed slowly, between the faculties of Clermont-Ferrand, Paris-IV and Amiens. Bernard Dompnier, Jean-Luc Fray, the late Annie Moulins-Bourret, Bernard Klein, Denis Crouzet and Giovanni Brizzi all contributed in their own ways, through their teaching and their discussions, to putting this work on the right track.

I have also benefited from the kind help of several scholars who shared their wisdom with me at the start of my research. It would be impossible to overstate what this work owes to Pierre Ayçoberry, who guided me through the maze of the bibliography on Nazism, in an erudite series of messages that I then had to include in my database. In Freiburg, Stuttgart, Hamburg, Vienna and Berlin, Gerhard Hirschfeld, Gerd Krumeich, Ulrich Herbert, Gerhard Botz, Reinhard Rürup and Michael Wildt made time to correspond with a student just starting a doctorate, and discussed my plans, unstintingly giving me their advice and criticism. At the Centre Marc-Bloch, Marie-Claude Lavabre and Peter Schöttler encouraged me, reading my work and opening up valuable theoretical horizons. I would also like to give warmest thanks to Gerhard Hirschfeld, who, one September day in 1997, saw a young Frenchman with shaky German landing in Frankfurt and asking him to co-supervise a thesis. He there-upon decided to give me his support, to supervise the German part of the work, and to open the doors of several archives, at the University of Stuttgart and the *Bibliothek für Zeitgeschichte*. My profound gratitude goes to him.

At the IHTP – as in Berlin – Florent Brayard was a pleasant travelling companion in the history of Nazism. He and I formed, together with Pieter Lagrou, Fabrice Virgili, Valeria Galimi and Benn Williams, a group that was agreeably able to mingle laughter with far-reaching discussions. Again at the IHTP, Danièle Voldman, Michel Trebitsch and Marc-Olivier Baruch read my work, listened to me and invited me, thus contributing to the progress of my research. And yet again at the IHTP, the group on 'wartime violence' was, together with the 'Monday seminars' and the 'Saturday seminars', the place for real scholarly work. Nicolas Werth, John Horne, Gerd Krumeich, Jean-Jacques and Annette Becker, and Denis Crouzet, Marc Lepape and Claudine Vidal, Luc Capdevila and all those who took part gave my work a decisive fillip. The same goes for Roland Beller and Jean-Jacques Pont, who guided me in the arcana of psychiatry and psychoanalysis. Thanks to all who showed confidence in me and answered my questions.

Nicolas Werth was probably the researcher with whom I worked most closely over the last two years. He read my work, and allowed me to discover the subtleties of his own and of the historiography in which he works. In short, he made time to bring me into his own field of research. I was exceptionally grateful for the warmth of his welcome. Christian Delage has also read my work – almost all of it – during my time at the IHTP. His generosity and his friendship have meant a great deal to me.

I found in Raphaëlle Branche the historian whose preoccupations were the closest to my own. The friendship that sprung up from our exchanges and my reading of her work have been most valuable. Her questions, as well as those of Anne Duménil, who also agreed to read part of my work and to annotate it, were crucial. From Berlin to Paris, 'Del' Corteel and Valentine Meunier initiated me into anthropology and ethnology, providing me with books, remarks and paths for research, during discussions which combined Claude Lévi-Strauss and Françoise Héritier with the fruits of the coast at Blaye.

The fact remains, however, that this work would never have seen the light of day without the confidence of Nadine-Josette Chaline, dean of the University of Amiens, who, when I was still a young Parisian student, ensured I received the first research grant awarded in ten years to the UPJV, only to see me head off straight away for Germany. At the Centre Marc-Bloch, the warm welcome of Étienne François, his advice, the 'seminar on method' that he started up, nursed my taste for teaching and an interdisciplinarity that, as practised in Berlin, hardly needs long and learned debates, but emerges from daily life.

Henry Rousso welcomed me when, as I was starting my research, I went to his office at l'Amiral-Mouchez for advice and addresses. He later continued at Cachan, thereby giving me the opportunity to finish writing this work, involving me in the activities of his research laboratory, full of indulgence for my inefficiency.

Finally, Stéphane Audoin-Rouzeau supervised my work with unique precision, constancy and scrupulousness, even though, as I was taking my DEA, the first task he assigned to me was that of finding . . . another thesis supervisor. If I have so far pretended to have forgotten him, this is doubtless because the *Book of Changes*, the *I Ching* of the Chinese, attributes the last place to the figure of the Waker.

Esteban and Nathan have nothing, or almost nothing, to do with all this. They are my armour, and the chink in it.

What I learn from them sustains my work.

Paris, 23 July 2001

In the gap that separates the present words from those of before, there is now Gaïa, the Heiress; in this gap, there are faces, figures, absences, names – all too numerous to mention all of them.

Eventually, all things merge into one, and a river runs through it.

To Esteban, Nathan and Gaïa: we are the Army of those who dream of Laetitia.

Paris, 26 January 2010

Glossary

Abteilungsleiter: head of department or section
Ahnennachweise: genealogical tree (as proof of ancestry)
Akademiker: person who has studied at university
alter Kämpfer: old fighter (i.e., generally speaking, someone who joined the Nazi Party before the elections of September 1930)
Amtschef: (another term for) head of department (*Amtsleiter* or 'office leader' was a specific rank in the Nazi Party)
Bildungsbürgertum: educated bourgeoisie
Burschenschaft: student association
Daseinskampf: struggle for existence
Ereignismeldung **(EM)**: report on activities
Gleichschaltung: coordination, bringing into line
gottgläubig: believing in God (but not a Christian)
Gruppenleiter: head of a group (*Gruppenführer*, 'group leader', was a rank in the SA and SS)
Judenräte: Jewish councils (especially those established by the Nazis in the ghettos)
Komilitonen: comrades
Landser: soldier(s) in the troops, private(s)
Lebensgebiet: life domain
Lebenslauf: life story, detailed curriculum vitae
Machtergreifung: seizure of power
Oberrealschule: technical high school
Promotionsordnung: text regulating access to a doctorate
Proseminar: seminar
Rassenwahn: racial madness
Sippe: lineage
Staatsexamen: state examination (at university, for entry to certain professions)
Trek: convoy of migrants
Umvolkung: ethnic dissemination
Vehme: secret organization practising political assassination

Vernichtung: annihilation
völkisch: ethno-nationalist
Wandervögel: youth movement ('migrating birds')

Part I

The young men of Germany

Chapter 1

A 'world of enemies' (I)

The first experience common to the members of the group we are studying (which I will henceforth simply call 'the group') was the First World
War. This formed the background to their childhoods, especially as it
was followed by several years of upheaval, up until 1924. This was a
decade in which everyday life was shaken from top to bottom – a decisive decade in which the members of the group grew from childhood to
adolescence.

Stéphane Audoin-Rouzeau and Annette Becker have sought to explain
how combatants as well as civilians expressed their thoughts with such
urgency after the Great War, pointing out that the hankering to give
words and narrative form to 'their' war had driven a great number of
Europeans in the nineteenth and twentieth centuries to take up their
pens for the first – and often the last – time to communicate the intensity
of their war experience. So one might have expected that SS *Akademiker*,[1]
being men of letters, would also have resorted to introspection, to communicate their wartime childhoods. Far from it: in fact they kept silent
about it, and it is this silence on which we first need to focus.

The outbreak of war

Every war opens up a breach in the slow unfolding of works and days.
Of course, it leaves certain times and spaces untouched: but, directly or
indirectly, it affects all the protagonists. In Germany, the war which broke
out in 1914 was no exception. Children – with a few rare exceptions – were
neither combatants nor labourers. Thus, future SS members played practically no part in the German war effort. They were, however, spectators.
They were central actors in family relations disrupted by the departure
of the menfolk; so their perceptions were mainly restricted to the private
sphere, to family emotions and intimate bonds. The fact remains that
western societies had decided to keep children under supervision from
an early age by subjecting them to the school system: all children went

to school – in Germany, from the age of five. Thus the perception of the event of the war also takes on a cultural and social dimension. How are we to grasp the 'wartime experience' of these children?

War meant that the men marched off to the front and entire populations were mobilized. In the immediate pre-war period, in the big German cities, populations lived in expectation of a Serbian reply to the Austrian ultimatum. The delivery of daily newspapers led to stampedes, with people elbowing each other out of the way to be first to read the headlines and get news of how the situation was developing, hot off the press. When war was declared, there were demonstrations of support, but seriousness and gravity were the dominant note rather than warmongering elation. A positive response was to be found elsewhere, in the sprawling suburbs, where most of the middle classes to which belonged the vast majority of the group we are studying were concentrated. So their own families probably experienced going to war as an occasion for wild enthusiasm and a sense of determination. Though they never mentioned it later on, we should nonetheless note that Jeffrey Verhey sees in this 'spirit of 1914' a crystallization of the basic *völkisch* (ethno-nationalist) desire to unify the nation, a desire which the members of the group were later to share uncompromisingly.[2] It is, then, surely permissible to speculate that, in spite of the silence they would observe on the outbreak of war in their later writings, this period may well have left an enduring impression on them.

The second salient fact of the war relates to the experience of loss and bereavement among the combatants, and even the suffering brought about when a family member was wounded. Such a trauma, though elusive for lack of any written account, doubtless left deep traces. Let us postulate, as demographers do, that every death in the Great War was at the very least surrounded by two concentric circles of sociability, each with perhaps ten people in it. The German Empire lost 2 million soldiers, so 18 million people were directly plunged into mourning. And some 36 million people may have been affected in the more distant circles of sociability.[3] In this way, half of the German population would have had to mourn a family member. And even this calculation fails to take into account reactions to the news of a wounded relative in the forces, and the stress of waiting for information about a missing person – an integral part of the mourning process[4] – whether he was later found on the list of prisoners or not. Thus everything suggests that the loss of men sent to the front, whether this loss was definitive or only temporary, was a mass trauma.

Then there were the food shortages. Though these affected all the societies at war, nowhere were they more intensely felt than in Germany. Right from the summer of 1914, in fact, the blockaded Reich was more or less forced to become self-sufficient. In 1914, Germany already seemed to have attained relative independence in food production. Over 90 per cent of basic foodstuffs were produced on Reich territory.[5] But this relative self-sufficiency was based on maintaining rates of agricultural production, which relied on the massive acquisition of fertilizer and keeping a large workforce busy in the fields. Furthermore, especially after 1916, supplies of food were mainly destined for the army. So the cities found it really difficult to get enough to eat. In Berlin, the reduction in daily rations became very serious; prices rose throughout the war. Potato and sugar rations were kept at sufficient levels to avoid famine, but meat, fish and fat – significant foodstuffs, the distinctive intake of the middle classes – more or less disappeared from market stalls and fuelled a flourishing black market. From 1916 onwards the Germans felt that they were literally earning their 'daily bread' by the sweat of their brows. The Allied blockade did not create problems of food supply for them, but it did contribute to exacerbating these problems by provoking panic among the working and middle classes.[6] After the war, this blockade was indeed seen as a direct Allied attack on the civilian populations, a war waged on women and children.[7] Hunger, bereavement, the sense of fighting for one's daily survival – these were the three main elements in children's experience of war, especially since these were part and parcel of a specific interpretation of everyday life.

German society, like the other wartime European societies, developed a system of representations to give meaning to the conflict. Once they were at war, the Germans considered the combats in Belgium and France to be profoundly defensive in nature: if the Reich had to invade Belgium to implement the Schlieffen Plan, this was so as to stop Britain invading Germany using Belgium as a bridgehead. On the basis of this model, newspapers, political commentaries and soldiers' letters constructed the image of a conflict into which Germany had found itself thrown unwillingly, and fighting for its safety alone. The song 'Die Wacht am Rhein' ('The Watch on the Rhine'), a great favourite among German troops facing the British during the great battles, is evidence of this set of ideas.[8] Likewise, the German army was fighting on French soil in order to protect the territory of the Fatherland. Susanne Brandt has shown how images of destruction, showing the damage caused by the war, always cast blame on an enemy who, if the Germans were defeated, would wreak similar havoc on their national territory.[9] The war was a question of security: final victory was necessary to break the strategy of encirclement set up by the Allies. And reporters vied with each other in expressing this: 'They [French civilians] do not or will not acknowledge that it is the ruling classes of their country who, last August, tried to break through into our territory and inflict on us the fate that they themselves are suffering today. Attack is the best form of defence.'[10]

In summer 1914, this representation was reinforced by events in the east. At the outbreak of war, Cossack troops invaded East Prussia, leading to a massive exodus of local populations. The devastation that followed aroused a wave of panic that intensified the representations created by the invasion of Belgium. In the east as in the west, whether invading or invaded, Germany was fighting to defend its *Kultur* and its territory, encircled and threatened as it was by a 'world of enemies'.[11]

The Germans were able to subscribe to this representation of an encircled Reich, forced to wage a total defensive war, mainly because of the way an inhuman image of the enemy had crystallized in the very first days of the conflict.[12] The Belgians and the Russians in particular were associated with countless acts of cruelty committed on wounded German soldiers and on civilians in the invaded regions. Thus the German units invading the territories of Belgium and the north of France were swept by waves of panic that led them to believe stories of the physical abuse perpetrated on their wounded comrades by civilians, women and children, which 'proved' the inhumanity of the enemy and legitimized the summary executions carried out by German troops. This 'body of evidence' – and this is the essential point – was spread throughout Germany by the press, by images and by schools. Also, many depictions focused on the dirtiness of the Russians and their backwardness, part of the cultural inferiority of the population: in the same spirit, a quasi-colonial set of images, made up of a sense of superiority and racial prejudice, presided over the plans laid by the *Oberost*, the German military administration on the Eastern Front.[13] The Great War was interpreted as a defensive struggle in which the fate of Germany was at stake, faced as it was with a ubiquitous enemy distinguished by the inhumanity of its fighting methods – an inhumanity that resulted at least in part from an essentially ethnic and biological hostility.[14]

Although it was defensive, the Great War was all the same endowed by the warring powers with great expectations that gave meaning to the sufferings experienced. Observers claimed that it was necessary to struggle through the misfortunes of the age. War was an ordeal in the medieval sense, and it paved the way to a new era: this was one of the themes that gave meaning to the conflagration, in the front lines as well as behind them.[15] For example, the historian Friedrich Meinecke resorted to the metaphor of the Roman *Ver Sacrum*, the ritual of human sacrifice prefiguring the fertility of a new spring,[16] as a way of expressing the mass deaths of the Flanders battlefields. It was the great millenarian expectation that gave meaning to the hecatomb:

> Our *Ver Sacrum* is now occurring on the canals of the Yser, where young reserve regiments of war volunteers have launched an assault. For us, their sacrifice means a new sacred spring for the whole of Germany.[17]

During the actual hostilities, soldiers created the myth of the battlefield as a place of initiation.[18] One young secondary school teacher, who had been a participant in the youth movements, tried to find adequate words to express this in a letter to his mother dated 26 May 1915:

> My dear Mother, I need to write you a really special letter and try to express what I'd like to say – as a sort of consolation, since [. . .] Erich too has now

become one of those who have helped to build the future of a greater Germany, with all the blood and the strength of his heart.

The war has powerfully shown us that our lives had a completely different meaning from that of simply unfolding along the normal paths of middle-class family life. They are part of a great and sacred aim. This aim we cannot know. It has been implanted in us from eternity, and is leading us on towards something great and eternal. We can sense it already.

God is now forging out great paths for world history and we are the chosen ones, the chosen tools. Should we really, truly be happy at this? Around me everything is verdant and blossoming, and the birds are exuberant and joyful in the light. How much more grand and beautiful will be the spring that follows the Great War![19]

The immanence of hope and the millenarian imaginings[20] here expressed are all the more powerful when we reflect that Walter I. was a product of that *Bildungsbürgertum* (cultivated bourgeoisie) that gave its consent to the conflict, as did European society as a whole. He was active in the pre-war youth movements that expressed a desire for social and intellectual renewal: this rekindled desire gave meaning to the conflict and fused warlike fervour with the militant tendencies of the *Wandervögel* (the youth groups or 'migrating birds').[21] Crucially, the author of this letter differs from the members of our group only by his date of birth: his precocious activism, his membership of the cultivated classes and his extreme youth give him an overall profile similar to that of the young adolescents who stayed behind the front lines. The few years' difference between them explains, nonetheless, why he actually underwent the baptism of fire, unlike the future SS intellectuals.

This letter, the hundred and seventh of those written in ten months by this young man to his family,[22] also shows how intense were communications between the front and the rear. In addition, the continual sending and receiving of letters, bringing hope, anguish, sorrow, millenarian expectations and daily worries, explains the extremely porous nature of the divide between the system of representations prevalent among civilians and that of their relatives living in the trenches. While the experience of combat, assault and interpersonal violence remained to a large degree unspoken, acquiescence in the conflict, its fluctuations, its crises and its resurgences, continued to circulate between the front and the rear throughout the war.[23] In this gigantic struggle against an enemy that was at least partly branded as barbarous and bestial, and utterly pitiless, the fate of the nation was being decided. In many of the well-off, cultivated homes that constituted, sociologically speaking, the heart of German consent to the conflict, the war thus became the site of a derivative form of millenarian utopia.

These issues were too important in the eyes of those involved for their children to be shielded from them. And indeed, the Great War was the first conflict in which children were 'mobilized', in the sense that they were the object of a specific discourse that provided them with an explanation of the war, its meaning and their enemies. Experience of the war took the form – in a way impossible to evaluate in general terms – of a dialogue between parents and children, but it also irrupted into the systems of perception prevalent among children and adolescents by means of toys, books and newspapers. As early as the autumn of 1914, the German toy industry, the biggest in the world in terms of production and global trade, fell into step with the culture of war.[24] Certain firms, such as Otto Maïer Verlag – the future Ravensburger – and the famous electric train manufacturer Märklin, produced toys that related directly to the war, or even to the fighting. In this way, violence was 'trivialized', as George Mosse likes to put it:[25] toys made it less real, while at the same time introducing it into children's daily lives. Toymakers, indeed, had fully realized the cultural issues at stake. At the end of 1914, their official organ declared:

> The toy industry is unfairly classified as one of the luxury industries. It has its own specific mission in wartime: it is important to make use of toys to imbue children with recent developments, and to inoculate [*verimpfen*] them with an upright, national and patriotic spirit.[26]

The pedagogical efforts made by society and state thus took the form of a discourse of legitimization of the conflict that was handed down to children and adolescents in primary and secondary schools. Textbooks, exercise books and lectures all started to discuss the war, its development and its meaning, by adopting and adapting a certain discourse that was placed in the service of definite aims and objectives. The ideal pursued by teachers was that of a serious, preoccupied generation of youngsters, filled with gratitude towards the heroes laying down their lives at the front in defence of the nation: 'mobilization of minds, mobilization of hearts', said one of the texts describing 'those who stayed in the rear'.[27] In 1917, this effort was taken over by the educational system via 'classes in patriotism' that summed up the culture of war. This sudden generalization of the effort of mobilization, evident in primary and secondary education thanks to the institutionalization of a pedagogy of conflict, formed the main way of transmitting a heroic sense of morality and applying it to the daily lives of children and young people.[28] The latter were urged to follow the events of the conflict, to communicate in thought with the combatants, and to act in a serious, responsible way in everyday life. A young boy found himself the oldest male member of the family and eventually had to transform himself into a hero of day-to-day existence, able to make up for the absence of his father and/or brothers. While the soldier was someone to admire, this discourse did not, however, encourage the young boy to imitate him by setting off for the front, even though the fantasy of the child-hero, so vivid in France, did have a few equivalents in Germany: certain illustrations in albums for young people showed children or adolescents guarding the frontier all by themselves, against the assembled Russian and French enemy,[29] while others had young people weeping with frustration at not being able to set off with their fathers, and yet others depicted the child in uniform, daydreaming.[30] All these illustrations insisted on the importance of the home front, a front on which the child had his rightful place.

The silence of the *Akademiker*

In spite of the high profile of the conflict and the efforts at mobilization deployed by the state, however, the members of our group who had an opportunity to relate their childhood experiences of war did not in fact do so. On entering the SS or getting married they were almost all impelled to set down their life story – a mixture of curriculum vitae and personal text in which were described the narrators' family backgrounds, their academic studies and sometimes even their emotional worlds. Even if only in cursory form, these *Lebensläufe* should logically have mentioned their wartime experiences. But only five of them make any mention of these, and even this is often a passing reference – to a father's death, exodus or captivity.

Ernst Turowsky was born in 1906, into a family of landowning farmers near Johannisburg, in East Prussia. When war broke out, he experienced the Russian invasion. Without going into too much detail, he mentions his status as a war refugee and the enlistment of his father. Turowsky also explains that his schooling was interrupted for nearly two years in succession following the invasion, and says that he had returned to his land with his family only in 1922 – in other words, as he himself put it, 'after the return of [his] father from the war and the stabilization of the situation on the borders'.[31] These are the only traces of the war that he was ready to divulge.

Thus, the SS candidate stuck strictly to the facts. He did not feel it necessary to talk about what he, as an eight-year-old boy, had thought about it. And yet we know that Turowsky's home town, Johannisburg, was one of the epicentres of the atrocities committed by the Cossacks and the ensuing panic. In line with a practice that spread during the first months of the war, the German government systematically collected evidence of the acts of brutality carried out by Russian troops. While a great deal of this evidence came from German soldiers and prisoners who had managed to escape, another series of statements was made by civilians, both men and women, who had witnessed – or claimed to have witnessed – enemy abuses. Stories of rapes, mutilations, summary executions of civilians and prisoners alike were thus spread by the classic institutional channels of blue books, but also via rumours, as the refugees streamed into German territory.[32] Turowsky belongs precisely to this category of persons who for a while found themselves trapped within the first circle of war. Nowhere, however, does the SS candidate mention the atrocities or the panic that presided over the exodus. Nowhere does he give any information on his family's state of mind. And nowhere, finally, does he explain how this family of refugees managed to subsist, having lost their lands and their means of earning a living, during the long years of exile. Is it unreasonable to think that, in spite of the adult's silence about his childhood, the 1914 exodus had been experienced by his family with such traumatic intensity that it took them eight years to return to East Prussia? However, Turowsky ignores this aspect, as if exile had not affected him in the slightest.

While Ernst Turowsky's war experience was that of a refugee and civilian victim, it also constituted the matrix of a 'border' identity: born in East Prussia, surrounded by Poles and Russians, Turowsky wrote his doctoral thesis in medieval history on the problems of border administration between Poles and Germans in the fifteenth century.[33] This surely showed a scholarly interest linked to his boyhood experience of the war. This thesis, a veritable attempt at a retrospective legitimation of the German identity of these border territories, doubtless marks a commitment to defence of one's territory – an intellectual defence, admittedly, but one directly related to the 'intellectual mobilization' (*geistige Mobilmachung*) initiated by the *Bildungsbürgertum* in the Great War.[34] While the traumatic experience of the war is not expressed, and while the war is not for the most part even mentioned, this silence does not mean that the experience was insignificant. Quite the opposite: silence is not a lack of something, but a sign – the sign of a trauma.

Another example was Heinz Gräfe, the son of a Saxon bookseller, the product of an educated milieu. Heinz's father, mobilized on the outbreak of war, was killed on the front in Flanders in 1914. Even though Heinz's *Lebensläufe* are among the most elaborate, this fact is mentioned in only one of them, and only in parenthesis (he had to give his father's occupation). So we have no idea what the death of Heinz Gräfe's father meant to him. However, he wrote that his mother took a job with the postal service, which involved abandoning the family bookshop, a loss of social status, and a loss of income. But Gräfe says nothing about this, or of his bereavement, or even of his life during the war, even though he was probably forced back onto his own resources since his mother was away, forced to work outside the home. He does, however, detail his career after 1918, discussing his discipline problems while at school, and providing us with the image of a disturbed adolescent – he was then fourteen – who nonetheless managed to make up for his lost time at school while beginning a political career dominated by rejection of the Treaty of Versailles and the Weimar Republic.[35]

The cases of Ernst Turowsky and Heinz Gräfe thus illustrate the fact that war could be implicitly present in people's *Lebensläufe*, but that its traumatic dimension ruled out any more substantial analysis of it.

These cases merely reflect a German society that passionately discussed the origins as well as the consequences of the conflict[36] – the question of responsibility – but not of its actual progress. This was a collective attitude close to psychological repression.

Even more disturbing is the universal absence of any mention of the German defeat in 1918. Unlike the war itself, this is *never* mentioned, even by people who were obliged to leave their homes after the armistice or the peace treaties.[37] In the *Lebensläufe*, the war does indeed exist as a fact, but not in discourse; as for the defeat, this has neither factual nor discursive existence. Between the two treatments of the event, there is the same difference of nature and degree as between repression and foreclosure in psychoanalysis, where the latter involves a splitting-off of material that cannot be expressed even indirectly.

There was some attempt to give expression to this trauma, almost impossible to speak of between the wars, during the period following the Second World War. Werner Best, for example, an ex-deputy leader of the RSHA,[38] tried to do so in 1947, while in prison. His biographer, Ulrich Herbert, correctly points out that these narratives of childhood echo both the real childhood experienced by Werner Best and the stylization that he, in common with others of his generation, wanted to impose on this story.[39] In the tales he tells of his life, the former Nazi dignitary always makes a very clear break between the years before and after 1914. The year of the war's outbreak became a year of bereavement as early as 4 October. This was when his father, mobilized at the start of the conflict, died from his wounds, in a Trier hospital.

> My father's heroic death [*Heldentod*] threw me back on myself when I was eleven. My mother collapsed and sought more support from her sons than she could bestow on them herself. As a result I was brought up by the family tradition rather than by the family itself [. . .]. My father had left us a letter in which he commended our mother to us and exhorted us to become men, Germans and patriots. At the age of eleven, I thus felt responsible for my mother and my young brother. And from the age of fifteen, I felt responsible for the new direction Germany should take. In my youth, all I knew was seriousness, worry, work and responsibility. [. . .] The financial hardship – my mother had no widow's pension – also cast a pall over my youth.[40]

What Best forgets to say here, though he mentions it in his 1965 account,[41] is that his paternal grandfather passed away a few weeks after his father's death: the bereavements came one on top of the other, with the first perhaps hastening the second.[42] Likewise, Best does not always manage to talk about the 1918 defeat. He does partly suggest it, saying that he felt 'responsible for the new direction Germany should take' at the tender age of fifteen, but he says nothing about his reaction to the catastrophe. For this too, one had to wait until 1965:

What a painful surprise the end of the war had been, with the November revolution – even in the very tame version which it assumed in Mainz – and especially the occupation of the city!

The fact that all those sacrifices had been proved futile seemed unimaginable to me. And when the conditions of the armistice in Compiègne were made public, I was so convinced that they could not be accepted and that the war needed to be continued that – from the lofty perch of my fifteen years – I decided with a friend to go to the Rhine to join some troops that would continue fighting.[43]

At almost fifty years' distance, the war retrospectively seemed intolerable, since the huge sacrifices that had been accepted – by him personally and by the population as a whole – had been useless. In another text, he uses the term *umsonst* ('in vain') in the same circumstances, identifying it this time just with his father's death. It was the combined impact of bereavement and defeat, private grief and collective trauma, that made the inexpressible intolerable. Refusal to accept defeat found a particularly clear expression in the young schoolboy: the defeat, unnamed, unnameable, was also unimaginable and made it obvious that hostilities should be continued. And indeed, what Best deemed to be the most painful aspect was the fact that the enemy was occupying *his* city. After communicating with the soldiers who, for four years, had brought the war into enemy territory, Best could logically perceive this occupation as an invasion, even though it had taken place *after* the cessation of hostilities.[44] This meant deciding that, to *his* mind, the defeat had not really happened. After all, the first sentence in his text basically states 'end of the war' while denying the real meaning of these words – defeat.

Such is this set of images embodying a longing to continue the struggle and a series of violent emotions: it involves the perception of a defeat that is mentioned only to be rejected immediately, even when the associated images have been entirely moulded by the culture of war. As well as bereavement and its economic and social consequences, Best's testimony provides evidence of his whole attitude during the struggle. And Best does indeed confess that he had followed 'with feverish interest' the events of the conflict, and experienced the 'greatest trauma' of his life at the fact that he had 'not been able to fight for a German victory'.[45] In 1947 or 1965, these accounts invariably portrayed a mature, serious, responsible child, whose behaviour conformed to the discourse of children's mobilization developed during the war.[46] This discourse, while presenting them with models of heroic children, continued to deny young people any possibility of heroism on the battlefield, so that the ideal of the child-soldier was consigned to fantasy.

On the other hand, these accounts of war and defeat bring out the way that the political and military field was invaded by individual passions. This process is attributable to the huge emotions invested in the war by the affected populations, caught up in a ubiquitous discourse of legitimation of the conflict, and able to experience its outcome only as a massive shock. Through Werner Best's story, however, this feeling becomes blurred, giving way to a chain of numerous events of which defeat is merely the trigger. Of course, Best cites the armistice first and foremost, but he also insists on the revolution and the occupation. This, in fact, is a constant element in German narrators: they cannot represent the defeat *in isolation*. The year 1918 means the defeat, but also the Communist revolutions, the French invasion, the dismembering of the eastern territories, and the separatist putsches; 11 November cannot be isolated from 9 November [the date of the Kaiser's abdication – *Tr.*] any more than it can from the occupation of the Rhineland and then the Ruhr in 1921–4. But while the war and the defeat fall prey to the silence we have mentioned, the troubles that followed them resurface all the more forcefully.

The 'time of troubles': an experience of war?

The *Lebensläufe* very often mention an active participation in one or other phases of the troubles that shook Germany after 1918. The narration of Richard Frankenberg, a future teacher and officer in RSHA *Amt* III B in charge of the surveillance of interethnic relationships in Nordic countries, provides us with a sort of inventory of the events that marked the period.

> [. . .] In Dortmund, during the putsch [*illegible*], I took part in the combats against the Red Army (I was in a militia of Dortmund residents, and batman with the Epp *Freikörper*). In 1919, I was co-founder of the National Youth League in Dortmund. In 1919, co-founder of the League of National Youths. [. . .]
> In 1923, during the occupation of the Ruhr, [*active*] in the organization of the propaganda service, and head of the department for combat on the Rhine with the *Deutsche Hochschulring* (DHR).[47]
> In Flensburg, co-worker in charge of border policies in the League of Schleswig-Holstein. [*Active*] as teacher in [Arg *illegible*] in Schleswig-Holstein when separated [from Germany and handed over to Denmark – *Tr.*] 1929: trip to Flanders to the home of the Flemish nationalist leader. In 1930, trips to Finland, Estonia, and Lithuania. In 1931, trip to Alsace to study the independence movement. In 1933, trips to Memel and Danzig. In North Schleswig, significant activity in border policies, leader of German boy scouts of North Schleswig.[48]

Richard Frankenberg was thus involved in many varied political activities, initially fighting the Communists, then joining the armed militias. He then moved to passive resistance and intelligence against the French during the occupation of the Ruhr, and finally worked towards the preservation of German identity in all the German communities separated from the Reich by treaties made in the suburbs of Paris. Like Frankenberg and Best, the vast majority of the members of the group encountered, during childhood or adolescence, one or other of the political crises engulfing Germany. The schoolboy Georg Herbert Mehlhorn, later head of the administration of the SD between 1932 and 1937, took part in various paramilitary nationalist organizations. At the age of sixteen, Mehlhorn, in conformity with the myth of the child-hero suggested by the war literature for children, participated in camouflaging weapons, thus acting against the Allied Disarmament Commission.[49] Too young to play any direct role in the fighting of German militias against Polish groups, he nonetheless reacted to the threat of annexation menacing Silesia by working underground in passive resistance.

Reinhard Höhn, a future professor of law in the universities of Jena and Berlin and head of the SDHA II/1 from 1931 to 1939, did not limit his activities to armed struggle and militancy:

> I studied at the secondary school in Meinigen and developed a certain precocious political competence. I first began to fight against vermin and filth when I was sixteen, as leader of the youth circle of South Thuringia. I was active in youth movements until I was eighteen, in my final school year. That was the time of the *Abwehrkämpfe* [defensive struggles – *Tr.*] against Communism. I was active in those combats and in 1922 entered the *Deutschvölkischer Schutz- und Trutzbund*.[50] I was jailed [. . .].
>
> When the NSDAP was banned, I became an active member of the *Jungdeutsche Orden* [Young German Order – *Tr.*] which was then attempting to unify the *völkisch* forces in Bavaria. I then lived for two and a half years in Munich [. . .]. This was when I first led an intelligence section and fought against separatist plots.[51]

The enemies – Communists and separatists – here described as 'vermin' and 'filth'; the defensive dimension of the combat; Höhn's extreme youth at the time he started to join the 'struggle' – all these show how the culture of war born from 1914–18 had been preserved intact. In his *Lebensläufe* of the 1930s, Werner Best also highlights his varied activities during the 'time of troubles'. His precocious militancy, his participation in the founding of the *Jungnational Partei* of Mainz, and his activism in the *Deutsche Hochschulring* are all detailed with the greatest care. The fact remains that he continues to keep silent about the images and representations that dictated this militancy.

It is in a tract of the *Deutsche Hochschulring* published at the time of the French invasion of the Rhineland that Best most clearly reveals his deeper motivations:

> *Komilitonen* [comrades]! We are again at war. The enemy is in the heart of Germany [. . .] Every French and every Belgian person is our enemy, a member of a people that has set itself above all law and all morality. Every

German who gives them the least support, tolerates them in his house, treats them on equal terms, will be struck down by the *Vehme* [a secret organization that organized political assassinations].[52]

The image of war is here quite explicitly placed at the heart of the author's representations. Franco-Belgian intervention, motivated by financial considerations,[53] is seen as an invasion without any prior declaration of war. The tract depicts an enemy behaving treacherously, which justifies the assertion that it has 'set itself above all law and all morality'. Best finally launches an appeal for resistance which, under these auspices, can only be an out-and-out fight. He reveals what is at stake here in two articles that were published in a Rhineland newspaper:

> However, the resolution to hold firm is present. But the Rhineland cannot succeed in this unless it is backed by a brave and resolute Reich. Defeatists should be brought before a war tribunal, or be struck down by the *Vehme*, since they are stabbing our western front in the back as it fights on [. . .]. On 4 February, the French entered Baden. Their aim is to divide Germany into three parts, one, the biggest possible, in the west under a French protectorate, a south under French influence, and a Prussian remainder, destined for the Poles to gobble up. The end of the world war is taking place at this moment. We need to throw our last strength into it – our physical strength but, even more, our moral strength.[54]

The issues at stake in this combat were vital, since it was a matter of fighting off a French army hell-bent on annihilating Germany. In the view of the student Best, partitioning Germany into multiple zones of influence would mean the end of Germany as a state and as a nation. At the beginning of the text quoted below, the activist expresses the risk of his nation completely disappearing in more precise and explicit terms:

> We are now confronted by an ambitious French plan of extermination [*Vernichtungsplan*]. Our government, thank God, is resolved to resist. It is doing only what is possible and thinkable. The German people, too, lives with the same desire. Social democracy fears national union in any case and sabotages it wherever it can. We need now to clarify for our people the consequences and the ruthless nature of the French extermination plan. Resistance and combat, or annihilation [*Vernichtung*] without mercy! For us, more than ever, one thing alone counts: to be ready. Nothing more need be said.[55]

Faced with what he thinks is the final phase of a concerted plan, Best vividly describes the ultimate aims of the French invasion. The *Akademiker* who became involved in the local militias or the *Freikörper* very largely internalized these representations.[56] This quasi-apocalyptic anguish surely forms the kernel of the images and representations that dictated the behaviour of the members of our group during this time of troubles. And it was doubtless also at the heart of the culture of war that coalesced during the great conflagration of 1914–18. The book *Sperrfeuer um Deutschland (Barrage Around Germany)*, by Werner Beumelberg, which saw the Great War as a 'decisive combat' against the 'desire for annihilation' of the Entente Cordiale, sets the tone for this – which explains its huge sales figures between 1929 and 1941.[57]

The shaping of a belief in the more or less imminent disappearance of Germany, as a state, of course, but also as a biological entity, thus seems, in the final analysis, to have lain at the heart of representations of the Great War and the 'time of troubles'. This was doubtless the very essence of the initial traumatic experience of the members of our group, an experience so painful that it made it practically impossible for them to describe their childhoods at all. Once they had become adults, they could rekindle their wartime lives by means of the *Abwehrkampf*, or defensive struggle, and thus manage at least partly to objectify it. The intensity of their perception of war seems to have comprised a crucial aspect of the choices made by the *Akademiker*.

Chapter 2

Constructing networks

Places to study

Once their secondary studies had come to a conclusion with the *Abitur*, or school-leaving exam, future SS intellectuals entered university and were faced with the need for geographical mobility. (This is actually the norm in German universities.) The need to change one's residence can be proved quite empirically from the *Lebensläufe* composed by SS intellectuals at the time they were recruited. Out of some eighty cases, seventy-two studied in at least two universities; out of the eight remaining cases, only three stayed in their home towns.

This mobility is fostered by the extreme decentralization of German space and the great number of universities in the Germanic world. It is quite common to see German students emigrating to Graz, Innsbruck and even Prague.[1] This mobility is even made obligatory in the *Promotionsordnungen* (the rules and regulations on doctoral studies). These rules stipulate that students must have studied at a minimum of two universities before taking a doctorate.[2]

The recurrent appearance of a certain number of major universities in the CVs of future SS intellectuals is striking – Leipzig, Munich, Göttingen and Heidelberg in particular. Nearly 80 per cent attended these universities. Only one of them, Leipzig, could draw on a local pool of students. And Leipzig was by far the most popular. The three other universities also mainly attracted students from other German *Länder*. So students could choose the university at which they would matriculate quite irrespective of any geographical criterion. The excellence and the prestige of a few major universities played a fundamental role in their choices.

In law and political economy, Halle, Göttingen and Heidelberg were also significant. Otto Ohlendorf (head of the *Inland*-SD from 1939 to 1945), Willy Seibert (head of the SD's economic bureaus), Georg Herbert Mehlhorn (head of the administration of the SD from 1935 to 1937), Heinz Gräfe (RSHA *Amt* VI G), Alfred Filbert (RSHA *Amt* VI A) and Paul Mylius

(Gestapo and later RSHA *Amt* VII) studied there.[3] Werner Best, Heinz Jost, Heinz Rennau and Alfred Filbert all spent time in Gießen, where student recruitment was both lower in numbers and more regional: Jost, Filbert and Best, Rhinelanders by birth, chose Gießen because the city was the main centre for law in their region. Werner Best, for example, combined a desire for a brilliant academic career with a commitment to radical militancy both *völkisch* and Rhinelandish (he was already a key figure in this movement), and he left to finish his state examinations in Gießen.[4]

In the human sciences, the pecking order was not so clear. Leipzig still led by a long way, ahead of Heidelberg and Berlin, then Königsberg, Tübingen, Kiel and Bonn, which also competed in the academic stakes. Paul Dittel, the future successor of Franz Six at the head of *Amt* VII of the RSHA, started studying history, geography and English at Graz before returning to Leipzig, the capital of his native Saxony. Here he was friends with Heinz Hummitzsch, one of those who would later be responsible for the *Generalplan Ost*, Emil Augsburg, who co-directed the Wannsee Institute,[5] Walter von Kielpinski, in charge of the human sciences in the SD, and Wilhelm Spengler.

There was another criterion of excellence that may have influenced academic choices: the prestige of great individual professors, especially when it came to the choice of university in which the subject of the *Dissertation* was registered.[6] The career of Heinrich Malz, who matriculated successively at Halle, Leipzig and Jena, would be puzzling if we did not take into account his choice of a thesis supervisor. This was Reinhard Höhn, who held the chair in public law at Jena, and whom Malz followed when he was elected head of the *Institut für Staatsforschung* (Institute for State Research) in Berlin.[7] The academic itinerary of Otto Ohlendorf could seem equally confusing since the guiding thread of his movements is even less easy to see than Malz's. Ohlendorf, in fact, never took his doctorate, and so did not convert his intellectual affiliations into academic success. However, after his studies in political economy and law in Leipzig, Halle and Göttingen, Ohlendorf settled in Kiel and then Berlin, following two renowned academics. He was appointed assistant to Jens Jessen at Kiel, before becoming – thanks to Jessen[8] – one of Reinhard Höhn's closest collaborators in Berlin. It was the latter who brought him into the SD in 1937.[9]

The attraction of an apparently brilliant individual mind thus sometimes determined the choice of university or the place in which one's doctorate was taken. These individual encounters sometimes went far beyond the limits of scholarly and personal exchange and involved direct supervision of militant activity. Königsberg is an exemplary if rather atypical case here. Among the future SS intellectuals, the students were found basically in two periods and two highly individualized departments. The men concerned were either historians living in Königsberg until 1934, or opportunists who arrived in 1936–7 to study journalism.

This concentration was the result of the presence of the historian Hans Rothfels and of Franz Six.

In both cases, scholarly ambition was combined with political activism. If Franz Six was described – especially after the war – as a scholarly usurper, the fact remains that at that time he cut the figure of an alluring young professor, with a brilliant career ahead of him.[10] As for Hans Rothfels, his work, both before and after the war, roused unanimous praise: he trained the future great figures of the German school of social history.[11] After 1934, however, Rothfels, being Jewish, was dismissed from his chair and forced to emigrate. The fact remains that he set up a national and conservative school of historiography. By linking studies in economic and social history with concepts rooted in the *volkisch* world, Rothfels attempted to demonstrate German socio-economic domination in the Baltic and turn it into a constant feature of the medieval and modern periods. While apparently defending the hypothesis that different ethnic groups could coexist in one and the same state,[12] Hans Rothfels planned study journeys for his pupils and structured *Deutschtumarbeit* (work on 'Germandom' – revisionist activism among the German minorities of the Baltic) by organizing 'work camps' for students.[13] He insisted on the importance of 'local re-educational work' in the *Volkstumskampf* or 'ethnic struggle',[14] and encouraged the Balts not to underestimate the German foundations of their culture.[15] The lure of Königsberg and Rothfels was thus twofold: a renowned centre of historiography was also the location of a militant organization.

Thus it was that Ernst Turowsky, later in charge of supervising *Ostforschung* (research on the east) within the RSHA,[16] chose Königsberg as one of his places to study. As is well known, he rapidly demonstrated a decided taste for German–Polish border territories.[17] His thesis was an opportunity for him to find a historical foundation for the superiority of Germans over Slavs in administrative institutions.[18] Born in 1908 in Hamburg, Hans Joachim Beyer decided to move to Graz immediately after his *Abitur* and went as a student to Königsberg in 1928.[19] While studying history, law and *Volkstumwissenschaften*, or 'ethnic sciences', Beyer moved in Rothfels' circle, but apparently never spoke of the influence this paradoxical professor (sometimes an intellectual guru for *völkisch* groups and sometimes a target for their anti-Semitism) may have had on him. Perhaps this was one of the reasons behind the insistent silence of the uncompromisingly anti-Semitic Beyer? The interest Beyer showed in the populations of Central Europe was aroused by contact with Rothfels and his pupils,[20] with whom Beyer kept up close contact throughout his career in the RSHA.[21] His militant activities began during his stay in Königsberg. He joined the Union for Germandom Abroad,[22] and on his return started to work for the DAI, a centre of documentation and research based in Stuttgart that coordinated attempts to revise the Treaty of Versailles and studies on the 'German-ness' of foreigners.[23]

For his part, having taken his doctorate and *Habilitation* in record time (just a fortnight elapsed between the two), Franz Six was in 1935 promoted to the post of director of the Institute of Journalism Studies at the University of Königsberg, which he was actually given the task of establishing. He headed it for nearly four years and attracted students from all across Germany. With the help of those young graduates who would later flock to *Amt* II of the SD and, after 1940, *Amt* VII of the RSHA, Six attempted to set up scholarly and ideological studies of the contents of the German, western and Polish press. He derived several publications from this work,[24] and many of his students did doctorates that focused on these press studies. Men like Rudolf Oebsger-Röder, Horst Mahnke, Kurt Walz and Herbert Hagen, future deputy director of the French Gestapo and a close associate of Eichmann, were led by Six to undertake studies in journalism. Of course, Hagen considered this just a form of postgraduate training necessary for his work in the SD, but Six's three other pupils combined university degrees, teaching careers and work in the RSHA.[25] A certain kind of academic excellence (as judged by Nazi criteria) and a marked political commitment were thus brought together, under the influence of a young mandarin (Six was still not yet thirty),[26] to turn Königsberg into a popular university.

The University of Bonn was of a similar calibre. The chair in 'local' history was occupied by Hermann Aubin, who also directed the *Saarforschungsgemeinschaft*, a Society for Research into the Saarland. Until 1935 he took part in German activism in the internationalized Saarland before the referendum on reintegration into the Reich. The *Saarforschungsgemeinschaft* maintained close contact with the representatives of *Ostforschung* but also with Walter Wüst, professor of history in Munich, SS *Sturmbannführer* and vice-director of the *Ahnenerbe* ['Ancestral Heritage', a Nazi body that promoted the study of so-called 'Aryan' and 'Nordic' civilizations – *Tr.*],[27] and Günther Franz, a young historian appointed professor at Marburg in 1934, SS *Hauptsturmführer* and director of studies in history at RSHA *Amt* VII from 1940 onwards.[28] In Bonn, Hermann Aubin and a geographer colleague created the *Institut für die geschichtliche Landeskunde der Rheinlande*,[29] or Institute for the Historical Geography of the Rhineland, a multidisciplinary institute devoted to the question of the western borders. Three SD cadres studied at Bonn during the most intense period of activity of Aubin and the *Saarforschungsgemeinschaft*. None of the three certified that they had attended any of these institutions. However, Hans Nockemann was one of the most active RSHA students in the *Abwehrkampf* in the Rhineland: arrested by separatists supported by the French at Aachen in 1929, he was exiled to Bonn, the city where he studied.[30] He mentions the fact that he belonged to the student corporation in Bonn, one of those most committed to the actions in the Rhineland: its 'border office', merged with the *Jugendgrenzlandarbeit* (a body promoting work for young people in German borderlands) of Friedrich Heiss, organized propaganda trips to the Saar.[31] Nockemann, given various responsibilities in this organization, played a part in these border activities and their institutionalization, of which Aubin and the University of Bonn were the theorists. However, his activism did not assume any concrete form in his CV: he studied law and political science and so had no visible connection with Aubin's 'local history'. This was doubtless not the case with Ernst Turowsky, Rothfels' pupil, who, before starting at Königsberg, matriculated at Bonn for two semesters. His itinerary is somewhat similar to that of Kleo Pleyer, who left Bonn in 1934, where he had been Aubin's assistant (and one of his closest disciples), to succeed Rothfels.[32] The common points in the historiographical practices of the two professors, their multidisciplinary ambitions, and their desire to combine history-writing with political commitment constituted a clear factor of continuity in Turowsky's career. He was thus one of the few historians of his generation to have combined the experience of *Westforschung* (research on the west) with that of *Ostforschung*. He therefore took over the coordination and surveillance of the whole range of institutes researching *Volkstumwissenschaften* within the SD.[33]

Lawyers, economists, geographers and historians matriculated at the University of Leipzig, as this was – together with Heidelberg – one of a handful of great universities that could lay claim to excellence in all domains. Three of the most eminent leaders of the SD or the RSHA, Mehlhorn, Ohlendorf and Gräfe, undertook part of their studies there. At the *Proseminaren* (seminars), they encountered Dr Lutz Richter, appointed to a post as assistant, who was interested in labour law and corporation law in Germany and fascist Italy and who, in 1930, left to give classes in one of the bastions of pro-German revisionism in the Baltic, the Herder Institute in Riga.[34] Gräfe and Mehlhorn were active in *Grenzlandarbeit*, 'border work', within the Leipzig student corporations, while Ohlendorf, like Richter, went to study fascism and its system of social surveillance in Pavia.[35] In German studies, the seminal role played by Karl Justus Obenauer has been emphasized by Gerd Simon, who demonstrates – though with some exaggeration – that Wilhelm Spengler, Walter von Kielpinski and Ernst Turowsky were influenced by the holder of the chair of Germanic literature.[36] Wilhelm Spengler was given a distinction (a mark of 'Très bien') for his doctorate,[37] partly thanks to the highly positive report of Obenauer, who had been his professor for four years and in whose house he had been a frequent guest.[38] At the same time, the young man made the most of his stay in Leipzig, joining student corporations active in *Grenzlandarbeit* and becoming involved in propaganda and the surveillance of written productions in Leipzig. He later resumed this activity in 1933, within the 'central office for surveillance of writing' of the SD.[39] The case of Walter von Kielpinski is similar to Spengler's, as both men shared the same masters, a few years apart. Von Kielpinski forged a professional career for himself in the Nazi press of Silesia, before joining the SD under the influence of Spengler during his first semester at the University of Leipzig.[40] It is no coincidence that, from their base in

Leipzig, the SD organized the surveillance of German literature, including both newspapers and books. Apart from the presence of the *Deutsche Bibliothek*, a sort of functional equivalent of the Bibliothèque nationale in France [or the British Library or Library of Congress – *Tr.*], the departments of philosophy and law were a breeding ground for young graduates distinguished both by their academic excellence and by their militancy.

These young men were trained in 'border universities'. Here they came into contact with non-German populations and with the controversial borders that emerged from the treaties after 1918. These border universities included Bonn, 'an intellectual border fortress', as Ernst Anrich,[41] a self-proclaimed Nazi and future rector of the German university of occupied Strasbourg (itself a combative border city), liked to put it;[42] Leipzig, a crossroads from which students headed off into the Sudetenland to spread propaganda; and Königsberg, an island of Germandom besieged by Poland and cut off from the Reich by the Danzig corridor. Studying at these universities was, for a great many future SS intellectuals, a fundamental act in their careers as militants, and this was probably because it led them gradually to consider these close borders as 'marches' of biological German identity which, when not correctly demarcated, left German islets abandoned in what were now foreign countries. In this sense, universities were not simply places of study.

Places of association

While classes and seminars may have contributed to the political education of future SS intellectuals, their commitment logically found a first home in student corporations, sports clubs and other associations. The trace of this can be found in the accounts of their lives that they wrote later, even though certain young SS officers mentioned the organization to which they belonged only if it was socially prestigious, if they had performed specific functions in it, or if its political trend corresponded to that of the SS and the NSDAP. Hermann Behrends, between 1934 and 1937 the leader of the *Inland*-SD,[43] then of the *Hauptamt Deutsche Mittelstelle* (also known as the *Volksdeutsche Mittelstelle* or VoMi: Main Welfare Office for Ethnic Germans) between 1937 and 1945,[44] as a law student in Marburg most probably joined a *Burschenschaft* (student association). Here he learned to fence, as was the tradition, and came away with a few scars that were judged a badge of honour,[45] but refrained from mentioning this in his *Lebenslauf*, as if the place or the activity struck him as likely to prejudice his image.[46] Hans Nockemann, on the other hand, emphasized his affiliation to the very prestigious *Burschenschaft* Alemannia, which gave him a position of responsibility in the student organizations of the University of Bonn.[47] He naturally went in for group activities, including fencing, and likewise picked up a few scars.[48] Like many of his comrades, he combined belonging to a *Burschenschaft* with activities of passive resistance against the French. Bruno Lettow (future director of the SIPO school in Prague, which trained members of the *Sicherheitspolizei* or Security Police) was a member of the *Burschenschaft* Teutonia. He occupied important positions in the federal association of student corporations.[49] However, most of the students do not specify what *Burschenschaft* they were members of. This is true of Gustav Jonack, a Sudetenland student and future Gestapo officer in Bohemia-Moravia, and of Paul Mylius, who worked successively for the Gestapo and *Amt* VII of the RSHA.[50] Literature students often opted for sporting associations. Heinz Hummitzsch was one of these. He studied history, philosophy and ethnology of folklore in Leipzig and Munich, and was a member of the Leipzig *Turnerschaft*, then *Bundesführer* (group leader) from 1933 to 1935, while also taking part in the activities of the university's *Studentenschaft* or student body. Here he was appointed 'head of land service' (*Landdienstführer*).[51]

In this way, SS candidates furnished proof of their ability to lead and organize teams. This shows how gratifying this type of commitment could be. However, if we read these biographical accounts carefully, it transpires that not all student organizations were seen as being on an equal footing: the *Studentenschaften* are readily mentioned, the *Burschenschaften* are regularly passed over in silence, while the *Turnerschaften* are spoken of only if they involved particular responsibilities. The former, recognized by the state, implied both responsibilities for management and administration of the university, organizational functions in the realm of student life, and representative functions. The *Burschenschaften* were the traditional student corporations, particularly widespread in law faculties. They were based on a communitarian principle: the property of a shared house acted as a place of residence for the active members and as a meeting place for the corporation. The oldest *Burschenschaften* – Germania, Alemannia or Teutonia – were present in every university. To mention them was a sign of social status. On the other hand, a veil of discretion was drawn over local corporations. Rolf Mühler, who studied at Heidelberg, Kiel and Leipzig, entered a *Burschenschaft* in his very first semester, though he does not give its name – the entire corporation joined the SA (*Sturmabteilung* or Assault Division) in May 1933. He was active for ten semesters within this corporation, a very clear sign of the way student sociability and student militancy could be combined.[52]

The *Turnerschaften* were sports societies that basically went in for gymnastics. The most prestigious were part of the *Studentenschaften*. This was the case with the *Turnerschaft* Mundenia, a major club in Leipzig, whose elitist quality was particularly in evidence and which associated its sporting activities with themed evenings which, far from being the classic student parties, could take the form of colloquia for the discussion of revisionist political subjects. Herbert Mehlhorn, a specialist in questions of armaments and military policy,[53] was one of the main speakers at these

meetings. Indeed, one of the decisive phenomena found in student movements between the wars was their increasingly radical politicization.

In 1919, the *Turnerschaften* 'professed [their] support for the *völkisch*
theory' and thereby endorsed the 'harshest and most inexorable struggle
against all trends promoting internationalization, against the appetite
for power of homeless Jewry, as well as an undying hatred for [their]
enemies, which stems not from a lack of fraternity, but from an awareness
of its historical necessity'.[54] The unusual nature of these remarks lay in the
juxtaposition of images of total war and anti-Communism with an anti-
Semitism different from the classic elitist anti-Semitism based on religion.
Student organizations excluded Jews on the basis of the *Ahnennachweise*
(genealogical tree) – this showed a biologically tinted understanding of
Jewishness.[55] This mapped an ethnically based interpretation of Jews and
Germans inherited from the Great War onto a pre-existing hostility to
Jews dating from Wilhelmine Germany.[56]

The sudden radicalization of the student sports movement was not
an isolated phenomenon. In 1921, the *Deutsche Studentenschaft* (German
Student Association), a body that represented students in the managerial
institutions of universities, also moved towards an elitist revolutionary
nationalism under the influence of radical student organizations. The
movement, common to all German universities, was admirably summed
up by the great German historian Friedrich Meinecke, who gave Berlin as
an example:

> Of the 10,000 students, 9,400 simply attend lectures, seminars and institutes
> and busy themselves with their studies and exams alone. Some 600 find
> themselves in *High Spirit* [in English in the original – *Tr.*], of which 400
> are hyper-nationalist and '*völkisch*', while the other 200 are split between
> Communists, Social Democrats and Democrats.[57]

This description fits the ultra-minority activism of the left but does not
account for the very widespread support of the silent majority for radical
völkisch ideas. The nationalist groups that were rapidly formed after the
war managed to get their representatives elected to the student councils.
Against the background of the occupation of the Rhineland and uprisings
in Silesia, there was a debate on the conditions of entry to the association at the congress of German students that had gathered in Erlangen.
The *völkisch* radicals, whether Germans, Austrians or Sudetenlanders,
raised the question of 'German descent' as a criterion of selection, as
well as wondering what should happen about Jews wishing to become
members of the association.[58] In 1922, at the Fourth Student Congress,
the *Deutsche Hochschulring*, which already formed the majority of the
Studentenschaft, imposed its racist and anti-Semitic positions by a majority
vote of more than two thirds.[59] It also set out this new line to be followed
at the next congress, held in Würzburg. At the Erlangen Congress, these

principles were included in the statutes of the Austrian and Sudeten *Studentenschaften* and forbade entry to any students who could not prove their 'German lineage'. However, the *Deutsche Studentenschaft*, financed and recognized by the state, could not by law lay down statutes that excluded Jews and foreigners. Nonetheless, in 1921, in spite of pressures from the Prussian minister for religious worship and education, successive student votes approved this *völkisch* and anti-Semitic line, with very large majorities – between 66 per cent and 90 per cent of the votes cast. Student participation stood at an average of around 70 per cent of the total of those registered, so that the silent majority was here expressing itself quite unambiguously.[60]

The relative failure of Rhineland activism and the debates about moving on to armed struggle put paid to the student organization, which lost ground to the *Nationalsozialistischer Studentenbund* (NSStB or National Socialist German Students' League) run by Dr Gustav Adolf Scheel, a doctor trained at Heidelberg, SS official and precocious student activist. From 1926 onwards, the success of the NSStB grew while the *Deutsche Hochschulring* saw its numbers fall. The older activists, born between 1900 and 1905, then left the universities, giving way to individuals who belonged directly to an NSStB that very soon made clear its ambition of unifying students who had hitherto been scattered across a whole range of *völkisch* parties and groupings into a single organization able to make a bid for power in universities as well as in the political arena.[61] Apart from differences in sensibility and outlook, these two bodies were part of the same world, the direct product of memories of the Great War and the *Abwehrkampf*. The rector of the University of Tübingen still maintained, in his speech at the start of the summer semester of 1929, that 'nobody should have the right to sing *Deutschland über alles* unless he is determined to reconquer what has been lost, and this can be accomplished only by force of arms [. . .]. Never will diplomats grant us freedom.'[62]

At the beginning of the 1930s, the support given by student milieus to nationalist and racist circles was thus already a fait accompli. The future SS intellectuals were witnesses of and, sometimes, actors in this decisive transformation. Individual men such as Werner Best, Georg Herbert Mehlhorn and Richard Frankenberg, born between 1901 and 1905, matriculated at university straight after the war and were important participants in the *Studentenschaft*'s lurch into right-wing radicalism. The majority of the group's members went to university *after* the *Studentenschaft* had moved into *völkisch* radicalism, *after* the rise to power of the NSStB, and even, in certain cases, *after* the *Machtergreifung* (Nazi seizure of power). Their paths then became more linear, their memberships more stable, their political quests more short-term. So Franz Six served his full period as a student in the NSStB after matriculating in 1929 while at the same time being an activist in the SA, and he had no opportunity to compare his Nazi political convictions with other alternatives on offer. At this precise moment, the *völkisch* bodies were melding together within the

Nazi organizations, one of the most dynamic of them being the very same NSStB that was led in Heidelberg by Gustav Adolf Scheel and threw itself into political activism, while attempting to bring the teachers into line with Nazi norms, setting up for example cabals against lecturers of Jewish origin.[63] Rolf Mühler studied at Heidelberg, Kiel and Leipzig. Younger than Franz Six, he matriculated for the first time in 1929 and left the university five years later. He joined a *Burschenschaft* in his very first semester, and left only after passing his final exam. On 20 May 1933, his *Burschenschaft* decided to join the SA, thereby making effective a Nazi normalization that would continue throughout the same year.[64] In university milieus, *Gleichschaltung* ('coordination', in which all institutions were brought into line with Nazi ideas) occurred without difficulties, and joining the NSDAP, the SA or the NSStB was often merely a confirmation of already long-standing ideological affinities. However, this normalization occasionally provoked resistance. In Leipzig, Heinz Hummitzsch became involved in the sometimes violent conflicts between the NSStB and student organizations reluctant to become merged with the Nazi organizations. In 1935, Hummitzsch was elected to the *Studentenschaft*, but distinguished himself by his pro-Nazi attitude and, although being the head of his *Turnerschaft*, was excluded from it for 'breaking the links of associative solidarity'.[65]

One constant feature marks student life throughout the interwar period: the pervasive importance of the memory of the Great War, and its role in the biologization of systems of representation and in a radical anti-Semitism, a common set of beliefs shared by the many nationalist *Bünde* and the NSStB, by the students of 1920 as well as by those of 1935. In order to get to the heart of the social images and representations at play, let us take a closer look at student activism.

Who now remembers the amazing assiduity shown by the *Studentenschaft* in its commemoration of the battle of Langemarck throughout the 1920s? [This battle took place in October–November 1914: a myth arose that German students made a fixed bayonet charge on the Allies while singing '*Deutschland, Deutschland über alles*' – Tr.][66] From 1932, furthermore, this commemoration was taken over by the NSStB of Gustav Adolf Scheel, who, not content with simply continuing the activity of remembrance, organized summer schools and training courses for activists, under the aegis of the great battle. In this way, the fundamental place of memory of the Great War in student representations was confirmed. The fact that celebrations based on Langemarck had little impact, or that the war did not, for the university rectors, constitute a major subject for their beginning-of-semester speeches, must not allow us to draw the over-hasty conclusion that memory of the war was fading. It is, rather, a sign of the repression of the memory of defeat, since the war's consequences still weighed heavily.[67] Why, after all, would students assiduously celebrate an episode – however emblematic it was, in their view – in a war that the vast majority of them considered as unfinished?[68]

The student associations were active in an even more visible way in the *Volkstumskampf*, a combat with and on behalf of the German minorities left outside the borders of the Reich by the peace treaties. The very term *Volkstumskampf* comes with marked biological connotations. In 1919, a multitude of organizations and associations was formed, creating a dense network of communication between the Reich and these German communities subjected to foreign political domination.

Within the Reich, student organizations were one of the main points of contact with the representatives of German minorities abroad. They frequently invited them to conferences where there were discussions of the situation – always described as alarming – of these communities. The case of the Saarland is a symptomatic example of this, for two reasons. Activism in the Saarland began only around 1925, in the period of diplomatic normalization in Germany; so the external causes are not very clear. Secondly, there is no question here of the start of any terrorist movements or of scuffles with the occupying power, as occurred from 1918 to 1924 in the Rhineland and the Ruhr. The *Bund der Saarvereine*, an umbrella association for the whole pro-German network in the Saarland, was from 1929 plunged into intense activity – conferences, slide shows, the forwarding of documentation and so on. Organizing information tours for its leaders, the *Bund der Saarvereine* covered the whole territory of Germany, sometimes returning to the same localities several times.

This burst of activity might have come up against bafflement or lack of interest on the part of students. But these conferences were actually organized at the behest of student associations themselves: they produced a stream of correspondence, requesting lectures, documentation or aid for the organization of an expedition of *Komilitonen* to the internationalized Saarland.[69] It is true that we have little concrete evidence of the enthusiasm of the students or the success of these conferences. However, in 1932, at a time when the Saarland was not really in the headlines and the members of the *Bund der Saarvereine* regularly complained that they could not arouse the same interest as the other 'oppressed minorities',[70] over 600 students from Berlin came to Charlottenburg to attend the lecture by the speaker from the Saarland, Vogel – which shows that there *was* a real interest on the part of students in the territories lost in 1918.[71]

The *Bund der Saarvereine* also welcomed delegations of students who had come to carry out fieldwork. This association investigated the situation of the communities there, or carried out activist work, though these two things were of course not mutually exclusive. The trip was seen by the student leaders as an introduction to the '*Grenzlandproblem*'.[72] This 'border problematic' included political, economic and social phenomena in border territories. However, the question of borders was not seen simply in economic or administrative terms; for these students, a border was also, indeed mainly, a cultural, national and even ethnic limit. The Berlin students thus thought that, in the Saarland, they would be able to study specific phenomena caused by a geographical and political situation conditioned by the proximity of a culturally and ethically different entity, a proximity viewed as a form of confrontation, as the term *Volkstumskampf* suggests.[73] And yet there were no clashes between the different communities in the Saarland. This was perhaps why the Berlin students opted to gain an initial understanding, in this rather quiet 'border territory', of problems that they considered to be crucial and that might lead them to change their behaviour in the future. Students from the universities of Graz, Innsbruck and Brunn organized, with comrades in the Reich, the visit of a representative of the *Bund der Saarvereine*. They themselves were a German minority: they could thus highlight their experience of the *Volkstumskampf*. They warned the speaker that they were under police surveillance and alerted him to the possibility of arrest if he agreed to speak of 'the Saar cause' on Czech territory.[74]

Student organizations were in regular contact with a 'Reich Committee for Border Work', run by the state, and discreetly coordinating border activism.[75] In addition, a Liaison Office for German Youth in Europe gradually gathered all the youth organizations, both student and religious groups, whose activities included a certain 'border activity' and turned them into a legal association.[76] Of interest in this connection is the career of its leader, Friedrich Heiss, who – like Werner Best and Richard Frankenberg – was active in the DHR,[77] became one of the *éminences grises* of the *Volkstumspolitik* or ethnic policies of the Weimar Republic, while publishing history books for a general readership.[78] From 1938 onwards, he played a part in Nazi expansionism, being closely linked with the SD and the VoMi, which was at that time led by a former member of the SD, Hermann Behrends. Around the latter there gravitated a remarkable number of SD intellectuals whom Heiss had frequented in his activist days on the border.[79] One of the reasons for this connivance between SS intellectuals and Friedrich Heiss doubtless lies in the latter's ability to bring out the connection between the Great War and his struggles in the 1930s. His publishing house, Volk und Reich, was one of the centres for bringing out accounts of the Great War and propaganda pieces to foster activism on the border. His personal written work, which brought Germany 'out of daytime into night',[80] called for a (Nazi) German revolution to consummate five years of national struggle.[81]

At meetings of the Office, statements remained confidential, and the lists of attendees conferred anonymity on the participants who had come from associations of *Volksdeutsche*, while the most prestigious names in German academia, in history, geography, sociology, and ethnology of folklore, appeared on them. This alliance, forged between the academic milieus of the Reich and activists adept in keeping a low profile or working underground, epitomizes the world of SD intellectuals. Young graduates such as Siegfried Engel, Richard Frankenberg, Hans Joachim Beyer and Heinz Hummitzsch entered the *Volkstumskampf* through organizations that supported the *Mittelstelle*.[82] One disturbing fact is that the four men, after careers that were basically very similar, ended up, in

Engel's case, providing ideological training for Gestapo and SD person-nel, while the three others took part, under the leadership of Hans Ehlich, in the development of the *Generalplan Ost*, the series of plans designed to lay down the future resettlements necessary for the Germanization of territories extending from Crimea to the Arctic Circle. It was as if, in the view of these Nazi militants, the *Generalplan Ost* was the ultimate aim of the *Volkstumskampf*.

Networks of solidarity

It can be an arduous task to try and grasp what created the hidden but perfectly real affinities between SS intellectuals. Everything seems to indi-cate the existence of networks based on a community of places of study and on shared activist, festive and corporatist experiences. It is hard to detect these networks actually being formed within student social groups. Nonetheless, the a posteriori confirmation of their existence allows us to localize them, to grasp their individual nature and to evaluate the environment in which they were shaped.

The only source that gives us any chance of recapturing the emo-tional ambience of SS intellectuals during their studies is, of course, their *Lebensläufe*. We can, however, draw on few infrequent mentions of *Komilitonen* (acquaintances who had acted as partners in some political activity) applying to a corporation or entering the SS.

References to these connections created during the period of study mainly concern early entrants into the SS and the SD: after 1937, only rare and atypical individuals felt any need to name acquaintances who might guarantee their doctrinal affiliations. Only individuals who considered themselves to be ideologically suspect mentioned character witnesses. Practically no SS intellectual ever mentions these links – which proves the activist character of the elite we are studying.

The personal file of Reinhard Höhn helps us piece together part of the network of acquaintances of an SS intellectual:

> I committed myself actively to these *Abwehrkämpfe*, and entered the *Deutschvölkischer Schutz- und Trutzbund* in 1922 in Meiningen. (Proof of this: the *Staatsarchivrat* [State Archivist – *Tr.*] Engel Weimar, Alexanderplatz 3, who was also active with me at that time.) I was arrested on the orders of Police Colonel Müller-Brandenburg, now head of the press and communi-cations office of the secretary of state at the Labour Department. Colonel Müller-Brandenburg, whom I met recently in the company of Dr Becker, inspector of schools for cadres in the Labour Department, remembers that period very clearly. I studied law and political economy. In the summer semester, I met Hans Kobelinsky, currently SS *Standartenführer*, who took over my training. [. . .] I entered the department [of the SD – *Tr.*] on the instructions of SS-*Standartenführer* Kobelinsky.[83]

Reinhard Höhn takes care to name the people with whom he had remained in contact and who could guarantee the veracity of his statements. It is impossible to date this document. It must, however, be later than 1932, when Höhn joined the SD, and before 1938, since it was then the object of disciplinary proceedings, with the file for an *ad hominem* investigation being opened. It thus seems that Höhn wrote his *Lebenslauf* at the very time he found himself in an uncomfortable position in the institution. Mention of this network of acquaintances, a network that was simultaneously militantly anti-French, anti-separatist and academic, seemed in his view to be a piece of evidence that would clear his name when his political attitudes were under investigation. To the names already quoted we should add those of Werner Best, Gerhard Klopfer and Jens Jessen, co-editors of the review *Reich, Volksordnung, Lebensraum* [*Reich, People's Order, Lebensraum – Tr.*], who were also the products of *völkisch* activism. It was this same group that, in 1941, published the *Festschrift* for the fortieth birthday of Heinrich Himmler.[84]

This network of Nazi intellectuals was one of the most important, both for its activities in the formulation of doctrine and for its position in the corridors of power of the Third Reich. Stuckart was one of the participants at the Wannsee Conference in 1942, Best was the deputy head of the RSHA until 1939, and Höhn head of the SD until 1938.

Other networks are identifiable if we focus on the combined criteria of age, geographical origin and party affiliation. The following men studied at Leipzig: Otto Ohlendorf, Emil Augsburg, Paul Dittel, Wilhelm Spengler, Rudolf Oebsger-Röder, Willy Seibert, Hans Ehlich, Helmut Knochen and Walter von Kielpinski. If we examine the dates of birth, we find a first sub-group composed of men born after 1908: Dittel, Spengler, Oebsger-Röder, Hans Rössner, Mühler, von Kielpinski and Gräfe. The last of these is the only lawyer in the sample. The others studied German language and literature, and history or geography, and matriculated at the same time. So we have a set of individuals taking the same courses and sharing the same expectations, even though there is nothing to prove that they actually knew each other. The fact remains that Spengler, von Kielpinski and Rössner had the same director of studies.[85] Spengler, two years older than the others, was the first to join the SD, recruited his comrades in the *Schrifttumstelle* [Bureau for Written Works – *Tr.*] of the SD in Leipzig and remained their superior in the hierarchy until 1945.[86]

Gräfe and Oebsger-Röder were exactly the same age and were both active in the Leipzig *Studentenschaft*,[87] the very one which undertook *Grenzfahrten*, border trips, so assiduously.[88] Probably their shared labours began in Poland, where they both went on secret missions to *volksdeutsch* groups among the *Einsatzkommandos* [i.e. individual units of the *Einsatzgruppen* – *Tr.*],[89] and, once they had rapidly become friends in Leipzig, continued in Russia. The tone of complicity in the administrative letters they exchanged on this occasion suggests as much.[90]

Other sub-groups can also be easily identified, such as the one formed by the economists in the circle of Otto Ohlendorf. Willy Seibert was probably close to the latter at Göttingen during his studies in economics.[91] He became his subordinate in the RSHA *Amt* III D, then his deputy when he joined *Einsatzgruppe* D.[92] Friedrich Tiedt was also one of the students whom Ohlendorf probably encountered fleetingly, though we know that he associated with the student agitator only when he joined the SD. The bond between the two seems this time to have been of a more militant kind, with the two men exercising regional responsibilities within the NSStB at the same time.[93]

If we examine the leaders of the *Inland*-SD – known after 1940 as RSHA *Amt* III – under the orders of Otto Ohlendorf, we can see that no fewer than twelve *Referente* or heads of department, in other words more than 50 per cent of them, studied at Leipzig between 1928 and 1932 and were part of the NSStB or a corporation. Two of Ohlendorf's most important collaborators are not included: Willy Seibert, who, as we have seen, got to know Ohlendorf at Göttingen; and Hans Ehlich, who studied medicine at Leipzig too early to have known Ohlendorf there.[94] Studying in the same places, moving in the same political milieus influenced by the NSStB, these men must have formed close bonds with the future head of RSHA *Amt* III – bonds which resulted in the remarkable homogeneity of the cadres gathered around him.[95]

Finally, one last Saxon network formed round the figure of Paul Dittel, the successor, from 1942, of Franz Six at the head of RSHA *Amt* VII. Dittel, a product of the faculty of history and German, joined the *Schrifttumstelle* in Leipzig and from 1943 gathered round himself collaborators such as Rudolf Levin, Ernst Merkel and Rolf Mühler: he knew the latter both from the lecture halls of the university and from the offices of the SD *Schrifttumstelle*. This network was distinguished from the others by the absence of any dominant individual who might have been able to recruit members to the group.

Chapter 3

Activist intellectuals

So far, we have seen the time spent by future SS cadres at university as an aspect of their social and activist education. But it was also the period of their professional and intellectual training. These young men provide no evidence at all for the clichéd image of the thuggish Nazi activist; they gained entrance to universities, and took – and generally passed – their exams. Nor were they the bad boys of a science that they 'perverted'.[1] The content of the courses they followed proves as much. Knowledge, activism and levels of cultural sophistication: it is in the interaction between these three dimensions that the specific character of these activist intellectuals (or, perhaps better, intellectual activists) can be identified.

The construction of academic knowledge

It was in their apprenticeships that future SD cadres were trained while at the same time they forged the specific nature of their group, in which their knowledge skills were remarkably well suited to their militant activities. They followed university courses that granted diplomas and conferred on each student the title of *Akademiker*:[2] this involved a series of hierarchies that are at first glance difficult to grasp. While the level of studies of these men may appear homogeneous, their level of cultural sophistication was less so, and this had an impact on their careers in SS organizations.

Did they study for a short or a long time? This is the first criterion. The records for brevity of academic career are held by Karl Burmester, Erich Ehlers and Paul Zapp. All three embarked on their studies but dropped out after a few weeks – or, in the case of Ehlers, a few days. Having registered to study German, history and philosophy, Burmester and Ehlers, in Hamburg and Kiel respectively, and Zapp in Leipzig,[3] all gave up: and in every case this seems to have been due to insurmountable economic difficulties. The three men then decided to start a business course. Their academic failures were in no way a bar to their being recruited into the repressive organizations of the Third Reich. But they had only average careers.

These three men excepted, the duration of study lasted between five to sixteen semesters, with the norm being eight semesters. The period of studies was punctuated by a series of demanding examinations. To obtain the *Staatsexamen*, the way into the civil service and the magistracy, lawyers had to follow eight semesters of training, validated by exams every semester. Based on the ideal of *Ausbildung* [literally, education and general cultivation – Tr.], which referred to the voluntary and independent training of the student, who could, within a predefined framework, choose his subjects for each semester, the law curriculum was taken over by the Nazis and subjected to greater supervision: from 1940, the contents of the eight semesters were laid down in advance.[4] Exams for entry into the teaching profession followed the same development. Richard Frankenberg, for example, studied history and German for eight semesters, from 1921 to 1925, before taking 'the scientific exam for teaching in higher education', which gave him access to teaching in a *Gymnasium* [roughly, grammar school or selective high school – Tr.] and in the *Hochschulen*.[5] Helmut Knochen (the future head of the Gestapo and the SD in France) studied German, English and physical education between 1930 and 1934, and after two years took his exam to be a sports teacher, but passed his final exams only at the end of his eight-semester course.[6]

The longest academic careers were often those of historians, geographers, Germanists and linguists. Rolf Mühler studied history, German and English for a full ten semesters in Heidelberg, then took two extra semesters at Kiel and Leipzig.[7] Herbert Strickner studied at Graz and Leipzig for sixteen semesters, between 1929 and 1937. The length of his stay in the groves of academia was due to his radical change of direction. His first eight semesters in Graz had been devoted to Protestant theology. The year 1933 was for him a complete break on the academic, personal and political levels. His pro-Nazi activism in Austria made him a wanted man and he took refuge in Leipzig, where he embarked on the study of history and German, continuing for a further eight semesters. This break provides us with a first clue as to the interaction between knowledge, political commitment and personal life.[8]

Georg Herbert Mehlhorn studied for eight semesters, from January 1923 to December 1926, in Göttingen, Munich and Leipzig, passed his exams and obtained his doctorate in 1928. The length of his studies was quite average, but Mehlhorn admitted that he had spent most of his first semesters on social and sports activities rather than training as a lawyer. Indeed, it is as if the students' first university years, undemanding in terms of personal work, allowed them to put their social lives and political activism first. Werner Best was himself a good example: he joined the DHR in his very first semester. All these students, or almost all, played a part in the life of associations, and were desirous, as newcomers, to join in student social and/or activist life. On the other hand, towards the end of their studies, the need to take exams or write a thesis slowed down their 'associative' activities. Thus Mehlhorn, after giving a long and detailed account of his political and associative commitments during his first two semesters, writes in his *Lebenslauf*:

> In the Munich period of my studies (1924), I had few political contacts. At that time I just had a few contacts with the circles of the *Stahlhelm* via a colleague, but I did not become a member. The following period, until my second *Staatsexamen*, was extraordinarily busy due to my professional work, which thus made any political affiliation impossible. It was only during my probationary period as a lawyer that I again started to become more particularly active in politics.[9]

Werner Best was also very actively involved in the DHR from his first semester onwards, for example as one of the leaders of the *Studentenschaft* who imposed the *völkisch* line at Würzburg; but he moderated his activism after spending six months in prison, and concentrated on his studies, finishing them in one semester. Freed in September 1924, he was able to rejoin the university only in the summer semester of 1925. Nonetheless, he moved straight into his *Referendar* [probationary period – *Tr.*] and finished his thesis at the same time. The image of an extremely active man, effortlessly succeeding in his studies, is unavoidable.[10] This impression of facility, and even dilettantism, might well be confirmed by the curriculum. In the course laid down for future cadres of the public professions, one semester was composed of twenty-four hours of classes and seminars.[11] In other words, the actual presence of students in the lecture halls could be sporadic: the bulk of their work lay in reading. Werner Best, absorbed in the Rhineland *Abwehrkampf*, seems to have undertaken only sketchy studies in law and economics. However, he drew from this a general knowledge that gave him the stature of a highly qualified intellectual in theoretical debates.[12] So we need to draw a different set of distinctions between the cultural levels of students who later became SS intellectuals.

It was the norm, in Germany, to choose two disciplines at the start of one's university studies. Lawyers generally opted for law and political economy, or even political science. In the case of law, their studies mainly led to the business world or the civil service. Only a few individuals such as Hans Leetsch set out from the start to undertake fundamental research in law or economy, and completed their legal training with work in the political sciences, going on to take a doctorate in the latter.[13] In all these cases it was a matter of a general training that produced professionals who could immediately be put to work in the law courts and the state apparatus, having as they did a good knowledge of the cogs of the economy. But they were not simply there to carry out orders: their training equipped them to pass judgments, to draw up regulations and reports, and to draft reforms; in short, to think in some depth about the practice of the law.

'Literary' subjects gave rise to a greater diversity, which did not exclude the presence of certain invariant features. The vast majority of students chose German literature. The hierarchy between major subject and minor subject was here less important than it was in law. Most of the students who opted for the 'faculties of philosophy' where one could study literature and the human sciences were heading for careers in secondary school teaching. But every teacher in a secondary school taught two subjects: though specialization in one subject was desirable, it was good to have more than one area of competence. German, a prestige subject, was usually optional. The subjects chosen were history and geography, more rarely philosophy. In some cases, another subject added to these was *Volkskunde*, German ethnology of folklore: this had nothing in common with, for example, the social anthropology that came into being in France at this time with the teams working at the Musée de l'Homme.[14] Foreign languages, taught in the departments of Romance languages and Anglo-Saxon studies (not just English – Dutch too was included), completed the range of choices made by future SS intellectuals.

Though we must not leap to any conclusions about the intellectual stature of the students, we can register the importance of the traditional humanist ideal in German universities. This is borne out by the frequent choice of German, and the popularity of philosophy and languages. The lack of taste for *applied* literary studies – nothing stopped a student combining, for example, public law with history, sociology with geography – also confirms the way literary studies dominated choices of university course: German universities were still the citadel of humanist scholarship that they had been since Ranke, and this was true even in the implicit choices made by the most fervently Nazi students. Some individuals did turn to a multidisciplinary course combining history or geography with economics, public law or political science. Hans Joachim Beyer, for instance, combined history and *Volkswissenschaften* with public law. At the age of thirty-three, he was appointed professor at Posen, then Prague: his career – like those of Franz Six[15] and Günther Franz[16] – was one of the most meteoric in the Third Reich.[17]

The subjects chosen by students on entering university mean that we can distinguish between the various members of the group, but do not allow us to evaluate the tenor of their studies, or even the judgements passed on these students by their teachers. Otto Ohlendorf, for example, seems to have pursued a perfectly ordinary course of studies: at Leipzig, Halle and Göttingen he took law and political economy, as did many intellectuals in the SD. At the end of his university career, he took the *Staatsexamen* without doing a doctorate. He did not enter the magistracy. This might be read as a failure to join the civil service, due to his mediocre track record. But this is not the case, although the reasons that led him not to take a doctorate remain obscure. He freed himself, for the first time, from the norm dictating that law students become lawyers, engaging instead in intense research in economics. He played a role in setting up a department in the Institute for World Economics in Kiel, one of the biggest German institutions, then left to work at the Institute for Applied Sciences in Berlin. In parallel, he took part in the major debates between the SS, the DAF [*Deutsche Arbeitsfront* or German Labour Front, the Nazis' trade union organization – *Tr.*] and the Quadrennial Organization on economic policy. His collaboration with two experts in Nazi economics and political science (Jens Jessen and Reinhard Höhn), his organization and administration of research centres, and his economic theorizing at the highest level of state[18] all indicate that he was an excellent figure in his field, rather than just being a typical product of the subjects he chose at the start of his studies.[19]

This leads us to a question that is often asked: were the future SS members brilliant students? Georg Herbert Mehlhorn wrote a thesis on the history of law and penal practices relating to poaching, and was given an outstanding grade. He was the sole lawyer in the group not to go into the civil service; on leaving university, he immediately joined one of the most renowned lawyers' practices in Chemnitz. The laurels awarded to his academic excellence were thus confirmed by an extraordinary start to his professional career.[20] As for Heinz Gräfe, his case is quite ambiguous. He was the only one to write about his schooling:

> My career as a schoolboy followed a surprising course. From the lowest forms onwards, I was a lazy, rebellious pupil, and constantly got a poor mark of 3, and was even threatened with being hauled up in front of the school disciplinary board. My results improved considerably in the upper fourth form, reaching 2a, and in the fifth form there was a complete change – a surprise for my teachers: I behaved irreproachably and was given a mark of 1b, ending my *Abitur* 'top in all subjects' [. . .].
>
> I studied law from 1928 to 1931 in Leipzig, with one semester in Heidelberg in 1930. I passed my degree with merit.[21]

Gräfe came from an educated home, but one that had been shaken by the death of his father at the front: his schooldays were difficult. The way he swung things round simply makes his career all the more exceptional. He went on to get a result only rarely achieved in the *Staatsexamen*. His path was that of a war orphan, a rebel from childhood onwards. Indeed, he claimed to have seen the labour organization as an 'opportunity for young people to establish a united front against the government of old men'.[22] This also found expression, perhaps, in his difficult school career. Gräfe stands out by the way he describes his path, but his career followed a quite common course: he entered the civil service and the magistracy before joining the Gestapo, then, in 1938, the SD. [23] Mentioning the marks he obtained in the course of his studies thus seems to have formed part of a strategy: like him, other SS candidates sought to highlight their achievements when writing their *Lebensläufe*. However, other men in his position did nothing of the kind. Wilhelm Spengler passed his doctorate summa cum laude,[24] but makes no mention of this in his autobiographical documents.[25] The image of the group is that of students who, in spite of the intensity of their associative lives and the financial problems that often obliged them to find work during their studies, had certain achievements under their belts: they were good pupils, in short. By the criteria of the time, some of them even enjoyed a reputation for brilliance.

This image, however, rests on the criteria laid down by their contemporaries. And, from 1933 onwards, these criteria could seem rather out of line with those of other European universities. The example of Franz Six is an example of this mismatch. He studied history, sociology and journalism in Mannheim and Heidelberg. His CV is unusual in that it seems based on an apparently very modern apprehension of the social sciences: indeed, there is something quite astonishing about it. Registering for eight semesters at two universities, he took his doctorate and *Habilitation* in rapid succession. When the Nuremberg judges read these theses, however, they were taken aback: the two documents combined amounted to no more than a hundred pages or so. Furthermore, the *apparatus criticus* of the dissertation was composed of quotations from Hitler and Goebbels, which led the American judges to view Six as a 'scholarly charlatan'.[26] Still, though he may occasionally have come under attack from Nazis who deplored the lack of rigour of his work, he still passed for a researcher of high calibre in Nazi academic circles. While he has become the typical example quoted every time people deny that Nazi 'scholars' had any real intellectual heft, his apparent mediocrity seems belied by his spectacular reinstatement after the war, and by the fact that his students occupied posts in the most prominent main media of Federal Germany.

But not all students saw their qualities questioned after the war. Wilhelm Spengler was born in 1907, in Ratholz in Allgäu. After secondary schooling in Catholic religious establishments, he pursued studies in electronics and engineering in an *Oberrealschule* (higher technical school). He then dropped these subjects and registered to read German history, philosophy, art history, linguistics and biology. So his CV had several centres of interest, with an unusual balance between sciences and humanities. His marked liking for the latter finally led him to choose a subject taken from German literature for his doctorate. On 16 and 17 July, Wilhelm Spengler, who had submitted his thesis a few months earlier, took his viva in front of the assembled faculty. He was questioned for two whole days on 'Merovingians and Carolingians', on the capitulary *De Villis*, on the reign of Louis XIV and on the nineteenth century. In literature, he sweated his way through questions on language in the Middle Ages, and had to translate passages from the Latin; in philosophy, he was asked about Kant's *Critique of Judgement*, Schiller's philosophical prose and Goethe's writings. In all these disciplines, Spengler obtained a distinction: his seventeen interrogators were unanimous. In tandem with this, his doctorate was

given two *Gutachten*, i.e. two highly flattering assessments.[27] The second
reader of Spengler's thesis wrote:

> In addition, the wealth of ideas put forward by the author can easily be seen
> from the table of contents. I entirely subscribe to the author's views. I have
> to say that the present thesis is among the best of anything I have ever read
> on the essence of tragedy in Schiller. I myself have learned a great deal from
> reading this thesis.[28]

Only some reservations about his style prevented Spengler from
obtaining a summa cum laude. All his examiners agreed on the exceptional character of the work and on the candidate's intellectual stature.
And yet Spengler was at that time far removed from the conservative
political culture of his interlocutors. From the very start of his literary
studies, he had set out the terms of his method: for him, the important
thing was to 'teach our ideological and ethical values linked to a Teutonic
and German spiritual heritage', in 'opposition to the Catholic supervision' prevalent in the technical school he had just left in order to enter
the philosophy faculty. On entering the SS, he continued to use this kind
of language to give meaning to his teaching activity: his 'main mission'
was 'to give the higher classes concrete connections with the ideological
value of the Teutonic-German spiritual heritage'.[29] His case illustrates
the specific character of a group of SS intellectuals who, as they built up
their knowledge base, combined academic excellence with *völkisch* and
Nazi political activism. It is this relationship between activism and the
academic disciplines that we now need to investigate, bearing in mind
that the major break of 1933 was really the initial step in merging the two
elements together.

Knowledge and activism, 1919–1933

One of the most stubborn prejudices about the history of academic
knowledge under the Weimar Republic and the Third Reich concerns the
way the disciplines were demarcated: it is claimed that one discipline,
either 'technical' or 'objective', resisted the rise of the Nazis and their
racial paradigms, while another, ideologically more 'susceptible', fell
prey to the elaborations of Nazi doctrine. Some academic subjects, on this
reading, represented a *via media*, which was perverted by a minority of
'black sheep'.[30]

Law, it is averred, was the archetype of a 'technical' subject that, before
1933, resisted the 'ideologization' of knowledge. In this respect, the attitude of the lawyers in our group has hitherto appeared as the model of a
discipline that was sheltered from the outside by the technical nature of
its themes.[31] In this way, Werner Best's doctoral thesis was an archetyp-
ally 'technical' thesis, quite unaffected by Nazi doctrine.[32] His doctorate

was an essay on the right to work: it was favourable to the rights of employers, but did not provide any theory in support of a Nazi right to work.[33] Hans Nockemann's thesis also produced an impression of technical objectivity and 'apoliticism'. It dealt with the economics of the Ruhr coal industry, but did not highlight its author's *völkisch* commitments.[34] The same applies to the theses of Alfred Filbert,[35] Ernst Hermann Jahr,[36] Friedrich Tiedt[37] and Hermann Behrends.[38] But this is not all we can say about the relationship between the academic discipline of law and Nazi doctrine. (And in any case, not all the subjects studied by lawyers confirm these initial observations.)

The economic sciences, an optional subject chosen by the majority of lawyers, sometimes revealed interests that were very focused on contemporary issues. Hans Leetsch's thesis on the role of public markets in the development of the financial crisis constitutes a good example of an attempt to theorize state planning conceived as an alternative to socialist planning, here seen as its foil.[39] Otto Ohlendorf's thesis did not show any sign of his link to Nazism. And yet he is known to have worked with Jens Jessen on a Nazi economic theory, based on logistical control and the inner market of the middle classes.[40] Appointed librarian at the Institute of Applied Sciences in Berlin, he took part in a research group investigating the political sciences and economics.[41] After the Nazis came to power, he thus legitimated policies of self-sufficiency, while recommending a reform of the circuits of distribution of consumer goods, so as to put into practice the ideal of a prosperous life for the Nazi *Volksgemeinschaft*.[42] Economics was not just an academic subject for Ohlendorf, but a front for militant activity. He does of course represent a particular type: his career, stamped from the start by the influence of Nazism, and the intensity of his work on establishing doctrinal formulae for economics made him into a very specific cog in the machine. Still, many academic economists were, as he was, involved in the Reich's economic policies, whether this means home policies or the economic mechanisms developed in order to legitimate the desire for expansion.[43] Götz Aly and Susanne Heim have brilliantly brought out the role played by the *Institut für Staatsforschung*, as well as the Institute for World Economy in Kiel and the universities of Königsberg and Breslau, in this development.[44] More broadly, the instrumentalization of economics, a subsidiary subject to law studies, undermines the image put forward by Ulrich Herbert of 'rational' lawyers pursuing 'apolitical' studies.[45] For them, economics comprised an intellectual bridge between contributing to academic disciplines on the one hand, and activism on the other. There was no distinction in such men between the serious, 'neutral' student and the Nazi activist: they were both of these things, simultaneously. Literary studies are evidence of this.

History, geography, sociology and ethnology comprised the spearhead of the 'sciences of legitimation'. Before 1933, the theses of future SS intellectuals quite often reflected preoccupations that betrayed their *völkisch* world-view. A good example is the Hamburg group of historians. Richard Frankenberg, Siegfried Engel and Hans Joachim Beyer all produced doctoral theses between 1927 and 1931. All three were, when they finished their theses, already involved in activist networks. But, leaving aside the positivism of their methods and problematics, their theses are imbued with the *völkisch* mental world in which they were immersed.

In 1927, Richard Frankenberg submitted a study on the 'non-renewal of the German–Russian treaty in 1890', at the University of Hamburg.[46] This seems far removed from the *völkisch* social history of Hans Rothfels: Frankenberg's work is in line with classical diplomatic history, though the subject of his thesis is not quite as 'apolitical' as its title suggests. The event in question, after all, played a decisive role in the changes in Germany diplomacy at the end of the nineteenth century. After the 1870–1 war, the German Empire set up a diplomacy founded on the alliance of the three emperors which, combined with mistrust of Great Britain, left France completely isolated. On 18 June 1887, Germany signed with Russia a so-called 'counter-assurance' treaty, stipulating that Germany would remain neutral if Austria attacked Russia. The subject of Frankenberg's thesis was an attempt to explain the mechanisms leading to the non-renewal of this treaty in 1890, which was the death knell of the Bismarckian diplomatic system: Russia, feeling threatened by Austro-Hungary, sought support in the west and in 1893 engineered a rapprochement with France. At the same time, England, worried by the change in German diplomacy and the *Weltpolitik* indicated by the expansion of the fleet, made overtures to the French–Russian alliance. So the non-renewal of this treaty thus entailed the formation of the Entente Cordiale and shaped the Triple Alliance, the system of forces that faced each other at the time of the Great War.[47] Frankenberg adopted a strictly causal approach to the formulation of his thesis: he viewed the non-renewal of the treaty as one of the causes of the 1914–18 war and the formation of the 'world of enemies' depicted by Beumelberg. On the other hand, the way the German attitude was seen as quite innocent in this affair contributed to minimizing the Reich's role in the polarization of international relations, and thus attenuating the German guilt which the Treaty of Versailles so heavily emphasized. So, in this apparently traditional thesis subject, issues regarding historical memory are crucial, and involve a struggle over the revision of the Treaty of Versailles.[48] Though Richard Frankenberg's thesis was not Nazified in the terms it used or the problematics it selected, it nonetheless reflected the world-view of *völkisch* students, as well as the continuing impact of the Great War on their behaviour.

The thesis of his colleague Siegfried Engel is astonishingly close to Frankenberg's preoccupations: Engel opted to study Austro-Hungary and Russia from 1870 to 1890,[49] in other words during the period immediately prior to that investigated by Frankenberg. The former sought to understand why Germany did not renew the treaty studied by the latter. In his view, the stumbling block of the Bismarckian system was the Balkan problem, which divided Russia's two allies: Austria had vital interests on the coasts of Dalmatia, in Bosnia and Croatia, while Russia had based autocracy on a pan-Slavic ideology and posed as a protector of Serbia. Germany's two allies had a tense relationship and in 1890 Wilhelm II decided to emphasize the alliance with Austria.[50] Engel, like Frankenberg, produced a causal study of German decisions and, like Frankenberg, cleared Germany of any blame.

Of course, nobody would claim that classical German historiography took the side of Nazism. However, these young intellectuals were not entirely innocent in their choice of subject. Such topics involved real issues, and led to conclusions which the entire German academic world, whether Nazi or not, could not fail to endorse. True, these theses contain no trace of Nazi racial determinism, but they were conceived as a commitment to 'the German cause'.[51] An attempt to demonstrate, through rigorous and 'objective' study, the absence of any German responsibility in the unleashing of war was surely one of the intellectual dimensions of the *Abwehrkampf*?

In short, the self-proclaimed objectivity of the subjects of doctoral theses in history here seems to have been symptomatic of specific academic practices. Ethnology, sociology and geography were increasingly involved in a study of the consequences of the war, including the preservation of *volksdeutsch* minorities outside the Reich's borders. As we have seen, future SS intellectuals did not remain aloof from these debates or from this political commitment. On this occasion, German academic productivity was invaded by the political sphere. However, it is almost impossible to detect any references to the NSDAP, to Hitler or to Nazi racial and anti-Semitic determinism. This absence suggests that we should ponder the nature of Nazism and political activism, and the relations between the construction of doctrine and the production of scientific and scholarly knowledge.[52] In every subject, with the exception perhaps of law, we have the impression that the themes chosen fitted in with contemporary debates in German society. So what happened was less a Nazification of scholarly practices than a clear politicization of research, combined with a continued endorsement of the ambition of scholarly objectivity. So the themes chosen for research reflected the preoccupations of committed *völkisch* students and demonstrated the kinship between the system of representations and Nazi racial fundamentalism.

One final case study will allow us to grasp more fully the relations between knowledge and political commitment, and to open up new perspectives on the objectivity of legal knowledge. Hermann Behrends and Georg Herbert Mehlhorn were both lawyers, and both took their doctorates before 1933, with very good marks. Their thesis subjects show no sign of Nazification, even though this is overt elsewhere.[53] Does this mean that we here have a case of a watertight separation between legal knowledge and political commitment? Not at all. In fact, at the end of their doctoral studies, both men, members of the NSDAP and the SS, placed their juridical expertise at the service of their Party activities: Mehlhorn became the official counsel of the NSDAP in Chemnitz, while Behrends became a legal advisor for the Party.[54] What we have here is an instrumentalization, not of legal theory, but rather of legal knowledge placed at the service of Party aims. The activism is that of experts giving the benefit of their knowledge to a particular cause – a counterpart to the politicization of knowledge. In the case of 'technical' knowledge, the relation between knowledge and activism is expressed mainly by the invasion of the political field by expertise, not by the invasion of the scholarly field by ideology. This explains the apparently apolitical quality of the legal work carried out by future SS intellectuals. After 1933, however, the latter, if they were still students, demonstrated their ideological commitments more overtly in their scholarship.

'Combative science' and SS intellectuals in the Third Reich

The Nazification of knowledge and its acquisition continued throughout the Third Reich, combining an institutional dimension (made concrete in the progressive takeover of the places of scholarly production), a scientific dimension (with major changes in the human sciences) and an individual dimension (thanks to the increased visibility of the Nazi belief system in the theses submitted). This process, given a different slant in each discipline and each institution, was characterized by an increasing permeability between the construction of knowledge, political commitment, and activity in the NSDAP or even the SD. It was embodied, for example, in a historical practice that was increasingly influenced by the SS and the SD: *völkisch* 'legitimating history' was thus transformed into Nazi 'militant science'.

In 1933, the student activist networks, academic institutions and organs of repression of the Third Reich pooled their resources, and together organized conferences and publications. The scholarly review *Volk im Werden* [*The 'Volk' and its Evolution – Tr.*] was founded by Ernst Krieck, who held a tenured chair in political science at Heidelberg, where he was also the rector. Krieck wrote several works on the construction of Nazi ideology and the education system.[55] The launch of *Volk im Werden* was aimed at sparking debate between Nazi theorists. Krieck himself set out to develop a Nazi theory of '*völkisch* political anthropology', which rapidly led to a confrontation with Alfred Rosenberg, the official theorist of the Nazi faith and future minister of the Reich's Occupied Territories.[56] In 1936, Krieck decided to widen the review's editorial board, drawing on the Nazi academic microcosm of the University of Heidelberg. Franz Six and Gustav Adolf Scheel were appointed to the committee, while Six became editor in chief. The journal published articles on political science, on 'literature', on *Auslandskunde* (the science of foreign countries and societies), on law and on anthropology. With Six and Scheel, a whole swathe of the young guard of SD intellectuals that had emerged from the NSStB published in *Volk im Werden*. Wilhelm Spengler and Walter von Kielpinski dealt with general scientific questions.[57] Franz Six – who delegated his editorial tasks to von Kielpinski – directed studies in *Auslandskunde*,[58] while Hans Joachim Beyer provided studies in the *Volkstumswissenschaften*. Spengler was mainly asked to provide pieces on 'creative liberty in the arts' and on 'woman in the image of the Germanic and Christian world'.[59] That title speaks volumes about the anti-Christian line of the review, which had chosen, to discuss this subject, an SS officer who was most eloquently averse to Christianity,[60] which he deemed 'contrary to the Germanic essence'. Six wrote about the Teutonic heritage in the German spirit,[61] Beyer pondered the relations between 'Germans in the Sudetenland' – who were of course described as oppressed – and the Czechs, considering them in the light of the laws governing individual peoples.[62] All these men opted for themes that were based both on their academic studies or centres of interest – such as Spengler, a specialist in literature and art – and on their work in the SD.

Entire disciplines were taken over – or taken back – and Nazified. A clear example of this phenomenon can be found in *Zeitungswissenschaften* [literally 'the sciences of newspapers' – *Tr.*]. As we have said, the material treated by this discipline could vary quite widely. It combined political science, history, civilization and languages. When Six was appointed to the chair in Königsberg, he took over the entire discipline, organizing a series of publications, and training a generation of young doctoral students who practised *Auslandskunde* under his direction. Several dissertation subjects clearly show the extreme Nazification of the subjects taught and the research problematics. The '*Gegner*', opponents against whom the SD collected documentation and compiled dossiers, became, under Six's guidance, the scientific objects of the ambiguous discipline of *Auslandswissenschaften*. Some theses were written on the basis of traditional forms of espionage and counter-espionage outside the Reich.[63] Other work was devoted to the scientific study of writings produced by 'enemies within'. Rudolf Oebsger-Röder's study, for example, was a statistical work on the journalists of the Weimar Republic, with data collected in files detailing the members of the profession when *Gleichschaltung* was imposed. Paul Mylius wrote a thesis on German jurisprudence and legislation regarding the Jews;[64] Horst Mahnke worked on the Freemasonic press.[65] Here, there was complete fusion between the repressive practices of the SD and a scholarly academic production that, by defining the enemy, played a part in the construction of Nazi doctrine. However, this process came to a conclusion only in 1940. The growing influence of the SD, as spread by younger SS intellectuals who had been students after the *Machtergreifung*, soon made teaching, research, activism and repression inseparable.[66] By this stage, academic knowledge was crucial to the ideological formulations of the SS.

The Nazification of knowledge was not always uniform in shape and intensity. It varied, of course, from subject to subject. Reinhard Höhn's political science, Martin Sandberger's social economics and Wilhelm Albert's 'sciences of education' all enable us to distinguish between more or less lengthy and successful processes. The oldest of them, who had completed their studies before the *Machtergreifung*, produced less Nazified work, even if, as we have seen in the case of Richard Frankenberg, it betrayed the *völkisch* commitments of its author. Reinhard Höhn embodies a second kind of figure, producing *völkisch* work that became progressively more Nazified after he joined the NSDAP and, even more, after the *Machtergreifung*. Sandberger's thesis is an example of a type of knowledge that had not developed in pre-1933 conditions, and so was fostered by Nazis who were already deeply committed or had even attained significant positions of power. After this, total orthodoxy reigned. In the particularly belated case of Wilhelm Albert, the officialization of a specifically Nazi form of knowledge, a knowledge that could be immediately mobilized by government practice, represents a final stage of Nazification, carried out via specialized institutional channels, including the NSStB, the Ministry of Education and, more and more frequently, the SS and the SD.[67]

The case of history and the *Volkstumswissenschaften*, to which I have often alluded in connection with future SS intellectuals such as Beyer, or institutions such as the universities of Königsberg or Bonn, is a perfect example of this phenomenon of Nazification. From the 1920s onwards, a scattering of semi-private foundations, university research institutions and associations of *Volksdeutsche* took over much of the academic research on the countries adjoining the Reich. Throughout the 1920s and 1930s, these institutions carried out work at the crossroads of history, geography, economics, ethnology, demography and sociology.[68] The coming to power of the Nazis was of course an important date for this movement. While these institutions had previously been frequented by the Nazis, these were simply one *völkisch* group among others. Nazi dominance, as embodied in a dual form of supervision, both activist and state-controlled, was only gradually established.

The example of the *Volkswissenschaftliche Arbeitskreise* (VWA) of the *Volksbund für das Deutschtum im Ausland* (VDA) is a perfect illustration of the development of revisionist historiography as a whole. This scientific circle, founded in 1934, was marked by the presence of the most prestigious academic founders of this *völkisch* historiography: Gunther Ipsen, Karl von Loesch, Walter Kuhn, Hans Schwalm, Albert Brackmann, Hermann Aubin and Max Hildebert Boehm.[69] Their presence means that we cannot describe the VDA as a specifically Nazi institution. Its director, Harold Steinacker, was eventually forced out of his post in 1938 by the SS, who wished to push a more radical line. The VWA were akin in every respect to the *Forschungsgemeinschaften* or research communities born in the Weimar Republic, and were thus part of the same tradition as the *völkisch* organizations in spite of their belated foundation, contemporary with the Nazi *Gleichschaltung*. However, the years 1934–9 were marked by the irresistible rise of a young generation of scholars who gradually modified their disciplines, dominating the secretariat of the organization while forging close links with new proponents of *völkisch* historiography. For instance, Alexander Dolezalek took over the organization of the VWA study days, while working towards his *Examen* in Schleswig.[70] He soon found himself working alongside the group of young SD intellectuals made up of Engel, Frankenberg and Beyer, who very frequently attended VWA meetings.[71] Between 1936 and 1939, the four men, to whom we might add Fritz Valjavec, Ernst Turowsky and Wilhelm Spengler, joined the SD, combining scientific research, activism, and surveillance and repression.[72] It was this generation that, as we shall see, after the invasion of Poland, found itself in a position where it could have a direct impact on reality, in so far as it was now presented with the possibility of applying its work to the reshaping of populations and areas in East Europe.[73]

This mechanism of Nazification by trans-generational renewal can also be observed in the development of the themes of conferences, as well as in the bibliographies of reference works appended to the circular letters sent out by the VWA.[74] One conference, held on 5 and 6 January 1939 in Bayreuth, is a good example of the degree of Nazification attained and its impact on the historiographical practice of VWA members. The main speaker at the session was Kleo Pleyer, the successor to Hans Rothfels at Königsberg. Trained in Bonn and Königsberg, Pleyer's appointment as head of the VWA marked the generational shift that accompanied Nazification.[75] Although he belonged neither to the SD, nor to the SS, his contributions to the conference and his discussions with participants such as Hans Joachim Beyer and Alexander Dolezalek show that the attendees shared a way of looking at, and writing, history, a common practice of providing evidence, and an identical, and total, support of Nazi racial determinism.

At this conference, Kleo Pleyer opened the proceedings with a paper on *'völkisch* policy' and the *völkisch* scientific mission in the Sudetenland. Exulting at the return of the Sudetenland to the bosom of the Reich, he emphasized that:

> The scientific labour of awaking the will, developed in border conflict and always evaluated by its criteria, has over the last twenty years been directed towards the south-east quarter of the Reich and of German territory, which is now incorporated [. . .]. What is needed now is to build up the Reich's inner unity from its borders and in particular to unify the *Deutschtum* [Germandom – *Tr.*][76] of the south-east with the old *Deutschtum* of the Reich.[77]

Pleyer went on to describe the task of each of the *Volkstumswissenschaften* in this 'mission'. As he enumerated them, he restored the hierarchy of knowledge within Nazi culture: the first 'science' mentioned was raciology; the second, history; then came sociology and ethnology, then Slavic studies, seen as an auxiliary science with a strong practical dimension. There was a general agreement on Pleyer's programme. The discussions that ensued did not question either its form or its content, and merely highlighted the delegates' endorsement of the biologism affirmed by Pleyer. In particular, there was a proposal to draw up the family tree of important foreign personalities to prove their Germanic origins. In reply to a Hungarian attempt to demonstrate the 'Magyar' ancestry of Dürer, the VWA decided to reply by drawing up a purely Germanic line of descent for the painter. At this point, we are in a world where proof of value is derived from one's bloodline and forebears. There was general assent to these measures – an assent which amounted to agreement.

This conference came at the end of the process of Nazification of knowledge. At that time, most SS intellectuals had left university and joined the SD. Those who wrote theses now did so within the framework of their work within the repressive bodies of the Third Reich. This was the case with a certain number of members of the RSHA *Amt* VII who, between 1940 and 1943, did their doctorates under the joint scholarly supervision of Franz Six and the historian and *Hauptsturmführer* SS Günther Franz.[78] But these limit cases do not demonstrate any ongoing construction of knowledge, let alone any process of Nazification, since these two mechanisms were now fully effective, as they had long been. In 1940, Hans Joachim Beyer submitted a *Habilitation* thesis on the processes of 'assimilation and dissemination'. His study was focused on racial and biological studies within populations, and made miscegenation one of the main factors in the history of the population of Europe, as well as the United States – which was doomed to mongrelization and decadence as a result of racial mixing.[79] This text, of course, comprises a stage in the construction of Nazi doctrine, but it cannot be considered to be an additional step in the process of Nazification, which was by now completely achieved. By now, this habitué of the VWA had already been a member of the 'Black Order' for five years. On the institutional level, Beyer now had nothing in common with those radical anti-Semitic students engaged in the *Volkstumskampf* of the years 1919–21: he had a doctorate and a *Habilitation*, and was appointed to a chair in Posen and then Prague. And, as an SS officer collaborating with one of the bureaus responsible for expelling *fremdvölkisch* elements, 'foreign to the people',[80] he was one of those who 'conceived the annihilation'.[81]

The shadow of the Great War

Once they had obtained their degrees, SS intellectuals found jobs without much difficulty. The lawyers, having taken their *Staatsexamen* and doctorate, joined the magistracy; the literary students became teachers in secondary schools and higher schools, while others aimed for a university career and continued their studies by taking a *Habilitation*, while occupying an assistant's post. All of them, in fact, soon found themselves in a position to join the Nazi Party and, even more, forced to confront the choice between *hauptamtlich* (professional) service in the SD and a professional career. Any sense of social failure, in any case, seems to have been quite foreign to them.

What is striking, in the final analysis, about their careers is the shadow cast by the Great War. Their time as children and students was spent in a Germany plunged into the First World War and then into a time of troubles that lasted until the apparent normalization of the Stresemann era. The latter has been basically well explored by the historians of diplomacy, but did it have the same meaning for the students of our group? These men experienced their studies as a fertile experience of acquisition of knowledge that, far from passing itself off as some mythical form of objectivity, was overtly a 'science of legitimation'. They became part of precociously radicalized networks of association, which deployed intense political activity presented as a defensive struggle against a universal and Protean enemy, an enemy which, on the 'home front', took the shape of the Spartacist, the Social Democrat, the separatist and – already – a Jewishness to which they were profoundly hostile. On the foreign front, it was the fight on behalf of 'oppressed' German minorities that focused most of the preoccupations of the *völkisch* students of the time. This commitment included armed struggle in the *Freikörper* between 1918 and 1921, in resistance to the French in the Rhineland and the Ruhr, and in activism on the borders of Germany throughout the period. In each case, the struggle was viewed as defensive in nature; in each case, the danger menacing Germany and the Germans was, in their opinion, a deadly threat that questioned the very foundations of the existence of Germany as a state, as a nation and even as a biological entity. No one can fail to see this as the simple transposition of the legitimating culture that took shape during the First World War. It is just as if this culture had emerged preserved and even reinforced from the Great War, to live on in a now vanquished Germany.

Did SS intellectuals, as children of that war, ever feel that they had 'emerged from the war'[82] during that period? We may well doubt this: the driving force behind their commitment and their attitudes seems to have been, in the final analysis, the interpretative grid that took shape in 1914, which gave meaning to the defeat, seeing the latter as part of the 'desire for annihilation' that in their view was harboured by the 'world of enemies'; such an interpretation led them to re-envisage, from the point of view of a defensive *Volkstumskampf*, the difficult inter-community relations in the countries created by the peace treaties, to decry the alleged impotence of the traditional parties to forestall the 'inexorable decline' they associated with a Weimar Germany bearing the brunt of the economic crisis, and, finally, to analyse the invasion of the Ruhr by France – an invasion mainly motivated by financial considerations – as the final blow meant to smash Germany and corrupt its biological substance by sending in colonial troops.

Was this period between the wars not actually an interminable war, a war that these men waged by their associative activism, but also, in certain cases, by their scientific careers? Did they not all try, to a greater or less degree, to choke off the rising panic of eschatological anguish that sprang from the Great War and seems never to have left them throughout their studies? And was it not precisely this muted anxiety that turned their adolescence and their years of study into an activist quest that found what it was looking for only when they endorsed the system of beliefs of Nazism?

Part II

Joining the Nazis: a commitment

Chapter 4

Being a Nazi

When interrogated by his judges at Nuremberg, Franz Six, the former director of *Amt* VII of the RSHA and chief of a commando brigade in *Einsatzgruppe* B, came up with an explanation of why he had committed himself to Nazism, and how he viewed it. His testimony, implicitly aimed at clearing himself – he was faced with a possible death sentence – was the product of a creative reshaping of his past, and deserves close analysis:

> In those years, for me and my whole generation, the NSDAP programme didn't mean anything, or not much [. . .]. There were the interpreters of Feder and the interpretation of Rosenberg, there was a Spann school, there was a Krieck school, *Westideologie, Ostideologie* [west ideology, east ideology – *Tr.*], there were those who supported a Germanic belief in God and positive Christians [. . .].[1]

One can see this statement as the first step in a defence strategy when faced with a court convinced, in Six's view, that the Nazis were bent on extermination right from the start. Certain historians have thought they could find in this kind of remark proof of the lack of any ideological content to Nazism.[2] And the movement did present itself in a way sufficiently loose to give rise to quite different interpretations. If we are to understand Nazism, we need to bring out the lowest common denominator which Nazis endorsed. If we look at the different 'interpretations' of Nazism quoted by Six, we find there is an extreme disparity between the various ideological trends. The highly economicist and socialist Nazism of Feder is at the opposite end of the spectrum to the Nordicist Nazi philosophy of Rosenberg; *Ost*- and *Westideologie* are diametrically opposed geopolitical theories;[3] while, on yet another level, the *völkisch* neo-pagans were quite different from German Christians, who tried to reconcile their support for Nazism with Protestantism. So can we still speak of *one* Nazism?

All these trends, whatever their influence, nonetheless share common points, inherited partly from the *völkisch* movement and reshaped.[4] They all have in common a way of basing their arguments on categories with a biological foundation.[5] They all formulate for the future a plan to reinvent a Germany perceived as diminished on a new sociobiological foundation.[6] These two characteristics comprised a consensus within the federation of groups around the NSDAP and its organizations, structuring the movement and forming the centre of its doctrinal constellation.

The foundations of the doctrine

I have no intention here of proposing a synthesis of the raciology deployed in the Nazi interpretation of facts. Instead, I wish to focus on a study of the way a raciological interpretative grid was used in the discursive practices of SS intellectuals. This discourse, even if it acquired specific characteristics through its scholarly and scientific formulation, was tailored into a flexible grid through which meaning could be given to the surrounding world, to history and to one's self.

The Nazi reading of the world found its referential system in the Nordicist raciology of Hans F. K. Günther.[7] In an attempt to differentiate between the concepts of race, *Volk* or *Völkergruppe* [people or group of peoples – *Tr.*], he borrowed from Eugen Fischer a normative definition of race: 'Anthropology includes race as a group of human beings bound together and differentiated from other groups by the common hereditary possession of a precise congenital physical and spiritual habitus.' From this he deduces that it is practically impossible to find anywhere on earth a 'human group that has remained closed', with a pure racial inheritance. 'All the peoples of western countries', he writes, 'constitute racially mixed populations, in which all the European races or at least several European races are represented in definite proportions.' The differences between peoples are thus, in his view, based on differences in combinations of miscegenation.

After these preliminary definitions, Günther continues his discussion with a description of the ideal racial types whose combinations have played a role in forming the population of Europe. He sketches a picture of a Europe that is an aggregate of peoples. Günther, a pupil of Gobineau, is hostile to miscegenation. He contrasts the supporters of a 'Germanic race' with the concept of an 'Aryan race' developed by his old mentor: this he calls the 'Nordic race'.[8] Seven races collectively comprise the population of Europe.[9] Günther first describes racial types on the basis of physical criteria. While he seems to insist on the specificity of each race by presenting them successively in terms of their abilities, the photographs that he uses to illustrate each racial type leave little mystery about his Nordicism and the aesthetic qualities he attributes to the Nordic and Falic races. In his view, these form the two proportionally dominant races among the peoples of North Europe, Germany and Scandinavia in particular. He then attributes to the various races 'spiritual' and intellectual characteristics and explains the excellence of the two major races that constitute the basis of the initial (because prehistoric) population of the German area of settlement.[10] In this way, a hierarchy is established between the peoples with a high number of individuals from the Nordic or Falic race, and the rest. The judgement of value is qualified by the higher or lower level of preservation of the purity of the original race: a country of western (Mediterranean) race with a low rate of interbreeding (perhaps he is here thinking of Italy) is given a higher rating than a region such as Galicia, which, having inherited a Nordic populace via German and later Austrian emigration, has still, in Günther's view, been the victim of miscegenation between 'Orientals', 'Ostics', 'Sudetens' and 'Dinarics' on the one hand, and Nordic elements on the other.

While Günther waxes very prolix on the races that populate Europe, he has hardly anything to say about the 'Jewish question'. The Jewish population of Germany, for example, is examined from the perspective of racial determinism and given a coefficient of miscegenation comprising 'Nordic, Oriental and Levantine contributions'. From 1930, Günther, who was at the time writing an entire book on the *Judenfrage*,[11] definitively rejected the idea of any Nordic contribution present in the Jewish 'racial hereditary heritage'. He warned against 'the universally harmful spirit of the Near Eastern race'.[12] Thus, with Günther, whose positions had triumphed in the years 1929–30 within the SS, the three components of the SS biological world-view fused together: racial determinism, Nordicism, and anti-Semitism couched in scholarly jargon. Even though he was far from being the sole point of reference for the SS's racial discourse, he remained the one who formulated the 'Nordic doctrine of races',[13] erecting it into a scientific norm and turning it into the main pillar of the Nazi system of beliefs.

How could this discourse, conceived as theoretical and scientific, condition the sensibilities of SS intellectuals, imbue their system of representations and form a basis for their relationship to the world?

When the Wannsee Institute, the centre for research on East Europe that was integrated into the RSHA, was requested, in spring and summer 1941, to compose a 300-page report on Ukraine, with a view to providing SS officers sent to the Eastern Front with a vade mecum, it opened its study on the geopolitical conditions of existence of Ukraine, before focusing on the racial spectre of the Ukrainian people: space first, then race. This pre-eminence of the geopolitical dimension over raciology should be enough to belie the determinist side of Nazi racism. But that is not really the case, for this geopolitical study actually consisted in establishing that state limits did not correspond to the territory occupied by the Ukrainians as an ethnic group: new borders were laid down, less in relation to the Romanian or Hungarian state than to isolate 'Ukraine-ness' (*Ukrainertum*) from Romanian-ness or Magyar-ness. These traces constituted biological frontiers: it was a matter for the *Ostforscher* of fitting geopolitics to biology.[14] Likewise, the different phases of Ukrainian history were measured by the criterion of the Ukrainian *Volkstumskampf*. There ensued phases of 'Ukrainization' and 'Russification', with this latter – corresponding to the Stalinist collectivization of 1929–30 – being grasped as a Bolshevik attempt to annihilate 'Ukraine-ness'.[15] This purely racial interpretation of an event – the great Ukraine famine of 1932-3 – while ignoring its political, economic and social character, constitutes an archetype of the SS interpretation of the world.

The system of beliefs internalized by the SS intellectuals reformulated history, transforming it into a succession of struggles, confrontations and combats over identity, all marked by the question of ethnicity. Racial determinism thus provided the SS intellectual with a representation of history imbued with immanence, transfigured by providence, and guided by a sense of purpose. Between 1937 and 1942, trainee officers of the SIPO and the SD could take courses on 'Charlemagne and Widukind', the Freemasons, or even Christianity and the movement of German believers.[16]

The course on Charlemagne was an SS staple, despite the obvious ambiguity of the topic. How was one to interpret the confrontation between Widukind, a pagan Saxon hero dear to Himmler, and Charlemagne, the herald of an empire that, for the first time, no longer seemed stained by a Roman-ness that could be integrated with Germandom only at the price of tricky ideological contortions? The author's main concern was to base his interpretation on the immanence of Charlemagne's racial mission, bringing together the Germanic *Sippen* [lineages – *Tr.*] and Nordic blood within a unified state launched into the conquest of the Slavic immensities – an immanence that was providentially embodied in the advent of the Nazi revolution.[17] The author erected these two moments into the foundational moments of a new era. This just left the author to deplore the way the German emperor still owed allegiance to Catholic Rome – an allegiance that led to the fratricidal struggle against Widukind's Saxons, whose paganism is presented as the bastion of resistance to a universalist Roman Christianity. 'Blinded by the Roman forces', Charlemagne, the author claims, 'almost exterminated one of the foundation stones of Germandom'. In short, Charlemagne's reign was, in spite of everything, a 'harsh but useful schooling' for the Germanic tribes who were then subjected to the *Capitulatio de partibus Saxoniae*.[18] This law, which forbade pagan religious practices and set up a new penal system, was analysed by the SS ideologue as a *Blutgesetz*, a law of the blood. He then established a very clear parallel with the *Blutschutzgesetzen* (laws for the protection of the blood) of Nuremberg. Thus the Nordic doctrine of races provided the Nazi discourse on history with two specific characters. In the first place, it turned the *Veniat Imperarii* of the emperor and the Führer into the accomplishment of providence. Then – and perhaps above all – this advent of empire legitimated the necessary racial refoundation: in the eighth as in the twentieth century the two potentates reorganized Germandom and laid down laws to protect its biological substance;[19] in the eighth as in the twentieth century, a purified Nordic Germandom was meant to march off and conquer Slavic immensities.

A second example to confirm this Nazi reinterpretation of history can be found in the Thirty Years War, that 'German catastrophe par excellence'. Franz Six, Günther Franz and Hans Joachim Beyer took an interest in this religious and political conflict that ravaged the Germanic space between 1618 and 1648.[20] From the start, the war was characterized as a Germanic revolution: all the German populations, in fact, united under Lutheranism, and the war was provoked by Catholic aggression. If the narrative took the form of a classically shaped 'evenemential' history, Nordicist providence was incarnated in the person of Gustavus Adolphus, who was discussed at length. The SS pedagogue relished painting the portrait of this blond, tall and slender monarch – one of 'the most honourable figures' ever to have existed – an archetype of the Nordic race who attempted, in the Thirty Years War, to free himself from Roman-ness and Catholic universalism. On the one hand, Gustavus Adolphus was the racially aware champion of a threatened Nordic identity; on the other hand, over and above religious and political factors, the war itself was interpreted as a racial conflict. For Siegfried Engel, the Thirty Years War set the Germanic world against Roman universalism, in this case embodied by the Austrians, whose empire was seen as the 'natural space' of the Alpine race designated by Günther as the immanent enemy of Nordic identity.[21]

After contrasting the opponents and describing Gustavus Adolphus as the sovereign of 'Germanic becoming',[22] the narrator sets out the Swede's plans in these terms:

> Behind this projected marriage lay the plan for a great Germanic Nordic empire that would doubtless have included the other Scandinavian states and the Baltic. [The question of knowing] whether the strong point of such an empire would have been situated in Stockholm or Berlin, whether it was at that time possible to think of uniting Germany and Scandinavia into a single state no longer requires any answer. Thanks to the powerful German cultural influence and the great awareness of a Germanic influence, the king's plan was, in spite of everything, not so far removed from reality as it might appear today.[23]

Interpreting the conflict in terms of the Nordic doctrine here consists of erecting the advent of an empire uniting Scandinavians and Germans into the ultimate aim of the rivalry between Roman universalism and Germandom. But internalizing the Nazi belief system did not merely lead the SS intellectual to racialize current forces and imperial utopias, as the conclusion to his lecture shows:

> Although three hundred years have gone by since the period of the Thirty Years War, the political problem and the aim of our enemies have remained

the same: the definitive partitioning of Germany, and the annihilation of the Reich.

A posteriori, the Thirty Years War can be characterized as the *first* Thirty Years War [. . .].

The period 1789–1815 represents the *second* Thirty Years War, in other words the period of the great French Revolution and the War of German Liberation. After its victorious outcome, the German national feeling was awakened. When the Prussian and Austrian soldiers of the first national-popular army [*Volksheer*] returned to their fatherland, they might have thought that German unity would now at last be realized. The new settling of diplomatic relations, however, preserved the principles of the Peace of Westphalia and Germany was still fragmented. The German tribes [*Stämme*] had seen their hopes for imperial unity stolen away by the nobility.

The foundation of the 'small German' Reich by Bismarck in 1870–71 was indeed a huge leap forward, but the aim was not attained, as Austria was left outside, and the nobles were still in power.

The *third* Thirty Years War started in 1914. The First World War did not reach any solution. The period of apparent laying down of weapons between 1919 and 1939 was the continuation of the war by other means: a political struggle. This was supplemented by open wars waged by the Reich, on the east against the Poles, on the west against France, in the Ruhr.

Today, in 1942, we have entered on the last stage of this third Thirty Years War.

The peace to come, which will bring the third Thirty Years War to a victorious conclusion, and thus the three-century-long struggle for German unity, will bring about at once the definitive surpassing of the Peace of Westphalia in 1648 and this time – as we all know – there will be no half measures.[24]

Siegfried Engel was no propagandist, he spoke as an SS intellectual to SS officers who had all been to university and acquired a historical culture. Germany, the place where there was still a maximum concentration of pure Nordic blood, was called to a providential destiny – whatever the period investigated through the lens of the Nazi belief system. For SS intellectuals, belief in the immanence of Nordic identity gave history its meaning, guiding its course and leading inexorably to the reign of the race, in an unpartitioned country, and regenerated in Germandom.

It was this faith in a collective salvation of Germandom that Otto Ohlendorf, this time expressing his thoughts in the name of his whole generation, formulated at Nuremberg:

We [. . .] studied the history of the human race, its religious history included, as well as the high and low points of states and nations, with the aim of finding an idea that would guide us in the rise and fall of peoples, and indications that would help us to fulfil the demands of our age, demands that issued from the experiences and sufferings of history.[25]

Describing Nazism meant describing the fervour that came with it, and the hope of finding an answer to the riddle of history. In Ohlendorf's case, Nazism was, even though he could not put it like this, a 'quest for race' in history. In the eyes of a generation for which the defeat of 1918 had been a scandalous, senseless absurdity,[26] endorsement of the Nordic racial doctrine provided those who subscribed to it with both a final explanation of the defeat *and* a providential means of redemption. It is futile to seek out any 'super-sense',[27] any interpretation for the initiated:[28] what can be read from the mere expression of the participants is a set of beliefs that belongs to the register of *affects*, producing, in turn, faith and anguish, hope and fervour. Nazism offered its supporters the feeling that the course of history involved a collective salvation through the coming of the empire. The Nazi faith was the 'promise of a reign':[29] a feeling that sprang from the ineffable and from a sense of certainty, mobilizing bodies and souls in the expectation of a racial utopia in which the elect would be made as one.

This system of beliefs, as a determinist grid of interpretation, did not simply set out the destiny of the Nordic nations and race. The need for smaller biological units made an appearance early on, units that linked the individual and his destiny to the great collective entities. The invention of family and lineage, missing links in the chain that bind an individual into history, thus gave the belief system its coherence. In Nazi doctrine, there was an inseparable solidarity between the individual, the family group and the nation, all brought together by genetic heritage.

Even before 1914, the biologist Heinz Weismann had formulated the theory of the 'continuity of the germ plasma', which made of each human being the depositary of the complete genetic inheritance of both mother *and* father. So the child was logically the heir, not just of the couple's genetic inheritance, but also of the set of ancestors on both sides.[30] All that was needed then was to officialize this bond between the individual, as carrier of the 'germ plasma', and his or her ancestors and parents who carried the same or kindred plasma. Seeking to move beyond the nuclear family that took no account of this inseparable mixture of blood and genetics, raciologists and racial hygienists drew on Weismann to remobilize the terms *Stamm* (tribe) and *Sippe* (lineage, kinship).[31] The tribe, a term taken from Germanic tradition, was a kinship whose members came from a single couple of original forebears (*Ureltern*). This tribe could itself be broken down into *Sippen*, lineages that issued from this same couple of original progenitors. An individual's *Sippe* brought together all his or her relations, on the male as well as the female side, both by marriage and by blood. It thus included his or her germ plasma and those acquired by marriage that were then integrated into the genetic inheritance resulting from 'births in becoming': the spouses of the individual's sisters or brothers were thus included in their *Sippe*, but only as a virtual part of it if the individual in question had as yet no nephews or nieces. In the Nazi belief systems, the *Sippe* became the individual's basic reference point, linking

together the living, the dead and the unborn, natural kinship and elec-
tive kinship – all of this suffused by awareness of biological and spiritual
kinship with Nordic identity.

Günther's works were to be found in all the libraries of the intelligence
branch of the SS.[32] The terms *Sippe* and *Stamm*, found infrequently in
doctrinal writings,[33] recur regularly in documents made available to the
Rasse- und Siedlungshauptamt (RuSHA, or SS Race and Settlement Main
Office), an organization which managed marriages within the SS and
granted permission to wed.[34] Some, such as Reinhard Höhn, head of
SDHA II, accepted this dimension of Nazi belief that consisted of making
an individual a present, living link in the immanent chain of germ plasma
that binds the dead 'to what is to come', what is no more with what is not
yet born.[35] After giving his date of birth, Höhn begins his *Lebenslauf* in
these terms:

> My father came from a lineage of peasants [*Bauerngeschlecht*] based in
> Thuringia, with its tribal stock [*stammesmässiger Sitz*] in Franconia. My
> mother is the daughter of the landowner and peasant Reinhard Schneider
> [. . .]. The Schneiders had for centuries lived in Lower Franconia. The
> Schneiders' *Sippe* is mainly comprised of well-off peasants, people who
> worked the land [. . .].
>
> My father's *Sippe* seems to have migrated from Dutch Friesland to
> Franconia. Documents relating to inheritance disputes seem to suggest as
> much, but we do not know. Only the tall stature of my relatives on my
> father's side, all about six feet, indicates as much.[36]

Reinhard Höhn has often been considered to be a *völkisch* lawyer who
was quite hostile to Nordic ideology, and a supporter of the idea of a
'German race'.[37] However, his *Lebenslauf* shows how he internalized the
supranational dimension of the genetic heritage, with his Aryan descent
being in no doubt as far as he was concerned, in spite of his Dutch roots.
After all, was he not the man to whom, in 1937, Himmler entrusted the
organization of the highly esoteric celebration of Henry I the Lion,
the emperor of the Nordicist *Drang nach Osten*? This made Höhn the
master of a ceremony to which only nineteen people were invited, including the dominant figures of SS Nordicism (the heads of the *Ahnenerbe*,[38]
the head of the RuSHA racial department, Professor Schulz, Reinhard
Heydrich, Friedrich Jeckeln[39] and Walter Darré, the minister for agriculture who became the apostle of 'Blood and Soil' ideology within the
Third Reich).[40] Reinhard Höhn was thus part of the very exclusive circle
of men who helped Himmler to carry out the most abstruse rituals of SS
Nordicism.[41]

Establishing the family tree of the *Sippe* at the time of marriage did
not consist merely in identifying one's ancestors, but in specifying their
social history and their health records, setting out dates and causes of
decease, serious illnesses, and deaths resulting from war: the SS aspirant

to marriage thus became the product of this history of health and race. Only a new rite of marriage could sanction this decisive change in lineage. In 1935, the Nazi authorities tried to create a liturgy that would set out an individual's racial responsibilities at the fateful moment when the couple arrived at the town hall to obtain the consent of the *Volksgemeinschaft*.

Here, then, is how the wedding of a young Nazi couple from Posen, a Germanic land won back from the foreign Slavs, was orchestrated in 1941–2.[42] The ceremonial chamber in the town hall was 'simple and dignified': Reich flags with their swastikas, portraits and busts of the Führer, flowers and oak leaves, and a torchère in the shape of the Nordic rune for life. In brown NSDAP uniform, the registrar welcomed the young couple and, in a short address, reminded them of the heritage of 'German man', celebrating the 'extraordinary events, periods and turning points of his life' with particular solemnity. He made of this pronounced taste for ceremonial an 'integral part of the German soul', which derived from his 'ardent desire for internalization and community'. An adolescent from the Hitler Youth and a young girl from the League of German Girls, its female equivalent, then recited in turn a poem by Herbert Menzel:

Look! We hold above you the Banner.
Look! We have lit the Flame.
God is here and Germany and the Ancestors,
You are captive to the eternal People [. . .].
To venture on plighting this troth
is granted to the pure in blood and soul alone.
He alone, having measured up to these demands, will dare
to say 'yes' here, before the People and before God.

Thus edified as to their responsibilities, the couple gave their consent in turn, gave each other their hands and, while the orchestra struck up Haydn's Emperor Quartet (the Reich national anthem), the registrar proclaimed, while giving the German salute, 'In the name of the Reich, you are now legitimate husband and wife.' They were given the 'booklet of the German family' on which two edifying sentences were written: 'Your life is bound to that of your people' and 'The earth will increase in your grandchildren.' The newlyweds signed the marriage certificate, while a representative of the Party, an activist of the Union of German Women and a soldier of the Wehrmacht stood up in turn and recited poetry by Menzel.

The Party member said:

Man awakens in the pact that binds him to his comrades.
His aim is honour and his glory lies in action.
Though young, he must already face up to heavy tasks,
as his people's soldier, he lays claim on them.
Thus man after man rises, disciplined, bearing a weapon,

and around him flourishes the growing lineage,
a people of men fighting on behalf of their honour,
a people of men fighting for what is theirs by right.

Then the Nazi woman recited:

In such a people, the women serve in silence.
They are the homeland and they are the house.
When men take on the risk, they offer them their trust.
They are the parents of the works accomplished by their men.
They are the joyous mothers of proud sons:
They desire them, the consummation of their glory.
They bear throughout the years all that is beautiful,
They labour for a higher humanity.

Finally, the soldier declaimed:

We are the people who await in the dawn;
we are the people of the great return.
He has come who will lead us to victory;
In his fist is the badge of our honour.
At this momentous hour, let us think great thoughts:
listen to God and Germany in the sounds of the lyre [. . .].

The registrar continued, declaring that the couple 'bear within them the idea of Germany', and he defined the roles of the man and the woman. The latter 'must make her home an expression of German identity'. He emphasized the 'need for women who recognize the divine order of the world', in other words for women who endorsed, as did 80 per cent of the wives of SS intellectuals, the neo-pagan *gottgläubig* doctrine (belief in God [albeit not of a Christian kind – *Tr*.]).[43]

Then came the most 'sacred' moment of the ceremony; the registrar addressed the couple:

In front of you burn two fires, one on each of the two arms of the rune of life. They symbolize the vital flux of the two lineages [*Sippen*] from which you sprang. By saying 'yes', you have declared that the vital fluxes are united, that they are to flow together into a new flame of life.

On the word of the celebrant, the newlyweds approached and lit the candles on the torchère. They listened to the final admonition, the one that instructed them from henceforth to be guardians of ancestral Nordic identity:

See at this sacred moment rising before your eyes the future and the past. It is there, before you, the endless chain of our ancestors. The blood that flows in your veins once belonged to them. Your faith was their faith, your will was their will. The ardent desire and the goal nursed in your hearts burned, in bygone days, in their hearts. Now they are turning on you their grave eyes, to see whether you are following and obeying the law from which you have sprung.

And the spaces are filled behind you: your hands can already sense the children and the children's children born from your blood. Their trust exhorts you to do your duty [. . .].

This moment that unites you is the minute [when] the dead ancestors hold out their hands to those who are not yet born.

After this solemn moment, the ceremony continued with the exchange of rings, in sign of the eternity promised by the Nordicist doctrine. Endorsing this racial doctrine meant finding within biological immanence a discourse on death, but also a discourse on the responsibility of the individual, who held the destiny of Germandom as well as that of his or her ancestors and descendants.

This type of ceremony, which remained optional throughout the Third Reich in spite of pressure from the local Party authorities, is one of the signs of the way the Nazi belief system was internalized. Furthermore, this was the moment when Nazism most clearly assigned a place to every individual, 'racially aware and militant'. Georg Herbert Mehlhorn, *Oberführer* SS and former head of SDHA I, later vice-director of the administration of the Warthegau, and thus one of those who drew up the policies of Germanization in that region,[44] married in the town hall of Posen.[45] *Gottgläubig* like his wife, how could he have failed to welcome with fervour this militant admonition, an invitation to listen to the voice of the ancestors and to conform to their heritage, offering them – as he did – a descendant who arrived exactly nine months after the wedding?[46]

The origins of Nazi fervour: planning a sociobiological re-establishment

In his 'Short raciology of the German people', Günther expressed for the broadest public the Nordicist vision of the Great War. He drew inspiration from the American Madison Grant, who stated in 1917: 'the present European conflict is essentially a civil war and nearly all the officers and a large proportion of the men on both sides are members of this [Nordic] race'.[47] As a civil war between Nordic peoples, the Great War was also a racial war in the sense that it set the French, 'westerners' and allies of the 'Ostic' Russians against the Austro-German Nordic bastion. It was the advanced level of miscegenation of the European peoples which, in Günther's view, transformed this racial war into a fratricidal war springing from the most tragic and complex causes: the best of each camp, represented by respective officer castes, was composed of those Nordic 'characteristics' (*Einschläge*) that every people bears within itself. At this point of his demonstration, Günther then disclosed what for him was the quintessence of European evolution.

> All races involved in the miscegenation of European peoples that led to the war took part in the world war to a tangibly equal degree, but the much higher proportion of losses among the officers signifies a much more profound annihilation caused by the war, as far as the Nordic race is concerned.[48]

In a word, the biological substance of the German people was in danger. Racial determinism illuminated this eschatological anxiety. It played a revelatory role, giving the conflict, for the Nordicists, a deeper meaning. But the war had not ended the process of de-Nordification of Germany: quite the opposite.

> The birth rate is rising in Europe from east to west and from south to north, unlike [the division of] the Nordic race. It is rising more in the lowest social classes than in the upper ones, again the opposite to [the division of] the Nordic race. There thus appears a counter-movement, directed against the ancient Nordic waves of settlement towards the west and the south, as well as an increase in the lower social classes of the western peoples, those poorest in Nordic blood.[49]
>   [. . .] The world war, seen raciologically, has led to [. . .] an acceleration in the process of de-Nordification [. . .]. It is clear that the loss of genetic heritage of the Nordic race [. . .] would also find expression in the spiritual behaviour of the German people.[50]

The spread of Nordicism – which was quite real, as witness the 43,000 copies of the 'Short raciology' sold by Günther[51] – thus seems to have been a reaction, then a re-establishment in accordance with a process of racial hygiene, eugenic selection and a spread of racial consciousness.[52]

In 1930, the dominance of Nordicists in the Party organizations became evident, especially after the split of the Strasser brothers and the arrival on the political scene in Thuringia of Wilhelm Frick. He was the first Nazi activist to obtain a major portfolio, in a *Land* that was very early distinguished by its eugenicist policies.[53] In 1931 and 1932, the SS, via Himmler and Darré, officialized support for the Nordicist doctrine by a series of directives on marriage and genealogical research.[54] The 'Black Order' or SS sought to pose as the cutting edge of a sociobiological re-establishment now seen as the distinctive badge of Nazism.

In fact, the SS embodied Germany's future. If we forget that, for the Nazis, what was valid for the SS today would be valid for the whole of Germany tomorrow, we will completely fail to understand what the Black Order could represent, including for the Party members most hostile to Himmler. In this way, SS candidates were instructed in the 1932 directives to take a raciological examination based uniquely on their phenotype. The candidate, classified on a scale of values with five levels, from 'pure Nordic' to 'traces of extra-European ancestry', then had his aptitude for entering the Black Order evaluated. Only those in the first two categories, which brought together those of mainly Nordic or Falic ancestry, were accepted. A 'Nordic appearance' meant a height of more than 1.74 metres, clear dolichocephaly and light-coloured hair. There was also an age limit (around thirty).[55] But over and above the rather summary examination of SS candidates, the Nordicist influence acquired a social dimension through the 'total registering' (*restlose Erfassung*) of SS members in a 'Book of *Sippen*'.[56] In its recruitment by physical examination and its use of a racial-ideological questionnaire, the SS sought to be avant-garde. By setting up so soon a registry of *Sippen*, it also claimed to be the first 'Nordic genetic continent' to be mapped completely, before Germandom as a whole, as a prelude to a great eugenic policy that, in the view of the Nazis, was to be 'scientific',[57] being founded on Günther's principles and the 'empirical cartography' of the Book of *Sippen*.[58]

The SS did not just assume a symbolic role as a precursor body: it wanted to play an active part. One of its first aims was to integrate the wave of Nordicist research and subsume it under its militant organizations. It thus took over the Faculty at Jena, a bastion of racial physical anthropology, and – thanks to Dr Frick – ensured that in 1932, Günther was appointed to a chair in racial anthropology. He trained pupils including Dr Hirt and Dr Beger, members of the *Ahnenerbe*, in charge of the 'collection of skulls of Jewish commissioners' of the University of Strasbourg. At Jena, Hans F. K. Günther was a colleague of Günther Franz and Reinhard Höhn. In 1935–7, Günther Franz and Franz Alfred Six had close ties with the men in the *Ahnenerbe*, the SS organization dealing with raciological studies, especially with Wolfram Sievers and Walter Wüst, who were responsible for the recruitment of Hirt and Beger. The intellectuals of the SD and the raciologists and anthropologists of the *Ahnenerbe* set up, for example, common scientific and cultural programmes. These links between Nordicist intellectuals, though they have left few traces in the archives, are highly significant and were very common: they can be considered as fully organic, if we take into account the SD bureaus that focused on racial policy. The practices of Germanization established in 1940 by the RSHA in occupied Poland and, more centrally, by the Reich Supreme Commission on Nationality represent an organic collaboration between the researchers of the *Ahnenerbe*, or the practitioners of racial investigation within the RuSHA, on the one hand, and SD intellectuals on the other.

The appropriation of a system of beliefs

We now need to try and understand the stages of the process by which SS intellectuals decided to join the NSDAP, the SS and the SD, and to internalize the Nazi belief system. One example, yet again, is Werner Best, who, in 1918, was already an activist confronted by a world of enemies who were, this time, hell-bent on destroying Germany once and for all – witness his pamphlet calling for resistance, in January 1923, which I have already quoted.

We are here facing an ambitious French plan of extermination [*Vernichtungsplan*]. Our government is, thank God, resolved to resist. It is thus doing the only possible and conceivable thing. The people, too, shares this same will. Social Democracy in every case fears national union and is sabotaging it wherever it can. We need now to make clear to our people the consequences and the unyielding nature of the French plan of extermination, which is now driving towards its conclusion. Resistance and struggle or ruthless annihilation [*Vernichtung*]! For us, more than ever, one thing alone counts: to be ready for everything. [. . .]

However, the resolution to hold firm is present. But the Rhineland cannot succeed in this unless it is backed by a brave and resolute Reich. Defeatists should be brought before a war tribunal, or be struck down by the *Vehme*, since they are stabbing our western front in the back as it fights on [. . .]. On 4 February, the French entered Baden. Their aim is to divide Germany into three parts, one, the biggest possible, in the west under a French protectorate, a south influenced by France and a Prussian remainder, destined for the Poles to gobble up. The end of the world war is taking place at this moment. We need to throw our last strength into it – our physical strength but, even more, our moral strength.[59]

All of Werner Best's anguish is expressed in this text: dread at the idea of a vanquished Germany being partitioned, the oppressive sense of being encircled, and the terror of racial dilution by the occupation of colonial troops. Given this, becoming an activist was also a way of making these apparently shared obsessions evaporate. His career as an activist soon led him towards the NSDAP. And yet, Best seems to have been a little hesitant about the Nazi Party, claiming that he dreamed of a 'revolution from on high', at least if we can trust what he wrote when he came out of prison after the war.

The beginning of the 1930s offered fewer encouragements and stimuli than the previous years for philosophico-ideological considerations, since the economic and thus political situation in Germany was growing ever more threatening.

The mass publicity campaign of the NSDAP and its whole style were not to my taste. But since the first solution, that of a 'revolution from on high', had not come about and was becoming more improbable by the day, the electoral successes of the NSDAP in September 1930 demonstrated that there was a possibility of attaining something by that route. So I entered the NSDAP, without knowing a single Nazi leader, and almost without having attended a meeting, on 1 November 1930, aware of my status as a 'September partisan'.[60]

The NSDAP programme posed no problems for me, since it corresponded to all the other programmes of national and *völkisch* movements and was nothing but a compilation of tendencies that were in the air at that time.[61]

But another *völkisch* intellectual, little involved with Nazi institutions, Ernst von Salomon, wrote about the same period:

> At that time it appeared that, in every discussion, there was someone there, a silent guest, not entirely visible even though he dominated the discussion, setting out the themes, describing the methods, defining the directions. And the name of this silent guest was Adolf Hitler.[62]

Written in 1965 with the obvious aim of making it all seem quite normal, and much more circumspect than von Salomon's text, Best's *Lebenslauf* shows the way Nazism was able to bring together revolutionary nationalist forces – and, above all, how the SS was able to play the role of an elitist organization capable of luring in the student or bourgeois *völkisch* activists who had hitherto frequented intellectual nationalist circles. In the SS, Werner Best found the organization that enabled him to reconcile racial *völkisch* commitment with elitism, all within a mass party.

If the NSDAP was thus able to win over these intellectuals via the SS, this was surely, in the final analysis, only because Nazism could reshape these 'tendencies that were in the air at that time' and combine them into a coherent system of beliefs: it thus endowed events with meaning and provided a road to salvation for those prepared to join it. Best brings out very effectively the providential dimension assumed by Nazism in power:

> The years 1933–1939 brought a series of successes, all of which benefited the German people. The deadly danger of increasing unemployment was overcome. The whole people – especially the workers and peasants – was doing better than ever in our history. After the 1933 revolution, the least bloody revolution in history, the humiliations that Germany had endured as a result of the Treaty of Versailles were eliminated without bloodshed. Only a few marginal groups had to suffer from the new regime [. . .]. Faced with these positive dimensions, the mistakes made or the arbitrary decisions – which they tried to correct – seemed without any doubt to be beginners' mistakes, the results of the passions of youth: they would quickly be overcome, spontaneously and organically.[63]

Here too, the retrospective point of view is a whitewash. And yet the sense that all the dangers that had been threatening the existence of Germany had vanished does not seem an a posteriori construction. Through the elements enumerated, the different dimensions of the underlying dread clearly appear, even though Best takes care to refrain from mentioning the laws on the protection of the blood, that rampart of the integrity of the German biological substance. In the postwar period when he was faced with several charges, Best could hardly highlight these. What is left is this feeling, expressed quite directly: Nazism had literally 'saved' him.

Werner Best focused on the career of an entire generation; Otto Ohlendorf brought out just what it meant to 'live as a Nazi', especially in his last declaration at the trial of the *Einsatzgruppen*. Accused of murdering over 90,000 people, the SS general was faced with the death penalty (he was indeed executed in 1951) when, on 13 February 1948, he spoke before the American Tribunal:

> If it please the Tribunal, all the serious literature on National Socialism, especially the religious literature, agrees in seeing it not as a cause, but as a consequence of a spiritual crisis. This crisis, which has unfolded over the last few centuries, in particularly acute form over the last decades, has two aspects. On the one hand, it is a spiritual and moral crisis, and on the other hand, a political and social crisis. Catholic and Protestant literatures agree in noting the growing elimination of the Christian religion, the final aim of mankind, from the sphere of the state, which forms the kernel of historical evolution. The end of the Christian idea as the common goal of mankind in its social system, and the end of the individual's yearning for the beyond and life in God, have had a twofold effect.
>
> 1) Man lacks absolute and unified values in his life. In his mind and his action, he can no longer find the unified, certain reference point that had motivated his actions before. Laws and religious values hold an ever more reduced place in his emotions, his thoughts, his actions. Christian values, though in the final analysis they are still important, cannot prevent a man from being split into a 'weekday individual' and a 'Sunday individual'. The working week motivates the individual with different aims from those of meditating, even just for a time, on God's will. Life this side of the grave has not only acquired its own self-contained meaning, but really dominates man, with its concepts of autonomy, wealth, social status, and so on.
>
> 2) Society, organized into different states, has not found in its development any uniform values that might comprise the constant objective of state or society. Once groups and individuals were in a position to make their own aims the objective of society and its policies, the inviolable and metaphysical coherence of the political realm was lost, as a consequence of which the existing political and social order was fought over by the ideas of different individuals and different groups. The aim of preserving the status quo between the state and different nations was replaced by the desire to eliminate this status quo by war or revolution.
>
> My generation decided that this spiritual, religious and social disintegration had a profound effect, once we had become aware of the social conditions in which it was entangled. For this generation, there was no value

beyond criticism. Thirty or more parties were fighting for state power and they all represented opposing interests. Those from this generation were not provided with any uncontested idea that could teach them how to live as human beings. Their social future was hopeless. It is understandable, given these conditions, that this generation did not regard wealth as an aim. In fact, material wealth became a problematic notion after inflation, the financial crisis and the years of economic troubles in which age-old fortunes had been wiped out.

A clever piece of pleading from a man who spoke of his acts without uttering a word about his genocidal action, and who described Nazism without mentioning racism. And yet his words, perhaps, suggest the essential aspect of the movement: its fervour.

Otto Ohlendorf analysed the appearance of Nazism while setting it back within the context of the period's 'ideas', trapping his audience inside an analysis that saw support for racial fundamentalism as a purely intellectual process. And this indeed was how the individual or generational dimension of Nazification was analysed. Do we not refer to the 'Nazification of minds'? By uttering the terms 'heroic realism',[64] and even 'romanticism', he turns Nazism into the final tragic avatar of a German *Sonderweg* [a 'special way': the word implies that German history is *essentially* different from that of the rest of Europe – *Tr.*]. To limit oneself to such terms, however, means that the collective ontological dimension of support for Nazism is obscured, and the fervour which the text allows us to glimpse is ignored.

Once it has been extricated from its conceptual dross, Otto Ohlendorf's apologia provides the observer with a tableau of the generational experience of the men in whose name he is speaking. He describes the existential nature of the crisis they faced, dwelling, however, on what he calls the 'lack of values' that German society at that time was experiencing. In his view, Weimar Germany – a society of chaos, poverty, war and revolution, a society in which the economic elites had been ruined – was a nation on its deathbed. Admittedly, Ohlendorf does not depict Germany as a citadel besieged simultaneously from both without and within (as does Werner Best), but how could he do so, when he is after all expressing his ideas in front of judges who come from the very same 'world of enemies' that defeated Germany in 1918 and seemed to attach such importance to vanquishing it definitively? To state any hostility was impossible for him: all he could do now was express adversity through the emotions of the accused. Germany, shrunk in both space and population, weakened on the international level, stripped of its army, is described as divided in its government and facing economic shipwreck. The loss described by Ohlendorf casts its shadow over entire centuries: with the disappearance of the empire and its economic and social elites, Germany has now been deprived of the essential underpinnings of its identity. From the despair of this realization was born the muted panic that seized on young SS intellectuals in the course of the 1920s. If we follow the lines of his argument, it was this profound anguish that gave birth to the quest of the activists:

> They [the men of this generation] were seeking a spiritual support, an aim that went beyond the social system in which they had been born, an aim that would promise them a real human dignity, real human goals, as well as a religious and spiritual basis for their development as human beings. This generation, by its sufferings, became too realistic to believe that in this period of history it would find the ethics and the social basis necessary for its human existence merely by directing its gaze to the Beyond. Confronted by everyday life and social activities, it found those different elements too transparent – they could not form any touchstone for life. In fact, the split between the 'weekday man' and the 'Sunday man' seems one of the deepest causes of material and moral suffering. So it becomes easy to understand that this generation should seek new religious values.
>
> On the other hand, the dependence of each individual on the constitution and conditions of existence of the society, state, and nation in which he lives was so very important for this generation that they could not fail to seek aims and means to replace the changing domination of special interest groups by an order based on an overall conception, relating to all individuals, without regard to their social status [. . .]

Ohlendorf is here communicating his own perception of a vital dimension in the activists' quest. But even here, he decides to give only partial expression to the expectations that marked his career. In particular, he does not mention the shared hope for the coming of an empire, in other words in the gathering of all Germans within a single state. However, he did express this idea elsewhere, in much more brutal terms, when detailing the Reich's needs for raw materials, which legitimated an expansionist policy that in his view was vital if the power of the new Germany was to be assured.[65] But expressing his hopes for the Reich amounted to confessing, in front of the Court, his ethnic conception of German identity, allowing them to glimpse its racial determinism and expansionist imperialism. This kind of language would have undermined his defence strategy while at the same time bolstering the certainty, expressed by his American judges, that Nazi Germany had 'conspired against peace'.[66] Ohlendorf's horizon of expectations, reduced to these limits, can be summed up in two dimensions: the one social and political, the other spiritual.

Ohlendorf claims to be seeking an order 'relating to all individuals, without regard to their social status'. This is a way of expressing his aversion to Communism which, in his view, is concerned only with the well-being of the working class. Thereby, he is trying to express surreptitiously the 'ambition of totality' which the Nazi belief system prided itself on.[67] This totality lay, of course, not in universalism, but in the ethnic dimension of the construction of identity. The belief system that he yearned for was meant for all *Germans*. However, his quest as an activist was not merely the quest of a Party member: he tried to make of it a spiritual movement. This emerges from the very next words of his declaration, in which the SS general finally talks of his own fervour:

> It was this idea which we found in National Socialism, and we counted on it to provide us with the basis for a new order. Talking in terms of a thousand-year Reich was not a frivolous gesture, since we knew that mankind's great developments take centuries and even millennia to ripen and give birth to the latest developments.
>
> Thus, we were not impatient in spirit, but we studied the history of the human race, its religious history included, as well as the high and low points of states and nations, with the aim of finding an idea that would guide us in the rise and fall of peoples, and indications that would help us to fulfil the demands of our age, demands that issued from the experiences and sufferings of history. From this quest across history, we drew the certainty that the great religious questions, the great moral and ethical problems were accompanying current events of great historical significance.

The Nazi belief system is here seen in two inseparable aspects. On the one hand, it is a discourse that puts forward interpretative frameworks for those men whose quest as activists is described by Ohlendorf, a quest itself provoked by the irrepressible anxiety that the *Volk* might disappear. Now this 'idea that would guide [them]' in history can be none other than Nordicist racial determinism, whose providential immanence designates the chosen race as well as its eternal enemies.[68] On the other hand, it expresses the millenarian dimension of the Nazi belief system.[69] The formula *'Tausendjähriges Reich'* ('thousand-year Reich'), which has too frequently been seen as a mere empty slogan, surely gives material expression to the immense expectations of a revolutionary and redemptive movement? This was the strange alchemy of the Nazi creed, which transfigured eschatological anguish into a powerful expectation of the Millennium; a strange alchemy which generated a visceral attachment on the part of these men to their own political commitment, demanding from them the ultimate sacrifice. This was a multifaceted, individual and collective reality, a 'kind of kingdom',[70] which only a social and political anthropology of emotion will perhaps enable us to grasp.

Chapter 5

Entering the SD

SS intellectuals came into Nazism in different ways, more or less quickly. Some of them, born between 1901 and 1905, entered the NSDAP before it seized power; others, born in 1910 or 1911, joined the Party or one of its organizations only later. In every case, the dates of joining as well as the itineraries followed by those entering Nazi organizations show different kinds of activism and modes of recruitment.

The clear change in the status of the NSDAP that occurred between 1930–2 and the end of the decade – a moment when, solidly installed in power, the Party became the obligatory channel for a career in administration – is a good reason for examining these itineraries. For why, after all, might entering Nazism not just have been an opportunistic career move? A study of the dates of recruitment and the institutions in which SS intellectuals became active suggests one answer. What emerges is the importance of recruitment networks, of powerful characters making their mark on different departments, and the institutional mechanisms that made it possible for individuals to be registered automatically in the SS and the SD.

Whether to enter the Party or not?

An examination of the recruitment dates stipulated in every personal SS file shows that the SD had peak periods of recruitment, especially between 1933 and 1938. This corresponded to an intense development in the intelligence services. After an initial phase that was cut short by the events of 30 June 1934 (the 'Night of the Long Knives'), and the SS seizure of power over the police, Heydrich organized the SD's central departments and covered the territory of Germany with local offices charged with the task of gathering information and transmitting it to Berlin.[1] The SD recruited, from every stratum of society, informers who worked for free and provided it with intelligence or studies of particular sectors.[2] It also employed young cadres, whether or not they had come up through the

SS. So, far from being the goal of an activist itinerary, recruitment into the SD seems to have been more the result of the SD needing fresh blood, and seeking graduate cadres to further its plans for restructuring. There was a first 'generation' of SD cadres composed of precocious activists working within an organization that was still coming into being, but opposed to this there was also a generation of 'technocrats', less committed, but possessing functional competences that would have been the main criterion for recruitment, rather than any long-established loyalty.

In fact, from 1931 to 1933, few SS intellectuals were recruited. The SD was at that time a tiny department, with no more than 400 members in the whole of Germany. The few SS officers recruited full time to work within it formed, however, the basic structure of the department, laying down its working methods and its organization. This shows how important they were. They included Georg Herbert Mehlhorn, Lothar Beutel, Hermann Behrends and Wilhelm Albert. Mehlhorn and Albert were given the task of organizing respectively the administrative departments and the internal SD. Beutel organized the SD in Saxony and seems in particular to have been the inspiration for the foundation of the Leipzig *Schrifttumstelle*, the SD office charged with keeping surveillance over all written productions in Germany. Finally, Hermann Behrends was the first head of the SD in Berlin, before moving into the *Inland*-SD.[3] While in post, he set up – together with Wilhelm Albert and Georg Herbert Mehlhorn – the general principles for managing the files of opponents.[4] If we add Reinhard Höhn and Heinz Jost to this group,[5] we find that all those in charge of SDHA II/2 (*Deutsches Lebensgebiet* [literally 'German culture or life domain'– *Tr.*], i.e. German gathering and assessment of intelligence on every sector of society, apart from opponents of the regime) and the SD's department of external intelligence were recruited during this period. These men established new working methods, and supervised local organization and recruitment in the following period. They created it from start to finish.

From 1934–5 and up until 1938, over 80 per cent of SS intellectuals forming the group we are studying entered the SD. The start of this second period corresponds to the arrival of individuals who organized the specialized bureaus and the local sections in medium-sized towns. Wilhelm Spengler, for instance, founded – at the request of Lothar Beutel – the Leipzig *Schrifttumstelle*; Erich Ehrlinger moved from the SA to the SS to organize the SD network in Nuremberg.[6] Martin Sandberger and Eugen Steimle, who both entered the SD at the request of Gustav Adolf Scheel so as to serve as liaison officers between the NSStB, the SD and the DAI,[7] quickly moved from the south-west SDHA to the central echelons at the request of Heinz Jost, who wanted them to organize the *Ausland*-SD: these cases all illustrate the general pattern of young experts entrusted with the task of sharpening up working structures and methods, so as to systematize the gathering and processing of information.[8]

Then, after 1936, came officers who no longer had any organizational responsibilities, apparently recruited solely as experts, such as Hans

Joachim Beyer and Walter von Kielpinski. The first succeeded Steimle in his role of coordination, giving this post a more scientific than activist dimension,[9] while the second joined the Leipzig SDOA, organized under the leadership of Wilhelm Spengler.[10] Practically all the SS intellectuals we are investigating were by then employed: were they taken on as specialists whose political tendencies were more or less a matter of indifference to their recruiters? The answer varies with their degree of Nazification, and their ideological profiles at the time they arrived.

We cannot trust appearances. Entering the SS and the SD, as we have just seen, was an ambiguous move. Studied in isolation, it could merely be evidence that the new recruits were technocrats avid for power who, sniffing the Nazi breeze that was blowing through society, were quick to join an organization which they sensed was going to be important in the future. Here, we need to link together all the signs of belonging to Nazism, to the NSDAP, to the organizations that kept the population under surveillance (especially the NSV, but the trade unions too), and finally the SD and the SS.

Being a member of the NSDAP cannot constitute a unique criterion. However, of the forty or so entry dates into the NSDAP gleaned from personal files, thirty came *before* the seizure of power, which suggests authentic activist support rather than opportunism. However, curiously enough, Jens Banach rejects this idea: he presents joining the Party as solely the result of wide-scale propaganda.[11] Does this mean that propaganda lured in only individuals without strong convictions? But joining the Party was, for these men, a sign of their activism: they were committed supporters from very early on, and they already had long careers as militants behind them: this was the case with Werner Best and Otto Ohlendorf, as well as Eugen Steimle and Herbert Strickner. However, these latter two did not join the SD until 1935 and 1938. But, far from being opportunistic technocrats, both demonstrated an early commitment, embodied in *Volkstumsarbeit* border work for the NSStB, in Steimle's case,[12] and Strickner's activities in the Styrian *Heimschutz* when he was only sixteen.[13]

The fact remains that a far from negligible number of men joined *after* the seizure of power. These can appear, more legitimately, as the result of more tactical than political decisions. But in that case, what are we to say of the many individuals who were members of the SS but not of the Party? This was, for a long period, the case of Hans Joachim Beyer, the historian who studied at Königsberg, where he encountered a German–Polish border that was perceived as a biological frontier, and started to militate in favour of German minorities beyond the borders of the Reich. Beyer was close to the *Die Tat* group, a member of the DAI and the *Volkswissenschaftlicher Arbeitskreis* of the *Deutscher Schutzbund* – this was a veritable seedbed for SS intellectuals – but he felt no need to join the NSDAP and did not become a member even when, in 1936, he joined the SD in Stuttgart to coordinate student activism, SS intelligence and the kind of historiography that legitimated German demands. He joined the NSDAP only in 1940, when – solidly installed both in the Nazi historiographical landscape and in the organizations that were planning population shifts – he was one of the men who thought through the ethnic reorganization of occupied Europe. His joining was not the same as adherence to Nazism: it was a mere formality.[14] And, in this respect, Beyer was no isolated case: nearly 15 per cent of the group's members were, at a given moment, members of the SS and not of the NSDAP, members of the elite corps and not of the mass organization. In the same bureau as Beyer (RSHA *Amt* III B), Heinz Hummitzsch, one of the organizers of the *Generalplan Ost* in 1940–2, joined the NSDAP in 1937 after two years in the SS;[15] Bruno Lettow, director of the Police and SD School in Prague, and thus responsible for the ideological training of officers, joined the SS a few days before the *Machtergreifung*, but joined the NSDAP only four years later.[16]

In any case, while holding a Party card did not necessarily mean that one was a political fanatic, we have to admit that *not* having one did not imply – far from it – any absence of support for Nazi anti-Semitism. In short, belonging or not to the NSDAP is not a definitive criterion, unless it is set back in the context of these men's entire activist career.

One of the means by which we can evaluate the degree of activism of SS intellectuals consists in trying to assess it within its more day-to-day dimension. None of them, for example, was active in local administration, assuming the functions of *Blockleiter* or *Gruppenleiter*, with the notable exception of Otto Ohlendorf. As we have seen, there can be no shadow of a doubt about his activism: he entered the Party in 1925 and was *Gruppenleiter* only during the phase when the NSDAP was not yet in power,[17] before the post became that of permanent officials charged with the task of overseeing the orthodoxy of the behaviour of the people in their apartment block, in other words a post for small fry – figures of often dubious morality.

Other organizations served as a framework for Nazi activism. They included trade union organizations (students and lawyers) and Nazi charitable organizations such as the NSV.

We have already looked at the case of the NSStB. Its activism was varied and changing. So one can observe a break between the student activist period, during which militancy was linked to the pressures brought to bear on Jewish and democratic teachers as well as to the many shows of strength put on by the Nazis in the universities, and the period after 1933, when the NSStB was transformed into a mass student organization. It then undertook propaganda campaigns, border activism and, later on, voluntary work in the Germanization of occupied territories. Of course, not all the SS intellectuals joined: only a quarter of the group's members did so. However, it needs to be pointed out that they then became active members, like Helmut Knochen, Siegfried Engel and

Friedrich Tiedt. All three assumed responsibilities in the administrative organizations of their respective universities, and also directed, within the NSStB, departments in the central administration. Knochen, for instance, found himself in 1935–6 at the head of the office in charge of media and written productions for the whole of Germany.[18]

As well as being involved in this student activism, Martin Sandberger joined the League of National Socialist Lawyers.[19] For a commissioner in the Gestapo, it is true that Emil Berndorff might seem to have become a member of the NSDAP only belatedly, in 1937. But he had been a member of the Nazi League of Employees since 1932.[20] As for Hans Leetsch, he had been a very early member of the NSDAP as well as of the DAF, the trade union for German workers.[21] And I could cite many other examples of Gestapo functionaries or SD officers who belonged both to the Party or the SS and to some corporatist association. None of them, on the other hand, assumed any significant responsibilities in these trade union corporations, so we know nothing of the militant activities which their membership entailed.

Fewer than a dozen SS intellectuals, finally, belonged to the NSV, the Party's charitable organization that helped in needy milieus and collected clothes or money.[22] However, this does not imply that this activism was not significant. In fact, it was mainly women who took part in it, and over half of the wives of the men in our group were members.[23] So if, instead of concentrating on individuals, we look at couples, the NSV played a major part in the activism of intellectuals' *families*. Here too, information on NSV membership comes from personal files and marriage files of the RuSHA, so it is extremely difficult to determine how much activism was involved. However, the case of Erich Ehrlinger provides us with some basic details. Ehrlinger, the last head of the RSHA *Amt* I,[24] gathered the different sections of his personal file and his correspondence into a special file that escaped the destruction of 1945. Apart from a very full correspondence and his schoolboy's file, it contains several NSV documents: cards, souvenirs of charity parties, records of gifts of tinplate, receipts for sums of money. These documents create the image of an activism that was close to bourgeois patronage, as if this SS officer, taking on the role of a 'benefactor', had poured out on the poor and needy of the Third Reich the largesse – which was quite real in the 1940s – which his status allowed.[25] As well as embodying a clear financial comfort and social success, he also took part in an activism that was far removed from his role in the SD. The latter endeavoured to put into practice the solidarity of the *Volksgemeinschaft*, the racial community comprising all Nordic Germans, in which – thanks to organizations such as the NSV – well-off individuals contributed to redistributing property, overcoming the division into social classes; a division symbolizing the capitalist societies which Nazism defined itself against, but also of the Communist society that was being built in the USSR in which, according to Nazi ideologues,[26] a single social class had, by means of a bloody civil war, confiscated most of the wealth and power.[27] Joining the NSV, for SS intellectuals, was a way of giving concrete form to the solidarity of the *Volksgemeinschaft*, and adding a 'fraternal' dimension to an SS commitment which, from the *Machtergreifung* onwards, was not exactly peace-loving.

The last militant framework was, of course, made up of the two major activist organizations in the NSDAP: the SA and the SS. The group can be subdivided into those men who passed from SA to SS activism and those who, for various reasons, joined the SS directly.

A certain number of individuals began their militant careers in the SA, sometimes, but not always, with membership of the NSDAP. Some passed through rapidly, registering in a *Standarte*, and perhaps playing a major part in the activism of the SA, but without leaving the slightest trace of this. These militants, whose time in the SA was short and discreet, joined after 1934 and soon left for the SS. One example was Karl Burmester. He joined the SA in April 1933, just as its numbers were swelling rapidly, and just as it was starting to focus on revolutionary activism; he then left it in April 1934, just before the movement was neutralized in the Night of the Long Knives. In spite of the ban on SA cadres moving to the SS, he joined the Black Order and the SD. We know nothing of his activities in the SA, or of the responsibilities he may have assumed while a member. At the most we can suppose that, since he was appointed to the rank of *Obersturmführer* in the SS, he may have already reached the same rank of subaltern officer in the SA.[28]

Several other SS intellectuals, such as Erich Ehrlinger and Martin Sandberger, stayed in the SA for a long period of time, and took part in its activities, assuming various responsibilities, and showing what an intellectual form of militancy could look like in these plebeian cohorts. Both worked in senior positions in the AW (*Ausbildungswesen*) department of the SA. This department provided political, paramilitary and physical training for cadres and militants. Sandberger and Ehrlinger, pedagogues of doctrine and street fighting, here had their first experiences of *Menschenführung*, i.e. exercising command. From 1931 to 1935, they directed training groups, inculcating into their recruits a minimum of discipline, useful in that time of intense and violent political struggles. In his *Lebenslauf*, Ehringer also states that he had taken part in street fighting in Berlin in 1931 and directed 'sports training' from 1931 to 1935.[29] Then, from 1934, when the organization was brought under control, the two men followed it as it evolved into a mass institution, transforming the movement's paramilitary dimension into a sporting vocation.[30]

A second group of SS officers is characterized by the sometimes surprising absence of any time spent in the SA. These included Nazi militants who joined very early on, but did not in spite of that join the SA. Examples included Hans Ehlich, Werner Best, Richard Frankenberg, Georg Herbert Mehlhorn and Reinhard Höhn. However, these men did not feel any particular revulsion for paramilitary activism. Mehlhorn and Best had undergone a military training with the clear intention of putting it to activist use,[31] Ehlich and Frankenberg had joined *Freikörper* or the Bavarian *Reichsflagge*,[32] while Höhn and Ehlich had for a while been active in the *Stahlhelm*.[33] Only the plebeian side of the SA seems to have put them off. Werner Best, for instance, expressed his revulsion for a movement whose 'mass publicity [. . .] and whole style' he disliked,[34] a movement that did not embody the 'revolution from above' that he yearned for, but was a quite different revolution, a proletarian one, which the SS elites could not fail to stamp out in June 1934, backed on this occasion by the traditional bourgeois and military elites.[35] Is it any coincidence, in this context, that Best, Behrends, Mehlhorn and Albert – all representative of the older fringes of the group of SS intellectuals who had emerged from the elite form of *völkisch* activism – did not just refuse to join the SA, but were also behind the repression of the so-called 'Röhm putsch'?[36]

The youngest of these intellectuals who had avoided the SA probably realized, after 1934, the uselessness of such a move. They had entered Nazism via the SD and were then automatically taken into the SS, before they had received their NSDAP cards – so they did not even have a chance of thinking of joining an SA *Standarte*. Several young Saxons fell into this category. They included Hans Rössner, an assistant professor in German literature who entered the Leipzig *Schrifttumsstelle* in 1934, and Heinz Hummitzsch, one of the closest of Hans Ehlich's associates in RSHA *Amt* III B.[37]

In short, Nazi activism was a form of commitment whose importance and meaning will escape us if we examine its elements only in isolation. In fact, there were few intellectuals who entered the SS before joining the SD, following the example set by Otto Ohlendorf and Günther Franz, Wilhelm Albert and Bruno Lettow, head of the Police School in Prague.[38] The case of the last of these is worth dwelling on. Lettow entered the SD only in 1937. In addition, he was in a Gestapo bureau where his functions were those of a practitioner of criminal law, a technician entrusted with the task of hunting down opponents with 'rationality' (*Vernunft*) and 'efficiency' (*Sachlichkeit*), following the principles of Werner Best. So he seems to have had nothing in common with those SS intellectuals who clung to their convictions out of a sense of panicky belief: Ohlendorf would be the archetype of these. However, Lettow shared with Ohlendorf a relatively early participation in SS activism. Indeed, his officer file presents us with the image of a man who, far from being a specialist of the 'rational repression' dear to the lawyer Werner Best, was initially a committed student who even became physically involved in the political studies internal to the academic world: indeed, he was given a suspended prison sentence for acts of brutality within the university. In fact, the lawyer had long been a Nazi activist by the time he joined the SD in 1937.

So his belated membership of the SD was in no way any proof of his endorsement of the '*Sachlichkeit*', the 'rational efficiency' that was, in Ulrich Herbert's view,[39] the mainspring of the behaviour of Gestapo and

SD cadres: on the contrary, he was a militant in the Nazi cause, a cause that for him was embodied in the struggle for power within the university, in the highly selective *Allgemeine* SS, in the police activity of the Gestapo and also, in a more anodyne way, within the NSV, in an intense activity of patronage of the NSVW and the DAF – an activity that he undertook in tandem with his wife, also a member of these organizations and the BDM.[40] In short, this was a case of activism within the family, combining violent militancy, charitable activism, a corporatist social bond and membership of the Black Order: is this not a good example of the way that we cannot grasp Nazi activism and its meaning unless we take into account *every* kind of membership and belonging that it involved? Bruno Lettow's activism was ambiguous, since it combined the violent forms of Nazi activism with a charitable and associative activity. This undermines the thesis of social atomization that, in Hannah Arendt's view, was generated by totalitarian regimes.[41]

The question of Nazi militancy – its forms, its extent, the strength of its roots in the minds of SS intellectuals – cannot be given any simplistic answer. We cannot hope to solve it by capturing it in some 'fanaticism versus opportunism' paradigm. The phenomenon was itself complex and variable enough not to be reduced to these terms, especially since these two concepts raise more questions than they answer. I will not here attempt to demonstrate the unproductive and scientifically dubious character of the term 'fanaticism'. That of 'opportunist' seems to be more interesting, in the sense that the Nazis themselves were aware of the reality of the phenomenon: indeed, in 1933 the NSDAP excluded several members and closed its doors until 1937.[42] These and similar measures show that the Nazis wished to protect activism and militancy, to emphasize conviction rather than calculation. Did the hierarchs of the SD share this point of view, trying to spot in the ranks of the SS intellectuals a lukewarm commitment allied with a sense of calculation? For if we look at the number of people who joined the NSDAP in the months following the *Machtergreifung*,[43] this opportunism seems to have been very common in the movement.

Among the eighty SS intellectuals I am studying here, only one aroused ideological objections in the course of his career through the Nazi agencies of repression. This was Heinz Gräfe.[44] On at least three occasions, his case was examined at the highest level of the Gestapo and the SD, going right up to Heydrich. In June 1936, Heydrich received from the personnel department of the Ministry of the Interior a letter questioning the firmness of Gräfe's 'ideological convictions' – a letter that requested that his political orthodoxy be re-examined if he were to be confirmed in his Gestapo position. Heydrich, springing to the defence of his trainee functionary, retorted that the latter had, through his time in the SD, given sufficient proof of his support.[45] However, Gräfe's problems were only just beginning. In 1943, when he was appointed to the rank of *Obersturmbannführer*

– a very belated appointment, since his last promotion dated back to
1939 – he saw the solidity of his convictions being cast into doubt yet
again. The proposal for promotion stated that in April 1938 the head of
the north-west region of the SS had drawn up a critical report on him,
depicting him as an 'intellectual who sticks to pacifist positions', and as
an 'adversary of National Socialism before the seizure of power, [who]
belonged to the working commission of the AstA for the self-management
and reform of the university system, within which [he] represented a very
democratic line, solidly on the left'. Again, the decision was taken at the
highest level: the marginal mentions point out, to begin with, that the
promotion needed to be 'submitted to C.' – it had been put forward by
Kaltenbrunner – but also that the document was to be 'transmitted to the
central department of SS personnel for transmission to the *Reichsführer*'
Himmler, before being returned to RSHA *Amt* I.[46]

The accusation was a serious one. However, it needs to be carefully
scrutinized. We also have the assessment report of the SS regional head
who had raised doubts about Gräfe. Dated April 1938, just as he was
coming out with these accusations, the personal assessment adopted a
noticeably less accusatory tone. The report stated that Gräfe 'is absolutely
bent on passing for a National Socialist but is perhaps not completely
convinced in his own mind' and that he is 'trying to build up his own
grasp of ideological issues'. The report's author, though critical of Gräfe's
'character' – he reproached him for his lack of military attitude and
openness, his egoism and his ambition – is forced to admit that he has an
irreproachable (*einwandfrei*) attitude and a remarkable intelligence.[47]

A committed student with left-wing leanings, who – in his boss's
words – had spent time in the SA after the *Machtergreifung*, and who was
doing his absolute best to pass as a Nazi (in order to disguise what past?):
Heinz Gräfe, as seen from this quotation from the report of April 1938,
embodies the figure of the opportunist. We should note in passing that
the admittedly more moderate remarks in the personal assessment are
evidence of the hierarchy's insistence that doctrine be internalized: it was
not enough to be competent, you had to be convinced if you were to be
given high marks. This is surely clear proof of the militant status that one
could acquire through work in the SD.

The case of Gräfe suggests that we ponder the components of Nazi
activism. Gräfe was an orphan of the Great War. Brought up in Leipzig,
he joined the local scouts very young, before he was eleven.[48] This commitment was a way for him to involve himself in border activism, in the
Abwehrkampf that was common in Leipzig, close to the Czech frontier.
He assumed the leadership of 300 young activists who, in the summer of
1928, undertook a propaganda mission into the cities of the Sudetenland.[49]
So, whatever the degree of his student activism, he was, as were other SS
intellectuals, a child of the Great War continuing the struggle begun in
1914. This student commitment, indeed, was something he drew on in an
attempt at self-justification he wrote in 1934.

I entered, via the Student Foundation of the German People, the independent organization of the student corporation [. . .]; I occupied the
posts of head of the free student corporation and was a member of the
Studentenschaft leadership. I organized, inter alia, two scientific work camps.
It was at that time my view that the freedom of the University should be
maintained against 'the stench of party politicking' – this was how all the
youth leagues viewed events in the Weimar state. This is why I found
myself opposed to the NSStB leaders who, furthermore, created a negative
image of National Socialism.

In the summer semester of 1931, I organized the first department for
student labour in Germany: the work camp of the Leipzig student corporation in Fehmarn (with 200 students). From then on, the Student Labour
Department assumed a great importance. At that time, I saw the Labour
Department as an opportunity for young people to present a united front
against the old folk's state [i.e. Weimar].[50]

Gräfe makes no secret of his hostility to a sector of National Socialism.
However, like the majority of *völkisch* students, he had a certain number
of points in common with Nazi students: the extreme hostility to the
democratic regime of Weimar, the use of a coarse vocabulary to denounce
it – which we find elsewhere, in the *Lebensläufe* of Reinhard Höhn and
Georg Herbert Mehlhorn, for example – the experience of an inter-
generational conflict, attachment to the Labour Department (a Nazi
creation), perhaps Labour Service, and protean activism. There was a
common cultural underpinning that allowed Gräfe to gain ready access to
the ranks of the SS and the SD. Whatever his true political colours, in fact,
he doubtless shared with Nazi students something that, in their heart of
hearts, determined their political commitments: the memory of the Great
War, the experience of the *Abwehrkampf*, activism in the anti-republican
opposition and membership of the youth leagues. All he needed to make
him a perfect Nazi was an internalization of racial determinism. Perhaps
it was precisely this gap that the SS head of the north-west region spotted
when he declared that Gräfe was 'trying to build up his own grasp of
ideological issues', but was afraid that he was 'not completely convinced
in his own mind'. In every case, Heinz Gräfe, who had begun his career
under the aegis of a scout movement strongly imbued with Protestant
religious fervour, left his Church to state that he was *gottgläubig* and to
pledge his support for the neo-pagan movement, an additional sign that
he had assimilated more Nazi doctrine than at first appears.[51]

Finally, his activity in the SD and the Gestapo makes clear his support
for the idea of racial determinism, a determinism that he was able to check
against the realities of wartime, first as head of an *Einsatzkommando* in
Poland,[52] then as leading a special action consisting in training activists
from national minorities of the USSR to send them on espionage missions behind Soviet lines, or to fight partisans and play their role in the
genocide campaigns.[53] In both cases, Gräfe demonstrated a violence that

stemmed from his racial determinism. In the second case, at least, he said he agreed with the SS that he had directed this revulsion in response to the 'Asiatization' that threatened him,[54] on contact with these natives whom he sent behind Soviet lines or in combat units against partisans, when he had not decided to subject them to 'special treatment'.[55]

Given these conditions, should we put down to pure hypocrisy Ohlendorf's speech, which he gave at Gräfe's SS funeral (he was cremated at the same time as Karl Gengenbach, head of RSHA *Amt* III A, with whom he had been killed in a car accident)? At any event, between two flags, with the colours of the Black Order and the NSDAP, amidst the wreaths sent by Himmler and Kaltenbrunner, Ohlendorf hailed the memory of the two dead men, and celebrated in them

> representatives of true German manhood, real comrades and real National Socialists, who, unyieldingly and without any other consideration, had chosen their paths. Faithful to the aims they had set out for their lives, faithful to their people, this people which was identical with these aims; faithful to their community in which they served these aims; faithful to their families from which they drew ever greater strength; and faithful, finally, to their fidelity to the path that led to the goals set before them.[56]

At the moment of his committal, Heinz Gräfe had, in the eyes of those bidding him farewell, joined the ranks of the martyrs of the Nazi belief system, even if, despite the grandiloquence of Ohlendorf's speech, the end of this particular martyr had nothing in common with the soldier's heroic death (*Heldentod*) which his father had met on the fields of Flanders in 1914.

Heinz Gräfe's 'opportunism', the only example of an accusation of this kind brought against an SS intellectual, illustrates the difficulty of passing any definitive judgement on the 'sincerity' with which men appropriated Nazi doctrine. This was gradual and changing, and Gräfe was doubtless 'more' Nazi in 1944 than in 1935. So he shared with the other SS intellectuals a memory of the Great War and a world-view of continued struggle, and, like his companions in the Black Order, he had conceived a profound aversion to a Weimar Republic which was an incarnation of the death agonies of a shrunken Germany. In such conditions, how could Gräfe have remained immune to the welling up of eschatological anguish that overcame Germany between the wars? Was it not precisely this anguish which found expression in border propaganda, aimed as it was at maintaining the Germandom of those countries on German frontiers that had come into being as a result of Versailles? The example of Heinz Gräfe seems to indicate that even a display of opposition to one or other aspects of the belief system was no barrier to internalizing other basic tenets of the doctrine. Cut-and-dried terms such as 'opportunism' and 'fanaticism' prevent us from realizing this; focusing on the signs of political commitment taken in isolation is not enough, and we need to see the different forms of commitment developed by young SS intellectuals within the full context of their careers as activists.

Towards the SD: Nazi careers

If we see the different forms of support for Nazism as part of the careers of these young intellectuals, we can identify three major paths they took. The first, probably the most common, led them from activism within the Party to officer rank in the Black Order; the second, less typical, reflected the opposite route; the third, which concerned many Gestapo functionaries but few SD cadres, consisted in moving from a job as a functionary to membership of the SS and the NSDAP.

Alfred Filbert was one example of the first path. He joined the NSDAP in 1932, before entering the SD in 1934. His case appears representative of the path taken by the greatest number: 50 per cent of the members of the group belonged to the Party before entering the SS; they were also in the Party before the seizure of power. Joining was, for them, a demonstration of their militancy, and entering the SS was the result of a previous career in Nazi organizations. Most of them joined the NSDAP before 1933, but most moved into the SS between 1934 and 1937. In spite of these two constants, the time lapse between entering the first and the second of these organizations could vary greatly: just a few days in the case of Hermann Behrends[57] and several years for others (eleven years in Otto Ohlendorf's case).[58] This latter was something of an exception – no other SS intellectual spent such a long activist career in the NSDAP. Henrich Malz and Ernst Hermann Jahr are examples of a more common type of 'old' NSDAP militants who joined the SS and the SD after a shorter period of activism. It is quite difficult to establish clearly the extent to which this delay between joining one organization and then another constituted a real progression for such activists, and whether it involved any overtures to the SD. The case of Erich Ehlers may help to answer these questions. Ehlers joined the NSDAP in January 1932 and the SD the following year.[59] Between these dates, Ehlers was a local Party official, successively *Blockleiter* and *Zellenleiter*, before entering, as did many members of the Party or the SA, as a police auxiliary at the time of the *Machtergreifung*.[60] He was then put to work hunting down Communists and Social Democrats. This was his first experience in the police.[61] Was this not a determining factor in his enlistment in the SD? Ehlers' lengthy discussion of this suggests that it was a significant element in his development. But the speed with which he moved towards the SD makes Ehlers an atypical example: just one year elapsed between his becoming a Nazi and his joining the nascent SDOA in Berlin.

This was not the case of most SS intellectuals. Much more typical was that of Eugen Steimle and Erich Ehrlinger, who joined the SD after four or five years in the NSDAP and other Nazi Party organizations. They very soon signed up for the SA and the NSStB, organizations in which their activism was sufficiently noteworthy for them to become permanent members. Steimle was given important posts in the NSStB, devoting his time to assisting *volksdeutsch* students in the Sudetenland, with the rank of head of a central department in the trade union,[62] while Sandberger was a trainer in the SA's training department (AW), and even directed one of the schools of physical education preparing men for the paramilitary organization. At the same time, he took on various jobs in the NSStB, and on that occasion collaborated with Steimle.[63] The time spent by these two men in the AW and the NSStB can best be explained by taking a quick look at their careers in the SD. Both initially joined the local section in Stuttgart at the beginning of 1936 and helped set up an intelligence and espionage network abroad, via *volksdeutsch* communities. They then left for central departments in Berlin, and ended their careers, after some time in the *Einsatzgruppen*, in *Amt* VI of the RSHA, the department in charge of espionage abroad. So there were two major elements in their career paths: the first was a field of investigation (abroad) that focused on *volksdeutsch* communities; the second was that of an intense activity, in parallel with the first, of both ideological and physical training, with both men very frequently teaching in SD schools.[64]

It is just as if they had both acquired an early experience of work that they were to complete in the SD. Does this mean that they were recruited only as technicians in a new organization? This does not seem very likely, as the militant dimension of these two activities was very pronounced. When they entered the SD, it was as experienced activists who had, in their careers so far, shown particular aptitudes for espionage.

Likewise, Heinz Ballensiefen joined the SD very belatedly, in 1939. He started his career in the Propaganda Ministry, as a specialist in anti-Semitic propaganda, before joining the RSHA *Amt* VII (in charge of theoretical studies), where he independently embarked on propaganda missions abroad, for instance in Paris.[65] Finally, in 1943–4, he founded the 'Institute for the Study of the Jewish Question' in Budapest.[66] The two successive heads of *Amt* VII, Six and Dittel, entrusted him with the task of leading scientific investigation into, and propaganda on, the Jewish question: this was the terrible period when the Hungarian Jews were being deported en masse and massacred at a rate of 10,000 a day in the gas chambers of Birkenau. Ballensiefen, a 'scientist' with a doctorate, a former functionary in the Propaganda Ministry, is thus evidence of a remarkable continuity in the actions he performed in both his ministry and the SD offices. Apart from his work in the Propaganda Ministry and the RSHA, he was an active member of the NSKK[67] and, even as a schoolboy, gave evidence of a Nazi fervour and a deeply rooted anti-Semitism, writing essays (for what readership?) on St Paul and De Lagarde, or on the Labour Service. We can see how feverishly dedicated he already was, and how eager to indulge in intellectual activity and 'propaganda':[68] the functional and militant dimensions were inseparable in the path that led from school to the SD, via the NSKK and the Propaganda Ministry.

Ballensiefen is an excellent representative of the way SS intellectuals made their way to the SD. They took the path of activism, in a real process of political evolution, marked by the gradual move into the SS and the integration of a Nordicism that was much less pronounced in other Nazi Party organizations. During their activist careers, all these men picked up know-how and techniques that would later be mobilized by the Third Reich's organs of repression. Thus, their activist and professional careers, their political evolution and their rise in society all merged together, so that it seems difficult to decide what factors stemmed from which of these dimensions when they finally joined the SD.

The second path taken involved some 25 per cent of SS intellectuals. In this case, they belonged to the SD and the SS *before* joining the NSDAP. They were mainly recruited by the SD before they started any professional activity, just after finishing their studies. These men joined the NSDAP belatedly for structural reasons. The NSDAP stopped recruiting between 1934 and 1937–8, in an attempt to preserve the activist dimension of the 'movement' (*Bewegung*). For example, an individual who joined the SD in 1934 was then automatically part of the SS, but not, paradoxically, of the NSDAP. He was part of the elite body without belonging to the mass movement. This was true of Walter von Kielpinski, Heinz Hummitzsch and Rudolf Levin. They all joined the NSDAP after 1937 – a sign of the efficacy of the measures banning new members, whose sudden new enthusiasm was the cause of some suspicion, from joining the Nazi Party. However, these men, whose careers sometimes began before they entered the SD, considered themselves to be authentic militants. Walter von Kielpinski contributed to the Nazi local press from 1931.[69] He joined the SA in 1933, by which time he had a good knowledge of the Nazi Party in Saxony.[70]

Heinz Hummitzsch, too, entered the Black Order before joining the Nazi Party. Like von Kielpinski, Hummitzsch was a Saxon, a member of the Leipzig SD: he entered the SD in 1935 and the NSDAP in 1937. He had by this time a long experience of militant activities, having played a part in the Nazification of the Leipzig *Studentenschaft*, via various student organizations and his own *Turnerschaft*. He joined the SA just a few weeks after the *Machtergreifung*, and could easily be viewed as one of the opportunists whom the NSDAP sought to exclude by closing its doors. The fact remains that his *völkisch* militancy had found expression at the beginning of the 1930s, in a very dynamic border activism in the student corporation. This was how he came into contact with SS officers from the Leipzig SDOA, with which he collaborated from 1933, finally joining its ranks in 1935. It was militant activity and the networks of sociability created within it that turned out, yet again, to be decisive for his recruitment. The only notable difference from the previous group is that this militancy

was not exercised in the NSDAP, but in *völkisch* student organizations.
However, it is not clear how much of a difference this really made, since
the *Studentenschaften* had been very largely Nazified since 1929–31. The
one in Leipzig was no exception and Hummitzsch, furthermore, had
played a significant part in its Nazification.[71] The absence of an NSDAP
card is thus no indication of any lack of enthusiasm for the Nazi Party.
That was an insignificant factor, even in the eyes of a man like him who
had very quickly taken up the cudgels in the *Volkstumskampf*, a commitment which he discusses at some length in his *Lebenslauf*, bringing out its
importance for his move to the central departments of the SD.[72]

Most men who fell into this category were Saxons, members, like von
Kielpinski, of the Leipzig *Schrifttumstelle*, as if the latter had recruited
young intellectuals without referring to the Party and without its
approval. In any case, these atypical paths were those taken by men
who had already proved their ideological orthodoxy: they had mainly
come up through *völkisch* student organizations, like Heinz Gräfe, Heinz
Hummitzsch and Rolf Mühler,[73] which was evidence of the constancy of
their commitment and ideological orthodoxy. This was evidence enough
in the view of the SD 'recruiters', who took them into the Leipzig SDOA
without being bothered by the fact they were not Nazi Party members.
For all these men, joining the NSDAP was a mere formality.

The third type of itinerary was that followed by men who joined the Third
Reich's police organizations via their bureaucracy, without being affili-
ated to the NSDAP or the SS. They included many of the young lawyers
recruited after their *Staatsexamen* at the behest of Werner Best, in the
years 1934–8, and then placed at the head of the local Gestapo sections.
Some of them went on to join the SD and worked on the formulating of
doctrine or on educational projects, so their case is similar to that of SS
intellectuals. Paul Mylius and Walter Zirpins fell into this group. The first
was a pure product of the Gestapo: Mylius was a lawyer who, after many
years of police activity, was transferred to RSHA *Amt* VII, after passing
through the training departments of RSHA (RSHA *Amt* I A). Later, under
the leadership of Franz Six and Günther Franz, he was one of the small
group of SS intellectuals who set up a study programme, and wrote a
thesis on 'anti-Semitic jurisprudence', which enabled him to gain the title
of doctor of law. Despite being an SD intellectual, Mylius had actually
entered the SS by the back door. Like many Gestapo cadres, he had for
long been a police functionary without actually being a member. Walter
Zirpins had a similar profile: he was a functionary in the criminal police, a
pedagogue who published various works and gave classes on the theory
of police action, both the criminal police and the political police. He was
logically linked to the activities of RSHA *Amt* I B, although he did not
join the SS until 1939, when he was sent to Poland. He was a member
of an *Einsatzgruppe*, and was made head of the criminal police in Łódź.
In each case, the impression that the men joined only late in the day is

reinforced by the fact that they did not do so on their own initiative. In fact, they were brought into the SS as part of the programme designed to standardize the Third Reich's repressive organizations, a programme implemented by Heydrich and Best. They were thus automatically given an SS rank and a registration number. This has led some historians to come up with the idea that there were less politicized, less 'Nazi' cadres in the Gestapo than in the SD:[74] but the cases of Mylius and Zirpins clearly show that this was not the case. Mylius had been a member of the NSDAP since 1931, so he was an *alter Kämpfer* (an old combatant) who had no need to prove his ideological orthodoxy. As for Zirpins, he had been active in the Silesian *Freikörper* ever since he had been a tender youth: his commitment was evidently a bridge to a Nazi belief system whose attractiveness lay precisely in its ability to federate the *völkisch* forces that had been born out of this wartime outlook. Zirpins and Mylius owed their membership of the SS to an automatic, collective process, but they were dyed-in-the-wool Nazis all the same.

Recruitment: a social mechanism of enlistment

In the first three years of the SD's existence, recruitment was the result of individual encounters, and can be attributed to a few individuals of strong personality who, being in charge of a department or a particular region, left their own enduring stamp on recruitment. In this respect, we can distinguish between two 'generations' of recruiters. The first, composed of a few individuals very close to Heydrich and Himmler, formed the initial nucleus of the SD. They included Wilhelm Albert, Georg Herbert Mehlhorn, Lothar Beutel, Ernst Damzog, Hermann Behrends, Hans Kobelinsky and Werner Best. They were not all SS intellectuals. Beutel and Kobelinsky were Nazi militants of very long standing, and they took over training for the SD in the two biggest *Länder* of Germany, namely Saxony and Berlin.[75] Albert was responsible for organizing the SD in Frankfurt, Beutel founded the SD in Saxony, while Kobelinsky and Damzog collaborated with Behrends in Berlin, and Georg Herbert Mehlhorn, one of the very first of Heydrich's collaborators (together with Kobelinsky), was later active in Silesia.[76] This meant that they were powerful local SD potentates, whose views carried considerable weight in the organization of the intelligence department. Mehlhorn, Behrends and Albert went on to head the central departments, once these had moved to Berlin.[77] All, in fact, were the first collaborators recruited by Heydrich in 1931–2.[78]

A particularly interesting example is Lothar Beutel. At the end of 1933, this Saxon was delegated to head the SD for Saxony and Silesia. Beutel was a very old acquaintance of Heydrich. Beutel, Heydrich and Mehlhorn belonged to the *Orgesch* (*Organisation Escherich*) in the 1920s and formed close bonds within this organization which fought against the commission of the Entente Cordiale in Upper Silesia, hiding weapons.[79] Does this explain Beutel's entry into the SS and the SD? We are reduced to guesswork. The fact remains that he did join it in 1931 and, while working for the SD, he was officially transferred there as SS-*Hauptsturmführer* and a permanent member in 1934, by which date the SD was already quite highly structured in Saxony. He was behind the organization of the Leipzig *Schrifttumstelle*, that surveillance centre for the written production of the whole Reich, which could draw on the *Deutsche Bücherei* in the city (a copyright library), and on a faculty of literature and human sciences dominated by the *völkisch* militancy so characteristic of this border university.[80]

So Beutel lay behind the specific character of the SD, which consisted in recruiting young arts and social sciences graduates and putting them in charge of surveillance of the written production in their fields. In June 1934, Beutel put the first of his recruits, the literature graduate Wilhelm Spengler, at the head of the *Schrifttumstelle*. Spengler, who had entered the SS in September 1933,[81] was recruited by Beutel just a few weeks later to keep the 'confessional opponents' of Nazism under surveillance. A convinced *Gottgläubiger*, particularly hostile to the Catholic educational system in which he had been brought up,[82] Spengler set up a surveillance network before becoming, at Beutel's behest, the recruiter of a whole generation of literature and history graduates from Saxony who flocked into *Amt* III C of the RSHA from 1940 onwards. In any event, Beutel was acting in concert with Spengler, one of the figures active in the SD policy of recruiting qualified personnel and putting them to work in assessment and surveillance in their fields of training. Indeed, in August 1939, some time before being subjected to disciplinary proceedings for 'embezzlement', Beutel was present at a debate on the organization of what was to become the RSHA, and here he urged that new graduates be enlisted:

> SIPO cadres must have a legal, political and criminological training. SD collaborators, on the other hand, must be trained either in politics and economics, or in politics and literature, and may be political and legal only in departments of law and administration. In every other case, the SD needs specialists. The most capable lawyers might conceivably be sent on a special course in the universities, but I believe this is the wrong answer, since it would at best give [them] a superficial knowledge and not the deeper understanding of the specialist [. . .].[83]

Beutel poses as a defender of the SD intellectuals as against the domination of legal magistrates of the Gestapo and the administration, but it is as if he were providing a synopsis of the recruitment policy applied by him in Leipzig between 1934 and 1938. The figure of the specialist, a graduate in literature and the human sciences, called on to lavish his academic expertise on SD activities in every branch of the German 'life domain', is perhaps best embodied in the person of Wilhelm Spengler, head of the *Schrifttumstelle*. He held a doctorate in literature, and also brilliantly passed exams in history and philosophy, which meant that he could draw on a wide classical culture.[84] He was mainly in charge of German literature, an area in which his judgement was considered reliable, thanks to his ideological orthodoxy. And finally, he turned out to be an excellent organizer, turning the Leipzig *Schrifttumstelle* into one of the three great intellectual centres of the SS.[85] So we can see how this officer and organizer made his mark in his choice of recruits. For example, Hans Kobelinsky recruited Reinhard Höhn, the future head of the SDHA *Amt* II, a department that focused on centralizing all the reports coming into the Reich on the 'life domain'.[86] These first appointments defined the working methods implemented in the SD. Its numbers grew extremely quickly between 1934 and 1937. This first generation of SD cadres thus played a considerable role in the arrival of SS intellectuals in the intelligence services.

The composition of the group of SS intellectuals was decisively shaped, however, by the choices of the second generation of recruiters, brought in by Beutel, Kobelinsky, Damzog and Behrends. A few powerful personalities recruited tens of young intellectuals into the SS and the SD, training tightly organized teams who in certain cases remained in place until 1945. These individuals, recruited between 1934 and 1937, were more concentrated in the central departments than those of the previous generation, and were sometimes tempted by the prospect of building up for themselves a regional fiefdom that would prove their independence from Heydrich. The generation that succeeded the SS activists who had contributed to bringing the SD out of its amateur phase was younger, more concentrated in Berlin, better educated and closer to Heydrich himself.[87]

In all these cases, these individuals took over a recruitment drive that reached its peak in 1935–7, a peak that was surpassed only in 1939–40 with the establishment of planned procedures for 'personnel acquisition'. Among the biggest recruiters in this second generation were Werner Best, Franz Six, Reinhard Höhn, Wilhelm Spengler, Otto Ohlendorf and Heinz Jost. In this respect, Best – like Jost – was a special case, since he was recruited directly by Heydrich and Himmler during a tour of inspection in the Rhineland. But while Höhn was enlisted by Hans Kobelinsky, and Spengler by Lothar Beutel, Six and Ohlendorf were brought into the SD by Höhn. These examples give us some idea of the hold these new recruiters had on the departments they set up on a firm footing when the RSHA was created.

The cases of Six and Best also help us to measure the volume of recruitment as well as its qualitative impact on the SD's development. Best entered the Third Reich's repressive organizations in 1934. He continued to move to and fro between the Gestapo and the SD, occupying in succession the post of head of the administration in both departments. This meant he could recruit the very young lawyers and economists who had emerged from the *Assessorat*,[88] and entrust them with local Gestapo or SD bureaus, and – more rarely – positions in the central departments. He thus contributed, as Herbert pointed out, to training RSHA cadres, both at local level and in the central offices: these cadres included Ernst Hermann Jahr, Bruno Lettow, Paul Mylius and Gustav Jonack. His recruitment policy was initially pragmatic but later became a planned process that had a major impact on the composition of the body of RSHA cadres. After the war, Best described his 'kindergarten for assessors in those days', emphasizing how 'efficient' they were,[89] as shown by the way they implemented the policy of genocide.[90] Hence the predominance of lawyers among the RSHA cadres: if we look at all the officers of the SIPO and the SD, 70 per cent of the graduates were lawyers or economists, and over 50 per cent of them were recruited by Best himself.[91]

However decisive the latter's role in RSHA and Gestapo recruitment may have been, this overall assessment does not apply to the SD, or even to the RSHA personnel department (*Amt* I). Indeed, the recruitment practices set up by Best tried to keep up with the exponential growth of the Gestapo to provide the political and criminal services (which until 1934 had been under the control of individual *Länder*) with a unified framework. Once Best had entered the lists, they came under the control of the SS, of Heydrich and Himmler, who relied on his recruitment policy to unify and control.[92] As for the SD, it was mainly immune to this phenomenon under the leadership of Reinhard Höhn, Otto Ohlendorf and Franz Six: the last is a perfect example of the role of recruiters from this second generation.

Six, then, entered the SD in 1935 at the urging of Reinhard Höhn. He was enlisted to set up, within the SD *Inland*, a department for the scientific study of the adversaries of Nazism (*Gegnerforschung*). This was a creation *ex nihilo*, for while the SD had hitherto gathered information on the enemies of Nazism, this had been in an unsystematic fashion, based on networks of amateur informants, and unable to investigate the written productions of the – real or supposed – opponents of the Third Reich. Six organized the department, setting up protocols of systematic surveillance and research programmes aimed at producing tables and diagrams showing the relations between adversaries. To carry out this programme, which required a significant number of qualified personnel capable of the work involved in 'intelligence treatment' (*nachrichtendienstliche Arbeit*) and integrating it into periodic syntheses on the activity of opponents, Six employed young graduates, historians, economists, literary specialists and publicists. In this way, the following men were recruited: Helmut Knochen, the future head of the SIPO and the SD in France, Herbert Martin Hagen, one of 'Eichmann's henchmen'[93] and Knochen's future deputy in France, Horst Mahnke, Heinz Ballensiefen, Waldemar Beyer, Karl Burmester and Emil Augsburg.[94] It was also Franz Six who had Erich Ehrlinger transferred from the south-west SDOA to the central departments, giving the latter's career a considerable fillip.[95]

The second – and principal – mechanism of recruitment of SS and SD intellectuals relied on the many varied networks of affinity and solidarity built up over their student and professional careers. Among these networks, the most homogeneous and efficient were those that could draw on student and activist solidarities, and add the charisma of a 'recruiter' distinguished by his responsibilities and his long career as a militant. Thus, Reinhard Höhn, who was at one and the same time a brilliant professor and a very precocious *völkisch* activist, could profit from the many networks to which he was linked – in academic, activist and state circles – to recruit a great number of intellectuals, including Six, Ohlendorf and Heinrich Malz – who were in a position to take over the assessment and observation of the economic, social and cultural facts of Nazi Germany. He shaped the core of what became *Amt* III of the RSHA. Together with Best and Wilhelm Stuckart, he founded the review *Reich, Volksordnung, Lebensraum*, created in 1939 and dedicated to problems in administrative theory linked to the emergence of a Nazi empire in Poland, in the west and – from 1941 – in the Balkans and Russia.[96] The very high level of coherence binding these various groups, all linked by solidarity, went far beyond the person of the young professor of public law – Höhn was thirty-six in 1940 – who was at the same time the deputy head of the *Inland*-SD.[97] These networks of activist solidarity – whose origins went back to the *Abwehrkampf* against separatists and Franco-Belgians in the Rhineland – a degree of academic sociability and SS loyalty all left a decisive mark on recruitment into the SD.

Certain local SD bureaus were distinguished by their situation and the presence of institutions with which intense cooperative activities could be organized. Universities or private institutions such as the *Deutscher Ausland-Institut* [German Foreign Institute – *Tr*.] in Stuttgart, the NSStB, or the *Deutsche Bücherei* in Leipzig set up a local organic cooperation with SD bureaus, especially those in Hamburg, Stuttgart and Leipzig. The SDOAs in Stuttgart and Leipzig organized specific activities – surveillance of migrants, activism in German minorities, specialization in the domain of culture – thus providing the best example of the action of networks of solidarity in recruiting intellectuals into the SD.

The aforementioned case of Leipzig is inseparable from the two specific activities of the SDOA: surveillance of written production in the Reich and border activism. Wilhelm Spengler, the patron of the *Schrifttumstelle*, could draw on the occasional collaboration of two academics, Karl Justus Obenauer and Andreas Jolle, who had been his German literature professors.[98] He then enlisted their assistant professor, Hans Rössner, as well as Ernst Turowsky, known to Spengler from the activist circles of the *Grenzkampf*. These two latter characters are a perfect example of the SD intellectual, and made their entire careers in the wake of Spengler in the RSHA. Walter von Kielpinski and Paul Dittel complete this muster of men met by Spengler in university activist circles, circles which were a breeding ground for the *Schrifttumstelle*. In March 1936, when the latter was transferred from Leipzig to Berlin, other young graduates were recruited in Leipzig, proof that the network did not depend on Spengler's personality alone, but had become an organic network, dominated by links between the SD and academic milieus in Saxony.

Border activism, in other words clandestine support for German minorities in the Sudetenland, was the second specific feature of the Leipzig SDOA's activity; witness Heinz Gräfe and Heinz Hummitzsch. Both these men joined student activist networks involved in *Grenzarbeit*, went on several trips to *volksdeutsch* communities in the Sudetenland and joined the SD in Leipzig immediately after their studies. In his *Lebenslauf*, Hummitzsch specifies that 'at the beginning of 1935, [he] had drawn the attention of the SD by his *volksdeutsch* activity [and that] after the completion of a mission to Czechoslovakia [he had been] summoned to the central department of the SD in autumn 1935'.[99] He then became a close collaborator of Hans Ehlich, another Saxon who had come from the Berlin SDOA. Rudolf Oebsger-Röder was also one of the Saxon activists who joined Ehlich in the departments specializing in racial policy and population displacements, as commander of the *Einwandererzentralstelle* [EWZ; Central Immigrants' Office – *Tr.*] in Łódź.[100] Previous to that, Oebsger-Röder had been head of the 'Press' service in the Königsberg SD, where he was a colleague of Heinz Gräfe, his friend from university days[101] and *Grenzarbeit* in Leipzig, now an SD member in Tilsit. So they both took up there the specific activities that came with their position in border territory, activities which they had first been introduced to in the militant networks of Leipzig. The two men were later to meet again in 1942–3 where they were both in charge of Operation Zeppelin.[102]

The men in charge of racial policy exploited this osmosis between intelligence activities and *Volkstumskampf* inaugurated by the Leipzig *Studentenschaften* and by the Stuttgart NSStB to recruit qualified personnel. In Stuttgart, the activism of the NSStB concerned, first and foremost, Martin Sandberger and Eugen Steimle but also, through the connections forged between the NSStB, the *Deutsche Stiftung* and the DAI, Alexander Dolezalek and Hans Joachim Beyer. All of these men came from activist and student networks and joined the SD at the behest of the *Reichsstudentenführer*[103] and head of the SDOA in Stuttgart, Gustav Adolf Scheel.[104] All, at a given moment, were employed by Ehlich and the RSHA *Amt* III B because of the on-the-ground skills they had acquired in the *Volkstumskampf*,[105] skills which – as the examples of Gräfe and Oebsger-Röder show – the RSHA *Amt* III B had to share with the *Ausland*-SD (RSHA *Amt* VI), which also employed Steimle, Sandberger, Filbert and Gräfe. After a promising early career in the Stuttgart SDOA, Sandberger directed the EWZ in Posen on behalf of Ehlich, then in 1941 left to direct Sk 1a of the *Einsatzgruppe* A in Russia,[106] returning, finally, to direct RSHA *Amt* VI A under the command of Schellenberg.[107]

Chapter 6

From struggle to control

From the 'Security Department of the SS' (SD) to the 'Reich Security Main Office' (RSHA)

The SD was created in 1931, under the name *Nachrichtendienst* ('News Service' or ND), by Reinhard Heydrich, at Himmler's request.[1] So it was an intelligence service that came into being within the NSDAP, more particularly the SS. Initially, the SD set out to be an instrument serving, first and foremost, the short-term aims of its two creators. From 1931 to April 1932, it was still overshadowed by the intelligence services of the SS and of the SA – in the latter case, the intelligence service did not survive when the SA itself was banned. Heydrich, with the help of a few collaborators – mainly Kobelinsky, Albert and Mehlhorn – then set down on paper the plans for an organization that he sought to provide with a network of informers. The latter were initially SS members, who gave their services for free (the ability of the SD to pay people was at that time practically zero) and gleaned information mainly on leftist political opponents.[2] Once he was rid of competition from the SA intelligence service, Heydrich was appointed 'head of the SD' on 19 July 1932 and, two months later, brought together the first members of the SD in a Munich apartment – which acted both as the residence of the Heydrich couple and as the SD's central office. Paul Leffler has left the only description of this meeting:

> On 11 September 1932, in an apartment on the Türkenstrasse in Munich, the first meeting of the heads of local offices from all over the Reich took place. They were joined by the collaborators designated as members of the central office in Munich. At this meeting, Heydrich and Himmler were present, and in their programmatic statements they claimed that the SD would become the Party's intelligence service; modelled on the Intelligence Service [probably of the UK – *Tr.*] and the *Deuxième Bureau* [the French equivalent – *Tr.*] it was to keep the leaders of the Party and, later, of the National-Socialist state, informed by systematically collecting documentation on the aims,

methods and plans of internal political enemies and, should the case arise, on problems within our own ranks.[3]

This curious account[4] brings out the very relative extent of the SD's development in summer 1932. Admittedly, Leffler's account suggests that the regional and local network of the SD was already partly established. But it is doubtful whether networks of informers were, at that precise moment, very extensive. And nothing suggests that the local network was complete: after all, three years later, Erich Ehrlinger was transferred to the SD to organize it in Nuremberg, the Party's main city, of crucial importance for SS dignitaries.[5] What we do know, at all events, is that the SD's 'central services' then numbered six members.[6] This did not prevent either Heydrich or Himmler from nursing great ambitions for this infant structure. Indeed, on this occasion they formulated the main lines of the activities assigned to the SD: surveillance of political enemies on the left, surveillance of the 'reaction' – the traditional parliamentary right – and surveillance in the NSDAP's 'own ranks'. The SD was to act as an intelligence service for a party, and play the role of an activist service engaged in the political struggle being waged by the NSDAP for the conquest of power. But the second source of the SD's usefulness could already be discerned in outline. Faithful to Himmler and Heydrich, who endeavoured to keep control over it,[7] the SD was to ensure that the SS retained its supremacy with the Nazi 'polycracy' and to establish itself as the Party's only intelligence service.[8]

Though it continued to develop throughout 1932 and 1933, the SD could not live up to its models: its numbers were too low, its information not reliable enough, and its working methods much too amateurish.[9] Nonetheless, it turned out to hold a strategic interest for Himmler, the one who apparently came off worst in the sharing out of powers that followed the *Machtergreifung*. Indeed, the *Reichsführer* had not obtained a ministerial portfolio, and had acquired a significant position only in the *Land* of Bavaria – he took over the Bavarian political police in March–April 1933.[10] Assured of his position in Bavaria, Himmler, who wished, as his own statements made clear, to found a 'defence body for the Reich' formed by a fusion between the SS and the police services (political, criminal and uniformed),[11] undertook to infiltrate their administration, constitutionally left in the hands of the *Länder*. Himmler's SS had some 52,000 men in its ranks,[12] with a body of qualified cadres[13] and in particular several graduates already recruited by Heydrich into the SD. The latter, in collaboration with the other services of the SS, introduced his own members into the political forces of the *Länder*, so as to prepare for Himmler's official appointment as their head and thus institutionalize SS control over police power. Walter Stahlecker, future head of *Einsatzgruppe* A, who entered the SS in 1932, was thus appointed vice-director of the Württemberg police in January 1933, thereby providing Himmler with decisive support a year before the latter succeeded in being made chief of police.[14] During the winter of 1933–4, then, the SD produced seven heads of the political police out of the existing sixteen.[15] At this date, Himmler was appointed chief of police over eleven of the *Länder*: only the police forces of the small *Land* of Schaumburg-Lippe and – much more important – the powerful political police force in Prussia were still beyond his grasp. This almost complete control over the German political police was to a great extent the work of the SD, of its nascent networks and of its files – even though the last were as yet not very voluminous. In April 1934, Himmler was the head of all the German police forces, and two months later the SD was confirmed as the sole intelligence service of the NSDAP by Rudolf Hess.[16] The SD had reached the goal set out for it by Himmler and Heydrich, and its existence and its permanence were now assured.

In addition, Werner Best, who had come under suspicion in a murder case and been relieved of his duties as head of the Hesse police, had a few months previously joined the intelligence service: promoted head of the SD for the whole of south Germany (SDOA south and south-west, from Stuttgart to Munich) by Heydrich and Himmler, Best had undertaken the task of reorganizing the security service, recruiting personnel for local offices, and trying to extend the scope of the central departments.[17] Known for his hostility to the SA, a hostility which played a part in his expulsion from Darmstadt, Best focused SD activity on keeping the rival organization under surveillance, at a time when it was dreaming of a 'second revolution',[18] especially by drawing up reports for Nazi Party dignitaries.[19] And it was on the occasion of the 'Röhm putsch' that the SD had really acquired, for the first time, its role as advisor to power, acting as an intelligence service and 'brains trust'[20] as Himmler and Heydrich wished it to be.[21]

There are many different accounts of the 'Röhm putsch' or 'Night of the Long Knives'. The impact of the event was considerable, on both the SD and its intellectuals, as it resulted in the first division of tasks between police organs and the intelligence service. The Gestapo was entrusted with arrests, round-ups and searches for individuals; the SD was involved with all intelligence, surveillance, file-keeping, and infiltration by unpaid agents. When, on 29 June, Werner Best announced the demonstration of an SA *Standarte* in the heart of Munich, this was the signal for the crack-down that followed the next day. This was minutely prepared beforehand by a meeting of SDOA chiefs from all over Germany, held in the head-quarters of the Gestapo that had only just been taken over by Heydrich in Berlin, and was led by the Gestapo and SS commandos placed under the orders of the heads of local sections of the SD.[22] The preparatory and triggering role assumed in the purge by the SD, symbolic as it was of the division of tasks between the police and the security service, also revealed the way the SD had been transformed from an amateurish outfit into an organized service: after all, in June 1934, the Leipzig *Schrifttumstelle* was founded.[23] The SD now had access to a hoard of documents that made of it a real intelligence service: it could provide jobs for many SS intellectuals

– in fact, from May 1934, it could finally draw on significant financial support[24] on the part of the *Reichsschatzmeister*, once the Party treasurer, had 'certified that the budget would be assured', so that Heydrich could order that they 'proceed to the recruitment of men who had hitherto worked so faithfully for no pay'.[25] In January 1935, the SD, now officially known as the *Sicherheitsdienst Hauptabteilung* (Security Service Main Department or SDHA), was consolidated, financed and given clear missions to fulfil; it was promoted to being the main office of an SS which, controlling the police and the concentration camps,[26] held all power of repression in Germany.[27] The time of political struggle for the SS's security service was over. It was now the age of surveillance (*Überwachung*) and investigation (*Forschung*).

The SD aimed first and foremost to be an instrument for 'investigating the adversaries' of Nazism (*Gegnerforschung*). More than the term 'adversary', it is the word 'investigating' that draws attention to itself: this is not an investigation confined to tracking down prey, with images derived from hunting or the world of the quest, but involves instead scientific research (*Forschung*). Of course, we are still in the field of struggle, since one 'investigates' the enemy only so that one can fight him more effectively.[28] This was the conclusion of one intellectual, employed by the *Reichsleiter* [National Leader, a rank in the NSDAP – *Tr.*] responsible for foreign affairs, the future minister, Joachim Ribbentrop, to compile scientific studies, after a visit to the offices of SDHA *Amt* II/1:

> We went through several rooms, stuffed with cupboards full of systematically numbered folders. On the empty walls, organization charts were stuck up showing, in differently coloured lines, the 'transversal links' [*Querverbindungen*] between the ideological enemies [of Nazism] and Communists, Freemasons, 'persons of Jewish descent' [*jüdisch versippten*][29] and Catholics.[30]

It was the systematization of working methods, the use of organization charts (taken from sociology), the claim to scientific status and the progress already made in the task that impressed the observer. In fact, Heydrich made this scientific dimension of intelligence work into one of the priorities when the SD was reorganized in 1935: in *Das Schwarze Korps*, the official publication of the SS,[31] he wrote a series of programmatic articles that set out the main lines.[32] It was mainly a question of launching a historically based 'investigation' into ideological adversaries, so as to study those adversaries' methods and tactics. The SD was also to set up a real 'didactics of investigation into adversaries'. Here too, Nazi practice derived its foundations from history – a sign of the doctrinal dimension assumed by *Gegnerforschung*.

Adolf Eichmann, who entered the SD in 1936, was also struck by this zeal for scientificity:

> Dr Six led the 'ideological struggle against opponents'[33] on a purely scientific basis. He had eyes and ears everywhere and knew perfectly who was in charge of this or that institution, who this or that person was. [. . .] Our task was to bring in acquaintances, and this activity went full steam ahead [. . .].

Whoever the adversary under surveillance was, the harvest of 'concrete' facts and the files kept on individuals involved along with him – the traditional dimensions of intelligence work – were always accompanied by the systematic scrutiny of all information published on him and by him. This information, integrated into the writing of reports, helped to create an image of the enemy, to bring written production into line with the formal criteria of scientific discourse, conferring on it that 'objectivity' on which the *Geisteswissenschaften* prided themselves in the 1930s. Indeed, these 'human sciences' were the very model of this activity. This, at least, was what *Sturmbannführer* Rudolf Levin, a historian and philosopher of history,[34] wrote in 1943, in a methodological lecture describing the methods employed by the SD over the past decade for 'studying' its opponents.[35]

In fact, the memorandums of the SDHA II/1 provided readers with a discourse filled with vivid concrete examples. They quoted the enemy's writings, giving references in footnotes. They drew a portrait of the adversary using the same discursive practices as historians, sociologists or philosophers describing social phenomena or groups: had not the latter, after all, inspired those 'sciences of combat'[36] that the social sciences had become at the end of the Weimar Republic?[37] Produced by the same universities as the assistant professors in the faculties, at times carrying out in tandem the two types of activity, the SS intellectuals of the SD formed an ideal group for giving *Gegnerforschung* the stamp of objectivity while setting up an academic science fully committed to the Nazi revolution.

This scientific revolution went far beyond the field of 'investigations into opponents': it extended across all the activities of the SD, whose young intellectuals identified with the programmatic remarks written by one of Franz Six's colleagues in Heidelberg:

> In a very highly differentiated society such as modern society, it is not possible to maintain complete order with unified, long-term leadership unless this leadership can call on a properly qualified security apparatus that must be completely independent of the economic and ideological groups that form the complete structure. Without an intimate awareness, and accurate assessment, of sociological factors, state security can be protected only by brutal authoritarian methods – and only until the forthcoming revolution! On the contrary: political vision and intelligence make necessary [the establishment of] a security apparatus that can reckon with sociological givens. A sociology of security, or a police sociology, becomes an inevitable necessity for our modern order as a whole.[38]

Published in *Volk im Werden*, this article was the manifesto of a new combative, activist science, the science of government and security,[39] as incarnated in *Gegnerforschung*. It was also embodied in the second concept developed by SD intellectuals, that of the 'surveillance of the domain of German life'.[40]

This second activity was the field of the SDAH II/2, directed by Reinhard Höhn and then Otto Ohlendorf. The complicity between the two men created a remarkable sense of continuity, with the result that the practices established by Höhn in 1934–5 lasted until the collapse of the Third Reich.[41] First and foremost, they both had to conform to the wishes of Himmler and Heydrich. Thus, in 1937, Himmler assigned to the SD the mission of 'drawing up regular and representative reports on the current situation for the information of the *Reichsführer*, the leaders of the state [and] the Party, concerning the political situation in the Reich and the morale [*Stimmung*] of its populations'. The SD '[took] an interest solely in major doctrinal issues that needed to be treated scientifically, like a general staff'.[42] When combined with the mobilization of the social sciences imposed by Höhn, Six and Ohlendorf, this normative definition drew its flexibility as well as its rhetoric from the practitioners of education. The concepts developed by SS intellectuals turned out to be rather hazy, however, and their authors often found them just as difficult to define as do the historians of Nazism. In reply to the question of an American interrogator asking him to define the term '*Lebensgebiet*', Ohlendorf, who was then a prisoner and waiting for his turn to testify at the International Tribunal at Nuremberg, replied as follows:

> It's very difficult to define, as it includes a whole world of ideas. Let's take the 'domain' of law, for example. We need to imagine that the life of the law includes all its institutions and their effects on the normal course of life. In our groups, we have always expressed the opinion that culture was wider than what is usually understood by this term, in other words that it includes all the manifestations of the life of a people. This means culture in the narrow sense, just like areas that are distant from it, such as economics, which are then included. This must not just include the superficial, but the whole human environment that springs from it. Thus, for us, public health,[43] law, administration, economics, the sciences, education, and religious life all composed the 'life domain'.[44]

This helps us to grasp the way the SD tried to act as a general observatory for the social and racial transformations brought along, in its view, by the Nazi revolution. Was not Ohlendorf proposing a remarkably modern – and erudite[45] – 'definition of culture', a definition which formed the basis for a practice of surveillance that was in other respects quite difficult to seize as a coherent whole? In any event, the SD had to provide the government figures of the Third Reich with information on every aspect of the country's social, cultural and economic life. It was also entrusted with the mission of treating the major ideological problems in a scientific way. In line with this extensive definition, the SDHA II/2 was divided into three sub-bureaus embracing culture, law and administration, and finally economics.[46] So this was the 'domain of German life', the categories of which were so fuzzy that SDHA *Amt* II/213 (the future RSHA *Amt* III B), in charge of the surveillance of politics and health, race and ethnic issues, was part of the bureau on 'culture', viewed, this time, in a limited sense: surely it should logically – in so far as there was any logic to the matter at all – have fallen to *Amt* II/2 2, in charge of law, administration and government policies?[47] There was no inconsistency here. The biological and organicist world-view of the Nazi system of belief led them to see in the 'ethnic', racial and 'hygienic' life of German Nordicity a phenomenon that was much more part of a *culture* seen in a very broad sense by Ohlendorf and his henchmen, a *government* policy, even a Nazi one, and thus in principle totally conditioned by overwhelming biological necessity. Apparently simple questions of labelling thus became an occasion for internal debates which contributed to the formulation of Nazi doctrine, as witness the definition formulated by Ohlendorf. These clearly referred to debates between the 'referents'[48] of the SDHA during the reorganization of 1935, and perhaps that of 1939 too, which led to the foundation of the *Reichssicherheitshauptamt*, the RSHA.

While this latter body was set up only at the beginning of 1940, it nonetheless required many months of preparation beforehand, and strenuous negotiations between department heads. All the debates that preceded the creation of the new central department of the 'state security body' focused on questions of personnel politics and the division of activities, but the concepts on which SD activity had hitherto been based now came under scrutiny. The observation of the 'domain of German life' was barely affected by these debates, in spite of the expansion of a Reich that had moved from being 'pan-Germanist' to European as a result of the conquest of Poland. The way of studying – and combating – opponents was, on the other hand, entirely a matter for the reorganization of the relations between the Gestapo and the SD. The means, the increase in manpower and funding for the spheres of intervention were obviously a powerful motive force in the fierce debates on this reform that preoccupied SS intellectuals and the lawyers of the Gestapo.[49]

Thus everything turned on the question of the recruitment and training of personnel – a question to which we shall return – and on the way in which opponents were to be observed and combated. Three writers, who all had experience of day-to-day intelligence and police work, played a part in this debate. The first was Franz Six, the theoretician of the concept of *Gegnerforschung*, head of SDAH *Amt* II/2. The second was Werner Best, the deputy – at that time in disgrace[50] – of Heydrich, the promoter of a 'state security body' to be entrusted to the lawyer functionaries of the Gestapo, and himself at the head of the administration of the Gestapo and the counter-espionage police. The third was Walter Schellenberg, a lawyer and politician with Gestapo experience, in charge of SDHA I/11.[51] Three men who were together faced with plans for revamping the Reich's organs of repression – plans which were all based on a different conception of 'investigation of and struggle against adversaries'.

The triangular debate was organized around two questions. The first concerned police and SD personnel – their training, career opportunities and status. On the one hand, Werner Best claimed pre-eminence for the practitioners of law known as the Gestapo's *Assessoren*, and tried to turn a course in law into an obligatory route into the positions of cadres of the future RSHA. Conversely, Schellenberg and Six, united on this question, found support in Lothar Beutel's memorandum. They wanted to create a body of cadres comprising graduates from the different *Geisteswissenschaften* rather than from legal studies – they preferred men who had come up through the activist networks rather than the civil service. This debate set the Gestapo at loggerheads with the SD and resembles a mere corporatist polemic, as the three writers were in other respects in agreement on the need to recruit men of an undeniable 'ideological soundness'.[52] However, the front presented by the SD was not unified: Six and Schellenberg defended very different visions of SD activity, and the stumbling block lay in *Gegnerforschung* and *Gegnerbekämpfung*.

On 24 February 1939, Schellenberg, requested to map out a fusion of the police forces with the SD, produced his 'plan for a reorganization of the SD' in which the Security Service and the police would indeed be merged.[53] In his view, intelligence, 'ideological investigation' and 'executive activity' should constitute different sectors, divided between three independent *Ämter* or departments: an internal intelligence service, an 'investigative' service, and an executive service for 'political defence'. In his memorandum, Schellenberg took care not to draw on the current terminology, and to avoid as much as possible the terms *'Sicherheitsdienst'*, *'Gestapo'*, *'Gegnerforschung'* and 'life domain': his project was bathed in the aura of functional efficiency, and led to profound changes in structures and concepts, and in particular a circulation of personnel between the SD *Ämter*, and between the Gestapo and the SD. Here, for example, are the 'two proposals' made by him on the development of *Abteilung* II/1:

> Either the *Abteilung* disappears, with the rest of the missions it fulfils, and is merged with a new *Amt* for 'Investigation', or else it preserves its outer form of organization, without carrying out any more thematic activities, in line with the missions of *Amt* III (external intelligence service), dedicating itself to the implementation of the service of information and in addition comprising a special network of observers for *Amt* II [*Lebensgebiet*].[54]

In fact, the main victim of Schellenberg's proposal was Franz Six's SDHA II/1: it was to be literally emptied of all content, and broken up between the Gestapo (the executive section) and the future intelligence service: all that remained of the *Gegnerforschung* and *Gegnerbekämpfung* was the first term – which, in fact, Schellenberg held in little esteem. Indeed, even though he did not formulate this explicitly, he considered that the activity of *Gegnerforschung* was 'outdated' and that Franz Six's department possessed neither the means nor the competences to abandon 'investigation' for pure intelligence work, a change that was implied by the alternative:[55] Schellenberg's plan meant the abandoning of the ambition, developed by Six, of combining scientificity, political commitment and police work, replacing these with a more traditional view of intelligence, a view that linked it to the secret services on the one hand, and to the political police on the other.

Franz Six, acknowledging the transfer – carried out at the behest of Schellenberg – of *Abteilung* II/112 (external ideological opponents) to the new *Ausland*-SD, sent a memorandum to Heydrich on 17 July 1939 proposing the reorganization of what he then called *Amt* III, '*Gegnerforschung*', in the future RSHA. This department was to combine its former bureaus[56] into one big service with four *Abteilungen*: the first was to focus on 'fundamental investigation', the second on 'ideological opponents', the third 'internal problems' and the fourth 'external problems'. By this logic, the *Gegnerforschung* proposed by Six entailed nothing more or less than the creation of a central office for theoretical investigation working in close collaboration with the other *Ämter* of the RSHA, such as the criminal police 'for scientific research' into criminology.[57] Six's plan left pure intelligence work to the other *Ämter* of the SD, and police work to the Gestapo and the KRIPO: in other terms, this was an intellectual office, a new SD that, in the long term, would be able to dominate other *Ämter*, whose work was narrower. This plan was quite well received by Heydrich,[58] but it came up against the fierce opposition of the five departmental heads,[59] who wished to keep the scientific dimension of the field of investigation under their own control.[60] The two solutions envisaged by Schellenberg were actually applied to Franz Six's department on the creation of the RSHA: part of the service was transferred to *Ausland*-SD, while another was handed over to the Gestapo[61] – in particular to Eichmann's department.[62] The rest was hived off to form RSHA *Amt* VII, dedicated to 'ideological investigation'. 'Investigation' into and 'combat' against opponents still fell to the powerful central office now coming into being, but were not carried out by the same men: as a result, investigation was marginalized.

When, at the beginning of 1940, the RSHA's structure had finally stabilized, it was composed of six *Ämter*: *Amt* I was the personnel department, *Amt* II was responsible for all the administration of the different departments: they both formed the administration of the two former main offices – Security Service and Security Police – which were now merged into a single unit. *Amt* III comprised the *Inland*-SD which, under the leadership of Otto Ohlendorf, took over the name 'domain of German life', and the activities of sociological, cultural, racial and economic assessment, observation and research previously carried out by Reinhard Höhn's service. *Amt* IV comprised a Gestapo that had a major influence now that it was enlarged by the addition of the old SDHA II/112 in charge of 'Jewish affairs'. The KRIPO, unchanged, constituted *Amt* V. *Amt* VI was formed from the *Ausland*-SD, while *Amt* VII was formed from the remainder of the activities of ideological investigation in Six's department. There was one constant feature: the need to 'struggle' against enemies – real or supposed, internal or external – and to 'control' the life domain of the Reich. These two notions remained the keywords of the Reich's main Security Office, the RSHA, which would soon fill occupied Europe from the Atlantic to the Polar Circle with its local offices.[63]

A 'world of enemies' (II)

The RSHA was, by definition and tradition, an organism of struggle against the enemies of Nazism and the Reich: it succeeded a series of institutions that had been 'struggling' ever since the period when the NSDAP – which remained one of its supervisory bodies – and the SS were still no more than militant organizations in a sovereign, democratic republic. 'To struggle', in the eyes of the RSHA and SD intellectuals, meant defining the enemy, and gathering intelligence so as to neutralize him. This last task, in theory, fell to the Gestapo: I will not discuss it in any more detail. To struggle meant to identify the enemy, both within and without the country, note down his characteristics and his various activities in reports that were then distributed to a more or less wide circle of readers. But defining the enemy did not just bring institutional traditions into play: it was anchored in previous activist practices and the internalization of the Nazi belief system. It drew nourishment from the memory of Germany between the wars.

At the end of 1940, the SIPO school, based at Charlottenburg, welcomed the first year of pupil officers from the new training course designed to provide cadres for the RSHA.[64] Legal training comprised a great number of historical and sociological lectures, all deeply imbued with 'ideological instruction': Siegfried Engel, Walter Zirpins and Bruno Lettow took over this didactics of persecution. University graduates and battle-hardened activists, the three men were not 'propagandists': they considered themselves, rather, to be SS officers who had decided to form a body that would be militant, of course, but also competent. One of the lectures given at the time discussed the 'enemies of the Third Reich and the struggle against them', and offered a first glimpse of the way the enemy was seen by SS intellectuals.[65] First there was a definition of the country's enemies, their aims, their modus operandi, and the goals and conditions of the struggle against them, as well as a discussion of those taking part in this struggle. Then came a quick typology of each adversary in turn. All that remains is a detailed plan of this lecture, but fortunately it enables us to grasp the structures of the world-view at work underneath what was ostensibly a mere description of Nazism's victorious struggle against its opponents. The lecture was given after the training period for the security organizations: the age of activist surveillance, when the SD did not have a sufficient number of networks of informers or of active officers, was now a thing of the past. However, this development was not confined to questions of increasing ramification or greater means: the adversaries themselves had changed, new ones had appeared, others had lost their importance and been dropped from the blacklists of SS officers.

There is, however, a remarkable continuity between the definition of the enemy laid down by the SD from 1931 to 1936 – a political, Party-based definition, without any real reference to the state as such[66] – and the definition formulated by RSHA *Amt* I in 1941: the author-lecturer here started out with a concept of 'enemy of the state', contrasting a definition proper to liberal states with a Nazi definition or, more precisely, perhaps, a different definition of the state enemies in each of the two systems. In the liberal state, says the author, 'the state enemy is one who opposes every system at the helm, every holder of power'; in the Nazi state, he is the enemy of the people, 'the opponent of the ethnic, racial and spiritual substance of our people'.[67] The difference between the two definitions was decisive for the SS pedagogue: in the liberal state, the enemy attacks only the system of government, and there was nothing illegitimate in this for the lecturer, who was after all the anti-democratic proponent of a 'total state'.[68] But the racial determinism to which he subscribed viewed hostility to the Nazi state as a mortal danger: to attack the 'ethnic, racial and spiritual substance of the people' was to strike at the essence of German Nordicity, to menace its very existence. The extent of the damage which the two types of adversary could commit was not the same and so did not call for the same response.

The lecturer ended with a typology of these enemies, in the front rank of which were Marxism and Communism. Then came what he called the 'three Ks',[69] in other words the Jews, the Freemasons and the 'politicizing churches' (Catholics, Protestants and 'sects'), then the 'reaction', and finally the 'agitators, malcontents and other parasites of the people': all formed the political and ideological wing of hostility towards Nazism. This group in turn was followed by the 'dangers stemming from the economic, social and cultural domains' and lastly by 'criminal delinquents'. In short, this list includes all the enemies that the Third Reich saw as a threat, without paying overmuch attention to categorization or to the various groups it left out: what did malcontents and Jews have in common, or homosexuals and 'traitors', Communists and reactionaries? Where is the coherence in this list that brings together political groups such as 'Marxists' and 'reactionaries', but leaves out separatists (even though these were the object of considerable interest to the SD)? To make confusion worse confounded, the list also enumerates religious adversaries (the churches and sects), as well as other groups then considered as racial (the Jews, of course, with the surprising omission of the Gypsies), and lastly milieus whose hostility to Nazism was more the result of their position in society (the malcontents) or the fact that they were criminals. Assembled in this way, these categories definitely do not seem to constitute a typology that would allow for a full-scale catalogue, and certainly rule out any coherent system of classification.

What we do find here, however, is an analysis of the phenomena considered to be transgressive by the Nazis. Let us take the example of the last category, including what the lecturer calls 'criminal transgressions' (*kriminelle Verbrechen*): his definition seems to be related to the juridical sphere. However, the delinquents occupy the last position in it: they are preceded by attacks on state security – a political act – as well as by homosexuality and abortion – essentially religious 'crimes'. How were such transgressions erected into criminal acts? In the view of SS intellectuals, were homosexuals 'social' enemies because of the 'disturbance' they caused, in the eyes of the KRIPO? Or were they racial enemies because of their supposed 'refusal to procreate'? The SS instructor's discussion refers neither to the first nor the second reason: could 'criminal transgression' be a catch-all category, in which the lecturer can place whatever has not fitted into any previous lists?

Nonetheless, the definition of this category of adversaries corresponds roughly to a division of tasks between the different organs of repression, a division that did not depend on the essential nature of the enemy but on the kinds of action to be taken against him. So the four types of phenomenon brought together under the rubric 'criminal transgression' are all, unlike the previous ones, the exclusive responsibility of the SIPO, even if they were not dealt with by the same body. They are basically transgressions to be tracked down. Attacks on state security, on the other hand, are the responsibility of the Gestapo: they are thus political in nature; the three others fall to the KRIPO. The common denominator between these four phenomena stems in fact from how they are committed: each of them is characterized by a *deed*. The police – criminal or political – intervene in an abortion, a sexual misdemeanour, a crime or an act of treachery. This is what radically distinguishes them from the other transgressions, which are all characterized by a way of *being* (Communist, Jew, Freemason, malcontent), a kind of language either spoken (criticism, the discourse of propaganda) or written (the tract, the book, the letter), by a social bond (membership of a lodge, a cell, a party) – all transgressions that are linked to identity, all analysable in terms of collective behaviour that, even if it is embodied in individualized acts, is not exhausted by them.

All the previous categories, then, can be traced in different ways, and in the first instance comprise collective realities, materialized by writings or reported utterances that are the objects of study for the SD, while the individualized cases, lifted from their collective background by denunciation or inquiry, become the domain of police investigation. They are also much more transparent, and clearly fall within the ideological, religious or racial sphere. We must, however, bear in mind that these categories are not mutually exclusive: someone who is an enemy because of religious affiliation may also be considered an enemy in the ideological and/or racial sense.

It is difficult to give a systematic overview of the way the Nazis built up an image of all the groups they considered hostile. However, there are some significant examples of how this happened that reveal the world-view that lay behind the process.

The lecturer left out one group of adversaries: the Rhineland separatists. And yet this group had attracted the closest attention on the part of the SD ever since its formation, and as late as 1941 was still the object of investigations and memorandums.[70] The reason behind the speaker's silence may have lain in the insignificance of the separatist movement. So the interest taken in this group by the SS's organs of repression, though perfectly real, was disproportionate to its objective existence.[71] It is noteworthy that Werner Best took personal charge of *Referat* IV E 3 of the RSHA, the very body that dealt with separatism, although this flew in the face of any hierarchical logic.[72] After all, what need could have impelled the second in command of the RSHA, *Amtschef* I and II, and director of the counter-espionage police, to concern himself with a *Referat* that was so marginal to the preoccupations of the RSHA? Of course, a functional logic may have been at work here: Best was himself a Rhinelander and had already combated the separatists, and had specific knowledge of the region and the milieus involved. However, he did not undertake any investigation that drew on his particular capacities. The real reason was doubtless his activist youth, his action in the *Abwehrkampf* and the first taste of violence experienced by this RSHA lawyer when, in 1924, at the age of twenty, he became involved in street fighting against these same separatists. They played a major role in Best's imagination, and crystallized some of the anguish he felt about Germany's possible disappearance, an anguish that he expressed in one political tract after another.[73]

A pamphlet on separatism, signed by Armin Bach – in actual fact *Hauptsturmführer* Biederbeck, an SD member – confirms the way certain images from the *Abwehrkampf* persisted in the construction of the image of the separatist by the Third Reich's repressive organizations. Biederbeck argued his case at length, attempting to prove the collusion between the French and the separatists, who were plotting together to dismantle Germany.[74] For him as for Best, separatism was also an attack on the 'territorial substance' of Germany. However, Best expressed his fears during the French occupation of the Rhineland, while Biederbeck published his brochure after the German remilitarization of this region. In fact, the circumstances were of little account: the enemy was branded as an essential, immanent threat, and represented at all times and in all places a danger which SS intellectuals needed to combat.

A second characteristic example of how the Nazis constructed an image of the enemy was the Freemasons. They were one of the groups considered most able to inflict damage. *Sturmbannführer* Paul Zapp, future head of *Einsatzkommando* 10 a and KdS [Kommandeur der Sicherheitspolizei und des SD, i.e. Commander of the Security Police and the SD – *Tr.*] in Crimea,[75] was one of the 'specialists' of the question. Thus, at the beginning of 1941, he drew up a memorandum setting out the main lines of the image of Freemasonry, which became one of the main documents used to train SD and Gestapo officers.[76] Its principal aim was to provide a general overview of the character of the Freemasons; it then studied the measures taken to counteract their influence, the structure of 'worldwide Freemasonry' and that of Freemasonry in Germany, going on to describe the 'working methods' of the latter and its links with other enemies of the state. Zapp took great care, right from the start of his discussion, to give quantitative details of what for him was the 'danger of Freemasonry', mentioning straightaway that between 50 and 70 per cent of the cadres of Freemasonry were, on his estimate, 'of the Jewish race'. On the one hand, Zapp wanted to demonstrate that the essence of the movement connected it to other adversaries of Nazism; on the other hand, he sought to bring out its malevolent intent and the real threat that it represented. He claimed that the hostility of the Freemasons to Germany stemmed from the attitude of Wilhelm II. Supporting his claims to objectivity by quoting the enemies' own words against them, he drew on a Genevan newspaper produced by the Freemasons in evidence of his views:

> Wilhelm I was still an fm [Freemason]. So was his son [. . .] but he had forbidden his own son, the current Wilhelm II, from entering a lodge.
>
> If Wilhelm believes he can govern without the lodges, he is mistaken. If he were to lose all sense of proportion and decide to govern against them, we would force a revolution on him.

Zapp used this text to view the thirty years between the declarations in this Genevan paper and the defeat of Germany as three decades of ceaseless Masonic plotting. These plots had, he claimed, led to the encirclement of Germany and even to the fact that Italy, once a faithful ally of the central powers, had entered the war on the side of the Entente Cordiale at the behest of the Italian Grand Orient. Putting an explicitly edifying spin on the examples that supported each of his arguments, Zapp gave Freemasonry a crucial role in the outbreak of the Great War (the assassination at Sarajevo had, in his view, been ordered by the Serbian Grand Orient) and in the inflation of 1923 (provoked by the 'Freemason' Stresemann). In this way he sought to interpret the time of troubles as having one single cause. Once these 'facts' had been presented, Zapp naturally considered the 'defence measures' implemented by Nazi Germany as legitimate. Zapp claimed that there was no united, centralized body controlling Freemasonry throughout the world – not that this undermined the idea of a plot, far from it: it made such an idea more alarming, in the sense that the plot was not due to a conscious strategy against Germany by a global enemy. Rather, it was part of the daily practices of the lodges, who behaved in ways so far removed from those promoted by Nazism that they constituted a complex of aggressive actions that forced Germany to defend itself. For Zapp, it was because Freemasonry was what it was, and not because it was a global organization, that it was hostile. When sifted through the racial determinism internalized by the SS officer, Freemasonry – mainly a 'Jewish' phenomenon, he claimed – was thus *naturally* (because *biologically*) an enemy of Germany.

Paul Zapp's discourse was clearly part of the culture of war that SS intellectuals had never ceased to fight. They sought to portray the Freemasons as the men who had really sparked off the Great War, and to prove that President Wilson belonged to a lodge – all part of the continued attempt to legitimate and prolong that war. Encirclement, a sinister plot, the defensive attitude of Germany in the face of a Freemasonry allegedly allied with the Jews, 'reactionaries' and 'Social Democrats' – these were the themes that fuelled the idea, close to the hearts of Werner Beumelberg and Hindenburg, of a Germany thrust into conflict by a 'world of enemies'. And, in the final analysis, it was the Jews who gave this 'world of enemies' its real meaning in the eyes of SS intellectuals.

The intellectuals of the SD wrote prolifically about Jewishness, its history, its characteristics, its supposed role in this or that domain.[77] The activities of control, education and *Gegnerforschung* are all evidence of the very early SD focus on this question.[78] The great mass of documents left behind by those who, from 1935 onwards, consistently bent their thoughts to anti-Semitic legislation and persecution makes it easier for us to form a clear idea of the image of Jewishness constructed by SS intellectuals. This image was very traditional in content, but still reflected the ambitions of scientificity. Disapproving of the extremist anti-Semitism of Julius Streicher and the SA, SS intellectuals mobilized anti-Semitic feelings by setting them within a historical discourse, interlarding their statements with footnotes and quotations from Jewish periodicals. So it was not just the form but the historicized expression of Judaeophobia that comprised the new twist in a discourse imbued with all the banality of Nazi anti-Semitism.

In February and March 1937, SDHA II/112 was asked to organize a series of lectures on 'Jewishness, the enemy of National Socialism'.[79] These lectures, an integral part of the task of building up and promulgating doctrine assigned to it by Himmler and Heydrich, were given to an audience of economics specialists, students of the NSStB and members of the RuSHA – an audience that came from the SS and other institutions, in whose view the members of SDHA II/112, Hagen, Eichmann and Schröder first and foremost, already counted as experts.[80]

On 8 February 1937, in front of an audience of twenty-five economists,[81] SS-*Hauptscharführer* Schröder delivered, in the name of his group, a lecture in which we can find all the elements of Nazi anti-Semitic rhetoric. Schröder took a causal approach as he sought to understand why the Jews were 'opposed' to National Socialism. This formula itself betrays the defensive world-view at work in Nazi anti-Semitism. SS intellectuals *believed* they were acting in self-defence against the Jews, thereby reactivating – whether consciously or not – the theme of the *Abwehrkampf* that had crystallized in the Great War and the turbulent years that had followed. For the SS NCO, there were two causes behind the way the Jews 'opposed' Nazism: 'racial otherness' and a 'different life domain'.[82] Schröder, drawing on racial hygienists without explicitly quoting them, contrasted the preservation of German Nordicity with a Jewishness composed down the centuries from several interbreedings. In line with Nazi racial determinism, Schröder used the biological dimension as a starting point for his discussion. However, race was soon followed, in his discussion, by the life domain, an 'unlimited space', described as the 'basis of Jewish life': 'in other terms,' says Schröder, 'the international spread of Jews lies behind the internationalism of their ideology'. It was on these two points that the Nazi view of the absolute otherness of Jewishness and its supposed malevolence was based: it was because 'the Jews [had] no land' and because, as a mongrel race, their racial identity was impure that they aspired to 'assimilation', the source of all Nazi anxiety. For Schröder, 'assimilation', in other words 'Jewish mingling with the ethnic life proper to a nation, must inevitably have a destructive effect. This [was] why the Jew [was] destructive throughout the whole world.'[83] He thus saw the assimilation of the Jews as an attack on the racial substance of nations, an attack that in his view was intentional – a ploy on the part of a people who would manage to preserve their ethnic identity even in interbreeding, while the latter would, in the view of the SS, spell the loss of Nordic identity. In this way, the Jews were biological enemies, whose action would threaten, or so the SD experts claimed, the foundation of Germandom: its racial substance. Do we not find here, set out practically in the same terms, the rhetoric of legitimation of the Great War, a defensive but vital struggle?

And yet the comparison needs to be qualified: the rhetoric of war, and the representation of the occupation of the Ruhr by foreign troops, had after all been a powerful source of anxiety during the youth of SS intellectuals. The Nazi representation of the Jews, however much it mobilized people against them, however alarming it could be, was now expressed through a system of beliefs that set out to bring the struggle to a triumphant conclusion. In fact, if the anxiety was clearly intimated in the first part of Schröder's lecture, his discussion was designed to lead to the providential coming to power of the Nazis: the second part began with a description of 'the Jewish influence in Germany' which, in 1933, [was] much more significant than [the] percentage [of Jews] in the population', but the *Machtergreifung* and 'the combat of the Nazi state against Jewishness, thanks to the retreat of Jewish influence and the promotion of emigration', allowed the speaker to conclude his lecture by setting out 'concrete examples' of defensive measures, as he described the struggle of fellow activists.[84]

This was a standard text by an SS intellectual, characteristic of a Nazi formulation of 'banal' anti-Semitism which it nonetheless emphasized with the aid of statistics and press quotations, channelling it into a form shaped by academic rhetoric. This lecture shows the emotions that gripped Nazi activists, underlining the function of anti-Semitism in the psychological make-up that was created when Nazi values were internalized. The representation of the enemy – Jew, Freemason and Communist – roused powerful anxieties and generated real hatred: it is particularly evident when Schröder, in his very first paragraph, makes the Jew into 'a potential bastard'[85] – and legitimates a Nazi policy profoundly marked by the *Abwehrkampf*. However, belief and fervour gave those activists the hope that the 'defensive combat' against the 'world of enemies' would end in triumph. And this was just what Zapp expressed when he finished his lecture on the Freemasons: 'The Freemasons, Jewry and other ideological enemies form, or rather *used to form*,[86] a united front of opponents!'[87]

This did not comprise any addition to pre-existing doctrine.[88] In this case, the contribution made by the men of the SD lay rather in the formulation than any ideological content: they were setting out to prove the accuracy of their ideological beliefs with the help of facts and figures. This was a 'scientific' variant of Nazism. SS intellectuals classified, cross-referenced, catalogued, enumerated and scrutinized masses of documents in order to verify the foundations of their beliefs in the investigations they carried out. But it was precisely because they interpreted the world as a 'world of enemies' leagued against their nation that they clung all the more obstinately to the Nazi belief system and the *Abwehrkampf* that activism in the SD represented in their eyes. 'Work' in the SD, a work in the formulation of doctrine and the 'empirical verification' of doctrine, was thus essentially a matter of finding the right arguments.

Control

The second activity carried out by the SD consisted in controlling and assessing the German 'life domain'. Aware of the weakness of the expression of opinion in the Third Reich, starting in 1936 and even more after 1939, Ohlendorf and Höhn set up a system of regular reports for the government and the NSDAP hierarchy: these reports were designed to act as opinion polls, press dispatches and information bulletins simultaneously.[89] These 'Reich dispatches' (*Meldungen aus dem Reich*) comprised a significant activity of RSHA *Amt* III, especially its group III A.[90] On the other hand, in the domains of health and race (*Amt* III B), culture (III C) and the economy (III D), the SD had taken on the function of assessment, giving its opinion on measures taken, advising the government, allowing the *Reichsführer* to call on a brains trust thanks to which it could keep the initiative within the Nazi polycracy.[91] Lastly, from 1937–8, the SD, together with other agents of repression in the Third Reich, played a part in the policy of expansion: to control, for SS intellectuals, meant testing public opinion and evaluating the findings, but it also meant getting their hands on Austria, the Sudetenland and the rest of Czechoslovakia between 1938 and 1939. This hankering for control led to the creation of the first commandos of intervention, the *Einsatzkommandos*.

Under the leadership of Höhn, Ohlendorf and his deputy Karl Gegenbach, the SD thus set up a regular system for the provision of information. The various statements made by Ohlendorf at the Nuremberg Trial give us a one-sided view of this activity. Ohlendorf said that he had been recruited by Höhn as the latter was looking for 'critical spirits' able to discuss current affairs, and able to become the spokesmen of a public opinion that was – to put it mildly – muzzled. At Nuremberg, attempting to pass himself off as a heterodox, critical Nazi, Ohlendorf posed as a marginal figure, the victim of the bullying tactics of Himmler and Heydrich,[92] as a result of these very same reports. This was a big part in his defence strategy,[93] and his version of the use and status of the *Meldungen aus dem Reich* and the polling and assessment activities of the SD thus need to be treated with caution.

The *Meldungen aus dem Reich* have nonetheless proved themselves as a providential source for the history of Nazism. Works by Ian Kershaw, Lawrence Stokes and Marlis Steinart[94] are very largely based on this long series of documents probing the Germans' 'morale' and 'attitudes'. The writers of the *Meldungen* compiled reports transmitted by the SDOA, and they of course sifted out from a mass of pre-selected information what would be to their advantage. So it is futile to try and find in them any 'objective' reflection of day-to-day life in Nazi Germany: they present us, instead, with the way it was received by the SS intellectuals – a reception that was all the more constructed in that it was far removed from their own daily lives. One example will illustrate this gap.

On 27 May 1936, the Stuttgart SDOA wrote that the courts were 'reaching incomprehensible verdicts in racial affairs' and that 'the sentences being handed down were extremely light', since 'up until now, no prison sentence has been handed down in spite of the instructions of the Code'.[95] It is difficult to see this as a faithful reflection of German opinion, which was not well versed in the Nordicism of the Nuremberg Laws.[96] On the other hand, intellectuals of the SD, who together with other groups had actually instigated these laws,[97] expressed astonishment at the slowness of the courts in bringing the *Blutschutzgesetzen* to bear on the process of law: the report of the SDOA (which was headed by Gustav Adolf Scheel, Sandberger and Ehrlinger) expressed the feelings of the young Nordicist intellectuals of the SD, and certainly not those of the Swabian populace.

However, it is perfectly true that the Nuremberg Laws necessitated a period of adaptation for the courts, who were initially disinclined to support the implementation of racial laws. Perhaps this report was simply the echo of the gap between Nazi racial 'law' and its application, a gap expressed with a hint of irritation by SD officers who would have liked it to be applied in full and immediately? It was in their discovery of the difficulties of implementing this and other laws that the *Meldungen aus dem Reich* were fulfilling the mission of control assigned to the SD by Heydrich and Himmler. The SD, the latter declared, 'is the Party's great ideological information service, and ultimately that of the State also'.[98] Writing these reports comprised a political act, since – in the name of the SD – they formulated a certain opinion that was then passed on to the hierarchy; it was also a militant act, the act of men who interpreted reality through their belief system, men who scrutinized daily life in Germany for signs of their hope. They were, in their very subjectivity, an exceptional source for the history of representations.

The SD's second function consisted in providing assessments for every domain of the *Lebensgebiet*. These assessments could be integrated into the *Meldungen aus dem Reich*[99] when they achieved a significant degree of generality, or be the object of memorandums written by the *Referenten* of the RSHA or their subordinates.[100] Questions of nationality, interethnic relations, 'public health'[101] and racial policy were the remit of RSHA *Amt* III B, directed by Hans Ehlich with the help of Heinz Hummitzsch; questions of culture were dealt with by RSHA *Amt* III C (Spengler, Turowsky, Rössner and von Kielpinski); economic questions, unless they were handled directly by Ohlendorf, were the province of RSHA *Amt* III D (Willy Seibert, Friedrich Tiedt and Hans Leetsch).[102] These offices were organized thematically, and behind this process there sometimes lay, after 1942, a geographical structure; the example of RSHA *Amt* III D is a good one.

This group, directed by Willy Seibert, an economist very close to Ohlendorf, provided economic assessments and contributed to the composition of special reports for the *Meldungen aus dem Reich*. The group was organized into five thematic *Referate*, numbered 1 to 5: there were also two geographical *Referate*, one concerned with the occupied territories in the west (III D W) and the other with the occupied territories in the east (III D E). *Referat* no. 1 was devoted to subsistence economy, no. 2 to 'commerce, craft industries and transport', no. 3 to 'financial economy, banks, stock exchanges and insurance', no. 4 to 'industry and energy', and the last, no. 5, to 'unemployment and social welfare'.[103] This specialization, apparently imbued with rationality and functionality, did, however, disguise one fundamental characteristic of the Nazi system of representations: the division did not correspond to the three major sectors (primary, secondary and tertiary) currently defined by economists, either in its internal hierarchy or in the taxonomy employed. Furthermore, the sector

labelled 'agriculture' (*Landwirtschaft*) was not really one: if we translate
the German term literally, this was a sector with the title 'economics of
food, of supplies' (*Ernähungswirtschaft*), a name which might simply have
reflected the Nazi focus on the food supply situation in Germany as well
as the occupied territories, a focus which played a decisive role in the
shape adopted by the war in the east, the policy of occupation in Poland
and Belorussia, and even the prosecution of mass murder. Perhaps we
can correlate this focus with the dread that the economic situation of 1918
might return – the near famine experienced by Germany at the time of its
capitulation.[104] In fact, and even before we take a closer look at the actual
contents of the assessments, we can emphasize that the shadow cast by
the Great War and the 'time of troubles' extended right into the names
given to different SD bureaus.

The SD piled up memorandum on memorandum, on industry, energy
and agriculture in one region of the Reich or another – or in the occupied
territories after 1939 – and various observations on social phenomena.
Under Ohlendorf's influence, the SD played a role in the Nazi economic
debate, which became increasingly virulent as the war progressed.[105] The
SD supported very doctrinal positions with the aim – in the words of
its own leader – of setting the economy 'in an ethnic context'.[106] By this,
Ohlendorf meant the establishment of a 'societal [*gesellschaftlich*], in other
words *völkisch*' economy:[107] an economy in line with racial determinism.
However abstruse such a programme may have been, it was embodied
specifically in the Nazi economic debate. As against the productivist
technocratic model of Speer,[108] on the one hand, against what Ohlendorf
called 'the collectivist trends of the Party', on the other,[109] the latter
defended a 'line that favoured the middle classes', in the words of one of
his opponents, *Sturmbannführer* SS Gunter d'Alquen, the editor in chief
of *Das Schwarze Korps*. Of particular interest is a letter from d'Alquen, a
young journalist recruited into the SD by Heydrich, who had emerged
from his own sphere of influence to join Himmler's entourage. In this
letter, d'Alquen summarized the terms of the debate that was shaking
economic institutions:

> Dear Comrade Ohlendorf, [. . .]
>
> [. . .] I feel that the time has come, dear comrade Ohlendorf, to discuss
> things together and clarify certain matters, especially since, in my view, the
> death of *Gruppenführer* Heydrich has laid on us the duty to be as united as
> steel [. . .].
>
> I have to tell you certain things very openly, and I must ask you not to be
> too prickly, and to discount in advance any ill intentions on my part.
>
> During our discussions over the past years, I have never been able to rid
> myself of a feeling that led to me posing myself the following question:
> 'Well, who are you talking to right now? With *SS-Oberführer* Ohlendorf,
> head of department in the SD, or with the secretary general of the trade
> department [*of the Ministry of the Economy*]?' [. . .]

> Dear comrade Ohlendorf, you view the sphere of trade from the point of view of the maintenance and advancement of a middle class to the detriment of any other factor. This may be fair enough. [. . .] But I think that [trade] plays a subordinate role in the whole question. For if National Socialism emerges from a biological foundation that the SS is striving to promote in its practical significance within a wider framework, I then feel that we cannot get away so easily from these racial preconditions. And I would claim that an instinct for trade is correlated with and indeed linked to racial inferiority. And I would claim that trade, in the current form of retail trade, is far removed from the aptitudes of Nordic man, in other words the Germanic.
>
> Of course, this has nothing to do with the small trader as a factor of division of wealth in the context of political economy[.].[110]

When seen in its context, Gunter d'Alquen's text resembles a pamphlet that remains quite faithful to the tone of the SS journal: the presentation paragraph, while apparently a 'clear and frank explanation worthy of SS dignitaries', lumps Ohlendorf together with functionaries who were often given a rough ride in the journal. In particular, by viewing Ohlendorf as a specialist in trade, d'Alquen forced him into the racially inferior role that such a branch of activity represented in his eyes. For an SS officer, d'Alquen's letter amounted to a real personal insult. Even more serious: the accusation of ignorance of the fundamental principles of Nazi racial determinism could, if bruited about by *Das Schwarze Korps*, considerably harm the position of the SD. So d'Alquen's letter was a not inconsiderable threat for the SS general and his department – a threat to which he had to reply both on the doctrinal and on the personal level. On the second point, Ohlendorf referred the affair right up to Himmler,[111] who did not, however, come down severely on what appears to have been his favourite journalist.[112] On the doctrinal level, the reply of Ohlendorf and the SD was more interesting, since it finally gave expression to what the SD intellectuals understood by the project of a 'Nazi economy'.

In a scathing reply, Ohlendorf reminded d'Alquen that 'after all, traders founded Bremen, Lübeck, Danzig and Riga, and laid the foundations of our colonial power[. . .]'. He added:

> The decisive fact that the German people does not comprise in itself a racial unity corroborates the fact that [. . .] it is not a race which expresses itself in its trading function, but expresses rather all the components of the racial heritage of the German people, represented in that same trading function.[113]

Ohlendorf set out to lambast d'Alquen's simplistic racism and to recentre his economic theory in an orthodox Nordicism. The middle classes that it was his aim to advance were, of course, the purified, Nordified middle classes: after all, this was the task of RSHA *Amt* III B, one of the most important groups under his direction. Under the leadership of Hans Ehlich, this *Amt* took on the never-ending task of selecting northern blood

– a 'quest for German blood' that was instigated by the desire for racial hygiene.[114] Once the 'German racial heritage' had been 're-Nordified', Ohlendorf aimed to give the middle class the task of redistributing wealth via trade, in a social economy which, in his view, needed to set itself apart from both capitalist and communist economies, those 'two admittedly extreme dimensions of a flat and simplified rationalism', one of which '[would] mechanize production in the course of technical progress while eliminating ever more of the workforce', while the other, Communistic economy, '[has] elevated a materialism and a rationalism that ignore culture and the human mind to the rank of economic and social system'. In contrast, the Nazi system should, in the view of Ohlendorf, Seibert, Leetsch and SD economic experts, represent 'truly human principles of organization', combating the forces of 'the autonomy of quantitative and calculative activity'[115] found in the capitalist and Soviet systems.

The economic assessments carried out by the SD thus reveal two levels of discourse. The first, more particularly based on the practical and sectorial dimension, reveals the continuing significance of the memory of the Great War through its obsession with potential food. The second, while not formulating any conceptualized project,[116] brings out fully the Nazi ambition to place the economy in the service of the 'forces of development of German man', who could not be 'the object of an anonymous economic market, but rather its Subject and thus the man who configures the economic domain and leaves his mark on it, as an integral part of his culture'.[117]

The SD's surveying and assessment activities thus led it to assume a high degree of control, enabling Nazi bosses to gauge people's reactions to their policies and to evaluate the efficiency of these policies. At the very heart of this activity, SD intellectuals continued to formulate doctrine and ideology: this did not always take the form of memorandums, but could also involve them, discreetly, bringing pressure to bear on the organs of government to try and impose *their* Nazism. The SD, an instrument of control, was transformed into an ideological apparatus and an instrument of power with which the state eventually had to come to a compromise: Ohlendorf, for example, became one of the dominant figures in the Ministry of Economy.[118] These activities of assessment and control, however, were always reinforced by intelligence activities that bordered on *Gegnerforschung*: in this realm, the SD still maintained its function of control, a function that took a decisive turn with the beginning of Nazi expansion.

The idea of training up groups composed of SD officers, of 'soldier activists' in the SS, and of Gestapo police officers was, as we have seen, put into practice at the time of the 'Röhm putsch'. The *Kommandos* of the Black Order proceeded to make arrests and execute a number of opponents of Nazism or the SS. In 1938, the SD was no longer a small group of amateurish activists, and the Gestapo had become one of the pillars of the Nazi state. The *Einsatzkommandos* active in the Sudetenland, in Austria and in Czechoslovakia are evidence of this increase in numbers and the growing sophistication and specificity of their methods of investigation: resort to an essentially politically motivated violence remained a constant feature. These *Einsatzkommandos*, in the final analysis, reflected the practice of control implemented by the SIPO and the SD in the years 1936–8.

Little information about the recruitment or training of these *Kommandos* has survived.[119] Their activities are somewhat better known, less as regards their repressive activities and more in terms of bureaucracy, at least in Austria – though we have facts and figures of arrests carried out in Czechoslovakia.[120] The practices developed in these 'non-violent' invasions emerged from the daily work of the SD. It is in this sense, but also for the precedents these practices created, that we need to focus on them here: with them, for the first time, conquest and control were merged in Nazi repressive practice.

A memorandum from Heydrich described the objectives of the *Einsatzkommandos* with great clarity:

In all previous actions – starting with the one in Austria – *Einsatzgruppen* acted with the troops, in line with the Führer's special order. On the basis of preparatory work, they carried out systematic arrests, and confiscated and sequestered the most important political documents; they hit hard against the Reich's enemies throughout the world, enemies who came from the camp of emigrant Freemasons, Jews, and the politico-religious opposition, as well as from the Second and Third Internationals.[121]

In the case of Austria, preparations for the action began in mid-March 1938 with the selection, on the basis of SD and Gestapo files, of '*Sonderfahndungslisten*', in other words special lists of wanted people;[122] this speciality, taken from *Gegnerforschung*, seems to have remained the province of the SD. In the field, however, the Gestapo took over the greater part of the systematic arrests mentioned by Heydrich. For its part, the SD concentrated on occupying strategic buildings, and on the confiscating and sequestering of the 'most important political documents'.

In Austria, the men were commanded by Franz Six, who, from his post in Berlin, entrusted the *Kommando* to Wilhelm Spengler and Erich Ehrlinger: while the former dealt with documentation, the latter operated more particularly in liaison with the Gestapo, while also taking charge of confiscations. After five days' work, the SD and Gestapo *Kommandos* were transformed into stationary units of the SIPO and the SD organized, as within the Reich, into SDOA and *Stapostellen*.[123]

Franz Six's men seized the archives of Jewish congregations, Masonic lodges, left-wing parties and 'suspicious' associations, as well as the holdings of many libraries whose books, carefully selected, ended up lining the shelves of the institutional libraries of the SD and the Gestapo.[124] The letters that went back and forth between the central office in Berlin and the men in the *Einsatzkommandos* detailing these operations speak volumes on the searches – they even mention one of the numerous suicides that occurred when the Nazis entered Vienna – but they are especially informative on the operations of selecting, archiving and packaging material for transport.[125] In sum, we can discern a clear continuity between the SD's missions of control and assessment and those of the *Einsatzkommandos* who entered Austria, while we have but a fragmentary and rather tenuous impression of the Nazi practices implemented in the takeover of these territories, given the absence of facts and figures on the number of victims arrested.[126] An analysis of the case of Czechoslovakia will enable us to fill in some of the gaps.

Preparations for the invasion of the Sudetenland were being made from the end of June 1938, with the first plans for the intervention of the SD and the SIPO if there were to be 'complications between Czechoslovakia and the Reich': this first plan made provision for the SD to follow directly after the troops entering Czechoslovakia to carry out a 'mission analogous [to that pursued in] the Reich', a mission designed to 'enforce the securing [*Sicherung*] of political life'.[127] Drawing on the documentation amassed by the SDOA working on the borders, the SDHA was to set up a general file, complemented by local files, two for each Czech district, one of them to be entrusted to the general staff of the *Kommando* that would be operating there. As well as lists of names, this file was to contain instructions on the treatment to be meted out to physical or moral persons: 'Imprison, liquidate [*Auflösen*],[128] suspend, observe, confiscate, keep under police surveillance, confiscate passports [. . .]'.[129] In a joint operation, the Gestapo was to set up, on the Austrian model, a 'special research list' of confiscations and arrests, even if their tasks overlapped. As units sent to specific localities, and given the names of their destinations, the *Einsatzkommandos* were meant to take over control of the territory as the troops advanced. The mobile phase was to be completed by the transformation of the *Kommandos* into SDOA and *Stapostellen*. But the objectives of the '*Einsatzgruppen* of the SIPO and the SD' – the first of that name – were given their final formulation in a retrospective circular, sent out by the Gestapo on 5 October 1938, at a time when the groups had already settled down in the Sudetenland. These objectives now had a programmatic character, with new *Einsatzkommandos* being trained with a view to the invasion of the rest of Czechoslovakia, on 15 March 1939. In both cases, the missions with which the *Einsatzkommandos* were entrusted were as follows:

a) rendering secure the new order against any attack or disturbance;
b) arrest of any person known to be hostile to the Reich;
c) safeguarding of all documentary evidence [*Unterlagen*] – written and other – produced by persons and organizations hostile to the Reich;
d) liquidation of organizations hostile to the Reich or used for purposes hostile to the Reich;
e) occupation of all official premises of the Czech state and criminal police,

and those of all organizations serving the purposes of the state and criminal police.[130]

The first article, which was in line with the Nazi world-view, described the actions of the *Einsatzgruppen* as preventive and ascribed to them a defensive character. So the *Kommandos'* missions were no different from those of the SD and the Gestapo in Germany. The state of exception, brought into force after the two successive invasions, gave the Nazis the opportunity for launching a wave of repression which we can measure thanks to the evidence provided by Helmut Groscurth, one of Wilhelm Canaris' deputies in the *Abwehr*. Appointed Wehrmacht liaison officer to the *Reichskommissar* for the Sudetenland, Canaris was unable to obtain an exact account of Nazi arrests. What we do know, thanks to his diary, is that the number of arrests rose to some 2,500 in a fortnight. He also noted that they mainly involved German Communists in the Sudetenland, but also members of the Social Democratic Party, the Germanophile independence party, and Czechs considered hostile to the Reich. In March 1939, Groscurth tells us, 1,600 people were arrested in the very first week of the invasion. This figure grew rapidly to 4,639 arrests. Of this total, 1,288 people were kept in prison;[131] it was as if the export of SD and SIPO security practices was more brutal in the Sudetenland than in Austria, and even more brutal in foreign Czechoslovakia than in the 'profoundly Germanized' Sudetenland. Was this 'brutalization' of *Einsatzgruppen* practices a result of Nazi racial determinism?[132]

Six months after the invasion of Czechoslovakia, occupied Poland was in turn the arena of a quantitative and qualitative leap in the violence meted out by the *Einsatzgruppen*, a decisive leap marked by the coalescence of political violence – to which the actions of the *Einsatzgruppen* had hitherto been confined – with a wartime violence that inexorably rekindled Nazi memories of the previous war. The new war would soon be viewed as a *Daseinskampf*, a 'struggle for existence':[133] the comparison would be more vivid for those young adults[134] who were now SS intellectuals, as the Great War had been the war of their childhood.

On 12 June 1944, the head of the RSHA, Ernst Kaltenbrunner, ordered Erich Ehrlinger to request the SSPHA to promote Walter Schellenberg to the rank of *Brigadeführer*. The argument set out by the departments of *Amtschef* I is quite remarkable:

> *SS-Oberführer* Schellenberg is the archetype of the indefatigable activist [. . .].
> Promotion of *SS-Oberführer* Sch. to the rank of *SS-Brigadeführer*, with effect
> from 21/6/44, is proposed in view of his attitude and his action, and in
> consideration of his function.[135]

A year before the collapse of the Third Reich, the men of *Amt* I of the RSHA were still using, in promoting the head of the *Ausland*-SD, the vocabulary of activism and political struggle to describe the candidate's 'virtues'. In a word, they continued to believe in what they were doing right to the bitter end.

Thanks to their role in carrying out assessments and formulating doctrine, SS intellectuals contributed to conceptualizing Nazism, propping it up with a discourse whose scientific ambitions were, they thought, not in doubt. And yet these ambitions were imbued with the ideas of verification and syllogism: SD intellectuals saw the world through the lens of racial determinism and each of the observations, each of the facts reported by them was erected into evidence confirming the validity of the doctrine. In this way, surveillance and assessment, conditioned by Nazi beliefs, contributed to reinforcing these same beliefs.

Scientific ambition was embodied in *Gegnerforschung*, the study of opponents. By opening files on everybody and constructing organization charts that gave concrete shape to the transversal links between those real or supposed adversaries, they could reveal the 'world of enemies' in league against the new Germany they hoped to build. However, the discourse of SS intellectuals was fundamentally different from that of the *völkisch* students of the Weimar Republic they had been before entering the SD. Their SS discourse was still, as in their student days, a fundamentally defensive discourse of mobilization and struggle, but in 1939 there was no trace of the eschatological anxiety felt at the end of the Great War: the 'world of enemies' was still dangerous, but it no longer ran the risk of destroying a Germany that had, in Nazism, found a millenarian providence. Nazism, too, had channelled eschatology into itself.

These men also faced a hierarchy that urged them to bring their practices into line with their convictions. They had to conform to a constrictive normative system, a system which, in the final analysis, expected them to turn their words into deeds, and commit themselves more deeply to a struggle that, in 1939, was still merely an attempt to avenge 1918. As the willing targets of a discourse presenting them with the myth of the intellectual as a man of action, an ideal for them to strive after, the SD intellectuals saw their world change significantly between 1939 and 1941.

Part III

Nazism and violence: the culmination, 1939–1945

Between 1 July 1939 and 22 June 1941, over a third of SS intellectuals received instructions to present themselves at the police school in Pretzsch or Düben. Here they found groups of Waffen SS, Gestapo and KRIPO functionaries, and a small number of SD employees, all undergoing military training as well as being given an introduction to the customs and way of life of the countries they would be invading. These troops formed SIPO and SD *Kommandos* whose task was to be that of protecting the rear of the invasion troops in the Polish and Russian campaigns. SD intellectuals headed off to war in the east.

The east symbolized a mythical space for the SS – a virgin land to conquer, a *tabula rasa* for Germandom to shape, a place rich with possibilities, precisely because it was occupied by ethnic groups considered to be inferior. Since these groups had not left their mark on the eastern immensities, they were open to Nazi activity. This was the message of one of the women's songs of the *Reichsfrauenführung*, which proclaimed:

To the East is our tomorrow, is the coming year for Germany;
There is a people's care, there await danger and victory.
There brothers were faithful, and never lowered their flags,
Five hundred years of fidelity: they kept watch and were given no thanks.
There are neither farms or hearths, there the earth cries out for the plough.
There we must conquer foreign lands that once belonged to the Germans.
There a new start can take place, so take up your weapons, Germans, and
　　listen![1]

This song, composed by Hans Baumann, captures in a nutshell the Nazi representations of the east, which are consistently set in the context of the history and evolution of Germandom. As is typical of such expressions of Nazi fervour, Baumann sees the east as a land in which the Germans already had a stake, from bygone days. It was in the east that were buried those ancestors who, 'faithful', had 'kept watch' with 'no thanks' for five hundred years. This is another example of the 'Blood and Soil' rhetoric that raised this land to a place of Germanic destiny.[2] Celebrating both the brotherhood of arms and the bonds between ancestors and Germans of the Third Reich in the conquest and conservation of the land, this text conforms to the three main functions assumed by Nazism in the outlook of its supporters: interpreting the world, interpreting history and giving the individual a place in the chain of ancestors. As an ancestral land, the east was also depicted as a land of 'care', a place where 'victory' and 'danger' were inextricably linked, thus combining belief in a victory that would mean the coming of the German Empire with an anxiety which is not expressed in any more specific terms.

After 1939, the east, imagined in this way, became the target of great projects that were all imbued with a utopian impulse. SD intellectuals, who played a fundamental role in this, were not alone: they were accompanied by other groups of SS intellectuals, expert developers and architects in other bureaus of the SS, especially the RKFdV. Henceforth, they would no longer be acting alone – they were now part of activities that went far beyond the context of the SD alone. In the formation of the *Einsatzgruppen* and in the *Osteinsatz* more generally, the 'active intellectuals' they aspired to be lost, as I have said, the specific characteristics of their original groups. They were now no longer very different from the young lawyers recruited by Werner Best to form the Gestapo cadres who comprised the major part of the *Einsatzgruppen*. The experience of the *Osteinsatz* was not confined to SD intellectuals alone: it was shared by most SS officers from the SIPO and the SD. So I have felt free to draw on sources from within this wider group to gain access to the words and actions that accompanied genocide.

Chapter 7

Thinking the east, between utopia and anxiety

In 1939, SD intellectuals had on average worked for the SS for only three or four years. The overall development of the political situation then gave their activities a decisive turn. The conquest – which, as it turned out, was to involve the conquest of the whole of Europe – led to a very great extension in their activities and their field of application.

For the Nazi leaders, the war was the era of every possibility: ethnic reorganization would come about under the aegis of the Nordic elite represented by the RSHA and the RKFdV.[1] The creation of these two bodies, at a week's interval in October 1939, was a response, in intention if not in reality, to Nazi expansion in Europe. The first real task of the RSHA, after all, was to settle the *Einsatzgruppen*, whose task it was, during the Polish campaign, to ensure that Germany had effective police control as it extended its occupation. Once the conquest was complete, the *Einsatzgruppen* were transformed into local Gestapo and SD offices:[2] after the time of conquest came that of administration and Germanization.[3]

In October 1939, the RSHA created special institutions charged with implementing Germanization and population displacements. Thus were created a *Sondergruppe* III E S (the future *Amt* III B of the RSHA) under the leadership of Hans Ehlich,[4] as well as a *Sonderreferat* IV R (the future *Amt* IV D-4 then IV B-4) under the leadership of Eichmann,[5] both officially in charge of population questions in the occupied territories. To complete the establishment of the central bodies, it was also decided to create two local specialized institutions, the *Einwandererzentralstelle* (EWZ) and the *Umwandererzentralstelle* (UWZ), the first focusing on the resettlement of *Volksdeutsche*, and the second on the expulsion of Jews and Poles.[6] Both were placed under the joint leadership of the departments of Eichmann and Ehlich.[7]

These were the organizations that produced plans for settlement and resettlement, and urban studies that were to form the context for Germanization. They selected the populations that were to be imported or expelled, in liaison with the local bureaus of the Gestapo and the SD.

Together with the RSHA there were several institutions for which

Germanization was a policy priority. In various ways, the civil administrations, the Reich ministries, the Ministry for Occupied Territories (*Reichsministerium für die besetzten Ostgebiete* or RMfdbO, also called *Ostministerium*) after 1941, and the *Rasse- und Siedlungshauptamt* (RuSHA) and *Volksdeutsche Mittelstelle* (VoMi)[8] played their part. For example, the VoMi was active in the administration of transit and selection camps, and the general staff of the RKFdV in the general planning of Germanization.

Collaboration between these different institutions involved both mutual support and rivalry,[9] but eventually they decided to complement one another.[10] It was common for a young specialist in questions of *Volkstumpolitik* to serve in the EWZ or a local SD bureau before joining the central departments of RSHA *Amt* III B, responsible for the overall planning of population movements. Thus Herbert Strickner was transferred to the Posen SDOA and the EWZ before being recruited in 1942 by Hans Ehlich in Berlin.[11] Likewise, *Hauptsturmführer* Alexander Dolezalek started his career in the general staff of the Posen *Ansiedlungsstab*[12] before joining the VoMi and the RKFdV.[13]

A regular exchange of men and ideas seemed to contribute to the development of successive consensuses,[14] based on a similar understanding of the situation and on a shared sensibility.[15] From 1939 to 1944, SS intellectuals would turn the RSHA into one of the most important bodies involved in laying plans for the east, one of the decisive protagonists in the Germanization that quickly constituted one of the ultimate aims of the Nazi utopia.

The field of competence of the RSHA was very broad, and its interventions in administrative plans and the management of territories in the east were just as diverse in nature. In the first instance, the RSHA produced a resettlement plan for different populations, to be preceded by a census and a process of selection. There are many archival traces of this work, in spite of the policy of systematic destruction implemented in 1945. These traces include statistics, memorandums, final reports and accounts of lectures delivered. These documents provide information on the practicalities and the concrete dimension of assessment and planning, while also revealing how the SS *Akademiker* apprehended space and understood human beings. These documents depict a demographic obsession and describe, each more vividly than the other, a Germandom isolated from the Reich, in small islands scattered across an ocean of hostile foreigners. The isolation of Germanic populations was seen as a curse that they had to try and remove by resettling populations and carrying out measures of spatial preventive hygiene.

The curse of Germanic isolation

One of the ubiquitous themes of the SD is the Germandom of Germans living abroad and involved in the *Volkstumskampf*. I cannot here embark on a history of the many confrontations – real or imaginary – between the German minorities of East Europe and the nations that had become states in 1918, or even that of the many ways they were represented. I will simply emphasize how, after 1918, the theme of the 'Germandom of the borders and foreign countries' became both an object of studies[16] for the new, politically committed 'human sciences' known as the *Volkstumswissenschaften*, and a focus for revisionist demands. These demands grew in the heart of *volksdeutsch* communities as well as in a host of scholarly societies discreetly financed by state institutions and then, after 1934, by the SS,[17] which eventually took over control during the final phase of the conflict.[18]

When, in December 1938, the SD produced a voluminous report describing Polish policies in the Baltic, it naturally described the diplomatic dimension of the Polish action in the three Baltic countries. But the decisive factor the report emphasized was of course the way Slavic, Jewish and Baltic populations were united in Germanophobia, thanks to Marxism or nationalism.

The author of the 1938 report claims that the belated fusion of the German Baltic community with the Latvian populations was biologically limited in character and concerned the elites and urban populations alone. Indeed, the SD considered the process as a Germanization of the Latvian elites – something which had been interrupted in the mid-nineteenth century by the Russification policies of the Tsarist governments. This, resulted, or so they claimed, in an 'alienation' (*Verfremdung*) of the two communities, while revolutionary Marxist ideology continued to reinforce Germanophobia. Surrounded by a Russophile administration, by Germanophobic revolutionary currents and Baltic nationalisms, the German community in the Baltic had been encircled by communities united by their Germanophobia alone.[19]

In 1940, a report drawn up by the *Amt Raumplanung* of the RKFdV depicted this Baltic Germandom as numerically small. It was noteworthy that its birth rate was lower than the Lithuanian average, but the community was described as being economically stable. This population was, according to the author of the report,[20] racially 'healthy and vigorous' but was being culturally suffocated by the constant pressure of foreigners. As a result, its situation was described as 'hopeless [for lack of] schools or of enough teachers and writings'.[21]

It was the same kind of description that the Petersburg *Sonderkommando* of the VoMi produced in the Leningrad region during the winter of 1941. Given the task of proceeding to an assessment of the situation of *volksdeutsch* communities, *Standartenführer* von Hehn, liaising with *Einsatzgruppe* A, carried out an investigation, village by village, that comprised a veritable racial X-ray of the German communities in the Leningrad area. He always went about his task the same way: he started by establishing the date of settlement of the *Volksdeutsche* so as to assess what state they were in. This allowed him to provide details of the conservation or decline of

Germandom as internalized by the *Volkstumswissenschaftler* of the SS. For instance, one village (Duga) still preserved German-style religious festivals; in another, the individuals in the community kept up relations with one another (Strelna colony, a suburb of Leningrad). The report on the town of Kiopen is representative: according to local memories, this was a colony that had been founded around 1610 by migrants from Darmstadt. It was no longer *reindeutsch*, as a result of frequent 'mixed marriages', and did not have a German school, even if the inhabitants still spoke German with a few Russian words incorporated in it, a result of the Russian desire to 'repress' Germanic culture.[22]

The German island in Slavic territory was thus threatened by interbreeding – and might find its very substance diluted as a result. Assimilation – whether social or cultural – was starting to accentuate the community's insular character, and villages were losing contact with each other. Now that it was an archipelago, it was seeing the external characteristics of its identity vanish: associations, schools, newspapers and religious festivals too. Finally, its 'racial purity' was vanishing, either by interbreeding or by the immigration of foreigners.

This is clear from the description of the 're-Polonization' of the Warthegau. The introduction to the report of the bureau of 'resettlement sciences' insisted on the development of ethnic relations in the Warthegau. The 'slow Germanization' of before 1900 had been transformed into a rapid 'Polonization'. The author, Dr Luise Dolezalek, the wife of the SS *Hauptsturmführer* of the RKFdV, attempted to bring out the Germanic presence through a study of the occupation of the land.[23] In a series of seven maps, she sets out a Nazi vision of the development of German–Polish relations between the fifteenth century and the 1930s. This analysis was inseparable from a history of German settlements until the eighteenth century, but changed in the twentieth. After the Great War, German communities suffered a significant drop in numbers thanks to the loss of Posnania, which had been ceded to Poland, but also thanks to the 'policy of cultural oppression' imposed by the latter. Luise Dolezalek restored a widespread vision dating from before the war in the institutions responsible for *Auslandsdeutschtum*:[24] that of isolated German communities gradually being assimilated as a result of the loss of their language,[25] by interbreeding, by dispossession of their land and by Polish immigration, which the Nazis claimed was significant in volume.

The signs of resistance to assimilation were also noted. The *Institut für Staatsforschung*, a branch of the University of Berlin directed by Reinhard Höhn, produced a memorandum on the struggle led by the German bishop of Posen/Gnesen. Between 1887 and 1907, he demanded that German clergy be retained so that German-speaking Catholics would not be subject to Polonization. Completely decontextualizing the bishop's actions, and forgetting to mention the *Kulturkampf* that Bismarck's administration was waging on the Catholic Church, Höhn's men turned this polemic into an interethnic confrontation, depicting German Catholic elites as seasoned warriors in the *Volkstumkampf*.[26] Nonetheless, in the eyes of Luise Dolezalek, the stand of the bishop of Posen did not hold up the Polish advance. The Polish people, 'particularly inclined to *völkisch* combat' in the view of SD intellectuals, were in 1939 – she claimed – in a position to do great damage to a Germanic population cut off from their native land.[27]

At a session of the *Akademie für deutsches Recht*, Professor Kurt Walz, invited to deliver a lecture on the condition of the German minority in Poland, came to the same conclusions:

> In Poland, demographic growth is so significant that the question of minorities is mainly the question of property. From the racial point of view [*blutmässig*], 'Polishness' thinks it can very quickly submerge and neutralize minorities by significantly increasing its own numbers. That's why the struggle is taking place decisively around economic positions [. . .]. And the struggle against German schools and the German language is grafted onto this [. . .].
>
> Germany has more to lose in this respect than Poland; Poland can take the loss of 10,000 Poles in Upper Silesia if, in exchange, she can liquidate the much more numerous group of Germans in Poland, a group that is much more significant culturally and economically. It is this calculation that seems to lie behind the Polish policies here described.[28]

This idea of a Germanity that was vanishing – or even being 'liquidated' – was internalized by the SS hierarchy to the extent that it influenced its policy decisively. Erhard Kroeger, one of the leaders of the *Volksdeutsche* in Riga, merely needed to spend a few minutes describing to Himmler the sense of danger felt by the Germanic minority in Estonia for the latter to decide on the evacuation of all German communities from Estonia and Latvia, and not just of 'persons under direct threat' (active Nazis and *Volkstumskämpfer*). On 26 September 1939, two days before the USSR and Germany signed the secret agreements dividing up the Baltic regions, Kroeger had described the situation to Himmler, insisting on 'the intense fear of Bolshevism in Riga [. . .] and the very vivid memory of the massacres of 22 May 1919 perpetrated at the last moment by the retreating Bolsheviks'. And he concluded 'by assuring the audience that the greater part of the Germanic community of the Baltic should be considered as under threat'.[29]

In this excerpt from Kroeger's memoirs we see everything that conditioned Nazi thinking about the east: a memory of the interwar period marked by violence and confrontation, the sense of danger run by people of Germanic stock living in a foreign country and – something which made the case of the Baltic lands even more crucial in the Nazis' view – the panicky, obsessional fear of 'Russian Bolshevism'. The facility with which Himmler and Hitler – informed overnight by the SS *Reichsführer* – allowed themselves to be convinced is surely proof of their susceptibility to the theme of an isolated Germandom in danger of being overwhelmed. The *Heim ins Reich*, in other words the emigration of *Volksdeutsche* to German soil, became the salvific operation par excellence.

In autumn 1939, the situation of Germandom abroad and the Nazi apprehension of the east underwent a decisive change. The conquest of Poland and the German–Soviet agreements on resettlements led to a double movement. On the one hand, Polish territory was incorporated into the Reich and, on the other, *volksdeutsch* communities from Hungary, the former Baltic countries and South Tyrol were welcomed in. The massive influx of German 'stock' was augmented by the annexation of territories 'conquered by force of arms',[30] to be appropriated from the foreign populations. Expulsion and resettlement were now inseparable from the issue of Germanization. For SS intellectuals, the desire voiced by Hitler on 6 October 1939 to 'reorder "ethnographic relationships" in Europe with the help of resettlements'[31] became an opportunity for reversing the fate that had until then seemingly weighed on the German communities that were lost amid the Slavic immensities: it announced the providential twist being assumed by Germanic destiny.

SS intellectuals tried to realize this attempt in the various resettlement plans drawn up between 1940 and 1942. In their projected reshaping of the eastern space, their aim was dominated by the desire to protect racial hygiene: 'to develop' a territory meant, first and foremost, 'to separate out' its populations.

In April–May 1940, *SS-Oberführer* Professor Konrad Meyer[-Heitling] produced the first plan for general reconstruction of the eastern territories 'taken back' from Poland.[32] His strategy of *völkisch* reconquest was aimed at reversing the relations of power between Poles and Germans in the conquered territories. The document contained two discourses: a discourse on the restoration of Germandom, with 1914 as its origin, as if the Great War had triggered a dysfunctional evolution of Germandom in Posnania; and a discourse on the overcoming of the curse of isolated Germandom, with the aim of reducing Polishness (*Polentum*) to a series of linguistic islands surrounded by 'walls' and 'Germanic bridges':

1) We should in the first place build a German ethnic wall along the border with the General Government, in the form of a broad cordon of *Germanic farms* [italics in the original]. This border wall will separate the Polishness still within the Reich from its hinterland, right from the start, once and for all.
2) There is an urgent need to populate the great basins of the biggest cities with German peasants.
3) There is also a need to found a broad German bridge, to some extent as an east–west axis, linking the border wall to the Reich. Finally, a more slender wall must be built across the old corridor, through the districts of Zempelburg, Bromberg, Kulm and Gaudenz. These ethnic bridges

separate the remnants of the Polish communities still there, thus forming Polish islands.[33]

The postulate of a strict segregation between Poles and Germans in these regions seemed such an obvious measure to the SS agriculturalist and geographer that he expressed it only between the lines. The two communities confronted each other, and the Poles, separated from their 'hinterland', were doomed to suffocation.[34] This technique of the cordon sanitaire and the penetrative bridge of resettlement was to be a constant feature in all the population plans of the RSHA and the RKFdV up until summer 1942.

Breaking the circle of isolation meant, as far as the SS developers were concerned, separating and isolating the Polish communities, but also organizing the old German islands so that they could emerge from the ocean of foreigners and, later on, be extended. This was the so-called policy of 'settlement and support points' (*Siedlungs- und Stützpunkte*) that was implemented from the summer of 1940. Meyer-Heitling's plan thus established a spatial typology: the border territories, those of the ancient territories of Posnania and the Danzig corridor[35] were designated as major settlement zones for intensive colonization.

The second version of *Generalplan Ost* was produced in July 1941.[36] The first category of settlement zones became 'zones for reshaping and reconstruction [of Germandom]' for immediate re-Germanization. They were complemented by zones of 'new construction' (*Neubauzonen*) which formed a 'Germanization front' embracing interstitial regions, namely the still Polish *Kreise* between East Prussia and Silesia. In the east, following the invasion of the USSR, a huge cordon sanitaire was to run from the north of the Baltic to the south of Ukraine, passing through Belorussia and Galicia. It was to be populated by colonies of SS soldier-peasants. Territories located between the 'ethnic front' and the sanitary glacis of the border, on the other hand, were to be Germanized more slowly, over a period of thirty years. This monumental plan required using 4.5 million Germans for colonization, and the displacement of over 31 million people[37] (Russians, Poles and Balts). Such plans did not go unquestioned. Calculations that had risen to a total of 4.5 million Germans had been revised given the lack of *Reichsdeutsche* and now included *Volksdeutsche* rendered available by their return to the Reich, but also the 'captured German blood', forcibly wrested away from the foreigners.[38] These aggressive, racially motivated plans were considerably extended.

This adaptation, however, was not restricted to a revision of mere numbers. Ehlich's plan, like Meyer-Heitling's, was also modified through the spatial organization of Germanization. Faced with a deficit of Aryans, the SS planners resigned themselves to a scattering of German islands set up on the model of Walter Christaller, thereby accepting Germanic insularity so as better to ensure – as they saw it – its victory by drawing on other variables applied this time to the 'foreigners'. Having started from

a policy applied to Nordic *Sippen* and described as 'positive', the planners now resorted increasingly to *Umvolkung* (ethnic dissemination). This
Umvolkung was of course present in the first plans, in so far as these made
provision for gigantic displacements of so-called foreign populations,
displacements which would entail serious demographic consequences
for the populations concerned. Nonetheless, the figures in the final plans
of the RKFdV and the RSHA, produced between mid-1942 and mid-1943,
involved even more than the displacement of 35 million people.

In fact, for SD intellectuals as for the agrarian experts of the RKFdV, the
stumbling block in all planning of German expansion to the east was the
'lack of men'. The *Rassenreferent* of the *Ostministerium* was perfectly well
aware of this when he addressed his criticisms to the RSHA's *Generalplan
Ost*. Ehlich's plan involved settling ten million German colonists in thirty
years. Taking a careful look at the figures of 'available strength', Wetzel
arrived at a total of 8 million people available over the period:

> The central question in the whole colonization of the East is [knowing]
> whether we will be able to awaken the urge to colonize the East in the heart
> of the German people. [The fact] that this urge is already to a large extent
> present cannot be doubted. But we must be aware that a great proportion
> of the population – especially in the western half of the Reich – nonetheless
> fiercely refuses to settle in the East – even in the Warthegau or in Danzig and
> Prussia. [. . .]
>
> As well as the question of the desire [of the Germans] to colonize, it is
> essential to awaken a 'desire for a child' [*Wille zum Kind*] in the German
> people, especially amid colonists in the east – to a far greater degree than
> previously. We do not have any right to conceal this from ourselves: the
> increased birth rate since 1933 is admittedly satisfying in itself, but can in no
> way be considered sufficient [. . .], especially if we examine the huge colo-
> nizing mission in the East and the monstrous way our neighbours in the East
> are increasing their numbers.[39]

Here, Wetzel is expressing the ambiguity of Nazi planning. All
the plans developed by the RSHA and the RKFdV were based on
the presupposition of a significant increase in the German birth rate.
Facing Germanic colonists, whether *Reichsdeutsche*, *Volksdeutsche* or (re-)
Germanized 'Slavs' of Nordic race, were 45 million foreigners, whom
the Nazis dreaded as a proliferating multitude. Insularity was not just a
matter of space: it depended too on the dynamics of number. The fateful
loss of Germandom in the immensities of the steppes was not the only
thing to haunt the SS's imagination: Nazi anxiety in the east was also
focused – perhaps more than on anything else – on the dilution of the
Nordic racial patrimony within the foreign multitudes. This legitimated
the expulsion of 31 million of those 'undesirables' (*Unerwünschte*), with 14
million others being forced, as the planners had decided, to stay put so as

to constitute a reservoir of manpower. Their fate was not decided in any greater detail.[40]

At a colloquium of RSHA *Amt* III B held in Bernau on 1 and 2 February 1943, led by Ohlendorf, Ehlich and Justus Beyer, Beyer presented the RSHA *Generalsiedlungsplan* to the *Referenten* III B of all the local SD bureaus, and retained the figures of the foreigners to be expelled.[41] While the number of individuals of Nordic blood was limited, Nazi plans for expansion continued to develop: Himmler[42] and the planners kept the Urals as their aim.[43] The threat of dilution thus became even greater. SS intellectuals then adopted a murderous logic. In the final RKFdV plan, dated 23 December 1942,[44] the number of people in the territories of the east to be Germanized – from which Russian territories conquered in 1941–2 were excluded – rose to 19,045 million people, a total that would soon, in the opinion of the experts, be brought back down to 10,234 million.[45] The Germans of the Reich counted for only 451,000 of these, and only 883,000 foreigners were considered as Germanizable, so 8.9 million colonists needed to be found to reach the objective. Out of the 19 million people originally present, only 1.2 million inhabitants could subsist on their land of origin or of election. Even if the plan did not envisage as such the means of getting rid of undesirables, the difference between the two figures naturally implied extremely high death rates. Konrad Meyer-Heitling's plan simultaneously took into account the state of the policy of extermination of the Jews in the east, the policy of food supply established by the Wehrmacht and the Ministry of Agriculture, and the concept of extermination through work (*Vernichtung durch Arbeit*) developed by the WVHA.[46] In spring 1941, Herbert Backe and the bodies directing Wehrmacht logistics had decided to make the army live off Russian resources, programming the murder by famine of 'tens of millions of individuals'.[47] It was this mechanism, called 'depopulation' (*Rückvolkung*) by the RKFdV and the RSHA, that was reflected in the figures of the *Generalsiedlungsplan*.[48] In any case, it comes as no surprise to see Konrad Meyer-Heitling appointed – following an inspiration of Himmler's – as head of planning under secretary of state Backe:[49] the man who had led negotiations between the Wehrmacht, the RSHA and the Ministry of Agriculture was the same man who had set up the 'famine plan'. The initial policy of spreading Germans across the sea of foreigners had given way to a policy of planned depopulation, so as to ensure – along with the expulsions – the 'ethnocultural survival' of Germanic communities amid the Slavs.

When, on 11 December 1942, Hans Ehlich, the head of RSHA *Amt* III B and overseer of the *Generalplan Ost*, delivered a lecture to the leaders of the NSStB on 'the treatment of foreign peoples',[50] he thus envisaged four methods of treating the 70 million people who lived in the territories that were to be Germanized: 'life in community with racially and ethnically close peoples, "dispersal" within Germandom, the spatial repression and physical extermination [. . .] of undesirable ethnic groups'. As far as

Ehlich was concerned, 'life in community' concerned only the essentially Nordic peoples, who were not to be found in the east. Dispersal, which involved a loss of ethnic identity prior to assimilation into Nordicity, was in his view conditioned by a selection that meant Nordic blood could be tapped. Now, very soon after, Ehlich, Ohlendorf and Justus Beyer organized a colloquium of *Referenten* III B of the SDOA,[51] during which they produced percentages of those *incapable* of being Germanized within each people:[52] by combining the numbers given by Ehlich in his lecture with the percentages of 'displaced persons' given by Beyer, we can finally discover the destiny of those foreigners whom the Nazis wanted to get rid of. Ehlich mentions 22.5 million Poles, 80–5 per cent of whom could, in Beyer's view, be expelled. Out of 7 million Czechs and 4.1 million Balts, 50 per cent could be expelled; out of 5 million White Russians, 75 per cent; and out of 30 million Ukrainians, 65 per cent (the figure concerned only the Ukrainians of Galicia, who were more 'Nordified' than the others, and so this figure was just a *minimum*). In this way, we have a total of 47,875,000 undesirable persons.

Generalplan Ost, however, planned on the expulsion – the 'spatial repression', in Ehlich's words – of 'only' 35 million people. This left nearly 12,875,000 'undesirables' who could not live 'in community with the Germans', could not be 'dispersed', and whose deportation was not planned. This left the fourth solution envisaged by Ehlich: physical elimination. This figure still did not include the Jews, whose number in East Europe was estimated at 8,391,000 individuals: all were destined to be exterminated. According to the report of the inspector general of statistics, SS Richard Korherr, their number had already been halved.[53] The plan thus seemed to be aiming at the expulsion of 35 million people and the violent death of 21,266,000 individuals, starved to death, exterminated by work, or killed by mobile killing units and in the death camps. The practice of genocide, which had been in operation since 1941, was not just integrated into the planning: it had even become a condition of Germanization, the final aim of the Nazi utopia.

The Nazi project for a sociobiological re-establishment

At the end of 1941, an exhibition was held in the Palace of the Princesses in Berlin. Its organizers were, to put it mildly, unusual. The RSHA, represented by *Amt* III B, the EWZ and the UWZ, here associated with the RKFdV, opened to the public an exhibition that included a great panoply of explanatory tableaux, maps, architects' plans and lectures. Its subject was planning and construction in the east (*Planung und Aufbau im Osten*). The exhibition was subsequently to be put on in Posen, right in the middle of the occupied territories. This confrontation with the *Reichs-* and *Volksdeutsche* of Posnania, major participants in the 'construction' of the Germanic east, shows clearly that this exhibition, above and beyond its propaganda value, had a programmatic dimension. After his visit, Heydrich insisted that the expulsion of Jews and Poles be included in the exhibition.[54] This is evidence of the Nazi desire not to conceal the concrete conditions of Germanization, which did not, of course, exclude the evident smoothing over of the process's rougher edges[55] – no mention was made of the violence being inflicted on the expelled Jews and Poles.[56]

The exhibition 'Planning and development in the east' shows how extensive and detailed the work of the RKFdV and the RSHA was. The exhibition catalogue, published at the beginning of 1942 on glossy paper with the RKFdV crest, was adorned with photos, maps and plans, and comprised one of the most complete representations of the SS project.[57] It provided – and herein lies its value – a mass of information on the world-view on which the SS plans drew. The plans for developing the boundaries of the Posnania villages reproduced schemes for a reconstituted and egalitarian open-field system and involved a total reshaping of landholdings by a policy of purchase and massive confiscation in the Warthegau and Posnania.[58] The east was to be reconstructed on a *tabula rasa*.

These territories, however, annexed in and after 1939, were already subjected to short-term policies by the civil administration. These policies represented both a starting point and a restriction for RKFdV developers. Thus *Gauleiter* and SS-*Obergruppenführer* Arthur Greiser, *Reichsstatthalter*[59] of the Warthegau, had some highly specific ideas about the future of the region and its place in the Reich's economy. In his view, the cereal production of the Warthegau was of vital interest for the Reich; it should become its 'granary'. Firmly opposed to any initiative that might disorganize production or lead to a flight of the workforce, he protested against the planned upheavals in landholding and the total reshaping of rural town planning in the Warthegau. One week before Himmler visited the exhibition, Alexander Dolezalek, the young SD historian transferred to the department of resettlement of the *Volksdeutsche* in SSPF Warthegau, had his request to expel Poles employed as rural workers turned down, a refusal which Dolezalek attributed to Greiser's 'reactionary agrarian advisors'.[60] Like the 'Solution of the Jewish Question', the realization of the planned millennium came up against the realities of local administration.[61]

For SS developers, the conquest of the east was a unique opportunity to build, out of nothing, an ideal society based on racial determinism. To design farms in the east, the new site of Posen or Litzmannstadt (Łódź), was to realize the millenarian dream, to express and implement the planned new Nazi sociobiological beginning. There were three main dimensions to the set of plans approved by the RSHA and the RKFdV. The first was to embody, in the shape of public places and buildings, the *Volksgemeinschaft*,[62] the community of blood which SD intellectuals hoped to organize as the basis of the thousand-year Reich. The second was to inject their world-view of racial hygiene into a compartmentalized space, as could be seen already in the planned settlements, rigorously separated from the rest of the population, and the inroads made in the *Generalplan Ost*. Finally the organization of houses and interiors displayed a representation of the family in line with Nazi discourse on the individual, controlled at every stage of his life.

The architectural practice of Roth and Schumann in Berlin, for example, drew up a blueprint and scale model for a typical colonization village in the shape of a *Strassendorf* (street-village) which it tried to provide with an attractive centre that could act as a way of organizing traffic flows. Thus, in the middle of the village, 'the street widens out into a public green space, with workshops, businesses, housing and a hotel and restaurant around it'. The centre was also the place for public buildings, the list of which clearly indicated the contents of the Nazi project: 'the town hall and the parade ground [or place for marches – *Aufmarschplatz*], with the belfry, the Party HQ, the HJ [*Hitlerjugend*] centre, the school, the NSV and the girls' work camp' were its main elements.[63] It may seem strange that the most visible surveillance structures of Nazi activism were not mentioned: neither the SA nor the SS was represented. The sole possible explanation lies in the locality of the villages: these were planned to be sited in the Warthegau or Posnania, regions destined for rapid Germanization, and not in border territories – so they had neither a defensive nor an invasive role. Their organization did not reflect the necessities of the Nazi *Volkstumskampf*: hence the absence of the Black Order. On the other hand, the frequent presence of youth organizations, Party headquarters and the NSV offices[64] revealed the preference for day-to-day activism linked to a pacified form of social life.

While these villages of colonization never became a widespread reality, experiments of the kind were carried out by the SSPF for the Lublin district, *Brigadeführer* Odilo Globocnick. He composed regulations for the economic life of the new villages of *Volksdeutsche*, making it obligatory to attend the *Julfeier* and the *Sonnenwendefeier*, both neo-pagan ceremonies. He thereby placed these new *Volksgemeinschaften* under the aegis of belief in an SS god.[65]

Plans for the Warthegau villages were an opportunity to develop a much more complex environment. One of the most complete sets of plans to have been preserved concerned the city of Łódź, which the Nazis renamed Litzmannstadt.[66] The plan was structured by a circular rail line separating the historic centre of the German city in the west from the two living colonies located to the north and south, thus excluding the three industrial zones and the Polish quarter. Redevelopment plans for the city did not envisage the total expulsion of foreigners, but the area of Polish settlement, shifted some five kilometres outside the historic centre, was enclosed between a German residential zone and an industrial zone which it was to supply with a workforce. The town plan reflected the overturning of German isolation.

The plans for the city centre revealed a clearly less idyllic representation of social life than that of the villages. One of the development quarters was devoted to police buildings – the size of this site (about half the surface area deemed necessary for an area of four thousand dwellings)[67] gives us some idea of the forces the SS wished to mobilize in what it conceived of as the final phase of the *Volkstumskampf*. Unlike rural space, urban space was the site of a final ethnic confrontation, where a subject population was to be maintained.

On the plans for the city's forum there appear streets with the names Adolf Hitler, Hermann Göring and Rudolf Hess, a sign of the Party's pre-eminence in toponymy.[68] The main square fulfilled two functions: the first was political and civil representation, with the buildings of the *Regierung* (government) standing next to the *Volkshalle* (the People's Palace). Its cultural and artistic function was represented by a museum, a concert hall, a theatre and a cinema, while to the south of the city a large stadium made it possible for sports activities and parades to be combined, in a familiar liturgy. Set back a little, the town hall linked the historic heart of the city to the forum quarter, created *ex nihilo*. To the south of the forum, clearly separating it from the historic city, an extensive park enclosed the *Hitlerjugend* centre, whose site was very clearly demarcated, as if young people – here established as major protagonists in the *Volkstumskampf* – were to be subject to careful supervision: the planners had made provision for no fewer than three HJ centres, one in the city centre and two in the 'German western city', the biggest district, separated from the forum by the railway: its outlying district was also given a *Gemeinschaftshaus*, a 'Community house'; probably designed to give some structure to internal relations within the German community. These collective rede-velopments of social space were already, so to speak, a response to the recommendations of Odilo Globocnick. He stated that he wished to turn cultural activity into the second main axis of his policy of Germanization, making community events into opportunities for bringing together the nascent *Volksgemeinschaft*.

All in all, RSHA intellectuals and the architects and developers of the RFKdV dreamed of a harmonious and ruralist *Volksgemeinschaft*, and factored in the Nazi activist organizations – the SS – only in places where there was a confrontation between Germandom and a foreign presence now rendered residual, but seen as a valuable labour force. The Nazi project imagined by the architect, implemented by the peasant and defended by the SS could be turned into a reality only through armed victory, the racial selection of the defeated, eugenic weeding-out, and the formation of the community by means of the social bond.

Redevelop and settle: forms of Nazi fervour

The Nazis' project was conceived during a very short period, and retreat and defeat did not allow them to realize more than a few significant aspects of their plans. Urban redevelopment and rural Germanization, in particular – with the notable exception of the *Wehrdörfer* of Zamość and its district,[69] and a few fledgling experiments in Belorussia[70] – did not get off the drawing board. Several thousand of the SS, however, found themselves involved in operations meant to lead to Germanization: the expulsion of Jews and Poles, the intake of *volksdeutsch* migrants. They were responsible for logistical control and administration in the provisional reception camps: they acted as 'cultural support' teams and encouraged the spread of literacy.

The reports written by SS officers on their return from operations to repatriate the *Volksdeutsche* are eloquent, as are the poems written by young activist women of the NSStB which demonstrate a real emotional investment in this land and the men who were to be 'Germany's future'. Here, for example, is SS-*Untersturmführer* Dr Wallrabe describing his trip to north-east Russia, a trip he carried out as part of *Sonderkommando* R of the VoMi, in charge of racial assessment and the evacuation of *Volksdeutsche*:

> On 10 January 1942, I was, at my request, incorporated into the *Volksdeutsche Mittelstelle* [. . .] I learned that I was to be assigned to the Petersburg *Kommando* of Sk 'R' [. . .]. On 12 January, I had to arrive in Kaunas by car before the *Kommando* with comrade Preusse [the leader of the *Kommando*; Wallrabe was chief of its general staff]. From that time, from the day we left Berlin to the day we returned, I was with the *Kommando* leader the whole time. His experience [*Erlebnis*] was mine, I shared joys and sorrows with him, and I hope I was a faithful companion and a good comrade. Our chauffeur, Martin Vosen, was an active part of this camaraderie.
>
> [. . .] The trip [to Petersburg] will remain unforgettable for me: I had not seen war from close up. I was amazed at the sight of the columns [. . .] of trains, I took in the fascinating spectacle of the countless Soviet tanks destroyed by the violence of the German attack and lying at the roadside. I was very taken aback by the towns: the closer we came to the front, the more they resembled huge entrenched camps. We also saw the signs of the great exodus of hunger – Russians dragging their carts along by hand, retreating to where they hoped they could find bread and lodging. As for us, we had undertaken this journey so as not to let our compatriots [*Volksgenossen*] fall into this wild and chaotic stream, but to get them out of the theatre of operations and take them by train to the Reich.

This new mission to repatriate the *Volksdeutsche* was, for the young SS anthropologist, an opportunity to discover war and Russia as he had doubtless imagined them, and at the same time. As a veteran of the 1940 missions, he was familiar with the Baltic States, but had never visited the Russian land which embodied the biologistic presuppositions of the Nazi belief system.

In Ivangorod, as nowhere else in Europe, East and West, the Germanic-Western and the Russian-Asiatic worlds stand menacingly opposite one another. It is lucky that our comrades have been able to fix this image in their minds.

Was this not just what he expected to find there? Russia: a land of hunger, barbarity and 'Jewish domination' – for Wallrabe had enjoyed a unique opportunity to visit Reval under the supervision of a 'Soviet Jew' during the *Umsiedlung* of Germans from the Baltic in 1940. And the Russia registered by the young anthropologist was merely the confirmation of his a priori representation of it, and in itself comprised a powerful reason for repatriating the *Volksdeutsche*. For the latter, the east in wartime was a place filled with danger.

The east, however, was not simply the vast and dangerous place depicted by Nordicist experts. Wallrabe himself, after this description, insists on giving voice to the fervour within him as the mission comes to an end:

> Anyone who has taken part in an *Umsiedlung* will remember those tough but wonderful times with nostalgia [. . .]. The *Kommando* in charge of the *Umsiedlung* then constituted a sworn community; this time, some [of us] first had to learn to become part of it and subject to its rules. You need to have *passion* [in French in the original] for the *Umsiedlung*. Wherever you come from, the essential thing is to be passionately in thrall to the mission of repatriating individual Germans to the Reich.

The myth of return and the experience of the front here merge in the expression of the anthropologist's feelings: *Umsiedlung* is both part of the combat – the semantic field associated with combative fraternity is very much in evidence – and of a redemptive adventure. At the same time that the *Trek* (migrants' convoy) of *Volksdeutsche* was setting off for the Reich, Wallrabe fell back on words from Exodus and the idea of the Promised Land to convey his fervour.

The experience of the repatriation of the *Volksdeutsche* also gave people the feeling that they were taking part in the reconstruction of the *Volksgemeinschaft* while also working towards the reconquest of the lost territory. These were, for instance, the two main axes of the way student action in the east was represented, as can be seen in the writings left by those rather idiosyncratic volunteers. So we see boys and girls giving a hand in the activities of naturalization, giving lessons, helping raise children, working in the fields and running the secretariat of the EWZ bureaus. Others performed missions to assist the *Volksdeutsche*, drew up plans, maps and projects, and thus found themselves in the epicentre of the Nazi construction of utopia. At the heart of this 'humanitarian' activity of the Nordic *Volksgemeinschaft*, a young girl student related her *Osteinsatz* in these terms:

As soon as we arrived in the village [of *Volksdeutsche*] we came across several children and peasants who clearly wished to attend our school show. On our arrival in front of the school, the group of schoolchildren waiting at the door quietened down a bit and observed us, partly curious and bold, partly cautious and even scared. The children had until then known only their 'mamoiselle' [*sic*] as they generally call the student girl who works in their village. Today we have come from the surrounding villages to help our friend Annelies in organizing and putting on a children's show. The ordinary run of mortals has no idea of what it means to organize a varied show with the children of migrants, an afternoon on which the children are not spectators, but actors.

In the classroom there was a throng of children, their brothers and sisters, and everyone who took an interest in the show [. . .]. Then the programme began. To begin with, children's songs and dances [. . .]. Then came the first piece [. . .]. Time then went by very quickly. [. . .] Then came the high point, with the children playing *Hansel and Gretel*. Of course, there wasn't much Grimm in it, but the old gentleman will surely not hold it against us: the children [. . .] played with such enthusiasm that everyone was clearly enthralled. One of the particular pleasures was for the main actors to eat a piece of real cake and real chocolate taken from the house of sweeties. The 'mamoiselle' had generously supplied the chocolate.

With this fairy-tale scene and a song, the afternoon had found its main tenor and its conclusion. [. . .] The mothers were very proud of their children, and we kept hearing: 'How well little Josef (or little Aline) performed!!!'[71]

Signed by 'a student on her *Osteinsatz*', this text might seem quite innocuous. The activist, aware of her racial and cultural 'value', makes sure she emphasizes twice over the exotic nature of the German pronunciation of the *Volksdeutsche* – people who had come from Romania, the Baltic States or the Volga – so as to bring out the task of Germanization that still needed to be accomplished. Behind the entertainment, the locals were thus surreptitiously being incorporated into what these Nazi activists considered to be German culture. The village community needed to be gathered in and integrated into the group of those who represented the future of Nordic identity: these children, in other words, to whom the students of the NSStB were teaching the new Germany and its 'age-old culture'. To organize, Germanize, create a sense of community: this was one of the axes of student action in the east. The same signature, 'a student on her *Osteinsatz*', is found beneath some poems that clearly suggest the emotions that presided over this voluntary action. They refer to a peasant of a new kind who sows the seeds in the lands that are to be Germanized, but also, symbolically, the *Ostland* itself, which is '[this] tomorrow, [this] year which is coming for Germany]':[72]

On certain days, the peasant is there, [. . .]
On Sundays, he counts the pages of the calendar,

The grandmother prays for the time of harvest.
The men are clever, but God even more so.
He makes the sky sometimes cloudy, sometimes clear,
And we human beings, we hunt, we pause, and we grow anxious:
Will the sun ripen the harvest?
[. . .]
The Lord God thinks: 'I too will show them'
And then he makes the sun to shine.
Skilfully, without dwelling on the effort, without counting,
The harvest will at last be brought home.
And then neither England nor Russia will make us yield.[73]

Apart from its obvious paltriness, the text shows the internalized elements of the Nazi belief: a recitative of the main markers of time by the description of the peasants' works and days, the union of the generations in family life, and the presence, at the end of the text, of the world of enemies against which German identity is to be constructed.

The activist student who signed the text was staying in East Prussia in summer 1942, just at the height of the extermination of the Jewish communities, victims both of the extermination camps that were working at maximum capacity,[74] and of the killing units that, like the 101st police battalion, were shooting entire communities in the whole of occupied Poland and Russia.[75] The Jewish villages were emptied under her eyes and promptly resettled by the *Volksdeutsche* waiting in the transit camps. Now, she designates her stay and her action in her own writings by the term *Osteinsatz*, the same term used by SD officers and the police of the Gestapo to label service in the *Einsatzgruppen*. It suggests the idea of action (*Einsatz*) in the east (*Ost*) and seems to link her Nordicist 'humanitarian activism' to a service that was involved in conquest and war. Fervour, utopia and war thus fused, transforming the activist's stay into a 'journey to the east' that had more than something of a crusade about it.

Chapter 8

Arguing for war: Nazi rhetoric

Drawing on historical memories as it did, the 'thought of the east' was inseparable from the previous war; but it was also part and parcel of the present war that dominated the horizon of SS intellectuals from 1939. The experience of war then tended to merge into the representation of the east and, from 1941, into the representation of extermination – all borne up by a constant desire for justification and interpretation. Initially, on the level of the combatant society as a whole,[1] the invasion was preceded and accompanied by a widespread enterprise of legitimation of the war in the east. One specific argument was formulated too, especially by SD intellectuals, for the SS and the police. Finally, the protagonists themselves – SS, officers, SD cadres – distilled their representations of the concrete practices implemented at ground level.

Though violence was perpetrated in obedience to orders, and though the decision to carry out massacres could be motivated by material arguments,[2] the means that made it possible for consent to be given to this violence pre-existed these 'orders', these 'impulses', these 'initiatives'. The discourse of war or the rhetoric of genocide were not a static construction, as an intentionalist *Geistesgeschichte* would have it, but rather a set of beliefs, of feelings, of emotions in constant tension with perceived reality. They were fluid mental representations – so fluid that they were sometimes fleeting: and yet they alone allow us to explain why people's behaviour changed so suddenly on the ground.

From the reparative war to the 'great racial war'[3]

The representation of the Polish attitude towards Germany, the Germans and the *Volksdeutsche* did not suddenly take shape with the Nazi attack in September 1939. The situation of the *Volksdeutsche* was the object of constant developments, widely broadcast in the German media. The war marked a significant qualitative leap. *Volksdeutsch* communities were not merely represented as the target of oppression, but rather as the target of widespread massacres, which legitimated Nazi aggression.

Very rapidly, the German authorities estimated the number of *Volksdeutsche* killed or missing as a result of Polish attacks during the campaign at nearly 58,000[4] in three weeks. The a posteriori legitimation of the German attack was thus essentially based on this estimate. Faced with this 'Polish violence', the *volksdeutsch* minority was deemed to have created self-defence units, actually organized secretly by the SD and Behrends' *Volksdeutsche Mittelstelle*.[5] The justificatory argument was here of a defensive order: it was a question of German troops bringing help to endangered communities.

The Poland campaign did, however, draw on more complex mechanisms of representation than those employed in the mendacious constructions of the 'propagandists'. Over six weeks, starting with the invasion, the SIPO and SD *Einsatzgruppen* sent daily reports on their activities to the central office of surveillance set up by the RSHA. These reports detailed the activities of groups in 'maintaining order', and justified the executions they carried out. Almost all of these executions, in fact, were responses to civilian firing, both in the daytime and at night. The line between civilians and soldiers does seem to have been extremely hazy. Polish soldiers, overwhelmed by the German attack, ended up in great numbers behind German lines. Badly equipped and badly informed, they were lumped together with civilians firing at troops from behind, and many of them were shot. The most frequent disturbances of order, such as shootings at night, pillaging and panic-stricken movements, were attributed to civilian combatants, or 'snipers'. Taken prisoner, they were immediately shot, sometimes after summary sentencing.[6] The representations of the German police played a decisive role in this: a psychotic fear of the sniper is something we have known about since the work of Alan Kramer and John Horne, and it was a constant feature in German armies from the invasion of France in 1870 onwards.[7] In summer 1914, this mechanism had produced a wave of summary executions and reprisals against the Belgian and French populations. It had remained one of the great questions aroused by the debate on responsibility for the war, a question on which historians and publicists avidly seized[8] and which 'naturally' became a live issue again in Poland.

While accounting for their police activity, the *Einsatzgruppen* expressed the conviction – fully internalized – that they were engaged in a just and lawful war against a barbaric Polish enemy that mutilated soldiers,[9] shot them in the backs, massacred *Volksdeutsche* and cut off children's hands. These reports, classified as secret, were communicated only to the eight most highly placed dignitaries in the RSHA[10] and so had no propaganda aim. They formulated an argument for German war in Poland unchanged since the Great War. But the Polish campaign was not simply a resumption of hostilities; true, groups were mainly pursuing the old insurgents of 1919 in Silesia and Posnania, but this practice, of course, had a utilitarian dimension to it. Repression of the former Polish activists of the 1919 movement meant forestalling the establishment of clandestine nationalist resistance movements, so as to nip in the bud any attempt on the part of the Poles to take up *Volkstumskampf* again. On a deeper level, SS relentlessness against these insurgents concealed a symbolic function of 'reparation' for 1918–19.[11] Waging war and serving in the *Einsatzgruppen* was thus, for SS intellectuals, a patriotic and political act, but also a rite of memory.

Apart from the obviously Machiavellian aspect of an aggression triggered by a fake assault – SD officials (Behrends, Mehlhorn, Otto Rasch, Heinrich Müller and Arthur Nebe) were involved in the attack on the Gleiwitz radio station[12] – the Polish campaign was the object of particularly intense emotions on the part of the Germans. This campaign, a war for justice and reparation, was not decisive, any more than were the wars in France and the Balkans: these were merely the endpoint of the 'apparent silence of weapons',[13] as Siegfried Engel would call it in his course on the Thirty Years War. The decisive conflict, of course, was the one unleashed in the summer of 1941.

The struggle against the USSR – as historians have said repeatedly – was a total war against the 'Judaeo-Bolshevik' enemy.[14] For the Nazis, the USSR was the land of Jewish domination and Bolshevik barbarity, the place where the two mortal and immanent enemies of Germandom were united. While it was SS intellectuals who often formulated these two dimensions of the Nazi world-view most clearly, this was probably because, experienced as they were in doctrinal formulation, they could make a great show of references, arguments and evidence in the memorandums they produced. Because they had been trained in the universities, and by quoting figures and citing sources could bend their doctrinal formulation to fit academic rules, these men highlighted the Nazi representations at work in Operation Barbarossa.

The representation of the objective alliance between Communists and Jews was rooted in the main theories developed by Hitler and the ideologists of the Nazi Party from the 1920s. More interesting, however, is the way this belief in the representations was so widespread. For it was a belief not just developed when memorandums were written specifically on the situation in the east: for the Nazis, it was a key factor in the analysis of events. Thus, even before the German authorities started to think of turning against the USSR, the collusion between Jews and Communists constituted an interpretative grid of the troubles suffered by the *Volksdeutche* of Bessarabia when this territory was occupied by the Red Army in July 1940.

> Frequent observations suggest a unified sub-system underlying these phenomena [of pillage]. Gangs of Jews and Communists are pillaging German farms and businesses and tormenting [*drangsalierten*] the *Volksdeutche*. The

Soviet troops entering [Bessarabia], who are in other respects behaving perfectly correctly, state however that they are powerless in the face of these riots. In *volksdeutsch* circles, however, people suppose that there is a link between these riots of Jews and Communists and the belated arrival of the Soviet troops.[15]

In the view of the *Volksdeutsche* – Nazified by the VoMi – there was a double collusion at work in this series of riots. The alliance between Jews and Communists, in the very heart of the territory, was not in doubt as far as the writers of the report were concerned, and was intensified by collusion with the outside – with the Russians of the Red Army. This highly concentrated representation of the 'world of enemies' can be reduced to two protagonists who are being melded together. The duplicity with which the Soviet army acted against the *Volksdeutsche* was, after all, a sign of the 'Jewish grip' on its command. It was an old cliché of anti-Semitism to make of Jews the 'puppeteers' of Communist action. The German term *Drahtzieher* means the one who pulls the strings, usually offstage: it was widely used to refer to the supposed action of the Jews between the wars[16] and gave rise to many letters on individual cases.[17]

At the start of the war, the RSHA, via Reinhard Heydrich, took pains to draw up an account of the Russian action that made aggression a legitimate response. On 10 June 1941, the head of the SIPO/SD sent the *Reichsführer* SS a summary of the Bolshevik 'work of destruction' carried out since the signing of the non-aggression pact. Heydrich carefully surveyed the territories occupied by the Germans – from France to the Government General – and detailed the 'plots' laid by the Comintern and the USSR, and carried out by local Communist Party branches and émigré German Communists. Precisely detailed, and based on all the documentation provided by *Ämter* IV, VI and VII of the RSHA,[18] Heydrich named names, and set out biographies, without ever omitting the Jewish ancestry of this or that activist.[19] Germany, thus enmeshed in countless plots, was in his view forced to break the non-aggression pact and plunge into war – a war which, in his mind, was indeed defensive,[20] though its aims were more ambitious:

> We are not waging war merely to beat England and America, but also to lay the basis for a new Europe united under German leadership.
>
> [The Bolsheviks] are currently seeking to bring Europe under the yoke [*unterjochen*] and Bolshevize it [. . .] so as then to turn this Bolshevik Europe against their present allies, and spread world revolution. [. . .] *In Russia, the fate of the world is being decided.*[21]

In these few lines we find, expressed in succinct form, the two main aspects of Nazi war rhetoric: the war in Russia was the object of a utopian construction that crystallized the imperial hopes of Nazism, while remaining a defensive war.

Until now, interest has been expressed only in the world-view fostered
by the central Berlin authorities. However, these bureaucratic institutions were in no position to interpret the experience of war and were
limited to confidential documentation. The men who, on 22 June 1941,
launched their attack on the immensities of Russia were, however, the
object of an intense mass communication on the part of the Wehrmacht.
The specifically SS discourse of the RSHA was in fact amazingly close to
the rhetoric developed by the army men. It was as if the actual doctrinal
formulation of SS and RSHA intellectuals were one of the basic elements
of war rhetoric – as if the world-view at work transcended the activist
membership that joining the SS still comprised; as if this argument for
war, more than being specifically Nazi, formed the context for *national*
consent to Barbarossa – witness the speech of General Hoepner to the
Fourth Armoured Group:

> The war against Russia is an essential part of German people's struggle for
> existence [*Daseinskampf*]. It is the old struggle of Germans against Slavs, the
> defence of European culture against the Muscovite-Asiatic invasion, the
> defence against Judaic Bolshevism.
>   This struggle must aim at the annihilation of today's Russia and must
> therefore be waged with unparalleled harshness. Every part of the strug-
> gle must be prosecuted with iron tenacity until the enemy is totally and
> ruthlessly annihilated. In particular, there cannot be any mercy for the
> proponents of the current Russo-Bolshevik system.[22]

The few phrases classified as 'defence secrets' and communicated as
such to the officers who were meant to pass them on to their men provide
valuable evidence of the degree of internalization of racial determinism
by a Wehrmacht general, even though he cannot be counted as one of
those closest to Nazi activist circles.[23] Apart from the evidence of Nazi
racism in a formulation of uncommon clarity, this text makes an explicit
link between war rhetoric and normative discourse on the practices to be
implemented on the ground. Because the Russian war was merely one
incarnation of a vital, age-old struggle, the demand for ruthless behaviour expressed by Hoepner could gain a hearing and be endorsed by his
audience. His speech provided a justifying context for all the practices of
extreme violence that his soldiers would – in the view of the author of this
order – be carrying out in Russia. In fact, these practices were, so to speak,
already hinted at in the more concrete directives given to their soldiers by
the commanders of regiments or divisions. A mimeographed leaflet was
distributed to the majority of soldiers. Called 'Do You Know the Enemy?'
it was designed to constitute a vade mecum for those fighting on the
Eastern Front:

> Soldiers! You will be fighting against an enemy from whom you cannot
> expect methods of combat [worthy of a] decent, chivalrous opponent. The

Bolshevik Red Army knows that it is facing certain annihilation by the German army, and will as a result employ the most repellent and most underhand methods.

[. . .]

You must expect night attacks on posts, small units, rearguard columns, and broken-down vehicles. Thus, vigilance during surveillance tasks can never be too intense. Anyone who strays from his troop without being on a special mission is in danger. Stick together like good comrades [. . .]. For every German soldier, not allowing any comrade to fall into the hands of the enemy is a matter of duty and honour.

[. . .]

You must also expect that the dead and wounded you encounter as you advance are merely pretending to be such so as to shoot you at point-blank range, or from behind. The Reds will also allow small units (infantry vanguard) through, so that they can attack the main forces. All of you be on your guard when you advance towards dead or wounded!

[. . .]

You are used to thinking that an opponent who advances towards you with his hands up must be intending to surrender. Among Bolsheviks, this can also often be a trick, so they can resume fighting behind your back. Treat someone as a prisoner only when you are sure he has been disarmed. Do not leave any prisoner unguarded.

[. . .]

We need to be clear that the Bolsheviks are using combat gas for the first time in this war – in all existing forms. If you are aware of this danger, our means of protection are effective against all types of gas. Gas masks [. . .] and anti-poisons must be constantly in reach and in working order. We will not be stopped by gas-infested roads. You know how they can be recognized and neutralized.

[. . .]

Do not eat anything you find; do not drink water from fountains before examining it. You have to expect that everything will have been poisoned.

[. . .]

The country and its population are contaminated by typhus, cholera and plague: diseases which, thanks to the hygiene of the German people, have long since disappeared from our land. You are vaccinated against contamination and have nothing to fear. In spite of everything, guard against any close contact with the population and do not drink any unboiled water.

[. . .]

Parachutists in civilian clothes will try to fight behind our backs. They are not soldiers, but snipers: they need to be liquidated. Take care! Be harsh and unyielding wherever you come across these methods of fighting – it matters little whether they be civilians or soldiers. Unless you observe behaviour of this kind among the enemy, behave as you did before. Whatever mode of combat the enemy adopts, your weapons are used to victory and will destroy him.[24]

Produced in great numbers,[25] these appeals for constant vigilance were of a kind to instil a sense of collective near-psychosis likely to produce behaviour of extreme violence from the very earliest days of the conflict.[26]

Barbarossa was indeed a 'great racial war', less because of the imperial hope with which the *Drang nach Osten* filled the victors than due to the fear generated by the discourse addressed to the combatants. This anxiety-arousing discourse, which promoted an animalistic vision of the adversary in line with Nazi racial determinism, insisted on the atmosphere of insecurity which would reign in wartime Russia, where the civilian could not be distinguished from the soldier.

From the discourse of security to the discourse of genocide

To grasp the second main aspect of the Nazi legitimizing rhetoric in Russia, we need now to concentrate on the discourse addressed specifically to the police and SD units formed in preparation for the invasion of June 1941. This discourse was produced, to a far from negligible degree, by SD intellectuals. Transferred to the headquarters of their units or to *Kommando* divisions, these intellectuals formed a major part of the staff of the *Einsatzgruppen* and wrote the reports. Indeed, this was an integral part of the functions of a head of *Kommando* and officer in the SD.

The name '*Einsatzgruppe*' has become so associated with the genocidal actions of the groups in the USSR that the term, however generic it may have been, tends to be applied indiscriminately to the four groups assembled for the invasion. However, in 1941, SIPO and SD *Einsatzgruppen* were not the only such groups to follow the Wehrmacht's troops: the Todt Organization and the VoMi in particular had their own mobile units, assigned to very different missions. Hence, in the vocabulary of the period, the term '*Einsatzgruppe*' did not designate 'mobile killing units'.[27] Also, the *Einsatzgruppen* in Russia were not the first to be organized by the SIPO and the SD: the first groups had been put together at the time of the *Anschluss*, and other formations of the same type followed at the time of the annexation of the Sudetenland and the invasions of Czechoslovakia and then Poland.[28] The groups formed for Operation Barbarossa were thus part and parcel of a practice already tried out by intelligence and police departments in the Third Reich. They were in any case intimately linked to Nazi imperial practice. These groups, the product of security bodies, and organized in view of the Reich's phases of expansion, were dependent both on the institutional discourse and on the activist discourse that, in the RSHA, overlapped.

The first real written account of the *Einsatzgruppen* missions came out only belatedly. On 5 November 1938, Heydrich issued a circular specifying a posteriori the activities to be carried out by the units that had been operating in the Sudetenland for several weeks. According to this circular, the *Einsatzgruppen* were to ensure:

(a) the protection of the new order against any attack and any disturbance;
(b) the arrest of all persons known to be hostile to the Reich;
(c) the confiscation of all archives and dossiers concerning the activities of persons and organizations hostile to the Reich;
(d) the liquidation of organizations hostile to the Reich or pursuing objectives hostile to it;
(e) the occupation of all premises of the Czech criminal and political police as well as of all organizations pursuing political or criminal police objectives.[29]

These directives remained valid in their general lines in both Poland and the USSR. They were actually imprecise enough to leave *Kommando* leaders with a margin of interpretation. In particular they sketched out a security-based order that constituted the common basis for the activities of all these units. The *Einsatzgruppen* were conceived as units meant to ensure the control of territories as the German advance, whether in the form of invasion or not, progressed. This discourse of preventive police measures, both political and racial, was in any case not specific to mobile units, as this type of argument had been introduced into Germany in both the criminal and the political police.

Indeed, in the KRIPO, sending 'professional or hereditary delinquents' to concentration camps was a consequence of the biologization of criminogenic factors. For KRIPO officers, this process comprised a way of internalizing Nazi racial determinism. This practice of preventive internment, carried out in two waves in the Reich, tended both to become more generalized and to become a constant feature of its activity.[30]

As for the political police, it had seen its action theorized under the impetus of Werner Best, who conceived of Gestapo practices from the point of view of discrimination. In his view, the Gestapo was an organization for struggle: like the Wehrmacht, it needed to keep its modes of action secret and lead the fight against political enemies in the way the Wehrmacht fought against outside enemies. The metaphor is evidence of the way the warrior world-view was injected into German society: in his theorization of Gestapo action, Best again drew on terms that, a decade previously, had been used to interpret the struggle against French occupation in the Rhineland. Fighting the French and fighting political crime were for him the two faces of the same *Abwehrkampf*. In this sense, operations in Czechoslovakia and Austria were no different, fundamentally, from repressive activities within the Reich: they were simply more intense, and carried out in the context of greater urgency:[31] they were preventive and defensive measures, perceived as a kind of reminiscence of the war.

It was the context of a *real* war that marked out Poland, the first true military campaign on which the Third Reich embarked: the internal organization of the groups showed as much. They were more militarized: SD and Gestapo men were accompanied by soldiers, Waffen SS and sections of the ORPO. It was still a matter of 'preserving the new order', but the action which had hitherto been essentially preventive now became curative. The practices of the *Einsatzgruppen* were now presented as a reaction against attempted disturbances.

In this way executions served mainly, in the view of the authors of the reports, to repress the threats being made against the *Volksdeutsche*, and pillaging and sniping. Arrests were of course police preventive measures, in the sense that they were targeted at social, political and racial groups seen as dangerous, but executions – aimed at the same groups – were always described as the results of enemy action. The violence deployed by the *Einsatzgruppen* was allegedly just a legitimate response to other violence. Police groups could interpret any incident as a threat of destabilization to the nascent occupation. Executions served both to neutralize enemies – real or imaginary, potential or immediate – and to represent German authority and the aspirations of the Reich to empire.

Refugees, soldiers who had quitted their units, local Jewish elites, panic-stricken rioters, runaways and Polish intellectuals were all identified either as the direct perpetrators of disturbances,[32] or as responsible for their outbreak. As I have said, they were sometimes given summary trials before being executed.[33] For the Poland campaign, the violence of the invasion, even though it was surreptitiously instrumentalized, was not planned in the sense that no directive for automatic execution seems to have been issued by the RFSS or Heydrich. The orders that came with the 1938 directives for Austria and Czechoslovakia remained the reference points for the hierarchy. This shows that the groups' practices had varied in between, and their interpretation of the hierarchy's discourse had been transformed. The *Einsatzgruppen* campaign in Poland was thus the ground bass of the radicalization of repressive practices implemented on the basis of the established rules and regulations of the Gestapo.

When the USSR was invaded, the *Einsatzgruppen* remained dependent on the discourse of security defined in 1938, though this was complemented by the hierarchy of new orders – often called 'criminal orders' – which, for the first time, defined the categories of individuals to be executed automatically by the groups. The original order defining these categories has not survived. But on 2 July 1941 Heydrich had made a copy for the use of the HSSPF newly appointed to Russia in one of his *Einsatzbefehle*. These orders, which have been studied frequently,[34] are not often quoted, and deserve closer examination:

Preliminary remark:
The short-term aim is the political pacification (in other words, essentially, the pacification by the political police) of the occupied territories. The long-term aim is economic pacification [. . .][35]
3) Searches
The Ek of the Security Police and the SD should take every necessary measure to seek out those on the special list issued by the RSHA. As it was

of course not possible to list all the dangerous people in the USSR, we also need, as a complement to this list of wanted persons, to perform all searches and [decisions to carry out] executions necessary for the political pacification of the occupied territories.

4) Executions

The following are to be executed: all officials of the Comintern (and, more generally, all professional Communist politicians), upper- and middle-ranking officials of the Central Committee, of committees of individual republics or Party branches, as well as the radical subaltern officials [of these institutions], Jews in state or Party positions, all other radical elements (saboteurs, propagandists, snipers, terrorists, agitators) *in so far as* [emphasis in the original] they are not needed to provide information on economic or political matters that could be of especial importance for future measures of political policing, or the economic reconstruction of the occupied territories.

It is important in particular not to liquidate definitively any economic, commercial or manufacturing organizations so as not to deprive ourselves of qualified personnel who can provide information. Attempts at purges carried out on their own number by Communist or Jewish groups are not to meet with any obstacles in these newly occupied territories. On the contrary: they are to be supported, even if this must be done *without leaving any traces* [emphasis in the original], so that these local self-defence groups cannot later appeal to political orders or assurances [that might seem to have been given to them at the time] [. . .]. In addition, prudence is needed in the execution of individuals working in medical milieus. The country has only one doctor for every ten thousand inhabitants, so the execution of a great number of doctors would create an inexorable vacuum if there were to be an epidemic[. . .].[36]

As in Poland, this discourse was based on considerations of security. The mission of the *Einsatzgruppen* was to 'pacify the newly conquered regions', but the imaginary representations of total war were injected into security practices. For the German members of the *Einsatzgruppen*, this war was to lead to the destruction of the Soviet state, and this implied the execution of its cadres. The orders issued by Heydrich were nothing less than a set of rules, formulated in detailed and categorical form, of the injunction addressed by General Hoepner to the men of the Fourth Armoured Group.

It is in the interpretation of this list by the cadres of the *Einsatzgruppen*, on a level with the psychosis instilled by the discourse of war, that we can discern the first step towards genocide. This, at all events, is what we find reflected in the daily reports compiled by the RSHA, based on information provided by the *Einsatzkommandos* and the *Einsatzgruppen*. Many of the executions carried out in the USSR in July 1941 are here legitimated. See, for example, how *Sonderkommando* 4a described his actions in Sokal and Luck:[37]

On 30/6/1941, 183 Communist Jews were arrested and liquidated with the help of trusted local Ukrainians [. . .].

A *Kommando* from the vanguard, who had been sent to Luck on 27/6, found a great part of the town in flames. According to information from the *Ortskommandant*,[38] the Jews were entirely responsible for this blaze. In the prison in Luck, the Bolsheviks had executed 2,800 of the 4,000 Ukrainians jailed. According to the statements of 19 Ukrainians, who had survived the massacre with more or less severe wounds, Jews had played an exemplary part in the arrests and executions. [. . .] In the town itself, everything was still upside down. All shops were pillaged by the population. To support [the action] of the *Ortskommandant*, all the forces of the available *Kommando* were brought in after the latter entered the town, so as to secure at least the major food warehouses.

Finally, the planned search of public buildings and the hunt for Jews responsible for the pillaging and the blaze began.

Three hundred Jews and twenty pillagers were successfully arrested: they were shot on 30/6.[39]

This type of document, studied quite frequently for the factual dimension of its content, also provides information – hitherto largely neglected – on the system of representations prevalent among the groups: belief in the collusion between Jewishness and Communism on the part of the *Sonderkommando* 4a officers, the conviction that Jews played a role in the violence and insecurity encountered by the groups on their arrival in the town, the execution of Jews seen as a way of keeping order. In this respect, the *Kommando*'s 'investigation' was merely the verification, on the ground, of the anxiety-arousing discourse of before the invasion.

This 'evidence' that Jews were troublemakers, perpetrators of atrocities, fire-raisers and major proponents of the Communist system marked them out as the main targets. This was why male adult Jews of between fifteen and sixty were more and more systematically shot during the first eight weeks of the conflict, as the idea that they were the spearheads of a potential resistance to the German invasion became increasingly internalized.[40]

Thus the security discourse of the Gestapo and the SD for the first time gave the missions of the police groups the task of physically neutralizing their opponents – who were clearly categorized and apprehended as capable of undermining the order imposed by the occupiers. But the racial determinism of the SS officers, in constant tension with experience on the ground, led them to subsume the categories defined by the regulatory framework issued by Heydrich, and to make automatic and systematic the violence against a racial adversary who, they thought, was directing all the forces in the USSR fighting against Germany: from July 1941, the war waged by the groups in the east was indeed a racial war.

A major priority, however, was still the hunting down of Communist officials. See, for example, how *Einsatzgruppe* C, which covered Ukraine and Galicia, summarized its first three weeks of action on 16 July 1941:

> Seven thousand Jews have been concentrated [*zusammengetrieben*] and shot in reprisal for inhuman atrocities.[41]
>
> Seventy-three men have been interrogated as NKVD bosses or officials and have also been shot.
>
> Forty men have been liquidated [*erledigt*] on the basis of well-founded denunciations from the population. They were mainly Jews of between twenty and forty, though on this occasion specialized workers and craftsmen were placed in reserve. As well as these executions in Lemberg, other reprisals were carried out, including in Dobromil, where one hundred and thirty-two Jews were shot.
>
> In Javorow, where thirty-two Ukrainians had been murdered, fifteen Jews were liquidated in reprisal.[42]

Einsatzgruppe C stated that craftsmen and specialized workers had been spared,[43] which shows that in spite of the hatred that played a part in the behaviour of those involved, the latter subordinated their feelings to the policies pursued by the authorities. This system of representations was a key mechanism in understanding what drove the protagonists – individual and collective – to consent to the genocidal instructions coming from Berlin, from local administrative chiefs, and from the SS hierarchy.

The radicalized security discourse of these first three weeks of conflict did, however, undergo rapid transformations, as is attested by the correspondence sent to Berlin in the second fortnight of July 1941. *Einsatzgruppe* B, for instance, sent a report on 'The Jewish question in the zones of settlement in White Ruthenia'[44] which, while reflecting the security practices set in place by *Einsatzgruppe* B, clearly shows the ambiguity of the system of representations that conditioned Nazi aggression:

> A solution to the Jewish question does not appear feasible during the war, since it could be achieved only by expulsion, given the very great number of Jews. To create a viable basis for the near future, the following measures have been taken in all the towns where *Einsatzgruppe* B has done its work:
>
> In every town a representative from the Jewish council has been appointed with the task of assembling a Jewish council of three to ten people. He alone bears the responsibility for the attitude of the Jewish population. Furthermore, it [the Jewish council] must begin registering the Jews resident in the given locality [. . .]. Also [. . .] orders have been issued everywhere that all Jewish men and women of ten years or over should immediately wear the yellow Jewish mark on their chests and backs.
>
> [. . .] Given their numbers, the enclosure of the Jews in a ghetto seems a particularly difficult and urgent task.[45]

The measures, admittedly conceived as temporary, aimed – as far as the SS cadres were concerned – at ensuring that Jewish communities were 'in no state to cause harm' by excluding, registering and enclosing them in ghettos: they revealed a preoccupation with separating out the Jews. However, the cadres of the groups and their Berlin hierarchy agreed (and this is the meaning of the expression 'viable basis for the future') that the Jewish communities comprised a danger for the security of the conquered zones.

Even if, however, the measures taken by the *Einsatzgruppen* – enclosure in ghettos, wearing of the yellow star, registration – were always aimed at 'making secure' the conquered territories by making those communities visible and hampering their margins of manoeuvre, it was perhaps another motivation that guided the RSHA cadres: maybe it was, for them, a way of modelling themselves on the SS experience in Serbia,[46] which consisted, from May 1941 onwards, in transforming Jewish communities into reserves of hostages. Deemed to be responsible for various acts of sabotage and for the slightest dysfunctions of incompetent administrations, the Jewish communities of occupied Russia needed, in the view of SS officers, to be 'intimidated' massively if calm were eventually to be restored. Every incident was, as before, interpreted by the SS as a trap laid by the Jewish community, and thus led to new shootings. However, in this new system, the community itself was considered as a hostage, and men were no longer the only targets. This argument doubtless enabled the cadres of the *Einsatzgruppen* to legitimate the execution of women and children so as to preserve order, or as a reprisal. Other passages of the abovementioned report, especially the introduction, bring out clearly the urgency of other representations:

> In the relatively narrow band of Central Eastern Europe, on either side of the line from Riga to Bucharest, in the so-called 'Jewish quarter' of Europe, lives over half of world Jewry. It is here that we should seek the human reservoir of western Jewry, which cannot renew itself and is continually being supplied by blood transfusion [*Blutzufuhr*] from the east. It is in any case impossible to go back very far in the genealogy of any person in a position of leadership in world Jewry without ending up, once or several times, in one of the ghettos of some town in Central Eastern Europe.[47]

The document insists from the start on the strategic place occupied by the region in the 'Jewish question'; the idea of dealing a fatal blow to Jewishness by striking it in its 'cradle' was growing. Holding the Jews of central Europe hostage was already a way of limiting the room for manoeuvre of 'world Jewry'[48] and destroying the capacity of the race's demographic growth as a whole. However, in July 1941, in spite of the many executions carried out by *Einsatzgruppe* B, there was still no question of complete destruction.[49] The text constituted a stage in the mental development that led from a world-view based on questions of security and segregation to a 'world-view of eradication' that led to genocide. Between the two, there was the same difference in nature and degree as between the concepts of prophylaxis and asepsis.[50]

When, a fortnight later, the sixteen *Kommandos* forming the four *Einsatzgruppen* started shooting women and children,[51] they forged the representations that would enable them to face this new radical demand, and to acquiesce in it.

Gerlach has demonstrated that there were two distinct stages leading the mobile groups from the execution of men to that of entire communities: the first stage, which occurred between 1 August and the third week of the same month, was the inclusion of a great number of women and children in the massacres; the second, starting in the first week in September and lasting until December, saw groups annihilating Russian Jewish groups *full-scale*, with the exception of a few tens of thousands of individuals selected for work.[52]

Two reports, important because of the details they give us about the operations described, provide information about the representations of the massacre: these are the reports of *Standartenführer* Jäger, head of *Einsatzkommando* 3, and his superior in the hierarchy, *Brigadeführer* Walter Stahlecker, head of *Einsatzgruppe* A, on the 'Final solution of the Jewish question in the Baltic'. This is what Stahlecker wrote on 15 October 1941:

> Jews
> In *Ostland*, systematic cleansing has included, in line with the orders laid down, the elimination – as full-scale as possible – of Jewry. This aim has been attained – with the exception of White Ruthenia – essentially by executing some 229,052 Jews (see appendices). As there is a crucial need for the rest to work in the Baltic provinces, they have been shut up in the ghettos [. . .].[53]

Stahlecker, however, does not specify what was to become of the 'labouring Jews'[54] whose lives were spared. Enclosed in the ghettos, they no longer, in his view, represented any danger for the occupying power. For if the SS officer had accepted the means of ensuring full-scale genocide, he continued to view it as a security measure:

> At the time of the entry of the German troops, there were seventy thousand Jews in Latvia. The rest had fled with the Bolsheviks. The remaining Jews were extremely active as saboteurs and fire-raisers. Thus, in Dunaburg, the Jews had started such a great number of those fires that much of the town burnt down.
> During the Judaeo-Bolshevik terror, 33,038 Latvians were deported, imprisoned or murdered, and a general pogrom might have been expected on the part of the population. However, just a few thousand Jews were spontaneously eliminated by local forces. In Latvia, it was necessary to

implement several cleansing actions, undertaken by a *Sonderkommando* with the help of forces selected from the Latvian auxiliary police (mainly relatives of deported or murdered Latvians).

Until October 1941, this *Kommando* executed nearly thirty thousand Jews. The remainder, Jews who are still indispensable given current economic constraints, have been brought together in ghettos set up in Riga, Dunaburg and Libau.

After punishment had been meted out, for failure to wear the Jewish star, black marketeering, theft and fraud, but also so as to avoid any danger of an epidemic, other executions were carried out subsequently. Thus, on 9 November, 11,034 [Jews] were executed in Dunaburg; at the beginning of December, on the occasion of an action led and performed by the HSSPF in Riga, 27,000 [Jews]; and in mid-December in Libau, 2,350 Jews. At present, in the ghettos, there are (apart from Jews from the Reich), in:

Riga, about 2,500

Dunaburg, 950

Libau, 300

These, as a qualified workforce, are indispensable for the preservation of the economy.[55]

This text presents all the arguments based on considerations of security, and is evidence of the way these considerations continued to play a role throughout the period when Jewish communities were being massacred. However, this line of argument seems, from October, to have relied less on images of war, and to have shifted to images of occupation, more adapted to the economic preoccupations of the administrative bodies. This classic phenomenon has been described by Gerlach, who sees economic considerations as one of the driving forces that led to the decision to carry out the genocidal operations, showing that the dates of liquidation of the Jewish communities of Belorussia were settled on the basis of a set of measures taken by local administrations – measures very often linked to the provision of food or to accommodation policies.[56] Gerlach presents genocide as the complex product of negotiations between, on the one side, officials from the Wehrmacht and the civil administration and, on the other, the *Einsatzgruppen* – who in the meantime had become stationary units with the name BdS.[57] While the former insisted on preserving a Jewish workforce, while refusing, most of the time, to feed and house these populations, the latter pushed for the total extermination of the Jews because of their potential harmfulness. There is consensus on one point: Jews were harmful, and this led local authorities to view the preservation of the Jewish workforce as a temporary measure.[58]

This aseptic imagination found expression, in December 1941, even in the modes of preservation of these 'labouring Jews', the rare survivors of the mass shootings of the autumn and the cold and famine of winter. This is how *Standartenführer* Jäger, head of *Einsatzkommando* (Ek) 3, put it:

I also wanted to shoot down those 'labouring Jews' and their families too, which led me into huge quarrels with the civilian administration and the Wehrmacht, who imposed the following ban: these Jews and their families must not be shot [. . .].

I consider 'Jewish actions' to be over, as far as their main phase is concerned, in the territory of the Ek 3. The labouring Jews still present are indispensable, and I imagine that after the winter this workforce will still be absolutely necessary. I am of a mind to begin sterilizing the male labouring Jews straightaway, so as to avoid any reproduction. If in spite of this a Jewish woman falls pregnant, she will be liquidated.[59]

We here encounter the cutting edge of the discourse of genocide in its institutional expression, in the sense that what counts for Jäger is no longer the harmfulness of Jewish communities that shootings have reduced to a low level that he considers acceptable, but their eventual extinction. In the last analysis, the striking thing about his remarks is this representation of an animalistic Jewishness.[60] This process of animalization echoes the representation of 'Jewish bestiality', discerned by the authors of the reports in the ruthless hostility shown to the bodies of soldiers.[61] In Jäger's *imaginaire*, the Jews are seen as domesticated wild creatures, useful for their work even if they are still harmful in his view, and thus distinguished from the representations of a population stigmatized for its alleged 'bestiality'[62] and savagery. In December 1941, Jews were no longer, in Jäger's view, something to be hunted down – they no longer seemed so dangerous.[63] By massacre, sequestration, reduction to labouring folk who wear a mark – the 'yellow Jewish mark'[64] – anti-Semitism had acted, in Jäger's eyes, as a substitute form of domestication, preceding the total annihilation of the species.

When all is said and done, should we see the psychological mechanisms at work in the conflict and the mass murders carried out as forms of certain major invariant factors of anthropological order? Perhaps, instead, the change in behaviour and representations that took shape in the mobile groups can be divided into two distinct processes of animalization of the opponent? It is as if the first phase of activity, a mobile phase marked by war, a phase in which male adults and activist women were actively tracked down and put to death, had been subtended by an *imaginaire* drawn from the world of hunting, in which the Jews were identified as wild beasts. The second phase, marked by the context of occupation, by the more settled existence of the groups and the fixation of the image of Jewishness in the ghettos, had been experienced by the *Einsatzgruppen* officers as a form of domestication, which ruled out hunting, but led to slaughter,[65] including that of very young individuals, even newborn infants.

Actually, such processes elude observation and are not susceptible to a completely reliable study. At the best we can, in the current state of documentation, suggest their existence, and try to discern their effects in the way our groups perpetrated violence.

The fact remains that the discourses of legitimation of genocide in the groups' reports were a mode of expression that remained essentially internal to the hierarchy: it was SS officers in post in Russia addressing Nazi dignitaries living in Berlin. When the action started, these discourses made way for another mode of expression that, this time, could indeed allow the emergence of those impulses that led to consent to genocide. This consent was given by men in the troop, by their officers, and also by local auxiliaries.

Expressing violence: defensive rhetorics, utopian rhetorics

The discourses developed on the ground itself, at the time of the massacres, by those who committed them, those who ordered them and those who were present at them – speeches made by Nazi bosses or RSHA cadres, judicial interrogations, letters from members of the *Einsatzgruppen* – form a heterogeneous corpus whose elements, taken one by one, seem singularly difficult to make use of. Judicial documentation, in particular, is a real trap for the historian: how can we distinguish between what is fact and what is a reconstruction of memory? How can we tell strategies that are pleas of innocence from confessions and evasions? How are we to interpret the silences, or the declarations of the accused casting suspicion on their comrades? How, finally, are we to separate statements produced by prior understanding from spontaneous utterances? For all these questions, there is no 'method'.[66] All the same, these sources are of crucial importance in grasping the psychological, individual and collective mechanisms at work in genocidal violence.

'Expert ideologues of the RSHA' trained the groups in their missions when they joined up and when they carried out their operations.[67] We also know for sure that the heads of the groups addressed their men on numerous occasions to explain why their activities had changed character;[68] we know, finally, that speeches were given on the sites of the massacres by the officers, from the most humble rank up to Himmler himself. The contents of these speeches are for the most part unknown to us; a few examples, however, will give us an idea.

From 28 to 31 August 1941, there took place one of the biggest mass murders of the war, on the outskirts of the town of Kamenets-Podolsk, in Ukrainian Podolia, where over 11,000 Jews expelled from Carpathian Ukraine by the Hungarians were gathered. In three days, the massacre took the lives of 23,600 Jews, of both sexes and every age.[69] Rounded up from the streets and squares of the town by the Ukrainian militia on the afternoon of 28 August, the victims were locked in a building for the night, and then led in columns by men of the police battalion to the places of execution that were located one kilometre outside the town, at the aerodrome. Led in small groups to deep ditches dug specially for the occasion, the victims were then executed by marksmen of *Einsatzkommando* 5 and the troops of the HSSPF. The executions lasted for two days – those who had not been executed by the evening of 29 August had to spend the night next to the ditches.[70]

Apart from the sheer extent of this mass shooting, rarely attained again subsequently, the attitude of the hierarchy on this occasion is extremely interesting to study. The execution actually took place at a time when the practice of exterminating entire communities was starting to emerge. The men in the police battalion, the Ukrainian militia and especially the SD *Kommando* were here, for the first time, the perpetrators of full-scale violence. They were actively followed by that master of murder, *Gruppenführer* Jeckeln. On the second evening, he organized a meal at which the honoured guests were the members of the SD *Kommando*. One of the eyewitnesses to the massacre – later interrogated as one of the accused – attended the meal. While he did not give details about the conversations there, he insisted on the modest ranks of the men in the *Kommando* of marksmen from the SD who were invited not because of the institution they belonged to, but because they were the ones who, during the afternoon, had been shooting. None of the guests, at least, could ignore this situation: the accused declared that he had been so ill at ease that he could not swallow a thing, both because of the images of the massacre and because of the 'repellent sickly-sweet smell coming from the SD men sitting next to him'.[71]

Jeckeln did not limit himself to organizing this meal: he arrived by plane in the morning, landing near the execution site, and watched as the shootings progressed, standing on the edge of the ditch into which the Jews toppled.[72] He had previously requested to harangue the marksmen who had volunteered.[73] This is how the narrative of a witness – an indirect one, he claimed[74] – was re-transcribed by the clerk:

> It occurs to me that I know by hearsay that *Obergruppenführer* Jeckeln brought ten representative [*prominenten*] Jews[75] to the execution site between the two bomb craters, and declared to the [persons] present that these people were typical representatives of Jewry. He designated one of the Jews by the name Bela Kun (phonetic),[76] and said that Bela Kun had organized an uprising in Hungary after the First World War. Apparently, he [Jeckeln] mocked the Jews with particular comments. After this scene, the Jews were shot.[77]

Here, Jeckeln sought out masculine incarnations of the enemy – he chose neither women nor children – thereby hoping to set the execution in the context of a war on Jews. We also find three crucial dimensions of the Nazi *imaginaire* in the reported words: Jeckeln sets the image of the enemy within a historical discourse, whose reference point in his men's memories was the Great War and the 'time of troubles', in which the image of Jewishness was inseparable from Communism. Massacring the Jews of Kamenets-Podolsk, Jeckeln seems to be saying, was simultaneously to make up for the vicissitudes suffered by those who were beaten in the Great War – Germans and Hungarians[78] – to continue, in the face of the same enemies, the conflict that had broken out thirty years previously and, of course, to wage the racial and ideological war embodied by the struggle with the USSR. Jeckeln was thus carrying out an act of genocidal pedagogy.

We can here doubtless grasp some of the reasons used to legitimate the events at the very place they were carried out. Jeckeln's speech was in line with the modes of internalization of the Nazi belief system,[79] and held up an image of the enemy's immanence, seeing the enemies from the Great War and the Revolution as akin to those of the conflict in the USSR, and thus turning racial determinism into the main link between the two periods. This speech, uttered by one of the most important officials in the SS formations engaged in the mobile killing operations,[80] seems not to have been the only one of its kind: already, at the end of June 1941, Jeckeln and the *Kommando* leaders of *Einsatzgruppe* C had taken pains to legitimate in detail the missions of the killing groups. It is striking to note how these speeches addressed to the *Kommandos* were given in the first week of their action, in other words just as the groups were *starting* to carry out the shootings,[81] and the speech in Kamenets-Podolsk was given just when Ek 5 was moving to the second threshold defined by Christian Gerlach: the extermination of entire communities.[82] We may well conclude that a discursive practice similar to the one developed by Jeckeln could be systematically carried out in front of killers, thus accompanying every advance in genocidal violence.

A second example gives further support to this hypothesis. On 16 August 1941, Himmler visited Minsk, where he met Erich von dem Bach-Zelewsky, Arthur Nebe and Otto Bradfisch, respectively HSSPF *Russland Mitte*, head of *Einsatzgruppe* B and head of *Einsatzkommando* 8. This interview has remained notorious in the historiography of genocide, since it has often been seen as the moment when it was decided to instigate research into setting up gas chambers,[83] and the moment when Himmler is said to have issued the order that henceforth, men, women and children were to be killed.[84] It is now known that these two claims are unlikely to have been true.[85] The fact remains that this interview gives us an essential perspective on the rhetorics of legitimation developed on the ground, in front of, and by, the killers. While several eyewitnesses confirm that Himmler was indeed there,[86] few detailed accounts of his visit have been written. Himmler did indeed on this occasion attend the execution of some hundred men, mainly Jews, carried out by the men of *Einsatzkommando* 8. Raul Hilberg has left a vivid description of this execution.[87] Himmler, clearly on edge, turned his eyes away. He shouted at a sergeant to finish off two victims and decided, at the end of the shooting, to address all who were there:

He [Himmler] pointed out that the Einsatzgruppe were called upon to fulfil a repulsive duty. He would not like it if Germans did such things gladly. But their conscience was in no way impaired, for they were soldiers who had to carry out every order unconditionally. He alone had responsibility before God and Hitler for everything that was happening. They had undoubtedly noticed that he hated this bloody business and that he had been aroused to the depth of his soul. [. . .]

The most primitive man says that the horse is good and the bedbug is bad, or wheat is good and the thistle is bad. The human being consequently designates what is useful to him as good and what is harmful as bad. Didn't bedbugs and rats have a life purpose also? Yes, but this has never meant that man could not defend himself against vermin.[88]

For the men of *Einsatzkommando* 8, this massacre was a small-scale, rather routine affair: over the first three weeks in August, *Einsatzgruppe* B eliminated an average of 295 people per day, and *Einsatzkommando* 8 alone was responsible for over half of the massacres.[89] We also know that, even if the order to include women and children in the massacres was not given by Himmler in Minsk, he did order, on 12 August, in an interview with Jeckeln, that the repressive practices of the SS units be made even harsher.[90] Be this as it may, Himmler's rhetoric here drew on a major guideline of legitimation. Even apart from the discourse of unconditional submission to orders – another theme harped on by the *Reichsführer* – genocide is here presented, as among many of those in charge of the *Einsatzgruppen*, as a defensive action: even more important, perhaps, it is seen as highly regrettable. Himmler attached considerable importance to the fact that this 'horrible task' should be carried out without any pleasure. This was a constant refrain in his discourse on genocide, a refrain that we find for example in the well-known speech he gave at Posen in October 1943. Himmler decided on that occasion to tackle the question of the Final Solution in front of an audience restricted to Nazi dignitaries:

The phrase 'The Jews must be exterminated' has few words in it, and is soon said, gentlemen. But what it demands from the person who puts it into practice is the hardest and most difficult thing in the world [. . .].

I must ask you simply to listen to what I am telling you here and never mention it again. The following question has been asked: 'What shall we do about women and children?' – I have thought this over and found an obvious reply. I did not, indeed, feel that I had any right to exterminate them – say, if you prefer, to kill them or have them killed – and to allow their descendants to grow up and later avenge themselves on our children and our descendants. The decision had to be taken to make this people disappear from the earth. It was, for the organization that had to carry out this task, the hardest thing it has known. I feel I can say that this has been accomplished without our men or our officers suffering from it in their hearts or their souls. And yet there was a real danger of this [. . .].[91]

One last characteristic, less visible, seems to emerge from these words: in his conclusion, Himmler reiterates what constituted for him, as for the SS intellectuals, the ultimate aims of the war: the Germanization of the occupied territories.[92] Six months after the almost total cessation of planning operations for resettlements, the Germanization and colonization of the east were still a millennial hope whose advent depended on the outcome of the war,[93] a war of which genocide was, in his own words, one of the fronts. And indeed, this paralogical reasoning, which turned genocide into a *sine qua non* for the realization of the Nazi millennium, was one of the factors that made the perpetrators acquiesce in genocide, just as it was one of the arguments developed by the officers on the ground.

On 26 March 1968, at a judicial inquiry opened against the members of *Sonderkommando* 1a, a master jeweller, Erich R., gave evidence. When interrogated on the activities of KdS Estonia[94] and the accusations brought against the main defendant, Heinrich Bergmann, R. replied without giving any factual information. Not that he knew nothing, nor that he refused to speak; but his information invalidated the statements of the defendant, and hardly encouraged him to speak out. From the clerk's transcription of his statement, his replies, short and precise, were those of a man whose memories were still vivid. Erich R. was soon diverted from the main business in hand and interrogated instead on the orders received by the groups in Russia:

> The principal order stating that all Jews, Gypsies etc. were to be annihilated for political reasons and in view of the permanent security of the eastern regions is known to me. [. . .]
>
> These orders, however, were not announced to the troop gathered together [for this purpose]. I remember that we [the anti-partisan *Kommando* of which he was part] were assembled at the beginning of August 41 in the area round Kostyi, the station in Jam. This was about 30 km from Narwa. It was here that Dr Sandberger visited us [KdS Estonia]. He was fêted by the whole Wehrmacht as the 'hero of lake Peipus' because he had come through the lake on an assault craft at a time when the lake was still under the control of Russian gunboats. That evening [. . .] we had a party, and drank alcohol. During the celebrations, Sandberger took off his jacket. When he did so, he became an ordinary soldier like us. That's how we understood it. So we told one another what you don't dare say on other occasions – the truth. I suppose it was on that evening that Sandberger or the head of our *Kommando* Feder revealed to us, in a small committee, these orders and the objectives of German policies in the East.
>
> These objectives were sketched out rather vaguely: we were aiming to colonize the eastern regions. This is why the local intelligentsia had to be exterminated [*ausrotten*]. It was better to shoot a superfluous Russian than not enough Russians. It was better to place an Estonian officer – even if he to some extent belonged to our unit – in a post where we were certain that he

would fall, than not to place anyone there at all. It would be all the easier to colonize the region and exploit it economically [. . .].[95]

This evidence is valuable in several respects. For one thing, Erich R. describes the evening with Sandberger as a mode of that SS brotherhood of arms built on the memories of the Great War: the reference point here is the *Fronterlebnis*, the experience of the front, mythified, reformulated and adapted by the Nazi paramilitary formations.[96] Genocidal activity – admittedly less evident in the case of *Sonderkommando* 1a[97] – was perceived and lived as an experience of war by the members of this *Kommando*. Also, the plans to Germanize the eastern regions seemed the main form of legitimation developed by the SS officers present. Indeed, Erich R., in spite of the (admittedly potential) menace of being investigated for his activities with the *Kommando*, remained faithful to the universe of mythical representations that prevailed during his *Osteneinsatz*. Did he not, after all, feel a need to express the fervour and the fascination that drove him, when – at the end of his questioning – he came back to the issue of the legitimation of the activities of SS officers posted to the Baltic? Here are his concluding remarks:

> I would like to add something: KdS Sandberger was a man of great intelligence. I belonged to his close guard during the invasion and we had travelled together by car for hours on end. On this occasion, Sandberger explained to us the political objectives of the Reich government for the eastern regions. The content was always the same: the colonization of the eastern regions. Pushing the frontier back to Leningrad, where a border commissariat under police responsibility was to be created. Elimination of the Russian intelligentsia. We knew that this meant shooting [these people]. That way, we should be able to control the territory better and more quickly. This was always the trend of conversations with Sandberger, conversations that he viewed in fact as a kind of political education. I'm quite certain that every member of the KdS present at Reval must have been acquainted with this type of conversation and the remarks Sandberger made.[98]

Let me simply add to this direct legitimation of genocidal violence by the utopian project of expansion to the east that Sandberger was doubtless one of the group's leaders who was most able to share Nazi aspirations for the Reich. This SS intellectual, an economist who was an expert on systems of social security,[99] and the organizer of colloquia on legitimatory history, took over the leadership of the EWZ (an organization charged with resettling *Volksdeutsche* on lands previously confiscated from expelled Poles or Jews).[100] Here, from 1939 to 1941, he played an important role in the Nazi policy of Germanization of the occupied territories. Sandberger's speech refers directly to the *Generalplan Ost*, a document designating the regions for colonization and the populations to be deported:[101] this was the racial millennium that served to legitimate genocide.

In the mobile groups, the SS intellectuals assumed the legitimatory function that was central in the eyes of men responsible for executions. It is worth noting that the officials from the EWZ, the UWZ and the RSHA *Amt III B* were present in the four groups operating in Russia. In *Einsatzgruppe A* – the one in which Sandberger operated – we can note the presence of Karl Tschierschky, his former deputy in the EWZ, but also that of the doctor Hanns Meixner, who supervised the process of Germanization. In *Einsatzgruppe B*, the presence of Albert Rapp, former head of the EWZ, speaks volumes about the connections between Germanization and the legitimization of extermination. In *Einsatzgruppe C*, Hans Joachim Beyer, professor at the University of Posen, who had worked very closely with Hans Ehlich, served, according to Karl-Heinz Roth, as an advisor to Otto Rasch. They all had functions of communication within the hierarchy of the groups. The argument of defence, regret and Nazi millennial hope thus formed the three fundamental dimensions of genocidal discourse on the ground. It does, however, seem that the utopian dimension of the projected sociobiological refoundation of Nordicity was a minority discourse when compared with the use of defensive rhetoric.

The few moments when the killers tried to explain the meaning of their practice in letters home provide us with an imperfect but revelatory image of the way a man was actually involved in the facts he related.[102]

One of the members of *Sonderkommando* 4a of *Einsatzgruppe* C, a *Kommando* already glimpsed during the shootings in Lemberg and Sokal, who on 29 and 30 September 1941 eliminated 33,371 Jews from Kiev in the ravine at Babi Yar, wrote to his wife, a month after the massacre:

> This war is one we are waging for the very existence of our people. Thank God that you, back in our Fatherland, aren't seeing this from too close. But the aerial bombardments have shown you what the enemy holds in store for us if he wins. Those at the front are ceaselessly experiencing this. My comrades are fighting literally for the existence of our people. They are doing to the enemy what he would do to them. I think you understand me. Because we consider this war to be a Jewish war, the Jews are the ones who are suffering its first impact. In Russia, wherever there is a German soldier, there are no longer any Jews.[103]

The imagine of annihilation, imbued with eschatological anxieties, here reveals its profoundly defensive dimension of a war to the death in which the existence of Germany is at stake. Thanks to this kind of document, we gain an idea of the subjective perception of genocide among the *Kommandos* who, from September 1941, were almost exclusively devoted to 'liquidating' the ghettos. For instance, the members of *Einsatzkommando* 8, already at work in Minsk when Himmler visited, took over most of the big genocidal operations in Belorussia in autumn

1941.[104] On the occasion of the first of these liquidations, that of the Moghilev ghetto, an officer in the Vienna police, Walter Mattner, wrote to his wife on 5 October 1941:

[5 October]: So I took part in the great mass death [*Massensterben*] the day before yesterday.[105] When the first vehicles [bringing the victims] arrived, my hands trembled a bit when I started firing, but you get used to it. At the tenth vehicle, I aimed calmly and shot with confidence at the women, children and numerous babies, aware that I have two babies of my own at home, and these hordes would treat them just the same, or even ten times worse perhaps. The death we gave them was nice and quick, compared [with] the hellish sufferings of the thousands and thousands [of people] in the jails of the GPU. The babies flew in great arcs and we shot them to pieces in the air before they fell into the ditch and the water. We need to finish off these brutes who have plunged Europe into war and who, even today, are prospecting in America [. . .].

Oh, Devil take it! I'd never seen so much blood, filth, flesh. Now I understand the expression 'blood-drunk'. The population of M. is now reduced by a number with three zeros. I'm really glad, and many people here are saying that when we get back to the Fatherland, it will be the turn of our local Jews. But anyway, I mustn't tell you any more. This is enough until I get back home.[106]

The singular brutality with which this Viennese policeman expresses the violence inside him probably expresses what was one of the most powerful motors of the murderers' consent to genocide: anxiety about collective disappearance, including one's own and one's family's, and the feeling of being engaged in a struggle for the biological survival of the 'race'.[107] Anxiety and fervour thus merged to generate an absolute violence. It is in the light of this that we can re-read Siegfried Engel's history course, given to the officers of the RSHA:

Although three hundred years have gone by since the period of the Thirty Years War, the political problem and the aim of our enemies have remained the same: the definitive partitioning of Germany, and the annihilation of the Reich.

A posteriori, the Thirty Years War can be characterized as the *first* Thirty Years War [. . .].

The period 1789–1815 represents the *second* Thirty Years War, in other words the period of the great French Revolution and the War of German Liberation. [. . .]

The *third* Thirty Years War started in 1914. The First World War did not reach any solution. The period of apparent laying down of weapons between 1919 and 1939 was the continuation of the war by other means: a political struggle. This was supplemented by open wars waged by the Reich, on the east against the Poles, on the west against France, in the Ruhr.

Today, in 1942, we have entered on the last stage of this third Thirty Years War.

The peace to come, which will bring the third Thirty Years War to a victorious conclusion, and thus the three-century-long struggle for German unity, will bring about at once the definitive surpassing of the Peace of Westphalia in 1648 and this time – as we all know – there will be no half measures.[108]

These remarks of Engel, the SD intellectual responsible for all the ideological training of the RSHA, assume even greater weight when we know that his audience probably included candidates in training courses for cadres brought together in 1941. They had returned to Berlin after being sent in groups to the east to train the officers of the *Einsatzgruppen* throughout the autumn of 1941. This shows how much the speaker and his listeners were communing in a shared set of expectations.

Millenarian fervour, eschatological anxiety and defensive *imaginaire*: did not this combination of effects lead the SS in the *Einsatzgruppen* to find in themselves the resources of hatred on which they could draw to murder other human beings?

Chapter 9

Violence in action

The experience of violence

In the Sudetenland, as we have seen, 2,500 people were arrested within a fortnight, then 4,639 in the rest of Czechoslovakia. In Poland, there was a change of scale: the six *Einsatzgruppen* active there were much better equipped and manned than the previous *Kommandos*. They were, in addition, largely militarized formations, in which police from the KRIPO and the Gestapo, or SD officers, worked next to men from the Waffen SS and uniformed police from the ORPO. They were recruited mainly from local bureaus on the borders, and this made it possible to draw on men already familiar with the Polish context. These groups were also the first to develop in the context of war. As a result, nearly 10,000 people were executed in six weeks.

When the USSR was invaded, the four *Einsatzgruppen* spread across the front comprised between 2,800 and 3,000 men,[1] as opposed to between 2,000 and 2,700 in Poland, where the groups had killed some 1,700 individuals on average per week, i.e. 280 individuals per group. As we know that every group included 300 SS,[2] we can estimate that every member of a group killed somewhat less than one person per week, over a period of six weeks.[3] In the USSR, the groups executed over 550,000 persons: 50,000 from 22 June to the end of August, and 500,000 between September and December 1941.[4] Thus, they killed 55 times more than in Poland: a number that, if projected to the individual level, would imply that each of the 3,000 men operating in Russia must have killed one person *per day* over six months.

These are just orders of magnitude, but they allow us to grasp the new qualitative and quantitative leap that took place between the campaigns in Poland and Russia. The average should not conceal either the threshold crossed in September, or the unequal division of violence between individuals: in Russia, the *Einsatzgruppen* combined the violence of war with the 'dirty work'[5] of genocide.

To set off as part of the *Osteinsatz* also involved joining units whose organization developed: initially mobile units, they became more stationary at the end of 1941. The *Einsatzgruppen* were fully motorized formations – indeed, a significant number of their personnel provided technical assistance. In a few days, these units covered great distances. *Sonderkommando* 4a, for instance, took just five days to cross the 417 km between Cracow and Sokal (Ukraine) – some 80 km per day, including missions.[6]

The *Einsatzgruppen* were organized around a headquarters that coordinated their activities. Like the RSHA, each unit comprised a bureau responsible for the administration and management of personnel (*Ämter* I and II), a bureau for intelligence work (*Amt* III), and a bureau that combined the two police forces (*Amt* IV Gestapo and *Amt* V KRIPO). In addition, it was supported by detachments from the ORPO and the Waffen SS for its protection and for the operations that it did not delegate to *Kommandos*. There are relatively few documents that enable us to form an adequate image of these headquarters, though they played a decisive role in the coordination of genocide and the fight against partisans. However, the groups did keep very careful records of their personnel: it is just that these records were completely destroyed, with the exception of the accounts book kept by *Einsatzgruppe* B throughout its period of activity. This book sheds valuable light on the movements of funds that it records, as well as on the lists of names of personnel who received payment: we can thus gain an idea of the numbers of people involved.[7] The headquarters of *Einsatzgruppe* B, for instance, had a staff of 150, including some twenty officers. The troops had come from local bureaus of the Gestapo and the SD, central offices of the RSHA, the Waffen SS, the EWZ and the ORPO. The headquarters was less well staffed than the *Kommandos*, but numbers in it were still surprisingly high, relatively speaking: it reserved to itself over 16 per cent of the total numbers of the group. So nearly one man in six was assigned to administrative tasks, or to the protection and transport of this administrative apparatus.[8]

So the groups comprised *Sonderkommandos* and *Einsatzkommandos*, autonomous units in terms both of transport and of the day-to-day organization of activities. The *Sonderkommandos* were smaller and more mobile units, designed to work alongside troops at the front. Their mission was to enter conquered localities at the same time as the Wehrmacht troops. The *Sonderkommandos* then had the task of moving into public buildings, archives and centres of power. They also immediately secured urban centres. These *Kommandos*, whose job was to spring into action in the hours following the seizure of these centres, were one of the favourite destinations for men from the SD, while officials from the KRIPO and the Gestapo were more often to be found in the *Einsatzkommandos*. The latter followed the troops of the Wehrmacht, advancing in the rear of the front to secure terrain: they had more men and weapons.[9] They were more particularly responsible for checks and arrests. These differences in mission may seem minor, but on the ground they were decisive. *Einsatzgruppe* B, for instance, divided its territory into two big sections with somewhat fuzzy boundaries, and decided to advance in two successive waves. One, composed of two *Sonderkommandos* (Sk), 7a and 7b, progressed at the same rhythm as the troops at the front, often entering towns with the reconnaissance units of the armoured divisions, setting up the first anti-Jewish measures, namely the establishment of *Judenräte* (Jewish councils), registration, enclosure within a ghetto – though this was not systematic[10] – and the wearing of the yellow star. All of this was carried through with the help of frequent executions, which often affected men of weapon-bearing age alone.[11] The *Einsatzkommandos*, who arrived with the rearguard, had the task of verifying the persons interned and carrying out selections in the ghettos, and very quickly transformed themselves into the main centres of execution for the *Einsatzgruppe*. For instance, they carried out most of the liquidations of ghettos in Belorussia in September. This was not always how the groups functioned: in the case of *Einsatzgruppe* A, Sk 1b and 1a, directed by Erich Ehrlinger and Martin Sandberger, assumed more particular responsibility for the fight against the partisans,[12] while *Einsatzkommando* 3, headed by *Standartenführer* Jäger, was the main perpetrator of the genocide of the Jews in the Baltic countries.[13]

There was considerable latitude in the way the groups organized their activities and their structures. For example, *Einsatzgruppe* C drew little distinction between its *Einsatzkommandos* and its *Sonderkommandos*, all in charge of a quarter of the territory devolved to the group.[14] Within *Einsatzgruppe* D, there was just one *Einsatzkommando* (Ek 12) and four *Sonderkommandos* (Sk 10a and 10b, Sk 11a and 11b), which was probably due to the specific nature of Ohlendorf's command and the rather larger number of SD men within it than in the other *Einsatzgruppen*.[15] The difference in the missions assigned to Sk and Ek cannot be systematized either: for, while Ek 3, 8 and 9 were indeed the central bodies of extermination for *Einsatzgruppen* A and B, this role fell to Sk 4a within *Einsatzgruppe* C, even in spite of the presence of Ek 5 and 6.[16] Finally, within *Einsatzgruppe* D, initiative in the liquidation of the ghettos seems to have fallen to Sk 10a and, to a lesser degree, to Sk 10b. However, the division of labour and territory had a decisive effect on the men composing these groups. It was a very different matter to be assigned to Sk 1a, operating in Estonia, a country in which Jewish communities were very few and far between,[17] or to Ek 8, which carried out over 65 per cent of the executions performed by *Einsatzgruppe* B in winter 1941–2.[18] In the first case, it was mainly the fight against the partisans that was important,[19] while in the second, it was the practice of genocide that occupied by far the greater number of the *Kommando*'s activities. This shows the impact of one's group assignment on the experience of the men who left for the *Osteinsatz*.

These differences in structure did tend to lessen, however, over time. In the autumn of 1941, the groups settled down as the advance of

Wehrmacht troops slowed and civil administrations were established. The *Kommandos* were initially fixed in a town and a region, and were gradually transformed into local bureaus for the police and the SD (KdS),[20] while the groups' headquarters became the central bureaus of the SIPO and the SD (BdS),[21] extending their jurisdiction across both of the *Reichskommissariate*.[22]

This apparently simple process of settling down did, however, entail a mixing of personnel, which contributed to a homogenization of men's experiences in the east. Each unit in *Einsatzgruppe* A apparently received one territory to control. Sk 1a became the KdS for Estonia, Ek 3 became the KdS for Lithuania, and Ek 2, KdS for Latvia. Belorussia should have fallen to Erich Ehrlinger's Sk 1b, and he was indeed appointed KdS for Minsk in October 1941,[23] but did not keep his old *Kommando* intact. This body gradually included more men from *Einsatzgruppe* B, who were used to Belorussia, where they had been operating since autumn 1941.

Both in Poland and in the USSR, different operational methods were adopted depending on whether these formations were still mobile or stationary. In their mobile phase, the groups began by arresting the entire male population and checking whether the men were included in their *Fahndungslisten* (wanted lists). If they were not, they were freed or, in some cases, detained as hostages. If they were, they were arrested, questioned and – usually – shot. In Gdynia (Poland), in September 1939, 5,000 officials were arrested by *Einsatzgruppe* 6; 2,000 were released without further investigation, 30 were on the *Fahndungslisten* and the remaining 2,970 were interned. The group had already been informed that plans had been laid to build a camp for the internment of Polish elites. Two days later, once identities had been checked, 1,500 arrested individuals were definitively interned: these constituted a reserve of hostages at the group's disposal. Eighty individuals were either brought before a military tribunal or shot.[24] While the procedure was identical, the outcome was less so: it shows that the levels of violence were far less in Poland in 1939 than in the USSR in 1941. The example of Gargzdai illustrates this. This small town in Lithuania, 150 km from Riga, had 3,000 inhabitants, including a Jewish community of a good thousand or so. Located on an important coastal route, the town was strongly defended by Soviet border guards. Heavy fighting, leading to a hundred dead on the German side, continued until 23 June. During the action, the German troops reported shooting coming from the civilian population. One of the districts where the confrontation was most intense turned out to be the 'Jewish quarter'. On the afternoon of 23 June, the Germans, soldiers of the Wehrmacht and SS of the *Einsatzkommando* who had occupied the town, assembled a large number of the population. With the help of native auxiliaries, they separated out the Jews from the Lithuanians (who were freed), and forced the 600 people remaining to sleep where they were. On 24 June, after an agreement between the head of the *Einsatzkommando*, the head of the Tilsit Gestapo and that of *Einsatzgruppe* A, the women and children were penned together, the women were made to do forced labour, and the two hundred men were shot.[25]

The internment of male suspects was the first step towards the registration and internment of Jews in ghettos, and their use as hostages when shootings were carried out as reprisals. Also, Wehrmacht and *Feldgendarmerie* units handed over several prisoners and individuals considered as suspect – vagabonds, refugees, fugitive Jews – to SS units who interned them or, more and more frequently, shot them on delivery.[26] The units implanted in the form of KdS or isolated local bureaus did not have to organize these prior, large-scale internments. Their much more routine activity consisted in questionings and individual arrests, and thus produced a more spread-out violence. Under Ehrlinger as under Strauch, the activity of KdS Minsk was punctuated by the arrest of suspects who were all incarcerated and subjected to questioning. The prison was drastically overpopulated, as the BdS officials themselves admitted: every week, they would execute forty or so people, once the interrogations had been completed. Violence occurred on a daily basis, but it was no longer marked by operations of cordoning off and internment, or by the shooting of snipers.[27] As they became stationary, passing from a context of combat to one of occupation, the SS units thus set up a procedure which transformed wholesale violence into a routine.

The liquidation of the ghettos, which usually occurred after the units had settled in one place,[28] interrupted this routine. Thus 15,000 people were executed in Równo by the troops of the KdS (Ek 5),[29] 8,000 in Polozk (KdS Minsk, Ek 8), 6,500 in Bobruisk[30] (KdS Minsk) and 18,000 in Winnitza (Ukraine) on 19 and 20 September 1941 (Ek 6).[31] This combination between a daily rhythm marked by a very great regularity in the violence of extermination, and a punctuated sequence of a more paroxysmal type, characterized the *Osteinsatz* experience of many SS transferred to these units after the first months of the conflict. This was clearly true in the case of Walter Mattner, a Viennese policeman from Ek8, the author of the letters already quoted above legitimatizing the murder of newborn infants. The day before the massacre, he wrote to his wife:

> [2 October]: I have volunteered for a special action tomorrow. [. . .] Tomorrow, I will have a chance to use my pistol for the first time. I have taken 28 bullets. This will probably not be enough. It concerns 1,200 Jews of whom, somehow or other, there are too many in the town, and who need to be killed. I'll have some nice things to tell you between now and when I get back. But this is enough for today, otherwise you'll think I'm bloodthirsty[. . .].[32]

The case of Walter Mattner is just one example, but far from unique. Most officials in the *Einsatzgruppen* were transferred to the groups at the start of Operation Barbarossa, but a minority of them were sent east in the autumn or winter of 1941. So they were, without any preparation, thrust into a universe of routine violence punctuated by sudden outbursts.

The importance assumed by the fight against the partisans from 1942 onwards also modified the routine nature of the occupation. This period was marked by major search operations,[33] which, in one sense, succeeded the liquidation of the ghettos. Jewish communities, in fact, were reduced to their lowest level, and now existed as no more than small ghettos in middle-sized towns.

Operation 'Marsh Fever' rather clearly shows how a maximum level of violence returned to the daily world of KdS Minsk officials. From 22 August to 21 September 1942, 244 NCOs and rank and file, and 32 officers from the SIPO and the SD, took part in a major operation against the partisans. This operation was organized by the HSSPF von dem Bach-Zelewsky with nine police battalions, 2,000 men from the neighbouring KRIPO or KdS, and an SS infantry brigade.[34] Plans had been drawn up over the previous three days, and the operation started on 25 August 1942, with skirmishes against partisan units who lost thirty-two men and one of their camps. But the partisan units made good use of the terrain and were spread out across vast swathes of territory: they thus largely evaded capture.[35] From 26 August to 5 September, one partisan unit of a thousand or so men was pursued, without much success. The next day, the first villages were burned down by German formations. From 8 September, partisan units started to lose men and sacrifice heavy weapons, but the partisans killed in combat could be counted in mere dozens, which meant that their units were far from being severely affected. Furthermore, most of the shootings carried out by members of the KdS did not concern militarized partisan units, but suspects and, in particular, the remaining Jewish communities. When the operation was halted on 22 September, 49 partisan camps had been destroyed, a sign that the terrain had been temporarily reconquered. But as far as the KdS were concerned, these results were disappointing: only 389 partisans had been killed in action, as against 1,274 suspects executed – mainly the inhabitants of burned-down villages – and 8,350 Jews exterminated as such. One thousand, two hundred and seventeen people, in other words the rest of the populations of the destroyed villages, were evacuated.[36] Compared with the weekly rhythm of execution of some forty or so individuals observed in Minsk, operations like 'Marsh Fever' represented, without any doubt, a significant moment in the intensification of the violence faced by the men involved. They also meant the return of a context of war to the world of occupation as experienced by the men of the KdS: to their minds, they were really involved in combat, even if, in many cases, this consisted almost solely in executing civilian hostages.

It is obviously difficult to draw up a synthetic picture of the factors that conditioned the experience of the *Osteinsatz* for SS transferred to the *Einsatzgruppen*. This experience assumed many different versions depending on the period, the type of unit and the type of activity – the maintenance of order, the liquidation of ghettos, the fight against partisans – it was all the same an experience of violence inflicted, lived as an experience of war. The intensity of this confrontation and the way in which it was apprehended, however, depended on the framework within which it occurred, and on individual psychology, group pressure and the hierarchical conditions existing in each of the units.

There was one last element that determined the experience of the *Osteinsatz*, that of the rhythm at which violence was pursued. It may be useful to outline this here. The *Osteinsatz* led to the killing of massive numbers of individuals from the Polish campaign onwards. From June to October 1941, however, there was an extraordinary escalation in the rate of executions, in two successive phases: the increasingly systematic murder of women and children with adult males, and then the liquidation of entire communities. From October–December 1941 until spring 1942, units that had become garrisoned when the ghettos organized in the summer were liquidated slowed down their genocidal activities. This rhythm, varying with the *Kommandos* and the regions, lasted until the end of the occupation. It brings out two major phenomena: the radicalization of practices, and the way these became taken for granted.

For those men who took part in Operation Barbarossa from its first day, the campaign opened on a confrontation with violence represented by the shooting of men in a context of war. The brutalization of practices leading to increased familiarity with violence entailed the broadening of the range of victims. A second turning point came when children were suddenly included among the victims of shootings, which marked the shift to a general massacre, one which became full-scale between the third week in August and September.

The collective experience of the violence of Barbarossa came to light with the discovery and display of the Russian 'atrocities' committed as they retreated. As one example among others,[37] here is how *Einsatzgruppe* C presented its discovery of Galicia in the two first weeks of the conflict.

> *Einsatzgruppe* C:
> Position: Zwiahel.
> (I) General situation on arrival.
> [. . .]
> The Bolsheviks also murdered many Ukrainians as they retreated, in liaison with local Jews. Their pretext was an uprising among Ukrainians in Lemberg on 25/6/41, part of an attempt to free their prisoners.
> 20,000 Ukrainians, 80 per cent of whom belonged to the intelligentsia, disappeared from Lemberg, according to reliable information.
> The prisons of Lemberg were filled with the bodies of murdered Ukrainians. [. . .]
> In the course of the massacres, Russians and Jews behaved with extreme cruelty. Bestial [*viehische*] mutilations were the order of the day. Women had

their breasts, and men their genitals cut off. The Jews also nailed children to the walls and killed them.[38] The shootings were carried out with a bullet into the back of the neck. Grenades were often used in the killings.

In Dobromil, men and women were killed by blows to their bodies from mallets used to slaughter cattle.

In very many cases, prisoners must have been slain in the harshest ways – their bones smashed, etc. [. . .]

Finally, the murder of 4 to 7 German aviators who had been taken prisoner has come to light. 3 of them were found in a Russian hospital, where they were killed in their beds by being shot in the lower abdomen. [. . .]

III) Measures of the *Einsatzgruppe*

The *Sicherheitspolizei* has concentrated [*zusammengetrieben*, i.e. driven together] and executed some 7,000 Jews in reprisal for the inhuman atrocities.

73 men have been questioned and they too were shot as members or officials of the NKVD.[39]

So these initial two weeks were presented to the Berlin authorities as a time when Russian violence was uncovered – a violence which could generate group reprisals.[40] However, the reports presented a merely partial dimension of the experience of the groups in these first weeks of action. Bureaucratic and hierarchical as they were, these documents might well fail to register what the men actually felt. The example of one soldier from Sk 4a, Rudolf W. – the same man who was active in Lemberg, Zwiahel and Sokal – does, however, enable us to give some indication of how far the representations distilled in these reports corresponded with the experiences on the ground described by the protagonists of the campaign. Rudolf W. was one of the marksmen of Sk 4a and, after his unit ceased to be mobile, he was assigned to KdS Kiev, under the command of Erich Ehrlinger. It was during the proceedings brought against the latter that Rudolf W. was heard as a witness by the West German authorities after the war, where he gave evidence about the first days of the Russian campaign. He relates his discovery of the prison of Dubno, captured by Sk 4a. After reporting the eyewitness account of a Ukrainian woman who had survived a massacre perpetrated by the NKVD, Rudolf W. adds:

I was there myself, and you could still clearly see the traces left in different cells, where the walls were covered by bullet holes, bloodstains and bits of brains. The prison had been turned into a prisoner of war camp.[41]

The *Kommando*'s report quotes the evidence given by the same Ukrainian woman survivor as Rudolf W. The report of the group and the evidence of the war criminal describe, in the same terms, the places where executions were carried out. What emerged from the institutional narration compiled for the Berlin hierarchy thus corresponded completely, in this case, with the experience at ground level as witnessed by the soldier in question.[42] The definiteness of his memory, even though he was relating events eighteen years after they took place, allows us to imagine the impact of this visit to the prison on a man who was 'experienced' and indeed hardened: he had, after all, already confronted the spectacles of war and death administered by firing squad, as he had been with the *Einsatzgruppen* sent to Poland, and in particular took part in executions in Radom in 1939.[43] Now, rank-and-file troops sent to Russia were often experiencing the *Osteinsatz* for the first time. The discovery of mass graves or mutilated bodies must have been a formative experience. One example – the letter from a soldier of the Sixth Army to his parents – gives an idea of the shock felt:

Tarnopol, 6/7/1941. Dear parents,

I have just returned from the funeral wake of comrades from the Alpine chasseurs [soldiers trained for mountain combat] and the Luftwaffe captured by the Russians. I cannot find words to express such a thing. Our comrades were tied up, and their ears, tongues, noses and genitals cut off: this is the state in which we found them, in the cellars of the Tarnopol law courts. We also found 2,000 Ukrainians and *Volksdeutsche* 'treated'[44] the same way. Such are Russia and Jewry, the workers' paradise. [. . .] Vengeance was immediately carried out. Yesterday, with the SS [of Sk 4a], we were merciful: we immediately shot all the Jews we caught. It was different today, since we found another 60 comrades mutilated. The Jews now have to bring the bodies up from the cellar, lay them carefully to rest, and then their shameful depredations are shown to them. Thereupon, after they have seen the victims, they are beaten to death with sticks and spades. Up until now we have dispatched into the Hereafter about a thousand Jews, but that's still too few, given what they have done.[45]

Apart from the – largely exaggerated – factual details mentioned by this soldier, it is his reading of events that comprises the heart of the mechanism of radicalization. The young soldier presents us with a narrative of the massacre that is swollen by rumour and marked by the internalization of the Nazi belief system. The USSR, so long depicted to the soldiers as vast and dangerous, did indeed seem a land of barbarity to them. The spectacle of violence verified this perception and endorsed their Nazi perspective: if what the SS and the soldiers found when they arrived in the conquered territory corresponded to the apocalyptic descriptions that had been dunned into them before the invasion, the racial interpretative grid – which explained in advance why, in the view of the Nazis, Russia was a savage country peopled with subhuman ethnic groups – was validated by their experiences on the ground. The spectacle of butchery and its interpretation in terms of a Nazi belief rooted more deeply than ever before now generated fear, anxiety and dread that in turn produced a twofold movement of brutalization.

On the one hand, in the young man's words, soldiers and SS *Kommandos* more and more systematically vented their anger on Jewish adult males. This development, as we have seen, is observable in the figures of executions reported to Berlin by the SS *Kommandos*. But, more decisively, the psychological mechanisms were unleashed that led to a second process of brutalization, which could not itself emerge in the reports. For the soldiers or SS in Tarnopol – as indeed for Walter Mattner in Moghilev – for victims to be shot by firing squad, a mode of execution generally employed by the troops, was felt to be a 'merciful' measure given the 'bestiality' perpetrated by the Russians. So it was – on occasion – replaced by having the victims beaten to death with spades and picks. This document shows that, from mid-July, shootings which individuals had found challenging just a fortnight earlier were now seen as commonplace.[46] As for the use of spades and picks, this new mode of execution could constitute a degraded and anomic – but doubtless conscious[47] – form of the butchery usually reserved for animals. On the other hand, this practice of beating people to death was rare in any massive and collective form: it was found only in a few localities in Ukraine – in Tarnopol and, in more limited measure, in Lemberg and Sokal[48] – and in Kaunas in Lithuania, in the territory allotted to Sk 1b and then, later on, to Ek 3.[49] The localities mentioned coincided with those in which the executions carried out by the NKVD were interpreted as a confirmation of the alleged savagery of the enemy. Not that the massacres performed by the NKVD were necessarily the most massive in those areas,[50] but because they were localities in which the practice of the NKVD was analysed as an empirical proof of the enemy's inhumanity.

Thereafter, the more intense the representations mobilized by the spectacle of death and mutilation, the more the instrument used to deal out death brought the killer close to his victim. Attacks on the body thus induced a growing proximity, transforming a violence administered from a distance – that of shootings – into an interpersonal violence inscribed on the victim's body, administered and received by groups of individuals. It did not emerge, however, solely from the psyches of soldiers or SS, but from the dread and hatred that were experienced collectively.

Demonstrative violence, violence of eradication[51]

In our study of the psychological economy of the processes of brutalization that were triggered at the very start of the conflict, the gestures of violence mobilized against Jewish victims have become mirrors of systems of representation. At a completely different time, and in radically different historiographical conditions, Denis Crouzet set out the intellectual foundations for this type of approach:

The postulate that governs this analysis – for such a postulate was necessary – is that the paroxysmal set of actions that comprise the repertoire of violence is the externalization or rather the precipitate of a culture that has encouraged or imposed violence, that it is a culturally coded system of meaning, on the basis of which it is possible to delineate the reasons for violence and thus for the religious crisis.[52]

To see violence as a language, to try to bring out the conscious and unconscious mechanisms that lie behind the gestures used by the groups, thus means that we need to describe the gestures and procedures deployed in the murder of Jewish communities, partisans and hostages.

The *Einsatzgruppen* and non-mobile formations sent to Russia were supplied with rules and regulations that at least partly set out the procedures for killing. On 8 July 1943, BdS *Ostland* and head of the *Einsatzgruppe* A received from the RSHA a letter containing the draft of a circular from the Ministry for Occupied Territories concerning 'the carrying out of the death sentence in the occupied territories', a draft that covered three pages in precise legal language.[53] The details of the procedure of execution show the thought that had been given to the reception of the death sentence among the native populations, with a desire to preserve the mode of execution in use in the territories concerned. In the second place, the document outlined a form of killing based on legality. So it implied a prior sentencing, which meant it had no impact in the case of executions carried out without a sentence – the overwhelming majority, in fact.

So this circular, concerning as it did just a tiny number of executions, can still be viewed as the basis of a normalizing fiction, a fiction which laid down regulations on the presence of a doctor and an interpreter (if the person sentenced did not speak German),[54] and on the communication of the verdict of execution to the condemned.[55] This fiction presents us with a world in which the practices that were actually being carried out were rendered unreal. It is a picture that could be a decisive proof of the duplicity of Nazi authorities, were it not that two crucial elements emerge from this too transparent, too artificial text.

The first concerns the modes of execution envisaged by the circular: shooting and hanging. If the traditional mode of execution in the territories in question was to be preserved, Germans of the Reich and *Volksdeutsche* could be executed only by shooting. The second fundamental element was this: the man performing the execution needed to be selected carefully, depending on the victim's nationality. In the case of Germans, there was no question: Germans could not be hanged, so they were executed by squads of police officers. 'Foreigners' were executed by police auxiliaries – if shot – and 'by a competent native ordered to act as executioner' in the case of a hanging. So a German could be executed only by a German. Appearances may suggest that a native could be executed only by compatriots, but the reason here seems different. Was it not rather, in the mind of the Nazi lawmaker, a way of ensuring that the execution would not be attributed to the occupier? Was he not striving to create the impression,

if not of a business internal to the community of the occupied, at least of
significant participation of the latter in the carrying out of punishment?
In fact, the document did not completely exclude the execution of natives
by German squads, but the execution of Germans by natives was quite
simply unimaginable. This first absolute prescription was combined with
a second impossibility: no German in uniform could carry out a hanging.
This second taboo was not formulated explicitly; it was quite simply not
even imagined. Was this an absolute social prohibition, or a mere impossibility generated by typological mechanics? A second set of rules and
regulations goes some way to answering this question, and also provides
us with a quite different image of legally administered death. This text,[56]
which apparently discusses all forms of execution, and not just those
carried out after due sentencing, was on this occasion drawn up directly
by the Berlin officials of the RSHA, since it concerned both the Reich and
the occupied territories.[57] It envisaged all cases of execution by hanging, a
penalty which, in concentration camps, could also be applied to detainees
of German nationality. The prohibition is here formulated in precise and
explicit terms: the hanging cannot be performed by a German in uniform:
it must be carried out by a detainee. So a 'free', i.e. non-detainee, German
cannot be hanged; a free German cannot hang another person. It was thus
the mode of execution in itself which was, for the legislator, a mark of
infamy. It is difficult to understand why it was seen as so besmirching,
especially since we know that hanging was frequently carried out.

Shooting was performed by militarized formations, in squads, under
the command of an individual. It was an extremely codified procedure,
and was also a collective mode of killing: the text stipulates that there
must be a minimum of six gunmen. This appears to have constituted
a display of military power and its punitive dimension. The taboo on
hanging was also perhaps a prohibition connected with the military
and paramilitary condition, implying a collective killing under orders.
Furthermore, shooting and hanging are different in that hanging, which
kills by causing the vertebrae of the neck to break, does not involve any
crossing of a corporal boundary. And a soldier commits violence only by
crossing this boundary, whatever weapon he may use. As we know from
the research of ethnologists in the circle of Françoise Héritier,[58] there is a
taboo on women using instruments that shed enemy blood.[59] The warrior,
who voluntarily sheds enemy blood and his own, is contrasted with the
woman who involuntarily sheds her own in order to give life. A bipolar
anthropological structure is here created on the basis of death accompanied by bloodshed. Thus military killing, it seems, does not require this
bloodshed, unlike a death given and received in conditions of (largely
unnamed) infamy: the latter death can concern only socially or racially
inferior categories. This would explain the Nazi hierarchy of punishments, executioners and victims, largely determined by a prohibition
reflecting the social and racial order implicitly embodied in these texts.

So at the summit of this hierarchy of punishments we have death by firing squad, imposed on German citizens, *Reichs-* and *Volksdeutsche*, executed in a military scenario, by a squad shooting to order, after a proper sentencing, the condemned being accompanied by a doctor and allowed to choose whether to stand with his back or his face to the rifles, and whether or not to wear a blindfold.[60] One level below, the shooting of free foreigners by their 'fellows', a case in which death may be administered by German paramilitaries to free civilians, albeit of inferior race, since bloodshed is effective. Then comes the execution by hanging of free men, from the occupied populations, by an executioner who is also a free foreigner. The occupying public power then carries out an execution that demonstrates German respect for the 'traditions' of the occupied peoples, although in fact it mirrors their inferiority.[61] Then comes the final case: that of execution in concentration camps, a sign of the summary dimension of the sentencing which, even if it involves a German, can then be carried out by hanging.

If we now envisage the case of a figure occupying the lowest place in the symbolic hierarchy established by the legislators – the execution by hanging of foreign detainees – the ritual killing should no longer see the intervention of any Germans: a prisoner, 'rewarded' with food or cigarettes, is charged with triggering the trapdoor of the gallows.[62] It would have been possible, for the legislator, to arrange for a non-German executioner to be provided, but he did not do so. Thus the victim and the executioner were, in his view, two inferiors, by virtue of being prisoners – an inferiority that was significant enough for the legislator to accept that a German could be hanged, a case that he excluded outside the bounds of the camp – and by virtue of their being foreigners. Was it not this 'infamy' which made execution by hanging possible, a death in which the protagonists were of the same rank and could display the mark imposed on them by the punitive power, the victim in his death and the executioner in the death he imposed on his fellow man? The fact remains that the execution of political prisoners as well as of common law prisoners by firing squad, in the Reich and in the occupied territories, was no longer (para)-military in nature, and yet was carried out by police units. So it was not the military dimension as such which determined the taboo. Of course, it had some influence on it, as is shown by the very elaborate codification to which the execution had to be subjected even within the camp, but it was not decisive for it. We must conclude that it was the anthropological dimension connected with shedding the blood of the condemned which determined the ban on hanging for (para)military personnel, implicitly formulated by the legislator.

This symbolic hierarchical construction, however complex it may appear, is still a matter of anecdote. For one thing, the texts that establish it include only a tiny number of cases – proper executions after due sentence, summary trials and trials in camps – in which units of the SIPO and the SD carried out killings. For another thing, the prohibitions set out by these texts were very widely transgressed: the SS hanged several of their compatriots, and even many foreigners in the occupied territories. Finally, these texts were put into practice between the beginning and the summer of 1943, much later than the inauguration of killings in the east. At the very same time that the second text appeared, almost 80 per cent of the victims of genocide had already been executed.[63] So these texts were belated documents which aimed at smoothing over the transgressions committed on the ground and re-establishing a fictitious norm.

In all cases, by creating a hierarchy between the different modes of execution, victims and circumstances of killing, they underline the heterogeneity of murderous practices. 'Carrying out a death sentence' and 'subjecting someone to special treatment' – both expressions referred to the practice of putting someone to death – were very different things, and this is what these texts were attempting to define, while ignoring most of these 'special treatments'. However, in the reports of the groups, the words 'special treatment', 'liquidation', and 'execution' did not seem to designate, for those carrying them out, clearly differentiated practices.[64]

Two major types of execution can, however, be differentiated by the degree of publicity imposed by the executing power. Indeed, while the groups involved in killing attempted most of the time to avoid having unwanted spectators present at massacres,[65] there were certain executions which were not in the least confidential. It was as if some of the violence carried out by the groups was deliberately displayed.[66] Sk 4a, responsible for the Tarnopol pogrom and, later, the massacre at Babi Yar, captured two men in Chernykov who, by status and ethnicity, were living proof, in Nazi eyes, of the rhetoric of war: Kiepert and Kogan were both Russian Jews, and officials in the Stalinist legal machine.[67] Having been arrested and probably tortured, the two men confessed to several 'crimes' and their execution was decreed. It took place in Jitomir, and was skilfully orchestrated by the men of the Black Order. They resorted to the *Propaganda-Staffel* of the Sixth Army, which mobilized its rotary presses to print pamphlets announcing, with details of the sentence, the public hanging of these two men, as well as sending lorries with loudspeakers announcing the news throughout the town. A report of the group that arranged the execution gives us a glimpse of what was announced:[68]

> Kiepert, led to confess his crimes, described his atrocities with Jewish cynicism. From the age of eighteen, he had acted as a Zionist agitator in 1905, in illegal gangs working against the existing order [. . .]. In the Chernykov region alone, between 1905 and 1917, he committed 25 murders; from 1917 to 1919, 500 more; and from 1919 to 1925, 800: all the people he killed were Ukrainians and *Volksdeutsche*, and he took this opportunity to express his hatred for everything that was not Jewish by using murder methods that were novel each time. He had a particular preference for killing by firearms and knives, and by striking down his victims, poisoning or drowning them. When he could not get close to his chosen victims, he attacked their

families in the most brutal ways. Thus in Chernykov, a small girl – now an adult – had her right foot broken by a blow from a rifle butt when she was still literally in her mother's womb: this was because [Kiepert was overcome by] rage at the fact that her father, a Tsarist officer, could not be found. In 1933, the year of the Great Famine in Ukraine, Kiepert again distinguished himself. [. . .]

In short, there are at least 1,350 murders, both as a terrorist in Tsarist Russia and as an agent of the GPU or a member of a Troika (court of justice), which need to be laid at his door.

One of his collaborators did not meet with the same success, but in spite of this, over four months in 1934, killed a total of 120 Ukrainians and *Volksdeutsche*.

Kiepert himself and his fellow assassin were hanged in public in the market square of Jitomir on 7/8/1941.[69]

When the time came, the two men were perched on a lorry positioned under a gallows, and the rope was tied round their necks in front of a crowd of Ukrainian spectators and soldiers of the Wehrmacht.[70] Eyewitness reports also insist on the fact that the Ukrainians dressed up as if they were on holiday, especially the women accompanied by their children, and emphasize the cameras carried by the Wehrmacht men who laughed and joked,[71] asking the driver of the lorry on which the two condemned men were placed to advance more slowly so that they could grab them as their bodies fell. The spectacle was treated by the Ukrainians as a sort of festive ritual celebrating 'freedom from Communism' and presented as such by the loudspeakers of the lorries of the *Propaganda-Staffel*: this public hanging of the two men, which was the legitimizing prelude to the execution of 402 Jews, embodied a liberating violence, desired as such by the Germans and – probably much more fleetingly – received as such by the Ukrainians.[72] Be that as it may, the report of *Einsatzgruppe* C shows that 'the reading of the sentence was interrupted by yells of approval and applause' and that 'the local population greeted this punishment for decades of Jewish cruelty with particular satisfaction'.[73]

This was but one aspect of the discourse that emerged from this public hanging. Was the macabre spectacle not also conceived as a discourse addressed to the German soldiers present in considerable numbers? They were being shown an incarnation of the enemy that confirmed the representations distilled during the preparation of the campaign; the two men were thus the victims of a pedagogic and demonstrative violence.[74] Did this display of violence represent a significant proportion of the practice of the *Einsatzgruppen*? Without being able to gauge its extent, we can still note that public executions were carried out by groups in Poland during the 1939 campaign.[75] Thus twenty hostages were shot in the street in Bromberg after a German soldier had been wounded. Photos of the event show that the condemned men were shot in an open square, in front of monumental buildings, in two groups of ten. We also have a series of photographs taken in Katowice at the time of another public execution, and on these we can see one of the victims walking in the middle of a large crowd, his arms raised and his face swollen – the man was obviously beaten before being taken to the place of execution. He has been identified, apparently, as one of the town doctors.[76] So while there is some evidence to suggest that this practice did not remain completely isolated, these shots cannot be taken as proof that it was widespread. Apart from the fact that it has not been possible to consult the original prints, and so there remain doubts as to their identification and the context in which they were taken, they do not constitute the slightest proof that shootings were generally carried out in public. The public nature of the execution in Bromberg has been emphasized by Czesław Madajczyk:[77] while he does cite other examples,[78] he does not reveal any systematic desire to display this type of violence. Public executions occurred at the end of hostilities, in the context of the establishment of an occupation viewed as definitive, and they demonstrate a clear wish to intimidate and to make a show of power on the part of the conquerors. However, the special commissions set up in September 1939 by Roland Freisler handed down several death sentences for the same reasons: it is just that they were only very rarely carried out in public.[79] This shows that this practice was uncommon.

One of the members of KdS Minsk recalled having taken part in a public execution during which two women were put to death after being convicted of killing, dismembering and selling the pieces of two children in the town market.[80] The reasons for the execution, here again, were carefully read out to the public before both women were hanged. While it is impossible to attempt to draw any systematic conclusions from the semiology of this hanging, on the basis of one eyewitness account, it does seem that the men of the KdS viewed it as a way of bringing out the inhumanity of the Russian populations and the way it could be regulated by the German powers who punished their cannibalism. Other examples give us some partial confirmation of this use of public hangings: the men of KdS Minsk mention the case of three men convicted of having spread the typhus bacillus in the hospital.[81] The soldiers confirmed the enemy's supposed cruelty, but also the way he was perceived in terms that reduced him to the lowest level of life and seen as a mere bacillus. So the hanging was conceived as setting a clear example, taking as it did the form of a particularly degrading punishment. Even if this type of punishment had other uses, this one brings out the demonstrative dimension of the violence of the groups. Whether the message was of a political order, staging as it did the authority of the Germans, or more doctrinal, illustrative of Russian savagery and the need to punish it, this message involved the executioner, the victim and the occupied society simultaneously.[82]

Most of the 500,000 executions carried out by the groups were dictated by other reasons than the occasional death penalties we have been discussing. These more commonplace executions were always carried out by firearms, usually took place on the outskirts of towns, and concerned much larger groups of victims than public executions. From August 1941, and even more in September–October, the four groups took over the liquidation by shootings of the ghettos that had been set up over the summer. The number of victims, which hitherto had already reached several hundred per day, now rose to several thousands, or even tens of thousands. The most striking examples are the two major executions carried out by the *Sonderkommando* 4a in Kiev (Babi Yar) on the one hand – 33,371 persons were executed in two days (29 and 30 September) – and the massacre of Jews in Carpathian Ukraine by personnel of the HSSPF for the south of Russia, *Einsatzkommando* 5 and police battalion 320 in Kamenets-Podolsk, a massacre during which 23,600 persons were executed in three days (28–31 August).[83] In Belorussia, the signal for the total destruction by shooting of the Jewish communities was given by the massacre of the 2,273 Jews of the Moghilev ghetto, while in the area occupied by *Einsatzgruppe* D, the killing of the 11,000 Jews of Nikolayev, on 14 September 1941, marked the shift to the total extermination of entire communities. The huge scale of these 'actions' struck executioners and witnesses alike.

We need to try and take the measure of the transformations caused by the change in scale of the massacres by comparing the modes of operation developed throughout the extermination campaign led by the groups. In his study of the execution carried out by the men of the 101st police battalion, *Ordinary Men*, Christopher Browning has provided us with a standard work on the way men involved in the shootings handled the violence they meted out. But he used one particular case: that of a first shooting. For the men of the 101st battalion had no idea of their mission when they arrived in Josefow on the morning of the action. They were given no instructions as to the practical problems of organizing the shootings. The officers made no preparations for this first massacre: the gunmen had to go and fetch their victims themselves, taking them into the woods one by one, and shooting them after a face-to-face confrontation that lasted the length of the journey; the units left the bodies out in the open after the massacre, and the officers were not present at the place of execution.[84] This set of factors explains both the extreme slowness of the 'novices' and their reactions: as gunmen forced to undergo a completely disorganized baptism of fire – and a genocidal action – they were immediately plunged into what Walter Stahlecker, the first head of *Einsatzgruppe* A, called 'spiritual exertions' (*seelische Anstrengungen*).[85]

A trace of this lack of experience can be found in the narrative of a shooting carried out by Sk 7a in Vitebsk in mid-July 1941, described in these terms by a former member of the *Kommando*:

As I said in the report, there was complete mayhem at the place of execution. People were shooting all around, in the greatest chaos. So the execution did not take place in military order. This may have been due to the fact that Dr Blume had placed himself in the background.[86] During this execution, the tasks were not divided out between the men so that some members of the *Kommando* could organize a line [of guards] while others could lead the Jews from the place [where the victims were being kept] to the execution ditches, and others would do the actual shooting. As I have already described, what actually happened was that the Jews had to lie down with their faces to the ground, some twenty or so metres away from the ditch. Individual gunmen then came to fetch them, leading them to the edge of the ditch and killing them with a revolver shot to the back of the neck. On this occasion, the chaos gradually grew worse as more and more victims defended themselves, crying and lamenting. It was not like in the later executions that the inves- tigating judge told me about, in which, as I have heard, the victims were led to the gunmen standing near the ditches, who shot the smallest number of shots until the magazine of their pistols was empty. Everything was so topsy-turvy that some men could get away without shooting. In my opinion, it is quite possible that some members of the *Kommando* might have fired fifteen to twenty shots while others did not fire any. [. . .]

The execution in Vitebsk was particularly distressing for all those who took part. The victims were not the only ones to suffer: the members of the *Kommando* were completely on edge. This meant that members of the *Kommando* coming back kept bumping into those who were advancing towards the ditch with a victim. Individuals reacted with considerable vehe- mence, and there were yells on all sides. The fact that no precise instructions were given as to the way the executions were to be carried out was partly responsible for all the chaos. The members of the *Kommando* thus found themselves suddenly subjected to a face-to-face encounter [*gegenüberstellt*] with the victims, they knew that the latter were to be killed in front of the defensive ditches and that they would have to do it with their pistols. They had been told nothing more than to shoot them in the back of the neck. But there were no instructions [specifying] how this could be done as quickly and precisely as possible.[87]

Claus Hueser describes an execution that, in his words, 'went badly'. He begins by emphasizing the fact that the men had not been divided into teams with well-defined tasks, a failure already observed in the killing carried out by the 101st police battalion in Josefow. Once the surprise of this first shooting had passed, the officers of the 101st battalion also set up a system, like the Sk 7a and the other *Kommandos*. The second point in common was the individual nature of the shootings. The gunmen had to walk alongside their victims during the journey from the place where they were awaiting their execution and the ditch, then they had to shoot them individually. The interpersonal nature of the violence was thus experienced with great intensity in both cases – especially as the gunmen had to face this situation again and again: there was no system whereby their places could be taken by others, no rhythm set by a hierarchy which was, indeed, remarkable by its absence.[88] In Vitebsk as in Josefow, some men may never have fired at all, while others may have executed tens of victims. In Josefow, the absence of ditches for execution and interment is additional evidence of inexperience. Here, the Jewish victims were executed lying down, and the battalion completely neglected to bury the remains. However new to the task the *Sonderkommando* may apparently have been, it had at least dug ditches into which the bodies of the slain toppled under the impact of the bullets. Thus the options set out by the organizers on the ground – namely, the officers of the units responsible for the shootings – provide us with information about their level of experience in killing.

This was not the first time that Claus Hueser, giving evidence in his own defence, provided an examining magistrate with the description of a shooting.[89] Summoned as a witness a few months previously, he had narrated a later execution – one that to his mind was more 'comfortable' and perhaps easier to admit to – one that also took place in Vitebsk. The killer's tone of voice was notably different in this earlier account.

Q[uestion]: What were the missions of *Sonderkommando* 7a?

A[nswer]: [. . .] Sk 7a also carried out the executions in every case. In my view, the first executions were carried out in Vitebsk. The Wehrmacht and we put up posters saying that the Jews and Communists had to turn up at a certain place and a certain time with brooms or spades.

These people duly arrived, and were assigned to work clearing up and smoothing the ground. The others, I don't know how many altogether, were shot outside the town by Sk 7a – this was in defence ditches that had already been dug. The execution *Kommando* was composed of six to seven men. Although there was an order stipulating that all the members of the *Kommando* had to take part in at least one execution, they looked for volunteers to make up the squad.

I myself took part in an execution only once, at which some hundred persons were shot. This was in Vitebsk. Those who were going to be shot had to lie on the ground. Machine guns had been set up all around, and the people – Jews and Communists – were kept under guard. There were men and women. There weren't any children. The *Kommando* keeping guard then took them, eight at a time, to the ditch. The people then had to stand at the edge of the ditch, facing into it. We stood behind these people and, when the order was given, each of us shot one of the victims. After the shooting, the victims fell into the ditch and we, the gunmen, had to turn round straightaway and take ten paces back. Dr Blume had given this order. It was his way of preserving us from the sight of the dead victims.[90]

Although the two shootings must have taken place no more than twelve days apart,[91] they were organized very differently. The second involved a division of tasks between two teams of killers, one being responsible for keeping guard over the victims and leading them to the place of execution, the other shooting them. The execution properly speaking was organized collectively, with a squad firing a salvo when the order was given. The tasks were automated so as to be carried out as quickly as possible and so that the gunmen would see as little as possible of the ditch. On an officer's command, they had indeed to retire ten steps after each salvo, check their weapons and reload, while another group of victims was led to the edge of the ditch. The killing on this occasion was carefully arranged – and this was probably the result of earlier experiences; in this way, a set of practices was established which seemed to comprise, as it were, an experience of genocide that could draw both on the skill and on the organizational structures developed by the killers themselves.[92]

We can draw a distinction between two types of empirical knowledge – i.e. knowledge born from the experience of genocide. The most obvious is logistical in nature. The establishment of procedures of killing based on a productivist logic required a division of tasks.[93] In the case of major operations such as those at Babi Yar or Kamenets-Podolsk, the logistical mechanisms mobilized whole regiments to assemble victims, supervise them on their march or when they climbed aboard the lorries that were to take them to the place of execution, form a cordon to keep watch over them and lead them to the ditches. These men were also responsible for gathering the personal effects, luggage and valuable objects that the victims had to hand over before being led to the places of execution. In Kiev, for instance, some 33,000 Jews who were to be executed in the ravine at Babi Yar were guarded by three police battalions,[94] while the Wehrmacht provided some hundred lorries to transport the victims and the tens of thousands of suitcases and valuable objects confiscated before they were murdered.[95] It also provided the material (loudspeakers, posters, etc.) necessary for announcing the 'expulsion' of the Jews, and placed at the disposal of Sk 4a a regiment of pioneers who blew up the edges of the ravine in which the Jews had been shot, so as to bury them.[96] The logistical systems were not always so highly developed, but this division of labour became general in the practice of the *Einsatzgruppen* from the last weeks of July 1941 onwards.[97]

The example of Babi Yar reveals a second dimension of this logistical planning: it concerns everything to do with the preparations for the execution, namely the digging of the ditches and the burial of the victims' bodies. In Babi Yar, the presence of a natural ravine determined the choice of the site of execution, which meant it was not necessary to dig ditches (which would have needed to be very large), and the burial of the dead. This latter operation also dictated the decision to execute the victims on the side of, or within, the ditches. The excavation was in fact never carried out by the SS, but usually by Russian civilians or, sometimes, by the victims themselves before their execution. The burial, too, was always carried out by Russians dragooned in to do the job. Apart from the physically laborious nature of the task and the need to be quick, a third, and no doubt decisive factor, explains why this work was assigned to civilians of 'inferior race': the gunmen and the guards found the idea of having to handle corpses quite repellent. This is suggested by the eyewitness accounts of the men of KdS Minsk who took part in the use of vans to gas victims. These men, who were obviously used to killing men, women and children, stated that the sight and handling of corpses, in particular the need to pull them out of the van to throw them into the ditches dug in advance, were 'barely tolerable'.[98] This reveals another empirical experience, that of the limit which men of the *Einsatzgruppen*, however used they were to carrying out mass murder, were reluctant to cross. This revulsion and sense of being sullied seems to have been a constant factor in the groups' behaviour. So their officers had a twofold interest in accelerating the rate of execution and improving the efficiency of the killings, while sparing their manpower. And this was doubtless the case for many of these logistical measures. They all had a functional meaning, fulfilling as they did the criteria of speed and efficiency; but the separation of the task of transporting the victims to the place of execution from that of actually killing them was evidence of a desire to limit any face-to-face encounter with the victims. This is shown too, in negative form, by the descriptions of the executions in Josefow and Vitebsk, which were particularly traumatic for the executioners. In the establishment of the logistical dimension of the violence of elimination, the demands of speed and exhaustiveness coexisted with the wish to spare the executioners psychologically.

The third dimension of the empirical knowledge developed by the killers, either within the hierarchy or, even more directly, among the troops themselves, concerns the action of killing as such. The hierarchical instructions specifying the manner of death were never transmitted in writing, hence the great vagueness of our understanding of this subject. For example, Michael Wildt could quite legitimately raise questions about the shooting exercises carried out by men incorporated into the groups in Pretzsch and Düben: did they, on that occasion, learn to kill as part of a squad, using a pistol, and did they learn to kill with a bullet to the nape of the neck as they were preparing to enter the USSR in the wake of the armies of Operation Barbarossa?[99] If we read the evidence of the men incorporated into the groups closely enough, it seems that we can reasonably answer this question in the negative. Claus Hueser's evidence on the first execution in Vitebsk is illuminating in this respect. As we have seen, Hueser notes, in his inventory of the organizational shortcomings that contributed to the inefficiency of the execution, that no precise instructions were given on how the victims were to be shot, other than that this was to be done with a pistol shot to the nape of the neck.[100] The exactitude of this recollection shows that orders were transmitted by the hierarchy to the troops, but also that no clear instructions were provided beforehand. The few testimonies on this question seem to corroborate this fact. We could also surmise a hierarchical vacuum in the area of techniques of slaughter: this was evident in Josefow as in Vitebsk, and seems to suggest that the officers in charge of the troops were novices – and, if we are to believe Hueser's description, the ignorance of the rank and file as to how to kill was soon overcome. A fortnight later, the gunmen of Sk 7a were killing more quickly, more accurately, in a firing squad, under orders. Instructions on the quickest and simplest way of killing were divulged by the officers supervising the groups. Some eyewitness accounts also state that the doctors in these groups managed to play a role. Here, for example, is a description of the first issuing of instructions to the gunmen of the 101st battalion:

> About Dr. Schoenfelder I recall with certainty [. . .] . We stood, as I said, in a semicircle round Dr. Schoenfelder and the other officers. Dr. Schoenfelder sketched on the ground – so that we could all see – the outline of the upper part of a human body and marked on the neck the spot at which we should fire.[101]

A second testimony gives further details:

> It was discussed how the shooting should be carried out. The question was whether [to shoot] with or without a bayonet mounted on the rifle [. . .] . The mounted bayonet would avoid misfirings and the man need not come too close to the victims.[102]

As far as the groups of the SIPO and the SD were concerned, there is little evidence about the hierarchical and medical transmission of instructions on how to shoot. What we do know is that the doctors in the *Einsatzgruppen* took part in research into gassing, considered as an alternative to shootings carried out in groups. The case of the doctor of *Einsatzgruppe* B, Hans Battista, who participated in the experiments with gassing and dynamiting the mentally ill organized in Minsk by the *Kriminaltechnisches Institut* of the KRIPO at the instigation of Arthur Nebe (head of *Einsatzgruppe* B), is a definite proof of the participation of doctors from the groups in the development of practices of killing.[103]

While the unfolding of the operation was generally controlled by the hierarchy, the acts of murder were also caught up in a logic of hearsay and looking-on: we sometimes see this from eyewitness accounts. In the first days of the *Osteinsatz*, both the rank and file and the cadres of the groups were confronted for the first time by mass executions, in a context marked by a speeding up of events and a need for haste that seem partly to have caught the hierarchies short. The case of Sk 1b, directed by Erich Ehrlinger, is interesting here. The men of the *Kommando* probably had their first experience of the *Osteinsatz* when, on 30 June, they entered the town of Kaunas, where the *Kommando* remained for several days. Kaunas was at the time the scene of intensely violent pogroms, with nationalists launching attacks on the Jewish quarters, beating several hundred men and setting up militias. The *Kommando*'s role consisted in taking back control of the town, which it did by disarming the militias, with the exception of one detachment assigned, under German control, to Fort VII, an old fortress on the Tsarist *limes*, now transformed into an internment camp for 'suspect elements' and a centre for executing Jews.[104]

Ehrlinger was no novice in using intervention groups to ensure security. This SS intellectual, a former deputy of Franz Six, had been involved in mobile units operating in Austria, in the Sudetenland, in Czechoslovakia and in Poland, where he was head of the SD for the Warsaw district. He was one of the most experienced cadres. However, even he was somewhat nervous at the prospect of organizing the first group shootings. One witness, recounting the first execution performed by men from the *Kommando*, described him as 'pushing [his men] to the extreme' (*äusserst betriebig sein*). Showing unmistakable signs of haste, he urged them to carry out the executions as fast as possible.[105] The SS did not really seem au fait with this type of mission. Eighteen years after the events, one of the gunmen of the *Sonderkommando* tried to justify his non-participation in these first executions with an, to put it mildly, unusual argument given the rather limited range of alibis put forward by the killers.[106] He stated that he did not need to take part since there were enough old hands from the Poland groups in the *Sonderkommando* to carry out the task.[107] So just as the *Kommando* was preparing for its first shootings, the experience of killing acquired in Poland was transmitted by these men who took over the executions performed in the town. They thus partly made up for the inexperience of the other group members, whom they initiated into the techniques of killing. It does seem that, on the execution sites themselves, between two shootings, the gunmen were able to discuss the quickest and most efficient means of killing their victims. One of the gunmen of Sk 7a testified that there were discussions between the gunmen as to the exact place on the nape of the neck where the bullet was to be aimed so as to cause instant death.[108] The knowledge involved, in this case, was not simply anatomical: it was also – and Christopher Browning, and then Daniel Goldhagen, have both demonstrated this[109] – a matter of avoiding too messy an explosion and spattering the gunmen's uniforms with bits of brain and bone.[110] Having a shooting squad, usually three to ten metres away from the victims, meant this drawback was avoided. In this case, the conversations, if we are to believe the evidence available, consisted in designating and dividing out the victims or targets between the gunmen: Sk 7a, which – at the instigation of Walter Blume – established a system of two gunmen per victim, had one of the gunmen aiming at the victim's head while the other targeted his or her chest. This meant that the two gunmen in each case needed to agree beforehand on their roles.[111] The same type of agreement was involved in the case of the execution of women accompanied by children too young to walk.

The fact remains that this type of dialogue no longer consisted in the exchange of information on how to commit genocidal acts. However, the way in which cadres, *Kommando* leaders, troop leaders or NCOs of firing squads, and even the killers themselves, reached certain decisions (whether or not to have killers doubling up, the simultaneous shooting of women accompanied by children or the successive shooting of first one and then another victim) shows that the procedures of killing were indeed established and then gradually developed. These procedures were far from being spontaneous, but form very specific constructions, which comprise the essence of the violence of elimination. In any event, they seem to have satisfied two of the imperatives of the aseptic imagination at work behind the hierarchical discourse: the imperative of productivity – it was necessary to kill a lot of people quickly – and the imperative of exhaustiveness – nobody could be left alive. These practices were arranged as compromises between often contradictory imperatives. If, in the view of the group cadres, the imperative of productivity had trumped any other criterion in the establishment of practices of extermination, they would have overwhelmingly gone for a shooting carried out with large-calibre automatic weapons, with a much higher rate of fire than an execution squad and, a fortiori, more efficient than non-synchronized gunmen killing with a bullet in the back of the neck. The method would have been much more efficient but, if we are to believe some eyewitness accounts, it had, in the view of these cadres, the crippling drawback of not guaranteeing that the killing would be full-scale. In Równo, Ek 5 tried to carry out an execution using machine guns, but decided to go back to 'targeted shooting' (*gezielter Schuss*) as there were too many survivors and wounded who then had to be finished off in the execution ditch.[112] This can be seen as a sign that they were becoming hardened – indeed, the phenomenon was no longer seen as traumatic, as was the case for the gunmen of the 101st battalion.

Thus, the organizational dimension of the genocide rapidly became the norm in all *Kommandos*, after a phase – lasting for ten or so days at most – marked by inexperience and improvisation, by the inefficiency and confusion of the supervisors. A series of rituals were chosen and soon became the invariant frameworks for massacres. Shootings were practically always carried out on victims with their backs to the gunmen, standing or kneeling on the edge of the ditches, or lying inside them one on top of another.[113] The development of these procedures by the hierarchy, and the on-the-ground experience of the gunmen, formed a set of murderous skills whose major invariants comprised the essence of the Nazi violence of elimination.

A transgressive violence

Until now, our investigation has focused only on collective ritualistic frameworks, in other words the cultural construction of a violence conditioned by representations. However, these frameworks assumed a great variety of forms when put into practice in reality. The great invariant factors left the protagonists with room for manoeuvre even within each unit – squad, detachment, *Kommando*, KdS, BdS, *Einsatzgruppe*. The experience of confrontation with death inflicted on others was often traumatic, and the measures taken by the officers in charge of the *Kommandos* were often the result of attempts to manage and master this confrontation.

With a few exceptions, SS intellectuals were incorporated into the mobile groups at the start of the hostilities. Otto Ohlendorf, Erich Ehrlinger, Franz Six, Hans Joachim Beyer, Fritz Valjavec, Martin Sandberger and various other qualified officers of the RSHA left for the *Osteinsatz* in June 1941. We need to remember that 40 per cent of men in the group (32 out of 80) left for the east, 25 of them for Russia.[114] They thereafter assumed the functions of *Kommando* leaders, or even group leaders.

Given their ranks, the mission of SS officers was in the first instance administrative and organizational. The trial of two *Kommando* leaders, Erich Ehrlinger and Albert Rapp, provides us with more detailed information on the activities of SIPO and SD units operating in Russia. The career of Erich Ehrlinger is well known: he was urgently called up in the last two days before the invasion of the USSR because of his experience of police action outside the Reich's borders, and took over command of Sk 1b: he then became KdS Ukraine, then BdS Belorussia and head of *Einsatzgruppe* B. He stayed in post in Russia without interruption from June 1941 to April 1944,[115] and enjoyed one of the longest careers of any SS intellectual. Albert Rapp was transferred to Sk 7a in January 1942, just as the latter was settling into barracks in Klincy, on the border between Ukraine and Belorussia. Coming into the *Kommando* to end an interim period, he stayed there until January 1943, taking over command for nearly a year after a period of uncertainty due to a very rapid rotation of commanders – Blume and Steimle – who stayed in post for four months or less.[116] The evidence of their collaborators, and their own declarations, give us a clear idea of what they did in the east. The difficulties involved in using judicial sources are well known. In this case, however, the archival documents available to investigators and magistrates were sufficiently compromising for the two defendants, who were initially entrenched in their denials, to be unable to dilute their responsibilities and to give up any attempt at disguising the murderous activities of the *Kommandos* they led. In addition, they had both made themselves so unpopular among the members of their units that the latter apparently did not raise a finger to protect them. In short, it seems that the evidence has not been overly softened.[117]

The daily work of the cadres in the *Kommandos* consisted essentially in organizing and planning activities. During the mobile phase of the units, their leaders often took responsibility for the 'security' of towns and the establishment of what reports called the first steps towards the 'solution of the Jewish problem'.[118] In towns such as Vitebsk, in tandem with the executions already mentioned, the head of Sk 7a, Walter Blume, created the *Judenrat*, made it obligatory to wear a yellow star, and decreed that the Jewish communities should be interned in ghettos. In Klincy, his successor, Albert Rapp, was also in charge of this type of measure, but he organized a considerable number of executions too. The SS officer, according to witnesses, refused to allow his subordinates to take any initiative, and himself chose the place and mode of executions that he had ordered.[119] Rapp arrived when the *Kommando* was resting in Klincy, and gave a new impetus to the murders. This, as well as his reluctance to give his subordinates any room for manoeuvre, explains – according to the witnesses – why he was so very unpopular. Both Rapp and Ehrlinger instigated the executions, coordinating the activities of their units and deciding where, when and how the actions were to take place. One of the NCOs of the Waffen SS assigned to Sk 7a stated that the orders always came from Rapp, but followed traditional hierarchical channels, from head of the *Kommando* to head of the Waffen SS section. He thought it was impossible that Rapp could have been ignorant, but he did claim that the latter could give orders directly to section leaders, without going through a special officer.[120] Rapp's method is confirmed by the evidence of one of his officers, who under questioning stated:

> Just like the other officers, I had absolutely no competence or room for command. [. . .] Preparations for an action were his responsibility alone. He himself was absent, making preparations, and we officers were glad that he was away from Klincy. During his absences, Rapp evidently prepared the executions with the Russian stewards. [. . .] In the executions which Rapp made me supervise, things were done in such a way that I had no room for command or manoeuvre. I received from Rapp the order to turn up with twenty men at a given place in the environs of Klincy, and Rapp told me: 'Thormann, you go out with the men, the driver is already informed, it's all been arranged.' On this order, I left with the men for the execution at which Glockmann was killed.[121]

Rapp, on arrival, issued a written order stipulating that no action was to be undertaken by Sk detachments without his consent. This order, in force even before his arrival, was thus confirmed, and the practice of the new commander, who did not delegate the functions of the organizations performing 'actions', tended to reinforce its impact.[122] The function of arranging the executions was specific to group leaders, and lasted beyond the mobile phase. Erich Ehrlinger, in post in the BdS Ukraine, also supervised all the procedures set up by his *Amt* IV. Thus he received all the records of questionings together with the proposed sentences – these were usually death sentences – and countersigned them before the lists of execution could be drawn up and sent to the detention centre, from where the condemned were taken to be shot, at a rate of some forty per week.[123] Supervising, organizing and ordering: these were the three first tasks of *Kommando* leaders. However, their work was not restricted to these functions. *Kommando* leaders often attended executions, presiding over them and sometimes taking part in them. Their function was thus one of representation and legitimation. The Gestapo boss in Kiev, one of Ehrlinger's deputies, gave evidence about one of the executions which, in his view, concerned only partisans:

> I know that Ehrlinger himself took part in the shooting in this execution. [He] arrived during the execution, accompanied by Munk [his aide-de-camp]. Deciding that the execution was not going fast enough, he was complaining loudly. Suddenly, he stood upright at the edge of the ditch with the pistol he was carrying and shot down the prisoners arriving at the ditch. But I can't say how many delinquents he shot.[124]

Later, Ehrlinger attended other executions and finished off prisoners, or executed with his own hands a 'spy', in other words a Jewish man working under a false name for the BdS.[125] His attitude was not, in fact, isolated: a certain number of *Kommando* leaders used their own weapons and killed with their bare hands.[126]

The case of the first leader of Sk 7a is interesting in this respect. Here is what one of his subordinates had to say about an execution carried out in Gorodok:[127]

> The execution *Kommando* comprised some 25 men. Dr Blume himself was present and he fired too. He had brought with him men belonging to the main *Kommando*, which was stationed at the lake. [. . .]
> I myself had to fire, until my weapon was empty. Only men were shot, some 150–200 of them. [. . .] before the execution in Gorodok, Dr Blume told us how to place the barrel of our pistols against the victims' necks, at the hairline. After shooting, the bullet was supposed to come out through the forehead.[128]

This evidence shows the head of a *Kommando* himself shooting, and emphasizes the role that SS intellectuals could play in the development of the skills of murder. It was Blume, in this case, who indicated to his men, with considerable anatomical precision, how the shootings were to be carried out. Note that the presence of *Kommando* leaders at the places of execution, and the fact that they directed firing squads in person, suggest how frequent murder was at this level of the hierarchy: it was leaders of the firing squads who were usually responsible for finishing off victims who had not been killed by the salvo.[129] It was in this precise context that Ehrlinger fired, even if his gesture was caused by anger or impatience. The second case, in which Ehrlinger shot the Jewish spy working for the KdS, stems rather from the function assumed by the victim in the eyes of the Nazis. In every case, it seems that *Kommando* leaders, forced to carry out murderous acts less often than their subordinates, sometimes fired shots in circumstances in which violence acquired an exemplary 'virtue' in their eyes.

The case of *Sturmbannführer* Bruno Müller illustrates this function of representation. On the night of 6 August 1941, he passed on to the men of his team the new orders to kill all the Jews in the town of Tighina (in southern Ukraine), women and children included.[130] Thereupon, Müller himself killed a woman and her baby with his service weapon in front of the assembled troops, giving his men the example of what would be their task.[131] As far as we know, this case was unique: Müller was legitimizing a major transgression of boundaries, namely the extermination of children. In all probability, he gave a legitimizing speech in front of the troops,[132] then put his murderous words into practice to display the exemplary nature of his attitude. Many *Kommando* cadres were convinced that they could not ask their men to do things which they themselves could not carry out.[133] In another context, Albert Rapp insisted on giving an example of 'bravery' to his men, leading from the front during an assault on a partisan camp, an occasion on which he was wounded. However, he was so unpopular that he failed to galvanize the men of the Sk 7a, who were profoundly convinced that he was incompetent in military matters, especially when it came to fighting partisans.[134]

The example of Walter Blume, however, shows how contradictory the attitude of SS officers could be. Blume undeniably saw genocide right up close. He inspired it, and took part in it. However, the eyewitness accounts of men of his *Kommando* describe him as being deeply uneasy about the 'mission' with which his superiors in Berlin had entrusted him.[135] One witness, in particular, describes how he vomited during one of the first executions by Sk 7a at the beginning of July.[136] Blume never attempted to conceal his revulsion at the executions carried out by the groups. He very soon tried to get himself transferred and, during the first execution in Vitebsk, he 'stood in the background', for no reason other than that he could not get over the initial shock of the spectacle.[137] Some men in the *Kommando* described him as 'a weak man',[138] but if we look at all the evidence, a quite different dimension emerges: we have an SS officer in the *Sonderkommando*, one who himself shoots at victims, while yet showing signs of revulsion at executions, and who metes out very severe punishment to his subordinates when they drink too much, even going so far as to parade in front of the assembled troops an officer found drunk, before having him transferred for disciplinary reasons.[139] An officer, in other words, who set in place the measures that gradually comprised genocide, subscribing to them and overcoming his repulsion to organize massacres.

This situation was not so uncommon.[140] Christopher Browning describes an officer who, while leading his men in shootings which he fully supported, still had to cope with psychosomatic digestive problems, signs of his difficulty in 'getting over' the murderous violence he inflicted.[141] Indeed, Walter Blume could not imagine any of the men in his group carrying out such tasks in any other frame of mind. Before the *Kommando* entered Soviet territory, he had been quite clear on this point:

> In Düben the future leaders of Sk 7a were also present. There were Dr Blume, Radel, Foltis, Stanke, Meyer[-Heitling], Hueser and Becker. Hueser took us out for a march on the exercise ground. He suddenly shouted 'Take cover!' and eventually ordered us to rest. [. . .] Dr Blume was with us outside, and he then told us that we were going to be entering Russia and difficult times were awaiting us there, and he told us that we needed to keep [intact our] spirit of fellowship. He then added, more or less: 'God help anyone I catch there actually enjoying his task.' We thought that Dr Blume was alluding to the general events of war awaiting us in Russia. None of us knew that one of our missions would consist in shooting Jews in Russia.[142]

Blume mentions one of the most powerful taboos at work in the *Einsatzgruppen*: that of 'cruelty', in other words violence inflicted just for its own sake, and giving the killers a certain pleasure. This was probably one of the sole collective barriers established by the discourse of the hierarchy throughout the operations of extermination by the *Einsatzgruppen*. One last example will enable us to gauge the effects of this taboo.

Eduard Strauch, a lawyer in the SD, succeeded Erich Ehrlinger at the head of KdS Minsk. Strauch assumed responsibility for the extermination of most of the Jewish communities in Belorussia and played a major role in setting up the Nazi policy of fighting the Russian partisan units, when over six hundred Russian villages were burnt and their populations massacred.[143] Strauch also urged the local institutions – with their consent – to get rid of the already decimated Jewish communities. In Maly-Trostinez, in the environs of Minsk, he organized a camp that became a veritable centre of extermination for Belorussian Jews. All in all, Eduard Strauch was probably one of the men most deeply compromised in genocidal policies. His brutality even drew down the complaints of a civilian administration that had instigated the massacre. At this point, there entered the scene a secretary of state from Berlin and the HSSPF responsible for Belorussia, *SS-Gruppenführer* von dem Bach-Zelewsky. In his self-defence, Strauch turned the trial for sadism launched against him by the administration inside out:

> I [added that I] could again and again see that my men and I are accused of barbarism and sadism. Even the fact that Jews meant for special treatment have their gold tooth fillings removed in an orderly manner by specialist doctors had been made the subject of conversations. Kube replied that the manner of our proceeding was unworthy of a German person and of the Germany of Kant and Goethe. If Germany's reputation throughout the world was being undermined, this was alone our fault. Apart from that it was also correct that my men got a downright hard-on with these executions (*dass meine Männer sich an diesen Exekutionen geradezu aufgeilen würden*).

I protested energetically against this depiction and emphasized that it was deplorable that we, on top of this nasty work, also had dirt poured upon us.[144]

Strauch made no bones about his revulsion at the massacres, even though he was the man mainly responsible for the tornado of death which swept across Minsk and its region from the winter of 1941–2 to the end of summer 1943. In fact, we have a vivid portrait of Strauch in a report by *SS-Oberführer* Dr Achamer-Pifrader, head of *Einsatzgruppe* A and BdS *Ostland*, dating from the end of this period.

His personality is imbued with the refusal to compromise and a harshness that is mainly expressed in the defence of ideological positions and their implementation. His ideas and his conclusions in this area are simple [. . .]. In the most difficult situations, he has constantly acted as a skilled and extremely cool and collected *Führer*. His emotional life is not specially developed. He does not really like getting close to other people, and so can rarely charm [his subordinates] or evaluate them correctly. This no doubt explains his lack of trust in them, which in turn makes him susceptible to stool pigeons. His behaviour most of the time is instinctive and rarely inclines to being understanding.

His way of reacting is impulsive and explosive, which leads to an unbalanced personality, a failure to lead his men properly, and a mismatch between his behaviour and his basic principles.

The constant and growing use of alcohol has an extreme impact on this dimension of his personality.

The personal attitude of the head of the Minsk bureau has had some influence on his subordinates, in particular due to his excessive use of alcohol. *SS-Sturmbannführer* Strauch is responsible for the unhealthy atmosphere in KdS [. . .] Minsk.

However, it needs to be borne in mind that the circumstances are not the same in White Ruthenia as they are in the three Baltic countries. Ruthenia has not been pacified. Minsk has nothing to offer. The members of the institution are almost without exception constantly employed in the struggle against the partisans. The constant danger, the irregular way of life, and sexual deprivation are the causes of these alcoholic excesses.[145]

So it seems that Strauch lost his bearings because he was confronted too insistently and for too long with the paroxysmal violence that the *Kommando* imposed at his behest in Belorussia. After all, Achamer-Pifrader requested Strauch's transfer in the conclusion of his report. A man who was 'sick' with his own violence, the SS general seems to be implying, is a man to get rid of as fast as possible, both in the interest of the service and in his own. It is notable that these observations coincided with the opinion of the American experts at the Nuremberg Tribunal, who deemed Strauch fit to stand trial, but not to serve his sentence, due to repeated 'epileptiform crises'.[146] Though this kind of analysis requires considerable caution, we need to focus on a few features of collective behaviour. For Strauch and Blume were not exceptional cases.

It does seem that the violence inflicted generated in some members of the groups, independently of their consent to genocide, a degree of psychological suffering. This was the case with those gunmen who, as they grew used to carrying out their crimes, nonetheless felt each time that they were 'crossing a line'. While it seems very difficult to reach a conclusion about the extent of this phenomenon, the postwar interrogations sometimes include remarks that were not part of a strategy of whitewashing: witnesses launched out on irrelevant descriptions, defendants accused themselves and recounted events that were of no help in their defence. Something closer to confession than the need to conform to legal procedure seems to have been at work here. However, what was said in the hearing of witnesses or defendants was very rarely expressed in the form of any moral self-scrutiny. The structure of statements followed a standard pattern: the description of a massacre was followed by that of the feelings, individual or collective, generated by these events. And sometimes the carapace would crack. The executioners confessed that they were traumatized by what they had *done*, by what they had *seen*, by what they had *heard* and by what they had *felt*.

Curiously, the violence of murder was not usually expressed as such. The gunmen generally considered that they were likely to be found guilty, and so most of them were cautious in relating their own deeds. However, it is possible to follow the shock experienced by those who carried out the executions. Certain members of the *Kommandos*, more involved with the executions than others, were described by their old fellow members of the unit as both particularly brutal and deeply affected psychologically. This, for instance, was the case of one of the NCOs of Ek 8, the *Einsatzkommando* B which carried out most of the executions of Belorussian Jews in autumn 1941.[147] Karl Strohhammer, armed with an automatic pistol, shot victims who had not been mortally wounded, administering the *coup de grâce* either alone or with men of his squad. To do this, he leapt into the ditch and finished them off point-blank. A hardened killer, he complained that he was 'always on the job', and showed signs of being psychologically disturbed.[148]

Adolf Harnischmacher, the officer in charge of planning the executions carried out by Ek 8 and Strohhammer's superior in the hierarchy, was also known for his harshness. He was one of those who, armed with a whip, showed a markedly cruel form of interpersonal violence, lashing out at Jews during the round-ups in ghettos being liquidated. Harnischmacher was labelled a 'sadist' by witnesses who agreed on his state of nervous collapse, demonstrated by his constant alcoholism and the melancholy tones in which he spoke of the daily shootings in which he took part.[149]

In spite of the mechanisms that made these events easier to cope with,[150] violence remained at least partly perceived and experienced as traumatic; it 'left its mark' on the psychology of the killers.

As in the case of the 101st battalion, the first experience of a shooting had a depressing effect on the gunmen. This was the case, for example, with the men of Ek 5, who carried out their first shootings in Lemberg at the very beginning of June 1941. One of the gunmen later recounted that 'after this shooting, all the men were depressed, and nobody so much as mentioned it'.[151] However, not all violence was followed by a period of silence. In Sk 7a, the executions of July had such an impact that one of the officers assisting Blume reported that 'he [had] the impression that liquidating the Jews was a frequent topic of conversation since the men of [his] detachment had not got over them inside their own heads'.[152] After the first experience of massacre, some acts more clearly had destructive psychological effects on the killers. The murder of children and infants in particular seems to have been a transgression that did not leave the killers unscathed. Erich B., one of the SS in charge of the KdS Kiev under Ehrlinger's leadership, related one of the shootings in which he took part:

> 30 people got out of the lorry. Among them were 15 persons of the mas-culine sex, 6 or 7 women and the rest were children between 4 and 6. [. . .] The execution must have taken place in April or May 43. My then superior, *Untersturmführer* Klemmer, was present at the execution. [. . .] The execu-tion *Kommando*, five men strong, was chosen by Klemmer, who supervised the execution. The *Kommando* [. . .] headed out to a previously dug ditch. Then the Ukrainian militia led up the five delinquents. The victims were fully dressed and had to lie down in the ditch with their faces to the ground. The shooting followed with no particular command being given. I took part in this execution of some thirty persons, and I myself killed five or six victims. I suppose it must have been a lorry load. The delinquents assigned to me for execution were varied. There were men, women and children. After this execution, during which I killed two children and perhaps two women as well, we were replaced by other members of the *Kommando*. [. . .]
>
> After the execution, Klemmer talked with me. He asked me, basically, whether I had found this shooting difficult, and I agreed. He then told me that he too had found this chore [*Aufgabe*] very unpleasant. Since we were both ashamed of our participation in this execution, we said no more about it than was absolutely necessary. This experience [*Erlebnis*] had personally affected me to such an extent that I could not eat or work for two days. On the first day, I stayed in bed. Completely by chance, Miss Sieck came into my room and saw the state of mind I was in. I still recall that we both wept. She was tactful enough to realize that she should not ask me how the operation had gone. The reason for the collapse of my morale was known to her, but, very deliberately, she did not mention it.[153]

Erich B. was a former member of Ek 5 who, in July 1941, took part in the shootings in Lemberg.[154] He also stated that he had stayed with the *Kommando* until Berdichev, which means he took part in its operations until the end of July 1941, when he was transferred to the personnel of *Einsatzgruppe* C. We know that, in this period, Ek 5 carried out operations in Dubno, Berdichev and Chmielnik. If the executions in Berdichev were carried out by a specialized detachment, the previous executions had been carried out by *Kommando* members without any particular assignments.[155] While Erich B. says that Lemberg was the only time he took part as a gunman, he does not state in how many executions he took part as a member of the guard teams. All in all, it seems likely that he was relatively familiar with group violence. However, in each of the executions in which he may have taken part or which he attended, only men were targeted. The Kiev execution was thus probably the first execution of women and children in which he participated. His evidence, given nearly twenty years after the event, thus seems to be a representative example of the reactions to the crossing of the threshold comprised by the murder of women and, in particular, children.

Among all the trials studied here, the case of Erich B. is, however, the only one involving a German official who confessed to the murder of children. Of course, we cannot claim to be comprehensive: only sixteen trials involving the four *Einsatzgruppen* have been scrutinized. This represents nearly nine hundred eyewitness accounts, out of which only a hundred or so mention the murder of children. And out of this hundred, only one involves admission of direct participation. This shows how heavy was the taboo on this act: even though the risk of being found guilty was, in actual fact, more or less non-existent,[156] the men never referred to it.[157] More precisely, while reference to the execution of children was, in the final analysis, quite frequent, it was still anonymous: the speaker states that he was struck by a scene involving children or infants, but he never gives the names of the murderers.[158] It is less easy than one might think to understand the reasons behind this veil of silence which the prosecutors, for all their efforts, never broke. While the men confessed quite readily to the shootings,[159] admitting to the massacre of children clearly seems to have been subject to a different logic of behaviour and, perhaps, to a 'conspiracy of silence'.[160] Perhaps, when all is said and done, it is this instinct which explains both the transgression and the trauma?

Other practices of violence apparently caused traumatic reactions. One of these was connected with the gassing vans delivered to the groups from spring 1942 onwards.[161] Initially invented to relieve the men of the tension generated by executions,[162] they soon led to unforeseen difficulties. The first head of the Gestapo of KdS Kiev, when questioned as part of the investigation into Erich Ehrlinger, emphasized that the gas vans came with one major disadvantage: they had to be emptied of the bodies. The members of the *Kommandos* assigned to this task could 'only just cope' with it, and the SS officer abandoned the use of the van, returning to execution by firearms, thus registering the fact that his men preferred to have to shoot.[163] This statement is confirmed in the case of other *Kommandos*. In *Einsatzgruppe* D, especially in Sk 10b, the gassing van was used, for example, in Simferopol, in Crimea. One of the *Kommando* cadres, when questioned for the first time after his arrest, described his impressions in these terms:

> The gassing van came from Simferopol. There wasn't one stationed in Kertsch. I no longer remember whether it was sent to us from headquarters, or whether it was requested by me on a trip to Simferopol when I was informed of its existence and the orders that governed its use. Either way, it arrived one day from Simferopol and stopped outside the former NKVD building to load up prisoners which it then took to anti-tank ditches in the environs of the industrial quarter. [. . .] The prisoners were essentially people identified as partisans or agents. There were, I believe, also some women among them. No child was gassed; I am completely sure that no child was gassed during the second occupation of Kertsch. As for the request for an estimate of the number of people who were gassed in van S, I can give only an approximate estimate of fifty or so, as the van was filled twice and twenty-five people were, I reckon, loaded into it each time [. . .].
>
> I am sure that the delinquents were not forced to get undressed before they got into the van. The cries [of the prisoners] when the doors were closed and the van set off are still ringing in my ears. This action with the gas van was probably one of the hardest things I ever had to live through. I was not present when the van was unloaded into the anti-tank ditch. So I can't say who carried this out or how it was done. However, I do know that the men who took part in such actions said they would rather have shot those people than be on duty during the use and emptying of the van.[164]

This is doubtless a vivid description of one of the most traumatic experiences of the *Osteinsatz*. The revulsion felt by these men needs, however, to be examined in more detail. Schuchardt blames the sense of hearing: it was the sound – the cries of the victims – which made the experience so 'hard'. It seems that the other SS responsible for the execution did not feel the same. It was, rather, the view of the bodies – all soiled and entangled – when the van was opened up, and even more when the corpses had to be manhandled on unloading, that traumatized them. When we read the evidence, the two main sources of psychological distress were in this case touch and sight. Be that as it may, the gas vans, designed to alleviate the 'psychological pressure' on the gunmen, turned out to have the opposite effect, which led – at least in Kiev – to their being gradually abandoned.[165] The transgressive dimension was not at all moral in nature: it stemmed, rather, from the somatic and sensory experience. We also see how traumatic it was to have to jump down into the ditch to finish off the still living victims, which forced the gunman to confront the consequences of his action even more than did shooting from a distance. The problem posed by having to finish off the wounded personally seems, in any case, to have been perceived so intensely that, in some *Kommandos*, the officers resorted to throwing grenades into the ditches at the end of the execution.[166]

The confrontation with the bodies lying in the ditch was a visual experience. The eyewitness accounts of certain officers and rank-and-file members of the *Kommandos* leave no doubt on this subject; here, for example, is the description given by Franz-Josef Thormann, one of the Sk 7a officers in Klincy:

It is true that when there was a major execution in which nearly 400 Jews, men, women and children, were shot, it was carried out in a savage way. The business was prepared by Rapp and by him alone. At any event, I personally had nothing to do with the preparations. He told us that a big business was coming up and we all needed to go out. [. . .] There was chaos at the place of execution. Several men felt sick. The victims fell into the ditch, some of them were still alive. In any case, I still have a horrible image in my mind's eye: there were still movements in the mass of bodies, and suddenly someone rose up from the mass of tangled bodies and lifted an arm. The execution was carried out by a bullet in the neck from a PPK.[167] I remember that the victims were also shot from a sub-machine gun. I think that Rapp fired at this execution. Other officers also fired, on Rapp's orders. I myself didn't fire. At the beginning, I was standing next to Rapp. But I felt sick when I saw the bloody mass moving in the ditch and I turned round, with my stomach heaving. I eventually drank a lot of schnapps. There was a lot of schnapps in Klincy after the executions.[168]

The attempt to let himself off the hook is amazingly naïve, but it must not disguise the force of suggestion of the visual impressions mentioned by a man who was, after all, involved in a great number of executions. He describes the gruesome scene at the ditch – such a terrifying spectacle that the men did not have the courage to go down and finish off the wounded at point-blank range.

Jacob B. was a professional police officer in Sk 10b, Paul Zapp's *Kommando*. Older than most of the gunmen, he described in his statement the action of the *Kommando* during the mass murders in Feodosia and Simferopol. This man seems to have become accustomed, at least passively, to murder: though his voluntary participation is not proven, he relates without any apparent emotion an execution in which women and children were killed. However, after the narrative of this massacre, the tone of his discourse, as captured by a clerk, changes, as he embarks on the story of a second execution, one which involved just men:

The ditch had already been used, and I could smell the sickly-sweet odour of decomposition wafted to me on the wind, and this was what led me to view the shooting of prisoners as particularly cruel.[169]

The striking thing about the narrative of this gunman is the combination of this precise description with the fact that it was perceived by the prisoners he was keeping guard over.[170] It is because the smell betokens death and all that goes with it, to the guard as well as to his prisoners, that Jacob G. stated that he was particularly affected by this execution. Can we completely exclude the mechanism of 'sensory reminiscence' here? As we said, Jacob G. was older than the average for gunmen in the groups. So he took part, as he himself said, in the Great War. The smell of corpses is so easy to recognize: could he have failed to encounter it between 1914 and 1918? Perhaps the renewal of the previous experience explains, all by itself, the impact on this man, used to violence, of an execution in which his participation was only passive.

In spite of the way it became habitual, and even, for some, a source of intense pleasure, genocidal violence always had a transgressive and traumatic dimension, embodied by sequences in which it broke through the defences of the executioner, inflicting a specific shock on him. Such a statement in no way undermines the consent to genocide on a mass scale among the groups; nor does it contradict the implementation of practices of extreme violence or cruelty.[171] The fact remains that there were acts, sensations and perceptions that brought men up against psychological suffering that stopped them neither from taking pleasure in murder – a pleasure which none of them ever admits to, but which can be sensed, for instance, in Walter Mattner's letter[172] – nor from getting, quite simply, used to it.

This psychological suffering was quite significant enough, however, and shared on such a huge scale, for the cadres of the groups to worry about it – very early on, in fact. We have seen the strategies of legitimation drawn up by those in supervisory roles to ensure that ethical boundaries were most dramatically crossed. But the officers did not simply talk to their men; some also tried to alter the practices of violence, and apparently tried to limit the destructuring effects of genocidal rituals. These alterations reveal three distinct strategies. The first, practically common to all *Kommandos*, was the sharing out of violence among group members. For the cadres, this involved sharing out the psychological burden of murder among as many individuals as possible, with the aim of alleviating it for each one.

So as to avoid too great a disparity in the confrontation with violence, as in Josefow, where some gunmen got away without firing, one of the solutions applied in many of the *Kommandos* was having teams work in shifts. Either the men continued firing until they had emptied their weapons, or they fired one salvo and were then replaced by a squad moving in from behind. The second division of labour, more formal in organization, involved all the members taking part in at least one execution. The existence of this directive is attested for over half of the *Kommandos*.[173] While group members sometimes ascribed it to Himmler,[174] we know that it actually came from the heads of the *Kommandos*. The latter sometimes supplemented this type of regulation with practices whereby new arrivals were initiated into violence straightaway. This was the case with Erich Ehrlinger, who sent his newly appointed officers to execution *Kommandos* who were responsible for executing by firing squad, every week, some forty detainees from the prison of KdS Kiev.[175] When Heinrich Seetzen learned that one officer in his *Kommando* had not taken part in an execution, he selected him to lead the next one.[176] It was also this desire to share out the burden of shootings that led certain cadres to modify the execution procedures by doubling up the firing squads. This involved sharing the act: as we have seen, one gunman would aim at his victim's head, another at his chest. This happened, for instance, in *Sonderkommando* 10b, in which Aloïs Pesterer decided that two gunmen per victim would fire in collective salvos.[177] This measure, which went against the objective of 'productivity' assumed by the groups, meant that the responsibility for inflicting death could be diluted between the men.[178]

It is also possible to see the strategies used to make killing commonplace. Ek 3, yet again, is a good example. Between June and August 1941, murder was gradually extended to women, starting with the execution of a small number of them, suspected of Communist activities. After a few weeks in which these women were shot in groups of ten or twenty, numbers rose steadily to over a hundred, when women were definitively included in the general massacre. However, this process raises certain questions. All historians now agree that the groups' mission was not to exterminate Jewish populations between July and August 1941.[179] What was the intention behind these executions? Perhaps – and this is just a hypothesis – it was done to accustom the men to shooting women, as preparation for a policy of executing hostages that would also include the families of jailed men.[180]

Sharing out the task of shooting and imposing a strategy of habituation to murder were, no doubt, the adjustments most often made within the *Kommandos*. They were often accompanied by highly codified procedures that aimed at ritualizing the acts of violence and making them automatic, so as partly to disguise their transgressive dimension.

We find them at work in Sk 7a when Walter Blume was in charge, and in practically all the *Kommandos* of the *Einsatzgruppe*. Firing squads were set up and then, on an officer's orders, fired a salvo. The commands were very unvarying: the order was given to take aim and fire. The men did not have to choose when to fire.[181] They fired as a group, and the salvo was a collective act of killing. Thus the rite was a form of regulation of the psychological burden imposed on the killers. In this way, an analogy was established between these executions and the ones carried out by execution squads set up after summary trials. Also, the rite was a way of remilitarizing the practices of genocidal violence. Through its 'ceremonial', it reinstated butchery as part of war, and gave support to the fiction that these massacres were acts of war. It was thus the pendant to the discourse of legitimation, and its extension into practices of violence.

The adjective '*militärisch*', indeed, often appears in the remarks of gunmen questioned after the war, and is a criterion for evaluation of the organization of the shootings. The evidence of Claus Hueser, already quoted, is a striking example of this militarization taken to an astonishing level of sophistication. In Vitebsk, the SS had to line up: on the word of command, they took aim, and fired. As the victims tumbled into the ditch and the men in charge of bringing up the victims led the next group along, the firing squad, again on the orders of an officer, did an about-turn, took ten paces back, and reloaded their weapons. Here, shooting became a highly codified manoeuvre, and it is useful to hear what meaning the gunmen gave to this complex ritual, which presupposed both a large degree of thought on the part of the cadres, and a permanent control of their own acts on the part of the gunmen.

Claus Hueser was perfectly well aware, as the judge interrogated him, that this ritualization was an attempt to preserve his troops' psychological well-being. Blume's objective was to spare his men the vision of the ditch and the disintegration of the bodies. However, we are here faced with a limit situation: few *Kommandos* drew up such elaborate procedures.[182] In the case of Ek 2, in Latvia, and Sk 1a, in Estonia, the squads were formed and immediately fired when the order was given. But the case of Sk 1a is highly unusual: most of its victims were not Jews, and its action mainly formed part of the fight against partisans and of the maintaining of order.[183] There was, finally, one group in which the shootings were to an overwhelming extent carried out by squads: this was *Einsatzgruppe* D. The five *Kommandos* comprising it apparently carried out collective executions by firing salvos.[184] The reason, perhaps, is to be sought in the attitude of its first leader, Otto Ohlendorf, the economist head of RSHA *Amt* III who commanded it from June 1941 to May 1942. In Nuremberg, he stated that his mission had mainly consisted in ensuring that victims were executed 'in military fashion' and, 'in these circumstances, humanely'.[185] The reference to 'military fashion' may reflect Ohlendorf's normative discourse aimed at his *Kommando* chiefs, a discourse that incited them to maintain a strong hierarchical presence in the face of a continuing confrontation with violence on the part of men whose mental health Ohlendorf was endeavouring to preserve. The SS intellectual seems to have grasped the anomic dimension of genocidal violence, and tried to counteract its effects by ritualizing the executions. Here is what he said when he was giving evidence to the International Tribunal at Nuremberg, in reply to questioning by Colonel Amen, one of the American prosecutors:

> Col. Amen: Can you explain in detail to the tribunal how a mass execution was carried out? [. . .] On what pretext were the Jews assembled?
> Ohlendorf: On the pretext that they were to be resettled.
> A.: Carry on …
> O.: After registration, the Jews were concentrated in one spot, from which they were later transported to the place of execution, which was, generally

speaking, an anti-tank ditch or a natural excavation. The executions were performed in a military manner, by squads, under orders.

A.: How were they transported to the place of execution?

O.: They were transported by lorry, always in small enough numbers to be shot straightaway. This was an attempt to reduce as much as possible the time delay between the moment when the victims knew what was going to happen to them and their actual execution.

A.: Was that your idea?

O.: Yes.

A.: And after they had been shot, what happened to the bodies?

O.: The bodies were buried in the anti-tank ditch or the excavation.

A.: How was it ascertained whether they were dead, if indeed this was checked?

O.: The head of the firing squad or the unit had orders to see to it and, if need be, to finish them off himself.

A.: Who was supposed to do that?

O.: The head of the unit or someone designated by him.

A.: In what position were the victims shot?

O.: Standing up or kneeling down. [. . .]

A.: Did this apply to your *Kommando* or to all the groups?

O.: These were the orders in my group. I don't know what they did in other groups.

A.: What did they do?

O.: Some *Kommando* leaders didn't carry out the liquidations in military fashion, but killed their victims with a shot to the back of the neck.

A.: Did you have any objections to this procedure?

O.: I was opposed to this procedure, yes.

A.: For what reasons?

O.: Because it was, for the victim as well as for the person carrying out the operation, a huge psychological burden to bear. [. . .]

A.: Were all the victims executed the same way?

O.: Until spring 1942, yes. After that, an order came from Himmler [stipulating] that women and children were in future to be executed in gas vans.

A.: Before that, how were women and children executed?

O.: The same way as the men: they were shot [. . .].[186]

Ohlendorf thus defined the practices implemented by *Einsatzgruppe* D as a veritable procedure for managing the transgressive nature of murderous violence. The militarization of the shootings implied the physical distancing of the victim from the executioner; it also implied the collectivization of the act of violence, for which no individual could be rendered responsible. It fed into the fiction by which genocide was a military act – part of the total war that Nazi Germany was waging against the world of its enemies.

This long eyewitness account, however, provided evidence of other strategies for managing genocidal violence, especially that constituted by the development of gas vans. These can quite easily be seen as a mere 'technical innovation', based on a functionalism that analysed the mechanisms of genocide from a productivist point of view. Ohlendorf's evidence presents its use more as a way of 'sparing' men, with the most transgressive acts being delegated either to protagonists from outside the groups, or – as in the case of the gas vans – to more impersonal means of killing.

The groups very soon started to rely on native auxiliary units to carry out the shootings. This policy, visible in the four *Kommandos*, cannot be attributed merely to the desire to spare the killers any psychological stress. The case of Sk 4a is illuminating: it used local militias, a practice that flew in the face of that of the other *Kommandos*. At Babi Yar, according to one of the most direct eyewitness accounts communicated by German justice,[187] local militias were entrusted with conveying the victims to the spot, guarding them, undressing them, and taking them to the ravine. After that, the cooperation between Germans in the Sk and Ukrainian militia took the opposite form – one that was in line with the practices of other *Kommandos* – and the Germans delegated the onerous task of shooting women and children to *Schutzmannschaften*, the Ukrainian and Belorussian militias that were incorporated into the ORPO.[188] The example of Babi Yar thus reveals the inexperience of the Sk in dividing out tasks and their weakness in logistics. In the following operations, the Germans grasped the advantages they could draw from this collaboration, and modified the organization of the killings. We observe this mechanism, which consisted in leaving the native militias to kill women and children, in Ek 3,[189] Sk 1b[190] and 7a,[191] Ek 2,[192] 5[193] and 6,[194] and the *Kommandos* of *Einsatzgruppe* D.[195] Here too, the practice was not general, but depended on the initiative of each unit's leader.

This room for manoeuvre also partly determined the way in which the men viewed their cadres. The SS officers appointed to head the units made certain choices in procedure and thus established a relationship with their subordinates. Blume, Ohlendorf and some other *Kommando* leaders opted to set up less demanding procedures for their men. Other unit heads seem to have ignored this aspect, and did nothing to manage the psychological dimension of the *Osteinsatz*. This was true of Erich Ehrlinger and Albert Rapp. Both men, who came from the SD, decreed the execution should be carried out by a shot fired point-blank into the back of the neck, often by one individual, with the officer present limiting his role to inspecting the ground and finishing off the wounded. If we are to believe the witnesses – who were thus largely shrugging off their own penal responsibilities – Rapp and Ehrlinger allowed the officers supervising the troops no room for manoeuvre. The officers were chosen on a basis which struck the men as quite random: and the only measure still aimed at managing violence was the fact that each man was obliged to take part at least once in the shootings. In addition, Ehrlinger was very satisfied by the presence of a gas van in his jurisdiction, and seemed quite unaware of the specific experience of this type of action. Both men, finally, were described by witnesses as very strict superiors, whose relation with their men was marked by severity and disdain.[196] In their *Kommandos*, violence was not managed with as much care as it was in *Einsatzgruppe* D, and the relations between the men and their leaders were clearly affected.

The description of executions in the two *Kommandos* – in which mentions of alcoholism and gambling for money occur very frequently[197] – invariably repeat the same basic pattern: the execution was carried out with a bullet in the neck, at point-blank range, by gunmen acting without orders, in a violence close to anomie. So is it surprising that, during their trials, the two men were rebuked for their excessive rigour and the fact that they forced their men to do more than was required by the competent authorities, in other words, in this case, the BdS or the HSSPF? While witnesses attributed the attitude of the two men to a mixture of opportunism and fanaticism,[198] this lack of solidarity on the part of the troops was doubtless mainly due to the failure on their officers' part to take into account the psychological burdens of the *Osteinsatz*.

A comparison from within the Sk 7a itself provides us with an additional clue. The evidence of Claus Hueser already quoted shows Walter Blume's revulsion at the violence deployed and the extremely codified nature of the executions that he established. He was thus described as humane, sensitive and kindly. His successor, Albert Rapp, took not the slightest interest in how the executions were carried out. Worse, while he depended very largely on Russian auxiliaries for the logistical dimension of the massacres, the gunmen he selected were never Russians,[199] but always Germans from his *Kommando*. He was even criticized for giving them no respite. Even if this criticism may have referred to their being constantly sent off on missions against the partisans, such remarks may surely have expressed, between the lines, resentment at his indifference to what the men in his *Kommando* felt about their task. While it seems impossible to come to a firm conclusion, Walter Blume's evidence on the period just after his *Osteinsatz* gives some idea. Under questioning about his successor, he described his return to Berlin in these terms:

> When I left the *Kommando*, I told my men that I would pick them up, and I told them they could always turn to me. That's why, when I came back to the RSHA, I received a series of visits from members of the *Kommando*, requesting to be transferred from the *Kommando*. They complained at the form the shootings now took, with women and children being included. The overall situation was presented to me in such a way that it was easy to understand why they wanted to leave the *Kommando*. One of them complained loudly about the head of the unit, namely Rapp. [He said that] what they were being made to do involved a psychological burden that made too many demands on their strength.[200]

This statement, though illuminating, was surely dictated by a strategy of defence.[201] However, the same men were indubitably describing two leaders whose consent to genocide is not in doubt: it is simply that one of them was carrying out his 'duty' by expressing the psychological difficulties it generated, and tried to smooth over them by codifying the actions, while the other refused to allow the men's revulsion due expression, and was, in the eyes of his men, an example of fanaticism and opportunism. Fanaticism and opportunism – those veils which evade definition and cast a pall of unreality over everything – thus became, for a long time, tools that were ceaselessly deployed in the analysis of genocidal violence, tools which outlined a radical otherness, an otherness that was reassuring in the eyes of the murderers – and, perhaps, in our eyes too.

Violence as rite of initiation

The violence of elimination carried out by the mobile extermination groups seems to have been a cultural construction that emerged from the aseptic imaginings we have been following in the discourse of SS intellectuals.

As we come to the end of our study of the practices of murder, two salient facts deserve to be emphasized. In the first place, the definition of the violence of elimination is normative. It results from the desire to subject the practices of violence to the imperatives developed by the hierarchy. But the directives issued to regulate the shootings were not always effectively followed on the ground. All the groups, for example, were instructed to finish off victims who were not killed outright, in cases where they were not shot point-blank in the neck. But we know that a significant number of these victims did not die from the shots. The Soviet commissions of inquiry into Nazi crimes started exhuming burial grounds in summer 1943. Having on this occasion performed autopsies on the victims, they established that some of them had still been breathing when they were interred, and that others had been simply buried alive,[202] information which comes as no surprise given the reluctance of the officers to finish them off. More surprising, no doubt, is the fact that some victims survived the shooting,[203] which is evidence that the command to kill everyone was not always respected by the murderers. Furthermore, on several occasions, the norms ritualizing the executions, which seemed so powerful in *Einsatzgruppe* D, did not resist the increasing brutalization of behaviour: some autopsies revealed that the practice of shooting into the nape of the neck, so severely condemned by the *Kommando* leader, was nonetheless used on a massive scale,[204] and ill-treatment preceding the execution was much more common than Ohlendorf was prepared to admit.[205] This shows that some officers in charge of the supervision of the killings tried in vain to impose norms on mass murder. This is not, however, the main area of uncertainty left by the documentation. In their evidence, the gunmen overwhelmingly express their sense of sorrow and transgression. These feelings, corroborated by other sources, seem not to have been questioned. And yet the same archives, contemporary with the acts perpetrated, show that several protagonists wallowed in the cruelty and pleasure of killing, and gave expression to these emotions. Indeed, acts of cruelty are notably less common in eyewitness accounts given after the event. The case mentioned by a man from *Einsatzgruppe* D, in which gunmen threw an old woman down a well and stood there laughing as they listened to the victim's cries until they died out, is extremely unusual.[206] Just as infrequent is any mention of acts of extraordinary brutality carried out by the men of Ek 8 (infants thrown against walls, for example),[207] or by the men of Ek 5 (entire families who had hidden in the eaves of blocks of flats were hurled from the rooftops).[208] These few cases, so rarely mentioned by the gunmen, but more often by surviving Russian and Jewish witnesses, appear only here and there in the inquiries. And yet everything indicates that cruelty, bloodlust and the sheer pleasure of killing were ubiquitous. However, in 1941, the Nazis tabooed these practices, and no archive enables us to gauge their extent with any precision. The fact remains that the most frequent types of direct encounter with violence seem to be outlined with some precision in the description of acts, the perception and experience of their implementation, and the social dynamics underlying them. Consent, anxiety, sorrow, revulsion, hatred and intense pleasure thus mingled together in the words and deeds of the *Osteinsatz*.

Such was the experience of the men who 'travelled to the east'. As we have said, the SS intellectuals who took part lost what had set them apart from other cadres in the RSHA and the SD. Abandoning their work in theoretical formulation, they joined the police and the Waffen SS who constituted the groups. It was indeed this state of affairs that has led us to examine sources that, however representative they may have been of their *Osteinsatz*, seemed not to concern them specifically, even if their names cropped up constantly, men such as Martin Sandberger, Erich Ehrlinger, Walter Blume and Otto Ohlendorf. It is time, now that the main characteristics of this experience have been explored in detail, to return to these figures.

SS intellectuals did indeed play a crucial role in the discursive practice of the legitimation of genocide, justifying – even within the *Kommandos* themselves – each new step in the rituals of genocide, and providing the perpetrators with doctrinal justifications. As supervisory officers, they were also a decisive factor in the organization and codification of the practices of violence, conceiving and developing the techniques of extermination, managing the transgressive nature of violence, and legitimating the acts of genocide. Finally, as a result of their very presence in the *Kommandos* and their involvement in the actions of murder, they were right at the heart of a total confrontation with genocidal violence.

One need refer only to the case of Fritz Valjavec, originally a professor of history at the University of Vienna, a specialist in modern

history, especially of the Enlightenment in Austria and the phenomenon known as Josephism. This *SS-Hauptsturmführer*, a promoter of
Volkstumswissenschaften, joined *Einsatzgruppe* D as an interpreter and,
perhaps, as an expert organizer in relations with *volksdeutsch* activists.[209]
He experienced his first execution in Czernowitz, a town in which he
commanded a firing squad and finished off half a dozen victims with his
service weapon.[210] Finally, there was the case of Bruno Müller, the young
SD lawyer who had already been with the *Kommandos* in Poland, and
who, on the night of 6 August 1941, used his revolver to kill a woman and
her child in front of his assembled *Kommando*, as a way of announcing that
women and children were now to be included in the massacres.[211]

It is, however, clear that this confrontation with the violence being
unleashed in the east varied widely from individual to individual. The
same applies to the careers of SS intellectuals when faced with the experience of the *Osteinsatz*. The first type of career was that of the men who
were confronted with the experience of paroxysmal violence for the
longest. They included Erich Ehrlinger, Martin Sandberger and Albert
Rapp, and also Hermann Behrends, even though he did not serve his
Osteinsatz in the *Kommandos* of the SIPO and the SD. This was also the case
with Paul Zapp, the intellectual of RSHA *Amt* I. These men had all spent
several years in the *Osteinsatz*. They often served with several units – Sk
1b, KdS and BdS Kiev, BdS Minsk in the case of Ehrlinger, Sk 11b and KdS
Crimea in that of Paul Zapp,[212] the *Das Reich* regiment in Ukraine, 13th
SS division of the Panzer Handschar in Yugoslavia, then HSSPF Serbia
in the case of Behrends.[213] And sometimes, this *Osteinsatz* represented
only a part of their service on the fronts outside the Reich.[214] This was
true of Sandberger, who moved from KdS Estonia to BdS in Italy after a
brief second period in *Amt* VI of the RSHA.[215] These men, in fact, seem to
have specialized in executive functions. Only rarely did they now carry
out any work in appraisement and intelligence, as had been their role in
the RSHA. Though they were confronted with violence for a long period,
they were apparently not affected by it. They never attempted to obtain
leave, and never pleaded family or health difficulties as a way of prolong-
ing their holidays in Germany. In their case, consent to violence seems
to have been enough for them to stay in the east without any apparent
problems. The case of Albert Rapp, however, shows that the difficulties
of coping with genocidal violence, difficulties that remained unexpressed
except in the form of an alcoholism that finally incurred punishment,[216]
had nothing to do with any flinching in their consent. Rapp is generally
mentioned in the evidence as an ambitious man, driven by firm Nazi convictions – a man who carried out his mission as completely as possible.[217]

We find some meteoric careers in this group. The example of Otto
Ohlendorf is very illuminating: the head of the SD *Inland*, urgently
transferred to the head of *Einsatzgruppe* D. which had just been formed
in response to the planned extension of the front at the end of May
1941, remained at the head of his group for a full year.[218] The reason for

his being sent to the east has been debated by historians. Raul Hilberg explains his transfer in these terms:

> Heydrich was a man who did not like subordinates with divided loyalties. Ohlendorf was too independent. Heydrich wanted no one who functioned in an honorary capacity. The 'executive measures' to be taken in Russia required complete and undivided attention. Thus it came about that the intellectual Otto Ohlendorf found himself in command of *Einsatzgruppe* D.[219]

Transfer to special extermination units was, for Hilberg – here following Ohlendorf's statements at his trial[220] – a way of punishing him by keeping him at a distance. This is quite probable for subaltern officers, as is shown by the case of Marcel Wutsch. As a young SS *Untersturmführer* in RSHA *Amt* I, he was the subject of a certain number of unfavourable reports even when he was recruited in 1939; he was then, as a disciplinary measure, transferred to the *Einsatzgruppen* in 1942, to Białystok, where he took part in mass executions.[221] The case of *Gruppenführer* Bruno Streckenbach, Werner Best's successor as head of RSHA *Amt* I, sent to Poland to direct the extermination of the Polish elites in 1940, makes it problematic to generalize Hilbert's interpretation.[222] Can this appointment be seen as punishment when it came with a promotion? With regard to Ohlendorf, Norbert Frei suggests a completely different interpretation. Referring to work by Ludolf Herbst[223] and Heinz Boberach,[224] he states that Ohlendorf had 'unambiguously confirmed'

> [t]hose basic ideological convictions [. . .] in the first year of the Russian campaign as head of Action Group D. With his involvement in the crimes committed in the East, Ohlendorf had proved himself to be a dyed-in-the-wool Nazi, 'worthy' of a high-ranking position in a post-war system controlled by the SS.[225]

A militant right from the start, Ohlendorf hardly needed to prove his ideological orthodoxy, and his status as an *alter Kämpfer* (old fighter) was recognized without demur.[226] So what he did prove in the east was not the quality of his militancy, but rather his psychological ability to become physically involved in the killings. For the SS, what was happening in the east was obviously not a mass crime, but rather a 'repellent task',[227] which, however repellent, still had to be completed. By taking part in the massacres at the head of *Einsatzgruppe* D, Ohlendorf proved that he was able to 'get over' any revulsion he felt at this task.

In the light of the example of Ohlendorf, it seems that participation in genocide in the *Einsatzgruppen* acted as a rite of initiation. The SS viewed Ohlendorf as a man capable of assuming the highest offices in postwar Germany because he was able to take on – thanks to his Nazi ideological training – and above all to complete the task of exterminating the Jews in southern Ukraine and Crimea. As a rite of initiation,[228] genocide enabled those who successfully 'underwent' it to prove not only that they had fully internalized Nazi beliefs, but that they would be able to fill the highest posts after the war, in a victorious Third Reich finally purified of the blood of its enemies.

The protagonists of a second group, by far the most numerous, also spent their time in the *Osteinsatz* 'successfully' – in the view of the Nazis. But the crucial difference from the men of the previous group lay in the fact that they were not in post in the east for a prolonged period. Franz Six, for example, remained in the *Osteinsatz* for three months;[229] Eugen Steimle stayed in the east for just two periods of a few months each.[230] As for Walter Blume, he stayed for just two full months at the head of Sk 7a.[231] The same was true of Fritz Valjavec, who seems to have been with *Einsatzgruppe* D only until the winter of 1941, and also of Heinz Rennau, who succeeded Albert Rapp in 1943 and stayed in post for less than six months. The behaviour of this second group of men is typified by Eugen Steimle, a historian of the NSStB, an associate of Gustav Adolf Scheel, who took part in the scientific legitimation of the revision of the treaties that ended the First World War, and was one of the leaders of the SD in Stuttgart.[232] He stated that he had volunteered to fight on the front and had been given orders to proceed to Belorussia. He was here sent to Arthur Nebe, the head of *Einsatzgruppe* B, who appointed him to succeed Walter Blume. After three months in the *Osteinsatz*, he went on leave at home with his family in Stuttgart and, with the help of a doctor, managed to obtain certificates attesting that he was ill – with a raging toothache, apparently – that stopped him returning to his post. He was then again sent to Ukraine, where he was head of Sk 4a between August 1942 and December 1943.[233] On his return to Berlin, Steimle never attempted to conceal his revulsion for the *Osteinsatz*. It is true that he had tried to get out of it, but he does not seem to have faced any major difficulties in adapting to it. While some members of his *Kommando* depicted him as an arrogant and 'delicate' man, none of them mentions any difficulty on his part in carrying out genocidal violence. Like the men in the first group, Steimle eventually 'succeeded' in his *Osteinsatz* and was given a note-worthy promotion on his return, to the rank of *SS-Standartenführer*, and appointed head of department in the RSHA *Amt* VI.[234] So his 'initiation' in the east was effective, even though rapid, and carried out with an intense and self-proclaimed distaste.

The men of a third group were those for whom the signs of a failure to adapt to the conditions of the *Osteinsatz* with all its violence can be discerned. Certain officers in SS groups did not manage to 'get over' the revulsion that seems to have been so general. The cases of Hans Joachim Beyer and Alfred Filbert can be seen as illustrative of this situation, but they also show that it is difficult to come to a firm conclusion on this subject.

Beyer, a historian with a chair at the University of Posen, and a collaborator of Sandberger and Steimle in Stuttgart, joined the *Kommandos* who arrived on 30 June at Lemberg Sk 4a, the headquarters of the group and Ek 5. According to Karl-Heinz Roth, he then served as an expert advisor in interethnic relations – particularly vexed in Galicia – and thus inspired the policy carried through by Rasch, the group leader, which consisted in channelling the riots and inciting the Ukrainian demonstrators to attack the Jewish quarters in the town. Beyer's *Osteinsatz*, was, however, interrupted a few weeks later by a digestive disorder, apparently hepatitis, which meant he could quickly return to Germany.[235] Beyer's medical file has not been consulted, so it has not been possible to come to a conclusion as to the authenticity of this illness. However, this hepatitis seems relatively suspect: it is not in the least comparable with the digestive pathologies observed among soldiers on the Eastern Front. We also know, from other cases, that functional problems of a psychosomatic nature were perfectly easy to identify for SS doctors, who tended to prescribe that the men suffering from them should go on leave.[236] Beyer's long convalescence – over two months – suggests that his symptoms were quite real while not allowing us to draw any conclusions as to their cause, whether infectious or psychosomatic.

Alfred Filbert's case is clearer. This Rhineland lawyer and young SD officer, present at Pretzsch from April 1941 and particularly close, at that time, to Heydrich, volunteered to go east.[237] He was appointed to the head of Ek 9 and, among other responsibilities, took over the task of exterminating the Jewish communities in Vilnius.[238] He remained at the head of his *Kommando* for only four months, however. He was sent back to Berlin because of nervous problems and severe depression. He was not present on RSHA charts for nearly two years, and reappeared there only at the end of 1943, brought back by his former head of *Kommando*, Arthur Nebe, who placed him in a central bureau of the criminal police with the task of fighting corruption.[239] This was, however, just a subaltern post, as if the 'confession of weakness' in 1941 now barred him from any prestigious career. The case of Filbert clearly shows that consent to murder was not enough to protect you from a nervous breakdown. The cadres of the group, indeed, were perfectly well aware of this. Thus Martin Sandberger, the head of *Sonderkommando* 1a, was forced to ponder the suicide of the head of his unit's SD.[240] He launched a brief but careful investigation into the causes, and took very seriously the possibility that confrontation with violence could lead to psychological collapse.[241]

These cases are few and far between, but they do show that, in spite of the internalization of Nazi beliefs among these men, their resistance to paroxysmal violence could not be taken for granted. Perhaps it is the very shape assumed by this internalization which sheds most light on the attitudes of SS intellectuals. If all, or almost all, of them had to go through the ordeal of the *Osteinsatz*, this was perhaps because those officer intellectuals whose work had hitherto consisted in developing the rhetorics of legitimation were the most able to express and transmit representations that, in their view, gave meaning to the act of extermination. Thus they were in a position to spread legitimating discourses and practices designed to lessen the shock of extreme violence, discourses and practices that – when reappropriated by the rank and file and combined with the process of habituation to violence – created and finally preserved intact the consent of all of them to genocide.

Chapter 10

SS intellectuals confronting defeat

From 1941 to 1945, the war followed a course whose outlines are well known. After a first phase of eighteen months distinguished by apparently dazzling successes, the capitulation of the Sixth Army, encircled at Stalingrad, coincided with the beginning of a relatively balanced stage in which the German troops retreated in good order, in a moderate but regular fashion, with the fronts becoming stabilized. This second phase, which lasted from the beginning of 1943 to the summer of 1944, was followed by the very rapid liberation of the USSR, the result of the collapse of the Centre armies in May 1944. Then it was the turn of Poland, the liberation of which, in January 1945, came just before the invasion of Germany, which began in March of that year.[1] On the level of events, the major phases of this chronology are uncontroversial. However, the first phase, that of German success, has been analysed in a remarkably different variety of ways by certain historians. Christian Gerlach, for instance, suggests that the Soviet counter-offensive of December 1941 ended any hopes of a short war in the east, and sparked off a profound crisis in the German command,[2] a logistical and psychological crisis in the course of which the policy of genocide was adopted. Christopher Browning, however, sets out a chronology based on the existence of a feeling of euphoria that overcame the government elites in the summer and autumn of 1941.[3] These differences of opinion – they are quite real, even though the two authors are not describing the same period – emphasize that, over and above a chronology whose transparency is something of a retrospective illusion, the analyses of representations of the outcome of the conflict had a considerable impact on Nazi activities. The same applies, of course, to the activities of SS intellectuals. From 1943 to 1945, the anticipation of a Nazi military defeat that seems to us – perhaps rather too hastily – to have been inevitable was subjected to a huge labour of mental reworking on their part. When faced with the increasingly frequent and serious reverses suffered by the Axis, they developed a specific analytical grid – one that came only very belatedly to the possibility of the Third Reich being defeated.

Defeat rendered unreal

The transaction between an initial belief in a thousand-year Reich and the actual facts announcing the meltdown of the Nazi empire, which became more than probable after 1944, determined the intensity of the reactions generated by the military collapse of autumn 1944 and the prospect of Reich territory being invaded. However, only three months after the surprise invasion of Soviet territory, representations of a quick German victory had come up against the stubborn resistance of the Red Army troops. Nazi representations, based essentially on racial determinism yoked with representations of the previous conflict (especially the Russian collapse in 1917), distilled an image of the Slav as inferior – someone who, although savage and barbaric, would be easy to beat. Amid a profoundly anxiety-inducing discourse, the leaflets distributed by the Wehrmacht claimed, after all, that the 'weapons accustomed to victory' of the German soldiers would 'wipe out' the Soviet enemy, while at the same time warning the same soldiers that this enemy would use every means at his disposal – including the most repellent – to kill them. The same text which distilled such terrifying representations of the Russians partly attributed their behaviour to the fact that the Red Army 'knew that it was facing certain annihilation'.[4] Anxiety and contempt thus coexisted in the same discourse. However, from the winter of 1941, the Germans discovered on the ground that the expected collapse had not occurred. At a date that it is difficult to specify exactly, RSHA intellectuals thus focused on the factors that might explain why it had not happened.[5] The reason was apparently to be sought in the 'fanaticism' of the Red Army soldiers, who were resisting the German advance to the bitter end. One report, which comprises a particularly clear illustration of the way Nazi racial determinism was brought into play, is one of the earliest pieces of evidence of this transaction effected by SS intellectuals between the initial imperial hopes and the reality of the strategic situation:

> During the period of hostilities with the USSR, we have constantly experienced the fact that the Russian soldier has fought up to the last moment, even though he must have realized that all resistance was vain and futile. The realization has thus spread that the political commissars have succeeded in instilling their soldiers with a truly panic fear of their German adversary. In any case, however, their fear of the Russian commissar is just as great.
>
> It is with this double fear at his back that the Soviet soldier goes into battle. The brutishness and insensitivity of the Soviets also explain their terrible losses. However, it is very superficial to try and explain [this resistance] by fear. It presupposes that the Soviet soldier blindly believes the ridiculously transparent statements of his superiors, and that at the same time he bows down before their gaze and their pistols. He [the Soviet soldier] is incapable of any personal opinion, since he is ignorant and not educated, imbued with

lies from his youth, rendered incapable of the slightest self-worth by unimaginable poverty and distress. Since there is practically no intelligentsia left [. . .], they [Soviet soldiers] form an amorphous mass.[6]

The image of the Russian army here seems rather paradoxical: it is simultaneously an amorphous mass incapable of thinking, and a fanatical troop, ready to sacrifice itself even if the sacrifice is in vain. Thus, Russian resistance was due – it was claimed – to the very great malleability of the masses. However, the report also indicates that it would be simplistic to explain everything by national characters: if the Russian Communists have managed to inspire the troops defending Soviet territory with such a will to resist, this is also because they have a very highly organized administration that alone can establish and maintain control over the inhabitants.[7]

The image of enemy resistance, as we can see, was not exempt from a sense of superiority. The fact remains that the idea of an easy success and a definite annihilation of the Red Army had just been dealt a first blow. While describing Nazi victory as inevitable, the report projected it into a much less immediate future than the first RSHA memorandums had done.[8]

Reports on opinion among the populations of the unoccupied USSR, however, continued at the same time to distil the image of a population whose morale was deeply undermined, swinging between hope and despair, and living in anxiety, discontent and hunger. In these conditions, this population could not fail to collapse and, as in 1917, end up imposing capitulation on Russia.[9] However, underneath the contradictory image of Russian public opinion contained in these reports, some indications of growing disquiet on the part of their authors could be read between the lines. A report dated 12 March 1943 notes the authorization given by Chiang Kai-shek to Stalin to recruit from the Chinese population fresh troops to form a barrier against the German forces.[10] The first volunteers, it claimed, had already appeared at the front, and the first transports of Chinese workers were heading to the Russian industrial basins. In tandem with this, the men of the SD described the fluctuating morale of the elites in the occupied territories and their dismay at the success of the Red Army. This shows that the SD were fully aware of the impact that developments in the war could have on people's opinions.

The theme of the alleged barbarity of the Russians was ubiquitous in the discourse of SS intellectuals, and gave the latter an opportunity to emphasize the Asian dimension of the Russians' 'personality':[11] the gunmen were always 'Mongols',[12] and their connection with Asia was endlessly underscored. One report on the Red Army, probably drawn up jointly by RSHA *Ämter* IV and VI, is the clearest example of this interpretative grid: racial determinism is systematically deployed, with the authors discerning the effect of race on the granting of promotions in the army. In their view, these promotions favoured Asians, Caucasians and Jews, to the detriment of 'Russian nationals'.[13] So the forces of the Red Army were comprised of vast swarms of Asiatics, which put up with terrible losses, sure as they were of their demographic supremacy, and brutalized by 'Bolshevik education'. They were barbarians who would not hesitate to commit any cruelty. The descriptions of atrocities depended on a particular chronology. As we have seen, they were particularly frequent at the time of the attack in 1941 and until autumn of the same year. In the following months, they seem to have been much rarer. From the beginning of 1943, they again became frequent in the documents issued by the security organizations. In other terms, dispatches of this kind became less common during the period of German success on the Eastern Front, and reappeared after Stalingrad, as the Russian armies advanced, posing a threat to German positions.[14] Perhaps this phenomenon reflected, over and above the influence of various rumours – which were, at least as far as 'germ warfare attacks' are concerned, unfounded – an increasing anxiety in the face of forces that seemed to be inexhaustible and, even more, were gaining in effectiveness as the German troops started to feel increasingly worn down. These documents were meant for restricted circles of readers, and were quite different from the mass communication set up by the Ministry of Propaganda. Indeed, the RSHA was soon being criticized for them, and in summer 1943 Goebbels suspended the circulation of the regular reports which the SD *Inland* distributed among the Party and government authorities of the Reich.[15]

In autumn 1944, once Soviet troops were in Poland, the RSHA again published reports on the state of opinion in that country. It tried to define a new political line to be followed towards the Polish communities; a line that, in the words of the RFSS, was to be 'strict but proper'. It described the wait-and-see opinion among the Poles, and the growing anxieties of the *volksdeutsch* milieus.[16] Nowhere, however, was the term 'defeat' used. While the SS ferreted out any sign of defeatism, and the Germans thought that victory was also a matter of moral mobilization, SS intellectuals refused, right up to the final months of the war, to call events by their proper name. This process of derealization, however, was only apparent: descriptions of the Russians, in constant tension with realities on the ground, had successively designated them as shapeless barbarians, then as barbarians resisting stubbornly, and finally as attacking multitudes. The SS simply could not envisage them 'flooding in' across the territory of the Reich.

The turnaround in the war situation was left unexpressed by the men of the Security Service of the SS, in spite of the tangible signs of what was happening. At the beginning of 1944, the RSHA found itself obliged to transfer some of its departments out of Berlin, to try and preserve them from Allied bombardments. *Amt* VII, the department of research and documentation that was now largely marginalized, reduced to managing the archives, had to organize its own move to Brandenburg, with the archives being sent into Saxony.[17] Rudolf Levin, one of the historians in the SD, was among the contingent of SS intellectuals who left for Schlesiersee. Throughout his stay, he exchanged letters with Günther Franz, professor of history at the *Reichsuniversität* of Strasbourg. These letters sometimes hint at the growing pressure of the Allies: in April 1944, Levin wrote to Franz that he had been obliged to travel to Munich to attend the burial of a department officer killed during an air raid.[18] The two men frequently mentioned family problems[19] or the bombing of houses. However, even after December 1943 and the Soviet reconquest of most of the territories occupied by the Germans in Ukraine and Crimea, most of the letters focused on Franz's scholarly supervision of Levin's *Habilitation* thesis.[20] As signs of the approach of the Russians and Americans became more frequent, the two men continued imperturbably to discuss their scholarly plans.[21] This was not because they were unaware of the total irrelevance of their work: it was just the choice they made.

From summer 1944, however, events speeded up with the collapse of the Centre group of armies, which led to the capture of over 200,000 men by the Red Army, which could now reconquer most of Belorussia. In just under six months, the local bureaus of the SIPO/SD in all the territories occupied in the USSR again became mobile, and beat a retreat. The German reverses thus started to be included in the organization charts of the RSHA. The new head of *Amt* I, Erich Ehrlinger, set up a procedure making it possible for the police units to retreat in good order. This procedure, which has left no traces in the archives, is known to us only through the evidence of Otto Ohlendorf, who gave a quick overview of its characteristics: the units were to retreat while 'securing' the channels of communication that the troops were to use.[22] BdS and KdS were travelling back the same way they had come in 1941.

One last example will demonstrate the undeniable existence of the harbingers of German defeat: that of Hermann Behrends. The former head of SD *Inland*, active throughout the war in the policy of Germanizing the occupied territories, later involved in the combat units on the Eastern Front and Yugoslavia, was appointed deputy to the supreme chief of police and the SS for Serbia and Montenegro in March 1944. Behrends replaced him in August 1944.[23] In this position, he was among the most powerful dignitaries of the Black Order. He had been appointed both because of his experience of the Balkan context and for his expertise in the fight against partisans, a fight that he directed from within a division of Albanian and Bosnian SS that ravaged the regions of Bihac and Tuzla. When he was officially appointed HSSPF in Serbia, the Eastern Front was giving way throughout its length. The situation in Serbia was extremely tense: Soviet troops were approaching and Communist partisans had liberated entire regions, forming autonomous zones over which the Germans no longer had any control. Indeed, the balance of forces was sufficiently compromised for underground fighters to launch major offensives throughout the winter, liberating Belgrade before the arrival

of the Red Army. The list of promotions won by Behrends provides us
with a sort of X-ray of the German retreat: appointed HSSPF Serbia at the
beginning of the capture of Belgrade by the partisans, Behrends, while
remaining HSSPF Serbia, was given a special proxy power and was sent
to France at the end of summer 1944, to Hungary at the end of November,
and to the Baltic States in December of the same year.[24] The reason for
his successive missions was never specified. It appears, however, that
he was sent to coordinate the evacuation of *Volksdeutsche*. Initially made
responsible for organizing expansion, he thus found himself with the
problem of preserving German 'racial heritage' in the face of the invasion.
At the very end of the Third Reich, the submersion of Germanic identity,
a source of old anxieties for the SS practitioners of Germanization, thus
became a possibility and indeed a reality. Thus defeat was daily reflected
in Behrends' activity. In his campaign to evacuate and save his charges,
he deployed such frenzied energy that the personnel department of the
RSHA itself found it difficult to keep in touch with him, and was not
even sure of the precise nature of his functions. The fact remains that he
became the man Himmler could trust when it came to evacuating ethnic
Germans.

Behrends, however, seems never to have shown the least sign of dis-
couragement. In a letter of good wishes sent to *Gruppenführer* von Herff,
head of SS personnel, Behrends was still expressing the idea that 1945
would be the 'decisive year', thanks to the 'miracle weapons' that would
soon be coming into service.[25] In the winter of 1944–5, while he himself
was organizing the panic-stricken retreat, and could not have failed to be
aware of the way significant swathes of *volksdeutsch* communities were
being abandoned behind him, Behrends was still, if we are to believe his
letter, confident of the outcome of the struggle – as was a great proportion of the German population.[26] We can of course still see this as an
artificial formulation, aimed for example at warding off any reproach for
defeatism,[27] as was so common in that period. This case of psychological
resistance to the evidence was not, however, an isolated one. Among the
SS intellectuals, it was embodied in collective behaviours. Indeed, everything suggests that, right up until the final months of the conflict, they set
in place mechanisms to make defeat seem unreal – in the activity of the
RSHA bureaus, and especially that of RSHA *Amt* VII.

Apparently, the bureaus of RSHA *Amt* VII, established in Schlesiersee as
we have said, acted up to the end of the Third Reich as if everything was
more or less fine. Paul Dittel's men continued to produce memorandums
on the attitude of the Vatican, on Freemasons' lodges or on the question
of 'humanism and fascism'.[28] From September to November 1944, the
intellectuals of *Amt* VII in particular exchanged a considerable number
of letters on the management of the departmental archives. These letters,
however, have nothing to do with the safeguarding of the archives in
the face of the Soviet advance, which was starting to have an impact on

Poland: instead, they concern the problem of how to classify the holdings. This task was entrusted to a nephew of Himmler.[29]

All the same, these men could perfectly well have had a grip on current realities. They published brochures on 'The Jewish question',[30] and even if they were politically marginalized they were among the best-informed men of the Reich. Heinz Ballensiefen, for example, had stayed in Budapest during the wave of deportations of Hungarian Jews organized by the RSHA in May–June 1944, and had even denounced the attempt carried out by Spanish diplomats to save a few Jewish children in the consulate.[31] One month previously, he had delivered a lecture to the RSHA *Rassenreferenten*.[32]

The work directed by the ex-head of department, now in the *Auswärtiges Amt* but still in very close contact with his former subordinates, illustrates the growing distortion between these men's behaviour and the realities of war. Franz Six continued to publish regularly until 1945. His works were mainly devoted to political science, and aimed to legitimize Nazi pretensions to *Imperium*: they discussed what Six called the 'process of European unification', studied 'Russia as a part of Europe' and proclaimed the 'unitary awareness' of a continent that was emerging as a world power.[33] In spite of a tone that remained obstinately confident in the victory of the Reich between 1941 and 1945, his last article betrayed some hints of his awareness that the situation had completely changed: he no longer adopted a martial accent or spoke of 'empire' but instead of a 'community of destiny of Europe', as if the author, in his presentiment of defeat, wanted to assure himself of an inevitable European unification by seeing this as independent of the vicissitudes of 'human history'.[34] Another sign of his blindness can be seen in his reaction to the discovery of the collection of skeletons of Jewish prisoners in the cellar of the University of Strasbourg in October 1944.[35] Six had the idea of setting up a commission formed of members of neutral countries to investigate, both in German territory and in the regions liberated by the Americans, the veracity of what the Germans essayed to portray as *Greuelpropaganda* (propaganda of horror). Six resorted to a practice whose origins went back to the Great War[36] and proved completely irrelevant given the imminent German collapse.[37]

Since 1943, however, the number of RSHA personnel had been in constant decline as more and more SS were called up into combat units ordered to stop the Russian advance. A total of over 10,000 men were in this way taken out of Gestapo and SS departments, both by the Waffen SS and by the Wehrmacht's recruitment commissions.[38] The first departments to be targeted were those which could not claim to have any immediate strategic importance, and *Amt* VII appeared on this list. Even the highest dignitaries of the RSHA were not safe from this measure: for example, Heinz Jost, former head of SD *Ausland*, and now a plenipotentiary of the RMfdbO with the southern army group, a post which had no raison d'être since all the territories of Ukraine and Crimea had been liberated in July 1944, was sent to the front.[39] But, faced with the growing shadow of defeat, SD intellectuals adopted an attitude of derealization that they would abandon only very belatedly, in the last months or even the last days of the conflict. This attitude, after all, was shared by a great number of SS departments, especially the Personnel Department, which until the very last days of the fighting continued to hand out decorations and promotions. For instance, Albert Rapp was promoted to the rank of *Standartenführer* SS on 29 April 1945,[40] at a time when the department was itself practically in shreds and forced to move on a daily basis because of the presence of Allied troops in North Germany, a region where the last fighting units were concentrated as were the last administrative organizations of the dying Reich.[41] Defeat, the prospect of which had been avoided by every means since Stalingrad, had at this precise moment to be confronted, and the shock was all the more brutal in that, to the minds of SS intellectuals, the disappearance of the Nazi *Imperium* and the disappearance of the *Volksgemeinschaft* were inseparable.

Finis Germaniae: the return of the old anxiety

The signs of growing anxiety appear very gradually in the sources left by the RSHA. For example, the institutional documents only very belatedly mention the worries that SS intellectuals might have felt, long after the first indications of an adaptation in the activity of the departments. From January 1943, the departments in charge of the Germanization of occupied territories slowed down their activities.[42] Indeed, Himmler showed less interest in plans to resettle Slav populations, and sometimes took weeks to reply to the letters sent by Konrad Meyer-Heitling requesting more details about the final shape to be taken by the *Generalplan Ost*.[43] While other forms of economic planning moved into the forefront, they were less a way of realizing this utopian project than a planning out of the total mobilization of the economic apparatus. Indeed, after the capitulation of the Sixth Army, the Germans seem, if not to have abandoned the realization of a racial millennium, at least to have subscribed to the idea that this was subordinate to victory and the cessation of hostilities, and would be concomitant with a general reconstruction.[44]

At the end of 1943, at least three factors crystallized the anxieties of SS intellectuals. First of all, there was the publicity, made general from the autumn of 1943, about the mass murders committed in the east. It was accompanied by a growing disquiet about the fate of German soldiers who had fallen into the hands of the Russians – a situation which, since Stalingrad, was the subject of various reports. Finally, from summer 1944 onwards, the awareness of Allied plans for the treatment of Germany after the war instilled the fear that Germany would disappear as a state entity, linked to its elimination as a racio-biological entity. The existence of Germany – what Hoepner, the general in command of the Fourth

Panzer Army, in June 1941 called the *Daseinskampf* of the Third Reich – was at stake. The difficulty – the impossibility – of imagining that the collective disappearance of the community was imminent may explain the strategies of derealization – more or less unconscious, more or less voluntary – that the SS developed so belatedly over the course of the war.

After the fall of Stalingrad, *Ämter* IV and VI of the RSHA were intensely preoccupied by the fate that the Russians might mete out to the German prisoners of war. The question had, until then, remained anecdotal since it concerned only very restricted groups of soldiers, who were victims (in the eyes of the SS) of dreadful tortures and did not remain alive for long once they had fallen into the hands of the enemy. The evocation of a profoundly mutilating violence, dehumanizing the bodies of German soldiers, had been a constant factor in the description of the corpses of soldiers taken prisoner. But after 1943, there appeared the question of the treatment of prisoners of war as a mass phenomenon.

In October 1943, after several months of investigation involving the collection of evidence, the departments of RSHA *Amt* IV A3, directed by Kurt Lindow, wrote the first general report on the treatment of prisoners of war by the Soviets. It insisted on the harshness of the interrogations, the violence of the guards, the frequency of summary executions, the back-breaking forced labour, and the Soviet attempt to win over both the rank and file and the officers by propaganda.[45] The executions revealed themselves to be both the expression of the 'bestial hatred' the Soviets were deemed to harbour for the Germans, and the elimination of the subjects who were the most recalcitrant to attempts at ideological indoctrination. Another report sheds a very clear light on this double representation of Soviet violence. An escaped German officer related how, immediately after his capture, he had attended the execution of a hundred or so German prisoners of war: the meaning of this execution was linked to the first motivation ('bestial hatred'). He then attended the interrogation by a political commissar of three members of the Waffen SS. The commissar ended up asking the three men why they were fighting. At the reply 'for Hitler' given by one of the Waffen SS, the commissar took out his pistol and shot the three men in the abdomen.[46] This act again demonstrated, for the author of the report, the deliberate decision to eliminate three SS of 'heroic courage' as well as the simultaneous upwelling of rage and hatred on the part of the representative of Stalinist power. Finally, inflicting death by shooting the men in the stomach meant both causing a mortal wound and postponing the moment of death of the three SS by making them suffer as much as possible: this was, in the view of the Gestapo men, a characteristic act of cruelty.

The SS attempted to gather proofs of the sadism and inhumanity of the Soviets with the help of many photos of corpses which, constantly collected by the units, found their way up to the *Reichsführer* himself, as if the hierarchy needed to illustrate its panic belief in Soviet inhumanity.[47] At all events, both rank and file and officers who resisted Soviet propaganda were, in the eyes of the Gestapo and the SD, doomed tb an unenviable fate, either forced to work until they collapsed, or rapidly killed by the Red Army men.

The second way in which defeat was represented was probably the bringing to light of crimes committed in the east. It is known that, in autumn 1941, figures of the number of victims of the huge massacres committed in Kiev or Kamenets-Podolsk spread across Europe. Then, in autumn 1943, a certain number of eyewitness accounts and rumours started circulating in Europe on the extermination camps. The intellectuals of the RSHA used surveillance of the press to keep track of the propagation of the news in the Allied camp.[48] So, in September 1943, members of the RSHA knew that the attempted genocide was known to the Allies, if only thanks to the discovery of the mass graves by the Soviets, in South Ukraine and Crimea.[49] The desire of the Allies to put on trial those responsible for war 'atrocities' already seems to have been known to them. From the beginning of 1944, Hans Frank, the governor general of Poland, knew for example that he appeared on the list of war criminals who would be tried after an Allied victory. However, it seems very difficult to determine how far SS intellectuals were aware of the degree to which they were implicated. However much they knew this, as we shall see later, they all, or almost all, chose – as far as possible – to keep silent the fact that they had belonged to the repressive organizations of the Third Reich, and some decided to go underground.

In September 1944, Himmler received from RSHA *Amt* VI a detailed report on the Soviet proposals for the treatment of Germany after the war. This document, written by *Sturmbannführer* Dr Paeffgen and addressed directly by Schellenberg to Himmler, studied the modes of territorial partition of Germany.[50] He established that the agreements drawn up between the Allies in Tehran had been rendered obsolete by the unilateral intervention of Stalin, who demanded large swathes of German territory as far as the Elbe, thereby separating Berlin from the rest of western Germany. Stalin declared he was in favour of a joint occupation of the capital of the Reich, and had also stated that he would present Germany with his 'best calling card'. While the report indicated that Stalin had pledged that he would not permit the German population to be pillaged or mistreated, its author used a formula which clearly intimated that Stalin's words were not to be trusted. Stalin specified that 'only those in charge of the Nazi regime and their deputies would be coldly wiped out [*auf kaltem Weg ausgemerzt*]'.[51] The documents in the appendix also emphasized the Russian desire to eliminate 'German capitalism', and used maps to show the partition of the Reich into zones of occupation.[52] While this plan corresponded in large part to the fate which Germany did indeed suffer after the defeat, we need, if we are to understand the way it was received by the Nazis, to put ourselves back in their context of memory: reference to the partitioning of Germany was one of the favourite themes of German activists between the wars, and also appeared in the discourse that legitimized war in the east.

Engel and Paeffgen may have been using the same terminology and drawing on the same historical allusions, but they were speaking in radically different circumstances. In 1942, the Wehrmacht, even when forced to retreat from Moscow, occupied nearly half of European Russia. Some soldiers on leave from *Einsatzgruppe* B were given orders to return with Moscow as their destination, and in the eyes of the Nazis victory seemed within grasp. Thirty months later, the Russians were in Poland, and besieging the Baltic States and East Prussia. If, between the wars, the theme of the partitioning of Germany had appeared the final objective of the 'world of enemies', the latter had never seemed so close as in 1945; never had the existence of Germany, as a territorial state, and perhaps as a nation, seemed so menaced. However, the report focused on proving that there were growing disagreements among the Allies, provoked by Stalin's imperialist appetite. For Paeffgen, faced with this plan for world-wide enslavement, the Allies could react only by declaring war on the Bolsheviks and forming an alliance with Germany. However, over the final few months, this terror at the prospect of collective disappearance welled up in a way that certain – rare – texts allow us to glimpse.[53]

Reports on opinion, as we know, had soon come to seem tendentious documents in the eyes of the hierarchy – so much so that the Ministry of Propaganda and the Chancellery had finally requested that they no longer be circulated. However, the SD continued to sound out the views of the population. Though it is difficult to distinguish between what came from the observation of the populace and what stemmed from the ideas and emotions of the intellectuals who wrote about them, it appears that in April 1945, these two points of view converged:

> The development of the military situation since the breakthrough of the Soviets from the bridgehead at Baranow to the Oder has burdened our *Volk* increasingly from day to day. Since then every individual sees him- or herself confronted with the naked question of life and death. [. . .] In this respect there are hardly any differences between the armed forces and civilians, Party and non-Party; those who lead and those who are led, between the milieu of ordinary folk and the educated, between workers and bourgeois, between town and country [. . .].
>
> The following basic facts stand out:
>
> [. . .] Since the invasion of the Soviets every national comrade knows that we stand before the greatest national disaster with the gravest consequences for every family and every individual. Without exception, the entire people is filled with an anxiety which becomes more oppressive with every passing day. With the evacuees and refugees from the East, the horror of the war has reached every town and village within the now narrower confines of the Reich. The air-raids have destroyed what had been a relatively normal

routine of daily life to such an extent that no single individual has remained unaffected. The population is suffering a great deal from the terror bombing. Contact between people has been extensively broken. Today, there are still tens of thousands of men at the Front who have no information about whether their relatives, their wives and children, are still alive and where they are. They do not know if they were slain long ago in the bombing or have been massacred by the Soviets. [. . .] There is a general trend that families and extended families are coming closer together; if the most extreme misfortune befalls Germany, people who belong together at least want to bear it together.

Here and there, no doubt, people desperately try to reassure themselves that perhaps, in the end, it will not be so bad. After all, a people of 80 million souls could not be wiped out to the last man, woman and child. The Soviets could not really turn against the workers and peasants, for they are needed in every state. In the West people listen attentively to everything which permeates through from the areas occupied by the English and the Americans. But behind all these so loudly expressed words of comfort lies a deep-seated fear and the wish that things should not go so far.

For the first time during this war the food question is becoming acutely noticeable. The hunger of the population is no longer assuaged by what they have. There are no longer adequate supplies of potatoes and bread. Women in the big cities are now having difficulty in getting food for their children. On top of all the misfortune comes the spectre of hunger. [. . .]

If defeatism is interpreted as superficially as has mostly been the case hitherto, since the Soviet offensive it has been a general phenomenon amongst the people. [. . .]

The most varied personal consequences are being drawn from the general hopelessness. A majority of the people have accustomed themselves to living just for today. They take advantage of every pleasure available. Any trivial excuse leads to the last bottle being drunk, originally kept for the victory party, for the end of the black-out, for the return of husband and son. Everywhere there is a great demand for poison, for pistols and other means of putting an end to one's life. Suicides from genuine despair at the inevitable catastrophe are the order of the day.[54]

Even if the next sentence goes on to say that people are trying to 'draw up plans to get away', anguish at the prospect of collective disappearance is here expressed in exemplary form, especially as the SS intellectuals must have subscribed to it absolutely. The author of the report, while writing that there were no more differences between classes or places, and that all Germans, convinced in their heart of hearts that a fragmented Germany was about to vanish as a state, were united in the same anguish, was doubtless expressing his own anguish too. It was the disappearance of the nation, 'extermination down to the last man, the last woman, the last child', that reveals the eschatological anguish of total disappearance. This anguish was exacerbated by the terror instilled by the raping of women. In fact, since the invasion of Poland and the need of the *volksdeutsch* and German populations to face the Soviet advance en masse, rumours concerning the systematic rape of women by the Soviets had been going round. Dispatches from the various KdS in Poland echoed these rumours,[55] and the stories of refugees fleeing from the territories undergoing invasion by the Russians helped to spread waves of panic. In fact, Soviet practice cannot be denied: while the figures vary from one author to another, all the evidence tends to indicate that nearly one out of three women was raped by Russian soldiers in the last months of the war, in Soviet zones of occupation. As convinced racial determinists, SS intellectuals deemed rape – especially if it led to pregnancy – to be a mortal blow to the racial substance itself.[56] The 'German essence', attacked by the disappearance of whole *Sippen* massacred by the Russians and by the sullying and bastardizing caused by rape, was thus doomed.

Finally, the author of the report discerned a veritable death wish in the population in this spring of 1945. Seeing suicide as a way out of the war could act as a psychological mechanism at work in the paroxysm of anguish that the last months of the war represented for the Germans.[57] To pursue the inquiry any further, however, means encountering great difficulties. How can we distinguish between suicides and violent deaths? How can we separate out, in the military losses, simple death in battle from the fact of getting oneself killed so as not to yield an inch of terrain? This latter practice was not really suicide strictly speaking, but it could be included in the series of acts that involved a voluntary death. Given the state of despair in which the German soldiers found themselves, this could not be a salvific sacrifice, to which the man performing it would give meaning because he would be helping to save his endangered country. It has, however, been established that over a third of the losses in battle in wartime Germany occurred in the final months of the conflict,[58] which seems to constitute evidence for the massive number of such phenomena of 'suicidal' resistance. If it had been a matter of the generalized massacre of a German army overcome by panic and succumbing to headlong flight, the Soviet losses would have dropped considerably. Far from it: the loss of life was still around 8,000 soldiers per day in the final months of the war, an even more significant number than during the first days of the conflict.[59] The German troops continued to inflict heavy losses on the Russians, even as they themselves were being torn to shreds where they stood. This is the only indication of behaviour dictated by the profound anguish sweeping through German society.

Likewise, the Russian invasion opened the door to suicidal practices in civil society. It is unfortunately impossible to gauge how common they were. One thing that appears beyond doubt, however, is that the Germans viewed the arrival of the Soviets as a deadly threat aimed at the physical existence of the German nation. In spring 1945 – this was doubtless one of the last consequences of Nazism – eschatological anxiety, the very same that had been born from the defeat of 1918, the very same that the Nazi belief system had taken over, re-emerged, as if multiplied tenfold by the internalization of racial determinism.

The denouement

How did SS intellectuals act and react to defeat – especially to its imminence? The question took the form, after 1945, of eighty individual destinies: confronted with the collapse of the Reich, institutions and groups of solidarity fell apart. Each reaction, each response was thus of an individual kind. However, these reactions were also a figure of the social structure, since they all fell within a typology of behaviour that needs to be analysed in collective terms.

It seems possible to distinguish between two attitudes. The first, by far the less common, was the pursuit of the struggle to the bitter end. In April–May 1945, this attitude took the form of participation in the *Werwolf* movement, an underground terrorist organization that tried to set up networks to keep the structures of the NSDAP and the SS going during the occupation in the west.[60] This logic of 'right to the bitter end' motivated the last destructive actions mounted by the SS and the Gestapo, notably those of the RSHA archives in the camp at Theresienstadt.[61] Certain SS cadres, finally, were involved in the last executions of condemned men and women judged to be too compromising to be left alive.[62]

In the winter of 1944, the schools of RSHA *Amt* VI had been transformed into sabotage schools, and *Sturmbannführer* Otto Skorzeny had been appointed to head a new department integrated with RSHA *Amt* VI, with a view to creating a guerrilla force operating behind the Russian and American lines. Some of the programmes for these schools have been found: they taught how to handle explosives, conduct interrogations and carry out guerrilla fighting.[63] The details of this programme had been drawn up by Martin Sandberger, who had taken part in negotiations with the soldiers of the *Abwehr*, an army intelligence organization that merged with the RSHA after the arrest of Canaris. The classes were combined with sessions of ideological instruction devised by certain SS intellectuals, including Professor Richard Frankenberg and Dr Wilfried Krallert.[64] The first, a professor of history in a superior technical school, had spent the whole war in the departments of Germanization of Hans Ehlich, while the second was involved in the networks of historians attempting to legitimize Nazism, where he had been a colleague of Sandberger, Steimle and the group of historians in Stuttgart. If the 'action' part of this instruction had fallen to Skorzeny, ideology had not lost its prerogative, since Schellenberg, Steimle and Sandberger still considered, as their millenarian dreams crumbled around them, that the SS man was first and foremost a political soldier.[65]

Thus the RSHA had laid plans for a possible continuation of the struggle by Nazi partisan movements. However, the *Werwolf* was not created under the aegis of the RSHA, but under that of an HSSPF, Hans Adolf Prutzmann, who, after having won his spurs by overseeing massacres in south Ukraine, had occupied the same post in East Prussia, a region that served as a laboratory for the *Werwolf* operation.[66] Prutzmann set up a 200-man headquarters, and tried to structure the movement around caches of weapons prepared in advance. One symptom of the kinship between the system inaugurated by RSHA *Amt* VI and the *Werwolf* movement is the way the organizational chart of its central department included two former pupils of the RSHA, Karl Tschierschky and Otto Skorzeny. The activities of the *Werwölfe* consisted in tracking down local cadres and officers who were inclined to collaborate with the occupiers. If, in the east, the *Werwölfe* were unable to carry out any very significant actions, thanks to the NKVD troops' expertise in the fight against partisans they did manage, between 1945 and 1946, to maintain a climate of insecurity that, despite the low impact of *Kommando* actions, hampered the occupiers.[67] More important, perhaps, was the fact that from November–December 1944 onwards, Prutzmann's department, together with the *Kriminaltechnisches Institut*, tried to develop plans for the mass poisoning of the occupying troops. In this way, about a hundred Russian and American soldiers were poisoned by carefully adulterated drinks.[68] The armed *Kommandos* of the *Werwolf* did not, however, survive for more than a few months after the war: in December 1945, most of them had been neutralized or had vanished. Ill-prepared for their task, and suffering themselves from demoralization, they did nonetheless continue, until at least 1947, to carry out propaganda activity, distributing leaflets inciting the Germans not to collaborate with the Allies and threatening young women who socialized with members of the forces of occupation. This activity soon fizzled out, however, when it met with little response from the population.

In the opinion of most observers, the *Werwolf* was a solution of despair.[69] No SS intellectual chose this solution: many, indeed, took stock of their military reverses and attempted to find a compromise solution that turned out to be illusory. They included Ohlendorf, Schellenberg, Ehlich and Rössner, all former members of the SD.

Schellenberg, probably at a very early date, tried to bring Himmler round to negotiating a separate peace with the western Allies. He convinced Himmler to start talks through the intermediary of Count Bernadotte, in the hope of obtaining a ceasefire in the west which would, in Schellenberg's view, make it possible for the German war effort to focus on the Russians. Himmler and Schellenberg hoped that the western powers would turn against the Russians, forming an alliance with the Germans against the 'Communist peril'.[70] This hope could already be seen, between the lines, in the report of Theodor Paeffgen, who tried to convince himself that the differences of opinion between the members of the opposite camp were growing worse, which would inevitably provoke war between them.[71]

This hope was shared by Hans Joachim Beyer, the professor of history who had moved to *Einsatzgruppe* C via the *Osteinsatz*, and who eventually became, in Prague, the *éminence grise* of the policy of intellectual and cultural Germanization implemented by the governor and *SS-Gruppenführer* Karl-Hermann Frank.[72] Beyer headed the *Reinhard-Heydrich-Stiftung*, a research centre that he created and named in honour of the head of the RSHA who had been assassinated by parachutists flown in from London. Beyer had written several articles on 'racial sociology' and set out the theories behind the Germanization of Bohemia. In 1945, he published his *Habilitation* thesis on processes of dissemination in Central Europe,[73] and he produced articles calling for a European civil war in defence of 'western European culture'. In the final days of the war, Beyer was still attempting to gather a delegation of entrepreneurs and politicians who, from Prague, were to march off to Bavaria to offer the Americans a separate peace.[74] The fiction of the 'western crusade' against Bolshevism was in fact the last stage in adapting Nazi racial determinism to the reality of the facts. If Nordicity had not been able to win the war in the east by itself, it would be necessary, in the view of SS intellectuals, to form an alliance with Europeans from different 'racial stocks' to beat the Soviets. Up until then, they clung to the racial fundamentalism through which they interpreted the conflict. They could not grasp the alliance between Soviets and westerners as an enduring alliance, since for them it was a fool's bargain, and made no sense in racial terms. This was no doubt the last fiction created by the Nazi belief system.

Ohlendorf, who wished to preserve the populace, seems to have opted for a cessation of hostilities. He reached Flensburg, the residence of the Dönitz government, and in this ephemeral regime became Speer's deputy in the Ministry of the Economy. It is interesting to note that this included a great number of intellectuals – Hans Ehlich, the former deviser of the RSHA *Generalplan Ost*, Rolf-Heinz Höppner, head of the UWZ, Willy Seibert, Ohlendorf's former deputy in *Einsatzgruppe* D and head of RSHA *Amt* III D, his former subordinates Heinrich Malz, Hans Leetsch and Hans Rössner, the former assistant professor at Leipzig who was now head of the department of surveillance of written artistic production (RSHA *Amt* III C2). In the Ministry of the Interior, there was Wilhelm Stuckart, the friend of Werner Best, co-editor of the miscellany in honour of Himmler, and of the review *Reich, Volksordnung, Lebensraum*, as well as Erhard Mäding, one of Konrad Meyer-Heitling's collaborators in the RKFdV.[75] At the very end of the Reich, in fact, quite a number of SS intellectuals thus found themselves participating in the last government, gaining appointment to fleeting political posts whose only role, in the event, was to manage the liquidation of the Third Reich.

Not all the SS intellectuals present in Flensburg, however, entered the Dönitz government. There was actually nothing automatic about this appointment. It was dictated, in the eyes of Dönitz and his advisors, by criteria of technical competence as proven by experience in the state apparatus, and a 'level of compromise' deemed to be reasonable. In the view of the admiral's advisors, men such as Kaltenbrunner and Himmler, who embodied the SS order and the violence of the last months of the regime, had no place in the government. This 'level of compromise', however, was 'reasonable' only in appearance: thus, Herbert Backe, who had planned the deaths of millions of individuals on the Eastern Front, did not seem 'compromised' to them; Otto Ohlendorf, who had spent a year at the head of an *Einsatzgruppe*, was in their view an 'honourable' economics expert; Hans Ehlich, who had formulated the plan to eliminate over 22 million Slavs and Jews, also kept his job. This shows how subjective these appointments were. Other men present in Flensburg, such as Erich Ehrlinger and Albert Rapp, were not given any position and, like many other SS officers, went underground.[76]

SS intellectuals thus reflected the new situation in their behaviour – a situation in which they were now under the scrutiny of the victors who, from 1942 onwards, had made it part of their plans to carry out justice on behalf of the victims of Nazism. Nazi executioners and those who had defeated them took on board the new factors of guilt and judgement. And only a few SS intellectuals escaped coming before the de-Nazification commissions or the law courts that sat in judgement on the attitudes they had adopted under the Nazi regime. But this stage was preceded by a time of captivity.

SS intellectuals almost invariably spent time in internment camps. Some of them, having chosen not to reveal their identities, emerged from them quickly and, under an assumed name, resumed civilian activities. This was the case of Erich Ehrlinger and Albert Rapp, Alfred Filbert and Paul Zapp. We can draw on several examples to evoke those periods of underground existence which, in most cases, ended in arrest.[77]

Until April 1945, Franz Six stayed in post at the Ministry of Foreign Affairs, before leaving Berlin, accompanied by his former assistant at the University of Königsberg, Horst Mahnke. Mahnke was one of Six's faithful supporters: he had followed him into the RSHA *Amt* VII, in *Einsatzgruppe* B, and had then become his deputy in the *Auswärtiges Amt*, combining these functions with those of a lecturer at the DAWI, the faculty of sciences of foreign culture created by Six in 1940. The two men headed for Garmisch-Partenkirchen, and then to Salzburg, the fief of Gustav Adolf Scheel. Their paths then separated in Baden. Six got back in touch with his sister in the American zone, and found work with a peasant in Kassel, under a false name. He managed to hide out there until January 1946, when a former SS member working for the Americans managed to worm his address out of his sister. Just before, the 'geopolitician' Karl-Heinz Pfeffer, who had collaborated with Six on certain of his projects and had got him a job and a place to stay, had been arrested. Ten days later, it was

Horst Mahnke's turn.[78] Thus began Six's captivity: it eventually led him to stand trial at the American Military Tribunal at Nuremberg, as part of the ninth series of investigations which passed sentence on crimes committed by the *Einsatzgruppen* in the east.

Erich Ehrlinger had also stayed at his post as head of personnel in the RSHA until the first days of May. The last three months of his activity had consisted in carrying out increasingly unreal missions, then in trying to preserve the coherence of his department by moving it from Berlin to Flensburg. On the day Germany capitulated, he made contact with the leader of a battalion in the same village and, through him, procured military papers giving him a fake identity and a rank as an NCO in the Wehrmacht. He stayed with the unit until Whitsuntide, then gave himself up to a British centre for POWs. After a few weeks in captivity, he was liberated, worked for a while in a farm in Schleswig, then managed to make his way back down to his own area, Württemberg, and found work in the American aerodrome of Karlsruhe, a post which he kept until 1951. He then worked as a cashier and croupier at the casino of Constance.[79]

In February 1945, Erich Ehrlinger had sent his wife and six children away from Berlin, accompanying them to his father's home. He had taken advantage of this occasion to destroy compromising documents, including an album of photos of executions. Then, Ehrlinger disappeared without giving any news to his family apart from a letter sent in March 1945 that reached them only a year later. On 8 April, Ehrlinger did visit his family when he was contacting 'atomic scientists' to send them to Flensburg. He left some *Panzerfäuste* (bazookas) with his wife, telling her to use them as soon as she saw American tanks, before hiding with their six children.[80] Throughout 1945, the only news Anna Ehrlinger had of her husband came through the secret visits of the latter's driver, who came to collect personal effects for him and a change of linen. She found her husband only two years later: he was living under his assumed identity, married to his former secretary of BdS Minsk with whom he had just had a child. She and he decided that he could not come back to live with his family, but that he was duty-bound to help her out, by paying her a small sum of money every month: this he did until March 1952. By this date, Ehrlinger had resumed his real identity for a year, and was making a comfortable living. However, he decided to reduce the alimony he was paying his wife and children. So Anna Ehrlinger went to see a lawyer. Convinced that her husband had decided to emigrate, she denounced him to the police and started divorce proceedings.[81] The authorities, though alerted, still took nearly six years to have him arrested.

Not all SS intellectuals managed to conceal their identities for so long. Martin Sandberger, Eugen Steimle and Walter Blume, for example, also spent time in American or British internment camps. They were identified by organizations investigating Nazi crimes. They were kept prisoner and brought before the American court at Nuremberg in 1947–8. Erich Isselhorst was handed over to the French for crimes committed in June

1944, Herbert Strickner was sent to Poland, while Hermann Behrends, extradited by the Americans, arrived in Belgrade in 1947 to be judged by the Yugoslavs. Otto Ohlendorf, finally, was arrested in Flensburg after the capitulation and interrogated for several weeks. Interned at Nuremberg in March 1946, he later became one of the most important witnesses for the prosecution in several trials. It was he, among others, who at a session at the great Nuremberg trial gave crucial evidence on what the *Osteinsatz* had been: a war crime. And even if the notion of a crime against humanity was never applied in proceedings held in Germany against former SS intellectuals, so as to avoid the accusation of retroactivity, many of them were judged either by the occupying forces, or at the insistence of investigators of the *Zentrale Stelle der Landesjustizverwaltungen* of Ludwigsburg.

The few SS intellectuals who chose to resist to the death found it in combat[82] or, more prosaically, in the bombings[83] or in sordid ambushes.[84] Suicide took place on a huge scale among older Nazi dignitaries, *Gauleiter*, heads of SS and HSSPF departments, who had already fought in the Great War, but we find it hardly at all in this group.[85] Most of the individuals studied here tried to preserve at least some semblance of a future, individual or collective. Most evaded trial straight after the defeat and occupation. But from the middle of the 1950s, a new generation of young German prosecutors decided to systematize proceedings against crimes committed by the Nazis in the Second World War. It was during these two waves of trials that SS intellectuals came face to face with their judges.[86]

Chapter 11

SS intellectuals on trial

The trials which the SS intellectuals faced after the war cannot be considered monolithically. Their characteristics depended on the circumstances in which they took place, the distance from events, the judges' nationality, and, of course, the accusations brought against the defendants. These trials comprise a field of research in themselves, since many historians rightly consider that they were one of the ways deployed by western societies to 'manage'[1] the traumatic past constituted by the Nazi period, the war, the occupation and the mass murders.[2] However, they do enable us to understand some of the behaviour of SS intellectuals after the war. They form a space of utterance that proved to be decisive, especially for the discovery – among the public as among historians – of the events that had occurred in the east.[3] What emerges was the sole characteristic apparently shared by all the defendants: the need to manage their memories of war, personal memories made up of violence, activism, utopia and anguish. We will not examine all the de-Nazification trials and the sentences handed down for crimes committed in the east, but we can nonetheless draw up a typology of the behaviour of SS intellectuals when facing their judges – in other words, facing their own deeds and their own guilt.

Strategies of negation

As we have seen, Franz Six had taken part in the *Osteinsatz* at the head of the *Vorkommando* Moscow, i.e. a special battalion of *Einsatzgruppe* B charged with the task of occupying the official buildings and the Kremlin if the plan to capture Moscow quickly was realized. He stayed at the head of the unit for only two months, and the Tribunal found it very difficult to find documents proving that the small group of police comprising it had been involved in murderous activities. He did not follow the line of defence generally put forward by the accused, and stated that he had been apprised of criminal orders only after he had entered Russia. He irritated his American judges by coming out with long speeches and trying to pass off his work in the *Kommando* as a piece of scientific research. For instance, he presented the programmes of teaching and research of the *Deutsches Auslandswissenschaftliches Institut* as an attempted 'east–west rapprochement'. There followed some unreal dialogues between Six and the president of the Tribunal, a former naval commander, a spare-time dramatist, whose taste for the theatrical left its mark on the questioning and on the justifications he gave for the sentences he handed down. Witness the following exchange where, after maintaining that the *Kommando*'s main activity in Smolensk had been protecting churches from pillage, Six found himself facing the following question:

> Q[uestion]: You knew what the aims of the *Einsatzgruppen* were in those territories. Did you know what the Führer had ordered, yes or no?
>
> A[nswer]: As I said in my direct interrogation, I learned of this order of the Führer's through the appointment of cadres from other *Kommandos*.
>
> Q.: Yes . . . So we are meant to understand that, once you had arrived, you immediately changed the nature of things and, instead of taking the Jews to camps to execute them, instead of oppressing the populations, you bent your efforts to reopening the churches and granting the greatest religious and cultural freedom to the civil population?
>
> A.: No, Sir, I don't see any causal link in this statement. I don't see any causal coherence in the fact that, on the one hand, executions had to be carried out and on the other that the churches were reopened to the populations.
>
> Q.: You did that of your own will. You've given us a very interesting little chat about your activity, and you've told us that you hoisted the flag of religious freedom and kindled the flame of development of cultural life.
>
> A.: Yes.
>
> Q.: You gave us a whole speech about it ...
>
> A.: Yes, of course.
>
> Q.: I'm now asking you if, when you were at the front, you made any effort on behalf of religious liberty, for cultural change, for political liberty.
>
> A.: Sir, I now have to give you some more details about my positions with respect to the war in Russia and the question of the treatment of the Russian people by the German troops. [. . .] My political views were as follows: as Germans, our mission consisted in bringing political, religious and economic liberty through our administration. As I crossed the German border, I had the deeply-rooted conviction that this was the programme of the German Reich in the territories conquered in the East. One of the greatest disappointments of my life was the realization – and until the last few days this was through documents that had previously been hidden from me, as well as through conversations between Hitler, Göring and Rosenberg – that from the first day of my service, terror took the place of political administration.[4]

Such was the dialogue of the deaf between the former professor of the University of Berlin, head of *Kommando* in *Einsatzgruppe* B, and the

American judge. Six's defence strategies are, however, interesting. Later in the dialogue, he was asked for his opinion of the executions carried out by the groups during his presence. While Six condemned the execution of women and children, he held it 'legitimate' to execute 'Jewish men of an age to bear arms' because of their capacity 'to be potentially active in the fighting'. While Six's reply might be seen as incoherent, it was in fact simply reflecting his own experience of the *Osteinsatz*: he had left Russia on 20 August 1941, a date at which the executions of women and children were still unusual in the territory that had fallen to *Einsatzgruppe* B. And yet Six was fully aware of what had happened in the east. He had been one of the addressees of the daily reports of the *Einsatzgruppen* in Poland and, as head of *Amt* VII, of the *Ereignismeldungen* (reports on activities) from the USSR: here he would have been able to read of the execution of 33,371 Jews in Kiev, including the execution of women and children that was clearly mentioned in certain cases from September 1941 onwards. Even more compromising was the fact that, from July, Six was perfectly well informed of Nazi plans concerning the future administration of the conquered territories. As the man was, before the American judges, defending an administration that would have brought 'religious, economic and political liberty',[5] he had used quite different terms when speaking to one of the officers of the *Abwehr* in charge of the Centre army group in July 1941:

> The frontier must be pushed back to a line through Baku–Stalingrad–Moscow–Leningrad. A protective glacis should be erected in the East, a 'strip of scorched earth' [*Brandstreifen*] in which all life should be extinguished. So we want to decimate the thirty or so million people who live in this zone, starving them to death by removing any supplies from this huge territory. All those who take part in this operation are to be threatened with a death sentence if they give even so much as a crust of bread to any Russian. In addition, the biggest cities, from Leningrad to Moscow, are to be razed to the ground.[6]

Six knew this and consented to it, despite what he told the Tribunal. His line of defence did not, however, change, and was helped by the uncertainties that hovered round the mission of the Moscow *Kommando*. Six claimed that this was merely a scientific mission, and, indeed, one of the only proofs of the executions was a report mentioning that the staff of *Einsatzgruppe* and the *Vorkommando* had carried out 114 executions between 22 June and 20 August 1941 – at precisely the time that Six had been its head. However, two units shared the responsibility for the executions. This piece of evidence was not enough, in the view of the prosecution, to incriminate Franz Six: his system of defence still held up. In spite of his consent to crime, in spite of the very clear impression of duplicity which he as a character gave the judges, the latter were forced to admit that they could not 'scientifically prove' that Six had taken part in the murderous programme of the *Einsatzgruppe*. The accusation was dropped, and Six was sentenced only for having been 'an active participant in an organization that had committed acts of violence and crimes, as well as inhumane treatment of the civil population':[7] complicity in war crimes, so to speak. He was sentenced to twenty years in jail.

Six, however, was a special case. He was at once one of the most highly placed officials in the RSHA, and had experienced a very specific *Osteinsatz*. Few officers of his rank could allow themselves to put up such a bold line of defence. Many subaltern officers in the SD or the administrative organizations of the RSHA, conversely, drew on their original posting to suggest that they had not taken part in mass murders. This was the case with Karl Tschierschky, Sandberger's deputy in the EWZ and head of the SD in the BdS *Ostland* (*Einsatzgruppe* B). In spite of his claims, his successive postings lead us to conclude that he had wide experience of the struggle against the partisans: after all, he had been one of the main participants among the *Werwölfe*.[8] In the Baltic, anti-partisan fighting was inseparable from the extermination of the last Jewish communities.[9] But he could not be charged with any of this, and was never sentenced for any crimes, only for having belonged to a criminal organization.[10]

In the case of other *Kommandos*, the evidence was much more compromising. Walter Blume, head of *Sonderkommando* 7a in *Einsatzgruppe* B, could not boast that his work had been simply scientific. But his *Kommando* had played a relatively secondary role in the genocidal campaign of summer 1941, especially if we compare the figures for executions carried out by the group's *Kommandos*. Sk 7a had executed just under 1,000 people between the launching of the attack and 20 August 1941, while Ek 8 had already killed nearly 7,000 victims, and Ek 9 had shot 8,100.[11]

Arrested and sentenced at the ninth trial of Nazi war criminals by the American Tribunal at Nuremberg, Walter Blume set up a system of defence that was very close to that of the other defendants. He claimed that an order to exterminate the Jews in the USSR had been broadcast when the units had been assembled in May 1941.[12] He acknowledged that he had commanded the executions carried out by his *Kommando*, but denied that he had consented to the wish for complete extermination. Sentenced to death and then reprieved,[13] he bore witness on several occasions at the trials of war criminals who had played a role in the organization of the *Einsatzgruppen*. In particular, he was involved in the investigation of Bruno Streckenbach and even more that of Albert Rapp. During these many interrogations, Blume showed remarkable consistency in his statements. Clearly fabricating a story based on a lie, he managed to set in place a strategy that denied several of the crimes committed at his command. Thus he stated that he had originally been given the order to kill all the Jews in Russia, but presented himself as the head of a *Kommando* who was reluctant to carry this order out. In his telling of events, the executions in Vitebsk became the result of a telex from Nebe, who, reacting to the news that the Jews were now to wear a yellow star and be confined to ghettos, handed on to him the order to 'indicate new measures against the Jews'.[14] Basing his actions on the so-called 'extermination order' of Pretzsch, he also cleverly created the impression that he had refused to have women and children killed. This alleged extermination order, which might have implied premeditation on the part of the accused, allowed him to fabricate an image of the *Kommando* as less submissive than others to the Führer's orders. He maintained his version of the facts throughout the interrogations to which he was subjected during the 1950s and 1960s. Unlike many of his ex-colleagues, he did not backtrack on his statements on the broadcasting of the order to exterminate all the Jews on the eve of the conflict: instead, Blume covered Streckenbach, saying that he did not have the main role in transmitting this order. He conveniently shifted this responsibility onto Heydrich. The absence of any massacre of woman or children under his command became, thanks to this order, a 'tangible' sign of reluctance towards the policy of extermination, an idea reinforced by the many witnesses who emphasized his revulsion at shootings and the mercy he could show to his own men. This was a fiction that he constructed on the basis of the statements of other defendants, but its sole aim was to get him off the judicial hook. When Blume produced his statements in the 1960s, he was indeed safe from being accused, at least as head of a *Kommando* in Russia:[15] sentenced at Nuremberg, he could no longer be prosecuted for the deeds that he had been accused of there.

His strategy of denial, as we can see, was both skilful and opportunistic: he shifted responsibility for the worst crimes onto the dead, avoided falling into the trap of denying the evidence – at least that of his involvement in the policy of extermination – and made the most of the grey areas in his file. There is, indeed, no document that proves that Sk 7a executed women and children under his command. So he denied this action, even if the Tribunal which found Albert Rapp guilty did not rule out the presence of women and children at the massacre of Gorodok, in which Blume had participated.[16] Blume tried to squeeze his denials through the narrow space between the intimate convictions of the judges and clear proof of murder – for motives quite different from escaping being sentenced by the tribunals.

The example of the attitude of Hans Ehlich before the American tribunals may, despite the decisive difference of context, shed more light on the strategies developed by SS intellectuals in front of their judges. After all, the American trials represented a mortal danger for the accused: sentences were severe, and Nazi war criminals were frequently executed.[17] Hans Ehlich was one of those who had most to fear from the tribunals: he had been head of Department III B, the organization whose task it was to plan resettlements. However, he slipped through the net, and appeared only as a witness at the trial of the RuSHA and the VoMi.[18] His evidence comprises an excellent example of a strategy of denial, based on the shortcomings of an American accusation that had prepared its proceedings in haste and had only an imperfect grasp of German administrative machinery.

In the witness box, Hans Ehlich described his functions at the head of RSHA *Amt* IIIB.

> Q[uestion]: Why were you interested in the planning activities of the defendant Meyer-Heitling?
>
> A[nswer]: Because the planning activity of the staff [of the RKFdV] was connected with the general development of the occupied territories in the east, and these areas were closely correlated with the ethnic questions that concerned the SD.
>
> Q.: Witness, do you know the document called *Generalplan Ost*?
>
> A.: Yes, I remember the *Generalplan Ost* in outline.
>
> Q.: Was the *Generalplan Ost* a plan, or did it consist of two plans?
>
> A.: If my memory serves me right, the *Generalplan Ost* consisted in a short-term plan and a long-term plan.
>
> Q.: Can you explain this short-term plan and this long-term plan?
>
> A.: Yes. The immediate plan, if I remember right, included all the questions that were the closest in time, the questions of expulsion and resettlement in the occupied territories incorporated into the Reich. It was a plan for the most immediate future, very short-term, while the long-term plan was concerned with fundamental questions to do with the population of all the territories in the east, and colonization in that part of the world.
>
> Q.: To what extent was *Generalplan Ost* applied?
>
> A.: In my view, the *Generalplan Ost* was applied only as regards the short-term plan.
>
> Q.: Can you tell us in which territories the plan was applied?
>
> A.: This plan was applied only in the incorporated territories in the east.
>
> Q.: What is applied in the so-called General Government?
>
> A.: I believe that the colonization measures carried out in the General Government were not implemented in the *Generalplan Ost*, but as special measures.[19]

This first evidence, requested by the Court, was immediately followed by the interrogation conducted by Meyer-Heitling's lawyer. The lawyer and the former head of RSHA planning then indulged in a florid duet, their mutual understanding being so finely tuned that they could add details to Ehlich's statements whose main purpose was to lose the judges in the labyrinth of SS planning:

> Q. (Dr Behling, Meyer-Heitling's lawyer): I would like to ask the Tribunal to continue the interrogation for the defendant Meyer-Heitling [. . .]. Witness, did you know that the defendant worked as a professor at the University of Berlin?
>
> A.: Yes.

Q.: Could you confirm that these tasks with the general staff [of the RKFdV] were a second job for him?

A.: No I can't, as I don't know anything about it.

[. . .]

Q.: Witness, you went on to speak about the *Generalplan Ost*, and you said that you could remember it in outline. Can you tell us at what date the plan was organized or established?

A.: The *Generalplan Ost* was produced in 1940.

Q.: In 1940?

A.: Yes, 1940.

Q.: Do you know which department drew up the *Generalplan Ost*?

A.: The *Generaplan Ost*, in so far as it concerned the deportation and evacuation of foreigners, in other words, in this particular case, the Poles, was established by RSHA *Amt* IV, which dealt with other participants when general matters and the overall structure were affected by the expulsions. I'm not sure I can remember, but I think I can say that certain parts of *Generalplan Ost* were discussed with Dr Fähndrich.

Q.: Can you tell us, witness, whether, apart from the *Generalplan Ost* of 1940, there were any other *Generalpläne Ost*?

A.: I couldn't tell you whether there were other plans called *Generalplan*, but there was definitely a series of plans for colonization and others in the eastern territories.

Q.: Oh, definitely, I see . . . And were these other plans drawn up and developed by various other departments, or: who did draw them up?

A.: Well, other plans were developed, I believe that in most cases they focused on certain questions of theoretical planning for new areas of colonization of different states. I think most of these plans were drawn up by the general staff [of the RKFdV].

Q.: Witness, I would like to remind you that the general plan known to this Court as the *Generalplan Ost* was composed in 1942 and was established by the department of agronomy and agricultural policy of the University of Berlin. Is my question justified, if I ask you whether the *Generalplan Ost* of which you speak, dating from 1940, established by RSHA *Amt* IV, was identical to those general plans?

A.: No, that's quite impossible, for we're talking about two completely different things, Sir.

Q.: Oh, I see . . . Do you know the plan dating from 1942, witness?

A.: No.[20]

These two long extracts enable us to reconstruct in all its complexity the Nazi mode of defence, which was fact-based. Ehlich, who was one of the most eminent leaders of the SD, and was thus a fine connoisseur of the labyrinth of Nazi institutions, took particular care to make his descriptions as complex as possible.[21] In his direct interrogation, he began by undermining any knowledge his American prosecutors may have had of the *Generaplan Ost* by describing it as formed of a long-term and a short-term plan. He thus managed to cover the tracks that might have led to his own department, by cunningly confusing the *Generalplan Ost* created by the departments of Meyer-Heitling with the *Generalsiedlungsplan* created by his own department. This second document had indeed been preceded by a double plan – one set of short-term plans (*Nahpläne*)[22] and one set of long-term plans (*Fernpläne*).[23] By mixing up these two plans, that of the RKFdV and that of the RSHA, he was protecting his own department – RSHA *Amt* IIIB – while avoiding accusing Meyer-Heitling. He shifted responsibility onto RSHA *Amt* IV: the Gestapo. Here too, he was being careful to tiptoe round making any false statements, since *Amt* IV had taken part in developing the *Generalsiedlungsplan*, as many documents could show.[24]

As if this first labyrinth were not enough, he also shed doubt on the veracity of the 1942 document: he dated the *Generalplan Ost* to 1940, and made it impossible for it to be equated with the 1942 plan. He then dated the period of maximum activity in deportations to 1940, which made this movement more innocuous, since it then excluded sending people to concentration camps, which were not built until the autumn of 1941. After that, he merely had to describe the 1942 plan – attributed to Meyer-Heitling – as 'theoretical planning' concerning new zones of colonization, and separating this latter from any implementation on the ground. This meant he had achieved two aims: he avoided appearing on the list of those responsible for the plan, and he disconnected the question of planning from that of extermination.

Never, indeed, did it seem as if Ehlich had played a highly important role in the planning of the Germanization of the occupied territories; never was this occupation seen in connection with the extermination; never, finally, was the function of Konrad Meyer-Heitling as central coordinator of all the Reich's planning bodies brought to light. The Americans could not fail to be baffled by this evidence, which seemed to be given in all good faith, as Ehlich said he clearly recalled what the *Generalplan Ost* had involved. When he left the courtroom, the prosecution had not succeeded in identifying its key evidence and might even have started to doubt its reality. The interweaving of red herrings and exact factual data skilfully elaborated by Ehlich had achieved its purpose: Meyer-Heitling was sentenced to nothing more than a prison term covered by the time he had already served in custody, while Ehlich himself was not harassed by the Americans and was later summoned before a tribunal only to be summarily de-Nazified.[25]

Ehlich here showed an uncommon cunning. Each of his answers was a model of ambiguity, each fact could be retracted on the basis of a mistake, a lapse of memory, an error, or a lack of precision in the terms. Each mendacious statement (on the date of the plan, on his appointment) was based on factual data that were verifiable from the archives seized by the Americans. This case clearly shows one of the strategies of negation deployed by the former SS.

These strategies could take many forms. Few SS intellectuals had the opportunity to deny en bloc the deeds of which they stood accused, especially when – as in the trial of the *Einsatzgruppen* – the prosecution could draw on a set of documents that delineated the evolution of the murderous activities of the groups. SS intellectuals were mostly former legal experts, past masters in rhetoric, aided by highly experienced lawyers, and they could thus draw up an initial strategy to manage the legal threat facing them. This strategy met with quite general success.

Strategies of evasion

The strategies of evasion deployed by SS intellectuals were probably those which most clearly betrayed the extent of their awareness of the crimes committed by the Third Reich. Indeed, they deployed a great deal of energy to hide, cover up and disguise the activities of their bureaus, to diminish their own responsibility and to exonerate their colleagues. In so doing, they showed their profound familiarity with the Nazi system, their intimate acquaintance with genocidal activities, and their rhetorical expertise. A few examples will enable us to illustrate this tactic, which was probably the one most frequently used by SS intellectuals at their trials.

We have already seen the lengths to which Hans Ehlich went to ward off any danger of prosecution. Such ingenuity would have failed, however, if the evidence of other dignitaries of the Black Order had pointed to his level of responsibility. The most critical evidence in this respect might well have been that of his superior in the hierarchy, Otto Ohlendorf, who was in fact the official best informed of the activities of RSHA *Amt* III B, and doubtless one of those most aware of Ehlich's role in planning and applying policies of Germanization. Ehlich, as we have seen, slipped through the net woven by the American investigators. They had, in spite of everything, guessed at the importance of the group led by the former doctor and hygienist from Saxony. They tried to separate out the strands of the institutional connections prevailing in the Germanization of the occupied territories, and on this occasion focused on the role played by RSHA *Amt* III B. Several times, in October 1947, Ohlendorf was interrogated about the activities of RKFdV and *Amt* III B of the RSHA. The matter was broached during the interrogations on executions carried out by the *Einsatzgruppen*.[26] In both cases, Ohlendorf replied with self-assurance, pretending to guide them through the meanders of the Nazi polycracy. He demonstrated a highly surprising familiarity with the men and institutions of the Reich, recalling the names of subaltern officers whom he said he had met only very rarely. He then explained, with considerable confidence, the functioning of institutions that, like the RKfDV, must have been relatively unfamiliar to him. On the other hand, he betrayed surprising gaps in his knowledge of executive organizations such as the EWZ and the UWZ, which were, however, antennae placed directly under the aegis of *Ämter* III B and IV B4 of the RSHA, in other words under the supervision of Ehlich and Eichmann. These two institutions, as the reader will remember, had taken over the tasks of expulsions and resettlements. These were all strategies of evasion, through which Ohlendorf sought to cover the compromised position of certain of his subordinates. This was an attitude that he frequently adopted. In his own words, he was eager to assume responsibility for his own actions and duties, and thus for the deeds committed by subordinates placed under his direct orders.[27]

But in another interrogation, Ohlendorf did not limit himself to protecting Ehlich and his men. When the American investigators asked him to inform them about the activities of Meyer-Heitling's department and thus about the very author of the *Generalplan Ost*, Ohlendorf drew up a protective ploy of considerable subtlety: when they asked him whether he was familiar with the *Generalplan Ost*, he answered in the affirmative, then launched out into a very vague account of the critiques he had made of the draft plans for expenditure and investment, then paused for a considerable length of time while he pretended to assign a date to the plan. This led the interrogator to give a date himself: 1940. Ohlendorf then seized on this reply, which actually enabled him to skirt round the murderous dimensions of the 1942 and 1943 plans. He said that the plan had been hatched in the bureaus of Meyer-Heitling, but emphasized with some vigour that the plan had remained a dead letter in the occupied territories. He was, at this precise moment of the interrogation, lying: a letter from Ohlendorf has been found in which he congratulated his men on Himmler's and Heydrich's behalf for putting into practice the short-term plans.[28] It was a question of keeping at bay any threat that may have been hovering over his men, but also of protecting Meyer-Heitling.

The interests pursued by Ohlendorf were not simply dictated by the immediate needs of the defence: Meyer-Heitling could indeed accuse the men in his department, but he could probably not provide proof that would be sufficient to accuse Ehlich. This strategy of Ohlendorf's was of a quite different order from the mere protection of his subordinates or of ex-members of the SS less close to him. To his mind, focused on the defence strategies currently being employed at Nuremberg, the aim was still basically that of political justification: even apart from the personal guilt of the SS, the planning of massacres, famines and extermination by forced labour was part of the 'Nazi plot' and might become a major argument in the demonstration by the Allies of the Germans' murderous intentions. By covering Ehlich, by concealing the extermination that was part and parcel of the *Generalplan Ost* of 1942, Ohlendorf was attempting to counter any demonstration of German guilt. He was a child of the Great War: did he remember the debates on the question of war guilt that raged fiercely in the Weimar Republic? We do not have enough evidence to assess his memories in more detail, but, in an article on German representations current at the time of the Treaty of Versailles, Gerd Krumeich

has shown that this type of strategy was already governing discourse on
the role of the Reich in unleashing the Great War: the guilt of the Reich
concerning the depredations committed in the occupied territories could
not be denied, and it was all the more important to prove that Germany
had played no part in triggering the conflict.[29] If this harmony between
the two rhetorical strategies does not constitute proof that the two defeats
were being remembered and processed in similar ways, it is not entirely
out of the question that the SS general attempted to interpret the event in
the light of historical references at his disposal.[30] Apart from this system
of references, the silence of the former head of SD *Inland* on the policies
of famine shows the full ambiguity that could unite, in one and the same
strategy, both decisive confessions and a stubborn silence on other issues
deemed to be even more sensitive for the Nazis. This brings out a hierarchy of what could be confessed and what needed to remain unsaid. On
the other hand, there is a striking concordance between the fictions forged
by Ehlich and Ohlendorf. It seems likely that Ehlich heard Ohlendorf's
statements and that he was able to stay faithful to them during his own
hearing. This was the first time that statements between ex-Nazis could be
coordinated in this way, and the case of Werner Best shows that this form
of evading responsibilities lasted up to the phase of the trials set up in the
years 1950–60 in the German Federal Republic.

Werner Best did not take part in the most murderous phase of the RSHA's
existence. He left in 1940, following disagreements with Heydrich.
Appointed successively to posts in France and Denmark, he did, however,
retain his close contacts with the members of his original organization, the
Gestapo.[31] Sentenced to death in Denmark after the war, he was quickly
pardoned and freed. In the German Federal Republic, he pursued a
career in business. When the wave of trials against former leaders of the
Gestapo began, he coordinated the defence of Gestapo officials accused of
activities that might have involved genocide.[32]

   In 1963, the wave of investigations being undertaken by the regional
bureaus of prosecutors was at its height. The Berlin bureau then launched
a major inquiry into the activity of the RSHA. Led by a group of eleven
magistrates, this wide-ranging trial immediately involved a very large
number of witnesses and defendants. Two thousand people were heard
by the commission, and the investigation covered all aspects of the activity of the Berlin central bureaus. Werner Best, who had long experience
as advisor to defendants and their lawyers, presented defence arguments,
and played on the degree of awareness of the genocide on the part of the
men in the Gestapo and the SD. After long trying to fall back on the argument of the 'state of emergency' necessitating unconditional obedience
to orders (*Befehlsnotstand*), and adapting this in line with the prosecutors' questionings, Best helped to set up a unified defence strategy for
former Gestapo and SD officers. He thus elaborated a series of judicial
quibblings that comprised a strategy of guilt avoidance. However, these

evasions could not conceal the facts, which the prosecutors in Berlin and Ludwigsburg tracked down with great persistence. What Best was seeking to avoid was having particular acts described as 'murders': he wanted the charge to be reduced to that of 'complicity in murder', which would have meant the ex-SS men got off with very mild sentences.

Thus Best claimed that the cadres of the political police had merely provided 'institutional aid' to those responsible – the dignitaries of the RSHA who were dead or missing, Himmler, Heydrich, Kaltenbrunner, Müller and Eichmann: these alone had known that the populations being sent to the east were doomed to extermination. Once the Gestapo cadres had been designated as ignorant accomplices, the Gestapo cadres could hope that their punishment would be greatly mitigated.

In the overall framework of these trials, the prosecutors did not fail to raise the question of the role *he* had played, and ordered a search of his home. They found what Best called his 'secretarial appendix' which contained all the correspondence between the former number two of the RSHA and his former subordinates. This brought to light Best's role as intermediary and coordinator. For several years, Best had been advising the defence, drawing on his long experience of law to counter the arguments of the prosecutors, writing to his former subordinates to coordinate their statements. Thus he wrote to one ex-officer of the Berlin Gestapo about the charges brought against Otto Bovensiepen, who had served on his staff:

> It seems important to me in this affair that the greatest possible number of heads of bureau in the Gestapo can attest to the fact that, at that time, they knew nothing of the 'Final Solution'. If the case arises, could you also attest to this?[33]

He also wrote to Gustav Noßke, the former head of an *Einsatzkommando* in *Einsatzgruppe* D:

> It is in the general interest that the greatest possible number of witnesses who, at the same time, occupied the same positions and took the same measures, can state they knew nothing about the 'Final Solution' and believed that the Jews were being concentrated in an eastern reserve so as to be resettled at a later date.[34]

The replies obtained by Best lived up to his expectations. Former SS officers such as Kurt Christmann certified in writing that they had not been aware of the Final Solution until after the war.[35] Christmann himself, it is worth pointing out, was eventually investigated, and was sentenced in 1984.[36] Christmann, Best and most of the men concerned were lying: the German prosecutors succeeded in proving that one, at least, of the SS intellectuals had acted in full awareness of the fate awaiting the Jews in the east: Knochen, the former BdS France, was put on trial for perjury.[37]

Best had thus reactivated the networks of solidarity of the Gestapo to coordinate the defence.[38] However, even though he was identified and criticized as a very high-ranking dignitary who had kept his influence over his former subordinates, Best escaped sentencing; his state of health deteriorated in the 1970s until he was, in the view of certain experts, unfit to stand trial.

Coordinating the defence in this way was, of course, nothing new. At the Nuremberg Trial, the defendants had prepared common statements and tried to define a line of argument that would convince the American judges. Historians have emphasized the role of Otto Ohlendorf in the construction of this line of defence. At the trial of the *Einsatzgruppen*, the SS officer assumed leadership of the defendants, advising them in their statements and strengthening their defence. Ohlendorf's lawyer, Rudolf Aschenauer, would say at the trial of Bruno Streckenbach that 'the defendants had connived to present a general line of defence' at the instigation of his former client.[39] The main decisions taken by Ohlendorf and his fellow defendants had a decisive impact both on the trials of the years 1950 and 1960 and on the historiography of the extermination of Russian Jews by the *Einsatzgruppen*.[40] The line of argument devised by Ohlendorf followed a particular strategy: it was not a matter of arguing over the materiality of the facts, but over the responsibility of the cadres in the various units. The judges had in their possession their daily reports, and thus had a relatively precise idea of the extent of the massacres committed in the east by most of the defendants. So there was no way of denying their reality: it was a matter of trying to demonstrate that the defendants had received precise orders before their entry into Russia, and that they had not had any opportunity to deviate from them. The argument of unconditional obedience to orders as imposed by an emergency situation became an essential moment in the defence put forward by ex-Nazis.[41]

The coherence of the idea that there was a *Befehlsnotstand* implied an order of total extermination dating from before the invasion of 1941. It also implied that the group cadres could not disobey these orders. As well, these orders must have been formulated at the highest levels of the hierarchy of the Third Reich, and transmitted by the main leaders of the RSHA. At the Nuremberg Trial, Ohlendorf and his companions stated that the order for extermination given by Hitler had been passed on by Bruno Streckenbach, head of *Amt* I of the RSHA, at a meeting of the groups in Pretzsch a few days before the invasion.[42] Ohlendorf was here setting out a fiction that would have a long series of consequences. For example, the description of how orders were passed on raises many questions. The order for extermination, which Ohlendorf consistently identified as an 'order of the Führer's', was supposedly transmitted to the group leaders by Bruno Streckenbach. The designation of the latter by Ohlendorf seems to have been the result of a careful calculation on the part of the former head of SD *Inland*: he might have been afraid that certain of Heydrich's written orders – the operation orders or *Einsatzbefehle*[43] – might be in the hands of the American investigators, which would have enabled them to pinpoint inconsistencies in the words of the RSHA leader. There was the same danger in the case of Himmler, who was absent from Pretzsch. Thus there was only one personage of the greatest importance present at Pretzsch who did not threaten to come along and contradict Ohlendorf: Bruno Streckenbach was at the time on the list of the missing, and everything suggested that he had been killed on the Eastern Front in the final months of the war.[44] Saying that he had played the main role in transmitting the orders for extermination by depicting these as word-of-mouth orders meant that the contradiction between the thesis of an extermination ordered in advance and the orders given in writing by Heydrich during the campaign could be resolved. Second, attributing the guilt to a dead man relieved the survivors of their responsibility; finally, with the orders being expressed at the highest level of the hierarchy, the context of the exterminating discourse assumed the character of emergency (*Not*) that formed the heart of the argument. The *Befehlsnotstand*, a fictitious construction, thus became one of the keys to the analysis of the entire behaviour of those who had perpetrated genocide in the east. The way in which historians insist on the SS's duty of obedience – a duty which, they claim, must have originated from the *perinde ac cadaver* of the Jesuits[45] – is of course linked to the normative way Himmler hammered out such demands in his countless speeches.[46] On the other hand, the judges very quickly started challenging the lawyers of the detainees who had held positions of responsibility in the mobile units of extermination to produce a single example of an individual who had been punished for refusing to kill. They could never produce a single case, which had ruled this idea out by the end of the 1950s, at least for the officers and the heads of section.[47] As far as the rank and file were concerned, the thesis of the *Befehlsnotstand* remained an incantatory formula in a great number of interrogations,[48] one which judges took into account until 1954–5.

But it never brought the exculpation that had been hoped for. At the Nuremberg trial, there were very many death sentences handed down, a sign of the futility of this strategy of defence. Though only four of these death sentences were actually carried out, this was not due to any change of heart based on the *Befehlsnotstand*, but rather because of considerations of a political order linked to the establishment of new institutions in the Germany of 1949. The American High Commissioner McCloy was fully convinced of the guilt of the men he was pardoning; he was simply pandering to German public opinion that still had no idea of the extent of the crimes committed in the east by the cadres of the units.[49] The *Befehlsnotstand* was inefficacious on the judicial level, and did not act as the basis for any mitigation of the sentences passed on Nazi war criminals. Indeed, those sentenced to death who went to the scaffold at Nuremberg in 1951 included the very 'inventor' of this strategy of defence, Otto Ohlendorf, who had not simply distinguished himself from

the other defendants in the trial by elaborating this defence. He had actually tried, throughout this long period of juridical and penal handling of
the sequence of genocidal crimes, to devise a much more complex strategy than the mere negation of responsibility or the evasion of crimes.

Strategies of justification: the Ohlendorf case

Ohlendorf was one of the most important Nazi officials to be interrogated
by the investigators, and he provided the latter with valuable information. After all, he had been simultaneously one of the representatives
closest to Himmler in the Black Order, and also an eminent member of the
ministerial bureaucracy.

He had been interrogated on very many occasions, with the questions ranging from the role of the *Einsatzgruppen*[50] to the functioning of
the *Freundeskreis* Heinrich Himmler, or even the supposed role of the
RSHA *Amtschef* in the formation of the *Werwölfe*.[51] On all these subjects,
Ohlendorf held information of the highest importance in the eyes of his
American interrogators. He could hold forth on the personalities he had
known, on the division of tasks between institutions and on the internal
organization of the different offices, as well as on the general lines of
Nazi policy. So it was that Ohlendorf soon became indispensable to the
American investigators, who would sometimes question him for just a
few minutes to complete the information supplied by other ex-Nazis.
Ohlendorf never seemed reluctant to give information, and his evidence
often had an informal character. The vocabulary he used was more that of
the expert than that of a prisoner being questioned.

For Ohlendorf, it was probably a matter of *seeming* to say everything,
and thus in fact filtering the information that reached the American prosecutors. Once he had become one of the 'sources' enabling the American
investigators to verify the statements made, Ohlendorf could at his leisure
devise defence strategies to face down the accusations.

The care with which the former SD head denied that his department
had any part in the economic activities of the SS, a subject that had not
had much importance in the trial of the *Einsatzgruppen*, may seem surprising. Ohlendorf, the main defendant in the trial, made it a point of honour
to say, from his first statement onwards, that the SD had no powers in
economic matters, since it had been obliged to abandon its claims in this
domain to the WVHA, the department of Oswald Pohl.[52] Unable to grasp
what exactly Ohlendorf was endeavouring to protect here, the investigators limited themselves to describing one of the files which might be of
interest to the judges at Nuremberg: that of the administration of the concentration camps. In 1939–40, the WVHA had taken over these camps and
organized the details of the Final Solution at least in so far as it concerned
the economic exploitation of genocide – in other words, 'extermination
through labour'.[53] Ohlendorf, insisting on this transfer of power, probably

wanted to protect his own department from this damning evidence. His department *must* have collaborated in the establishment of this complex system. At the very least, it had coordinated the planning of resettlements with that of the flow of population into the concentration camps and the extermination camps.[54]

So Ohlendorf was trying to give a singularly aseptic image of his department: in his remarks, everything seemed to suggest that the SD had been in charge only of economic theory and ideological construction. The SD, in other words, was meant to be simply the eyes and ears of the Nazi government. To make such a claim was literally to conceal any function of persecution of opponents and assistance to the Gestapo assumed by the intelligence service. This was because Ohlendorf wished to disclose only a part of his personal activity to the judges. And in fact the way he depicted himself in his statements was quite idiosyncratic. The young SS general did not conceal his exceptionally precocious activism in the Nazi Party, but he turned it into a factor of marginalization. He indicated that he had tried to defend heterodox ideological positions within the hierarchy, and claimed that he had been penalized for this reason. Ohlendorf maintained that Himmler and Heydrich had plotted to send him to the east so as to 'destroy him psychologically'.[55] He thus decked himself out in the image of a doctrinaire idealist struggling within the most orthodox bodies to preserve the original ideology of National Socialism: an idealist whom Himmler and Heydrich had tried to drag back down to harsh reality by forcing him to take part in the policies of extermination in the east.

Apart from the factual defence represented by the *Befehlsnotstand* and the denial of his consent to the *Osteinsatz*, the SS general, however, adopted a very firm attitude in claiming responsibility for his own actions, acknowledging that he had ordered executions and stating that the murders committed by *Einsatzgruppe* D had been carried out under his command.

Ohlendorf was in a tricky position when he appeared at the trial of the *Einsatzgruppen*. He had been a privileged and compromising witness for the prosecution at the Grand Trial, then at the trials of I.G. Farben and the Wehrmacht, and might have thought that he had tacitly acquired the status of a 'Crown witness', which would have guaranteed him a certain indulgence from his American judges.[56] However, his rank, the importance of his responsibilities and the extent to which he was compromised also weighed against him. His role in the coordination of the defence of his fellow accused also designated him as the most eminent defendant in this trial.

When, on 13 February 1948, Ohlendorf made his final statement before sentencing, he was probably aware – as he had been since the start of the trial – that he was in grave danger. He was the first defendant to stand up and he was the only one who made a long statement, going into minute detail over the different elements of his defence.[57] For nearly an hour,

Ohlendorf started by shifting the debate outside the field of investigation of the Tribunal, focusing on different interpretations of Nazism. The tone of his address, indeed, clearly showed that he had moved beyond the factual defence he should have been formulating:[58] he spoke in his own name, but also in that of his fellow defendants and, at certain moments, he acted as the spokesman for his entire generation.

Ohlendorf structured his speech in several parts. In the first, he expressed the Nazi fervour with which he was imbued, and reformulated the utopian promise that had metamorphosed the eschatological anguish born of the Great War into an imperial hope. He pursued his defence by recalling what in his view constituted the moral heritage of human-ity, quoting the Greek and Roman philosophers, Buddhist wisdom, the Roman and Persian mystery religions and the 'great Protestant and Catholic impulses', and tried to demonstrate that the era that was coming to an end with the defeat of Nazism should not be judged on the basis of moral precepts from outside it.[59]

It was from this angle that he introduced what he considered to be the justification for his acts:

> Our most recent history is no different from other periods simply because a combat took place for moral principles and, as a consequence of certain historical conditions, for the survival of nations, even if the appearances seem to suggest otherwise, after a superficial examination. I consider myself to be one of those who have become aware of the contrast between these two forces in history. I have experienced this contradiction within myself and tried to find a solution. I have said and repeated that I was tormented by fear of the punishment which those who were in charge of Germany [. . .] seemed to be seeking through their words and actions. Their frank contempt for human life, their rudimentary idea of their own religion and of the people's moral conceptions meant that this fear grew within me. But today, my fear of the future punishment entailed by current events is greater still.
>
> I have now been in the Nuremberg law courts for two and a half years. What I have seen of the spiritual forces here has increased my fear. Human beings who, in normal conditions, were respectable citizens of their coun-tries have been deprived of their fundamental conception of law, of custom and of morality by the power of the victors. The fact that they have been deprived of a conception which, in the absence of a lost religion, gave a majority of human beings a moral and ethical support, and the fact that the life they led was justified by conceptions that are now being called criminal, have led them to abandon their human dignity, which they never should have done. While they awaited a verdict which, in reality, was already known, once the victorious power had condemned their conception of life, history has not come to a stop. In its consequences [. . .], history contradicted the courts even before they reached their verdicts.
>
> I am driven by the desire that the court will wish to go beyond the out-rageously simplified and generalized formulae of the postwar period, and

look at the events of that period from the point of view of the two forces that have always decided the flux of events. No nation is solely guilty, but ideas, and the weight of concrete circumstances during the struggle of nations for their survival and their future, reveal leaders who are able to unleash this pent-up tension. The concrete situation faced by nations shows that the tension that persists and grows each day arises long ago in the past, far from the German people and its intentions.

This is why I ask the court, in its deliberations, to take into consideration the fact that the defendants here present have been placed within a historical development that they did not cause and was independent of their will. They were the target of impulses that led them to act independently of their own life plans. They entered their units convinced that they were sustained and driven on by an authentic and true moral force. They thought that their work was necessary even if it went against their own tendencies and interests, because the existence of their people was facing a deadly threat. They were the same good citizens who are found in their millions in every country. They never conceived of any criminal activities or intentions. They had the feeling that they were being flung into a gigantic, inevitable and horrible war that would decide the survival of their nation, their family and themselves; not only that – they also saw themselves as the shield that could protect other nations against a common enemy. They were not in a position to judge the necessities and methods of this war. Any attitude would have come into contradiction with the administrative state that had been in force for centuries, as well as with the responsibilities of the most eminent leaders of the nations. They had to accept the orders and methods of this war, just as all soldiers of all countries had to do. [. . .] The passion of their moral existence included the metaphysical condition that the existence of their people must be protected.

I have never lost my faith in a God present in history and even if we cannot understand His ways, no situation will deprive me of the certainty that life and death in this world obey a reason and must be regarded in an 'affirmative' manner. At no moment in my life have I failed to compensate for the submerging forces of history with religious, moral and ethical principles, every time that life expected something from me. I have always regarded history as the realization of ideals of which human beings are simultaneously subjects and objects – ideals which nonetheless seem to point to something beyond them. I think that the court will take into account the events which threaten not just the existence of the German people, but comprise a threat for the whole world, with the aim of fully understanding the realities of history, in its ideological and material implications. The fact that the victorious power declares the German people to be guilty and has declared that the moral and ethical basis of its past was illegal, immoral and contrary to ethics has disconcerted the German people and cut it off from its roots, as much as the individuals who have been heard here as representatives of this people. Thus, this legal, ethical and moral suffering of the German people has become more intense than the material suffering that

threatens its physical existence. May the court's verdict take into account
the reality of historical evolution and give the Germans, individually and
collectively, the opportunity to realize themselves fully, lest they fall prey
to despair because their existence will have been brought to unfold outside
historical reality and their destiny will be based not on the firmness of law,
but on power and force.

If it please the court, I will not conclude this final statement without
expressing my gratitude for the very generous way in which you have
treated the problems that we have considered important in these debates.[60]

On the personal level, Ohlendorf's self-justification was essentially
spiritual. He reaffirmed his faith, and claimed in advance that no situation
would ever make him lose his beliefs. Did Ohlendorf mean his belief in
God or his adherence to Nazi racial determinism? The paragraphs leading
up to this statement do not mention belief in God, but he regrets that the
Tribunal and world opinion have condemned Nazism, and at the same
time expresses sorrow that his companions' system of beliefs has been
stigmatized. The vagueness of Ohlendorf's declarations enables him here
to reaffirm the strength of the two beliefs that he does hold.

Just as he was expressing his own thoughts in the name of all the
defendants, Ohlendorf really set out his strategy for the justification of
the activities which the groups had taken part in. He explained that the
cadres 'had entered their units convinced that they were sustained and
driven on by a moral force [. . .]. They thought that their work was necessary even if it went against their own tendencies and interests, because the
existence of their people was facing a deadly threat', and he continued in
these words: 'they had the feeling that they were being flung into a gigantic, inevitable and horrible war that would decide the survival of their
nation, their family and themselves; not only that – they also saw themselves as the shield that could protect other nations against a common
enemy.' What Ohlendorf meant by these words, almost literally so, was
an argument in favour of total war – an argument that had remained
unchanged after three years of captivity. If Ohlendorf remained, right to
the end, faithful to the genocidal policies implemented by *Einsatzgruppe*
D, if he covered for his subordinates and acknowledged that he himself
had ordered the executions, was this not precisely because the rhetorical
language that had played such an active role during the war was still, in
his view, valid? Choosing to affirm its legitimacy, in this context, implied
for Ohlendorf both that he had remained a Nazi and that he was still with
hindsight convinced of the necessity and inexorability of the genocide of
the Jews. This choice, however, came with an extremely heavy price: by
acknowledging and justifying the murders, Ohlendorf was being defiant,
'managing' his guilt by preserving the arguments that had enabled him to
be convinced of the 'correctness' of his task, but he was thus – as he was
inevitably aware – accepting that he would be sentenced to death by the
American Tribunal.[61]

Nonetheless, the SS general did not simply harbour the ambition of remaining loyal to the Nazi belief system, even if this cost him his life. In the final analysis, he was defending not his own cause, or that of the former cadres in the groups, but that of Germany as a whole. And he finished his statement by adjuring the judges not to condemn his entire country.

Ohlendorf, in short, was thinking about the future of Germany and the question of collective guilt. In particular, he was reflecting on the stigmatization of Germany as a criminal, warmongering people – a stigmatization that had been developed during the negotiations preceding the signing of the Treaty of Versailles, and was embodied in article 231 of the Treaty, to the intense resentment of the Germans.[62] Ohlendorf, whose first experiences as an activist had been in a postwar context marked by the demand for revision of the Treaty of Versailles, was haunted by the prospect of collective condemnation: in his eyes, it would prevent the Germans from 'self-realization' as a nation and would lead them to found their destiny 'not on the firmness of law, but on power and force'.

At the very same time that he was appearing in court to answer for his actions, Ohlendorf was still drawing on the intellectual arguments that had inspired his career as an activist. This was a quasi-suicidal strategy, but one that enabled this man to remain convinced that his actions had been well founded.[63]

This attitude, in which Ohlendorf could justify his actions with the help of Nazi beliefs to which he was still loyal, was extremely rare,[64] but it did give him the means of describing his criminal acts and thus disburdening himself of the weight of genocide. This may, on the face of it, appear doubtful in the case of Ohlendorf at his trial, but the examples of other men will provide evidence for this interpretation.

On 2 November 1962, a former member of the Waffen SS, Peter E., testified for the second time in the proceedings against Albert Rapp. After a brief recap of the biographical information, he stated:

I have correctly described what I knew [about *Einsatzgruppe* B before it was stationed in Smolensk] in my statement of 11 October 1962. For the following period, certain things are mixed up. There are some things that I didn't describe very well. It's only when I was questioned three weeks ago that a weight was lifted from me, a weight that had been burdening me since that time. Only during this questioning was I able to talk with my wife about it, and she told me that certain things in my behaviour after the war were now becoming understandable. I have always suffered from my experience with *Einsatzgruppe* B. But I've never been able to talk to anybody about it. None of my work comrades has any understanding of what happened at that time. They would have told me, 'with me they'd never have done such a thing'. I've always expected that something would happen because of what happened then, and that those responsible would pay for this whole dirty business.[65]

While Peter E. did not justify the crimes committed in the east, his evidence brought out one of the involuntary functions assumed by the Nuremberg Tribunals. Apart from the function of punishment assumed by the juridical authorities, certain war criminals saw it – many of them fleetingly, no doubt – as a space for them to express themselves and unburden themselves of the weight of silence, thus giving an almost cathartic function to the admissions they made in court. Hence, perhaps, the occasionally surprising confessions, the recounting of executions – even when these stories could be of no avail to the narrator and might well be dangerous for him.

There was, however, a fundamental difference between the former Waffen SS man and the SD general, Ohlendorf. The latter had chosen to acknowledge the crimes so as to preserve his Nazi beliefs and keep up the rhetoric of legitimation. Although Peter E. had been an SS activist before the *Machtergreifung*, he showed no internalization of Nazi beliefs. He tried to find relief by expressing the grave trauma caused by the extremity of the violence that had been inflicted. In both cases, it was surely a question of 'managing' the guilt linked to genocide, on the one hand by *denial*,[66] on the other by speech.

In 1948, Otto Ohlendorf was still in a position to confront the American court of justice with his own unchanged system of beliefs. The end of his statement, predicting famine, revolution and national dereliction, nonetheless betrayed his ignorance of the realities of postwar Germany.[67] Perhaps Ohlendorf was already part of a bygone world? What could he know of the frenzied activity of reconstruction that had swept across Germany between 1945 and 1948? What could he understand, from his jail in Landsberg, of the political renaissance of Germany – a Germany without an army, with its Christian Democratic government in the Rhineland and a federal system, prosperous and industrial, turned towards the west?

The words he uttered seemed to have emerged from a text written in 1918: they no longer had, and *could* no longer have, the same resonance in 1948. The Nazi belief system, which so clearly lay behind his words, could not resist the miraculous political and economic rebirth of the two Germanys. It was this rebirth, indeed, which once and for all invalidated the imaginings, suffused with eschatological panic, that had arisen from the ruins of the Second Reich in 1919 – imaginings that were both exacerbated and repressed by the victory of Nazism and that eventually resurfaced with renewed vigour in the final months of the Second World War.

The renewal of democracy brought about by the death of the Third Reich led, perhaps, to the stifling of the memory of that anguish. Perhaps this meant that Nazism – already, in 1945–9, a historical object – was not fully understood?[68]

Conclusion

Memory of war, activism and genocide

After the Nuremberg Trials and those of the immediate postwar period, there was a period of silence: the silence of the scaffold, for a dozen or so SS intellectuals; the silence of prison, for most of them; the silence of nostalgia[1] and, for some, that of a new activism.[2] The history of Nazism comes to a close with this epilogue: the past becomes something to be managed, and national identities that had suffered during the Second World War were restored.[3] This restoration was, in Germany, very much determined by a form of collective amnesia, not so much of Nazi crimes as of the imaginings that had preceded them. After the Adenauer years, the memory of Nazi crimes crystallized in a stop–start fashion, punctuated by trials that were followed by huge audiences. There were the trials in Ulm, the trial of Eichmann, the Auschwitz trials . . . all of which marked the various stages of a shift in mentality that, in the context of a profoundly democratized Germany, involved forgetting the culture that had presided over adoption by SS intellectuals of the Nazi world-view. Indeed, in the last trials of crimes committed in the east, some of the accused, far from expressing their experiences as Nazis, refused to do so, quoting the work of Hannah Arendt or of German historians.[4] The trials were an opportunity for society as a whole to develop its own interpretations of the 'German tragedy'. Accusers and accused, investigators and spectators, basically no longer knew anything about Nazism. Supporting democracy as they did, they had internalized the outlook of western societies whose cultural demobilization had been a fact of life for three decades. These were societies which, in order to express what they understood by the Nazi enemy so as to beat it, had been forced to develop a war culture that was radically different from that of 1914–18.

SS intellectuals had emerged from the middle classes. This was one of the main vectors of the system of representations that had presided over the great conflagration of 1914–18. This culture of war was transmitted from the front to the rear, from the upper and middle classes to the working classes, from adults to children, in a movement that affected European societies as a whole. It was characterized by specific representations that gave a meaning to the conflict and enabled civilians as well as combatants to consent to huge sacrifices. For contemporaries, this war was a war of civilization against barbarism. If the former won, the war would mark the advent of a new era, a great and divine transformation for Christians, an era of fraternity and social justice for those on the social-democratic left, and a crusade for all.[5] Imbued with millenarian hopes that transcended religious affiliation, war and its paroxysmal violence, as well as its privations, were justified, especially as a defeat would have meant a deadly threat hanging over the heads of the populace. What, indeed, would have been the value of life under the domination of an enemy whose vileness, lust for destruction and attacks on women and children were not in any doubt? This argument explained the conflict in essentially defensive terms, as a way of protecting the nation's vital functions. Presented this way, the issues at stake in the conflict were too important for societies to imagine that they could spare their children from it. This explains why German society – like the other belligerents – inflicted, at home and at school, a pedagogical discourse of conflict on its children.

After four years of this discourse, Germany lost the war. Defeat was no isolated trauma; it was followed by continuous violence. Between 1918 and 1923, Germany fell prey successively to revolutionary upheaval, both Communist and separatist, to localized conflicts provoked by clashes between Polish and German communities in Silesia and to putsches launched by an extreme right that had been transformed by the conflict. Its surface area shrunk by the treaties that brought the conflict to an end, stripped of much of its territory in the east but also on the German–Danish border, Germany saw the Rhineland occupied, the Saar and the Rhine placed under international control, its economic sovereignty questioned and its prosperity in hock to reparations. The Germans, first and foremost the schoolboys and students who would be the intellectuals of the SS, interpreted this series of events through the discourse of war that they had internalized over four years of conflict. Every external event was attributed to a 'world of enemies', every uprising was an episode in the plot hatched by Germany's enemies – a plot that aimed at its annihilation. The students of the years 1918–24, often too young to have fought, expressed this eschatological anxiety most clearly, and formed the bulk of the *Freikörper* and the many paramilitary formations which aimed to defend Germany and continue the vital combat of which the Great War had been the alarming precursor. In 1919, the student corporations shifted to the *völkisch* far right, and their successes at elections with mass participation left little doubt about the political positioning of the young elites of the Weimar Republic.[6] The future SS intellectuals played an important role in this shift to right-wing radicalism. Their activism was a continuation of the fight against the Treaty of Versailles and its consequences – an attempt to safeguard the Germandom that was under siege from the 'world of enemies'. The career as activists on which they embarked was a quest, and it led to joining the Nazi Party – both a system of beliefs and an elite institution embodied by the SS.

Nazism, characterized by the extreme flexibility of its dogmas, was distinguished by the importance it assigned to the racial way of reading the world that it erected into a determinist system of interpretation. By explaining the defeat of 1918 and giving a meaning to the events that seemed to presage the *Finis Germaniae*, it provided an ultimate account in which the enemy was ever present and the struggle eternal. Its force of attraction resided in the plan to refound Germandom in a more Nordic form, by building a new community, purified and victorious over its enemies. Nazism gave expression to the hope of empire and the aspiration to renewal. In this way, it became the 'promise of a reign'.[7] As a form of the promise of salvation deeply rooted in human beings, the Nazi hope for the millennium stirred bodies and souls in the expectation of a 'beginning of the reign'.[8] The internalization of the Nazi belief system was thus a matter of fervour even more than of a political and activist calculation. In this sense, only a social anthropology of Nazi emotions seems able to grasp such realities.

For the future SS intellectuals, the years of university were the time of their political social training as well as of their – often brilliant – intellectual formation.

While law studies may have given the impression that the activist and intellectual aspects of their careers were relatively separate, the example of other disciplines – from economics to linguistics, via history – shows that this was not the case. As they built up their knowledge, so this became politicized. It was a slow process, which became completely effective only with the outbreak of war. However, it did lead SS intellectuals to consider themselves both as experts in the service of the SS and as theorists incorporating the reality of their dogmas into the furthering of their disciplines. History became a 'science of legitimation',[9] or even a 'combative science',[10] which from 1939 onwards mobilized racial determinism to justify war and to produce an image of the enemy.

Activist militants, committed scientists: SS intellectuals found in the SD an institution that enabled them to ally scientific rigour with the demands of Nazi elite militancy as embodied in the SS. The activities and membership of the SD were constantly being analysed by the hierarchy, judged to see how militant they were and how devoted to the Nazi cause; the men who entered became part of this mechanism of surveillance, and left their mark on the different departments, playing a decisive role in organizing the repressive bodies of the Third Reich. Under the influence of men such as Reinhard Höhn and Franz Six, SD missions were defined by two leit-motivs: control and struggle.

The function of control touched every area – economic, cultural and racial – of the *Lebensgebiet*, as ideological evaluation went hand in hand with keeping opinion under surveillance. The doctrinal training of SS intellectuals was best expressed in this function of control. Under the leadership of men such as Otto Ohlendorf, Reinhard Höhn, Wilhelm Spengler, Hans Rössner and Hans Ehlich, they did important work in the production of ideological tenets. Whereas Ohlendorf, for example, tried to formulate a Nazi theory of wealth distribution, and Reinhard Höhn theorized the legal and political aspects of *Volksgemeinschaft*, Wilhelm Spengler sought to specify what Nazi cultural policy would look like. Even if their reports were in complete agreement with racial determinism, they comprised the outline of a Nazism whose originality lay in its erudite formulation and the great variety of subjects it could tackle. In this way, the SD succeeded in answering the 'demand for totality' for which Nazi theorists wished.

The function of keeping 'enemies' under surveillance (*Gegnerforschung*) was also given a scientific spin, under the leadership of Franz Six. This ideological surveillance, based on the systematic scrutiny of everything written by groups of opponents, was one of the ways of defining who the enemies were – both as individuals and as a group allied against the Reich. When judged by the criterion of racial determinism, they were all – Freemasons and Social Democrats included – enemies in an essentially racial sense. So, in their reports, the departments of *Gegnerforschung* gradually built up a new picture of the 'world of enemies'.

Gegnerforschung also followed the formal requirements of university discourse, footnoting the sources that apparently proved the degree of collusion between Jews, Communists, Freemasons and Social Democrats. It was because the SS intellectuals had internalized racial determinism that they believed in this collusion between Jews and Communists and could spot it in every action carried out by the people they were keeping under surveillance. But it was precisely because they thought they could verify it in *Gegnerforschung* that this belief was even more strongly internalized. Thus, *Gegnerforschung* had a syllogistic essence – which yet again highlighted the basically militant dimension of membership of the SD and the work it performed.

The SS intellectuals had joined an elitist body, and now found themselves dealing with a hierarchy that managed their careers, promoting them and penalizing them. They were thus subjected to the same normative discourse as the other members of the SS. To this was added a discourse that was fundamentally aimed at intellectuals, which may seem paradoxical: Nazism comes across as an ideology that was profoundly hostile to thought. The image of the book-burnings carried out by the SA has long encouraged observers to believe that Nazism was a form of anti-intellectualism that back-footed anyone who might claim to be a thinker in Germany. Indeed, the Nazis took particular care to get rid of cultural elites that were hostile to them, but they also developed a new image of their profession destined for those who, within their own ranks, performed intellectual functions. While continuing to criticize the sterile intellectualism of their political adversaries, the Nazis – the SS hierarchy in especial – produced, albeit in the form of scattered statements, a normative discourse setting out the ideal figure of the committed intellectual. This alliance between theorist and man of action was fleetingly incarnated in Hitler, thereby moving from the status of a norm to that of an almost ineffable myth. So SS intellectuals found themselves being assessed simultaneously for their physical and military capacities as well as for their intellectual excellence or their academic performance: this evaluation imposed the norm of the 'intellectual as man of action', a norm implicit in the sense that it was never depicted as such. Rather, it was an unconscious norm.

SS intellectuals conformed to it more or less completely, in particular by taking on various different functions within the Nazi repressive apparatus. Moving from central SD departments in Berlin to the leadership of local bureaus, they became involved both in investigating opponents of Nazism, in the function of assessment and dogmatic formulation in central departments, and in intelligence work in missions abroad.

The most brilliant careers – those of Hermann Behrends, Otto Ohlendorf, Walter Schellenberg – indicated that these men had managed to identify with this norm, by embodying both dimensions in succession. At the summit of the hierarchy in 1943–5, a group of nearly 10 per cent of SS intellectuals reached the rank of officer generals, sometimes working with Himmler, occupying positions of responsibility (such as Ohlendorf, promoted head of department in the Ministry of the Economy, or Hermann Behrends, head of staff at the VoMi). On a lower rung, a group of nearly 20 per cent of SS intellectuals had distinguished themselves sufficiently to reach positions of importance without actually being officer generals. Erich Ehrlinger, Martin Sandberger, Eugen Steimle, Hans Ehlich and Willy Seibert were all promoted colonels, and appointed *Amtschef* – this was the case with Ehrlinger – or *Gruppenleiter* – as with Sandberger or Steimle. All these men had successfully assumed executive functions requiring action, and positions deemed to require great intellectual abilities or specific academic skills. All of them, in fact, conformed almost perfectly to the model of the 'intellectual as man of action'.

A second group, found in the local SD bureaus, was trained up in the Waffen SS or the Wehrmacht, and could demonstrate both intellectual excellence and a capacity for action. These men frequently ended their careers with the grade of *Obersturmbannführer* and the rank of *Referent* or head of a local bureau.

One final group comprised men who never served in the armed forces or carried out missions abroad: they did not, in other words, conform to the activist dimension of the model. Some of them, in addition, did not satisfy one of the demands made by the SS, in particular the requirement concerning the number of children produced by SS couples. Nearly 20 per cent of men thus found themselves marginalized: their advance was blocked, or they were penalized for failing to observe some norm. One remarkable fact is that the bureau of 'scientific' and ideological research

of the SD, the bureau most capable of fulfilling the idea of 'scientificity'
of the SD, was completely marginalized: under the command of a mere
Sturmbannführer, stripped of its staff, it had lost any strategic importance
by the end of the war, and was reduced to producing abstruse reports that
nobody ever read. Heinz Ballensiefen, Paul Dittel and Rudolf Levin fell
into this category

From 1934 to 1939, the functions of control, observation, *Gegnerforschung*
and action of the SD hardly changed in their form or their content, with the
notable exception of the bureau in charge of the 'Jewish question', which
was increasingly involved in finalizing the government's anti-Semitic
policy. The year 1939 marked the start of a new phase of expansion of the
departments, marked by the reshaping and combining of their central
departments, which became effective with the creation of the RSHA. In
1939, SD intellectuals announced a dual victory: against the enemy within
(muzzled) and against unemployment (eradicated). They described the
international resurgence of Germany thanks to the remilitarization of the
Rhineland and the occupation of Austria, the Sudetenland and the rest of
Czechoslovakia. In their view, Nazism was keeping its promises. There
was no trace, here, of the collective eschatology internalized during the
Great War; it was the illustration of how the Nazi belief system could
soothe anxieties.

The war was a decisive turning point in the tasks of SS intellectuals. More
particularly, the Polish campaign melded together three crucial elements
in the imaginings of SS intellectuals: the culture of war, with its many references to memories of the Great War, the utopia that crystallized round
the eastern territories, and the security measures taken by the organs of
repression.

For SS intellectuals, 1 September 1939 marked the end of the 'apparent silence of weapons'[11] of 1918–19. They set off for the *Osteinsatz*, amid
groups whose task was to maintain security in the territories occupied by
the Wehrmacht. The war on the 'world of enemies' had resumed in the
east – the very area where, between the two world wars, there had been
so much anxiety about the possible disappearance of *volksdeutsch* communities, which the SS felt duty-bound to rescue. The SD's resettlement
plans originally reflected these representations; they developed with
Nazi policy, and eventually took over the genocidal aims and planned
murder of some 21,266,000 individuals, starved, worked to exhaustion,
shot and – if they came from Jewish communities – gassed in the death
camps.

If they were to arrive at a position where they could legitimate mass
murder, the SS intellectuals had to experience the *Osteinsatz* – and,
between Poland and the USSR, this underwent a decisive change. During
Operation Barbarossa, every instruction issued to the group, every
warning against the enemy's wiles, emphasized a little more the bestiality and inhumanity of the Russians, who were surreptitiously being

controlled by the Jews. With this anxiety fed into them, the soldiers of the German army entered Russia in an advanced state of psychosis. The members of the *Einsatzgruppen* were no exception, and the reports of July 1941 outdid each other in describing the depredations committed by the NKVD as Jewish atrocities. During their advance through Poland, the Germans had rediscovered all the memories of invasion dating from the Great War, with the figure of the sniper and the image of severed hands. But the frenzied march that led them into Russia brought them brutally up against a violence that they read as confirmation of the anxiogenic discourse distilled before the campaign. In their view, Russia was indeed a land of subhumans and bestiality, a land of famine and Jewish domination. The war they were waging was indeed a 'great racial war', and the enemy was largely depicted as animalistic and perceived as a savage beast. These representations, distilling anguish and hatred in the minds of killers and their officers, made it possible for the men to acquiesce in genocide. They did so on a massive scale.

It is also in this light that we need to read the fundamental shift in the activities of the groups, a shift that came about from mid-July to the end of September 1941. Until mid-August, the *Einsatzgruppen* set up security measures consisting in the wearing of the yellow star, confinement to ghettos, obligatory labour – all underpinned by the execution of very many members of the Jewish elites. Might these practices be correlated with the animalistic vision that the men in the groups had internalized? This could help us sketch out an anthropology of the acts of violence perpetrated by the *Einsatzgruppen*. Seen from this angle, such practices consisted in confining, branding and setting to work Jewish populations perceived as wild animals. Perhaps this was a way of taming them, consciously or not? As these measures continued to be applied, the cruelty and danger attributed to the Jews in the reports of the *Einsatzgruppen* so far faded, to be replaced by an equally dehumanized image that did not see them as wild beasts but reduced them to cattle, whose sole vocation was labour, and whose reproduction the SS could control.

Such a model, however difficult it may be to put it into words, casts considerable light on the mental processes at work when people committed murder, as when – in mid-August 1941 – women and children were included in the butchery. When the SS perceived the Jews as wild animals, the mode of killing they applied to them necessarily drew on images of hunting, which presupposed a strict respect for the ban on killing infants. The shift from images of hunting to pastoral images, made possible by the substitution of domestication mentioned above, also changed the method of killing applied to the victims: hunting was replaced by slaughter, a mode of butchery that could encompass very young individuals, and even babies, in very great numbers.[12] The transformation of the practice of the groups, still apprehended in political and functional mode by historians, was perhaps also determined by a major, if probably unconscious, anthropological shift, which presided over the aseptic mentality that grasped the killers and alone made it possible for them to envisage the comprehensive dimension of the genocide.

As they led the extermination units, the SS intellectuals set in place a discourse that legitimated the activities of the groups, and found verbal expression each time there was an escalation in the violence of murder.

Thus, two lines of argument were developed. The first, less common, was utopian: it presented the genocide as the essential precondition for the Germanization of the occupied territories. It thus connected the millenarian promise to the total extermination of the Jewish communities. This argument became widespread thanks to the presence – remarkable among the groups – of intellectuals who had come from bodies whose task it was to develop and implement the *Generalplan Ost*: these included Hans Joachim Beyer, Karl Tschierschky, Martin Sandberger, Albert Rapp and the doctor Hanns Meixner, who had all emerged from RSHA *Amt* III B, the EWZ or the UWZ.[13] The second, much more frequent, line of argument tended to see genocide as a defensive action; it drew yet again on the eschatological anxieties that gripped men, appealed to the dehumanized image of the enemy, and turned genocide into one of the conditions necessary for the survival of the German nation and the Nordic race. This argument was deeply internalized by the killers and is often encountered in their writings.

These two dimensions combined into a discourse of legitimation and constituted the main ways in which the killers acquiesced in butchery. It should be emphasized as much as possible that these two lines of argument, the one defensive and the other utopian, did *not* arise in Russia. This was no doubt the first place where they were applied to legitimize the comprehensive massacre of civilian populations, but the fact remains that they had already in 1914 formed the basis of representations presiding over the explosion of violence seen as an ordeal. One might think that the cadres of the groups, children of the Great War, were here again drawing on representations which they had internalized in that first conflict. My suggestion, again, is that the culture of the 1914–18 war may indeed have re-emerged, but in a form made more systematic and radical by the racial determinism and millenarianism of the Nazis.

As heads of units, the officers of these groups also took over the organization of the killings. They ordered them and often took part in them. In the first weeks of Operation Barbarossa, they were taken unawares on several occasions by their own mission, by its bloody character. The troop was sometimes left to its own devices, and organized the killings in chaotic fashion. However, after a few days, a certain number of logistical arrangements were made in every *Kommando*. The victims were executed in front of ditches that had been dug in advance, by Russian civilians or by the victims themselves. Several teams of killers shared out the tasks of bringing the victims to the spot, keeping guard over them near the execution grounds, and actually shooting them. This way, the murders were carried out more quickly, and the number of victims killed each day increased dramatically. The killers simultaneously used certain skills in butchery that enabled them to perform their task more rapidly, and to kill more efficiently. Gradually, the use of firing squads, executing the victims at the edge of a ditch or as they lay within them on top of one another, became general. If the method of shooting the victims in the neck spread through the *Kommandos*, this was because it assured the killers that they had really finished off each victim and that the deaths of the latter would be quick. The violence unleashed in the east was thus a culturally constructed set of activities, on the basis of which it is possible to identify and analyse the thinking behind it.

This thinking, which aimed at annihilation, was not the only set of ideas at work in the murders. Unlike the massacres of Jewish communities, hangings were explicitly conceived as demonstrations of violence. The attitudes here had many meanings: they involved a ritualistic liberation from Communism and 'Jewish domination', a ritual performed for the sake of the local non-Jewish populations, and the discourse of syllogistic confirmation of the image of the enemy, meant for the killers themselves. Killing was here its own justification.

The cadres of the groups, however, who had to a large extent inspired these paroxysmal practices of violence, were faced with the problem of managing the transgressive nature of the genocide. They sometimes managed to accustom their men to murdering women, but killing children was still taboo. The killers were traumatized by their task and this transgression could produce many different effects: there were nervous breakdowns, massive alcoholism, acts of cruelty, all of which needed to be brought under control. The officers sometimes tried to modify the violence so as to lessen this traumatic dimension. One strategy consisted of dividing the 'burden' as much as possible between the groups, forcing everyone to take part in an execution. This practice became general; it was sometimes accompanied by rituals that made the killing a more communal activity, with more of a military aspect: a firing squad was formed, the men shot their victims when ordered, they about-turned and moved back at the officer's command – all of which showed a desire to protect the soldiers from responsibility for murder, but also a more complex wish to make genocide a military action. This meant that the action was congruent with a discourse that made genocide one of the fronts of a defensive war that the Third Reich was waging in Russia. This second strategy was sometimes accompanied by a third type of arrangement, in which the killers in the groups were replaced by Russian auxiliaries entrusted with tasks that the German killers were reluctant to perform, such as the killing of children. Another method consisted in developing the use of gas vans. But, as this example shows, such a response was not inevitably crowned with success: in several *Kommandos*, the men, repelled by having to handle corpses when the vans were emptied, refused to use them – and in at least two places, this led to their being abandoned.

In spite of the traumatic dimension of the experience of genocide, there was never any exception to the men's consent to murder. This was partly due to the legitimating discourse set up, for example, by SS intellectuals, partly to the way these actions were stage-managed by these same SS officers, and, finally, to the fact that the men just got used to it. The most hardened killers did not emerge unscathed from the violence inflicted. They said as much during the questionings to which they were subjected in the postwar investigations of crimes committed in Russia.

SS intellectuals were no exception, and experienced their *Osteinsatz* in the mode of revulsion and lamentation. The latter occupied a capital place in the economy of the discourse that legitimated genocide: it was, indeed, the criterion that enabled the executioners to preserve, in their own eyes, the humanity they refused to attribute to their Russian enemies, or to the Jewish communities. Conscious as they were that the mode of execution current in the genocidal campaign was the 'bullet to the back of the neck' (*Genickschuß*) that proved the inhumanity of Bolshevism, SS intellectuals thought that the main factor that distinguished the Russian from the SS in the *Osteinsatz* was the pleasure taken by the Russian in killing.[14] Apart from the border between the human and the animal, the SS were thus expressing what was doubtless one of the most powerful taboos current in the *Osteinsatz* and its activities: the cruelty and the pleasure to be found in butchery. Neither this discursive structure nor the control of the hierarchy, however, managed to keep the mobile killing groups free of this type of phenomenon, as the sources sometimes demonstrate.

Whether they wanted to or not, the SS intellectuals expressed the experience of genocide and that of paroxysmal violence. If the discourse of legitimation that they had contributed to producing was sufficiently internalized for belief in the absolute necessity of killing to be beyond doubt, some of them nonetheless betrayed the revulsion with which they were carrying out their task. The violent digestive disorders experienced by Walter Blume in Vitebsk were an involuntary manifestation of this, but the warning which this same man issued to the troops of Sk 7a, which was a clear expression of his lamentation over this act and his forbidding of any cruelty, was another sign. The fact that Erich Ehrlinger was edgy and distraught in Kaunas is further evidence, as is Albert Rapp's alcoholism in Klincy and the psychosomatic problems that Hans Joachim Beyer suffered in Lemberg. And yet these men repressed their revulsion, 'got over' it, in the view of their superiors, so as to lead their men on in the task of genocide.

Not all those implicated in genocide were involved to the same degree. If we know, in the cases of Erich Ehrlinger, Albert Rapp, Alfred Filbert, Bruno Müller, Fritz Valjavec and Walter Blume, that they killed with their own hands, this is not proven for Hans Joachim Beyer, Otto Ohlendorf or Martin Sandberger. In August 1941, Bruno Müller went so far as to exploit his own involvement in murder by killing a woman and her baby in front of his assembled troop, so as to demonstrate what the *Einsatzgruppen* were now expected to do.

Some SS intellectuals adapted to this extreme violence without any apparent sign of difficulty. Indeed, in the cases of Ehrlinger and Sandberger, they became veritable specialists of the *Osteinsatz*. Eugen Steimle, historian of RSHA *Amt* VI, is an example of their careers: he was stationed in the east twice, showed no reluctance in joining in with the practices of the *Einsatzgruppen*, but did not conceal his revulsion at genocide: so he would use the excuse of the slightest little health problem to take extended leave in Germany.

The *Osteinsatz* was to some extent a rite of initiation for the SS intellectuals. For those who managed to 'get over' the trauma it constituted, returning to Berlin often brought crucial promotion: it was because they had proved their psychological capacity to become physically involved in the violence being committed in the east that they were deemed worthy of responsible positions. However, those who did not return unscathed and those who never went to the east at all were not promoted. This phenomenon can be correlated with the normative discourse of the intellectual as a man of action, and we can see the *Osteinsatz* as the final test that allowed the SS intellectual to incarnate his belief in this action itself. Those who conformed to the image even more completely, becoming specialists of the *Osteinsatz*, needed no further ideological training. In the east, the intellectual as man of action lost what actually comprised the essence of his status. Conformity to this image was impossible in real life; thus it was transformed into a myth.

Most SS intellectuals survived the apocalypse of 1945. Admittedly, they experienced this, Germany's second defeat in less than thirty years, with all the intensity of their Nazi feelings, and with the anguish that had arisen in 1918. The first defeat may have constituted an original trauma, but they were not to blame for it. Unlike the generation of their elders, who had fought in the First World War and were in power during the Second, and who were now suffering a new defeat for which they were obliged to assume responsibility, they did not commit suicide. In this way, war played a crucial formative role twice over. It had formed an image of war that was in 1918 transposed into a Germany in turmoil; and it formed a genocidal violence marked by the ideas of defensive war and utopia. The two were combined in the terrible destinies of these children of war who went on to become killers.

Finally, the fate of these children of the 1914–18 war assumes another dimension if we linger over the case of Hermann Behrends, the former SD head who sent the *Kommandos* of the VoMi to the Russian Front. In 1943, this consummate theorist and practitioner of Germanization enlisted in the Waffen SS and, after a short stay in Kiev, rapidly obtained a post as commander in Serbia in the 13th division SS *Handschar*. Made up of Croats, Bosnians and Muslim Kossovars, the division distinguished itself for its quite particular savagery against local resistance.[15] Having thus acquired an incomparable practical experience of the Balkan context, Hermann Behrends was appointed HSSPF for Serbia and Montenegro in 1944. Arrested by the Americans in the summer of 1945, he was extradited to Belgrade, where he was put on trial, sentenced to death and executed in 1948.[16] In towns such as Mostar, Tuzla and Bihac, the *Handschar* units had left a bloody trail, begetting yet more children of war, of whom the Europeans of the end of the twentieth century, 'perpetrators, victims and bystanders'[17] of the drama of Yugoslavia, were, no doubt unwittingly, the heirs.

Afterword

Since I wrote my thesis, many controversies have arisen, including over the publication of Jonathan Littell's *The Kindly Ones*. This was a particularly interesting case, since the novel was a thematic fictional work that paralleled my own work, and made possible some highly instructive ethnographic observations. Many scholarly works have been published, tackling the Nazi policy of extermination of European Jewry from the point of view of the perpetrators. It is not possible either to take into account or even to master the flood of publications that, for over twelve years now, has fed this field with its waters. Several hundred books, thousands of articles, the huge effort of a community to try and understand the logics that presided over the behaviour of thousands of German soldiers who experienced the terrifying circumstances of death and genocide meted out on the Eastern Front.[1]

Yes, rarely will a community have made such an effort to understand and objectify a historical problem. And the main points that have been investigated have now become, as it were, entire fields within the discipline. Let us make a survey of the challenges that arose at the time.

A piece of research and its context

When, following the implosion of the Soviet bloc between 1989 and 1991, historians of Nazism gained access to new archives documenting the so far unknown dimensions of the war and the Nazi occupation, they refocused their attention and, turning away from the last phases of the quarrel between intentionalists and functionalists, developed new types of history. From the start of the 2000s, it was possible, for a well-informed observer, to draw up an overall if not exhaustive picture of the evolution in the historiographical field.[2] Three major tendencies could be discerned, which enduringly affected the structure of the historiography of Nazism. The first concerned the form of the historiographical renewal. The new generation of researchers had for the most part been trained in German universities, in particular by Wolfgang Scheffler at the Technical University of Berlin, and/or had worked with Ruth Bettina Birn at the Canadian Ministry of Justice. These young scholars were first and foremost explorers of archives, and their work was based on a self-declared empiricism that called for a move beyond the functionalist/intentionalist quarrel, and a neo-positivism that mistrusted speculative constructions. They called first for the painstaking reconstitution of facts based on many archives.[3] This generation, in the front ranks of which were Christian Gerlach,[4] Dieter Pohl,[5] Andrej Angrick,[6] Peter Klein,[7] Jan Erik Schulte[8] and Ralf Ogorreck,[9] made intensive use of the newly available archives in the east, but also of the legal archives of the *Zentrale Stelle der Landesjustizverwaltungen* of Ludwigsburg, or of the archives of the intelligence services of East Germany. The extensive mastery of the traditional archives, combined with the contribution of these new sources, gave birth to a wave of publications whose levels of evidence and erudition were unsurpassed. They were the object of careful reviews in France, especially on the occasion of controversies that shook German historiography during this second intense phase of research.[10]

One of the main stumbling blocks of this historiography is the study of the process whereby the decision to carry out genocide was taken, with, in between the lines, the question of the relation between the Berlin centre and the periphery of local organs of occupation. This problem was identified by Philippe Burrin in his classic work *Hitler et les Juifs. Genèse d'un génocide*, which dated the decision to autumn 1941. Christopher Browning replied by postulating a decision taken in the 'fateful months' of the summer euphoria of the same year.[11] The contribution of the new wave of scholarship was expressed in the work of Christian Gerlach, who, in a brilliant article, came down in favour of a 'Final Solution' that was decided on even later, a series of local decisions forming a continuum that led to an overall decision on principle taken by Hitler in December 1941, under the impact of the declaration of war against the United States.[12] This work, extended in a very fine thesis written by Florent Brayard,[13] meant it was possible to establish a careful chronology for the decision to launch the Final Solution. This has recently been questioned by Édouard Husson, the author of a *Habilitation* thesis on Reinhard Heydrich, who inclines to a decisive intervention made by the Führer in November 1941.[14] The technical nature of the evidence in this debate, the complexity of the arguments brought forward by Christopher Browning, Christian Gerlach and Florent Brayard, and the intervention of Édouard Husson have in practice so obscured the issues of this question as to make them difficult to grasp.

The second field of research is focused on the perpetrators of mass murder. The first historian to have posed the question of individual and collective mass murder during the violence was without doubt Christopher Browning, in his famous work *Ordinary Men*. The controversy triggered by Daniel Goldhagen echoed this. In *Hitler's Willing Executioners*, he presented – on the basis of the same archives – a radically different interpretation from Browning's. While the latter, relying on a social psychology dating from the 1970s, insisted not so much on the ideological factor as on the collective phenomena of group obedience and the pressure of this on individuals, Goldhagen set up a concept of 'eliminationist anti-Semitism', and turned the desire to kill into the mainspring of the actions of both groups and individuals.

However specious the quarrel between Browning and Goldhagen, it had the advantage and the consequence of leading a growing number of historians of Nazism to take an interest in the perpetrators of genocide, especially those on the Eastern Front. Admittedly, the work of Hans-Heinrich Wilhelm and Helmut Krausnick,[15] and of Ralf Ogorreck, the documents published by Peter Klein, the syntheses of Christian Gerlach and Dieter Pohl, and the thesis of Andrej Angrick all comprised excellent bases for work; but focusing on institutions debarred them from any fine-grained study of the behaviour of social groups and individuals. Studying the *Sicherheitspolizei* in Russia meant studying an institution, with its chain of command, its place in a local institutional landscape; it also often meant lacking conceptual tools and the right focus to grasp sequences of events and behaviours. Realizing this, perhaps, the specialists of what is now known as research on the perpetrators (*Täterforschung*) set out to try and understand the behaviour of men who, on the ground, embarked on a huge killing spree, mainly in the USSR and Poland. These specialists' work, begun in 1995–2000, could now fill an entire library. They have contributed a great deal to our understanding of behaviour. They are, however, the active members or heirs of that generation of neo-positivist scholars who combed through the archives of the former Soviet Union and the German legal archives of the ZStL. While they were excellent specialists of the primary documentation, they often demonstrate a certain lack of conceptual rigour. As opposed to Daniel Goldhagen, they draw on a multi-causal explanation of behaviour, and often indulge in the use of a kind of conceptual 'black box', with obscure terms such as 'fanaticism', 'ambition', 'careerism', indoctrination', 'obedience' and 'conformism'.

It was in this particular context that the present work was undertaken. It was far from isolated at the time: begun in 1995, it was written at a time when other historians were specializing in the personnel of police forces and Nazi secret services. Jens Banach, a historian who has worked in Hamburg and Kiel, wrote a thesis in quantitative social history that focused on the group of Gestapo and SD cadres, trying to write a sociography of them – i.e. to lay out a statistically informed social profile.[16] Michael Wildt, meanwhile, was completing a *Habilitation* on the cadres of the *Reichssicherheitshauptamt* (RSHA), the Berlin-based institution that controlled, centralized and administered the organs of repression of the Third Reich, the Gestapo (political police), the KRIPO (criminal police) and the SD (security service).[17] This led me to take up my own stance towards this work and to most of that produced by the previously mentioned *Täterforschung*.

A specific conceptual framework

The writing of the present work started with the realization that two dead ends had been reached. The first was the fact that there were just too many archives. The myth of archival exhaustiveness did not really tempt me. It seemed more interesting to probe more deeply into archives that were diversified but not all that numerous,[18] and to construct a line of argument that drew more on analysis than on narrative, unlike the German historians' usual method. Michael Wildt's work, whose themes were basically similar to those of the present work, comprised an excellent example of this. Based on a great number of archives by a sensitive historian well aware of the questions raised by the sociology and the history of everyday life, his *Habilitation* thesis, which I consulted after writing my thesis, seemed overly tied down to institutional logics and chronologies, even when he was drawing on the narrations of individual careers that he examined in depth. Individual destinies and institutional destinies were also very much in evidence in the narration, perhaps to the detriment of analytical profundity.[19]

The second dead end was historiographical. Quantitative social history had formed its hypotheses on the commitment and the behaviour of the group of RSHA cadres. It presented an explanation that drew on notions of resentment, of the 'fear of falling from one social class to another', seeing in the 1929 crisis one of the key factors in the way certain intellectuals committed themselves to the SS. So this commitment expressed a desire for social status and a channel for social frustrations. After drawing up the statistical social profile of the men he studied, Jans Banach embarked on a psychologistic interpretation of the data he had accumulated. Or rather, he moved somewhat artificially from his statistical data to a somewhat abstract interpretation of the mental universe of the men he was investigating. To support his conclusions, he quoted Herbert Ziegler,[20] one of the historians of these social generations, who analyses the commitment of these men thus:

> While one group of young men developed their animosity toward the older generation during their baptism of fire at the front, a cohort of adolescents cultivated its own peculiarly determined alienation, rancor, and resentments toward their fathers. Because of their young age, these individuals had to remain at home with their mothers [. . .]. Marked by sickness, nutritional deprivation [. . .] they became estranged from their fathers and developed an abnormally close relationship with their mothers, becoming in fact rivals to their fathers for the love of their mothers. The defeat of their fathers represented nothing short of a catastrophe to them.[21]

The influence of the Frankfurt School and a degraded Freudianism is obvious here, but the problem is that no source supports this shift from socio-statistical reality to the study of these men's psychological lives. How, for example, can we sense their rancour and frustration? How can we evaluate the 'right distance' between them and their fathers and mothers? Banach and Ziegler 'pathologize' the men of an entire generation, branding them with an Oedipal neurosis that these writers claim explains in full the men's political commitments.

These two critiques – that of the artificially bridged gap between statistical reality and psychological life, and that of a summary analytical apparatus – have led me to try and find new tools and thus turn to other historiographical reference points. In short, to examine the paths these men took to Nazism and involvement in genocide from a new angle.

Notes

Preface

1 The thesis viva was held at the University of Amiens on 21 December 2001, in front of a jury of examiners comprising Stéphane Audoin-Rouzeau, Gerhard Hirschfeld (chairs), Henry Rousso, Nadine-Josette Chaline, Philippe Burrin and Gerd Krumeich.

2 On the historiographical context and the way it has developed, see p. 261.

3 For a survey, see Jean-Jacques Becker and Stéphane Audoin-Rouzeau, *Les Sociétés européenes et la guerre de 1914–1918* (Paris: Université de Paris X and Armand Colin, 1990). The ideas of these historians were set out by Stéphane Audoin-Rouzeau and Annette Becker in *1914–1918: Understanding the Great War*, tr. Catherine Temerson (London: Profile Books, 2002).

4 Stéphane Audoin-Rouzeau, *La Guerre des enfants, 1914–1918. Essai d'histoire culturelle* (Paris: Armand Colin, 1994).

5 Stéphane Audoin-Rouzeau, *Cinq deuils de guerre 1914–1918* (Paris: Noësis, 2001).

6 For an overview of the present research, see the book that initially led these historians and their colleagues in the Institut d'Histoire du Temps Présent to pool their investigations: Stéphane Audoin-Rouzeau, Annette Becker, Christian Ingrao and Henry Rousso (eds.), *La Violence de guerre. Approches comparées des deux conflits mondiaux* (Brussels: Complexe, 2002).

7 Alphonse Dupront, *Le Mythe de croisade*, 4 vols. (Paris: Gallimard, 1997); Denis Crouzet, *Les Guerriers de Dieu. La violence au temps des troubles de religion*, 2 vols. (Paris: Champs Vallon, 1990).

8 Édouard Conte and Cornelia Essner, *La Quête de la race. Une anthropologie du nazisme* (Paris: Hachette, 1995).

9 Françoise Héritier, *De la violence*, 2 vols. (Paris: Odile Jacob, 1996, 1999).

10 Véronique Nahoum-Grappe, 'Les usages politiques de la cruauté', in Héritier, *De la violence*, vol. I.

11 Noëlie Vialles, *Animal to Edible*, tr. J. A. Underwood (Cambridge: Cambridge University Press; Paris: Éditions de la Maison des Sciences de l'Homme, 1994).

12 Élisabeth Claverie, *Les Guerres de la Vierge. Une anthropologie des apparitions* (Paris: Gallimard, 2003).

13 Catherine Rémy, *La Fin des bêtes. Une ethnographie de la mise à mort des animaux* (Paris: Économica, 2009).

14 Crouzet, *Les Guerriers de Dieu*.

15 Gerd Krumeich, 'Der Krieg in den Köpfen', in Krumeich (ed.), *Versailles 1919. Ziele – Wirkung – Wahrnehmung* (Essen: Klartext, 2001).

Chapter 1 A 'world of enemies' (I)

1 I use this term to refer to people who had studied at university.

2 Jeffrey Verhey, *The Spirit of 1914. Militarism, Myth and Mobilization in Germany* (Cambridge: Cambridge University Press, 2000) – see especially the chapter on *Volksgemeinschaft*, pp. 213–18.

3 This approximation is based on figures quoted by Audoin-Rouzeau and Becker, *1914–1918*, pp. 240–1.

4 Stéphane Audoin-Rouzeau emphasizes the importance of this in one of the narratives, that of the bereavement of Jeanne Catulle-Mendès (*Cinq deuils de guerre*).

5 Thierry Bonzon and Belinda J. Davis, 'Feeding the cities', in Jean-Louis Robert and Jay Winter (eds.), *Capital Cities at War. London, Paris, Berlin, 1914–1919* (Cambridge: Cambridge University Press, 1997), pp. 305–41; p. 310.

6 Belinda J. Davis, *Home Fires Burning. Food, Politics and Everyday Life in World War I Berlin* (Chapel Hill: University of North Carolina Press, 2000). Davis discusses difficulties in maintaining food supplies from the point of view of *Alltagsgeschichte*, which leads her to see them as one of the factors of dissolution of the existing links between the Germans and their government. She analyses hunger as a cause of the breakdown of consent. However, she also highlights the factor of anxiety that the question of food aroused in the system of representations of the middle and lower classes.

7 Werner Schaeffer, *Krieg gegen Frauen und Kinder. Englands Hungerblockade gegen Deutschland 1914–1920* (Berlin: Deutsche Informationsstelle, 1940). This source is particularly interesting in that it represents a reshaping of the culture that emerged from the Great War in the service of the Second World War. Far from reflecting the experience of the Great War, it clearly shows how the memory of this conflict was reactivated so as to serve as a crucial reference point in the discourse of legitimation of the second great global conflict.

8 Anne Duménil's thesis on 'Le soldat allemand' ('The German soldier') is yet to appear. Meanwhile, see Gerd Krumeich, 'Le soldat allemand sur la Somme 1914–1916', in Becker and Audoin-Rouzeau, *Les Sociétés européennes*.

9 Susanne Brandt, *Vom Kriegsschauplatz zum Gedächtnisraum. Die Westfront 1914–1940* (Baden-Baden: Nomos, 2000); see especially pp. 17–18 and 37–8.

10 Fritz Mittelmann, *Kreuz und quer durch Belgien*, quoted in Brandt, *Vom Kriegsschauplatz*, p. 25.

11 On this question, see Vejas Gabriel Liulevicius, *War Land on the Eastern Front. Culture, National Identity and German Occupation in World War I* (Cambridge: Cambridge University Press, 2000). The invasion lasted only a few weeks, and was halted by the autumn offensives and the victory of Hindenburg and Ludendorff over the Russian armies of Samsonov and Rennenkampf, a battle that was renamed 'the battle of Tannenberg'. The impact of this invasion on people's memories was, however, incomparably more extensive than its length, even if its appalling brutality should not be underestimated. The invasion and the salvific dimension of the battle also triggered the veritable personality cult which the two victorious German generals subsequently enjoyed.

12 On the image of the enemy internalized by the combatants, there is a systematic if somewhat abstract study of soldiers' letters: Klaus Latzel, *Deutsche Soldaten – nationalsozialistischer Krieg? Kriegserlebnis – Kriegserfahrung 1939–1945* (Paderborn: Schöningh, 1998). In spite of its title, this tries to draw a comparison between the war experiences of German soldiers in the two world wars (see especially pp. 191–4, 200–1 and 211–19). However, the analytical categories which the author has chosen prevent him from interpreting in a coherent way how the war was presented, and do not take into account the defensive character of the war as it was seen by German soldiers.

13 Liulevicius, *War Land on the Eastern Front*, pp. 29–30 and 54–88.

14 Ibid., pp. 174–7.

15 On this point, see ibid., pp. 134–56.

16 Jacques Heugeon, *Trois études sur le Ver Sacrum* (Brussels: Latomus, 1957).

17 Quoted in Gerhard Hirschfeld, foreword to Gerd Krumeich and Gerhard Hirschfeld (eds.), *'Keiner fühlt sich hier mehr als Mensch . . .'. Erlebnis und Wirkung des Ersten Weltkrieges* (Frankfurt: Fischer, 1996), p. 7.

18 Bernd Hüppauf, 'Schlachtenmythen und die Konstruktion des "Neuen Menschen"', in Krumeich and Hirschfeld, *'Keiner fühlt sich hier mehr als Mensch . . .'*, pp. 43–84.

19 Letter no. 107 from Walter I., Knoch private collection, BfZ, quoted in Peter Knoch, 'Erleben und Nacherleben. Das Kriegserlebnis im Augenzeugenbericht und im Geschichtsunterricht', in Krumeich and Hirschfeld, *'Keiner fühlt sich hier mehr als Mensch . . .'*, pp. 235–59; p. 244.

20 On this type of problematic, see Audoin-Rouzeau and Becker, *1914–1918*, and Annette Becker, *War and Faith: The Religious Imagination in France 1914–1930*, tr. Helen McPhail (Oxford: Berg, 1998), as well as Dupront, *Le Mythe de croisade*, vol. 2.

21 See Gudrun Fiedler, *Jugend im Krieg. Bürgerliche Jugendbewegung, Erster Weltkrieg und sozialer Wandel 1914–1923* (Cologne: Wissenschaft und Politik, 1989).

22 At a rate of about one every three days.

23 Becker and Audoin-Rouzeau, 'Violence et consentement. La "culture de guerre" du premier conflit mondial', in Jean-Pierre Rioux and Jean-François Sirinelli (eds.), *Pour une histoire culturelle* (Paris: Le Seuil, 1996); and Audoin-Rouzeau and Becker, *1914–1918*, especially p. 50.

24 Heike Hoffmann, '"Schwarze Peter" im Weltkrieg. Die deutsche

Spielwarenindustrie 1914–1918', in Gerd Krumeich, Dieter Langewiesche, Hans Peter Ullmann and Gerhard Hirschfeld (eds.), *Kriegserfahrungen. Studien zur Sozial- und Mentalitätsgeschichte des Ersten Weltkrieges* (Essen: Klartext, 1997), pp. 323–35.

25 There is an interesting discussion of toys and the world of children in wartime in George Mosse's study of the way the conflict was turned into an everyday phenomenon: *De la Grande Guerre au totalitarisme. La brutalisation des sociétés européennes* (Paris: Hachette, 1999), pp. 145–79.

26 *Deutsche Spielwaren Zeitung*, 10/9/1914, vol. 18, folio 3. Quoted by Hoffmann, '"Schwarze Peter" im Weltkrieg', p. 325.

27 *Ferdinand Hirt's Kriegslesestücke. Erlebnisse und Darstellungen aus dem Jahre 1915*, 3rd edn (Breslau: Hirt Verlag, 1917).

28 E. Matthias and H. Meier-Welcker (eds.), *Quellen zur Geschichte des Parlamentarismus und der deutschen Parteien*, vol. I/II: *Militär und Innenpolitik im Ersten Weltkriege 1914–1918*; vol. VIII: *Die Propaganda im Zeichen des 'vaterländischen Unterrichts', April 1917–Oktober 1918* (Düsseldorf: Droste, 1978), pp. 803–985.

29 Ludwig Pronold and Albert Henselmann, *Weltkriegsbilderbuch. Franzl-Michl-Mohammed* (Straubing: Attekoffer, 1916), p. 12; quoted in Audoin-Rouzeau, *La Guerre des enfants*, p. 68.

30 See the numerous engravings and lithographs by Rudolf Grossman, especially 'Celui qui veut être soldat' ('The lad who wants to be a soldier'), reproduced in Mosse, *De la Grande Guerre au totalitarisme*, p. 160.

31 *Lebenslauf*, 24/5/1938, folio 2 (BAAZ SSO Turowsky).

32 A significant number of eyewitness accounts of Cossack atrocities – rapes, executions, mutilations – come from refugees or *Landser* (soldiers) who were posted to Johannisburg. See *Greueltaten russischer Truppen gegen deutsche Zivilpersonen und deutsche Kriegsgefangenen*, Blue Book, 1915. Thanks to Anne Duménil for alerting me to this document.

33 Ernst Turowsky, *Die innenpolitische Entwicklung Polnisch-Preußens und seine staatsrechtliche Stellung zu Polen vom 2. Thorner Frieden bis zum Reichstag von Lublin (1466–1569)* (Berlin: Trilitsch und Huther, 1937). See also below, chapter 3, on 'The construction of academic knowledge'.

34 Kurt Flasch, *Die geistige Mobilmachung. Die deutsche Intellektuellen und der Erste Weltkrieg: ein Versuch* (Berlin: Alexander Fest Verlag, 2000). See also, for the French side of things, Christophe Prochasson, *Les Intellectuels, le socialisme et la guerre* (Paris: Le Seuil, 1993); Christophe Prochasson and Anne Rasmussen, *Au nom de la Patrie. Les Intellectuels et la première guerre mondiale (1910–1919)* (Paris: La Découverte, 1996).

35 *Lebenslauf* Gräfe, n.d. (BAAZ, RuSHA Akte, Gräfe).

36 See Ulrich Heinemann, *Die verdrängte Niederlage. Politische Öffentlichkeit und Kriegschuldfrage in der Weimarer Republik* (Göttingen: Vandenhoeck und Ruprecht, 1983).

37 This was the case of Emil Augsburg, a future researcher at the Wannsee Institute, a member of *Einsatzgruppe* B, and a *Volksdeutscher* from Łódź (BAAZ RuSHA Akte Augsburg), and also of Erich Ehlers, whose father, a

pastor in North Schleswig, said he wanted to move so as not to become a Danish civil servant, and to be able to give 'his seven children a German upbringing' (*Lebenslauf* Ehlers [BAAZ, RuSHA Akte Ehlers]).

38 A second case is comprised of the final statements made by Otto Ohlendorf and Heinz Jost at the Nuremberg Trials. I return to the first document in chapter 6, below.

39 Ulrich Herbert, *Best: Biographische Studien über Radikalismus, Weltanschauung und Vernunft 1903–1989* (Bonn: Dietz, 1996), p. 45.

40 Best questionnaire, 1947, p. 5, in BABL, Nachlass Best. Quoted from Herbert, *Best*, p. 47.

41 Werner Best, *Lebenslauf*, 1965; quoted by Herbert, *Best*, p. 2.

42 Jay Winter has shown that this was a widespread phenomenon, and one that largely explained the excessive death rates of the oldest tranche of the populations in the three capitals at war, namely Paris, London, Berlin. See Robert and Winter, *Capital Cities at War*; Audoin-Rouzeau and Becker, *1914–1918*, ch. 3.

43 Best, *Lebenslauf*, 1965; quoted by Herbert, *Best*, p. 48.

44 The entry of French troops into Mainz took place between 5 and 10 December 1918. See Herbert, *Best*, p. 30.

45 Ibid., p. 47. See also Shlomo Aronson, *Heydrich und die Frühgeschichte von Gestapo und des SD 1931–1945* (Berlin: Ernst Reuter Gesellschaft, 1967), pp. 144ff.

46 Audoin-Rouzeau, *La Guerre des enfants*.

47 The *Deutsche Hochschulring* was the biggest student union in Germany between 1921 and 1926, and had a very pronounced *völkisch* tendency. See the next chapter.

48 *Lebenslauf*, n.d. (BAAZ, SSO Akte Richard Frankenberg; the manuscript file and *Lebenslauf* have been badly damaged by fire and water).

49 *Lebenslauf*, 2/11/1932 (BAAZ, SSO Akte Georg Herbert Mehlhorn).

50 'Nationalist League for Defence and Attack', a radical anti-Semitic and *völkisch* group. See Uwe Lohalm, *Völkischer Radikalismus. Die Geschichte des deutschvölkischen Schutz- und Trutzbundes 1919–1923* (Hamburg: Leibnitz Verlag, 1970).

51 *Lebenslauf*, n.d. (BAAZ, SSO Akte Reinhard Höhn; non-folioed document).

52 Jungakademische Pressedienst, 29/1/1923 (BABL, R-16.03/2748, folio 160); quoted in Herbert, *Best*, p. 74.

53 Jean-Claude Favez, *Le Reich devant l'occupation franco-belge de la Ruhr en 1923* (Geneva: Droz, 1969); Denise Artaud, 'Die Hintergründe der Ruhrbesetzung', *VfZ* 27, 1979.

54 *Rheinlandumschau* 7, 25/1–8/2/1923.

55 Best, *Rheinlandumschau* 6, 10–25/1/1923, p. 64. Quoted by Herbert, *Best*, p. 74.

56 Bernd Weisbrod also noted this phenomenon. He wrote: 'All these formations [i.e. the neighbourhood militias, the student volunteer reserve units and the *Freikörper*] drew a terrifying portrait of their political adversary; and another feature they had in common was their legitimation of a potential resort to violence by an anti-Bolshevik propaganda fuelled by alarming stories and calls for murder' ('Violence et culture politique en Allemagne

entre les deux guerres', *XXe Siècle – Revue d'histoire* 34, 1992); see also Mosse, *De la Grande Guerre au totalitarisme*, on the brutalization of the political field in Germany and the ways this discourse was thus adapted to the militant forces of every political persuasion.

57 Written in the 1920s and published in 1929, *Sperrfeuer um Deutschland* (Oldenburg: Gerhard Stalling Verlag, 1929) was one of the bestsellers in Germany between the wars. The edition used here, that of 1941, raised the number of copies printed to 353,000, making this book the Bible of historical accounts of the war.

Chapter 2 Constructing networks

1 See *Lebenslauf* Strickner (BAAZ, SSO Herbert Strickner; Graz); *Lebenslauf* Beyer (BAAZ, SSO Hans Joachim Beyer; Graz); *Lebenslauf* Jonack (BAAZ, RuSHA Akte Gustav Jonack).

2 See BABL, R-4901 (Alt R-21)/11096: *Satzungs- und Promotionsordnung*, University of Gießen; BABL, R-4901 (Alt R-21)/11101: University of Heidelberg; BABL, R-4901 (Alt R-21)/11117: Prague; BABL, R-4901 (Alt R-21)/11123: Tübingen; BABL, R-4901 (Alt R-21)/11110: Leipzig.

3 See *Lebensläufe* and corresponding personal files: BAAZ, SSO Heinz Gräfe; RuSHA Akte Gräfe; SSO Alfred Filbert; RuSHA Akte Alfred Filbert; RuSHA Akte Paul Mylius; SSO Personal Akte Paul Mylius.

4 Herbert, *Best*, p. 89, for the CV and an evaluation; see also *Lebenslauf* Best, 1/8/1937, folio 2 (BAAZ, SSO Best).

5 The Wannsee Institute was a research centre providing expert reports in the human sciences for the RSHA. Dependent on the SD II and so directed by Franz Six, it came under the control of the RSHA *Amt* VI in 1942. See Michael Fahlbusch, *Wissenschaft im Dienst der nationalsozialistischen Politik? Die 'volksdeutschen Forschungsgemeinschaften' von 1931–1945* (Baden-Baden: Nomos, 1999); Michael Burleigh, *Germany Turns Eastwards. A Study in 'Ostforschung' in the Third Reich* (Cambridge: Cambridge University Press, 1991); BADH, ZR/758, A.7: files on the people in the Wannsee Institute; archives of activities in BABL, R-58/131, 237, 238 and 390; incorporation of SDHA *Amt* II with RSHA *Amt* VI: protocol of a discussion between Six (*Amt* VII) and Jost (*Amt* VI), 29/2/1940 (BADH, ZR/920, A.62, folios 19–21).

6 *Dissertation* is the German term for 'doctoral thesis'.

7 *Lebenslauf* Malz, 24/6/1940 (BAAZ, SSO Malz); on the election of Höhn to Berlin, see Anna-Maria Gräfin von Lösch, *Der nackte Geist. Die Juristische Fakultät der Berliner Universität im Umbruch von 1933*, Beiträge zur Rechtsgeschichte des 20. Jahrhunderts, 26 (Tübingen: Mohr, 1999).

8 Jens Jessen was one of the main pro-Nazi figures in the extremely prestigious Institute for World Economy in Kiel and one of Reinhard Höhn's closest friends. The two men, collaborating with Werner Best and Wilhelm Stuckardt, one of the participants in the Wannsee Conference, founded one of the reviews of public law and political sciences that were used by the SS

to conduct theoretical debates: *Reich, Volksordnung, Lebensraum,* published by Wittich Verlag, the company that in 1940 published the *Festschriften* in honour of Himmler's fortieth birthday. See Herbert, *Best,* pp. 284–5.

9 Ludolf Herbst, *Der totale Krieg und die Ordnung der Wirtschaft. Die Kriegswirtschaft im Spannungsfeld von Politik, Ideologie und Propaganda 1939–1945* (Stuttgart: DVA, 1982).

10 See Lutz Hachmeister, *Der Gegnerforscher. Zur Karriere des SS-Führers Franz Alfred Six* (Munich: C. H. Beck, 1988), pp. 275–9. Symptomatic of the vision of Six as an academic charlatan is François Bayle, *Psychologie et éthique du national-socialisme. Étude anthropologique des dirigeants SS* (Paris: PUF, 1953).

11 See Peter Schöttler, 'Von der rheinischen Landesgeschichte zur nazistischen Volksgeschichte oder die "unerhörbare Stimme des Blutes"', in Winfried Schulze and Otto Gerhard Oexle (eds.), *Deutsche Historiker im Nationalsozialismus* (Frankfurt: Fischer, 1999).

12 Letter from Hans Rothfels to the rector of the University of Königsberg, 31/5/1931 (GStA Berlin-Dahlem, Rep 76 Va, section II, title IV, department IV, no. 21, vol. 23, folios 299ff). Quoted by Ingo Haar, '"Revisionistische" Historiker und Jugendbewegung: das Beispiel Königsberg', in Peter Schöttler (ed.), *Geschichtsschreibung als Legitimationswissenschaft 1918–1945* (Frankfurt: Suhrkamp, 1997).

13 Haar, ibid., pp. 70–81.

14 Hans Rothfels, 'Universität und Auslandsdeutschtum', in *Ostraum, Preussentum und Reichsgedanke. Historische Abhandlungen, Vorträge und Reden* (Leipzig: Hinrich, 1935).

15 Remarks reported by one of Rothfels' pupils, Klaus Bicke, 'Deutscher Besitz in lettischer Hand', in *Unsere Baltikumfahrt 1933* (account of a trip to the Baltic made by the *Werwolf* of Berlin), pp. 7ff.

16 Personal report submitted for promotion, n.d., signed Franz Six, folio 2 (BAAZ, SSO Turowsky).

17 *Lebenslauf,* 24/5/1938 (BAAZ, SSO Turowsky). See also Gerd Simon, *Germanistik in dem Planspiel des Sicherheitsdienstes der SS,* vol. 1 (Tübingen: Gift Verlag, 1998), p. xxvii.

18 Turowsky, *Die Innenpolitische Entwicklung Polnisch-Preussens.*

19 BABL, R-4901 (Alt R-21)/10001: files on teachers in higher education.

20 In 1940 and 1941, Beyer wrote a *Habilitation* thesis strongly influenced by *Ostforschung* and the *völkisch* 'human sciences' (Hans Joachim Beyer, *Umvolkungsvorgänge in Ost-Mitteleuropa* [Leipzig: Teubner, 1944]), for which he requested a subsidy for publication from RSHA III B5. See Ehlich's letter to the RKFdV of 17/2/1941 (BAAZ SSO Beyer).

21 Beyer taught in 1941 at the same university as Werner Conze (BABL, R-4901 [Alt R-21]/10303: occupation of the chairs in the philosophy faculty of Posen: *Volkstumwissenschaften*: BABL, R-57/743: Beyer's correspondence with the NSStB). See also the lists of participants at the conferences of the *Deutsche Stiftung* and the VDA: here, Beyer came across the most eminent of the revisionist historians (BABL, R-8043/62731: correspondence of the *Deutsche Stiftung* with the VDA).

22 *Vereinigung für das Deutschtum im Ausland.*

23 Ernst Ritter, *Das deutsche Ausland-Institut in Stuttgart 1917–1945. Ein Beispiel deutscher Volkstumarbeit zwischen den Weltkriegen* (Wiesbaden: Steiner, 1976); Karl-Heinz Roth, 'Heydrichs Professor: Historiographie des "Volkstums" und der Massenvernichtungen. Der Fall Hans Joachim Beyer', in Schöttler, *Geschichtschreibung*, p. 271.

24 See especially the works by Franz Alfred Six: *Freimaurerei und Judenemanzipation* (Hamburg: Hanseatische Verlagsanstalt, 1938); *Die Presse in Polen* (Berlin: Deutscher Verlag für Politik und Wirtschaft, 1938); *Pressefreiheit und internationale Zusammenarbeit* (Hamburg: Hanseatische Verlagsanstalt, 1937).

25 Rudolf Oebsger-Röder finally joined RSHA *Amt* VI, and on its behalf carried out commando operations against the Poles and the Russians; Kurt Walz and Horst Mahnke – the latter after a period in the *Einsatzgruppen* – for their part joined RSHA *Amt* VII, where their work was of a scientific and doctrinal nature (see BAAZ, SSO Mahnke, Walz and Oebsger-Röder). For traces of Mahnke's time with the mobile extermination groups, see the list of personnel and tables of funds paid to *Einsatzgruppe* B, folios 267ff (BADH, ZR. 125).

26 Hachmeister, *Der Gegnerforscher*, pp. 77–144.

27 On the *Ahnenerbe*, see Michael Kater, *Das 'Ahnenerbe' der SS 1935–1945. Ein Beitrag zur Kulturpolitik des Dritten Reichs* (Stuttgart: DVA, 1974).

28 Correspondence of Aubin/Franz and Aubin/Wüst in BABL, R-8037/1: correspondence of the *Saarforschungsgemeinschaft*. On Günther Franz, see Wolfgang Behringer, 'Von Krieg zu Krieg. Neue Perspektiven auf das Buch von Günther Franz', in Benigna von Krusenstjern and Hans Medick (eds.), *Zwischen Alltag und Katastrophe. Der Dreißigjährige Krieg aus der Nähe* (Göttingen: Vandenhoeck und Ruprecht, 1999); by the same author, 'Bauern-Franz und Rassen-Günther. Die politische Geschichte des Agrarhistorikers Günther Franz (1932–1992)', in Schulze and Oexle, *Deutsche Historiker*, pp. 114–41.

29 See Peter Schöttler, 'Die "historische Westforschung" zwischen "Abwehrkampf" und territorialer Offensive', in Schöttler, *Geschichtsschreibung*, pp. 204–61.

30 *Lebenslauf* (BAAZ, SSO Nockemann).

31 Report on the conference of the *Mittelstelle deutscher Jugend in Europa*, a decision to join the bureau of border work of the student corporation of Bonn (BABL, R-8043/62732, folio 51).

32 See Schöttler, 'Die "historische Westforschung"', p. 229.

33 *Lebenslauf*, 24/5/1938 (BAAZ, SSO Turowsky).

34 *Lebenslauf* and exchange of correspondence between Richter and the director of the Herder Institute (BABL, R-8021/2). In 1939, the Herder Institute formed the backbone of the University of Posen, under the supervision of the SS and the RSHA; see the correspondence between G. A. Scheel (*Reichsstudentenführer* and *Oberführer* SS), Ohlendorf (*Standartführer* SS, *Chef* RSHA III) and Martin Sandberger (*Chef* EWZ), especially the teletype from Sandberger to Ohlendorf and Scheel, 14/10/1939 (BABL, film no. 14906).

35 See also the biographical details given by Ohlendorf (letter from Ohlendorf

to SS-Sturmbannführer Prof. Dr Höhn, 18/5/1936, folio 2; BAAZ, SSO Otto Ohlendorf). *TMWC*, vol. 3, pp. 244ff; *Lebenslauf* Mehlhorn 2/11/1932 (BAAZ, SSO Mehlhorn); *Lebenslauf* Gräfe, 21/8/1938 (BAAZ, SSO Gräfe).

36 Simon, *Germanistik in dem Planspiel*, pp. ix–xlvii.

37 Diploma and reports on the thesis viva of Wilhelm Spengler, 16 and 17 July 1931, UAL (*Universitätsarchiv Leipzig*), Phil. Fak, 2570, folios 1–6.

38 See Spengler's statement made under oath concerning Obenhauer, 30/5/1949 (HStA Düss. NW 1049/4268). Quoted by Simon, *Germanistik in dem Planspiel*, p. xxxviii.

39 Aronson, *Heydrich und die Frühgeschichte von Gestapo*.

40 *Lebenslauf*, 20/11/1937 (BAAZ, SSO Kielpinski).

41 Ernst Anrich, *Universitäten als geistige Grenzfestungen* (Berlin; Stuttgart: Kohlkammer, 1936).

42 On Anrich in Strasbourg, and his highly ideological policy of Germanization and recruitment, see Schöttler, 'Die "historische Westforschung"', p. 213.

43 See Aronson, *Heydrich und die Frühgeschichte von Gestapo*.

44 Ruth Bettina Birn, *Die höheren SS- und Polizeiführer, Himmlers Vertreter im Reich und in den besetzten Gebieten* (Düsseldorf: Droste, 1986); the biographies of Behrends and all the HSSPF are given in the appendix.

45 See the photo of Behrends in Hachmeister, *Der Gegnerforscher*, p. 174.

46 *Lebenslauf*, 16/12/1933 (BAAZ, SSO Behrends, folio 53757).

47 *Lebenslauf*, n.d. (probably 1935), folio 1 (BAAZ, SSO Nockemann).

48 These can be seen on the anthropometric photos (RuSHA Akte Nockemann).

49 *Lebenslauf*, n.d. (BAAZ, RuSHA Akte Lettow). It should be noted that his membership of the *Burschenschaft* is not mentioned in his *Lebenslauf* of 10/10/1938 (BBAZ, SSO Lettow).

50 Jonack: *Lebenslauf*, 3/4/1939 (BAAZ, SSO Jonack); Mühler: RuSHA questionnaire of 15/8/1941 (BAAZ, RuSHA Akte Mühler); Mylius: *Lebenslauf* n.d. (BAAZ, SSO Mylius).

51 For all of this, see *Lebenslauf* Hummitzsch, 12/7/1938 (BAAZ, SSO Hummitzsch).

52 *Lebenslauf*, 13/1/1934 (BAAZ, SSO Mühler).

53 *Lebenslauf*, 2/11/1932 (BAAZ, SSO Akte Georg Herbert Mehlhorn).

54 Quoted by Jürgen Schwartz, *Studenten in der Weimarer Republik. Die deutsche Studentenschaft in der Zeit von 1918–1923 und ihre Stellung zur Politik* (Berlin: Duncker und Humblot, 1971), p. 240.

55 This was the case for a great many of the *Burschenschaften*. See Heike Ströle-Bühler, *Studentischer Antisemitismus in der Weimarer Republik. Eine Analyse der burschenschaftlichen Blätter 1918–1933* (Frankfurt: Suhrkamp, 1991); this movement was theorized by Oskar Franz Scheuer (*Burschenschaft und Judenfrage. Der Rassenantisemitismus in der deutschen Studentenschaften* [Berlin: Verlag Berlin-Wien, 1927]).

56 See Audoin-Rouzeau and Becker, *1914–1918*; Michael Jeismann, *Das Vaterland der Feinde: Studien zu nationalen Feindbegriff und Selbstverständnis in Deutschland und Frankreich, 1792–1918* (Stuttgart: Klett-Cotta, 1992). As opposed to Daniel Jonah Goldhagen (*Hitler's Willing Executioners: Ordinary*

Germans and the Holocaust [London: Little, Brown, 1996]), who inclines to a very early biologization of anti-Semitism, the thesis of a biologization dating from the war and postwar period is largely shared by specialists. On this point see, in French, Conte and Essner, *La Quête de la race*; Christian Ingrao, 'Le nazisme, la violence, l'anthropologie. Autour de Daniel Goldhagen', *European Review of History – Revue européenne d'histoire* 4/1, 1998; Herbert Strauss and Norbert Kampe (eds.), *Antisemitismus. Von der Judenfeindschaft zum Holocaust* (Frankfurt: Campus, 1985); Werner Jochmann, 'Die Ausbreitung des Antisemitismus in Deutschland 1914–1923', in Werner E. Mosse and Arnold Paucker (eds.), *Deutsches Judentum in Krieg und Revolution 1916–1923* (Tübingen: Mohr, 1974); Shulamit Volkov, 'Kontinuität und Diskontinuität im deutschen Antisemitismus, 1878–1945', *VfZ* 33, 1985.

57 Friedrich Meinecke, 'Der Geist der akademischen Jugend in Deutschland. Zur Erklärung der politischen Ursachen des Rathenau-Mordes (1922)', in Georg Potoski (ed.), *Friedrich Meineckes politische Reden und Schriften* (Darmstadt, 1968), pp. 338–43; p. 340. Quoted by Herbert, *Best*, p. 65.

58 See Norbert Kampe, *Studenten und 'Judenfrage' im deutschen Kaiserreich. Die Entstehung einer akademischen Trägerschicht des Antisemitismus* (Göttingen: Vandenhoeck und Ruprecht, 1987).

59 Herbert, *Best*, p. 68.

60 Results of the votes and rates of participation in J. H. Mitgau, 'Studentische Demokratie', in *Süddeutsche Akademische Stimme, 1/3/1921, Nachrichtenblatt des DHR*, February/March 1921. Quoted by Herbert, *Best*, p. 551, note 69.

61 Herbert, *Best*, p. 69.

62 Speech for the new academic year, *Tübinger Chronik*, 22/6/1929, quoted by Mathias Kotowski, 'Noch ist ja der Krieg gar nicht zu Ende', in Krumeich, Langewiesche, Ullmann and Hirschfeld, *Kriegserfahrungen*, pp. 424–38; pp. 432–3.

63 See *Lebenslauf* Scheel (BADH, ZM/1455, A.3 [a collection of short *Lebensläufe* of high-ranking SS officials], folio 106); and Hachmeister, *Der Gegnerforscher*; signs of Scheel's collaboration with the SD, especially Six: BABL, R-4901 (Alt R-21)/10961 (lists of doctoral and *Habilitation* theses awarded prizes by the *Prüfungskommission zum Schutz des NS-Schrifttums*): Scheel played an active part with Six in the choice of the prize-winning theses; BABL, R-153/1625: inaugurations at the *Reichsuniversität* Posen: opening speech given by *Reichsstudentenführer* SS *Oberführer* Dr Scheel; BABL, film no. 14906 (documents from EWZ Posen and Gotenhafen): Scheel played a role in the foundation of the University of Posen by authorizing the use of professors from the Herder Institute of Riga.

64 *Lebenslauf* Mühler, 13/1/1934 (BAAZ, SSO Mühler).

65 *Lebenslauf*, 12/7/1938, folio 1 (BAAZ, SSO Hummitzsch).

66 There is in fact only one article that specifically discusses this theme: Hüppauf, 'Schlachtenmythen', pp. 43–84.

67 Heinemann, in *Die verdrängte Niederlage*, had already defended the idea that the defeat had been psychologically repressed.

68 On Langemarck and its heritage, see Hüppauf, 'Schlachtenmythen'; for the

lack of impact of the celebrations of Langemarck, see Kotowski, 'Noch ist ja der Krieg gar nicht zu Ende', pp. 428–9.

69 BABL, R-8014/716 to 719 (*Bund der Saarvereine* and student corporations: correspondence on the various collaborations and conferences 1929–35); in total, over 1,000 pages of a correspondence comprising invitations, student requests and organized trips.

70 At a conference of revisionist associations and representatives of the Ministry of the Interior and the *Auswärtiges Amt* dating from 1924, the representatives of the *Bund der Saarvereine* stated they had the impression they had been eclipsed by the Ruhr and were not gaining enough attention: BABL, R-8014/758 (correspondence between the *Bund der Saarvereine* and the *Deutscher Schutzbund*).

71 Letter from Vogel to the president of the Sarrois Senate, Andres, of 11/5/1932 (BABL, R-8014/758; non-folioed).

72 Correspondence in BABL, R-8014/716 (*Bund der Saarvereine* and student corporations: correspondence on various collaborations and conferences).

73 In *völkisch* ideology, border territories were the main geographical framework of the *Volkstumskampf*. See the scholarly analysis of the *völkisch* movement: on Franz Petri's historiographical work, by Peter Schöttler, in Schöttler, 'Von der rheinischen Landesgeschichte'; see also Haar, '"Revisionistische" Historiker und Jugendbewegung', pp. 70–81; and, more generally, Burleigh, *Germany Turns Eastwards*.

74 BABL, R-8014/717.

75 Traces of its activity under the aegis of the German League of Protection (*Deutscher Schutzbund*) are noted in BABL, R-8039/80 (correspondence between the *Deutscher Schutzbund* and the *Jugendbünde*).

76 Activity of the *Mittelstelle* documented in BABL, R-8043/62732 (correspondence between the *Deutsche Stiftung* and the DAI of Stuttgart); see for example the report on this conference's activities, folios 343–51.

77 Heiss was the head of the *Grenzamt* of the DHR in 1925 (BABL, R-8043/62732, folio 347).

78 On the links between the publishing house Volk und Reich and the *Publikationsstelle* Dahlem, see BABL, R-153/1190; see also Ingo Haar, *Historiker im Nationalsozialismus: Deutsche Geschichtswissenschaft und der 'Volkstumskampf' im Osten* (Göttingen: Vandenhoeck und Ruprecht, 2000).

79 On Nazi *Volkstumpolitik*, see Hans-Adolf Jacobsen, *Nationalsozialistische Aussenpolitik 1933–38* (Frankfurt: Alfred Metzner Verlag, 1968).

80 Friedrich Heiß, *Deutschland zwischen Nacht und Tag* (Berlin: Volk und Reich Verlag, 1934).

81 Friedrich Heiß, *Deutsche Revolution. Die Wende eines Volkes. Fünf Jahrzehnte deutschen Volkskampfes* (Berlin: Volk und Reich Verlag, 1933 (?)).

82 They took part in the conferences of the *Volkswissenschaftlicher Arbeitskreis*, which brought together members of *volksdeutsch* organizations, Nazi or *völkisch* academics, members of the VoMi and the leaders of the *Deutsche Stiftung*, the Puste Dahlem, the DAI and the *Mittelstelle*. For reports on the conferences, and lists of attendees, see BABL, R-8043/62731 (correspondence

between the *Deutsche Stiftung* and the VDA), especially folios 177–95 and 220–39.

83 *Lebenslauf* Höhn (copy), n.d. (BAAZ, SSO Höhn, folios 1–2). The cut was made by the author.

84 Werner Best, Reinhard Höhn, Gerhard Klopfer, Wilhelm Stuckart and Werner Wittig (eds.), *Festgabe für den Reichsführer SS und Chef der Deutschen Polizei Heinrich Himmler zu seinem 40. Geburtstag und ihm am fünften Jahrestag der Übernahme der Deutschen Polizei am 17. Juni 1941 überreicht* (Darmstadt: Wittich, 1941).

85 See Simon, *Germanistik in dem Planspiel*.

86 For administrative charts of the RSHA, see BADH, ZR-257; BABL, R-58/840 (charts: paraphs of the SDHA in 1937, RSHA charts for 1940, 1941 and 1943).

87 For Gräfe, *Lebenslauf*, BAAZ, SSO Gräfe; for Oebsger Röder, DZAP, RFM/868, folios 147 and 197: *Studentenschaft in Leipzig: Leiter der Hochschulschaft, Candidat Phil.*

88 BABL, R-8043/62732, folio 65.

89 On Oebsger-Röder's activities, see: *Einsatzkommando* from Woyrsch to Bromberg (ZStL, 203 AR-Z 313/39); see also Christian Jansen and Arno Weckbecker, *Der 'volksdeutsche Selbstschutz' in Polen 1939/40* (Munich: Oldenbourg, 1992); as head of a bureau of the EWZ in Łódź: BABL, DAI-Film no. 2185 (documents from VoMi, DAI and RSHA on the *Umsiedlungen*): for Gräfe, *Einsatzkommando* 1d in Poland: DZAP RSHA Film 2436, clips 420 and 879.

90 BADH, ZR-920, A.1, folios 187 and 193 in particular.

91 BADH, ZB-II/4776, A.15: Willy Seibert, personal SA and postwar file.

92 Until publication of his thesis, see Andrej Angrick, 'Die Einsatzgruppe D', in Peter Klein (ed.), *Die Einsatzgruppen in der besetzten Sowjetunion 1941/42. Die Tätigkeits- und Lageberichte des Chefs der Sicherheitspolizei und des SD* (Berlin: Edition Hentrich, 1997).

93 Letter from Ohlendorf to *SS-Sturmbannführer* Prof. Dr Höhn, 18/5/1936, folio 2 (BAAZ, SSO Otto Ohlendorf); *Lebenslauf*, n.d., BAAZ, RuSHA Akte Friedrich Tiedt.

94 Karl-Heinz Roth, 'Ärzte als Vernichtungspläner: Hans Ehlich, die Amtsgruppe III B des Reichssicherheitshauptamtes und der nationalsozialistische Genozid 1939–1945', in M. Hubenstorf et al. (eds.), *Medizingeschichte und Gesellschaftskritik. Festschrift für Gerhard Baader* (Husum: Matthiesen, 1997).

95 The importance of Leipzig is brought out in an impressionistic way by Jens Banach in *Heydrichs Elite. Das Führerkorps der Sicherheitspolizei und des SD 1936–1945* (Paderborn: Schöningh, 1998), p. 256, without any analysis in terms of networks.

Chapter 3 Activist intellectuals

1 This thesis was represented in the scholarly sub-literature produced by Christian Bernadec and the reviews *Historia* and *Historama* in the 1960s in

France. The thesis of perversion was also subscribed to by François Bayle (*Psychologie et éthique*); generally speaking, historical works on the sciences under the Third Reich do not manage to study the conditions of production of knowledge, restricting themselves to regretful or horrified denunciations of the scientific depredations of the Nazi regime. More satisfactory, even though very descriptive, are: Jeanne Olff-Nathan (ed.), *La Science sous le Troisième Reich* (Paris: Le Seuil, 1993); Benno Müller Hill, *Murderous Science: Elimination by Scientific Selection of Jews, Gypsies, and Others, Germany 1933–1945*, tr. George R. Fraser (Oxford: Oxford University Press, 1988) – this is more an anthology of documents than a work of synthesis; and the research pro- gramme drawn up by the Max-Planck-Institut für Wissenschaftsgeschichte of Berlin on the history of the Kaiser-Wilhelm-Institut under the Nazi regime.

2 Reminder: an *Akademiker* is a person who has studied at university.

3 *Lebenslauf* Ehlers (BAAZ, SSO Ehlers); RuSHA *Fragebogen* (BAAZ, RuSHA Akte Burmester); synoptic file on advance (BAAZ, SSO Zapp).

4 Study plan for the training of the department of surveillance of the civil service in BABL, R-18/3776 (Dr Stuckart's files), non-folioed, 12 pages.

5 *Lebenslauf* Frankenberg (BAAZ, SSO Frankenberg); appointment to the post of *Dozent* in BADH, ZA-V/179 (appointment proposals put forward by the minister president of Prussia), folios 389–90; appointment to a chair in his *Hochschule* (higher school of pedagogy) in BADH, ZA-V/171 (list of appointment proposals put forward by the minister president of Prussia, folio 233).

6 See in BADH, ZR-545, A.4; Ministry of the Interior, order of appointment as *Regierungsrat*.

7 RuSHA *Fragebogen* Mühler (BAAZ, RuSHA Akte Mühler).

8 *Lebenslauf*, 2/6/1942 (BAAZ, SSO Herbert Strickner); RuSHA *Fragebogen*, RuSHA Akte Strickner.

9 *Lebenslauf*, 2/11/1932 (BAAZ, SSO Mehlhorn), folios 1–2; see also his questionnaire RuSHA (BAAZ, RuSHA Akte Mehlhorn), as well as the bio- graphical file composed by Aronson, *Heydrich und die Frühgeschichte von Gestapo*, p. 59.

10 This is how he presented himself elsewhere; see *Lebenslauf*, 1/8/1937, folio 1 (BAAZ, SSO Best).

11 BABL, R-18/3776.

12 One should recall at this point that his publishing activity shows more than seventy references between 1929 and 1945: see Herbert, *Best*; bibliography of Best's work, pp. 647–9.

13 *Lebenslauf*, n.d., folioed 6274 (BAAZ, SSO Leetsch).

14 Benoît Massin, 'Anthropologie raciale et national-socialisme: heurs et mal- heurs du paradigme de la race', in Olff-Nathan, *La Science sous le Troisième Reich*; on the birth of anthropology in France, see François Dosse, *History of Structuralism*, tr. Deborah Glassman, 2 vols. (Minneapolis; London: University of Minnesota Press, 1997): vol. 1: *The Rising Sign, 1945–1966*; vol. 2: *The Sign Sets, 1967–Present*.

15 Hachmeister, *Der Gegnerforscher*.

16 Behringer, 'Von Krieg zu Krieg'; and, by the same author, 'Bauern-Franz und Rassen-Günther'.

17 Roth, 'Heydrichs Professor'.

18 BABL, R-3101 (Alt R-7)/2016, 2017, 2024 and 2049, where Ohlendorf's working files – conference speeches, notes, papers and reviews – are collected.

19 On Ohlendorf, see Herbst, *Der totale Krieg*, pp. 181–8, and, for the record, Bayle, *Psychologie et éthique*.

20 *Lebenslauf* Mehlhorn 2/11/1932 (BAAZ, SSO Mehlhorn).

21 *Lebenslauf* Gräfe (BAAZ RuSHA Akte Gräfe).

22 *Lebenslauf* Gräfe, non-folioed document, page 5 (BAAZ, RuSHA Akte Gräfe).

23 *Lebenslauf*, 21/8/1938 (BAAZ, SSO Gräfe).

24 Diploma and reports on the thesis viva of Wilhelm Spengler, 16–17/7/1931, UAL (*Universitätsarchiv* Leipzig), Phil. Fak., 2570, folios 1–6.

25 *Lebenslauf*, 13/7/1936 (BAAZ, SSO Spengler); see also Simon, *Germanistik in dem Planspiel*; Aronson, *Heydrich und die Frühgeschichte von Gestapo*, pp. 162–3 and 295–6.

26 The investigator at Nuremberg submitted his final report with the statement that Six's academic career was 'an imposture, and should be linked to the threat of terror on the part of his SS masters' (*IfZ* Interrogation Six/Mahnke, pp. 20–1).

27 Wilhelm Spengler's thesis was published under the title: *Das Drama Schillers. Seine Genesis* (Leipzig: Weber, 1932).

28 Thesis report, 22/5/1931, UAL, Phil. Fak., 2570, folios 2–3.

29 Quotations from his *Lebenslauf*, 13/7/1936 (BAAZ, SSO Spengler).

30 Typical of this presentation of facts is the tableau of the history faculties under Nazism drawn up by Helmut Heiber, who depicted a handful of char-latans usurping academic power through their slavish attitude towards the NSDAP, leaving the rest of the profession intact: see Heiber, *Universität unter dem Hakenkreuz*, 2 vols. (Munich: Saur, 1991–2); and the same author's *Walter Frank und sein Reichsinstitut für Geschichte des neuen Deutschlands* (Stuttgart: DVA, 1966); see in particular the critique by Peter Schöttler and the con-troversies that ensued: Schöttler, 'Von der rheinischen Landesgeschichte'. See also Christian Ingrao, 'Les historiens et le nazisme. Pratiques historio-graphiques, légitimation et engagement', *Sociétés contemporaines*, 2000.

31 See Ulrich Herbert, 'Weltanschauungseliten. Ideologische Legitimation und politische Praxis der Führungsgruppe der nazionalsozialistischen Sicherheitspolizei', *Potsdamer Bulletin für Zeithistorische Studien*, 9, 1997, pp. 4–18.

32 Werner Best, *Zur Frage der 'gewollten Tarifunfähigkeit'* (Mainz: Eis, 1927).

33 Herbert, *Best*, p. 89. Herbert describes Best's thesis as 'apolitical' and 'rational'.

34 Hans Nockemann, *Einige Streitfragen aus dem Kohlenwirtschaftsgesetz und den dazu ergangenen Ausführungsbestimmungen und ihre Beurteilung in der Praxis der ordentlichen Gerichte und der Organe der Kohlenwirtschaft* (Cologne: Welzel, 1930).

35 Alfred Filbert, *Kann das Ablehnungsrecht des Konkursverwalters des*

Vorbehalterskäufers mit der Anwartschaft des Käufers auf den Eigentumserwerb ausgeräumt werden? (Gießen: Meyer, 1935).

36 Ernst Hermann Jahr, *Das Regierunsgesetz* (Bochum-Langendreer: Pöppinghaus, 1935).

37 Friedrich Tiedt, *Die Haftung des Beamten und seines Dienstherrn für Amtspflichtverletzungen nach geltendem Recht und Gedanken über ein neues Amthaftungsrecht* (Seestadt Rostock: Hinstorff, 1939).

38 Hermann Behrends, *Die nützliche Geschäftsführung* (Marburg: Trute, 1932).

39 Hans Leetsch, *Die Bedeutung der Aufträge der öffentlichen Hand für den Ablauf der Konjunktur* (Geinhausen: Kalbfleisch, 1936).

40 Evidence given by Ohlendorf, in *TMWC*, vol. 3, pp. 244ff.

41 Notes of the working group of the Institute in BABL, R-3101 (Alt R-7)/2149, folios 74ff.

42 Paper on 'The SD man and the economy' given to the trainee officers of the Bernau SD; lecture on 'Ideology and economy', both in BABL, R-3101 (Alt R-7/2149) (files of Otto Ohlendorf, conference papers, notes).

43 This was the case, for example, of Helmut Meinhold and Theodor Oberländer. See Susanne Heim and Götz Aly, *Helmut Meinhold oder der Zusammenhang zwischen Sozialpolitik und Judenvernichtung* (Hamburg: Institut für Sozialforschung, 1986).

44 See Götz Aly and Susanne Heim, *Vordenker der Vernichtung. Auschwitz und die deutschen Pläne für eine neue europäische Ordnung* (Frankfurt: Fischer, 1993), especially p. 333 on the Kiel Institute.

45 Ulrich Herbert has analysed the profiles of a bigger number of SS lawyers, especially those of the Gestapo, who, being younger and employed as practitioners of penal law and police work, probably had different profiles from those of SD lawyers. His analysis seems invalid as far as the SD lawyers are concerned. For those of the Gestapo there is still a conceptual problem: Herbert presupposes an irrationality in the Nazi system of beliefs, which sets the terms of rationality and irrationality up as historical concepts without really defining them. Classifying attitudes in advance debars him from bringing out their coherence. Together with the omission of reference to the experience of the Great War and the underestimating of the significance of memory in the analysis of the behaviour of Best and the men of his generation, this is the main failing of a work that is still one of the best studies of Nazism produced in the last few years. See Herbert, 'Generation der Sachlichkeit', in Herbert, *Arbeit, Volkstum, Weltanschauung. Über Fremde und Deutsche im 20. Jahrhundert* (Frankfurt: Fischer, 1995); his *Best*; and his more recent 'Weltanschauungseliten'. See also, for a more detailed critique, the present author's 'Conquérir, aménager, exterminer. Nouvelles recherches sur la Shoah', *Annales. Histoire, sciences sociales*, 2001.

46 Richard Frankenberg, *Die Nichterneuerung des deutsch–russischen Rücksichtsversicherungsvertrags im Jahre 1890* (Berlin: Deutsche Verlagsgesellschaft für Geschichte und Politik, 1927).

47 On these diplomatic aspects, see Jacques Droz, *Histoire diplomatique de 1648 à*

1919 (Paris: Dalloz, 1972), and Jean-Baptiste Duroselle, *Europe. A History of its Peoples*, tr. Richard Mayne (London: Viking, 1990).

48 Heinemann, *Die verdrängte Niederlage*.

49 *Österreich-Ungarn und Russland, 1870–1890*, thesis viva held at Innsbruck in 1934. I have not managed to track down a copy; the title is mentioned in *Lebenslauf*, n.d. (BAAZ, SSO Engel, folios 1–2).

50 See Droz, *Histoire diplomatique*; Duroselle, *Europe*.

51 Engel showed his interest in these questions in his *Lebenslauf* (BAAZ SSO Engel).

52 See the theoretical discussions in Schöttler, 'Von der rheinischen Landesgeschichte'.

53 Behrends, *Die nützliche Geschäftsführung*; Georg Herbert Mehlhorn, *Die Bestimmung der Strafe für die Wilderei* (Teplitz-Schönau: Schmoll, 1929).

54 *Lebenslauf* Mehlhorn, 2/11/1932 (BAAZ, SSO Akte Georg Herbert Mehlhorn); *Lebenslauf* Behrends, 16/12/1933 (BAAZ, SSO Hermann Behrends, folio 53757).

55 Ernst Krieck, *Leben als Prinzip der Weltanschauung und Problem in der Wissenschaft* (Leipzig: Armanen Verlag, 1938); Bernhard Rust and Ernst Krieck, *Das Nationalsozialistiches Deutschland und die Wissenschaft* (Hamburg: Hanseatische Verlagsanstalt, 1936).

56 Ernst Krieck, *Völkische-politische Anthropologie* (Leipzig: Armanen Verlag, 1937). See also Hachmeister, *Der Gegnerforscher*, p. 113.

57 Walter von Kielpinski, 'Der Einbruch des Katholizismus in die Wissenschaft', *Volk im Werden* 5, 1937; 'Deutsche Wissenschaft und Sowjetunion', *Volk im Werden* 5, 1937.

58 Wilhelm Classen, 'Das Ausland und die nazionalsozialistische Wissenschaft', *Volk im Werden*, 1933; 'Politische Auslandskunde', *Volk im Werden* 4, 1936.

59 Wilhelm Spengler, 'Die schöpferische Freiheit in der Kunst', *Volk im Werden* 5, 1937; 'Die Frau im germanischen und christlichen Weltbild', *Volk im Werden* 5, 1937.

60 In other words, Wilhelm Spengler. See also Simon, *Germanistik in dem Planspiel*; Aronson, *Heydrich und die Frühgeschichte von Gestapo*, pp. 162–3 and 295–6.

61 Franz Alfred Six, 'Germanisches Erbe im deutschen Geist', *Volk im Werden*, 1937.

62 Hans Joachim Beyer, 'Sudetendeutsche und Tschechen im Völkerrecht', *Volk im Werden* 6, 1938.

63 Emil Augsborg, *Die staats- und parteipolitische Bedeutung der sowjetischen Presse in ihrer geschichtlichen Entwicklung*, typewritten thesis (n.p. (Berlin), 1941). Franz Six's work on the press in Poland is governed by the same questions: *Die Presse in Polen*.

64 Thesis not consulted: Paul Mylius, *Die juristische Darstellung der jüdischen Gesetzgebung*, quoted in AGKBZH, 362/298 (protocols of 'scientific' lectures given by Prof. Franz).

65 Horst Mahnke, *Die freimauerische Presse in Deutschland. Struktur und Geschichte* (n.p., 1941).

66 I am here thinking of the generation of SS intellectuals who filled the ranks

of the RSHA *Amt* VII during the war and who, all pupils of Six, pursued a thesis or *Habilitation* in tandem with 'research and ideological assessment' under the leadership of Six and of Günther Franz. See Hachmeister, *Der Gegnerforscher*, pp. 225–8; on Günther Franz see Behringer, 'Von Krieg zu Krieg'; and Behringer, 'Bauern-Franz und Rassen-Günther'.

67 On the role of the SD in scientific politics, see Kater, *Das 'Ahnenerbe' der SS 1935–1945*.

68 For the fusion of disciplines, see Willy Oberkrome, 'Geschichte, Volk, Theorie. Das Handwörterbuch des Grenz- und Auslandsdeutschtums', in Schöttler, *Geschichtsschreibung*.

69 On these men, their *völkisch* conceptions and Nazification by generational change, see Ingo Haar, 'Kämpfende Wissenschaften. Entstehung und Niedergang der völkischen Geschichtswissenschaften im Wechsel der Systeme', in Schulze and Oexle, *Deutsche Historiker*, pp. 215–41; pp. 224–5.

70 Report on a meeting between the *Reichsstudentenführung* and the SDHA II/211 on *Ostforschung*, stating that Dolezalek is to produce a report on Carpathian Ukraine. Non-dated meeting, probably from the second half of 1938: Dolazelak completed the report in January 1939 (BADH, ZR/921, A.2: archives of the administration of the SDHA 121, folios 134–5). On Dolezalek, see also Roth, 'Heydrichs Professor', pp. 269–70.

71 They occur regularly in the lists of speakers and attendees at the VWA conferences (BABL, R-8043/62731: correspondence between the *Deutsche Stiftung* and the VDA).

72 See the list of friends and promoters of the VWA in BABL, R-153/96 (correspondence between Puste Dahlem and the *Volksbund für das Deutschtum im Ausland*), non-folioed. All are mentioned in it, with other SD intellectuals such as Reinhard Höhn. On Valjavec, see Roth, 'Heydrichs Professor', p. 270; Michael Fahlbusch, 'Die "Süddeutsche Forschungsgemeinschaft". Politische Beratung und NS-Volkstumspolitik', in Schulze and Oexle, *Deutsche Historiker*; and Fahlbusch, *Wissenschaft im Dienst der nationalsozialistischen Politik?*

73 See below, chapter 7; see also Roth's excellent article, 'Heydrichs Professor', pp. 262–80.

74 Lists of works published by members of the VWA in BABL, R-153/96, non-folioed document.

75 On Kleo Pleyer, see Schöttler's article in *Geschichtsschreibung*, pp. 229ff.

76 [*Deutschtum* means 'Germandom', but, as Ingrao points out, Pleyer preferred not to emphasize the 'Germanic' aspects, otherwise he would have used the word *Germanentum*: so I have kept the word *Deutschtum* – *Tr.*]

77 Report on the session of the VWA, 5–6/1/1939, folio 1 for my quotation, folio 32 for the genealogical survey (BABL, R-153/95).

78 See AGKBZH, 362/298 (protocols of 'scientific' lectures given under the direction of Günther Franz). On Franz, see Behringer, 'Von Krieg zu Krieg', and his 'Bauern-Franz und Rassen-Günther'.

79 Letter from Ehlich to the RKFdV of 17/2/1941 (BAZ SSO Beyer).

80 Populations ethnically different from the Germanic. This word is best kept in German.

81 Roth, 'Heydrichs Professor'; see also his '"Generalplan Ost" – "Gesamtplan Ost". Forschungsstand, Quellenprobleme, neue Ergebnisse', in Mechtild Rössler and Sabine Schleiermacher (eds.), *Der 'Generalplan Ost'. Hauptlinien der nationalsozialistischen Planungs- und Vernichtungspolitik* (Berlin: Akademie Verlag, 1993); on the role of the RSHA *Amt* III B2 in population movements, see also Götz Aly, *Final Solution: Nazi Population Policy and the Murder of the European Jews*, tr. Belinda Cooper and Allison Brown (London: Arnold, 1999); the expression 'conceived the annihilation' is based on the title of the seminal study by Aly and Heim, *Vordenker der Vernichtung* (literally, those who 'thought out in advance' the annihilation).

82 I am here drawing on the concept developed by Stéphane Audoin-Rouzeau on the occasion of the seminar held at the EHESS, and which studied the material and psychological ways in which the emergence from and aftermath of conflicts was managed.

Chapter 4 Being a Nazi

1 StA Nuremberg, *TWC*, case 9, ZB-I, pp. 1335ff.

2 Characteristic of this type of thesis is Martin Broszat, *The Hitler State: The Foundation and Development of the Internal Structure of the Third Reich*, tr. John W. Hiden (London: Longman, 1981). However, Broszat's attitude was not always the same (cf. for the record his article 'Die völkische Ideologie und der Nationalsozialismus', *Deutsche Rundschau*, 84, 1958), which is not to impugn the merits of the functionalist school which he helped to found.

3 See Fritz Stern's work on Moeller van de Brück, *The Politics of Cultural Despair: A Study in the Rise of the Germanic Ideology* (Berkeley: University of California Press, 1961), and Gilbert Merlio, *Spengler, témoin de son temps*, 2 vols. (Stuttgart: Heinz, 1995).

4 On *völkisch* trends and their connections with Nazism, a traditional field of study for traditional *Geistesgeschichte*, see: Louis Dupeux (ed.), *La 'Révolution conservatrice' dans l'Allemagne de Weimar* (Paris: Kimé, 1992); Stefan Breuer, *Anatomie der konservativen Revolution* (Darmstadt: Wissenschaftliche Buchgesellschaft, 1993); Stern, *The Politics of Despair*; Broszat, 'Die völkische Ideologie'; Jost Hermand, *Old Dreams of a New Reich: Völkisch Utopias and National Socialism*, tr. Paul Levesque in collaboration with Stefan Soldovieri (Bloomington: Indiana University Press, 1992).

5 All authors emphasize the importance of the racial foundation of Nazi ideology, so there is no need to try and prove it, even if people often fail to describe its complexity, preferring to speak of *Rassenwahn* (race madness) rather than going into debates over doctrine. See the introductory remarks by Conte and Essner, *La Quête de la race*.

6 See in particular James Rhodes, *The Hitler Movement: A Modern Millenarian Revolution* (Stanford: Stanford University Press, 1980).

7 On Hans F. K. Günther, see Behringer, 'Bauern-Franz und Rassen-Günther', as well as Massin, in particular 'Anthropologie raciale et national-socialisme'.

8 Hans F. K. Günther, *Rassenkunde des deutschen Volkes*, 12th edn (Munich: Lehmann Verlag, 1928); Conte and Essner, *La Quête de la race*, pp. 70–1.

9 Hans F. K. Günther, *Kleine Rassenkunde des deutschen Volkes* (Leipzig: Lehmann Verlag, 1930), pp. 18–19 and 98, for a map of the theoretical original settlements of European, Asian and African races; pp. 86–7 for maps of miscegenation in Germany.

10 I will not here go into the details of Günther's raciology and his work on miscegenation; for all this, see Conte and Essner, *La Quête de la race*, pp. 79–116.

11 Günther, *Rassenkunde des jüdischen Volkes*.

12 See Conte and Essner, *La Quête de la race*, p. 76.

13 This is the expression used by Conte and Essner as the title of their ch. 2, ibid.

14 'Ukraine'. Draft memorandum of the Wannsee Institute (May–June 1941), BABL, R-58/37; folios 7–18 for the geopolitical presentation.

15 Documents of the same type (this is not a full-scale list): BABL, R-58/238: 'The new agrarian order in the occupied eastern territories' (position adopted by the Wannsee Institute); BABL, R-3101 (Alt R-7)/2151 (Ohlendorf files); BABL, R-58/19 (Wannsee Institute memorandum: 'Agrarian reorganization in the occupied territories of Eastern Europe'); BABL, R-58/13 (memorandum on the Russian question); AGKBZH, 362/236 (memorandum: 'The French Revolution in the light of the history of France'); AGKBZH, 362/45 (historical research into Emperor Otto I the Great. Memorandum on 'The SD and its activity').

16 BABL, R-58/844; pedagogic material for the SD.

17 Lesson no. 6 (BABL, R-58/844, folio 37).

18 Lesson no. 6 (BABL, R-58/844, folios 39–41).

19 Ibid., folio 38.

20 Lesson no. 15: *Der Dreissigjährige Krieg, die Katastrophe der deutschen Geschichte* (BABL, R-58/844, folios 97–124). See also Günther Franz, *Der Dreissigjährige Krieg und das deutsche Volk* (Jena: Fischer, 1940); Franz Alfred Six, *Der Westfälische Friede von 1648. Deutsche Textausgabe des Friedensverträge von Münster und Osnabrück* (Berlin: Junker und Dünnhaupt, 1940); and Hans Joachim Beyer, in a book of biographies: Otto Lohr and Hans Joachim Beyer (eds.), *Große Deutsche im Ausland. Eine Volksdeutsche Geschichte in Lebensbildern* (Stuttgart: Union, 1939).

21 It is worth noting the fundamental contradiction in Nordicist theory, which made Austria an empire with an Alpine centre even though it was hostile to Germany and saw the hereditary Habsburg lands (Styria, Carinthia and Carniola, today Slovenia) as the cradle of Austria only when the latter again allied itself with Germany. Günther was then obliged to invent, from observations made in the POW camps of 1914–15, a 'Dinaric race' (with its cradle in Carinthia), which enabled him to include the Austrians in the Nordic camp.

22 BABL, R-58/844, folio 110.

23 Ibid., folio 111.

24 Ibid., folios 123–4.

25 Otto Ohlendorf's final statement at the trial of the *Einsatzgruppen*, 13/2/1948 (*TWC*, vol. II, p. 386).

26 This absurdity is embodied in the word *umsonst* (in vain), which recurs like a leitmotiv in the accounts of the experience of defeat; see above, chs 1–2.

27 The term, coined by Hannah Arendt, designates the hidden meaning of Nazi ideology that, in her view, impelled individuals to pledge their support for it. It is the search for this 'super-sense' that the intentionalists seek to investigate. Like the latter, Arendt sees Nazism as an 'ideology', a mechanical system of ideas that unfolds logically and leads to total terror. But the philosopher thereby loses, perhaps, any way of linking ideological internalization to psychological life and personal emotions? See Arendt, *The Origins of Totalitarianism*, new edn (New York: Harcourt Brace Jovanovich, 1973).

28 Typical of this kind of analysis is Nicholas Goodrick-Clarke, *The Occult Roots of Nazism: Secret Aryan Cults and their Influence on Nazi Ideology* (New York: New York University Press, 1992).

29 Dupront, *Le Mythe de croisade*, vol. 2, pp. 1210–11.

30 Conte and Essner, *La Quête de la race*, pp. 120–1.

31 This was the case, for example, with Hans F. K. Günther in *Führeradel und Sippenpflege* (Munich: Lehmann, 1936) and *Gattenwahl zu ehelichem Glück und erblicher Ertüchtigung* (Munich: Lehmann, 1941). The meaning of these titles is: 'The nobility of leaders and the cultivation of lineage' and 'The choice of a spouse for conjugal happiness and the reinforcing of heredity'. Günther himself had married a Danish woman. See Conte and Essner, *La Quête de la race*, pp. 74–84 and 138–9.

32 Catalogues of the SD libraries: AGKBZH, 362/367; AGKBZH, 362/363 (schools of the SIPO and SD); AGKBZH, 362/308; AGKBZH, 362/368 (inventories of the books in the Stapo-libraries of several towns). No borrowing slips have been found for these books in AGKBZH, 362/342 (borrowing slips for books by collaborators of the RSHA), but these slips record only very occasional institutional investigations and not 'detailed' readings by SS intellectuals.

33 For example, the *Stammen* are mentioned in the *Denkschriften*, already cited, of the RSHA on Ukraine, Russia, the Caucasus and the Cossacks, as well as in training files on racial doctrine, but these files do not reflect the intimate internalization of this dimension of racial determinism. See, for example, the text describing education in 'race duties' and the 'racial consciousness' of children, in AGKBZH, 362/263 (non-folioed); BABL, R-58/37 ('Ukraine'. Draft memorandum of the Wannsee Institute); BABL, R-58/370 ('The Cossack nation' [*Das Kosakentum*], work produced by the Wannsee Institute); AGKBZH, 362/766 (work on the history of Ukraine and Poland).

34 On RuSHA, see Isabel Heinemann, *'Rasse, Siedlung, deutsches Blut': das Rasse- und Siedlungshauptamt der SS und die rassenpolitische Neuordnung Europas* (Göttingen: Wallstein, 2003).

35 Nazi ideologues vie with each other in trotting out this expression, starting with Hitler, in *Mein Kampf*, and in Walter Eggert, who in 1938 wrote a programmatic article requesting the establishment of a national ancestor cult that would intensify awareness of *Sippe*: 'Die deutsche Ahnenhalle. Eine Anregung', *Rasse* 5, folios 63–4.

36 Höhn's *Lebenslauf*, n.d. (BAAZ, SSO Höhn).
37 There is a similar analysis of the group that included Best, Höhn and Stuckart in Herbert, *Best*, pp. 284–7; Conte and Essner give a different analysis of Stuckart in the chapters on the marriage with the dead soldier (*La Quête de la race*, pp. 151–88).
38 Wolfram Sievers and Walter Wüst, and also Prof. Hirt, who in 1942 was requested to set up a collection of skulls from a contingent of Soviet prisoners for a 'museum of the Jewish race'. See Kater, *Das 'Ahnenerbe' der SS 1935–1945*, and especially the chapter in Conte and Essner, *La Quête de la race*, entitled 'Au terme de l'horreur' ('At the end of the horror'), pp. 230–64.
39 Jeckeln was later HSSPF in Russia, and coordinator of the Final Solution in Ukraine and the Baltic countries. See Birn, *Die höheren SS- und Polizeiführer*.
40 On Darré, see the discourse analysis in Mathias Eidenbenz, *'Blut und Boden'. Zu Funktion und Genese der Metaphern des Agrarismus und Biologismus in der nationalsozialistischen Bauernpropaganda R. W. Darrés* (Berne: Lang, 1993).
41 Notice of 15/6/1937 in BADH, ZM/1457, A.2, folio 65 (Himmler's timetable and *Reisepläne*).
42 The following account is drawn entirely from the description of the rite in Conte and Essner, *La Quête de la race*, pp. 143–9. It corresponds to the codification drawn up by a registrar, *Stadtamtsmann* Rieve, 'Eine Hochzeitsfeier im Standesamt der Gauhauptstadt', in *Zeitschrift für Standesamtswesen*, 1942, pp. 189–91.
43 The calculation was made on the basis of RuSHA preparatory marriage files. For lack of time, and to my great regret, I have not been able to delve into the question of 'belief in God' (*Gottgläubigkeit*) among SS intellectuals.
44 See the minutes of the session on the classifying of Poles into categories for Germanization or exploitation, 28/3/1942, signed by Strickner (BABL, SSO Strickner).
45 BAAZ, RuSHA Akte Mehlhorn (pre-marriage questionnaire and role of promotion, non-folioed).
46 Date of wedding: 6/6/1941; first child born on 5/3/1942, second child born on 11/6/1943 (*Stammrolle* SS, act of promotion, BAAZ, SSO Mehlhorn, non-folioed).
47 Madison Grant, *The Passing of the Great Race or the Racial Basis of European History* (New York: C. Scribner's Sons, 1917), p. 230. Günther quotes him in *Kleine Rassenkunde*, p. 141.
48 Günther, ibid., p. 134.
49 Ibid., p. 133.
50 Ibid., pp. 134–6.
51 To these one should add the 50,000 copies of *Rassenkunde des deutschen Volkes* and the 10,000 or so copies of the essay on the Nordic Doctrine (*Der Nordische Gedanke*): in terms of sales, the Nordic idea counted for only a fifth of the memory of the Great War as represented by the absolute bestseller that was Beumelberg's *Sperrfeuer um Deutschland* (Oldenburg: Gerhard Stalling Verlag, 1929), but was one of the most powerful commercial props of *völkisch* committed literature under Weimar. The figures are drawn from

the presentation of books published by Lehmann Verlag in Günther, *Kleine Rassenkunde*, folios 156–62 (non-paginated).

52 The Nazis also used the term *'Auslese'*, a term that can be literally translated into Latin by *electio*. See Günther, *Kleine Rassenkunde*, pp. 147–8.

53 Paul Weindling, '"Mustergau" Thüringen. Rassenhygiene zwischen Ideologie und Machtpolitik', in Norbert Frei, *Medizin und Gesundheitspolitik in der NS-Zeit* (Munich: Oldenbourg, 1991).

54 Heinz Höhne, *The Order of the Death's Head: The Story of Hitler's SS*, tr. Richard Barry (London: Secker and Warburg, 1969), pp. 156–7, and Robert Koehl, *The Black Corps: The Structure and Power Struggles of the Nazi SS* (Madison: University of Wisconsin Press, 1983).

55 Bernd Wegner, *Hitlers politische Soldaten: die Waffen SS 1933–1945* (Paderborn: Schöningh, 1982), p. 132.

56 'SS-Wiege- und Sippenbuch', *Das Schwarze Korps*, 19/5/1938.

57 Paul Weindling, *Health, Race and German Politics between National Unification and Nazism, 1870–1945* (Cambridge: Cambridge University Press, 1993).

58 Though the intentions of such intellectuals may have seemed quite coherent on paper – within the racist belief system – Conte and Essner have shown how defining the frontier between Nordics and foreigners led them into a 'labyrinth of racial logic' that in fact governed an endless selection, a *circulus diabolicus* (*La Quête de la race*, conclusion, pp. 347–69).

59 Werner Best, article in the *Rheinlandumschau* 6, 10–25/1/1923, p. 64. Quoted in Herbert, *Best*, p. 74.

60 Best uses this expression to mean that he entered the NSDAP as a *völkisch* opportunist.

61 Best, *Lebenslauf*, 1965, quoted in Herbert, *Best*, p. 102.

62 Ernst von Salomon, *Der Fragebogen*, quoted in Herbert, *Best*, p. 102.

63 Best, *Lebenslauf*, 1946, quoted in Herbert, *Best*, p. 202.

64 See Herbert, *Best*, and the same author's 'Weltanschauungseliten'.

65 Lecture on economics, in BABL, R-3101 (Alt R-7)/2149.

66 Charge no. 4 (conspiring against the peace) of the Nuremberg International Tribunal (*TMWC*, vol. 1).

67 There is a typical presentation of the *'Totalitätsanspruch'* in a lecture on the 'Nazi *Weltanschauung*' (AGKBZH, 362/347, folios 1–27; folio 1).

68 I am here using the neologism formed, in a totally different context, by Denis Crouzet (*Les Guerriers de Dieu*).

69 Rhodes, in *The Hitler Movement*, formulated this hypothesis but did not manage to contextualize it within early twentieth-century Germany and studied it only on the level of ideas.

70 The term, used in a quite different context (that of the USSR), comes from Alphonse Dupront (*Le Mythe de croisade*). This 'kind of kingdom' designated the way Communism had appropriated the Christian millenarian perspective of a heavenly order on earth; it seemed legitimate for Dupront to use it for Nazism too. Indeed, Dupront had been quite aware of what he called a 'perversion' of the crusading outlook which he discovered in Nazism and set out in a brief, brilliant passage in the abovementioned work.

Chapter 5 Entering the SD

1 Höhne, *The Order of the Death's Head*, p. 184.
2 See Jacques Delarue, *The History of the Gestapo*, tr. Mervyn Savill (London: Macdonald, 1964), p. 189.
3 Höhne, *The Order of the Death's Head*, p. 89; BAAZ, SSO Behrends.
4 This at least is what Delarue writes, though unfortunately he does not cite his sources (*History of the Gestapo*, pp. 190–1).
5 They were recruited in the first half of 1934.
6 See the personal SA file of Erich Ehrlinger in BADH, ZR/555, a.14; BAAZ, SSO Erich Ehrlinger; BABL, R-58/Anh.14 (file and personal correspondence of *Standartenführer* SS Dr Erich Ehrlinger).
7 See above, chapter 4, and Roth, 'Heydrichs Professor'. On traces of their SD activities in Stuttgart: for Steimle, BABL, RSHA film 4054, A.9181; for Sandberger, BABL, film 16982.
8 Organization chart SDHA III and RSHA VI, BABL, R-58/840 (organization charts: division of tasks and signatures of the SDHA in 1937, RSHA 1940, 1941 and 1943; the same documents cover the Havel Institut).
9 See Roth, 'Heydrichs Professor'.
10 Simon, *Germanistik in dem Planspiel*, pp. ix–xlvii.
11 Banach, *Heydrichs Elite*, p. 135.
12 See the grounds for the awarding of medals (these grounds are not specified, only one category is cited) for the NSStB and border activism (BADH, ZA-V/230, A.4).
13 *Lebenslauf* Strickner, BAAZ, SSO Strickner.
14 See Roth, 'Heydrichs Professor'.
15 *Lebenslauf* and notification of promotion, BAAZ, SSO Hummitzsch.
16 *Lebenslauf* and notification of promotion, BAAZ, SSO Lettow.
17 Letter from Ohlendorf to Höhn, 18/5/1936 (BAAZ, SSO Ohlendorf).
18 Questionnaire, n.d. (probably 1937, date of Knochen's marriage), BAAZ, RuSHA, Akte Knochen.
19 SA questionnaire, BADH, ZR-544, A.3 folio 16.
20 Synoptic file, BAAZ, SSO Berndorff.
21 Synoptic file, BAAZ, SSO Leetsch.
22 On the NSV, see Herwart Vorlander, *Die NSV: Darstellung und Dokumentation einer nationalsozialistischen Organisation* (Boldt: Boppard, 1988).
23 This calculation is based on data from the personal files of the RuSHA.
24 Personnel department of the Gestapo and SD, whose task was to plan personnel matters throughout occupied Europe. Order appointing Ehrlinger in BABL, R-58/467 (personnel management).
25 BABL, R-58/Anh.14 (file and personal correspondence of *Standartenführer* SS Dr Erich Ehrlinger).
26 See in particular Reinhard Höhn, *Rechtsgemeinschaft und Volksgemeinschaft* (Darmstadt: Wittich, 1935).
27 See Ohlendorf's declaration quoted in the previous chapter, as well as Franz

Six's declaration at the trial of the *Einsatzgruppen* (StA Nuremberg, KV Prozesse, Fall 9, ZB-1, folio 1335).

28 BAAZ, SSO Burmester.

29 *Lebenslauf*, 1/4/1935, BAAZ SSO Ehrlinger.

30 BADH, ZR/55. A.14 (personal file of Erich Ehrlinger); BADH, ZB-II/4776, A.15 (personal SA and postwar file of Martin Sandberger).

31 *Lebenslauf*, 2/11/1932, BAAZ, SSO Mehlhorn; *Lebenslauf*, 1/8/1937, BAAZ, SSO Best.

32 On Ehlich, see SSO Ehlich, and Roth, 'Ärzte als Vernichtungspläner'; for Frankenberg, see his *Lebenslauf* (badly damaged by fire, n.d., BAAZ, SSO Frankenberg).

33 *Lebenslauf*, n.d., BAAZ, SSO Höhn.

34 Best, *Lebenslauf*, 1946; quoted in Herbert, *Best*, p. 202.

35 See the account of the Night of the Long Knives in Norbert Frei, *National Socialist Rule in Germany: The Führer State, 1939–1945*, tr. Simon B. Steyne (Oxford: Blackwell, 1993), ch. 1.

36 See Aronson, *Heydrich und die Frühgeschichte von Gestapo*, p. 191ff.

37 *Lebenslauf*, 18/1/1939, BAAZ, SSO Rössner; *Lebenslauf*, 12/7/1938 BAAZ, SSO Hummitzsch.

38 *Lebenslauf*, BAAZ, SSO Lettow.

39 Herbert, 'Weltanschauungseliten', pp. 4–18.

40 Nazi League of Women. The details on Lettow's wife appear in his marriage questionnaire (BAAZ, RuSHA Akte Lettow).

41 Arendt, *The Origins of Totalitarianism*.

42 For the perception of opportunism by militants of the NSDAP, see Pierre Ayçoberry, *La Société allemande sous le Troisième Reich* (Paris: Le Seuil, 1998), pp. 98–100.

43 Frei, *National Socialist Rule in Germany*, pp. 244–5: table of departments of the NSDAP.

44 Short CV of Gräfe, born in Leipzig in 1906; studies in law and economics in Leipzig, *Staatsexamen* in 1932, doctor of law with a thesis on economics and labour law in 1937; joined the SD in 1935, various positions as head of local Gestapo sections (1937–40); September 1939: *Einsatzkommando* in Poland, then counter-espionage activities with the Gestapo in Tilsit; transferred at the end of 1941 to RSHA *Amt* VIC specializing in espionage in the USSR; in charge of Operation Zeppelin (from 1942 until his death in January 1944).

45 Letter from the Ministry of the Interior of the Reich and Prussia, II G 114 to Heydrich, and Heydrich's reply, June 1936, in BADH, ZR/48 (files of personnel in the Ministry of the Interior).

46 Proposal for promotion, signed by Schulz, 15/3/1943 (BAAZ, SSO Gräfe).

47 Personal assessment (ibid.).

48 *Lebenslauf*, 14/8/1938 (BAAZ, SSO Gräfe).

49 *Lebenslauf*, n.d. (BAAZ RuSHA Akte Gräfe).

50 Ibid., folios 3–4.

51 Personal assessment (BAAZ, SSO Gräfe).

52 *Einsatzkommando* 1d in Poland (BABL, RSHA film 2436, clips 420 and 879).

53 Implementation of the operation and general organization: BADH, ZR/920, A.2.
54 Notice reporting a staff meeting of the Zeppelin units (BADH, ZR-920, A.1, folio 453. Various documents RSHA Amt VI, DAWI).
55 Occurrence of the execution of a partisan of Operation Zeppelin in the report on the operation, 27/1/1943 (BADH, ZR-920, A.1, folio 453. Various documents from Operation Zeppelin).
56 Speech by Otto Ohlendorf, quoted in the *Völkischer Beobachter*, municipal edition of 30/1/1944. Reproduced as a press cutting in BAAZ, SSO Gräfe.
57 Entry into NSDAP: 1/1/1932; entry into the SS: the next day. Synoptic file in BAAZ, SSO Behrends.
58 Letter from Ohlendorf to Höhn of 18/5/1936 (BAAZ SSO Ohlendorf).
59 Synoptic file in BAAZ, SSO Ehlers.
60 *Lebenslauf*, n.d., ibid.
61 We should note that Ehlers did not fall into the category of those unemployed activists who were integrated into the police by the NSDAP, and that he had to request leave of absence from his business to enter it as a police auxiliary (ibid., folio 3).
62 BABL, Film 40737 (*Reichsschatzkammer*), A 225; BABL, R-47.01/868, folio 251; BADH, ZA-V/230, A.4: list of names for the medal of 1 October 1938.
63 BADH, ZA – V/230, A.4; list of names for the medal of 1 October 1938; Steimle and Ehrlinger obtained the same medal with the same justification and were both put forward by the Baden-Württemberg section of the NSStB.
64 For Steimle: BABL, Film (SS Versch. Prov.) no. 2705, A.1323; BABL, R-58/117 (from 1937–45: plans on training and division of recruitments between the SIPO and the SD). From 1944 to 1945, Sandberger was director of the school of 'Intelligence services abroad' (GMD, an organization – which existed only on paper – produced by the fusion of the military *Abwehr* and RSHA *Amt* VI): BABL, Film (SS Versch. Prov.) no. 2705, clips 1138, 1148, 1187, 1194, 1199, 1220, 1223, 1323 and 1341. At the same time, Sandberger was BdS in Italy and Steimle was probably Schellenberg's right-hand man taking over the direction of the RSHA *Amt* VI A (General questions of espionage abroad). Sandberger: BABL, film (SS Versch. Prov.) no. 2935, A. 9/342 045, 9/342 047ff; 9/341 985; Steimle: BADH, ZR-257 (RSHA organization chart for 1944–5).
65 Nur. Dok., NG-1730, BABL, film no. 58005.
66 Nur. Dok., NG-2980, BABL, film no. 58016.
67 An automobile association very close to the SS.
68 Dissertations and newspaper articles from the period of his *Gymnasium* in BADH, ZB-II/2956, A.12.
69 He collaborated on the Nazi paper *Chemnitzer Tageszeitung* (*Lebenslauf*, 20/11/1937, folio 1, BAAZ, SSO von Kielpinski).
70 Ibid., folio 2.
71 *Lebenslauf* 12/7/1938, folio 1 (BAAZ, SSO Hummitzsch).
72 Ibid., folio 2.
73 Gräfe and Hummitzsch were enlisted in the *Volkstumskampf* of the Leipzig

Studentenschaft, while Mühler joined a *Burschenschaft* that was collectively absorbed by the SA in 1933.

74 This is true, for instance, of Shlomo Aronson (*Heydrich und die Frühgeschichte von Gestapo*) and Heinz Höhne (*The Order of the Death's Head*, and *Canaris*, tr. J. Maxwell Brownjohn [London: Secker and Warburg, 1979]). We should note that both these authors drew, in their successive investigations, on information provided by Werner Best. See Herbert, *Best*, pp. 501–2.

75 Kobelinsky was designated as director of the Berlin SDOA by Aronson (*Heydrich und die Frühgeschichte von Gestapo*, p. 151) who refutes (in note 61) Orb's statement that Behrends headed the Berlin SDOA until the outbreak of the war. The fact remains that the latter worked with the Berlin SDOA when the central departments of the SD – the SD II directed by Behrends – were, like the SDOA, still embryonic and were taking over intelligence work for Berlin so as to take some of the burden off the SDOA. See the letter of office JI to the *SS-Staf*. Behrends. Object: list of informers in response to a request from the Chancellery, BABL, NS-34/2, non-folioed (personnel affairs, proposed nominations, statistics concerning the SD and RSHA): two thirds of the informers were from Berlin and seem to have been taken on by the SDOA and not by the central department.

76 See Aronson, *Heydrich und die Frühgeschichte von Gestapo*, pp. 156–63.

77 Organization chart of the SD for 1935–6 in Herbert, *Best*, note 153, p. 578. Note that it is impossible to establish with any certainty a reliable organization chart for the SD before 1934.

78 See Aronson, *Heydrich und die Frühgeschichte von Gestapo*, pp. 55–65.

79 *Lebensläufe* in BAAZ, SSO Beutel and SSO Mehlhorn; Aronson, ibid., note 111, pp. 295–6.

80 See above, chapters 3 and 4.

81 Aronson, *Heydrich und die Frühgeschichte von Gestapo*, pp. 162–3. *Lebenslauf*, 13/7/1936, BAAZ, SSO Spengler.

82 Ibid., and Simon, *Germanistik in dem Planspiel*, pp. xxii–xxiii.

83 Memorandum sent by Beutel to Heydrich on 10/8/1939, folio 25, AGKBZH, 362/93 (debate on the reorganization of the SD and the SIPO following the creation of the RSHA).

84 Diploma and reports on the thesis viva of Wilhelm Spengler, 16 and 17/7/1931, UAL (*Universitätsarchiv Leipzig*), Phil. Fak., 2570, folios 1–6.

85 With, in 1940, the RSHA *Amt* VII, the Wannsee Institute and the *Deutsche Auslandswissenschaftlicher Institut* of the University of Berlin. For a similar opinion, see Banach, *Heydrichs Elite*, p. 289.

86 See the *Lebenslauf* n.d., folio 1, BAAZ, SSO Reinhard Höhn.

87 This statement is based, in Shlomo Aronson's work, on the fact that the eviction of the 'founding figures' mentioned above seems to have been caused by Heydrich taking the services back under his control in 1939–40. It needs to be treated with caution: each of the departmental heads of the SD claimed to have hated Heydrich, which could have been part of a strategy designed to clear their names and portray themselves as victims, but was probably more a matter of their having a bone to pick with the SD leader. Ohenldorf claimed

that he had left for the *Einsatzgruppen* because of Heydrich (cf. Ohlendorf's evidence in *TMWC*, vol. 3; see also Raul Hilberg, *The Destruction of the European Jews* [London: W. H. Allen, 1961]). Franz Six left the RSHA straight after Heydrich's death and experienced the latter as a liberation, according to Hachmeister (*Der Gegnerforscher*, pp. 217 and 238); see also Best's quarrels with Heydrich in the correspondence between Best, Heydrich and *SS-Gruf.* Karl Wolff, Himmler's aide-de-camp, in BAAZ, SSO Best; Herbert, *Best*, pp. 314–23.

88 Probationary period of three years in the administration and obligatory period in the magistracy after the *Staatsexamen.*

89 Best, *Heydrich*, ms, p. 163 (BABL, NA 23).

90 Herbert, *Best*, p. 195.

91 Figures quoted in Banach, *Heydrichs Elite*, p. 79.

92 See Herbert, *Best*, pp. 133–91; and, for a detailed account of the process, Aronson, *Heydrich und die Frühgeschichte von Gestapo*, pp. 217–32.

93 This is the phrase used by Hans Safrian in *Eichmann und seine Gehilfen* (Frankfurt: Fischer, 1995).

94 This is not an exhaustive list, and merely notes a few of the most important SS intellectuals. For a good survey of the men recruited by Six, see the organization chart of the SD in 1937, in BABL, R-58/840 (organization charts: division of tasks and signatures of the SDHA in 1937, RSHA 1940, 1941 and 1943) and the organization chart published in part in Hachmeister (*Der Gegnerforscher*), pp. 177–8.

95 On Ehrlinger's career, see Christian Ingrao, 'Culture de guerre, imaginaire nazi, violence génocide. Le cas des cadres du SD', *Revue d'histoire moderne et contemporaine* 47/2, 2000.

96 See Herbert, *Best*, pp. 275–97.

97 Höhn was gradually relegated to the margins from 1937, but did not leave his post as head of the SDHA *Amt* II/2 until the RSHA was organized, at the end of 1939.

98 See Simon, *Germanistik in dem Planspiel*, pp. xxiv–xlii.

99 *Lebenslauf*, 12/7/1938, folio 2, BAAZ, SSO Hummitzsch.

100 There is evidence of his activity in BABL, DAI-film no. 2185 (documents VoMiU, DAI and RSHA concerning the *Umsiedlungen*).

101 They were activists together in the *Studentenschaft*; for Oebsger-Röder, see BABL, R-49.01 (Alt R-21)/ 868, folios 147 and 197; for Gräfe: *Lebenslauf*, 23/8/1938, BAAZ, SSO Gräfe.

102 See the various letters in which, despite the generally formal tone, the great complicity between the men can be sensed: BADH, ZR/920, A.1, 45, 49 (various documents of Operation Zeppelin).

103 Head of the NSStB.

104 See – despite its hagiographic character – Georg Franz Willing, '*Bin ich schuldig?' Leben und Wirken des Reichsstudentenführers und Gauleiters Dr. Gustav Adolf Scheel 1907–1979. Eine Biographie* (Leoni: Druffel Verlag, 1987).

105 See Roth, 'Heydrichs Professor' and his 'Ärzte als Vernichtungspläner'.

106 See Hans-Heinrich Wilhelm's thesis on *Einsatzgruppe* A published in the first part of Helmut Krausnick and Hans-Heinrich Wilhelm, *Die Truppe*

des Weltanschauungskrieges: Die Einsatzgruppen der Sicherheitspolizei und des SD 1938–1942, 2 vols. (Stuttgart: DVA, 1981); for details see too the excellent article by Wolfgang Scheffler, 'Die Einsatzgruppe A', in Klein, *Die Einsatzgruppen in der besetzten Sowjetunion*, pp. 29–52.

107 BABL, Film (SS-Versch. Prov.) no. 2431, folios 922, 926, 1001, 1193 and 1213.

Chapter 6 From struggle to control

1 On all the following, see the works by George C. Browder: *SIPO and SD, 1931–1940: Formation of an Instrument of Power*, PhD thesis (Madison: University of Wisconsin, 1968); *Foundations of the Nazi Police State. The Formation of SIPO and SD* (Lexington: University Press of Kentucky, 1990); *Hitler's Enforcers: The Gestapo and the SS Security Service in the Nazi Revolution* (Oxford; New York: Oxford University Press, 1996); also his 'The SD: Significance of Organization and Image', in George Mosse (ed.), *Police Forces in History* (London: Sage, 1975); and his edition of documents, 'Die Anfänge des SD. Dokumente aus der Organisationsgeschichte', *VfZ* 27, 1979. See also Alwin Ramme, *Der Sicherheitsdienst der SS. Zu seiner Funktion im faschistischen Machtapparat und im Besatzungsregime des sogennanten Generalgouvernements Polen* (Berlin: Deutscher Militärverlag, 1970); the introduction to Lawrence Stokes, *The Sicherheitsdienst (SD) of the Reichsführer SS and German Public Opinion, September 1939–June 1941*, PhD thesis (Baltimore: Johns Hopkins University, 1972); and finally, Aronson, *Heydrich und die Frühgeschichte von Gestapo*.

2 Aronson, *Heydrich und die Frühgeschichte von Gestapo*, p. 57.

3 Report written by Paul Leffler, passed on to Aronson and quoted by him in *Heydrich und die Frühgeschichte von Gestapo*, pp. 60–1.

4 This evidence was not directly given to Aronson by its author, but by . . . Werner Best, who, in the 1950s and 1960s, tried to influence the historiography of Nazism by granting several interviews, which the historians Helmut Krausnick and Shlomo Aronson sometimes used in a rather undiscerning way.

5 BADH, ZR-555, A.14 (personal file of SA Erich Ehrlinger).

6 Letter from Heinrich Heindorf to Aronson, May 1964, quoted in *Heydrich und die Frühgeschichte von Gestapo*, p. 62.

7 The fact is noted by Herbert, in his analysis of the reasons for the misunderstanding between Heydrich and Best. See Herbert, *Best*, pp. 228–30; see also Hachmeister, *Der Gegnerforscher*, p. 146.

8 Koehl, *The Black Corps*.

9 Ramme, *Der Sicherheitsdienst der SS*, pp. 33–43; Browder, *Hitler's Enforcers*, pp. 105ff, p. 140; Banach, *Heydrichs Elite*, pp. 94–6.

10 See Aronson, *Heydrich und die Frühgeschichte von Gestapo*, pp. 98–103, and Browder, *Foundations of the Nazi Police State*.

11 For a retrospective programmatic formulation, see, for example, Himmler's speech of 5/5/1936, at the *Haus der Flieger* (BABL, NS-19/4003).

12 Exact figure: 52,048, given by Richard Korrherr, SS inspector, in a

note addressed to Himmler on 1/3/1943, folio 4 BABL (*Sammlung* Schumacher/436); Wegner, *Hitlers politische Soldaten*, pp. 80–1.

13 On this, see the various statistical series in Herbert F. Ziegler, *Nazi Germany's New Aristocracy: The SS Leadership, 1925–1939* (Princeton, N.J.: Princeton University Press, 1989), p. 115, and Gunnar Boehnert, *A Sociography of the SS Officer Corps, 1925–1939*, PhD thesis (London, 1977), p. 123. See also Banach, *Heydrichs Elite*, pp. 80–1.

14 Aronson, *Heydrich und die Frühgeschichte von Gestapo*, p. 138.

15 Browder, *Hitler's Enforcers*, pp. 140 and 156–60.

16 Höhne, *The Order of the Death's Head*, pp. 97 and 215ff; Herbert, *Best*, pp. 135–8.

17 Ibid., pp. 141–2.

18 Ayçoberry, *La Société allemande*; Richard Bessel, *Political Violence and the Rise of Nazism. The Storm Troopers in Eastern Germany, 1925–1934* (New Haven; London: Yale University Press, 1984).

19 This activity became really intensive only after 1938.

20 The expression is used by Herbert in 'Generation der Sachlichkeit'.

21 Herbert, *Best*, pp. 138–43.

22 Ibid., p. 144; Aronson, *Heydrich und die Frühgeschichte von Gestapo*, pp. 191–5.

23 *Lebensläufe*, 3/8/1936 and 5/2/1936, respectively BAAZ, SSO and RuSHA Akte Spengler.

24 Even though this represented only half of what Heydrich wanted, this budget reached RM375,000 in July 1934. See Aronson, *Heydrich und die Frühgeschichte von Gestapo*, p. 199.

25 Private letter from Reinhard Heydrich to Franz Xaver Schwarz, *Reichsschatzmeister*, 14/5/1934; quoted in Aronson, ibid.

26 See the institutional studies in Ulrich Herbert, Karin Orth and Christoph Dieckmann, *Nationalsozialistische Konzentrationslager. Entwicklung und Struktur*, 4 vols. (Munich: Wallstein, 1999).

27 Koehl, *The Black Corps*.

28 The exact title Franz Six wanted to give a new *Amt* II within the RSHA was '*Gegnerforschung und -Bekämpfung*': 'Research into and struggle against opponents'. Cf. SD organization chart for 1940, BABL, R-58/840 (organization charts and signatures of the SDHA in 1937, of the RSHA for 1940, 1941 and 1943); BADH, ZR-257 (estimated RSHA organization chart for 1940); AGKBZH, 362/270.

29 The term *jüdisch versippt* is difficult to translate: we need a word that expresses the idea of 'people related to Jews'.

30 Leopold Caprivi, *Erinnerungen, 1933–1945, IfZ* ZS 3070, quoted in Hachmeister, *Der Gegnerforscher*, p. 23.

31 The writer/editor Gunter d'Alquen was for a time one of its recruits, before coming into direct confrontation with Ohlendorf. See the correspondence between d'Alquen and Ohlendorf in BABL, R-58/951 (SD reports on the press, especially 'Les tendances de *Das Schwarze Korps*') and Hachmeister, ibid., p. 159; Höhne, *The Order of the Death's Head*, pp. 201 and 218.

32 Reinhard Heydrich, *Wandlungen unseres Kampfes* (Munich; Berlin: Eher, 1936).

33 This is a translation of Eichmann's term *Weltanschauliche Gegnerbekämpfung*. It almost exactly repeats the official title of Six's *Amt* – extra proof of the way inner Nazi terminology was both natural and performative: the Nazis believed in 'doing things with words'.

34 On Rudolf Levin, see BAAZ, RuSHA Akte Levin; AGKBZH, 362/219, 380, 390 (professional and private papers of *SS-Sturmbannführer* Levin [RSHA VII], on academic work and review plans).

35 Lecture by *SS-Sturmbannführer* Levin, 'Geisteswissenschaftliche Methodik der Gegnerforschung', *IfZ* DC15/33, folios 1–27, n.d. (probably 1943).

36 See above, chapter 5, and the conference of the VWA, which ended with a 'profession of faith in the combative sciences' (account of the conference of 30–1/5/1936 in BABL, R-8043/6273, folio 122).

37 Haar, 'Kämpfende Wissenschaften', pp. 224–5.

38 Andreas Pfenning, 'Vom Nachteil und Nützen der Soziologie fur die Politik', *Volk im Werden* 7, 1939, p. 126.

39 On the complex relations between sociology and SD, see the conference organized by Ohlendorf on sociology in the BABL, R-3101 (Alt R-7)/2024: protocol of the sociology conference on 9 December 1944 at the Wannsee Institute; on this latter, see Carsten Klingemann, 'Les sociologues nazis et Max Weber, 1933–1945', *Genèses* 21, 1995, and the same author's 'Die deutsche Sozialwissenschaften zwischen den beiden Weltkriegen. Mythos und Realität von Kontinuitätbrüchen', in Gerhard Göhler and Bodo Zeuner (eds.), *Kontinuitäten und Brüche in der deutschen Politikwissenschaft* (Baden-Baden: Nomos, 1991).

40 This is an attempt to translate the German '*Überwachung des deutschen Lebensgebiets*'. *Überwachung* has connotations of observation, surveillance and keeping watch.

41 See the introduction to Heinz Boberach (ed.), *Meldungen aus dem Reich, 1938–1945. Die geheimen Lageberichte des Sicherheitsdienstes der SS*, Herrsching, 17 vols. and Index, 1984, vol. I; and Herbst, *Der totale Krieg*, pp. 181–8.

42 Himmler's lecture for a course on politics for the Wehrmacht, January 1937 (*TMWC*, PS-1192 A). Quoted in Herbert, *Best*, p. 579.

43 *Volksgesundheit* in German. This word needs to be taken in its sense of 'public health', but also and above all in terms of racial hygiene. See Robert Proctor, *Racial Hygiene. Medicine under the Nazis* (Cambridge, Mass.: Harvard University Press, 1988); Paul Weindling, *L'Hygiène de la race*, vol. 1: *Hygiène raciale et eugénisme médical en Allemagne, 1870–1933*, pref. Benoît Massin (Paris: La Découverte, 1998).

44 Interrogation of Ohlendorf on 29/5/1947, *IfZ* 832/53, vol. IV, folio 255. I am grateful to Carsten Schneider for having forwarded details of this document to me.

45 Here, Ohlendorf's words were very close to those of E. B. Tylor, who saw culture as a complex that included the knowledge, beliefs, art, morals, laws and customs that a person picked up as member of a society (E. B. Tylor, *Primitive Culture* [London, 1871], vol. 1, p. 1).

46 SDHA *Referaten* II/2 1; II/2 2 and II/2 3. See following notes.

47 See organization charts, n.d., of SDHA II/2 (probably 1938 or 1939), and of SDHA *Amt* II/2, AGKBZH, 362/41.

48 Translation of *Referent*, i.e. the SD officer in charge of a specialized bureau in a specific field; his hierarchical superior was an *Abteilungsleiter* (head of bureau), himself under the orders of an *Amtschef* (head of department), who reported directly to Heydrich; the structure in the RSHA was the same; the Roman numerals corresponded to *Ämter*, the letters (in the SDHA these were already Arabic numerals) to *Abteilungen*, the Arabic numerals to *Referaten*. Example from the SDHA: Eichmann's 'sub-bureau' was SDHA *Amt* II/112: a product of *Amt* II: SD *Inland*, *Abteilung* II/1: *Gegnerforschung und -Bekämpfung* and *Referat* II/11: ideological opponents, of which it constituted the second bureau (II/11–2). After 1940, this sub-bureau was promoted to *Referat*, namely *Referat* RSHA IV B 4, a product of *Amt* RSHA IV: Gestapo; from *Abteilung* IV B: 'religious opponents'. *Referat* B-4: 'Jewish affairs; expulsions, management of confiscated goods from enemy states and peoples. Granting of Reich nationality', which was soon transformed into *Judenangelegenheiten* (Jewish affairs). See SDHA and RSHA organization charts in BABL, R-58/840, folios 159 and 323. For an analysis of changes in the name of Eichmann's *Judenreferat*, see Aly, *Final Solution*, pp. 99–100, and, more generally, Safrian, *Eichmann*.

49 See Herbert, *Best*, pp. 182–95 and 225–9; Hachmeister, *Der Gegnerforscher*, pp. 203–17.

50 Herbert, *Best*, pp. 228–31.

51 Supervision of the operation of the departments (*Dienstaufsicht*). On Schellenberg, see Hachmeister, *Der Gegnerforscher*, pp. 201–2.

52 Best's memorandum and Schellenberg's annotations in BABL, R-58/826 and 827 (juridical-type works on recruitment of the leaders of the SIPO/SD); Beutel's memorandum to Heydrich, 10/8/1939, AGKBZH, 362/93 (debate on the reorganization of the SD and the SIPO following the creation of the RSHA); memorandums and organizational suggestions from Six to Heydrich, AGKBZH, 362/295.

53 Memorandum SDHA I/111, 'Reorganization of the SD of the RFSS with a view to an organizational and personal homogenization with the SIPO', signed Schellenberg, 24/2/1939, BABL, R-58/826.

54 Ibid.

55 See Hachmeister, *Der Gegnerforscher*, p. 208.

56 SDHA I/311, SDHA I/32 (bureau on the press and museums), SDHA II/1 (Research into ideological opponents), SDHA II/2 (German life domain, taken over after the departure of Höhn, head of the general staff: Ohlendorf and even Six took no interest in it). Hachmeister, *Der Gegnerforscher*, pp. 164, 173 and 177–8; organization charts SDHA 1937 and RSHA for 1940, BABL, R-58/840.

57 Memorandum from Six, 17/7/1939, AGKBZH, 362/295.

58 The report was annotated in the margins by Heydrich, who added a few approving comments, though these concerned only the 'applied research' aspects (supplementary files, for example) of the project, and betrayed a complete lack of interest in Six's 'fundamental research'. The idea which

Heydrich most appreciated seems to have been that of an *Amt* that would act as an auxiliary for the other departments.

59 Ohlendorf for the SD *Inland* (RSHA *Amt* III, created from SDHA II/2); Jost for the *Ausland*-SD (RSHA *Amt* VI, former SDHA III + SDHA II/2 1); Heinrich Müller for the Gestapo (RSHA *Amt* IV); Arthur Nebe (Kripo, *Amt* V of the RSHA); and Franz Six (RSHA *Amt* VII). For institutional studies, see Reinhold Schattenfroh and Johannes Tuchel, *Zentrale des Terrors. Prinz-Albrecht-Strasse 8. Hauptquartier der Gestapo* (Berlin: Siedler, 1987); Reinhard Rürup (ed.), *Topography of Terror: Gestapo, SS and Reichssicherheitshauptamt on the 'Prinz-Albrecht-Terrain': A Documentation*, tr. Werner T. Angress, 3rd edn (Berlin: W. Asrenhövel, 1993).

60 Hachmeister, *Der Gegnerforscher*, p. 213; the best proof of this is the way the *Volksdeutsche Forschungsgemeinschaften*, which should theoretically have come under *Amt* VII, was taken over. And it was a new *Abteilung*, answering jointly to the RSHA *Ämter* III B (Racial Policies) and VI G (Sciences), that made this control effective. See letter RSHA III B/VI G to the *Nord- und Ostdeutsche Forschungsgemeinschaft* of 19/11/1944, signed by SS *Stubaf.* von Hehn, summoning the representatives of the *Volksdeutsche Forschungsgemeinschaften* to a meeting in Prague (BABL, R-153/1283, non-folioed document). Von Hehn legitimated the holding of this conference by the RSHA takeover, which necessitated the setting of new aims and objectives. See the articles by Roth and Haar in Schöttler, *Geschichtschreibung*, and above, chapter 5.

61 This was the 'Ideological enemies abroad' department, led by Helmut Knochen; the counter-espionage police, allied to the former SDHA *Amt* I/1 2 (Political enemies), was merged with the Gestapo after the departure of Best from the RSHA. See organization charts in BABL, R-58/840 (organization charts, division of tasks and signatures of the SDHA in 1937, RSHA 1940, 1941 and 1943).

62 Aly, *Final Solution*, p. 145, and, more generally, Safrian, *Eichmann*.

63 On the level of the biggest entities occupied (mainly whole countries, witrh the notable exception of the partially occupied USSR), the SD and the SIPO were grouped into *Befehlshaber der Sicherheitspolizei und des SD* (BdS, e.g. BdS France, BdS Greece, BdS Italy) who commanded KdS (*Kommandos der Sicherheitspolizei und des SD*), set up in the main cities (KdS Minsk or Kiev, KdS Bordeaux, KdS Marseilles, KdS Prague) and controlling the main rural areas.

64 On this course, see Banach, *Heydrichs Elite*, pp. 312–24.

65 'The enemies of the Third Reich and the struggle against them'. A detailed plan of the lecture, n.d. (probably between the end of 1940 and the beginning of 1942 because of the presence of a class on foreigners in the Reich, a phenomenon that was significant only in 1941), folioed from 1 to 3, BABL, R-58/779 (pedagogic materials on the political churches, foreigners in the Reich and sects).

66 It seems that the shift from one definition to the other occurred in 1936, in particular with an article by Reinhard Heydrich, 'Die Bekämpfung der Staatsfeinde', published in *Deutsche Recht* 6, 1936, pp. 121–3.

67 'The enemies of the Third Reich', BABL, R-58/779, folio 1.

68 See, for example, the debate on the total state and the total *Weltanschauung* in 'Totaler Mensch' and 'Totaler Staat', articles by *SS-Hstuf.* Knochen (*Abteilungsleiter SDHA* II/22), AGKBZH, 362/513 (memorandums, lectures on Freemasonry, political Catholicism and Jewishness), folios 90–8 and 98–100.

69 *Kaftan, Kubus, Kutte*: 'the caftan, the cube, the habit'.

70 AGKBZH, 362/433.

71 Cf. in particular AGKBZH, 362/432, 433, 437, 440 and 441 (separatism, trial reports, inventories of the scientific work of the SDHA, organization of the *Separatistenbekämpfung*).

72 Letter RSHA IV E 3 of March 1940 in AGKBZH, 362/440 (separatism, inventory of scientific work of the SDHA and of the organization of its activity in that area).

73 Herbert, *Best*, p. 78.

74 Armin Bach, *Frankreich und Separatismus*; copy of the brochure in AGKBZH, 362/440.

75 On *Einsatzgruppe* D, read Andrej Angrick, *Besatzungspolitik und Massenmord. Die Einsatzgruppe D in der südlichen Sowjetunion 1941–1943* (Hamburg: Hamburger Edition, 2003). See also Krausnick and Wilhelm, *Die Truppe des Weltanschauungskrieges*; Ralf Ogorreck, *Die Einsatzgruppen und die 'Genesis der Endlösung'* (Berlin: Metropol, 1996); Angrick, 'Die Einsatzgruppe D'.

76 Paul Zapp, RSHA *Amt* I B1, 'Die Freisauerei', BABL, R-58/779, folios 48–67 (folioed from 1 to 24: mistake in folio numbers).

77 See, for example, BABL, R-58/623, 779, 844 (SD pedagogic material for ideological education) and the texts collected by the SDHA II/112 in BABL, R-58/987, in particular the book written under a pseudonym by a collective of SD intellectuals under the leadership of Herbert Hagen: Dieter Schwarz, 'Das Weltjudentum: Organisation, Macht und Politik' (Berlin: Zentralverlag der NSDAP Franz Eher NF. GMBH., 1939). See also BABL, R-58/565 (collaboration of the SD with other institutions for tackling the Jewish question); AGKBZH, 362/156, 180, 184, 198, 202 and 218 ('preliminary writings' concerning Jewish matters; press cuttings, memorandums, work files and lectures by Helmut Knochen [SDHA II/2], census statistics); BADH, ZR-811, A.3: reports on the Jewish question (correspondence of RSHA *Amt* VII with different institutions); BADH, ZB-II/2956, A.12 (literary and propagandistic works); BADH, ZB-I/1099 (documentation on the *Skalde Orden* [a *völkisch* esoteric order]). This represents merely part of the SD's activity in this domain, and we have not even mentioned the documentation concerning the 'practical work' carried out by the SD, or the memorandums in which Jewishness is not the main theme, but in which it is all-pervasive. Finally, we ought to mention the archives of institutions that were offshoots of the RSHA and that played a major intellectual role, with SS intellectuals at their head, in the discussion of Jewishness: here I am thinking of the EWZ, the UWZ, the Wannsee Institute and, of course, the *Einsatzgruppen*.

78 See Michael Wildt, *Die Judenpolitik des SD, 1935–1938. Eine Dokumentation* (Munich: Oldenbourg, 1995), and his 'Avant la "Solution finale". La politique juive du service de sécurité de la SS, 1935–1938', *Genèses* 21, 1995.

79 BABL, R-58/623.
80 On this group, see Safrian, *Eichmann*; Wildt, 'Avant la "Solution finale"'; and Claudia Steur, *Theodor Dannecker. Ein Funktionär der Endlösung* (Essen: Klartext, 1995).
81 Provisional plan for the lecture of 8/2/1937 (BABL, R-58/623, folio 42).
82 Ibid.; provisional plan, folio 42; text of the lecture, folio 47.
83 Ibid., folio 48.
84 BABL, R-58/623, folios 43–4 and 49–50.
85 Ibid., folio 47.
86 My emphasis.
87 BABL, R-58/779, folio 65 V.
88 This was not always the case; see, for example, the memorandums on Freemasonry in BADH, ZB-I/1099 (documentation on the *Skalde Orden*) as well as the thesis of SS-*Sturmbannführer* Hans Schick, *Das ältere Rosenkreuzertum. Beitrag zur Entstehungsgeschichte der Freimaurerei, Habilitation* thesis (Berlin: Nordland Verlag, 1942); the Jesuit Order (see in particular AGKBZH, 362/219: professional and private papers of *SS-Hauptsturmführer* Levin [RSHA VII] on academic work and review projects) or the different countries of East Europe (BABL, R-58/13, 19, 390: memorandum on the Russian, Ukrainian and Caucasian question). I do not here have the time or the space to discuss the significance of this ideological contribution. But the doctrinal formulation in itself, the transcription of the belief system into a construction based on levels of language considered as elevated from an activist and police point of view, already forms a highly original complex.
89 On this, see Ohlendorf's evidence, *TWC*, case IX, vol. I.
90 I have consulted these dispatches, published by Boberach, as microfilms in the Berlin archives.
91 Koehl, *The Black Corps*.
92 In particular, Ohlendorf declared that Himmler often rebuked him for his defeatism and that Heydrich wanted to transfer him to the *Einsatzgruppen* to 'destroy' him. See Ohlendorf's testimony, *TWC*, case IX, vol. I.
93 I will return to this point in my last chapter.
94 Ian Kershaw, *Popular Opinion and Political Dissent in the Third Reich: Bavaria 1933–1945*, new edn (Oxford: Clarendon Press, 2002); Stokes, *The Sicherheitsdienst of the Reichsführer SS*; his 'Otto Ohlendorf, the *Sicherheitsdienst* and Public Opinion in Nazi Germany', in Mosse, *Police Forces in History*; and Marlis Steinert, *Hitler's War and the Germans: Public Mood and Attitude during the Second World War*, ed. and tr. Thomas E. J. de Witt (Athens, Ohio: Ohio University Press, 1977).
95 Telex from the SDOA South-West to SDHA II/22, 27/5/1936; quoted in Höhne, *The Order of the Death's Head*, p. 157.
96 On the indifference of public opinion to the Nuremberg Laws, see Kershaw, *Popular Opinion*, pp. 231–46 and 257–72 (part of his study of the measures taken to persecute the Jews).
97 The group that developed around Höhn and Stuckart, but also the experts on Judaism around Hagen, Wisliceny, Eichmann and Ilges, played a significant

role in the suggestions put forward by Heydrich in 1935 and then in 1938, after *Kristallnacht* (a hateful term, which recycled an SA term, used to designate the pogroms of 9/11/1938); on this, see Uwe Dietrich Adam, *Judenpolitik im Dritten Reich* (Düsseldorf: Droste, 1972), and in particular Wildt, 'Avant la "Solution finale"'.

98 Speech by Himmler at Bad-Tölz, 1935; quoted by Höhne, *The Order of the Death's Head*, p. 125.

99 For example, 'The image of Russia among the populace', *Meldungen aus dem Reich*, 1942 (BABL, R-58/174).

100 Memorandum on the 'reorganization of Polish politics', written by *SS-Sturmbannführer* Dr Herbert Strickner (RSHA *Amt* III B2 d): '*Referent*; III B 2: *Stubaf.* Dr Buchardt: *Abteilungsleiter*; III B: Hans Ehlich: *Gruppenleiter*; III: Ohlendorf: *Amtschef*' (copy of the heading), copy, 19/10/1944 (BABL, R-58/1002, folios 15 to 24).

101 The term used by Ohlendorf to categorize the work of RSHA *Amt* III B in its definition of the *Lebensgebiet* is *Volksgesundheit*, which should be translated as 'racial hygiene' (interrogation of Ohlendorf, 29/5/1947, IfZ 832/53, vol. IV, folio 255).

102 See the complete organization chart of the RSHA, as of the end of 1942 and beginning of 1943 (BABL, R-58/3529 [affairs concerning the personnel of the RSHA]).

103 BABL, R-58/3529, folios 59–61.

104 This fact is noted in passing by Christian Gerlach, for example. He demonstrates that there was a factual correlation between a 'serious situation' on the level of food supplies and the *Hungerplan*, i.e. the plans to impose a famine in the USSR drawn up by the Germans in the spring of 1941. What Gerlach does not discuss is the extent to which memories of the Great War played a role. This might have activated a – more or less justified – fear in the assessment (which he views as objective) of the food supply situation ('Die Ausweitung der deutschen Massenmorde in den besetzten sowjetischen Gebieten im Herbst 1941. Überlegungen zur Vernichtungspolitik gegen Juden und sowjetische Kriegsgefangene', in Gerlach, *Krieg, Ernährung, Völkermord. Forschungen zur deutschen Vernichtungspolitik* [Hamburg: Hamburger Edition, 1998], pp. 10–84; p. 15).

105 Herbst, *Der totale Krieg*.

106 'Wirtschaft in völkischen Zusammenhängen', BABL, R-31.01 (Alt R-7)/2018, folios 47–53.

107 Ibid., folio 47.

108 See the *Memoirs* – a veritable apologia – of Albert Speer: *Inside the Third Reich*, tr. Richard and Clara Winston, intro. Eugene Davidson (New York: Macmillan; London: Weidenfeld and Nicolson, 1970); Frei, *National Socialist Rule in Germany*, p. 141; and Herbst, *Der totale Krieg*, especially pp. 341–52.

109 Testimony of Ohlendorf, *TWC*, case IX, vol. I.

110 Letter from Gunter d'Alquen to Ohlendorf, 22 July 1942 (BABL, R-58/951, folios 1–5; 1–3).

111 He sent all the letters to the head of Himmler's general staff, Wolff, with a complaint about d'Alquen's attitude (letter to Wolff, 14/12/1942, BABL, R-58/951, folio 31).

112 Wolff sent a letter to Ohlendorf exhorting him to make up with d'Alquen, to talk to him and 'draw a line' under everything that had been said (BABL, R-58/951: SD reports on the press, in particular 'The tendencies of *Das Schwarze Korps*, the organ of the SS', by d'Alquen, as editor, and Ohlendorf. Wolff replied to Ohlendorf on 6/4/1943, BABL, R-58/951, folio 32).

113 Letter from Ohlendorf to d'Alquen, BABL, R-58/951, folios 7–12; folio 9.

114 Conte and Essner, *La Quête de la race*; Michael Burleigh and Wolfgang Wippermann, *The Racial State: Germany 1933–1945* (Cambridge: Cambridge University Press, 1991).

115 'Report on economic policy', 28/12/1944 in BABL, R-3101 (Alt R-7)/2018, folios 32–7; here, respectively, folios 35–7.

116 Ohlendorf and his *Referenten* did this within the *Reichsgruppe Handel*, i.e. within the practical economic bodies: the SD here merely played a theoretical lobbying role, especially as it had no economic power in itself, this area being devolved (in the SS) to the WVHA; see Herbst, *Der totale Krieg*, and Koehl, *The Black Corps*.

117 'Report on economic policy' (see note 115 above).

118 See Herbst, *Der totale Krieg*.

119 Symptomatic of this is the fact that in the best-informed work on the *Einsatzgruppen*, the article on these groups before the invasion of Russia dedicates only two pages to the *Kommandos* who acted in Austria and Czechoslovakia: Peter Klein, 'Einleitung. Die Einsatzgruppen bis zum Überfall auf die Sowjetunion', in Klein, *Die Einsatzgruppen in der besetzten Sowjetunion*, pp. 9–28; pp. 11–13.

120 Estimates in Hans Umbreit (*Deutsche Militärverwaltung 1938/39. Die militärische Besetzung der Tschechoslowakei und Polens* [Stuttgart: DVA, 1977], p. 41) for one group of armies out of three.

121 Notice of 2/7/1940, transcribed by Krausnick, 'Hitler und die Morde in Polen. Eine Dokumentation', *VfZ* 11 (1963), pp. 196–209; pp. 206–7.

122 The lists drawn up for Austria and Czechoslovakia have not been preserved. However, we can gain some idea of them by consulting those established for a hypothetical landing in England or for the planned Operation Barbarossa (respectively, BABL, R-58/75 or 636 and R-58/574).

123 Decree of the RFSS, 17 March 1938, mentioned in Krausnick and Wilhelm, *Die Truppe des Weltanschauungskrieges*, p. 13.

124 AGKBZH, 362/369 (lists of books in the library of the SIPO/SD); examples of confiscations (not just those from Austria) in ibid., 362/363 (correspondence on the library and the archives of SIPO and SD schools).

125 AGKBZH, 362/150 and 151 (*Sonderkommando* Vienna; report on the confiscation of books, archives and works of art).

126 The only indication – though it does not even provide any figures – of the number of arrests is contained in a letter of 15/6/1938, from the head of the SS administration in charge of the management of concentration

camps, stipulating that 'as a result of the invasion of Austria, the number of concentration camp detainees has increased considerably'; letter quoted in Krausnick, *Einsatzgruppen*, p. 250, and Martin Broszat (ed.), *Studien zur Geschichte der Konzentrationslager* (Stuttgart: DVA, 1970), p. 79.

127 Memorandum SDHA II, Nbrg Dok URSS-509, reprinted in *TWC*, vol. XXXIX, pp. 537ff.

128 *Auflösen* means 'to dissolve', 'disperse', 'annul', 'cancel'. Translating it as 'liquidate' is unusual, and closer to everyday language. The term remains ambiguous, since the author does not specify whether he is referring to organizations, businesses or individuals (the latter, though possible, is unlikely, though murders were probably frequent).

129 Nbrg Dok URSS-509, *TWC*, vol. XXXIX, pp. 537–45.

130 Gestapo circular on 'Directives for the activity of the *Einsatzkommandos* of the *Geheime Staatspolizei* in the Sudetenland' (BABL, R-58/241).

131 Helmut Groscurth, *Tagebücher eines Abwehroffiziers 1939–1945*, ed. Helmut Krausnick and Harold C. Deutsch (Stuttgart: DVA, 1970), pp. 132, 327–8 and 331.

132 We are far from able to give any kind of an answer to this question. At most, we can venture to put forward the following hypothesis: a biological understanding of the adversary may have played a part, and other factors (the intensity of the *Volkstumskampf*, the shape taken by the invasion and the degree of resistance to the German advance) may have concealed the very existence of any dimension of representations drawing on and conditioned by material circumstances. However, the way the conquest was carried out seems, over and above the simplistic quarrel between intentionalists and functionalists (here in the form 'aimless expansion' versus 'preconceived programme'), to allow of an 'ethnic gradation' that drew on representations and then conditioned behaviour. Thus the Nazis proceeded from the most Nordic (the Saar, the Rhineland, Austria, the Sudetenland, etc.) to the most 'radically foreign' (Czechoslovakia, Poland, the Balkans, the USSR, etc.), and their behaviour displayed a corresponding 'brutalization' that seems not to have resulted from any cumulative radicalization (Mommsen) unconnected to representations.

133 The term '*Daseinskampf*' was in current use. Here are just two examples: an order from the general in command of the 4th Panzer group, General Hoepner, in the *Bundesarchiv-Militärarchiv* Freiburg (BA-MA), LVI. AK., 17956/7a; quoted in Gerd R. Ueberschär and Wolfram Wette (eds.), *'Unternehmen Barbarossa'. Der deutsche Überfall auf die Sowjetunion 1941. Berichte, Analysen, Dokumente* (Frankfurt: Fischer, 1997), p. 251: the general declared that 'the war against Russia is an essential part of the struggle for existence [*Daseinskampf*] of the German people'; 'Report on economic policy' by Ohlendorf, 28/12/1944 (BABL, R-3101 [Alt R-7]/2018). See below, chapter 8.

134 They were then between twenty-seven and twenty-eight years old.

135 Proposal for promotion, signed by Ehrlinger, 12/6/1944 (BAAZ, SSO Schellenberg).

Part III Nazism and violence: the culmination, 1939–1945

1 Hans Baumann, *'Im Osten'*, in Reichsfrauenführung (ed.), *Gemeinschaftslieder. Lieder für Frauengruppen* (n.p.: 1940).
2 The link between *Blut und Boden* and colonization in the east has been described in several detailed accounts. Its main proponent within the Third Reich, Walter Darré, was the first head of the *Rasse- und Siedlungshauptamt*, the Central Office for Race and Colonization. See Eidenbenz, *'Blut und Boden'*; see also the chapter 'Sang et sol. Action Zamość' in Conte and Essner, *La Quête de la race*, which shows the consistency between the *Blut und Boden* ideology and the most successful site of colonization in the Third Reich.

Chapter 7 Thinking the east, between utopia and anxiety

1 The *Reichskommissariat für die Festigung deutschen Volkstums* (Reich Commission for the Reinforcement of Germandom), created in 1940 with Himmler at its head, was responsible for the entire resettlement policy. See Robert L. Koehl, *RKFDV: German Resettlement and Population Policy, 1939–1945. A History of the Reich Commission for the Strengthening of Germandom* (Cambridge: Cambridge University Press, 1957); and the essential works by Aly, *Final Solution*, and Roth, '"Generalplan Ost" – "Gesamtplan Ost"'.
2 BABL, R-58/1082, folio 675: report on the activities of the SIPO and SD *Einsatzgruppen* in Poland, 6/10/1939; AGKBZH, 362/101: directives concerning the organization of the SIPO in Poland, folios 3ff: order RSHA IV A1, 20/10/1939, on the dissolution of the *Einsatzgruppen*.
3 The chronological coincidence between the creation of the RSHA (1/10/1939), Hitler's announcement that he intended to reorganize 'ethnic relations' with the aid of expulsions (6/10/1939) and the creation of the RKFdV (7/10/39) is striking.
4 See Roth, 'Ärzte als Vernichtungspläner'. *Sondergruppe* III ES (the future III B) was a branch of the SD *Inland*.
5 Eichmann's *Referat* was mainly in charge of executive functions and logistics. He had not produced any 'thinking on space' and so was not subjected to the same attention as *Amt* III B, even if its function in the Shoah had been more decisive. See Aly, *Final Solution*, pp. 63–6; Safrian, *Eichmann*; Steur, *Theodor Dannecker*.
6 On the birth of these institutions and the origin of resettlement, see Roth, '"Generalplan Ost" – "Gesamtplan Ost"', pp. 33–5, and Aly, *Final Solution*, pp. 21–4 and 49–58. The EWZ was based in Posen and the UWZ in Litzmannstadt (Łódź): they were complemented by external data-gathering operations in Gotenhafen (Gdynia) and Łódź (for the EWZ).
7 In other words, under the exclusive leadership of the RSHA, with a personnel taken mainly from the SD; see Aly, *Final Solution*, pp. 20–4.
8 Heinemann, *'Rasse, Siedlung, deutsches Blut'*. On the VoMi, see Valdis O. Lumans, *Himmler's Auxiliaries: The Volksdeutsche Mittelstelle and the German*

National Minorities of Europe 1933–1945 (Chapel Hill: University of North Carolina Press, 1993). These two bodies were merged with the RKFdV in 1939.

9 This was a very frequent phenomenon in the Third Reich, and government 'polycracy' and genocidal policies at the local level in the eastern territories have been decribed in detail: on 'polycracy', see Broszat, *The Hitler State*, and for the local level, see in particular Dieter Pohl, *Von der 'Judenpolitik' zum Judenmord. Der Distrikt Lublin des Generalgouvernements 1939–1944* (Frankfurt: Lang, 1993), and the same author's *Nationalsozialistische Judenverfolgung in Ostgalizien 1941–1944. Organisation und Durchführung eines staatlichen Massenverbrechens* (Munich: Oldenbourg, 1996). See also the articles by Christian Gerlach, Christoph Dieckmann and Thomas Sandkühler summarizing their ideas in Ulrich Herbert (ed.), *National Socialist Extermination Policies: Contemporary German Perspectives and Controversies* (New York; Oxford: Berghahn Books, 2000).

10 See for example the circular RSHA III B, January 1941, concerning the division of labour between the RSHA, the RuSHA and the VoMi (BABL, DAI-Film no. 2185, non-folioed document). See also BABL, R-59/53 and R-59/46 (various letters between the VoMi and the RSHA *Amt* III B).

11 BAAZ, SSO Dr Herbert Strickner. Though Strickner was only thirty-one when he was summoned to the central offices in Berlin, he was already well versed in *Volkstumpolitik*, since before being transferred to Posen he had taken over this brief in Tilsit, before the invasion of Poland.

12 This was a bureau of the Posen HSSPF responsible for questions of resettlement. Its executive functions were at the level of the Warthegau alone; here it represented the RKFdV.

13 The establishment of contact between Dolezalek and the SD is documented in the report on a working session between an NSStB representative and men from the SD (BADH, ZR-921, A.2, folios 134–5); for the VoMi, see the letter from Martin Sandberger (head of the EWZ) to *Reichsstudentenführer SS-Brigadeführer* Gustav Adolf Scheel, 27/10/1939 (BABL, R-49/304); letter from the VoMi to the DAI (BABL, DAI-Film no. 2185, folio 2393549). See also Roth, 'Heydrichs Professor', pp. 269–70.

14 This does not mean that the initiatives of one or other of these institutions did not arouse sometimes lively debates; witness the assessment of Erhard Wetzel, in charge of racial policy in the *Ostministerium* in the *Generalplan Ost* of the RSHA, reproduced in Czesław Madajczyk (ed.), *Vom Generalplan Ost zum Generalsiedlungsplan* (Munich: Saur, 1994), pp. 50–81. See too the criticisms expressed by one of the EWZ leaders, *Obersturmbannführer* Tschierschky, concerning the competence of the RuSHA members in charge, as part of flying commissions, of the racial selection of Polish *Volksdeutsche* with a view to their naturalization (BADH, ZR-890, A.2 [GKBZH-Sammlung zum Krumeys Prozess], correspondence between RuSHA and EWZ, folios 4–13).

15 This means we are right to draw on the archives of the UWZ (BABL, R-75), the EWZ (BABL, R-69), the RKFdV (BABL, R-49) and the VoMi (BABL, R-59) in order to supplement RSHA sources.

16 The German name was *Grenz- und Auslandsdeutschtum*. This became such a common research topic that scholars decided to dedicate an encyclopedia (*Handwörterbuch*) to it, which necessitated, until the last year of the war, a gathering of most of the *Volkstumswissenschaftler*.

17 One very concrete example of a liaison between the SS and the study circles involved in the *Volkstumswissenschaften* (here the *Handwörterbuch des Grenz- und Auslandsdeutschtums*) is the appointment procedure of Prof. Schwalm to the Posen *Reichsuniversität* in 1941 (BABL, R-4901 [Alt R-21]/10303, folios 8 and 109–15). Schwalm was one of the editors of the encyclopedia, and was discreetly paid by the Ministry of the Interior. On his appointment, the management of his salary was entrusted to the Ministry of Education, at the same time that he was informed he was being given leave to take part in a 'special mission' with the RKFdV. See the basic work on this subject: Burleigh, *Germany Turns Eastwards*; Schöttler, *Geschichtschreibung*, particularly the articles by Oberkrome, 'Geschichte, Volk und Theorie', and Roth, 'Heydrichs Professor'.

18 Letter from the RSHA III B/VI G to the *Nord- und Ostdeutsche Forschungsgemeinschaft*, 19/11/1944, signed by *SS-Stubaf* von Hehn, summoning the representatives of the *volksdeutsche Forschungsgemeinschaften* to a working meeting in Prague (BABL, R-153/1283, non-folioed document): von Hehn legitimated this colloquium by placing it under the supervision of the RSHA, which meant that new objectives neeed to be decided on.

19 AGKBZH, 362/209: *Sonderbericht* (special report): 'Die Politik Polens im Baltikum', pp. 33–8 (folios 38–43); folio 58 for the Jews.

20 Probably Alexander Dolezalek.

21 BABL, R-49/159: 'La germanité en Lituanie', memorandum of the *Amt Raumplanung* of the RKFdV, 1940, folios 31–2.

22 BABL, R-59/409: report of the Petersburg *Sonderkommando* of the VoMi: 'La germanité dans la région de Leningrad': folio 10 for the example of Kiopen.

23 *Kurzbericht* (short report) no. 8 (3/6/1942): 'Die Wiederverpolung des Netzgaues unter preussischer Herrschaft mit 7 Karten', BABL, R-49/3040, folios 37–56; folio 37.

24 See, for example, the colloquium organized by the working group for *Auslandsdeutsche Volksforschung*: led by Hans Joachim Beyer, who was active in RSHA *Amt* III B and the *Einsatzgruppen* in the USSR, this colloquium was dedicated to the processes of Polonization and the question of assimilation (*Umvolkung*) (programme of the colloquium for 11–13/8/1937 and 2/8/1937 in BABL, R-153/108; non-folioed document).

25 This linguistic takeover was discerned by the Germans, for example, in the way the Poles had in their view 'Polonized' local dialects such as Silesian, or tried to prove the Polish origins of the Silesian dialect. A German 'press agency' in Allenstein kept this type of activity under surveillance and issued reports on it (BABL, R-153/1655: 'Volkstumskampf in Polen').

26 BABL, R-153/1178a, folios 1–11 (*Institut für Staatsforschung* in Berlin and *Publikationsstelle* in Dahlem, various communications), *Auswertung der Erfahrungen der deutschen Ostsiedlung bis zur Machtergreifung* (analysis of

the practice of German settlement until the assumption of power). Archival report no. 6 on the action of the bishop of Posen/Gnesen between 1887 and 1907. On this aspect of the relations between Poles and Germans in Posnania, see Thomas Serrier, *Entre Allemagne et Pologne. Nations et identités frontalières, 1848–1914* (Paris: Belin, 2002).

27 AGKBZH, 362/766, folio 30 for the Poles' capacity for *Volkstumskampf* and folio 123 for the accusations of being dispossessed of one's own land (SD reports on political life and the conditions of possibility for the existence of a Polish or Ukrainian-Russian state to the east of Germany, dated 1939, before the September invasion).

28 K. Walz, 'Die Entwicklung der deutschen Volksgruppen in Polen und in Ungarn', a lecture delivered at the 7 May 1938 session of the *Akademie für deutsches Recht* (BABL, R-8043/1333; folios 128–9). He drew the same alarmist conclusions in the case of Hungary. The chairman of the session was *SS-Oberführer* Hermann Behrends; the audience included Carl von Loetsch (*Institut für Grenz- und Auslandsstudien*) and Reinhard Höhn: this shows how close the links between the SS, the SD and the *Volkstumswissenschaften* actually were.

29 Erhard Kroeger, *Der Auszug aus der alten Heimat* (Tübingen: Veröffentlichungen des Instituts für Nachkriegsgeschichte, 1967), pp. 4ff, quoted in Aly, *Final Solution*, p. 20.

30 This expression is drawn from the *Generalplan Ost* (BABL, R-49/157a, folio 1); quoted in Madajczyk, *Vom Generalplan Ost*, pp. 91–129; p. 91.

31 Quoted in Aly, *Final Solution*, p. 34.

32 Plans were already being laid in November 1939, but this document, which historians call the 'first *Generalplan Ost*', was the earliest to emerge from a central body dealing with the displacement of populations and Germanization and quoting actual figures. See Karl-Heinz Roth, '"Generalplan Ost" und der Mord an den Juden: der "Fernplan um der Umsiedlung in den Ostprovinzen" aus dem Reichssicherheitshauptamt vom November 1939', *1999* 2, 1997, and Aly, *Final Solution*, pp. 33–58 (Chronology).

33 'Principles of the plans for the reorganization of the territories in the East', memorandum of *SS-Oberführer* Meyer-Heitling, n.d. (BABL, R-49/157, folios 1–21; folio 6); also quoted in Madajczyk, *Vom Generalplan Ost*, pp. 5–6.

34 Meyer-Heitling estimated the proportion of Poles in these territories at approximately 81 per cent, and that of Germans at 11 per cent, with Jews comprising the remaining 8 per cent; the second paragraph of the memorandum sets out as a prior condition *sine qua non* their expulsion from the territory (Madajczyk, *Vom Generalplan Ost*, p. 1).

35 Meyer-Heitling's argument is supported by a map of those zones which gives remarkably clear shape to the policy of the cordon sanitaire and the highways of settlement (BABL, R-49/157, folio 7).

36 Roth, '"Generalplan Ost" und den Mord an den Juden', p. 60. This second plan has not survived – all we know are the general figures, from the memoirs written by Konrad Meyer-Heitling after the war.

37 The planners of RSHA *Amt* III B agreed on this figure and used it in the

Generalsiedlungsplan: 'Stellungnahme und Gedanken von Dr Erhard Wetzel zum *Generalplan Ost* des RFSS', Nur. Dok. NG-2325, in Madajczyk, *Vom Generalplan Ost*, pp. 50–81; Roth, '"Generalplan Ost" und der Mord an den Juden', p. 41.

38 See Conte and Essner, *La Quête de la race*, pp. 327–36, and BABL, R-49/3533, 'Fahndung nach deutschem Blut'. Action Zamość.

39 Erhard Wetzel, 'Stellungsnahme und Gedanken zum *Generalplan Ost* des Reichsführers SS', 27/4/1942, Nur. Dok. NG-2325; quoted in Madajczyk, *Vom Generalplan Ost*, pp. 50–81; pp. 51–2.

40 Wetzel points out that the RSHA plan does not specify whether these 14 million people are to be Germanized or 'made away with' (Madajczyk, *Vom Generalplan Ost*, p. 51).

41 Notes taken by Hermann Krumey, head of the UWZ, from Beyer's lecture (AGKBZH, 358/82). Document discovered and published by Madajczyk, *Vom Generalplan Ost*, pp. 261–6; p. 265.

42 Himmler's speech, 16/9/1942, to the SSPF at Hegewald (AGKBZH, NTN, vol. 253, folios 93–139); quoted in Madajczyk, *Vom Generalplan Ost*, p. 173.

43 *SS-Standartenführer* Bruno Schulz, head of the racial department of the RuSHA, indicated this limit during a discussion with officials of the RSHA and the *Ostministerium* in November 1941 (protocol of the meeting in BABL, R-6/159).

44 BABL, R-49/984.

45 Ibid., tables I and V. See also Madajczyk, *Vom Generalplan Ost*, pp. 236–41.

46 On this last point, see Miroslav Karny, 'Vernichtung durch Arbeit. Die Sterblichkeit in den NS-Konzentrationslagern', *Beiträge zur nationalsozialistischen Gesundheits- und Sozialpolitik*, 5, Berlin, 1987, pp. 133–58; Hermann Kaienburg, 'Vernichtung durch Arbeit'. *Der Fall Neuengamme* (Frankfurt: Fischer, 1998); Ulrich Herbert, 'Arbeit und Vernichtung. Ökonomisches Interesse und Primat der "Weltanschauung" im Nationalsozialismus', in Herbert (ed.), *Europa und der Reichseinsatz. Ausländische Zivilarbeiter, Kriegsgefangene und KZ-Häftlinge in Deutschland 1933–1945* (Essen: Klartext, 1991).

47 Roth, '"Generalplan Ost" und der Mord an den Juden', p. 53; Aly and Heim, *Vordenker der Vernichtung*, pp. 365–76; Christian Gerlach, *Kalkulierte Morde. Die deutsche Wirtschafts- und Vernichtungspolitik in Weißrußland* (Hamburg: Hamburger Edition, 1999), pp. 44–94.

48 Roth, '"Generalplan Ost" und der Mord an den Juden', pp. 72–3.

49 Letter from Backe to Himmler, 6/6/1942 (BABL, NS-19/3418); published in Madajczyk, *Vom Generalplan Ost*, p. 133.

50 *SS-Standartenführer* Hans Ehlich, 'Die Behandlung des fremden Volkstums', lecture delivered at Salzburg, 11/12/1942: *Der Reichsstudentenführer. Volkspolitisches Referat* (ed.), *Vertrauliche Berichte*, BABL, R-4901 (Alt R-21)/764, folios 3–9.

51 Signed notification from Ohlendorf, 28/12/1942 (AGKBZH, 358/82). Document discovered and published by Madajczyk in *Vom Generalplan Ost*, pp. 261–6.

52 Krumey, notes on Beyer's lecture (ibid., p. 265).
53 The calculation is based on statistics drawn up by RSHA *Ämter* IV B-4 and III B and used by Heydrich at the Wannsee Conference in January 1942. Protocol of the conference and statistical data published in English translation in Rürup, *Topography of Terror*, pp. 146–50; see also the report of *SS-Oberführer* Richard Korherr, January 1943 (BABL, NS-19/1570). I am grateful to Florent Brayard for a copy of this document.
54 BABL, R-69/554, folio 75.
55 The *Aussiedlungen* are represented by tables representing maps and figures, without photos. Expulsions are symbolized by trains (!); see Rössler and Schleiermacher, *Der 'Generalplan Ost'*, p. 333.
56 See Aly, *Final Solution*, pp. 214–42.
57 BABL, R-49/157, folios 47–73.
58 Heinemann, '*Rasse, Siedlung, deutsches Blut*', and Roth, '"Generalplan Ost" und der Mord an den Juden'.
59 Head of the civil administration.
60 Note by Dolezalek: '*Gauleiter* Greiser [. . .] on the forthcoming plans to colonize the Warthegau', 12/2/1941 (BABL, R-49/Anh. I/34, folios 43–7); remarks made by Greiser and Dolezalek quoted by Aly in *Final Solution*, pp. 144–5.
61 This thesis is defended by Aly (ibid.) and, for the *Hungerplan*, Gerlach, *Kalkulierte Morde*.
62 The main Nazi theorist of *Volksgemeinschaft* was Reinhard Höhn, first head of the SD *Inland*, Ohlendorf's superior and recruiter. Höhn also worked on the problems of managing the occupied territories (Höhn, *Rechtsgemeinschaft und Volksgemeinschaft*; 'Volksgemeinschaft und Wissenschaft', *Süddeutscher Monatsheft* 32, 1934). On Nazi imperial power, see also Höhn, *Reich – Großraum – Großmacht* (Darmstadt: Wittich, 1942), and the review *Reichs, Volksordnung Lebensraum*, third year, 1943: the issue is entirely devoted to the problem of Nazi imperial administrative practice. See Herbert, *Best*, pp. 291–8.
63 BABL, R-49/157, folio 59.
64 See in particular ibid., folios 55, 56, 57 and 59.
65 Directive of department no. 7, 12/5/1943 (BABL, R-49/3533 [Action Zamość, 'Fahndung nach deutschem Blut'], folio 32).
66 The plans and sketches for the development of Łódź have been published by Niels Gutschow in 'Stadtplanung im Warthegau', in Rössler and Schleiermacher, *Der 'Generalplan Ost'*, pp. 232–58; pp. 245–51.
67 Approximation based on sketch for the forum (ibid., p. 248).
68 Ibid.
69 Conte and Essner, *La Quête de la race*; Czesław Madajczyk, *Zamojszczyzna. Sonderlaboratorium des SS: Zbiór dokumentów polskich i niemieckich z okresu okupacji hitlerowskiej* (Warsaw; Ludowa: Spółdzielnia Wydwanicza, 1977).
70 See Gerlach, *Kalkulierte Morde*, pp. 1036–54.
71 BABL, R-49/3044, folios 96–7.
72 Baumann, '*Im Osten*'.

73 'Die Stunde des Bauern' ('The Peasants' Hour'), BABL, R-49/3044, folios 98–9.

74 For an overall chronology, see Ulrich Herbert (ed.), *Nationalsozialistische Vernichtungspolitik 1939–1945. Neue Forschungen und Kontroversen* (Frankfurt: Fischer, 1998), and Christian Gerlach, 'Die Bedeutung der deutschen Ernährungspolitik für die Beschleunigung des Mordes an den Juden 1942. Das Generalgouvernement und die Westukraine', in Gerlach, *Krieg, Ernährung, Völkermord*, pp. 167–257.

75 Christopher Browning, *Ordinary Men: Reserve Police Battalion 101 and the Final Solution in Poland* (London: Penguin, 2001); and, drawing on the same sources and with more facts and figures on the action of the police battalions, even though its conclusions are in general to be rejected (see my next chapter), Goldhagen, *Hitler's Willing Executioners*.

Chapter 8 Arguing for war: Nazi rhetoric

1 By the phrase 'combatant society' I mean all the groups of individuals taking part in the campaign, i.e. the Wehrmacht, the SIPO and the SD, but also the *Kommandos* of the VoMi, the RuSHA, the Todt Organization, and the members of the NSV who set off with an *Osteinsatz*.

2 Pohl, *Von der 'Judenpolitik' zum Judenmord*; Pohl, *Ostgalizien 1941–1944*; Gerlach, *Krieg, Ernährung, Völkermord*; and his important thesis, *Kalkulierte Morde*; Herbert, *Nationalsozialistische Vernichtungspolitik*.

3 The expression is taken from the publication of an RSHA intellectual, too young to fit the group's criteria, *Hstuf* Dr Hess, who wrote an article of this title in the annual issue for 1943 of the journal of the *Sicherheitspolizei* and the SD. This journal can be consulted in the library of the German Federal Archives in Lichterfelde.

4 Czesław Madajczyk, *Die Okkupationspolitik Nazideutschlands in Polen 1939–1945* (Berlin [GDR]): Akademie Verlag, 1987), pp. 12–13; see also Werner Röhr, 'Die faschistische Okkupationspolitik in Polen 1939 bis 1945 und die Stellung dieses Landes in den Plänen für eine "Neuordnung" Europas', *1999* 7/3, 1992.

5 Directives ordering the disarmament of the militia mentioning the past work of the VoMi with some of these militia in BABL, film no. 13917, clips 274 035, 274 042 and 274 126; see also and especially Madajczyk, *Die Okkupationspolitik*, pp. 11–18, and Jansen and Weckbecker, *Der 'volksdeutsche Selbstschutz'*.

6 See BABL, R-58/1082: reports on the activities of the *Einsatzgruppen* in Poland, especially folios 36, 40 and 58. Note the use of the term *Aufständische* ('insurgent'), which in 1920 had designated the Polish activists of the uprising in Upper Silesia: the re-use of terms which had previously designated different realities sheds light on the way war was perceived through the prism of memory.

7 See the crucial work by John Horne and Alan Kramer, *The German Atrocities 1914. Meanings and Memory of War* (Cambridge: Cambridge University

Press, 2001). See also Kramer, 'Greueltaten. Zum Problem der deutschen Kriegsverbrechen in Belgien und Frankreich 1914' in Krumeich and Hirschfeld, *'Keiner fühlt sich hier mehr als Mensch . . .'*, pp. 104–39, especially pp. 106–23; Kramer, 'Les "atrocités" allemandes: mythologie populaire, propagande et manipulation dans l'armée allemande', *Guerres mondiales et conflits contemporains* 171, 1993, pp. 47–67.

8 See, for example, Bernhard Heinrich Schwertfeger, *Belgische Landesverteidigung und Burgerwacht 1914* (Berlin: Ghobbing, 1920); Otto von Stulpnagel, *Die Wahrheit über die deutschen Kriegsverbrechen* (Berlin: Staatspolitischer Verlag, 1920); Lothar Wieland, *Belgien 1914: Die Frage des belgischen 'Franktireurkrieges' und die deutsche öffentliche Meinung von 1914 bis 1936* (Frankfurt: Lang, 1984). See also Heinemann, *Die verdrängte Niederlage*.

9 There are several occurrences (ibid., especially folios 58 and 59).

10 The files on the addressees stipulated that the reports of activities were for the eyes of Heydrich, his aide de camp, Werner Best, Heinrich Müller (Gestapo), Arthur Nebe (KRIPO), Heinz Jost (*Ausland*-SD), Otto Ohlendorf and Walter Rauff; even Franz Six could not see them (ibid., especially folio 59).

11 BABL, R-58/1082, folio 150.

12 I here refer to Madajczyk, *Die Okkupationspolitik*, pp. 12–13; see also Röhr, 'Die faschistische Okkupationspolitik in Polen', and Martin Broszat, *Nationalsozialistische Polenpolitik, 1939–1945* (Frankfurt: Fischer, 1965).

13 BABL, R-58/779.

14 Intentionalist historians were the first to bring this to light and, while remaining on the level of conscious, formulated ideas, made this representation the main argument for the long-standing existence of a plan for the extermination of the Jews. It is my aim here to shed light on the mental dynamics – and not just those that were conscious or formulated – that presided over the apprehension of war, to rehistoricize them by setting them in a context of memory, and to present them as linked to concrete practice. For the intentionalist reading of the facts, see Andreas Hillgruber, 'Die "Endlösung" und das deutsche Ostimperium als Kernstück des rassenideologischen Programms des Nationalsozialismus', *VfZ* 20, 1972; Hans-Adolf Jacobsen, 'Krieg in Weltanschauung und Praxis des Nationalsozialismus (1919–1945)', in Karl Dietrich Bracher et al. (eds.), *Nationalsozialistische Diktatur 1933–1945. Eine Bilanz* (Bonn: Dietz, 1983); Arno J. Mayer, *Der Krieg als Kreuzzug. Das deutsche Reich, Hitlers Wehrmacht und die 'Endlösung'* (Reinbeck: Rowohlt, 1989); and the historiographical discussions in Ian Kershaw, *The Nazi Dictatorship: Problems and Perspectives of Interpretation*, 4th edn (London: Arnold, 2000).

15 *Meldungen aus dem Reich*, 18/7/1940 (BABL, R-58/149, folio 69).

16 Wildt, *Die Judenpolitik des SD*; and especially his 'Avant la "Solution finale"'. The paradigmatic expression of the SD's anti-Semitism can also be found in a brochure published under a pseudonym by SD intellectuals including Franz Six, Herbert Hagen and Helmut Knochen: Schwarz, 'Das Weltjudentum' (BABL, R-58/987); appendices and statistical tables used by SD officers in BABL, R-58/995.

17 See for example a solemn report addressed to Himmler requesting the

execution of a Czech secret agent of the Jewish religion, a report character-istic of Nazi anti-Semitism: secrecy, manipulation, the use of seduction to lure women into espionage. According to the authors of the report, the man, described as a charmer, revealed the abject depths of his character when he forced the German girl he had seduced to betray her country (report to the RFSS, 18/10/1940, BABL, R-58/459, folios 107–15).

18 This is not the only time when documents were gathered by the RSHA in view of a report from Heydrich to Himmler. As is known, the census figures for Jews in Europe advanced by Heydrich at the Wannsee Conference had been provided to him by RSHA *Amt* VII (AGKBZH, 362/218: an attempt at a census of Jews living in every country); see also Christian Gerlach, 'Die Wannsee-Konferenz, das Schicksal der deutschen Juden und Hitlers politische Grundsatzentscheidung, alle Juden Europas zu ermorden', in Gerlach, *Krieg, Ernährung, Völkermord*, p. 112.

19 This was nothing new: in 1938, a report discussed the 'Russian propagandist preparation for a war against Germany'; half of the contents of this report tried to prove the perfect collusion between Jews and Communists (BABL, R-58/597).

20 BABL, R-58/569, especially folios 3 and 33–5.

21 RSHA memorandum on the Russian question (BABL, R-58/13, folio 2): emphasis in the original.

22 Order of the general in command of the Fourth Panzer group, General Hoepner, *Bundesarchiv-Militärarchiv* (BA-MA) Freiburg, LVI. AK, 17956/7a; quoted in Ueberschär and Wette, *'Unternehmen Barbarossa'*, p. 251. The Fourth Panzer group, active on the northern part of the front, had Leningrad as its objective.

23 This type of phenomenon has already been emphasized by Gerlach, in Hannes Heer and Klaus Naumann (eds.), *War of Extermination: The German Military in World War II, 1941–1944* (New York; Oxford: Berghahn Books, 2000), in an article on the generals involved in the plot of 20/7/1944 who had served in the *Heeresgruppe Mitte* where they had signalized themselves with acts of great brutality: as if anti-Nazism did not inevitably stop the rhetoric of total war from being internalized.

24 BA-MA, RH 23/218; quoted in Ueberschär and Wette, *'Unternehmen Barbarossa'*, p. 264. The text is quoted in full. The cuts correspond to the intertitles.

25 See, for example, the *Merkblatt* of the HQ of the army in Norway (June 1941; BA-MA, RW 39/20), which states: 'The Russian is a master at all the arts of guerrilla warfare, and highly inventive in devising ever newer ploys, in the employment of which he acts without scruple and shows himself ready for every bestiality.' Quoted in Ueberschär and Wette, *'Unternehmen Barbarossa'*, pp. 262–4.

26 This is the main objection to the hypothesis put forward by Omer Bartov on the unleashing of behaviour by the demodernization of war, with the high rates of loss atomizing the primary groups and the fact that depreda-tions on Russian civilians were instrumentalized by the hierarchy as an

outlet for a troop that was subject to a wartime justice that carried out huge nunbers of shootings. Bartov's account fails to explain the outbreak, from the very first week, of extraordinary acts of violence among the divisions of the Wehrmacht. But see Omer Bartov, *The Eastern Front, 1941–1945. German Troops and the Barbarisation of Warfare* (Oxford: Macmillan, 1985); more questionable is his *Hitler's Army: Soldiers, Nazis, and War in the Third Reich* (Oxford: Oxford University Press, 1992). For an example of the extremely rapid brutalization of behaviour in the first week of the war, see the case of the 530th infantry regiment, discussed by Bernd Boll and Hans Safrian, 'On the way to Stalingrad', in Heer and Naumann, *War of Extermination*, p. 267.

27 This is how the term is translated by Hilberg in *The Destruction of the European Jews*. He also states that the *Einsatzgruppen* were for the most part deployed in the USSR during Operation Barbarossa.

28 See the classic account in Krausnick and Wilhelm, *Die Truppe des Weltanschauungskrieges*, and the introduction by Peter Klein in Klein, *Die Einsatzgruppen in der besetzten Sowjetunion*, pp. 9–28; pp. 11–16.

29 Circular entitled 'Directives for the activity of the *Einsatzgruppen* of the *Geheime Staatspolizei* in the Sudetenland', 5/11/1938 (BABL, R-58/241). Quoted in Krausnick and Wilhelm, *Die Truppe des Weltanschauungskrieges*, p. 17.

30 Ibid., pp. 254–98.

31 See Herbert, *Best*, pp. 163–79, on Best's theorizing, and Krausnick and Wilhelm, *Die Truppe des Weltanschauungskrieges*, pp. 13–25, for Austria, the Sudetenland and Czechoslovakia.

32 The view that refugees were all potential pillagers is clear, for instance, from the report of 9/9/1939 (BABL, R-58/1082, folio 40): the report of *Einsatzgruppe* z.b.V. enumerates, without putting them into order of importance, insurgents, refugees and attempted pillagers.

33 From many examples, see the report of 10/9/1939 on the execution of twenty Poles as reprisals for night shootings which provoked a joint operation between the Wehrmacht and *Einsatzgruppe* IV in Rybnik (BABL, R-58/1082, folio 58). For examples of executions after sentencing, see the case of the officials at the post office in Danzig, who resisted during the invasion and were put on trial, sentenced to death and executed on 9/9/1939 (ibid., folio 41). It is worth noting that one of those shot was Günther Grass's uncle.

34 See Ogorreck (*Einsatzgruppen*, pp. 19–47) on the negotiation of modes of intervention of the *Einsatzgruppen* between the SS and the Wehrmacht.

35 Two passages were cut from the preamble. The first established the balance between the short-term and long-term aims; the second defined relations with the Wehrmacht and the organization of the composing, addressing and circulating of *Einsatzgruppen* reports.

36 Letter from Heydrich to the HSSPF of the east, 2/7/1942 (BABL, R-70 (SU)/32 [collection of directives from the head of the SIPO/SD to the *Einsatzgruppen*, published 2 March 1942]); copy in BABL, R-58/241 (same archive call number as for the directive of 1938); this document is also

reproduced and annotated in Klein, *Die Einsatzgruppen in der besetzten Sowjetunion*, pp. 323–8; pp. 324–5.

37 Small cities in Ukrainian Galicia, located respectively 80 and 210 km north of Lwów. For the itinerary of *Sonderkommando* 4a, see Ogorreck, *Einsatzgruppen*, pp. 130–2.

38 The *Ortskommandant* was in charge of the *Kommandantur*, i.e. a local bureau of the Wehrmacht's occupation troops, established straight after the arrival of the army in the city.

39 EM 24, 16/7/1941, BABL, R-58/214, folios 191–2.

40 It is known that Otto Rasch, head of *Einsatzgruppe* C, had to give the order to execute all male Jews not involved in strategic industries during the last week in July. See Dieter Pohl, 'Die Einsatzgruppe C', in Klein, *Die Einsatzgruppen in der besetzten Sowjetunion*, pp. 71–87; p. 74.

41 The author of the report, an officer of Rasch's general staff, had just given a description of the massacres committed by the NKVD in Galicia at the time of the invasion.

42 EM 24, 16/7/1941 (BABL, R-58/214, folio 191).

43 This was a general practice in the killing groups: *Einsatzgruppen* A, B and D did the same; see the articles by Scheffler, Gerlach and Angrick in Klein, *Die Einsatzgruppen in der besetzten Sowjetunion*, and Gerlach, *Kalkulierte Morde*, pp. 521ff and 574ff for *Einsatzgruppe* B, and Jäger report on the Jewish question in the Baltic States (BABL, R-70 [SU]/15, folio 87, for the mention of keeping the 'labouring Jews' alive.

44 Report used in several archives. See following note; situation and activity report (*Tätigkeits- und Lagebericht*) no. 1, 31/7/1941, reprinted in Klein, *Die Einsatzgruppen in der besetzten Sowjetunion*, pp. 112–33; p. 117.

45 EM no. 33, 25/7/1941 (BABL, R-58/215, folios 45ff).

46 Christopher Browning, 'Wehrmacht reprisal policy and the mass murder of Jews in Serbia', *Militärgeschichtliche Mitteilungen* 31, 1983; Walter Manoschek, 'Serbien ist judenfrei'. *Militärische Besatzungspolitik und Judenvernichtung in Serbien 1941–1942* (Munich: Oldenbourg, 1993); see also Manoschek, 'Die Vernichtung der Juden in Serbien', in Herbert, *Nationalsozialistische Vernichtungspolitik*, pp. 209–34; pp. 214–18.

47 EM no. 33, 25/7/1941 (BABL, R-58/215, folio 41).

48 Nazi anti-Jewish policies have been analysed in these terms by Philippe Burrin in *Hitler and the Jews: The Genesis of the Holocaust*, tr. Patsy Southgate (London: Arnold, 1994), especially in his conclusion.

49 *Einsatzgruppe* B was already responsible for the deaths of over 11,084 people, which meant a 'daily average' of 360 murders since the start of the conflict. Cf. EM no. 43, 5/8/1941 (BABL, R-58/215); see also Gerlach, 'Die Einsatzgruppe B', in Klein, *Die Einsatzgruppen in der betsetzen Sowjetunion*, p. 62.

50 This last concept is one of those which can explain a very specific feature of the Nazi system of representations, one which enables it to imagine the full-scale dimension of the genocide. This is why I have taken the liberty of calling the Nazi system of representations an 'aseptic mentality'.

51 Ogorreck, *Einsatzgruppen*.

52 See Gerlach, 'Die Einsatzgruppe B', pp. 57–60, and *Kalkulierte Morde*, pp. 585–608.

53 Stahlecker's report, December 1941 (BABL, R-70 [SU]/15, folio 27).

54 The term 'labouring Jews' translates the German word *Arbeitsjuden*.

55 Stahlecker's report (BABL, R-70 [SU]/15, folios 29–30).

56 Christoph Dieckmann, 'Der Krieg und die Ermordung der litauischen Juden', in Herbert, *Nationalsozialistische Vernichtungspolitik*, pp. 292–329; for the impact of the economy, especially of food supplies, on genocidal operations, see Gerlach, *Krieg, Ernährung, Völkermord*, and *Kalkulierte Morde*.

57 See below, p. 323, n. 77.

58 See Aly, *Final Solution*, especially the conclusion; and Gerlach, *Kalkulierte Morde*, pp. 1139–49, on the attitude of local administrations towards local populations.

59 Jäger report, December 1941 (BABL, R-70 [SU]/15, folios 87–8).

60 For one example of violent acts as a way of turning the victim into an animal, see the analysis of Catholic violence perpetrated in the sixteenth-century Wars of Religion in Crouzet, *Les Guerriers de Dieu*.

61 There is a whole sheaf of evidence on this: see for example BABL, NS-19/2442 (acts of violence and murder carried out by the SS in Karkov); and reports of the *Einsatzgruppen*, especially EM nos. 6, 10, 14, 15, 17, 24 and 28 (BABL, R-58/214). Most of the time, this concerns German soldiers, sometimes Ukrainians. The representation of bestiality lies in the descriptions of 'Jewish violence'. These diminished in the autumn of 1941, but reappeared in the *Meldungen aus den besetzten Gebieten* (see in particular BABL, R-58/224, folio 18); reports nos. 9 and 10, May 1943 (BABL, R-58/697).

62 This term, rarely used, is taken from a leaflet handed out to Wehrmacht soldiers (*Merkblatt* from the HQ of the army in Norway, June 1941, BA-MA, RW 39/20, quoted in Ueberschär and Wette, *'Unternehmen Barbarossa'*, pp. 262–4).

63 On the connections between animality, hunting, savagery and domestication, see Bertrand Hell, *Entre chien et loup. Faits et dits de chasse dans la France de l'est* (Paris: Éditions de la MSH, 1985); and Hell, *Le Sang noir. Chasses et mythes du sauvage en Europe* (Paris: Flammarion, 1994).

64 As we have seen, this was the name given to the yellow star by the author of the report on the 'Jewish question in White Ruthenia' (see above, p. 147).

65 See the crucial work by Vialles, *Animal to Edible*, which is quite unique in its anthropological approach to livestock, though it does not fully explore the killing of young specimens of the particular animals concerned. I am grateful to Delphine Corteel and Valentine Meunier for their extremely helpful ethnographic and anthropological expertise.

66 See the methodological surveys in Gerlach, *Kalkulierte Morde*, pp. 28–33; Norman G. Finkelstein and Ruth Bettina Birn, *A Nation on Trial: The Goldhagen Thesis and Historical Truth* (New York: Metropolitan Books, 1998), especially pp. 101–2 and 117; and Michael Wildt, 'Des vérités *différantes*. Juges et historiens face aux crimes nazis', *Genèses* 34, 1999; see also Wolfgang Scheffler, 'NS-Prozesse als Geschichtsquellen. Bedeutung und Grenzen ihrer Auswertbarkeit durch den Historiker', in Wolfgang Scheffler and Werner

Bergmann (eds.), *Lerntage des Zentrums für Antisemitismusforschung V* (Berlin: Metropol, 1988), pp. 14ff.

67 For Pretzsch, see Klein, *Die Einsatzgruppen in der besetzten Sowjetunion*, p. 23; see also, for example, the interrogation of G.B., 2/3/1960, ZStL, 207 AR-Z 246/59 (affair Sk 1a), vol. 2, folios 247–51, especially folio 248, in which G.B. says that his *Kommando* chief verified the weapons and gave ideological lectures.

68 For the *Einsatzgruppen*, and probably even more for the police battalions, see Browning, *Ordinary Men*, p. 163; we also have the papers detailing delivery of arms and equipment for propagandists in the *Einsatzgruppen* (BABL, R-58/857).

69 BABL, R-58/857, and Pohl, 'Die Einsatzgruppe C', p. 75.

70 Statement by the defendant Eduard Best, 17/5/1960, ZStL, 204 AR-Z 48/58 (investigation into police battalion 320 and KdS Równo [hearing of witnesses]), vol. 14, folios 2082–5; evidence of defendant Hans Bogdan, ibid., folios 2219–20.

71 Statement by Eduard Best, ibid., folio 2083. The mention of this 'sickly-sweet smell' coming from the corpses as they went cold and decomposed is found in statements by other witnesses. It should also be noted that Best says that the HSSPF was Prützmann, while this was actually Jeckeln – the posts were exchanged between the two men only a month later, at the beginning of November 1941. See Pohl, 'Die Einsatzgruppe C', p. 76.

72 Statement by A.Z., 3/10/1962, and evidence of W.F.W., 4/10/1962, ZStL, 204 AR-Z 48/58 (investigation into police battalion 320 and KdS Równo [judicial hearings]), vol. 27, respectively folios 4354–99 and 4459–62.

73 Evidence of G.B., 12/10/1962, ZStL, 204 AR-Z 48/58 (investigation into police battalion 320 and KdS Równo [judicial hearings]), vol. 37, folios 7033–69; folio 7037.

74 It should be noted that the witness, Z., who was here giving evidence, was interrogated again on two further occasions over the next eighteen months, that he was almost prosecuted, and that he was extremely careful about what he said. It was not at all in his interest to say that he was the direct witness of these events: this would mean that he was one of the marksmen and had indeed volunteered for the task, since his regiment had not as such taken part in the shootings, but only in surveillance activities in the area and the establishment of security cordons.

75 There is an ambiguity here: *prominenten* means both 'typical', 'exemplary' and 'first-rate': was the reference here to persons of a definite phenotype or to community notables? Without being entirely sure, I would suggest that Jeckeln's manner suggests that he had chosen physically representative men of what he conceived as being examples of individuals of the Jewish race from East Europe.

76 Added by the clerk.

77 Evidence of A.Z., 3/10/1962, ZStL, 204 AR-Z 48/58 (investigation into police battalion 320 and KdS Równo [judicial hearings]), vol. 27, folios 4354–99; folio 4358.

78 Remember that 11,000 of the 23,600 Jews slaughtered in Kamenets-Podolsk had come from sub-Carpathian Ukraine, a territory then under Hungarian rule: they had been expelled from it by Hungarian troops. See Pohl, 'Die Einsatzgruppe C', pp. 74–5.

79 See chapter 7, above.

80 On Jeckeln, von dem Bach-Zelewsky and Prutzmann, the three main HSSPF in Russia, see Birn, *Die höheren SS- und Polizeiführer*.

81 Pohl ('Die Einsatzgruppe C', p. 72) gives precise dates for the four units forming *Einsatzgruppe* C: 28 June for Sk 4a in Sokal; between 1 and 6 July for Sk 4b and Ek 5 in Lemberg; and 30 June for Ek 6.

82 For the move from shooting men to shooting women and children – the first stage defined by Gerlach – see Ogorreck, *Einsatzgruppen*.

83 Explanation given by one of the protagonists, Erich von dem Bach-Zelewsky, given in evidence at the first trial of the *Einsatzgruppen* in Ulm (StA Munich, I 22 Ks 1/61, appendices); quoted in Gerlach, 'Die Einsatzgruppe B', pp. 57 and 67.

84 Ogorreck, *Einsatzgruppen*, pp. 179–83; for a critique, Gerlach, 'Die Einsatzgruppe B', p. 57.

85 See Volker Riess, *Die Anfänge der Vernichtung lebensunwerten Lebens in den Reichsgauen Dantzig Westpreussen und Wartheland 1939–40* (Frankfurt: Fischer, 1995), pp. 273–81, for the question of gassings, and previous note for the *Einsatzgruppen*.

86 Interrogation of G., ZStL, 202, AR-Z 81/59 'g' [Ek 8, Harnischmacher], vol. 1, folios 2–7; Peter Witte, Michael Wildt, Martina Voigt et al. (eds.), *Der Dienstkalender Heinrich Himmlers 1941/42* (Hamburg: Hamburger Edition, 1999), p. 195.

87 Hilberg, *The Destruction of the European Jews*, pp. 136–7. The author drew on a description of the massacre by the former HSSPF von dem Bach-Zelewsky that was published in the New York review *Aufbau* on 23 August 1946 (pp. 1–2). I have not been able to see this document. The journal of von dem Bach-Zelewsky, always quoted in connection with this episode, contains just a mention of the *Reichsführer*'s visit to Minsk, with an imprecise date (BABL, R-20/45b).

88 Hilberg, ibid., p. 137.

89 Gerlach, 'Die Einsatzgruppe B', p. 67, note 38, and p. 69, note 60.

90 Ogorreck, *Einsatzgruppen*, pp. 190–1, based on statements made by the head of Ek 5 at Nuremberg and at several hearings throughout the 1960s in Germany.

91 Himmler, speech to the *Reichsleiter* and *Gauleiter* in Posen, 6/10/1943, published in Heinrich Himmler, *Geheimreden 1933 bis 1945 und andere Ansprachen*, ed. Bradley F. Smith and Agnes F. Peterson (Frankfurt: Propyläen, 1974), pp. 162–83.

92 Ibid., pp. 182–3.

93 See Roth, '"Generalplan Ost" – "Gesamtplan Ost"'.

94 See below, p. 324, n. 82.

95 Interrogation of Erich R., 26/3/1968, ZStL, 207 AR-Z 246/59 (affair Sk 1a), vol. 7, folios 1303–6; folio 1304.

96 Hüppauf, 'Schlachtenmythen'.

97 Scheffler, 'Einsatzgruppe A'; for Sk 1a, see p. 42.

98 Interrogation of Erich R., 26/3/1968, ZStL, 207 AR-Z 246/59 (affair Sk 1a), vol. 7, folios 1303–6; folio 1305.

99 Martin Sandberger, *Die Sozialversicherung im nationalsozialistischen Staat. Grundsätzliches zur Streitfrage: Versicherung oder Versorgung?* (Unrach im Württemberg: Bühler, 1934).

100 On the EWZ and resettlements, see Aly, *Final Solution*.

101 See above, previous chapter. Sandberger refers, for example, to the plans developed by RSHA *Amt* IIIB and reported by the *Rassenreferent* of the Ministry for the Occupied Territories: 'Stellungnahme und Gedanken von Dr Erhard Wetzel zum *Generalplan Ost* des RFSS', Nur. Dok. NG-2325, reprinted in Madajczyk, *Vom Generalplan Ost*, pp. 50–81; see also Roth, '"Generalplan Ost" – "Gesamtplan Ost"', pp. 41ff.

102 The theme of murder is present in only four series of reports, and seems never to concern the massacre of civilians.

103 Letter from Karl Kretschmer, 30/9/1941 (ZStL, 204, AR-Z 269/60, vol. of documents KA, folio 13). Quoted in Goldhagen, *Hitler's Willing Executioners*, though Goldhagen completely misses the way the letter is part of the culture of total war. For a critique of Goldhagen's work, which I do not have the time or space to investigate further here, see Finkelstein and Birn, *A Nation on Trial*. Perhaps I can also mention my 'Le nazisme, la violence, l'anthropologie', which summarizes the critiques which my present work is implicitly making of Goldhagen's (in my view) misguided work.

104 Gerlach, 'Einsatzgruppe B'.

105 3 November 1941: liquidation of the Moghilev ghetto by *Einsatzgruppe* B: 2,203 Jews were executed in the course of the day (Gerlach, *Kalkulierte Morde*).

106 Letter from Walter Mattner of 5/10/1941, *IfZ* Fb/104/1, non-folioed; quoted in Gerlach, ibid., pp. 588–9.

107 This eschatalogical anxiety seems to have been generated by the First World War. It is found in various texts produced by students in the *völkisch* far right during the 1920s, and Nazism seems to have played the role of a belief system that contributed to tapping this anxiety. See Ingrao, 'Culture de guerre'.

108 RSHA *Amt* IB, lecture course on the Thirty Years War given in 1942 (BABL, R-58/844, folios 123–4).

Chapter 9   Violence in action

1 *Einsatzgruppe* A: 990 men; Eg B: 655; Eg C: 700 to 800 men; Eg D: approx. 500 men; figures in Klein, *Die Einsatzgruppen in der besetzten Sowjetunion*, pp. 29, 52, 71 and 90.

2 The total manpower of the groups was 2,000 men (see *Bundesarchiv* Dahlwitz-Hoppegarten [henceforth BADH], ZR-521, A.9 [preparation of the provisional central office for Poland and the *Einsatzgruppen*]); the figure given by Krausnick and Wilhelm (*Die Truppe des Weltanschauungskrieges*, p. 28) is

higher. It is based on estimates made after the war by the *Zentrale Stelle der Landesjustizverwaltungen*, but includes recruitments of *Volksdeutsche* in situ. The figure quoted is just a virtual average.

3 Approximate figure based on reports giving updates and details of activities sent daily to Berlin (BABL, R-58/1082). The average was 0.93 persons killed per week by every SS member. A figure closer to the human realities would be that every SS killed, on average, 5 individuals every six weeks.

4 The figures are put forward by Burrin, *Hitler and the Jews*, p. 109. See also Aly, *Final Solution*, p. 217.

5 This was the expression used by Marshall von Bock, head of the group of Centre armies – to which *Einsatzgruppe* B was attached. He stated to Himmler: 'Yes, Herr Himmler, we are grateful to you that we don't have to do this dirty [or impure: *unsaubere*] work' (statement of von dem Bach-Zelewsky, 22/8/1947. ZStL. 202 AR-Z 52/59, volume of exhibits III/4, folio 92). Quoted in Gerlach, *Kalkulierte Morde*, p. 593; see also p. 58.

6 Cf. Krausnick and Wilhelm, *Die Truppe des Weltanschauungskrieges*, p. 162; Ogorreck, *Einsatzgruppen*, p. 130.

7 BADH, ZR-125 (list of personnel and tables of payment. *Einsatzgruppe* B). Document found in the Stasi archives by the author, photocopied and deposited in the archives of the IHTP and the Holocaust Memorial Museum of Washington. The list is not complete, and needs to be combined with the group's organizational charts, for the activities of the officers. The document's value lies precisely in the way it gives us access to information on the subaltern personnel in the group, even if I cannot systematically explore this document's implications here. For an organizational chart of *Einsatzgruppe* B, see Gerlach, 'Die Einsatzgruppe B', p. 63, based on investigations carried out after the war by the ZStL.

8 For the figures concerning the RSHA, see Rürup, *Topography of Terror*.

9 See the graphical appendices to Stahlecker's report (BABL, R-70 [SU]/15 [General directives to the *Einsatzgruppen* and 'Treatment of the Jews']); Gerlach, *Kalkulierte Morde*, pp. 594–5, and 'Die Einsatzgruppe B', p. 59.

10 The creation of the Moghilev ghetto dates from the week before the massacre which led to the extermination of its entire population (see Gerlach, *Kalkulierte Morde*, p. 589).

11 A typical example of this development is the case of Vitebsk (Belorussia): the town was first occupied by Sk 7a, which ran the processes of internment and registration from 14 to 31 July 1941, executing some 400 adult and adolescent Jews. At the beginning of August, Sk 7a was replaced by Ek 9, which liquidated the ghetto in September. See Ogorreck, *Einsatzgruppen*, pp. 109–11 and 114; Gerlach, *Kalkulierte Morde*, pp. 569 and 596–7. Executions perpetrated by Sk 7a in Vitebsk: interrogation of Claus Hueser on 4/7/1961 (ZStL, 202 AR-Z 96/60 [affair of Sk 7a, Rapp and others], vol. 4, folios 749–54); interrogation of Hueser, ibid., vol. 7, folios 1831–44.

12 This statement needs to be qualified as regards Sk 1b, active in Belorussia, a country where there were many Jewish communities, and where the work of Sk 1b was very similar to that of the Ek.

13 See Scheffler, 'Die Einsatzgruppe A', pp. 35–8.

14 Pohl, 'Die Einsatzgruppe C', pp. 71–2; detail already noted by Gerlach, 'Die Einsatzgruppe B', pp. 59 and 69.

15 See Angrick, 'Die Einsatzgruppe D', pp. 88–110; pp. 88–90.

16 Pohl ('Einsatzgruppe C', p. 75) attributes this to the radical fervour of those in charge of the *Kommando*, especially Blobel.

17 Sandberger's Sk 1a was 'credited', on 1 February 1942, with 'only' 963 executions of Jews in Stahlecker's report (appendix 7: chart of operations carried out by Eg A; BABL, R-70 [SU]/15, folios 572 and 573).

18 The group claimed to have executed 91,012 people, and Ek 8 was responsible for the death of 60,811 people (report on the activities of Eg B, 16–28/2/1942, BstU, ZUV 9, vol. 31, folio 166). Quoted in Gerlach, 'Die Einsatzgruppe B', p. 60 and p. 69, note 63.

19 See the figures of executions quoted in Scheffler, 'Einsatzgruppe A', p. 42: there were 921 Jews executed (468 men, 453 women) and 4,691 Communists.

20 KdS: *Kommandeur der Sicherheitspolizei und des SD*; this designates the head of the police and the SD and the organizations he directed, attached to a town and the region around it. For example: KdS for Belorussia, KdS Estonia for Reval, in the whole of occupied Europe.

21 *Befehlshaber der Sicherheitspolizei und des SD*: there were three BdS in occupied Russia: BdS Ostland (head: Eg A) in Riga; BdS Minsk (head: Eg B, autumn 1943); BdS Ukraine (head: Eg C from April 1942). See Klein, *Die Einsatzgruppen in der besetzten Sowjetunion*, pp. 44, 63 and 83.

22 Namely the *Ostland*, which included the three former Baltic States and Belorussia, and Ukraine.

23 BABL, film no. 2425, clips 7613 to 7983. Proposed appointment to the rank of *SS-Oberführer*, signed by Kaltenbrunner, June 1944 (BAAZ, SSO Ehrlinger, non-folioed, and BABL, R-58/appendix 14).

24 BABL, R-58/1082 (reports on activities of the *Einsatzgruppen* in Poland), folio 159.

25 EM no. 2, 23/6/1941 (BABL, R-58/214); see also Dieckmann, 'Der Krieg und die Ermordung der litauischen Juden', which gives an account of the massacre. In mid-September, the group of men and women was in turn shot by Ek 2.

26 Examples of the collaboration of the *Feldgendarmerie* and Sk 11b in the report on activities of local bureaus of the Wehrmacht in Crimea for March 1942 carried out on 26 March 1942 (NOKW 853, ZStL, 213 AR-1899/66 [affair of Pesterer and others, Appendices to documents], vol. 2, folios 361–4.

27 Interrogation of Wagner, *Abteilungsleiter* IV of KdS Minsk, 17–18/12/1959 and 15/1/1960 (ZStL, 2 AR-Z 21/58 [Ehrlinger, BdS Kiev, Sk 1b], vol. 10, folios 47–75 and 203–9) on the executions, the taking of decisions and the management of the execution *Kommandos*; see also the evidence of former members of the KdS in ZStL, 2 AR-Z 21/58 (Ehrlinger [BdS Kiev, Sk 1b]), vol. 9.

28 The standard counter-example is, of course, the massacre at Kiev (Babi Yar), carried out by Sk 4a when it was still mobile. See Pohl, 'Die Einsatzgruppe

C', pp. 75–6 and 81–2. This was, however, the case for the massacre at Równo, carried out by Ek 5 when it was transformed into KdS Równo. Eyewitness accounts in ZStL, 204 AR-Z 48/58 (investigation into police battalion 320 and KdS Równo [hearing of witnesses]), vol. 2, folios 406–27; final report of the preliminary investigation, ibid., vol. 10.

29 ZStL, 204 AR-Z 48/58.

30 For Ek 8 and Belorussia, see Gerlach, *Kalkulierte Morde*, pp. 585–609.

31 Letter from HSSPF *Russland-Süd* to the RFSS headquarters, 19/9/1941 (BABL, NS-33/293, folio 53).

32 *IfZ* Fb/104/1, non-folioed; quoted in Gerlach, *Kalkulierte Morde*, p. 588.

33 The policy of the war on the partisans has still not been systematically studied. And yet it was a touchstone of Nazi repressive practices, mingling genocide, war and violence perpetrated against the Russian civilian populations. For a very full overview of the facts, see Gerlach, ibid., pp. 859–1055. See also Rudolf Aschenauer, *Krieg ohne Grenzen. Der Partisanenkampf gegen Deutschland 1939–1945* (Leoni: Druffel Verlag, 1982); Matthew Cooper, *The Phantom War. The German Struggle against Soviet Partisans, 1941–1944* (London: Macdonald and Jane's, 1979); Heinz Kühnrich, *Der Partisanenkrieg in Europa 1939–1945* (Berlin: Dietz, 1968) – this last work is representative of East German historiography. A study of this policy, an indispensable stage for a cultural anthropology of the Nazi practices of violence, is in preparation.

34 Gerlach, *Kalkulierte Morde*, p. 899.

35 Operational journal of the Minsk headquarters (BABL, R-70 [SU]/16).

36 Ibid., and Gerlach, *Kalkulierte Morde*, pp. 899 and 930–2.

37 Especially EM nos. 6, 10, 14, 15, 17, 24 and 28 (BABL, R-58/214).

38 Nothing allows us to reach any decision as to the veracity of the descriptions given by the *Einsatzgruppen*. The elements of the investigation suggest that the report of the Eg very greatly exaggerated the figures put forward – one of the protagonists states that he helped bury some hundred bodies (interrogation of Rudolf W. on 18/6/1959, ZStL, 2 AR-Z 21/58 [Ehrlinger, BdS Kiev, Sk 1b], vol. 3, folios 1817–61; folio 1829); see also Bogdan Musial, *'Konterrevolutionäre Elemente sind zu erschiessen'. Die Brutalisierung des deutsch-sowjetischen Kriegs im Sommer 1941* (Berlin: Propyläen, 2000). When we remember that the NKVD did carry out executions, the violence described here seems to have resulted more from a dynamics of massacre that involved the large-scale participation of local populations, more frequent on the occasion of pogroms, and recurrent in the region ever since the Great War and the pogrom of 1919. In the absence of additional information, it is quite possible that the groups wished to see the acts of paroxysmal violence carried out against the Jews by the Ukrainians between the 25 and 30 July as depredations committed by the NKVD. Be this as it may, the decisive element is the interpretative grid adopted by the SS, and not the violence committed by the Soviets or the Ukrainians.

39 EM 24, 16/7/1941 (BABL, R-58/214, folios 188–91).

40 See above, chapter 8.

41 Interrogation of Rudolf W. on 18/6/1959 (ZStL, 2 AR-Z 21/58 [Ehrlinger, BdS Kiev, Sk 1b], vol. 3, folios 1807–61; folio 1833.

42 Report on the 'Dubno bloodbath' on 25 and 26 June 1941. Appendix EM no. 28, 20/7/1941 (BABL, R 58/214 folios 256–63).

43 Interrogation of Rudolf W. of 18/6/1959 (ibid., folio 1833).

44 The verb used by the soldier and translated as 'treated' is *zurichten*, a term from cookery that means 'to season or prepare' food.

45 Letter sent from Tarnopol (BA-MA, RW 4/v.422), quoted in Boll and Safrian, 'On the way to Stalingrad', p. 247. The letter closes with a request to relatives to disclose the contents of the letter and to send it to the local Nazi Party boss (in Vienna); a marginal mention added to the letter by an official in the investigative services of the Viennese command of the Wehrmacht proves that this was done and the letter was – by the standards of the period – reproduced on a massive scale.

46 On 31 July 1941, the first report on the situation and activities of the *Einsatzgruppen* described the 'mental' dimension of the state of health of the members of the groups in these terms: 'We must not underestimate the extreme psychological [*seelische*] effort that was imposed on them [i.e. on the members of the groups] by the great number of liquidations. Minds and attitudes were kept alert by permanent personal interviews bearing on the political necessity [of these liquidations]' (report on situation and activity no. 1, 31/7/1941, published in Klein, *Die Einsatzgruppen in der besetzten Sowjetunion*, pp. 112–33; p. 114.

47 A report by the groups connects the fact of beating someone to death and placing oneself in the stance of someone carrying out the activities of, and using the tools of, an abattoir – even if the report puts this fragment in the context of representations of the violence carried out by the NKVD on the Ukrainians: the report accuses the Russians of extreme brutality, as we have seen above (EM 24, 16/7/1941. BABL, R-58/214, folios 188–91). For the materials used here, see the discussion in Vialles, *Animal to Edible*.

48 See the report of Eg C (EM 24, 16/7/1941. BABL, R-58/214, folios 191–2).

49 See the article by Scheffler, 'Die Einsatzgruppe A', p. 47, note 27; for the succession of *Kommandos*, see p. 49, note 36, and also the evidence of a photographer from the German army, who in Kaunas took photos of a young man who beat people to death with an iron bar, and then played the harmonica sitting on the mountain of bodies (interrogation of Wilhelm Gunsilius of 11/11/1958. ZStL, 2 AR-Z 21/58 [Ehrlinger, BdS Kiev, Sk 1b.], vol. 2, folios 785–93.

50 This was the case for Lemberg and Tarnopol, but not for Sokal; logically, we should have found this practice of beating up the Jews in Dubno and Jitomir if it had been automatically provoked by murders committed by the NKVD as it retreated.

51 I am here adopting the categories of analysis developed by Denis Crouzet in his study on the acts of violence committed during the Wars of Religion. Alphonse Dupront and Denis Crouzet are the two great models for any study of systems of representation generating paroxysmal sequences of violence.

While there is no question of comparing the quantitative or qualitative dimensions of the rituals of violence that became common in the France of the Wars of Religion and in the USSR during the 1941–5 war, the adoption of schemes of analysis or categories produced by religious anthropology remains a heuristic choice whose legitimacy has been taken as unproblematic. On this whole question, see Alphonse Dupront, *Du sacré. Croisades et pèlerinages: images et langages* (Paris: Gallimard, 1987); Paul Alphandéry, *La Chrétienté et l'idée de croisade*, 2 vols., ed. Alphonse Dupront (Paris: Albin Michel, 1954, 1959); and, in particular, Dupront's *Le Mythe de croisade*, which inspired many of the themes discussed by Denis Crouzet in *Les Guerriers de Dieu*.

52 Crouzet, *Les Guerriers de Dieu*.

53 Draft circular RMfdbO, n.d., with accompanying letter, 7/7/1943 (BABL, R-58/3568, folios 10–13).

54 Ibid., §4, folio 11.

55 Ibid., §6, folio 12.

56 Document of RSHA IV D 2, 6/1/1943, signed Himmler (BABL, R-58/3568, folios 15–20).

57 It thus concerns the police offices in the occupied territories, as well as the local bureaus of the SIPO/SD in the Reich.

58 Françoise Héritier, 'Le sang des guerriers et le sang des femmes. Notes anthropologiques sur le rapport des sexes', *L'Africaine. Sexes et signes. Cahiers du GRIF* 29, 1984, p. 21.

59 Alain Testard, *Essai sur les fondements de la division sexuelle du travail chez les chasseurs-cuilleurs* (Paris: Éditions de l'EHESS, 1986); see also Vialles, *Animal to Edible*, p. 105.

60 Document of RSHA IV D 2 of 6/1/1943, signed by Himmler (BABL, R-58/3568, folios 15–20; folio 16).

61 Draft circular RMfdbO, n.d., with accompanying letter of 7/7/1943 (BABL, R-58/3568, folios 10–13; folio 12); even if this inferiority is not explicitly stated in the text, the fact that it is absolutely forbidden to have Germans executed by natives clearly shows that the relations between them were not viewed as transitive.

62 Document of RSHA IV D 2 of 6/1/1943, signed by Himmler (BABL, R-58/3568, folios 15–20; folio 16).

63 The text dates from July 1943. On the figures, see Browning, *Ordinary Men*, p. xvi.

64 In the circular RSHA IV D-2, the terms of executions by the *Sonderbehandlung* do not seem to refer to two different realities, and while the phrase 'execution of a death sentence' is never used for 'special treatment', this is because the *Sonderbehandlung* never follows a proper criminal trial. On the other hand, it may result from a summary procedure (cf. R-58/3568, folios 15–20; folio 15). These different labels do not seem to have led to any lessening in the ritualistic nature of the executions: the mode of operation by firing squad employed in the case of a *Sonderbehandlung* was defined just as carefully by the legislator in this case as in the case of a military execution.

65 This, for instance, is the meaning we should give to the oft-reiterated ban on photographing executions, except 'for reasons connected with the service'.

66 For Denis Crouzet, the demonstrative nature of Protestant violence did not essentially lie in its more public nature, but rather in the fact that the acts carried out were meant to bear witness to the Protestant identity of the authors and the religious content of this identity (see *Les Guerriers de Dieu*). For a summary of these ideas, see also Pierre Chaunu, *Église, culture et société. Essais sur Réforme et Contre-Réforme, 1517–1620* (Paris: SEDES, 1981), pp. 449–56.

67 Report on situation and activities no. 3, period 15–31/8/1941 (*Politische Archive des Auswärtigen Amtes* [PAAA], InlIIG, Regal 32, Fach 200, no. 431), reproduced in Klein, *Die Einsatzgruppen in der besetzten Sowjetunion*, pp. 155–80; p. 161.

68 The execution is discussed in EM 47 (BABL, R-58/215), in the report on situation and activities no. 2, passim, in Klein, *Die Einsatzgruppen in der besetzten Sowjetunion*, p. 139 and note 11, p. 152, and in report no. 3, ibid., pp. 160–1.

69 EM 58 (BABL, R-58/215, folios 102–3).

70 The report mentions a crowd of several thousands of people (ibid., folio 104).

71 In confirmation of this evidence, we have a certain number of photographs of the execution, published together with a detailed narrative of the event by Ernst Klee, Völker Riess and Willy Dressen (eds.), *'Schöne Zeiten'. Judenmord aus der Sicht der Täter und Gaffer* (Frankfurt: Fischer, 1988), pp. 105ff.

72 Description of the execution in ibid. and in Boll and Safrian, 'On the way to Stalingrad', p. 267.

73 EM 58 (BABL, R-58/215, folio 104).

74 A memorandum of the RSHA, dated 1943, indicates that the '*Einsatzgruppen* have been able to verify the Jews' domination of the USSR' (BABL, R-58/68 [general comments on the organization of the USSR. Works on the 'mentality' of the Russians and the NKVD]). One important fact is that the same text was used in the guide published by the RSHA for the SIPO officers sent to Russia (BABL, R-58/3506 [information on the USSR for local heads of the SIPO/SD]).

75 Evidence of O., 17/7/1962 (ZStL, 202 AR-Z 81/59 'g' [Ek 8, Harnischmacher], vol. 2, folios 688–94).

76 Published in a French review – a popularizing work whose quality, it has to be said, leaves a great deal to be desired – some of the shots have been wrongly labelled, and while some of the originals are credited to the CDJC, it has not been possible to assign them to a locality. Illustrative photos in Alain Pierre, 'Commandos SS in Poland', *Historia* 22 (special issue on the SS), 1971, pp. 172–89; pp. 179–80.

77 Madajczyk, *Die Okkupationspolitik*, pp. 12–13.

78 Ibid., p. 18.

79 Ibid., p. 12.

80 Interrogation of Karl-Heinz B., 9/10/1962 (ZStL, 202 AR-Z 96/60 [affair Sk 7a, Rapp and others], vol. 8, folios 3009–16).

81 Interrogation of Heinrich Bergmann, 1/6/1960 (ZStL, 207 AR-Z 246/59 [affair Sk 1a], vol. 2, folios 457–63.

82 This is a somewhat traditional situation, already emphasized in the – allegedly secret – practice of torture carried out by the French army in the Algerian War. See Raphaëlle Branche, *La Torture dans la guerre d'Algérie. Les soldats, leurs chefs et les violences illégales* (Paris: Gallimard, 2001).

83 See the notice of the investigating magistrate (ZStL, 204 AR-Z 48/58 [investigation into police battalion 320 and KdS Równo; judicial hearings], vol. 30); see also Pohl, 'Die Einsatzgruppe C', p. 75, and chapter 8.

84 Browning, *Ordinary Men*; the officers were not all absent, and company commanders often stayed with their men.

85 Report on situation and activities no. 1, 31/7/1941 (PAAA, In1IIG, Regal 32, Fach 200, no. 431), reproduced in Klein, *Die Einsatzgruppen in der besetzten Sowjetunion*, pp. 112–33; p. 114 (under the rubric 'state of health of the unit'). Stahlecker was not the only one to be worried by the psychological state of his troops: Ohlendorf (Eg D), von dem Bach-Zelewsky (HSSPF) and even Himmler took measures to try and manage the 'problem'.

86 Blume was not present (it seems he was on leave); there is, however, no definite proof.

87 Interrogation of Claus Hueser, 6/9/1962 (ZStL, 202 AR-Z 96/60 [affair Sk 7a, Rapp and others], vol. 7, folios 1831–44.

88 Browning, *Ordinary Men*.

89 This interrogation followed those of 28–9 August and 5 September 1962. Hueser had initially been questioned as a witness, then as a defendant. He was in fact sentenced, for the executions to which he confessed, to two years' jail, covered by preventive detention. Verdict in ZStL, 202 AR-Z 96/60 (affair Sk 7a, Rapp and others [verdicts]), vol. 16.

90 ZStL, 202 AR-Z 96/60 (affair Sk 7a, Rapp and others), vol. 4, folios 749–54; folio 752.

91 The *Kommando* actually arrived in Vitebsk on 14 July, and was replaced in the town by Ek 9 at the end of the month. We also know that the group did not start to carry out shootings in the town until 18 July. The executions in Vitebsk were spread out over two weeks, from 14 to 31/7/1941, at which date the Sk 7a left the town, and was replaced by Ek 9. Blume, the first commander, left the *Kommando* a month later (see Ogorreck, *Einsatzgruppen*, p. 114). It may appear doubtful whether the group carried out any executions before those in Vitebsk, even if Sk 7a apparently did not have any highly defined mission to perform executions, as is supposed by Gerlach on the – contested – basis of Blume's postwar declarations (see Gerlach, *Kalkulierte Morde*, p. 536). It is, however, quite possible that these latter executions were the first to be carried out by Hueser. Apart from this assertion on the dating of the first shootings carried out by the *Kommando*, nothing, in his evidence, allows us to throw any doubt on his remarks, especially as he accuses himself, at a critical moment for the continuing investigation. We should also recall that the second execution confessed to was revealed when Hueser was a defendant in the trial of Albert Rapp, and he was indeed sentenced for the

deeds reported here. Could the second description – that of the first killing – have comprised a strategy of defence if Hueser had been accused of cruelty towards the victims of the shootings? This seems not to have been the case. An examination of the complete procedure has brought out several accusations of this kind, but they were never brought against Hueser, or against any of those who knew him. It seems more likely that the modus operandi of killing by firing squad was to his mind easier to admit to in that it respected a sort of military norm for execution.

92 This was a skill which they transmitted by word of mouth, sometimes just as the executions were being carried out: an example of such discussions on the best way of taking aim to inflict an instantaneous death in Klincy, Belorussia, can be found in the interrogation of Ludwig S. on 5/12/1962 (ZStL, 202 AR-Z 96/60 [affair Sk 7a, Rapp and others], vol. 8, folios 3029–38).

93 There is quite a typical example of the system set up for the massacre in Równo in the interrogation of Oelenhafen, ex-BdO Ukraine, on 7/5/1946 (folios 38–40; folio 39). Fifteen thousand Jews were murdered in Równo on 6 and 7 November 1941. See Pohl, 'Die Einsatzgruppe C', p. 77.

94 Ibid., p. 75.

95 Boll and Safrian, 'On the way to Stalingrad'. Raul Hilberg reports that this was also the case in the major operation carried out by Sk 11b in Simferopol in December 1941 (Hilberg, *The Destruction of the European Jews*, p. 115).

96 See Klaus Jochen Arnold, 'Die Eroberung der Stadt Kiev durch die Wehrmacht im September 1941: Zur Radikalisierung der Besatzungspolitik', *Militärgeschichtliche Mitteilungen* 58/1, 1999, pp. 23–63.

97 This is emphasized by Hilberg in *The Destruction of the European Jews*, p. 121.

98 See for instance the testimony of Hans Schumacher (ZStL, 2 AR-Z 21/58 [Ehrlinger, BdS Kiev, Sk 1b.], vol. 7, folios 1–87; folio 51).

99 Wildt, 'Des vérités *différantes*', pp. 104–13.

100 Interrogation of Claus Hueser on 6/9/1962 (ZStL, 202 AR-Z 96/60 [affair Sk 7a, Rapp and others], vol. 7, folios 1831–44; folio 1839).

101 Evidence of E.H. quoted in Goldhagen, *Hitler's Willing Executioners*, p. 217.

102 Evidence of K.D., ibid.

103 See Gerlach, *Kalkulierte Morde*, pp. 648 and 1069.

104 On all this, see the report on the situation and activities of Sk 1b, 1/7/1941, signed by Ehrlinger (BABL, R-70 [SU]/15, folios 1–5; folio 3), and Scheffler, 'Einsatzgruppe A', p. 49, note 36.

105 Interrogation of Hellmann, 1/2/1959 (ZStL, 2 AR-Z 21/58 [Ehrlinger, BdS Kiev, Sk 1b], vol. 2, folios 353–579; folio 551).

106 To try and get themselves off the hook, the men always put forward two points: their assignment, as when they tried to pass themselves off as drivers or administrators, an argument that the prosecutors made short work of by retorting that in all the *Kommandos* both these categories of personnel took part in executions. The second argument was transfers, illnesses and periods of leave, which were indeed very frequent, but strangely enough particularly frequent around the time of the major massacres committed by the troops. The – very unusual – argument used here by a former Waffen SS by the

name of Hermann Z. seems quite convincing, especially as he subsequently confessed that he had taken part in other shootings – which suggests that he was not on this occasion trying to excuse himself, but simply explaining why he had not taken part in this particular execution.

107 Interrogation of Hermann Z., 8/12/1959 (ZStL, 2 AR-Z 21/58 [Ehrlinger, BdS Kiev, Sk 1b], vol. 8, folios 441–91; folio 450).

108 Interrogation of Ludwig Sparrwasser, 5/12/1962 (ZStL, 202 AR-Z 96/60 [affair Sk 7a, Rapp and others], vol. 8, folios 3029–38; folio 3033).

109 Browning, *Ordinary Men*, p. 64; Goldhagen, *Hitler's Willing Executioners*, p. 218.

110 This detail recurs frequently in the eyewitness accounts of the executioners, but not always with the same element of revulsion as in the case of the 101st battalion; these accounts are also a sign of the refusal to use a firing squad in executions. See the interrogation of Ernst Willnow, 9/10 and 7/11/1961 (ZStL, 213 AR-1899/66 [affair Pesterer and others; investigations], vol. 4, respectively folios 819–38 and 872–91; folio 884).

111 Interrogation of Ludwig Sparrwasser, 5/12/1962 (ZStL, 202 AR-Z 96/60 [affair Rapp], vol. 8, folios 3029–38; folio 3031).

112 ZStL, 204 AR-Z 48/58 (investigation into police battalion 320 and KdS Równo [hearing of witnesses]), vol. 2, folios 406–27.

113 This latter technique, frequently employed, was treated by the gunmen as like packing sardines into a tin. Raul Hilberg describes it in *The Destruction of the European Jews*.

114 The calculation was made on the basis of the personal files of SS officers. The others operated in Poland and Yugoslavia, in less intense but similar conditions.

115 See the interrogation of Ehrlinger, 9 and 10/12/1958 (ZStL, 2 AR-Z 21/58 [Ehrlinger, BdS Kiev, Sk 1b], vol. 1, folios 9–10 and 40–2); synoptic career overview in BAAZ, SSO Erich Ehrlinger; BABL, R-58/Anh. 14: file and personal correspondence of *Standartenführer* SS Dr Erich Ehrlinger; order of appointment as head of *Einsatzgruppe* B in BAAZ, SSO Ehrlinger.

116 Gerlach, 'Die Einsatzgruppe B', p. 63; interrogation of Steimle, 26/2/1960 (ZStL, 202 AR-Z 96/60 [affair Sk 7a, Rapp and others], vol. 1, folios 87–97); interrogation of Rapp, 21/8/1961 (ibid., vol. 3, folios 620–30); interrogation of Blume, 19/12/1962 (ibid., vol. 9, folios 3104–24).

117 The hostility generated by these men was sometimes so intense that the expression of hatred led to nervous breakdowns among former members of their *Kommandos*. This was the case for Curt K. (ZStL, 202 AR-Z 96/60 [affair Sk 7a, Rapp and others], vol. 9, folios 333–41); as for Rapp, his attitude inspired such dislike among the rank and file and the officers of Sk 7a that the latter tried to have him transferred for disciplinary reasons by getting him compromised in a sex scandal. He was actually transferred for alcoholism. These details are mentioned in the verdict in ibid. [verdicts], vol. 16.

118 This was the expression used in all the *Kommandos*; see, for example, the report on activities of Sk 11a from 22/8 to 10/9/1941 (NOKW-636, ZStL,

213 AR-1899/66 [affair Pesterer and others; Appendices to documents], vol. 2, folio 230). See also the report of *Einsatzgruppe* B on the Jewish question in White Ruthenia, EM no. 33, 25/7/1941 (BABL, R-58/215, folios 45ff).

119 Interrogation of Franz-Joseph Thormann, 12/11/1962 (ZStL, 202 AR-Z 96/60 [affair Sk 7a, Rapp and others], vol. 8, folios 1986–97; folio 1990).

120 Interrogation of Johann B., 19/2/1962 (ibid., vol. 5, folios 1265–80).

121 Interrogation of Thormann, 12/11/1962, cited in note 121 above. Thormann's claims can be read as an attempt to clear his own name, but the mass of concurring eyewitness accounts tends to diminish the possibility of any prior agreements reached by the different witnesses. They all emphasize Rapp's great harshness, and all insist on his inability to delegate the least responsibility.

122 Interrogation of Eduard Spengler, 13/11/1961 (ZStL, 202 AR-Z 96/60 [affair Sk 7a, Rapp and others], vol. 3, folios 808–29; folios 815–16). The statement made by Spengler needs to be treated with maximum caution: he was gravely compromised in the affairs he mentions, something which the investigators did not know at this precise moment in his interrogation. It may have been a cover-up, but his statement was corroborated by other witnesses. Furthermore, his defence, on this occasion, did not concern orders, but activities: Spengler claimed that he had taken part only in the *Partisanenbekämpfung* (ibid., folios 817–20).

123 Interrogation of Eduard B., 2/7/1959 (ZStL, 2 AR-Z 21/58 [Ehrlinger, BdS Kiev, Sk 1b], vol. 4, folios 2337–419; folios 2343–7).

124 Interrogation of Reinhold Brünnert, 24/7/1959 and 3/8/1959 (ZStl, 2 AR-Z 21/58 [Ehrlinger, BdS Kiev, Sk 1b], vol. 5, folios 3121–51 and 3239–61; folio 3243).

125 Interrogation of Hella H., 2/11/1959 (ibid., vol. 7, folios 467–81; folios 473–5). The evidence, we should point out, is indirect.

126 We have evidence of this for several *Kommando* leaders: in the case of Sk 7a and Rapp or Blume, see the interrogation of Franz-Joseph Thormann, 12/11/1962 (ZStL, 202 AR-Z 96/60 [affair Sk 7a, Rapp and others], vol. 8, folios 1986–97; folio 1990); Kurt Christmann (Sk 11b), who shot at victims to set an example; cf. the letter of the *Staatsanwalt* of the ZStL to the Soviet authorities, re the request for a hearing of Soviet witnesses (ZStL, 213 AR-1898/66 [affair Seetzen and others; files on correspondence of StA], vol. 2, folios 102–12; folio 109); Bruno Müller (Sk 10b), who shot down a woman and a newborn child in Tighina, stating that the unit would now need to kill all children too, an example quoted by Angrick, 'Die Einsatzgruppe D', pp. 94–5, and see below.

127 It has not been possible to localize and date this shooting more precisely: Gorodok is a locality between Minsk and Vilnius, towns where the *Kommando* stayed between 7 and 14 July, the date on which Sk 7a entered Vitebsk. See Krausnick and Wilhelm, *Die Truppe des Weltanschauungskrieges*, p. 156; Ogorreck, *Einsatzgruppen*; Gerlach, however, dates to August 1941 an execution that took place in Gorodok (*Kalkulierte Morde*, p. 536). This would seem to be the execution described by the defendant, since he also mentions

the participation of men from the Wehrmacht. It is, however, imposssible to come to any firm conclusion about this date.

128 Interrogation of Karl Sonntag, 15/7/1962 (ZStL, 202 AR-Z 96/60 [affair Sk 7a, Rapp and others], vol. 7, folios 1724–31; folio 1725).

129 For the KdS Kiev, Sk 1b and Ek 5, see the interrogation of Reinhold Brünnert, 24/7/1959 and 3/8/1959 (ZStL, 2 AR-Z 21/58 [Ehrlinger, BdS Kiev, Sk 1b], vol. 5, folios 3121–51 and 3239–61; folios 3242–3); on *Einsatzgruppe* D, see also Ohlendorf's statement, 3 January 1946 (*TMWC*, vol. 3, folios 245–75).

130 Krausnick and Wilhelm, *Die Truppe des Weltanschauungskrieges*, p. 174.

131 Quoted in Angrick, 'Die Einsatzgruppe D', pp. 94–5.

132 He assembled the troops after a discussion with the officers: it was apparently at the end of the gathering that he executed this woman and her child.

133 This was one of the arguments developed by Reinhold Brünnert, Ehrlinger's deputy, 24/7/1959 and 3/8/1959 (ZStL, 2 AR-Z 21/58 [Ehrlinger, BdS Kiev, Sk 1b], vol. 5, folios 3121–51; folios 3242–3).

134 See, in patricular, the interrogation of Wilhelm S., 19/1/1962 (ZStL, 202 AR-Z 96/60 [affair Sk 7a, Rapp and others], vol. 4, folios 1107–14; folios 1111–12); another gunman, with the same initials, even called him a 'pipsqueak' and a 'wanker' (*Niete*) in military matters: interrogation of Wilhelm S., 4/1/1962 (ibid., folios 1080–97).

135 Several eyewitness accounts show Blume – who, when he left, supposedly promised to take the members of his *Kommando* with him – trying to have some of them transferred on his effective return to the Berlin headquarters. Interrogation of Blume (ibid., vol. 9, folio 3109). See also Ogorreck, *Einsatzgruppen*, p. 184.

136 Interrogation of Emil W., 12/10/1961 (ZStL, 202 AR-Z 96/60 [affair Sk 7a, Rapp and others], vol. 3, folios 694–701).

137 This, at least, is what is suggested in Claus Hueser's evidence of 6/9/1962 (ibid., vol. 7, folios 1831–44; folios 1832ff): the execution described was one of the first carried out by the *Kommando*, and Blume told Hueser that he would have to take part, this time, while making no attempt to conceal his revulsion at this procedure. See Hueser's letter to the investigating magistrate, 5/9/1962 (ibid., folios 1838–41).

138 Interrogation of Heinrich K., 10/10/1961 (ibid., vol. 3, folios 655–62; folio 657).

139 Ibid.

140 See the remarks of Hilberg, who quotes, in dispersed form, and without any analysis, the case of perpetrators of genocide expressing their revulsion (*The Destruction of the European Jews*, pp. 135–8).

141 Browning, *Ordinary Men*, ch. 8.

142 Interrogation of Ludwig Sparrwasser, 5/12/1962 (ZStL, 202 AR-Z 96/60 [affair Sk 7a, Rapp and others], vol. 8, folios 3029–37; folio 3031). Blume announced the *Kommando* missions immediately after they had entered Soviet territory: interrogation of Heinrich S., 15/2/1962 (ibid., vol. 5, folios 1179–89; folio 1180).

143 On the *Partisanenbekämpfung* and its record in Belorussia, see Gerlach, *Kalkulierte Morde*, pp. 955–8.

144 Report of KdS Minsk to HSSPF *Russland-Mitte* (Nur. Dok. NO-4317). Quoted in Hilberg, *The Destruction of the European Jews*, p. 136. However, Hilberg mistakenly attributes an almost philo-Semitic attitude to Kube, the head of the local administration, when he was in fact one of the instigators of an acceleration of the genocide in Belorussia; see Gerlach, *Kalkulierte Morde*, pp. 692ff.

145 *Beurteilung*, 1/4/1943 (BAAZ, SSO Strauch), published in extracts in Konrad Kwiet, Jürgen Matthäus and Wolfgang Benz (eds.), *Einsatz im Reichskommissariat Ostland. Dokumente zum Völkermord im Baltikum und in Weissrussland 1941–1944* (Berlin: Metropol, 1998), pp. 235–6.

146 Strauch had been sentenced to death at Nuremberg, and sent to Holland, where he died in prison before sentence could be carried out. For a description of Strauch's troubled mind, see Bayle, *Psychologie et éthique*, p. 147.

147 Gerlach, 'Die Einsatzgruppe B', p. 60.

148 Interrogation of Hans B., 8/12/1961 (ZStL, 202 AR-Z 81/59 'g' [Ek 8, Harnischmacher], vol. 2, folios 323–31; folio 328).

149 Interrogations of W., S. and K., 7/2/1962 (ibid., folios 400–5).

150 Browning, *Ordinary Men*, p. 77.

151 Interrogation of Erich B., 20/8/1959 (ZStL, AR-Z 21/58 [Ehrlinger, BdS Kiev, Sk 1b], vol. 6, folios 3907–25; folio 3925).

152 Interrogation of Spengler, 16/11/1961 (ZStL, 202 AR-Z 96/60 [affair Sk 7a, Rapp and others], vol. 3, folios 731–47; folio 738).

153 Interrogation of Erich B., 7/11/1959 (ZStL, 2 AR-Z 21/58 [Ehrlinger, BdS Kiev, Sk 1b], vol. 9, folios 37–53; folio 40–2).

154 Interrogation of Erich B., 20/8/1959 (ibid., vol. 6, folios 3907–25; folio 3925).

155 See Ogorreck, *Einsatzgruppen*, pp. 146–7. Pohl ('Die Einsatzgruppe C', p. 72) emphasizes the brutality with which the *Kommandos* of Eg C operated in the first three weeks and the fact they were all the object of a sort of legitimation of the murders by the leaders of the *Kommandos* and Rasch himself. See also Krausnick and Wilhelm, *Die Truppe des Weltanschauungskrieges*, pp. 164–5.

156 They all had the possibility, if they were rank-and-file soldiers, of pleading *Befehlsnotstand*, i.e. the fact that they could not disobey orders given by superiors, which was generally the case for all other acts of murder. So their silence about the murder of children was not part of an attempt at evading responsibility. On the juridical arguments of *Befehlsnotstand*, see Christoph Bitterberg, *Die Richter und ihre Historiker. Zum Umgang mit NS-Prozessmaterialen als historische Quellen* (Hamburg: typescript, 1997), and Herbert Jäger, *Verbrecher unter totalitärer Herrschaft. Studien zur nationalsozialistischen Kriminalität* (Frankfurt: Suhrkamp, 1982).

157 This was not the general case: one of the gunmen of the 101st battalion stated that he had forced himself to shoot only at children, since he thought that the deaths of their mothers meant they had no chance of survival, and that he was thus reducing their sufferings (see Browning, *Ordinary Men*, p. 73). No statement of this type has been met in the trials studied.

158 One case is quite striking. During the trial of former members of Ek 8,

one witness, Kurt L., accused Karl Strohhammer, one of the NCOs in the company of Waffen SS accompanying the *Kommando* (see above), of violently separating mothers and children before the execution, and killing the children in a privileged way. The accused man defended himself, and, shortly afterwards, the witness invalidated his own testimony – which, in any event, had been formulated in such a way that the (admitted) responsibility of the NCO was not categorically questioned. Statement of Strohhammer and evidence of Kurt L., 9/8/1965 (ZStL, 2020 AR-Z 81/59 'f' [Ek 8, Strohhammer], vol. 1, folios 1–5).

159 One of the gunmen in Ek 5 admitted, for example, to killing fifty people during his *Osteinsatz*; interrogation of Renner, 6/2/1959 (ZStL, 2 AR-Z 21/58 [Ehrlinger, BdS Kiev, Sk 1b], vol. 2, folios 639–76). However, he did not specify whether there had been women or children among them.

160 The term 'conspiracy of silence' was used by the very great war historian Paul Fussell in *Wartime: Understanding and Behavior in the Second World War* (Oxford: Oxford University Press, 1989). On this point, see the chapter on violence in Audoin-Rouzeau and Becker, *1914–1918*, where this instinct is studied at work in narratives of violence among the combatants of 1914.

161 On gas vans, see Hilberg, *The Destruction of the European Jews*, p. 561.

162 Ohlendorf made statements to this effect: see that of 3 January 1946 (*TMWC*, vol. 3, folios 245–75), which claimed that Himmler had taken the decision.

163 Interrogation of Schumacher, 15/9/1959 (ZStL, 2 AR-Z 21/58 [Ehrlinger, BdS Kiev, Sk 1b], vol. 7, folios 1–87).

164 Interrogation of Siegfried Schuchardt, 14/5/1962 (ZStL, 213 AR-1899/66 [affair Pesterer and others; investigations], vol. 5, folios 1087–1130; folios 1124–5.

165 Interrogation of Schumacher, 15/9/1959 quoted in note 163 above. The vans, indeed, were mechanically unreliable and often broke down, which was the official reason very often mentioned for using them much less than had been originally planned. See Pohl, 'Die Einsatzgruppe C'.

166 This practice was rarely mentioned in the evidence and statements of former members of the groups, but it is attested; see for example the evidence of Ernst D. (ZStL, 213 AR-1899/66 [affair Pesterer and others; investigations], vol. 2, folios 357–60) on executions in Crimea: the victims jumped into the ditch before being shot, and the gunmen threw grenades in after them.

167 Pistol.

168 Interrogation of Franz Joseph Thormann, 24/9/1962 (ZStL, 202 AR-Z 96/60 [affair Sk 7a, Rapp and others], vol. 7, folio 8).

169 Interrogation of Jacob G. (ZStL, 213 AR-1899/66 [affair Pesterer and others; investigations], vol. 8).

170 This was not the only time this phenomenon occurred: there was also, as we have mentioned, the officer of the Schupo who attended the meal organized by Jeckeln at the time of the shooting in Kamenets-Podolsk and said he had not been able to eat because of the 'sickly-sweet' smell of the SD gunmen who had been executing Jews. Statement of the defendant Eduard Best, 17/5/1960

(ZStL, 204 AR-Z 48/58 [investigation into police battalion 320 and KdS Równo; hearing of witnesses], vol. 14, folios 2082–5).

171 The practices of cruelty were present in the the eyewitness accounts, but in such a way that this source cannot contribute either to any evaluation of the spread of such behaviour, or to the study of what the direct protagonists said about it: this specific kind of violence was always mentioned by spectators or by men who, perhaps, merely said they were spectators. Cases were reported of children whose skulls were smashed, old women thrown down a well, gunmen attempting to inflict painful injuries without immediately causing death, or whole families thrown from the roofs of houses during the liquidations of ghettos. References are given in notes 208–10 in this chapter.

172 Cf. p. 159.

173 Sk 1b: interrogation of Rudolf Müller, 6/2/1959 (ZStL, 2 AR-Z 21/58 [Ehrlinger, BdS Kiev, Sk 1b], vol. 2, folios 1245–69; folio 1255); Sk 7a: interrogation of Eischenescher, 21/12/1961 (ZStL, 202 AR-Z 96/60 [affair Sk 7a, Rapp and others], vol. 4, folios 970–84); interrogation of Otto Bradfisch, 1/10/1961 (ZStL, 202 AR-Z 81/59 'e' [Ek 8, Hans Graalfs], vol. 1, folios 11–16); *Einsatzgruppe* D, Sk 10a and 10b: interrogation of Erich Bock (ZStL, 213 AR-1898/66 [affair Seetzen and others. Defendants' statements], vol. 1, folios 20–33).

174 Interrogation of Rudolf Müller, 6/2/1959 (ZStL, 2 AR-Z 21/58, vol. 2, folios 1245–69; folio 1255).

175 Interrogation of Rudolf Brünner, 24/7/1959 (ibid., vol. 5, folios 3121–261).

176 Erich Bock (ZStL, 213 AR-1898/66 [affair Seetzen and others. Defendants' statements], vol. 1, folios 20–33).

177 Helmut Führer, 12/9/1961 (ZStL, 213 AR-1899/66 [affair Pesterer and others; investigations], vol. 3, folios 676–97).

178 This kind of situation is encountered in the interviews carried out by Noëlie Vialles with the staff of the abattoirs in the Adour: when one group was made responsible for stunning the animal and the other group for bleeding it, they no longer really knew who was causing death. Such a division of tasks, traditional in the sector studied by Vialles, was neither new to, nor specific to, the practice of genocide (Vialles, *Animal to Edible*).

179 See Ogorreck, *Einsatzgruppen*, and the articles by Scheffler, Gerlach, Pohl and Angrick in Klein, *Die Einsatzgruppen in der besetzten Sowjetunion*.

180 Some gunmen explained that, at the time, they viewed the executions as legitimate, since they believed that the men were delinquents and the women and children were being executed as hostages with their families. Interrogation of Klaus Z. (ZStL, 2 AR-Z 21/58 [Ehrlinger, BdS Kiev, Sk 1b], vol. 11).

181 This is quite striking, for instance, in the account given by Erich B., as part of the evidence on the shootings carried out by Ek 5 in Lemberg: interrogation of Erich B., 20/8/1959 (ibid., vol. 6, folios 3907–25; folio 3925).

182 This codification can be found, in isolation, in Ek 8 and Sk 10a; for the first, see the interrogation of Ströh, 17/10 and 21/11/1963 (ZStL, 202 AR-Z 81/59 'b' [Ek 8, Schönemann], vol. 1, folios 1–32); for Sk 10a: interrogation of Kurt

K., 28/3/1962 (ZStL, 213 AR-1899/66 [affair Pesterer and other investigations], vol. 4, folios 929–43).

183 Interrogation of Wilhelm Groh, 28/3/1961 (ZStL, 207 AR-Z 246/59 [affair Sk 1a], vol. 3, folios 709–14).

184 Interrogation of Helmut F., 12/9/1961 (ZStL, 213 AR-1899/66 [affair Pesterer and other investigations], vol. 3, folios 676–97).

185 Statement by Ohlendorf, 3 January 1946 (*TMWC*, vol. 3, folios 245–75).

186 Ibid., pp. 245–65.

187 Interrogation of Fritz H., 27/8/1959 (ZStL, 2 AR-Z 21/58 [Ehrlinger, BdS Kiev, Sk 1b], vol. 6, folios 4013–35.

188 Hilberg, *The Destruction of the European Jews*, p. 205, and EM 80, 12/9/1941 (BABL, R-58/215).

189 ZStL, 207 AR-Z 14/58 (Jäger, Ek 3 [correspondence]), vol. 7: translated statement of a Lithuanian defendant from the Aray *Kommandos*, which formed the kernel of those battalions of Lithuanian auxiliaries (report on Jäger, BABL, R-70 [SU]/15, pp. 24–38). See also Scheffler, 'Die Einsatzgruppe A', pp. 41–2.

190 Report on situation and activities of Sk 1b, 1/7/1941, signed by Ehrlinger (BABL, R-70 [SU]/15, folios 1–5; folio 3). See also Scheffler, 'Die Einsatzgruppe A', p. 49, note 36.

191 See the evidence of men from the *Schutzmannschaften* in ZStL, 202 AR-Z 96/60 (affair Sk 7a, Rapp and others [Soviet witnesses]), vols. 17 and 18. All in all, over twenty members of these units were apprehended by the Russians, and had to make statements as defendants.

192 EM 24, 16/7/1941 (BABL, R-58/214).

193 Interrogation of Paul D., 14/3/1961 (ZStL, 204 AR-Z 48/58 [investigation into police battalion 320 and KdS Równo; judicial hearings], vol. 31, folios 5080–7); interrogation of Willy R. (ibid., vol. 22, folios 3670–8); all these witnesses insisted on the extraordinary violence deployed by these militias.

194 Statement of Ernst Biberstein, former head of Ek 6, 20/6/1947 (Nur. Dok. NO-4997); quoted in Hilberg, *The Destruction of the European Jews*, p. 206.

195 Ibid., and interrogation of Spittermann, 17/10/1961 (ZStL, 213 AR-1898/66 [affair Seetzen. Defendants' statements], vol. 2, folios 269–82); and evidence of a Russian *Volksdeutscher*: interrogation of Nikolai Wassiliewitch Winokurow, 17/10/1964 (ZStL, 213 AR-1898/66 [*Sonderband* UdSSR, *Einsatzgruppe* D], vol. 2, folios 14–53).

196 For Ehrlinger, see the evidence of his head of staff: interrogation of Rudolf Müller, 6/2/1959, quoted in note 175 in this chapter, vol. 1a, folios 459–84. For Rapp, see the interrogation of Thormann, 12/11/1962 (ZStL, 2020 AR-z 96/60 [affair Sk 7a, Rapp and others], vol. 8). I am quoting only the examples of men very close to them in their work, and who seem very representative of the opinions of men in their troops.

197 See the interrogation of Stedry, 10/7/1963 (ZStL, 202 AR-Z 96/90 [affair Sk 7a, Rapp and others], vol. 10, folios 3693–5; folio 3694). Stedry mentions sums of money received by the men, as well as the booty they picked up from the executed Jews. Alcohol was also very much in evidence, even though Blume

had strictly banned it; see interrogation of Thormann, 24/9/1962 quoted in note 170 above.

198 For Ehrlinger, see the interrogation of Karl Boll, 2/7/1959 (ZStL, 2 AR-Z 21/58 [Ehrlinger, BdS Kiev, Sk 1b], vol. 4, folios 2337–419; folio 2343). For Rapp, among many other eyewitness accounts, see the interrogation of S., 13–15/2/1962 (ZStL, 202 AR-Z 96/60 [affair Sk 7a, Rapp and others], vol. 5, folios 1166–71; folio 1171).

199 This was markedly different from Ek 3, in which the executions of women and children were always carried out by Baltic auxiliaries. Cf. many interrogations of Lithuanian defendants in Soviet trials (ZStL, 207 AR-Z, 14/58 [Jäger, Ek3; correspondence], vol. 7).

200 Interrogation of Blume (ZStL, 202 AR-Z 96/60 [affair Sk 7a, Rapp and others], vol. 9, folio 3109). See also Ogorreck, *Einsatzgruppen*, p. 184.

201 Blume was here passing on the message that he had not had women and children executed: this was never proved. He was also attempting to show that he half-sabotaged the orders of Heydrich and Streckenbach which, in his view, were orders for total destruction, even dating to before Operation Barbarossa. See Ogorreck, ibid.

202 Final report of the Russian commission of investigation in Ukraine, 11 March 1944, exhumations of burial grounds (ZStL, 204 AR-Z 48/58 [investigation into police battalion 320 and KdS Równo; evidence translated from Russian], vol. 53, folios 9721–47); commission of exhumation, 4/10/1943, ZStL, 213 AR-1898/66 (*Sonderband UdSSR [Einsatzgruppe D]*), vol. 2, folios 117–29; also, ZStL, 213 AR-1898/66 (*Sonderband I UdSSR [Einsatzgruppe D]*), vol. 1.

203 We may quote the particularly heart-rending evidence of the 'Pinchuk Jewess' who, questioned by the Soviets, related that a bullet had been shot into the nape of her neck, but had blown off her ear without touching her spine, while her two children died in front of her (ZStL, 213 AR-1898/66 [Seetzen affair and others, correspondence files of the StA], vol. 2, folios 217–36).

204 Ibid.

205 Evidence of this is the corpse of a young woman whose ribcage had been staved in, probably by a rifle butt, before she was executed with a bullet to the neck. The angle of the bullet, which followed a path upwards through the skull, from the nape to the forehead, suggests an execution carried out point-blank (commission of exhumation ZStL, 213 AR-1898/66 [Seetzen affair and others, correspondence files of the StA], vol. 1).

206 Interrogation of Herbert Hofmann, 5/4/1961 (ZStL, 204 AR-Z48/58 [KdS Równo, judicial hearings], vol. 32, folios 5138–6147), who also mentions torture by fire.

207 Interrogation of Helmut Seitz, 8/2/1962 (ZStL, 2020 AR-Z 81/59 'g' [Ek 8, Harnischmacher], vol. 2, folios 408–11).

208 Interrogation of Paul D., 14/3/1961 (ZStL, 204 AR-Z 48/58 [KdS Równo, judicial hearings], vol. 31, folios 5080–7).

209 This, at least, was the idea put forward, without much in the way of evidence, by Roth in 'Heydrichs Professor'; corroborating evidence: interrogation of

Emil Greil, 25/10/1961 (ZStL, 213 AR-1899/66 [affair Pesterer and other investigations], vol. 4, folio 861); interrogation of Karl Finger, 16/5/1962 (ibid., vol. 5, folio 1175).

210　See the interrogation of Karl Finger, 16/5/1962 (ibid.).

211　Quoted in Angrick, 'Die Einsatzgruppe D', pp. 94–5.

212　Synoptic file in BAAZ, SSO Zapp.

213　For the Handschar: BABL, film no. 3355, clip 369 (film call number from holding NS-19 of Himmler's personal staff); note of change of address on 16/6/1943 in BAAZ, SSO Behrends, non-folioed. Telegram RFSS to SSPA, SSO Behrends, folio 59787: appointment to post with HSSPF Serbia.

214　This was the case, for instance, of Walter Blume, who ended up as BdS Greece.

215　Sandberger's career: RSHA *Amt* VI: BABL, film no. 2431, folios 922, 926, 1001, 1193 and 1213; Italian BdS: BABL, film no. 2935, 9/342 045, 9/342 047ff; 9/341 985; director of the school of intelligence services in 1944–5: BABL, film no. 2705; clips 1138, 1148, 1187, 1194, 1199, 1220, 1223, 1323 and 1341.

216　Letter from Himmler to Kaltenbrunner, re the intensification of disciplinary measures taken against Rapp for alcoholism (BABL, NS-19/2199 [new appointments and promotions within the RSHA by the RFSS]).

217　Interrogation of Heinrich K., 10/10/1961 (ZStL, 202 AR-Z 96/60 [affair Sk 7a, Rapp and others], vol. 3, folio 657); interrogation of Thormann, 24/9/1962 (ibid., vol. 7).

218　Angrick, 'Die Einsatzgruppe D', and Herbst, *Der totale Krieg*, pp. 341–52.

219　Hilberg, *The Destruction of the European Jews*, p. 288.

220　Statement by Ohlendorf, *TWC*, case IX, p. 513.

221　BABL R-58/850: documents concerning personnel business. This call number, as well as the whole personal file of Marcel Wutsch, can be consulted at the *Topographie des Terrors Stiftung* in Berlin.

222　It is also discussed by Angrick in 'Die Einsatzgruppe D', pp. 74–5.

223　Herbst, *Der totale Krieg*, pp. 341–52.

224　Boberach, *Meldungen*, vol. 1.

225　Frei, *National Socialist Rule in Germany*, pp. 104–5.

226　BAAZ, SSO/32205: *SS Personal-Akte* of Otto Ohlendorf, *Lebenslauf*, 18 May 1936.

227　As we have seen, Himmler called genocide 'the most dreadful task', as Frei states in *National Socialist Rule in Germany*, p. 136. There are several speeches by Himmler in which he voices his revulsion at extermination, a revulsion which he claimed was shared by SS officers; see in particular the Posen speeches in Himmler, *Geheimreden 1933 bis 1945*, pp. 162–83.

228　It also happened that certain cadres in the groups quite consciously reproduced on the ground the habitus of the hierarchy. Ehrlinger, for example, as we have seen, liked to require SS officers who had just arrived in the *Kommandos* to take part in the execution squads: see the interrogation of Reinhold B., 27/1/1960 (ZStL, 2 AR-Z 21/58 [Ehrlinger, BdS Kiev, Sk 1b], vol. 10, folios 227–33).

229　See Hachmeister, *Der Gegnerforscher*.

230 See Gerlach, 'Die Einsatzgruppe B', p. 63, and Pohl, 'Die Einsatzgruppe C', p. 83.

231 Interrogation of Blume, 19/12/1962 (ZStL, 2020 AR-Z 96/60 [affair Sk 7a, Rapp and others], vol. 9, folios 3104–24.

232 See Roth, 'Heydrichs Professor', pp. 269–70.

233 Interrogation of Steimle, 26/2/1960 (ZStL, 202 AR-Z 96/60 [affair Sk 7a, Rapp and others], vol. 1, folios 87–97).

234 Ibid.

235 Roth, 'Heydrichs Professor'.

236 Interrogation of Stedry, 4/1/1962 (ZStL, 202 AR-Z 96/60 [affairs Sk 7a, Rapp and others], vol. 4, folios 1080–97.

237 See on this subject the various statements made by Filbert about Pretzsch, studied by Ogorreck in *Einsatzgruppen*, pp. 74–5.

238 Filbert verdict published in *Justiz und NS-Verbrecher*, vol. XIX, pp. 771 873. See also, for Vitebsk, Gerlach, *Kalkulierte Morde*, pp. 596–7.

239 See the interview – which tries but fails to be anonymous – carried out by the Adornian psychiatrist Henry V. Dicks, *Licensed Mass Murder: A Socio-Psychological Study of Some SS Killers* (London: Chatto; Heinemann Educational for Sussex University Press, 1972): Nebe is discussed on pp. 205 and 211. Thanks to Raphaëlle Branche for drawing my attention to this work.

240 On the suicide of Burmeister, head of the SD in KdS *Ostland*, see the interrogation of Waldemar Stange, 8/6/1960 (ZStL, 207 AR-Z 246/59 [affair Sk 1a], vol. 2, folios 495–503).

241 Evidence of Hans E.K., 8/5/1968 (ibid., vol. 7, folios 1350–5).

Chapter 10 SS intellectuals confronting defeat

1 For the general chronology of events, see Richard Overy, *Russia's War 1941–1945* (New York: Penguin, 1997).

2 Gerlach, 'Die Wannsee-Konferenz'.

3 Christopher Browning, 'Beyond "intentionalism" and "functionalism". The decision for the Final Solution reconsidered', in *The Path to Genocide. Essays on Launching the Final Solution* (Cambridge: Cambridge University Press, 1992), pp. 86–123; pp. 118–19. Browning's thesis is more subtle than that of euphoria – he writes, for example, that the Führer's morale oscillated; but he does not distinguish the crisis to which Gerlach refers. Gerlach studies the months of November and December 1941, and Browning, rather, the period from July to September. The fact remains that the two theses lead the historians to refine the chronology, at the price of a complexification of the processes involved.

4 BA-MA, RH 23/218; quoted in Ueberschär and Wette, *'Unternehmen Barbarossa'*, p. 264.

5 The report pertaining to it, quoted in note 6, chapter 10, is not dated: we can simply suppose that it is later than December 1941 and the Russian counteroffensive, which would explain why the Nazis were interested in the Russian

resistance. It does seem to precede the discovery of the mass graves in Katyn, to which the document would not have failed to allude. These, however, are mere suppositions, which mean we cannot date the document with any certainty.

6 BABL, R-58/68 (General remarks on the organization of the USSR. Work on Russian 'mentalities' and the NKVD), folios 12–13.

7 Ibid., folio 15.

8 See, for example, the reports on the Russian question and Ukraine, which show that preparations were already being made to set out borders: BABL, R-58/13 (memorandum on the Russian question); BABL, R-58/37 ('Ukraine', draft memorandum of the Wannsee Institute).

9 Report on the situation in the occupied territories (*Meldungen aus den besetzten Gebieten*, henceforth MbG) nos. 51, 52 and 53 of 12, 16 and 20/3/1943; no. 55 of 21/5/1943 (BABL, R-58/224).

10 MbG of 12/3/1943 (ibid., folios 43–4).

11 Evidence of this is found, for example, in the collection of eyewitness reports on the famine in Ukraine, an inquiry carried out by the *Forschungsgemeinschaften* (BABL, R-153/1680) and the different reports on Ukraine produced by the RSHA or the Wannsee Institute (BABL, R-58/37 ['Ukraine', draft memorandum of the Wannsee Institute]; AGKBZH, 362/766 [Work on the history of Ukraine and Poland]; AGK-BZH, 362/289 [Work on the development of agriculture in Ukraine]; BABL, R-58/135 [Carpathian Ukraine]).

12 EM no. 3, 26/6/1941 (BABL, R-58/214).

13 BABL, R-58/68 (General remarks on the organization of the USSR. Works on the 'mentality' of the Russians and the NKVD), folio 17.

14 One example of this phenomenon: BABL, NS-19/2504 (reports on ill treatment and murder of German POWs in the USSR), which contains a report and a text presenting photos of the mutilated bodies of German prisoners. The photos are not in the collection.

15 Evidence of Ohlendorf (*TWC*, case IX).

16 See memorandum RSHA III B signed by Ehlich and Strickner, as well as the reports on situation and activities of the KdS in Poland, in BABL, R-58/1002.

17 On this, see the overview in Götz Aly and Susanne Heim, *Das Zentrale Staatsarchiv Moskau ('Sonderarchiv'). Rekonstruktion und Bestandsverzeichnis verschollen geglaubten Schriftguts aus der NS-Zeit* (Düsseldorf: Hans-Böckler-Stiftung, 1993). There is a thesis by Jörg Rudolph on the archival practices of RSHA *Amt* VII (forthcoming).

18 Letter from Levin to Franz, 5/4/1944 (AGKBZH, 362/219, folio 146).

19 But also births – Levin had a daughter in March 1944.

20 Correspondence in AGKBZH, 362/219, folios 135–46.

21 This is especially surprising given that Franz was a professor at the German university of Strasbourg, a border establishment exposed to American attacks.

22 Interrogation of Ohlendorf (*IfZ* 852/53, vol. IV).

23 Telex from RFSS to SSPA (BAAZ, SSO Behrends, folio 59787).

24 See the various telegrams indicating Behrends' changes of address (BAAZ, SSO Behrends).
25 Letter from Behrends to von Herff, SSPA (BAZ, SSO Behrends, non-folioed). On the Baltic, see BABL, R-49.01/9019–14.
26 See Steinert, *Hitler's War*, and, for a completely different general interpretation of the way opinion was led, though it agrees with Steinert on this point, Ulrich Heinemann, 'Krieg und Frieden an der "inneren Front". Normalität und Zustimmung, Terror und Opposition im Dritten Reich", in Christoph Kleßmann (ed.), *Nicht nur Hitlers Krieg. Der zweite Weltkrieg und die Deutschen* (Düsseldorf: Droste, 1989).
27 This criticism was made, for example, of *Regierungsrat* Neifeind, one of the SD lawyers, sentenced to death for cowardice in the face of the enemy and defeatism for his attitude during the campaign in France in 1944 in the BdS Paris. See Banach, *Heydrichs Elite*, p. 244.
28 See the conference on 'Bolshevism as a worldwide danger', December 1944 (AGKBZH, 362/633), or the plans devised by Levin for a review on the history of ideas (ibid., 362/219).
29 Letter from Rudolf Levin to Paul Dittel, October 1944 (BADH, ZR-115 [Documents of RSHA *Amt* VII and SDHA *Amt* II 122]).
30 Correspondence and complete series of reports in BADH, ZR/811, A.3.
31 BABL, film no 58005, folios 1094–5; film no. 58016, folio 866. See also Hachmeister, *Der Gegnerforscher*, p. 226. For other actions abroad, see BABL, film no. 8477, Aufn. Nr. E420, 812ff, 861.
32 *TWC*, case XI, p. 361; Nur. Dok. PS-3319, p. 57.
33 See four articles by Franz Alfred Six: 'Das Einsheitsbewußtsein Europas', *Zeitschrift für Politik* 32, 1942; 'Rußland als Teil Europas', *Zeitschrift für Politik* 32, 1942; 'Die Binnenkriege des europäischen Kontinents und der Einigungskrieg der Gegenwart', *Zeitschrift für Politik* 33, 1943; 'Der Wandel des europäischen Staatensystems zum Weltstaatensystem', *Zeitschrift für Politik* 34, 1944.
34 Six, 'Europäische Schicksalsgemeinschaft', *Zeitschrift für Politik* 35, 1945.
35 See Kater, *Das 'Ahnenerbe' der SS 1935–1945*, pp. 211–55.
36 On the commissions of inquiry into the atrocities, see John Horne and Alan Kramer, *German Atrocities 1914: A History of Denial* (New Haven; London: Yale University Press, 2001), especially the third part, 'War of Words'.
37 On all this, see Conte and Essner, *La Quête de la race*, pp. 260–1.
38 Over 7,000 from 1943 onwards, mobilized by the Unruh Commission in the Wehrmacht units. The movement gathered speed in 1944 and even more in 1945 (BABL, NS-19/2201 [Availability of personnel of the SIPO for the Waffen SS, the *Einsatzgruppen* or the army]).
39 Letter from the SSFHA to Himmler's head of staff, Brandt, 4/6/1944 (BABL, NS-19/1207: affair Dirlewanger) (special SS unit criticized even within the SS for its cruelty). At the trial of the *Einsatzgruppen*, Jost tried to persuade people that he had been sent to the front as an ordinary soldier for opposing the genocidal activities of the BdS that he was in charge of. The source quoted proves that this was not the case.

40 Verdict on Rapp (ZStL, 202 AR-Z 96/60 [affair Sk 7a, Rapp and other verdicts], vol. 16).

41 On the last days of the Reich, see – in spite of its lacunae – Marlis Steinert, *Capitulation, 1945: The Story of the Dönitz Regime*, tr. Richard Barry (London: Constable, 1969).

42 See details in Roth, '"Generalplan Ost" – "Gesamtplan Ost"'.

43 See the successive letters from Meyer-Heitling to Himmler in Madajczyk, *Vom Generalplan Ost*.

44 See the plans of WvHA *Amt* IV under the leadership of Hanns Kammler evaluating the investments that would be necessary for the reconstruction of the east after the war. Roth, '"Generalplan Ost" – "Gesamtplan Ost"', pp. 75–80; see also Herbst, *Der totale Krieg*.

45 BABL, R-58/3521 (on the treatment of German prisoners by the Soviets), folios 4–6; folios 9–10 for the shootings. An entire section of the report is devoted to the propaganda addressed to the prisoners and that addressed by prisoners who had rallied to German opinion (folios 53–65).

46 BABL, NS-19/2504 (reports on the ill-treatment and murder of German POWs in the USSR), folios 1–2.

47 Letter accompanying the report of KdS Karkow, sending the photos of German corpses to the RFSS, 21/3/1943 (BABL, NS-19/2442). The photos are not in the collection.

48 AGKBZH, 362/322 (international press cuttings; surveillance RSHA *Ämter* VI and VII), folios 3–4.

49 Cf. the Soviet commissions of exhumation (ZStL, 204 AR-Z 48/58 [investigation into police battalion 320 and KdS Równo; evidence translated from the Russian], vol. 53; ZStL, 213 AR-1898/66 [*Sonderband I UdSSR; Einsatzgruppe D*], vol. 1; ibid., vol. 2). The first exhumations took place in May 1943. They indirectly proved that gas vans had been used. A special *Kommando* of the SD, under the command of *Standartenführer* SS Blobel, had in June 1942 begun to exhume the mass graves and burn the corpses, with the evident intention of effacing any traces, though the decision was not taken under the pressure of any potential Soviet advance. The *Kommando* obviously did not have the time to carry out its task in Crimea or in the Baltic States. There are very few sources on Sk 1005; nevertheless, Dieter Pohl has managed to trace its activities in Galicia (*Ostgalizien 1941–1944*); see also Yitzhak Arad, *Belzec, Sobibor, Treblinka. The Operation Reinhard Death Camps* (Bloomington: Indiana University Press, 1987), p. 170.

50 Report RSHA VI D, 18/9/1944, on the Soviet proposals for the treatment of Germany after the war (BABL, R-58/1121, folios 29–33).

51 Ibid., folio 31.

52 This partitioning is shown on a map accompanying an article by Alexander Dallin, 'Russia's plan for Germany', *American Mercury*, folios 139–42. Map, folio 140.

53 They were especially rare because the repressive organizations of the Third Reich had completely broken down and ceased to function from March–April, and the sources concerning this period are very few and far between.

54 *Meldung aus dem Reich*, March 1945; Boberach, *Meldungen*, vol. 17, pp. 6734–70, quoted in Frei, *National Socialist Rule in Germany*, pp. 198–9.
55 Reports on situation and activities of KdS in Poland in BABL, R-58/1002.
56 See the chapters in Conte and Essner, *La Quête de la race* (pp. 65–116 and 119–50), which do not discuss the end of the war, but give a subtler analysis of Nazi racial beliefs.
57 The reader can consult Heinz Boberach, 'Die Stimmung in Deutschland im letzten Kriegsjahr 1944–1945', *Studien und Forschungen des Instituts für Niederösterreichische Landesgeschichte* 20/1, 1995; although Boberach completely ignored the emotions and his reading left out people's opinions, not to mention the anguish they felt at the prospect of collective doom.
58 Rüdiger Overmans, *Deutsche militärische Verluste im Zweiten Weltkrieg* (Munich: Oldenbourg, 2000); tables on pp. 266 and 278. I am grateful to Pieter Lagrou for indicating this work to me.
59 See G. F. Krivoieva, *Grif Cekretnsoti sniat, poteri voorujnickh cil SSSR v vounokh boeviskh deistviakh I vioennikh konfliktach* (Moscow: Voennoe Izdatelstvo, 1993), pp. 143–4. Thanks to Nicolas Werth, Pieter Lagrou and Gabrielle Muc for their help in seeking out and deciphering this work; see also Audoin-Rouzeau et al., *La Violence de guerre*; Christian Ingrao, 'Le suicide comme sortie de guerre', in Stéphane Audoin-Rouzeau and Roland Beller (eds.), *Annales. Histoire, sciences sociales* (forthcoming).
60 Perry Biddiscombe, *Werwolf! The History of the National Socialist Guerrilla Movement 1944–1946* (Toronto: University of Toronto Press, 1998).
61 On this point, see the article by Josef Henke, 'Das Schicksal deutscher zeitgeschichtlicher Quellen in Kriegs- und Nachkriegszeit', *VfZ* 30, 1982; and the introduction by Heinz Boberach, *Inventar archivalischer Quellen des NS-Staates. Die Überlieferungen von Behörden und Einrichtungen des Reichs, der Ländern und der NSDAP*, 2 vols. (Munich: Drost, 1986–94).
62 This was the case, for example, with Walter Huppenkothen, recruited into the Gestapo by Best and appointed head of an *Einsatzkommando* in Poland. Huppenkothen chaired the commission of inquiry into the plot by *Abwehr* officers. He attended the execution of the conspirators, including Wilhelm Canaris and Dietrich Bonhoeffer, in the yard of the concentration camp at Flössenburg, a few hours before the Soviets reached it (Höhne, *Canaris*). I have not been able to consult the proceedings against Huppenkothen after the war, led by the prosecutor of Ludwigsburg.
63 Training activity in BABL, R-58/117 (from 1937 to 1945).
64 Lists of those present and lists of teachers in BABL, R-58/117 and R-58/115.
65 See Wegner, *Hitlers politische Soldaten*, and the memorandum on the training of intelligence officers, October 1944, unsigned (probably by Schellenberg or Steimle), in BABL, R-58/117.
66 On Prutzmann, see Birn, *Die höheren SS- und Polizeiführer*.
67 Ibid., pp. 252–74.
68 Ibid., pp. 36–7.
69 Ohlendorf declared, for example, that he expressly forbade the men in his

department to take part in this operation. Cf. interrogation (loose note), *IfZ* 832/53, vol. 5, folios 24–8.

70 Cf. Walter Schellenberg, *Aufzeichnungen. Die Memoiren des letzten Geheimdienstchefs unter Hitler* (Wiesbaden: Limes, 1979).

71 Report of RSHA *Amt* VI D, 18/9/1944, on the Soviet proposals for the treatment of Germany after the war, in BABL, R-58/1121.

72 Roth, 'Heydrichs Professor'.

73 Beyer, *Umvolkungsvorgänge in Ost-Mitteleuropa*.

74 Roth, 'Heydrichs Professor', pp. 312 and 341.

75 Cf. the list of members of the Provisional Government of the Reich in BABL, R-62/3: *Varia* of the Dönitz government, folios 72–6.

76 Interrogation of Ehrlinger, 9 and 10/12/1958 (ZsTl, 2 AR-Z 21/58 [Ehrlinger, BdS Kiev, Sk 1b], vol. 1, folios 11–25 and 41–3). For Rapp, interrogation of Maria Lisa Hesse, 22/6/1961 (ZStL, 202 AR-Z 96/60 [affair Sk 7a, Rapp and others], vol. 3).

77 This was indeed the case for the four men cited here, who were arrested in 1958, 1966, 1962 and 1967.

78 On Six's wanderings, see Hachmeister, *Der Gegnerforscher*, pp. 269–78.

79 Interrogation of Ehrlinger, 9/12/1958 (ZStL, 2 AR-Z 21/58 [Ehrlinger, BdS Kiev, Sk 1b], vol. 1, folios 11–29; folios 15–17).

80 There is a clear destructive drive at work here, expressed in entrusting a woman responsible for six children with anti-tank weapons while knowing that she cannot use them – especially as the *Panzerfaust* caused a good many fatal accidents by emitting, when fired, a cone of flames that decapitated anyone who happened to be behind the person firing. In any case, it was useless to try and flee with children in tow. Ehrlinger could not have failed to know that he was condemning his wife and children to death by requesting that his wife use these weapons. She was well aware of this herself and said that his behaviour was crazy (*wahnsinnig*).

81 On all this, see the interrogation of Anna Ehrlinger, 23/1/1959 and 18/2/1952 (ZStL, 2 AR-Z 21/58 [Ehrlinger, BdS Kiev, Sk 1b], vol. 1a, folios 293–303 and 305–17).

82 This was apparently the case of Rudolf Levin, the historian of *Amt* VII, who was declared missing after the Russians launched an attack on an artillery school in the environs of Prague in which his Waffen SS unit was entrenched. In the absence of any document, my thanks go to Jörg Rudolph, archivist and author of a thesis on the archival practices of the RSHA, for passing on this information to me.

83 This was the fate of Karl Murawsky, a young doctor in history in RSHA *Amt* VII, killed at the end of 1944.

84 This is probably what happened to the former head of KdS Równo, Karl Hermann Putz, found dead with a revolver in his hand and identified by his wife in Württemberg. See the Note by the examining magistrate in ZStL, 204 AR-Z 48/58 (investigation into police battalion 320 and KdS Równo [localization of suspects]), vol. 1.

85 If we except the case of Rudolf Lange, lawyer, a former member of Ek 2,

responsible for the development and use of gas vans in the Warthegau. He was seriously wounded in Posen at the beginning of 1945 and, realizing that his wound would make it impossible for him to be transported, he committed suicide (ZStL, 204 AR-Z 48/58 [investigation into police battalion 320 and KdS Równo; hearing of witnesses], vol. 11, folios 1592–1610). See Ingrao, 'Le suicide comme sortie de guerre'.

86 See Florent Brayard (ed.), *Le Génocide des Juifs entre procès et histoire* (Brussels: Complexe, 2000).

Chapter 11 SS intellectuals on trial

1 I am here borrowing the term from the German *Vergangenheitsbewältigung*, 'management of the past'.

2 See Norbert Frei, *Adenauer's Germany and the Nazi Past: The Politics of Amnesty and Integration*, tr. Joel Golb (New York: Columbia University Press, 2002); Peter Kielmansegg, *Lange Schatten. Vom Umgang der Deutschen mit der nationalsozialistischen Vergangenheit* (Berlin: Siedler, 1989).

3 Ibid., and Heinz Bude, *Bilanz der Nachfolge. Die Bundesrepublik und der Nationalsozialismus* (Frankfurt: Suhrkamp, 1992).

4 StA Nuremberg, *Kriegsverbrecher Prozesse*, case IX, p. 1392. Quoted in Hachmeister, *Der Gegnerforscher*, pp. 289–90.

5 StA Nuremberg, p. 1392.

6 [Gerlach, *Kalkulierte Morde*, p. 51 – Tr.]

7 Hachmeister, *Der Gegnerforscher*, p. 292.

8 Biddiscombe, *Werwolf!*

9 See Gerlach, *Kalkulierte Morde*.

10 Questioning of Tschierschky, 14/8/1959 (ZStL, 2 AR-Z 21/58 [Ehrlinger, BdS Kiev, Sk 1b], vol. 8, folios 1–105).

11 List of executions carried out by *Einsatzgruppe* B, arranged by *Kommando*, as of 20/8/1941. EM 73, 4/9/1941 (BABL, R-58/214, folio 310).

12 Statement of Blume, 2/8/1958 (StA Hamburg, 145 Js 31/67, folios 307–8), quoted in Ogorreck, *Einsatzgruppen*, p. 69.

13 Frei, *Adenauer's Germany*, p. 106.

14 Questioning of Blume, 19/12/1964 (ZStL, 202 AR-Z 96/60 [affair Sk 7a, Rapp and others], vol. 9, folios 3104–24). See also Ogorreck, *Einsatzgruppen*, p. 115.

15 It would have been easy to bring proceedings against him for the crimes committed in Greece while he was BdS there. Apparently, any attempt to do so was not successful.

16 Verdict in the affair Rapp in ZStL, 202 AR-Z 96/60 (affair Sk 7a, Rapp and others [verdicts]), vol. 16.

17 There were some fifty or so executions from 1945 to 1951 in the American zone after the Nuremberg Trials. As far as the *Einsatzgruppen* were concerned, only five death sentences were not commuted and were actually carried out, in Landsberg. On the debate in West Germany, see Frei, *Adenauer's Germany*, p. 106.

18 See above, chapter 7. See also Roth, 'Ärzte als Vernichtungspläner'.
19 *TWC*, case VIII, vol. 3, pp. 573–635.
20 Ibid., and Madajczyk, *Vom Generalplan Ost*, pp. 314–19.
21 He thus helped to mislead a whole generation of historians, including Helmut Heiber ('Der *Generalplan Ost*', *VfZ* 6, 1958): his introduction repeats the commonplaces uttered at Nuremberg. Even more erroneous, albeit more cautious, is Wolfgang Benz, 'Der Generalplan Ost. Germanizierungspolitik in den besetzten Ostgebieten', in Benz (ed.), *Herrschaft und Gesellschaft im nationalsozialistischen Staat* (Frankfurt: Suhrkamp, 1990). Only in the 1990s was the question stated more precisely: see Madajczyk, *Vom Generalplan Ost*; Rössler and Schleiermacher, *Der 'Generalplan Ost'*.
22 On the *Nahpläne*, see Aly, *Final Solution*.
23 The *Fernplan Ost* was identified only in the middle of the 1990s by Aly (*Final Solution*) and was published by Roth in '"Generalplan Ost" und der Mord an den Juden'.
24 The division of tasks is discussed in Aly, *Final Solution*, who insists more on Ehlich's responsibility: Roth, '"Generalplan Ost" –"Gesamtplan Ost"'.
25 Ehlich was sentenced by an East German court to just one year and nine months' jail – which he had already served in custody – for belonging to a criminal organization. Sentence of 1/11/1948 in BADH, ZR/810, A.2, folio 22.
26 Ohlendorf replied to these three points during several questionings, especially that of 14/11/1947 (*IfZ* 832/53, folios 264–85).
27 Questioning of Ohlendorf, 16/10/1947 (*IfZ* 852/53, vol. IV, pp. 267–93). Thanks to Carsten Schriber for the photocopy of these documents.
28 Ohlendorf's correspondence with *Amt* III B in BADH, ZR-890, A.2, folios 1–3.
29 Krumeich, 'Der Krieg in den Köpfen'.
30 See Heinemann, *Die verdrängte Niederlage*.
31 See Herbert, *Best*.
32 Ibid., pp. 495–500.
33 Letter from Werner Best to Oldach, 29/3/1967 (HstA Düsseldorf, Re. 242/295), quoted in Herbert, *Best*, p. 499.
34 Letter from Best to Noßke, ibid.
35 Letter from Kurt Christmann to Werner Best, 21/4/1967, ibid.
36 Verdict in ZStL, 213 AR-1898/66 (affair Seetzen and others [correspondence files of the StA]), vol. 4, folios 1–71.
37 See Herbert, *Best*, p. 500.
38 Ibid., p. 501.
39 Note of the prosecutor in the investigation into the Streckenbach affair in StA Hamburg, Streckenbach proceedings, vol. 5, folio 803; quoted in Ogorreck, *Einsatzgruppen*, p. 54.
40 The first version of the book by Krausnick and Wilhelm was indeed based on the implicit supposition that Ohlendorf's statement concerning the promulgation of orders was authentic (*Die Truppe des Weltanschauungskrieges*, p. 182). Alfred Streim was the first to cast doubt on the version put forward by Ohlendorf and his fellow accused, in a well-documented study,

'Zur Eröffnung des allgemeinen Judenvernichtungsbefehls gegenüber der Einsatzgruppen', in Eberhard Jäckel and Jürgen Rower, *Der Mord an den Juden im Zweiten Weltkrieg* (Stuttgart: Klett-Cotta, 1987), pp. 107–19.

41 See the definition given by Adalbert Rückerl in *NS-Verbrecher vor Gericht. Versuch einer Vergangenheitsbewältigung*, 2 vols (Heidelberg: Müller, 1982), p. 282. For a discussion of the notion, see Jäger, *Verbrecher unter totalitärer Herrschaft*.

42 Ogorreck, *Einsatzgruppen*, pp. 48–53. See also Streim, 'Zur Eröffnung'.

43 Published in full in Klein, *Die Einsatzgruppen in der besetzten Sowjetunion*.

44 On this whole calculation, see the very interesting, if extremely cautious, remarks in Wildt, 'Des vérités *différantes*'.

45 For a study of the reference to' the Jesuits in the SS, see the first part of Wegner, *Hitlers politische Soldaten*.

46 Yoash Meisler, 'Himmler's doctrine of the SS leadership', *Jahrbuch des Instituts für deutsche Geschichte* 8, 1979; Himmler, *Geheimreden 1933 bis 1945*.

47 See Herbert, *Best*, pp. 494–5.

48 See in particular the several eyewitness accounts of the gunmen in ZStL, 202 AR-Z 96/60 (affair Sk 7a, Rapp and others), vols. 5, 7 and 8; 2 AR-Z 21/58 (Ehrlinger [BdS Kiev, Sk 1b]), vols. 9 and 11; 207 AR-Z 246/59 (affair Sk 1a), vol. 2. The list is not, of course, full-scale.

49 See Frei, *Adenauer's Germany*, p. 165.

50 Questioning of Ohlendorf, 16/10/1947, *IfZ* 832/53, folios 264–93.

51 See in particular the questionings on 15/11/1946, *IfZ* 832/53–69; for the *Werwolf*, non-dated questioning, ibid., vol. 5, folios 16–28.

52 Evidence of Ohlendorf, 8/11/1947 (*TWC*, case IX).

53 On 'extermination through labour' (*Vernichtung durch Arbeit*), see Karny, 'Vernichtung durch Arbeit', pp. 133–58; Kaienburg, '*Vernichtung durch Arbeit*'; Herbert, 'Arbeit und Vernichtung'.

54 It is probably on this kind of subject that the lacuna left by the destruction of archives is most difficult to fill. In fact, there is no source that establishes any connection between the departments of Hans Kammler in the WVHA and the SD. And yet we know that these connections were perfectly real, if only because both departments collaborated in costing in advance the *Generalplan Ost*. See Roth, '"Generalplan Ost" – "Gesamtplan Ost"'.

55 Evidence of Ohlendorf, 8/11/1947 (*TWC*, case IX).

56 The psychiatrist François Bayle, who followed Ohlendorf throughout the whole trial, wrote that the latter greeted his death sentence with the words: 'You don't mean you're going to execute me?' (Bayle, *Psychologie et éthique*, p. 86).

57 Bayle casts doubt on the improvised character of this statement, in spite of what Ohlendorf told him (ibid., pp. 49–51).

58 This was also a means of defence. Ohlendorf, of course, had no interest in mentioning the number of the group's victims, or the way the groups had operated. The mere fact of not mentioning these details, or even the victims, was thus conditioned by making a statement in his own defence.

59 Statement of Ohlendorf, 13/2/1948 (*TWC*, case IX, folio 386).

60 Ibid., pp. 388–90.
61 Indeed, he spoke of a 'verdict known in advance', given that the victorious power had condemned Nazism (ibid., p. 388).
62 See Krumeich, *Versailles*, and Heinemann, *Die verdrängte Niederlage*.
63 Actually, this strategy was neither understood nor even identified by the judges or indeed by the psychiatrist François Bayle. The latter all saw in Ohlendorf's attitude an incarnation of 'Nazi fanaticism' and attempted to see its characteristics as something pathological. Musmano, the president of the Tribunal, compared Ohlendorf to a Jekyll and Hyde character in the preamble to the death sentence (Bayle, *Psychologie et éthique*, pp. 78–90).
64 As far as I know, Ohlendorf is the only SS intellectual to have adopted this attitude. Only one other member of the groups, forced onto the defensive by the compromising details gathered by the German judges, was obliged to state the bases of the war mentality and tried to legitimate his attitude: see the questioning of Schönemann, 5/4/1963 (ZStL, 202 AR-Z 81/59 'b' [Ek 8, Schönemann], vol. 2, folios 366–84). The fact remains that this attitude was less dangerous for Schönemann, who did not risk being sentenced to death.
65 Questioning of Peter E., 2/11/1962 (ZStL, 202 AR-Z 96/60 [affair Sk 7a, Rapp and others], vol. 8, folios 1975–82; folio 1976).
66 I am taking the term 'denial' (*Verneinung*), sometimes translated as 'negation' (Tr.), from Freud, who wrote a short text on it ('Die Verneinung', in *Gesamtwerk*, vol. XIV, 1925). Denial occurs when a statement reaches consciousness in a negative form. When analysed as a denial, Ohlendorf's text becomes an expression of guilt in a negative form. Thanks to Roland Beller for telling me about Freud's text and explaining the mechanism of denial to me.
67 Ohlendorf's final statement, already quoted, folio 392.
68 See Jean Solchany, *Comprendre l'Allemagne de l'année 0. Les historiens face au nazisme dans l'Allemagne d'après-guerre* (Paris: PUF, 1999).

Conclusion: memory of war, activism and genocide

1 Such was the case of Walter Blume, who, in an interview, sang the praises of the 'Prussian *völkisch* ethic' and deplored the fact that the 'Solution of the Jewish question' had not been postponed to after the war. Quoted by Michael Wildt in 'Das Führungskorps des Reichssicherheitshauptamtes. Eine Kollektivbiographie' (Freiburg im Breisgau, paper given at the seminar of Prof. Herbert, 1996), p. 9. Thanks to Michael Wildt for passing this text on to me.
2 That of Werner Best in the FDP, in particular. See Herbert, *Best*, pp. 461–5.
3 See Frei, *Adenauer's Germany*, and Pieter Lagrou, *The Legacy of Nazi Occupation. Patriotic Memory and National Recovery in Western Europe, 1945–1965* (Cambridge: Cambridge University Press, 2000).
4 This was true of one of the officers – and SS intellectuals – in Christmann's *Kommandos*: questioning of Pratz (ZStL, 213 AR-1898/66 [affair Seetzen and others. Statements of the accused], vol. 1, folios 200–17).

5 See Peter Knoch, 'Erleben und Nacherleben. Das Kriegserlebnis im Augenzeugenbericht und im Geschichtsunterricht' in Krumeich and Hirschfeld, *'Keiner fühlt sich hier mehr als Mensch . . .'*.

6 See Herbert, *Best*, pp. 68–9; Schwartz, *Studenten in der Weimarer Republik*, pp. 232–44.

7 This is the phrase used by Dupront, *Le Mythe de croisade*, vol. 2, pp. 1210–11.

8 Ibid.

9 Schöttler, *Geschichtschreibung*.

10 Haar, 'Kämpfende Wissenschaften'.

11 Quotation from Siegfried Engel's lectures on the Thirty Years War (BABL, R-58/779).

12 Vialles, *Animal to Edible*.

13 Many orders were issued for a transfer: see BADH, ZR-890, A.2, for the men of *Einsatzgruppe* A.

14 Diary of Hanns Pilz, 'Als das Grauen triomphiert', ZStL, 204 AR-Z 48/58 (investigation into police battalion 320 and the KdS Równo [localization of suspects]), vol. 1, folios 50ff. Pilz relates dialogues between killers as to the reponsibility of the Russians in the invention of shooting people in the back of the neck.

15 Ole A. Hedegaard, 'SS-Division "Handschar" – en militær og etnik tragedie', *Militært Tidsskrift* 124/3, 1995.

16 Birn, *Die höheren SS- und Polizeiführer*.

17 Cf. the title of Raul Hilberg's work, *Perpetrators, Victims, Bystanders: The Jewish Catastrophe 1933–1945* (London: Secker and Warburg, 1995).

Afterword

1 Gerhard Paul (ed.), *Die Täter der Shoah. Fanatische Nationalsozialisten oder ganz normale Menschen* (Göttingen: Wallstein, 2003), is a good survey of the field, though it is already somewhat dated. See also a key work of the last years: Harald Welzer, *Täter. Wie aus ganz normalen Menschen Massemörder werden* (Frankfurt: Fischer, 2005). For a bibliographical overview, see the annual bibliographies of the *Vierteljahreshefte für Zeitgeschichte, Holocaust and Genocide Studies* and Michael Ruck, *Bibliographie zum Nationalsozialismus* (Darmstadt: Wissenschaftliche Buchgesellschaft, 1995), 2 vols.: this is updated annually, and currently has details of over 37,000 titles.

2 Perhaps I can refer the reader to my 'Conquérir, aménager, exterminer', for an admittedly incomplete survey.

3 I should here emphasize the seminal importance of the work of Götz Aly, which lies behind many of the insights on which the present generation has worked. See his collaboration with Susanne Heim, *Vordenker der Vernichtung*; crucial for an understanding of the sequence of later events is his *Final Solution*; and finally, his more controversial *Hitlers Volkstaat. Raub, Rasenkrieg, und nationaler Sozialismus* (Frankfurt: Fischer, 2005).

4 Gerlach, *Kalkulierte Morde* and *Krieg, Ernährung, Völkermord*.

5 Pohl, *Von der 'Judenpolitik' zum Judenmord; Ostgalizien 1941–1944; Verfolgung und Massenmord in der NS-Zeit 1933–1945* (Darmstadt: Wissenschaftliche Buchgesellschaft, 2003); *Die Herrschaft der Wehrmacht. Deutsche Militärbesatzung und einheimische Bevölkerung in der Sowjetunion 1941–1944* (Munich: Oldenbourg, 2008).

6 See Angrick, *Besatzungspolitik und Massenmord*.

7 Klein, *Die Einsatzgruppen in der besetzten Sowjetunion 1941–42*.

8 Jan Erik Schulte, *Zwangsarbeit und Vernichtung. Das Wirtschaftsimperium der SS. Oswald Pohl und das SS-Wirtschafts-Verwaltungshauptamt* (Paderborn: Schöningh, 2001).

9 Ralf Ogorreck, *Die Einsatzgruppen und die 'Genesis der Endlösung'* (Berlin: Metropol, 1996).

10 See in particular Dominique Vidal, *Les Historiens allemands expliquent la Shoah* (Brussels: Complexe, 2002).

11 Browning, *The Path to Genocide*. The author developed this hypothesis rather less convincingly in *Die Entfesselung der 'Endlösung'. Nationalsozialistische Judenpolitik 1939–1942* (Berlin: Propyläen, 2003).

12 Gerlach, 'Die Wannsee-Konferenz'.

13 Florent Brayard, *La 'Solution finale de la Question juive'. La Technique, les temps et les catégories de la décision* (Paris: Fayard, 2004).

14 Édouard Husson, *Heydrich et la solution finale* (Paris: Perrin, 2008).

15 Krausnick and Wilhelm, *Die Truppen des Weltanschauungskrieges*.

16 Banach, *Heydrichs Elite*.

17 Michael Wildt, *Generation des Unbedingten. Das Führungskorps des Reichssicherheitshauptamtes* (Hamburg: Hamburger Edition, 2002).

18 Eighty-three archives representing some hundreds of thousands of pages, consulted in Berlin, Koblenz, Warsaw, Ludwigsburg and Washington.

19 Wildt, *Generation des Unbedingten*.

20 Herbert F. Ziegler, *Nazi Germany's New Aristocracy: The SS Leadership, 1925–1939* (Princeton, N.J.: Princeton University Press, 1989).

21 Ibid., p. 71.

Sources and bibliography

List of archival collections consulted

Bundesarchiv Berlin-Lichterfelde

NS-2/: SS Rasse- und Siedlungshauptamt (RuSHA)
NS-7/: SS- und Polizeigerichtsbarkeit
NS-19/: Reichsführung SS (RFSS)
NS-32/: SS–Junkerschulen
NS-33/: Persönlicher Stab RFSS
NS-34/: SS–Führungshauptamt (SSFHA)
NS-48/: other SS organizations

R-18/: Reichsministerium des Innern (RMdI)
R-20/: Chef der Bandenkampfverbände
R-30/: Reichsprotektorat Böhmen und Mähren
R-31.01 (Alt R-7)/: Wirtschaftsministerium
R-49/: Reichskommissariat für die Festigung deutschen Volkstums (RKFdV)
R-49.01 (Alt R-21)/: Wissenschafts- und Erziehungsministerium
R-49.02/: Deutsches Auslandswissenschaftliches Institut (DAWI) (Berlin)
R-57/: Deutsche Ausland-Institut (DAI) (Stuttgart)
R-58/: Reichssicherheitshauptamt (RSHA)
R-59/: Volksdeutsche Mittelstelle (VoMi)
R-69/: Einwandererzentralstelle (EWZ) (Posen/Gotenhafen)
R-70 (P)/: Polizeidienststellen in Polen
R-70 (Sl)/: Polizeidienststellen in Slowakei
R-70 (SU)/: Polizeidienststellen in Sowjetunion
R-75/: Umwandererzentralstelle (UWZ) (Posen)
R-76 II/: Universität Graz
R-76 III/: Universität Innsbrück
R-76 IV/: Universität Straßburg
R-153/: Publikationsstelle Dahlem
R-8014/: Saarverein

R-8021/: Herder Institut Riga
R-8025/: Baltische Landwehr
R-8033/: Osteuropa Institut Breslau
R-8035/: Ruhrkämpfer Bund
R-8037/: Saarforschungsgemeinschaft (Bund der Saarvereine)
R-8038/: Schlageter Gedächtnismuseum
R-8039/: Deutsche Schutzbund
R-8043/: Deutsche Stiftung
R-8056: Volksbund für das Deutschtum im Ausland (VDA)

Some hundred or so microfilms from the Zentralstaatsarchiv at Potsdam (Central Archives of the Former GDR, ZstAP) have also been consulted:
Film No.
DAI-Film No.
SS-versch. Prov. No. (from various sources in the SS)
RSHA-Film No.

Bundesarchiv Außenstelle Zehlendorf

(transferred since 1997 to Lichterfelde)
SSO: personal files of SS officers
RuSHA Akten: file on marriages of SS members
Ordner No. (folders of documents from different sources, frequently RSHA and RKFdV)

Bundesarchiv Dahlwitz-Hoppegarten (former Stasi archives)

Classified by names, the collections have no thematic or institutional coherence.
ZA-I
ZA-II
ZA-III
ZA-IV
ZA-V
ZA-VI
ZB
ZB-I
ZB-II
ZC
ZD
ZM
ZR
ZR-I
ZR-II
ZWM
ZX
Dok-P

Archivum Glownie Kommisija Badania Zbrodni Hitlerowskie (Archives of the Commission of Inquiry into Nazi Crimes in Poland [Warsaw])

167: EWZ RuSHA Litzmannstadt
349: GFP 30 Nancy
350: BdS Frankreich
362: Reichssicherheitshauptamt

Zentrale Stelle der Landesjustizverwaltungen (Ludwigsburg)

Polen-Ordner (collection of documents on Nazi crimes in Poland)
RSHA-Ordner (documents of the RSHA; copy from the *Bundesarchiv* and from Warsaw)
Tschechoslowakei-Ordner (collection of documents on Nazi crimes in Czechoslovakia)[1]
UdSSR-Ordner (collections of documents on Nazi crimes in Russia)
2 AR-Z 21/58
114 AR-Z 269/60
202 AR-Z 81/59
202 AR-Z 81/59 'a'
202 AR-Z 81/59 'b'
202 AR-Z 81/59 'c'
202 AR-Z 81/59 'd'
202 AR-Z 81/59 'e'
202 AR-Z 81/59 'f'
202 AR-Z 81/59 'g'
202 AR-Z 96/60
204 AR-Z 48/58
207 AR-Z 14/58
207 AR-Z 246/59
213 AR-1898/66
213 AR-1899/66

Printed sources

This is a list of all the theses, including *Habilitation* theses, and published works by SS intellectuals found in the collection of the Berlin *Staatsbibliothek*. It also includes various important works by individuals who gravitated around them.

Albert, Wilhelm, *Auslese Ausbildung und Beruf. Ein Sozialpedagogischer Beitrag auf der Grundlage einer Reihenuntersuchung berufstätiger Erwachsener*, printed copy, Erlangen, 1941, 58 pages.

Aubin, Hermann and Otto Brunner (eds.), *Deutsche Ostforschung. Ergebnisse und Aufgaben seit dem ersten Weltkrieg* (Leipzig: Hirzel, 1942).

Augsburg, Emil, *Die staats- und parteipolitische Bedeutung der sowjetischen Presse in ihrer geschichtlichen Entwicklung*, typed thesis, n.p. (Berlin), 1941, 208 pages.

Ballensiefen, Heinz, *Juden in Frankreich. Die französische Judenfrage in Geschichte und Gegenwart* (Berlin: Nordland-Verlag, 1939), 149 pages.
—*Die englisch-amerikanische Rivalität in Palästina* (Frankfurt: Welt-Dienst Verlag, 1944), 42 pages.
Behrends, Hermann, *Die nützliche Geschäftsführung* (Marburg: Trute, 1932), 43 pages.
Berndorff, Emil, *Die persönliche Rechtsstellung der Reichsbankbeamten*, typescript, Berlin, 1922, 90 + 17 pages.
Best, Werner, *Zur Frage der 'gewollten Tarifunfähigkeit'* (Mainz: Eis, 1927), 60 pages.
—*Die Verwaltung in Polen vor und nach dem Zusammenbruch der polnischen Republik* (Berlin: Verlag Deecker, 1940), 258 pages.
Beumelberg, Werner, *Sperrfeuer um Deutschland* (Oldenburg: Gerhard Stalling Verlag, 1929), 542 pages.
Beyer, Hans Joachim, 'Zur Lage der auslandsdeutschen Volksforschung', *Volk im Werden* 5, 1937.
—(published in collaboration with the *Deutsche Ausland-Institut*), *Schriftenreihe der Stadt der Auslandsdeutschen* (Stuttgart: Kohlhammer, 1938).
—'Sudetendeutsche und Tschechen im Völkerrecht', *Volk im Werden* 6, 1938.
—*Das Schicksal der Polen. Rasse, Volkscharakter, Stammesart* (Leipzig: Teubner, 1942), viii + 166 pages.
—*Aufbau und Entwicklung des ostdeutschen Volksraums* (Danzig: Danziger Verlagsgesellschaft, 1935), 124 pages.
—(ed.) (working group of the *Hochschule für Lehrerbildung Danzig*, with Annelie Kuhbier), *Städte an der Weichsel* (Danzig: Danziger Verlagsgesellschaft, 1935), 35 pages.
Beyer, Hans Joachim and Otto Lehr (eds.), *Große Deutsche im Ausland. Eine volksdeutsche Geschichte in Lebensbildern* (Stuttgart: Union, 1939), 390 pages.
Beyer, Justus, 'Die Staatslehre Ernst Kriecks', *Volk im Werden* 3, 1935.
—*Die Ständeideologie der Systemzeit und ihre Überwindung* (Darmstadt: Wittich, 1941).
Classen, Wilhelm, 'Das Ausland und die nationalsozialistische Wissenschaft', *Volk im Werden* 5, 1933.
—'Politische Auslandskunde', *Volk im Werden* 4, 1936.
Dittel, Paul, *Die Besiedlung Südnigeriens von den Anfängen bis zur britischen Kolonisation* (Leipzig: A. Pries, 1936), 75 pages.
Ehlers, Erich, *Freimaurer arbeiten für Roosevelt. Freimaurerische Dokumente über die Zusammenarbeit zwischen Roosevelt und die Freimaurerei* (Berlin: Nordland Verlag, 1943), 70 pages.
Ehlich, Hans, *Febris intra Partum* (Freiburg: Maukisch, 1927), 25 pages.
Filbert, Alfred, *Kann das Ablehnungsrecht des Konkursverwalters des Vorbehalterskaüfers mit der Anwartschaft des Kaüfers auf den Eigentumserwerb ausgeraümt werden?* (Gießen: Meyer, 1935), vi + 20 pages.
Frankenberg, Richard, *Die Nichterneuerung des deutsch–russischen Rücksichtversicherungsvertrags im Jahre 1890* (Berlin: Deutsche Verlagsgesellschaft für Geschichte und Politik, 1927), 176 pages.

—*Das Grenz- und Auslandsdeutschtum im Geschichtsunterricht der höheren Schulen* (Berlin; Leipzig: Teubner, 1930), 68 pages.

Franz, Günther, *Der Dreissigjährige Krieg und das deutsche Volk* (Jena: Fischer, 1940).

Greiser, Arthur, *Aufbau im Osten* (Jena: Fischer, 1942).

Guett, Arthur, *Bevölkerungs- und Rassenpolitik* (Vienna; Berlin: Späth und Linde, 1942).

—*Die Rassenpflege im Dritten Reich* (Hamburg: Hanseatische Verlagsanstalt, 1940).

Hammer, Wilhelm, *Nießbrauchbarstellung für mehrere Personen als Gesamtbrechtige im Sinne des §428 BGB* (Altenburg: Bonde Verlag, 1935), 38 pages.

Hansen, Wilhelm and Erich Windt, *Was weißt du vom deutschen Osten? Geschichte und Kultur des deutschen Ostraums* (Berlin; Ulm: Verlag Ebner und Peter, 1942), 196 pages.

Heiss, Friedrich, *Deutsche Revolution. Die Wende eines Volkes. Fünf Jahrzehnte deutschen Volkskampfes* (Berlin: Volk und Reich Verlag, 1933 (?)), 124 pages.

—*Deutschland zwischen Nacht und Tag* (Berlin: Volk und Reich Verlag, 1934), 287 pages.

—*Der Sieg im Norden* (Berlin: Volk und Reich Verlag, 1942).

Höhn, Reinhard, 'Volksgemeinschaft und Wissenschaft', *Süddeutsches Monatsheft* 32, 1934.

—'Der Führerbegriff im Staatsrecht', *Deutsches Recht* 5, 1935.

—*Rechtsgemeinschaft und Volksgemeinschaft* (Darmstadt: Wittich, 1935).

—'Volk, Staat und Reich', *Volk im Werden* 4, 1936.

—'Das Heer als Bildungsanstalt', *Volk im Werden* 6, 1938.

—*Reich – Großraum – Großmacht* (Darmstadt: Wittich, 1942).

—*Frankreichs Demokratie und ihr geistiger Zusammenbruch* (Darmstadt: Wittich, n.d.).

Höhn, Reinhard and Werner Wittig, 'Staat, Volk und Führung als Rechtsprinzip', *Deutsche Recht* 4, 1934.

Jahr, Ernst Hermann, *Das Regierungsgesetz* (Bochum-Langendreer: Pöppinghaus, 1935), iv + 83 pages.

Kalbrunner, Josef and Franz Wilhelm (eds.), *Quellen zur deutschen Siedlungsgeschichte in Südosteuropa* (Munich: Reinhardt; Deutsche Akademie und Gesamtvereine für deutsche Geschichte und Altertumsvereine, n.d.).

Kielpinski, Walter von, 'Deutsche Wissenschaft und Sowjetunion', *Volk im Werden* 5, 1937.

—'Der Einbruch des Katholizismus in die Wissenschaft', *Volk im Werden* 5, 1937.

—'Das Ende der Ost-ideologie', *Volk im Werden* 6, 1938.

Klebel, Ernst, *Siedlungsgeschichte des deutschen Südostens* (Munich: Schick, 1940).

Knochen, Helmut, *Der Dramatiker George Coleman* (Göttingen: Göttinger Tageblatte, 1935), 83 pages.

Krieck, Ernst, *Das nationalsozialistische Deutschland und die Wissenschaft. Heidelberger Reden von Reichsminister Rust und Prof. Ernst Krieck* (Hamburg: Hanseatische Verlagsanstalt, 1936), 35 pages.

Kumsteller, B., et al., *Geschichtsbuch für die deutsche Jugend 1. Klasse* (Leipzig: Verlag von Quelle und Mener, 1941), 133 pages.

Leetsch, Hans, *Die Bedeutung der Aufträge der öffentlichen Hand für den Ablauf der Konjunktur* (Geinhausen: Kalbfleisch, 1936), 52 pages.

Mahnke, Horst, *Die freimaurerische Presse in Deutschland. Struktur und Geschichte*, n.p., 1941, ix + 201 pages.

Mehlhorn, Georg Herbert, *Die Bestimmung der Strafe für die Wilderei* (Teplitz-Schönau: Schmoll, 1929), 140 pages.

Nockemann, Hans, *Einige Streitfragen aus dem Kohlenwirtschaftsgesetz und den dazu ergangenen Ausführungsbestimmungen und ihre Beurteilung in der Praxis der ordentlichen Gerichte und der Organe der Kohlenwirtschaft* (Cologne: Welzel, 1930), 45 pages.

Oebsger-Röder, Rudolf, *Vom Zeitungsschreiber zum Schriftleiter*, typed thesis, Leipzig, 1936.

Ohlendorf, Otto, *Das deutsche Binnenhandel. Wesen und Aufgabe* (Berlin: Elsner, 1942), 62 pages.

Pfeffer, Karl-Heinz, 'Begriff und Methode der Auslandswissenschaften', *Jarhbuch der Weltpolitik 2*, 76 pages.

Rang, Fritz, *Untersuchungen über die Isohaemagglutinationen im Blute des Schweines und Rindes mit eingeengten Seren* (Wilhelmshaven: Tapken, 1931), 27 pages.

Reichsführung Schulungsamt (ed.), *Der Kampf um die deutsche Ostgrenze* (Berlin: Nordland Verlag, 1941).

Rössner, Hans, *Georgekreis und Literaturwissenschaft. Zur Würdigung und Kritik der geistigen Bewegung Stefan Georges* (Frankfurt: Diesterweg, 1938), 227 pages.

Sandberger, Martin, *Die Sozialversicherung im nationalsozialistischen Staat. Grundsätzliches zur Streitfrage: Versicherung oder Versorgung?* (Unrach im Württemberg: Bühler, 1934), vii + 93 pages.

Schick, Hans, *Das ältere Rosenkreuzertum. Beitrag zur Entstehungsgeschichte der Freimaurerei*, Habilitation thesis (Berlin: Nordland Verlag, 1942), 338 pages.

Schwarz, Dieter (pseud.), *Angriff auf die nationalsozialistische Weltanschauung im deutschsprachigen Schrifttum seit 1933* (Berlin; Munich: Eher-Verlag, 1936), 44 pages.

Six, Franz Alfred, 'Die erste Zeitschrift für Studenten', *Zeitungswissenschaft 9*, 1934.

—'Nachwuchs und Auslese auf den deutschen Hochschulen', *Der deutsche Student*, March 1935.

—*Die politische Propaganda der NSDAP im Kampf um die Macht*, doctoral thesis, Heidelberg, Winter, 1936, 76 pages.

—*Die Presse der nationalen Minderheiten in Deutschland*, Habilitation thesis, typewritten copy, Heidelberg, 1936.

—(ed.), *Studenten bauen auf! Reichsleistungskampf. Ein Rechenschaftsbericht* (Marburg; Berlin, 1936).

—'Germanisches Erbe im deutschen Geist', *Volk im Werden 10*, 1937.

—*Pressefreiheit und internationale Zusammenarbeit* (Hamburg: Hanseatische Verlagsanstalt, 1937), 38 pages.

—*Die Presse in Polen* (Berlin: Deutscher Verlag für Politik und Wirtschaft, 1938), 42 pages.

—*Freimaurerei und Judenemanzipation* (Hamburg: Hanseatische Verlagsanstalt, 1938), 38 pages.

—*Der Westfälische Friede von 1648. Deutsche Textausgabe der Friedensverträge von Münster und Osnabrück* (Berlin: Junker und Dünnhaupt, 1940), 117 pages.

—*Freimaurerei und Christentum. Ein Beitrag zur politischen Geistesgeschichte* (Hamburg: Hanseatische Verlagsanstalt, 1940), 107 pages.

—*Reich und Westen* (Berlin: Junker und Dünnhaupt, 1940), 30 pages.

—'Das deutsche Auslandswissenschaftliche Institut im Jahre 1941', *Zeitschrift für Politik* 31, 1941.

—'Das Einheitsbewußtsein Europas', *Zeitschrift für Politik* 32, 1942.

—'Rußland als Teil Europas', *Zeitschrift für Politik* 32, 1942.

—*Studien zur Geistesgeschichte der Freimaurerei* (Hamburg: Hanseatische Verlagsanstalt, 1942), 176 pages.

—(ed.), *Das Reich und Europa. Eine politisch-historische Skizze* (Berlin: Nordland Verlag, 1943).

—'Die Binnenkriege des europäischen Kontinents und der Einigungskrieg der Gegenwart', *Zeitschrift für Politik* 33, 1943.

—'Der Wandel des europäischen Staatensystems zum Weltstaatensystem', *Zeitschrift für Politik* 34, 1944.

—'Europäische Schicksalsgemeinschaft', *Zeitschrift für Politik* 35, 1945.

Six, Franz Alfred and Kurt Hancke (eds.), *Beiträge zur Entstehung des europäischen Liberalismus* (Berlin: Junker und Dünnhaupt, 1942).

Spengler, Wilhelm, *Das Drama Schillers. Seine Genesis* (Leipzig: Weber, 1932), 152 pages.

—'Die Frau im germanischen und christlichen Weltbild', *Volk im Werden* 5, 1937.

—'Die schöpferische Freiheit in der Kunst', *Volk im Werden* 5, 1937.

Tiedt, Friedrich, *Die Haftung des Beamten und seines Dienstherrn für Amtspflichtverletzungen nach geltendem Recht und Gedanken über ein neues Amthaftungsrecht* (Seestadt Rostock: Hinstorff, 1939), 99 pages.

Turowsky, Ernst, *Die innenpolitische Entwicklung Polnish-Preußens und seine staatsrechtliche Stellung zu Polen vom 2. Thorner Frieden bis zum Reichstag von Lublin (1466–1569)* (Berlin: Trilitsch und Huther, 1937), 114 pages.

Weifert, Ladislaus, *Die deutschen Siedlungen und Mundarten im Südwestbanat* (Belgrade: Südost, 1941).

In the library of Berlin-Lichterfelde there is also the series of *Reichsdrücke* (RD): RD 19/9 1 to 10 (Deutsche Polizei), which contains official texts for internal usage of the SIPO and the ORPO, their budgets, and course materials.

I have also consulted the following reviews:
Das Schwarze Korps (official organ of the SS).
Sicherheitspolizei und SD (internal newspaper of the police and the SD, in which certain members of the group, such as Walter Zirpins and Heinz Ballensiefen, wrote).

Bibliography

I have decided to present a bibliography ordered thematically. Thus, the bibliographical, archival and historical sources are followed by references that contextualize the epistemological stance adopted in the thesis. Then come references to the cultural history of the early twentieth century. Then the history of Germany after the Great War, with an emphasis on references to the student world. Finally, works on the Third Reich and specialized literature on the SS organs of repression and Nazism at war are listed, followed by a bibliography on de-Nazification and the postwar trials.

This is, of course, not an exhaustive bibliography, since such a thing is practically impossible to assemble.

Working instruments: archives: bibliography, published sources

Ayçoberry, Pierre, *The Nazi Question: An Essay on the Interpretations of National Socialism (1922–1975)*, tr. Robert Hurley (London: Routledge and Kegan Paul, 1981).

Boberach, Heinz, *Inventar archivalischer Quellen des NS-Staats. Die Überlieferungen von Behörden und Einrichtungen des Reichs, der Länder und der NSDAP*, 2 vols. (Munich: Drost, 1986–94).

Dennecke, Ludwig and Tilo Brandis, *Die Nachläße in den Bibliotheken der Bundesrepublik Deutschland* (Koblenz: Boppard, 1981).

Henke, Josef, 'Das Schicksal deutscher zeitgeschichtlicher Quellen in Kriegs- und Nachkriegszeit', *VfZ* 30, 1982.

Kershaw, Ian, *The Nazi Dictatorship: Problems and Perspectives of Interpretation*, 4th edn (London: Arnold, 2000).

Kurschner, Joseph, *Deutscher Literatur-Kalender* (Munich: Saur, 1900–43).

Mommsen, Wolfgang, *Die Nachläße in den deutschen Archiven, mit Ergänzungen anderer Beständen*, 2 vols. (Koblenz: Boppard, 1971–83).

— (ed.), *Das Bundesarchiv und seine Bestände* (Koblenz: Boppard, 1977).

Rückerl, Adalbert, *NS-Verbrecher vor Gericht. Versuch einer Vergangenheitsbewältigung*, 2 vols. (Heidelberg: Müller, 1982).

Seelinger, Rolf, 'Doktorarbeiten im Dritten Reich. Dokumentation mit Stellungnahme', *Braune Universität* 5, 1966.

History and anthropology: main references outside the chronological field

Alphandéry, Paul, *La Chrétienté et l'idée de croisade*, 2 vols., ed. Alphonse Dupront (Paris: Albin Michel, 1954, 1959).

Backo, Bronisław, *Les Imaginaires sociaux. Mémoires et espoirs* (Paris: Payot, 1983).

Boureau, Alain and Daniel S. Milo (eds.), *Alter Histoire. Essais d'histoire expérimentale* (Paris: Les Belles Lettres, 1991).

Cabannes, Bruno, Fabrice Lascar and Philippe Grandcoing, 'Traces et silences des sens. Propositions pour une histoire impossible' (interview with Alain Corbin), *Revue européenne d'histoire – European Review of History* 2/1, 1995.

Chaunu, Pierre, *Église, culture et société. Essais sur Réforme et Contre-Réforme 1517–1620* (Paris: SEDES, 1981).

Crouzet, Denis, *Les Guerriers de Dieu. La violence au temps des troubles de religion*, 2 vols. (Paris: Champs Vallon, 1990).

Delumeau, Jean, *History of Paradise: The Garden of Eden in Myth and Tradition*, tr. Matthew O'Connell (New York: Continuum, 1995).

Dosse, François, *History of Structuralism*, tr. Deborah Glassman, 2 vols. (Minneapolis; London: University of Minnesota Press, 1997): vol. 1: *The Rising Sign, 1945–1966;* vol. 2: *The Sign Sets, 1967–Present*.

Dupront, Alphonse, *Le Mythe de croisade*, 4 vols. (Paris: Gallimard, 1997).

—*Du sacré. Croisades et pèlerinages: images et langages* (Paris: Gallimard, 1987).

Eliade, Mircea, *A History of Religious Ideas*, tr. Willard R. Trask, 3 vols. (London: Collins; Chicago: University of Chicago Press, 1979.)

Guilaine, Jean and Jean Zammit, *Le Sentier de la guerre. Visages de la violence préhistorique* (Paris: Le Seuil, 2001).

Hanson, Victor Davis, *The Western Way of War: Infantry Battle in Ancient Greece*, intro. John Keegan (London: Hodder and Stoughton, 1989).

Hell, Bertrand, *Le Sang noir. Chasse et mythe du sauvage en Europe* (Paris: Flammarion, 1994).

—*Entre chien et loup. Faits et dits de chasse dans la France de l'est* (Paris: Éditions de la MSH, 1985).

Héritier, Françoise, *De la violence* (Paris: Odile Jacob, 1996).

—*De la violence II* (Paris: Odile Jacob, 1996).

—'Le sang des guerriers et le sang des femmes. Notes anthropologiques sur le rapport des sexes', *L'Africaine. Sexes et signes, Cahiers du GRIF* 29, 1984.

Rioux, Jean-Pierre and Jean-François Sirinelli (eds.), *Pour une histoire culturelle* (Paris: Le Seuil, 1996).

Sironi, Françoise, *Bourreaux et victimes. Psychologie de la torture* (Paris: Odile Jacob, 1999).

Sironneau, Jean-Pierre, *Sécularisation et religions politiques* (Paris; The Hague: Mouton, 1982).

Spitzer, Alan B., 'The historical problems of generations', *American Historical Review* 78, 1973.

Testard, Alain, *Essai sur les fondements de la division sexuelle du travail chez les chasseurs-cuilleurs* (Paris: Éditions de l'EHESS, 1986).

Vialles, Noëlie, *Animal to Edible*, tr. J. A. Underwood (Cambridge: Cambridge University Press; Paris: Éditions de la Maison des Sciences de l'Homme, 1994).

Cultural history of the first half of the twentieth century

Amberger, Waltraud, *Männer, Krieger, Abenteuer. Der Entwurf des 'soldatischen Mannes' in Kriegsromanen über den Ersten und Zweiten Weltkrieg* (Frankfurt: Fischer, 1984).

Audoin-Rouzeau, Stéphane, *Cinq deuils de guerre 1914–1918* (Paris: Noësis, 2001).

—*L'Enfant de l'ennemi, 1914–1918* (Paris: Aubier, 1995).

—*La Guerre des enfants, 1914–1918. Essai d'histoire culturelle* (Paris: Armand Colin, 1994).

—'Guerre et brutalité (1870–1918): le cas français', *Revue européenne d'histoire – European Review of History* 0, 1993.

—'Violence et consentement. La "culture de guerre" du premier conflit mondial', in Jean-Pierre Rioux and Jean-François Sirinelli (eds.), *Pour une histoire culturelle* (Paris: Le Seuil, 1996).

Audoin-Rouzeau, Stéphane and Jean-Jacques Becker, *1914–1918: Understanding the Great War*, tr. Catherine Temerson (London: Profile Books, 2002).

Becker, Jean-Jacques and Stéphane Audoin-Rouzeau, *Les Sociétés européennes et la guerre de 1914–1918* (Paris: Université de Paris X and Armand Colin, 1990).

Burrin, Philippe, *La Dérive fasciste: Doriot, Déat, Bergery, 1933–1945* (Paris: Le Seuil, 1986).

Christadler, Marieluise, 'Politik, Mythos und Mentalität. Französische und deutsche Jugendliteratur vor dem Ersten Weltkrieg', *Politik und Zeitgeschichte*, 1978.

—*Kriegserziehung im Jungenbuch. Literaturmobilmachung in Deutschland und Frankreich vor 1914* (Frankfurt: Haag und Herchen, 1978).

Eksteins, Modris, *Rites of Spring. The Great War and the Birth of Modern Society* (New York: Anchor Books and Doubleday, 1990).

Fiedler, Gudrun, *Jugend im Krieg. Bürgerliche Jugendbewegung, Erster Weltkrieg und sozialer Wandel 1914–1923* (Cologne: Wissenschaft und Politik, 1989).

Gestrich, Andreas, 'Jugend und Krieg: Kriegsverarbeitung bei Jugendlichen in und nach dem ersten Weltkriege', in M. Kintzinger, W. Stürner and J. Zahlten (eds.), *Das andere Wahrnehmen. Beiträge zur europäischen Geschichte* (Cologne; Weimar; Vienna: Böhlau, 1991).

Hervier, Julien, *Deux individus contre l'histoire. Pierre Drieu La Rochelle, Ernst Jünger* (Paris: Klincksieck, 1978).

Jeismann, Michael, *Das Vaterland der Feinde: Studien zum nationalen Feindbegriff und Selbstverständnis in Deutschland und Frankreich, 1792–1918* (Stuttgart: Klett-Cotta, 1992).

Kaschuba, Wolfgang, 'Volk und Nation. Ethnozentrismus in Geschichte und Gegenwart', in Heinrich-August Winkler and Hartmut Kaelble (eds.), *Nationalsozialismus – Nationalitäten – Supranationalität* (Stuttgart: Klett-Cotta, 1993).

Krumeich, Gerd and Gerhard Hirschfeld (eds.), *'Keiner fühlt sich hier mehr als Mensch …'. Erlebnis und Wirkung des Ersten Weltkrieges* (Frankfurt: Fischer, 1996).

Krumeich, Gerd, Dieter Langewiesche, Hans Peter Ullmann and Gerhard Hirschfeld (eds.), *Kriegserfahrungen. Studien zur Sozial- und Mentalitätsgeschichte des Ersten Weltkrieges* (Essen: Klartext, 1997).

Lebzelter, Gisela, 'Die schwarze Schmach. Vorurteile, Propaganda, Mythos', *Geschichte und Gesellschaft* 11, 1985.

Lindenberger, Thomas and Alf Lüdtke (eds.), *Physische Gewalt. Studien zur Geschichte der Neuzeit* (Frankfurt: Suhrkamp, 1995).

Liulevicius, Vejas Gabriel, *War Land on the Eastern Front. Culture, National Identity and German Occupation in World War I* (Cambridge: Cambridge University Press, 2000).

Maier, Hans, 'Ideen von 1914 – Ideen von 1939? Zweierlei Kriegsanfänge', *VfZ* 38, 1990.

Marten, Heinz-Georg, *Sozialbiologismus. Biologische Grundpositionen der politischen Ideengeschichte* (Stuttgart: Klett-Cotta, 1983).

Mosse, George, *Fallen Soldiers. Reshaping the Memory of the World Wars* (Oxford; New York: Clarendon Press, 1990).
—*The Nationalization of the Masses. Political Symbolism and Mass Movement in Germany from the Napoleonic Wars through the Third Reich* (New York: Grosset and Dunlap, 1975).
Mühlen, Patrik von, *Rassenideologien. Geschichte und Hintergründe* (Berlin; Bonn: Dietz, 1977).
Ostenc, Michel, *Intellectuels italiens et fascisme* (Paris: Payot, 1983).
Prochasson, Christophe, *Les Intellectuels, le socialisme et la guerre* (Paris: Le Seuil, 1993).
Salomon-Bayet, Claire (ed.), *Pasteur et la révolution pastorienne* (Paris: Payot, 1986).
Wall, Richard and Jay Winter (eds.), *The Upheaval of War: Family, Work and Welfare in Europe, 1914–1918* (Cambridge: Cambridge University Press, 1988).
Wohl, Robert, *The Generation of 1914* (Cambridge, Mass.: Harvard University Press, 1979).
Zmarzlik, Hans-Günther, 'Sozialdarwinismus in Deutschland als geschichtliches Problem', in Hans-Günther Zmarzlik, *Wieviele Zukunft hat unsere Vergangenheit?* (Munich: Piper, 1970).

War, defeat, Abwehrkampf and period as students

Altgeld, Wolfgang, 'Volk, Rasse, Raum. Völkisches Denken und radikaler Nationalismus im Vorfeld des Nationalsozialismus', in Rudolf Lill and Heinrich Oberreuter (eds.), *Machtverfall und Machtergreifung. Aufstieg und Herrschaft des Nationalsozialismus* (Munich: Bayerische Landeszentrale für politische Bildungsarbeit, 1983).
Anderbrügge, Klaus, *Völkisches Rechtsdenken* (Berlin: Duncker und Humblot, 1978).
Arndt, Helmut, 'Niedergang von Studium und Wissenschaft, 1933 bis 1945', in Lothar Rathmann (ed.), *Alma Mater Lipsiensis. Geschichte der Karl-Marx-Universität Leipzig* (Leipzig: Edition Leipzig, 1984).
Artaud, Denise, 'Die Hintergründe der Ruhrbesetzung', *VfZ* 27, 1979.
Baumgart, Peter, *Vierhundert Jahre Universität Würzburg. Eine Festschrift* (Neustadt an der Aisch: Degener, 1982).
Becker, Heinrich, et al., *Die Universität Göttingen unter dem Nationalsozialismus. Das verdrängte Kapitel ihrer 250–jährigen Geschichte* (Munich: Saur, 1987).
Berghahn, Volker R., *Der Stahlhelm. Bund der Frontsoldaten, 1918–1935* (Düsseldorf: Droste, 1966).
Bessel, Richard, *Political Violence and the Rise of Nazism. The Storm Troopers in Eastern Germany, 1925–1934* (New Haven; London: Yale University Press, 1984).
Bleuel, Hans-Peter and Ernst Klinnert, *Deutsche Studenten auf dem Weg ins Dritte Reich. Ideologien, Programme, Aktionen, 1918–1935* (Gutersloh: Mohr, 1967).
Böhles, Hans-Jürgen, et al., *Gießener Universität und Nationalsozialismus. Erfahrungen mit einer Ausstellung*, vol. 2 (Gießen: Institut für Soziologie, Soziologisches Forum, 1982).
Bollmus, Reinhard, *Handelshochschule und Nationalsozialismus. Das Ende der*

*Handelshochschule Mannheim und die Vorgeschichte der Errichtung einer staats-
und wirtschaftwissenschaftlichen Fakultät an der Universität Heidelberg 1933/4*
(Meisenheim: Hain Verlag, 1973).

Bracher, Karl Dietrich, *Die Auflösung der Weimarer Republik. Eine Studie zum
Problem des Machtverfalls in der Demokratie* (Düsseldorf: Droste, 1978).

Brandt, Susanne, *Vom Kriegsschauplatz zum Gedächtnisraum. Die Westfront 1914–
1940* (Baden-Baden: Nomos, 2000).

Breuer, Stefan, *Anatomie der konservativen Revolution* (Darmstadt: Wissenschaftliche
Buchgesellschaft, 1993).

Carmon, Arye Z., *The University of Heidelberg and National Socialism, 1930–1935*,
PhD thesis (Madison: University of Wisconsin, 1974).

Chroust, Peter, *Gießener Universität und Faschismus. Studenten und Hochschullehrer
1918–1945* (Münster: Waxmann, 1994).

—'Studentischer Alltag in Gießen vor und nach 1933', in Hans-Jürgen Böhles,
Frontabschnitt Hochschule. Die Gießener Universität im Nationalsozialismus (Gießen:
Anabas-Verlag, 1983).

—'Gießener Studentenschaft vor und nach 1933', in Norbert Werner (ed.), *375
Jahre Universität Gießen 1607–1982. Geschichte und Gegenwart. Ausstellung im
oberhessischen Museum und Gail'sche Sammlungen 11. Mai–25. Juli 1982* (Gießen:
Verlag der Feber'schen Universitätsbuchhandlung, 1982).

Dülffer, Jost, 'Die französische Deutschlandspolitik nach dem Ersten Weltkrieg',
Archiv für Sozialgeschichte 21, 1981.

Dupeux, Louis (ed.), *La 'Révolution conservatrice' dans l'Allemagne de Weimar* (Paris:
Kimé, 1992).

Eckhard, John, *Die Freiburger Universität in der Zeit des Nationalsozialismus*
(Freiburg; Würzburg: Ploetz, 1991).

Edmondson, Nelson, 'The Fichte Society. A chapter in Germany's conservative
revolution', *Journal of Modern History* 38, 1966.

Eick, Hans-Joachim, *Geschichtsbewußtsein und Gegenwartsdeutung Jugendlicher in
der Weimarer Republik im Spiegel der Zeitschrift 'Junge Menschen', 1920–1927.
Darstellung und Interpretation quellenbezogener Kulturaspekte* (Aix-la-Chapelle:
Shaker, 1994).

Faber, Karl Georg, 'Die südlichen Rheinlande von 1816 bis 1965', in F. Petri and
G. Droege (eds.), *Rheinische Geschichte*, 3 vols., vol. 2: *Neuzeit* (Düsseldorf:
Schwann, 1976).

Faust, Anselm, *Die nationalsozialistische Studentenbund. Studenten und
Nationalsozialismus in der Weimarer Republik*, 2 vols. (Düsseldorf: Schwann,
1973).

Favez, Jean-Claude, *Le Reich devant l'occupation franco-belge de la Ruhr en 1923*
(Geneva: Droz, 1969).

Fließ, Gerhard and Jürgen John, 'Deutscher Hochschulring (DHR) 1920–1933',
in Dieter Fricke (ed.), *Lexikon zur Parteiengeschichte*, 2 vols. (Cologne: Pahl-
Rutgenstein, 1983–6).

Fritzsche, Klaus, *Politische Romantik und Gegenrevolution. Fluchtwege in der Krise
der bürgerlichen Gesellschaft: Das Beispiel des 'Tat'-Kreises* (Frankfurt: Suhrkamp,
1976).

Geissler, Rolf, *Dekadenz und Heroismus. Zeitroman und völkisch-nationalsozialistische Literaturkritik* (Stuttgart: DVA, 1964).

Geyer, Michael, 'Der zur Organisation erhobene Burgfriede', in Klaus-Jürgen Müller and Eckardt Oppitz (eds.), *Militär und Militarismus in der Weimarer Republik* (Düsseldorf: Droste, 1978).

Giovannini, Norbert, *Zwischen Republik und Faschismus. Heidelberger Studentinnen und Studenten 1918–1945* (Weinheim: Deutscher Studien Verlag, 1990).

Golczewski, Frank, *Kölner Universitätslehrer und der Nationalsozialismus. Ein person-geschichtlicher Ansatz* (Cologne: Böhlau, 1988).

Götz von Olenhusen, Irmtraud, 'Vom Jugendstahlhelm zur SA. Die junge Nachkriegsgeneration in den paramilitärischen Verbänden der Weimarer Republik', in Wolfgang R. Krabbe (ed.), *Politische Jugend in der Weimarer Republik* (Bochum: Brockmeyer, 1993).

— 'Die Krise der jungen Generation und der Auftstieg des Nationalsozialismus', *Jahrbuch des Archivs der deutschen Jugendbewegung* 12, 1980.

Grimm, Reinhold and Jost Hermand (eds.), *1914–1939. German Reflections of the Two World Wars* (Madison: University of Wisconsin Press, 1992).

Gruchmann, Lothar, *Nationalsozialistische Großraumordnung. Die Konstruktion einer deutschen Monroe-Doktrin* (Stuttgart: DVA, 1962).

Haar, Ingo, *Historiker im Nationalsozialismus: Deutsche Geschichtswissenschaft und der 'Volkstumskampf' im Osten*, typewritten thesis (Halle-Wittenberg, 1998); (Göttingen: Vandenhoeck und Ruprecht, 2001).

Hammerstein, Notker, *Zur Geschichte der Johann Wolfgang Goethe-Universität zu Frankfurt am Main. Von der Stiftungsuniversität zur staatlichen Hochschule*, vol. 1: *1914–1950* (Neuwied: Metzner, 1989).

Hartung, Günther, 'Arthur Dinter. A successful fascist author in pre-fascist Germany', in John Milfull (ed.), *The Attractions of Fascism. Social Psychology and Aesthetics of the 'Triumph of the Right'* (New York: Berg, 1990).

Heinemann, Ulrich, *Die verdrängte Niederlage. Politische Öffentlichkeit und Kriegsschuldfrage in der Weimarer Republik* (Göttingen: Vandenhoeck und Ruprecht, 1983).

Heither, Dietrich, et al., *Wegbereiter des Faschismus. Aus der Geschichte des Marburger Vereins deutscher Studenten* (Marburg: Geschichtswerkstatt Marburg, 1992).

Hermand, Jost, *Der alte Traum vom neuen Reich. Völkische Utopien und Nationalsozialismus* (Frankfurt: Athenäum Verlag, 1988).

Hoepke, Klaus-Peter, 'Die SS, der "Führer" und die Nöte der deutschen Wissenschaft. Ein Meinungsbild aus dem Senat der technischen Hochschule Karlsruhe vom April 1942', *Zeitschrift für Geschichte des Oberrheins* n.s. 96, 1987.

Hof, Walter, *Der Weg zum heroischen Realismus. Pessimismus und Nihilismus in der deutschen Literatur von Hamerling bis Benn* (Tübingen: Niemeyer, 1974).

Hoffmann, Lutz, 'Das "Volk". Zur ideologischen Struktur eines unvermeidbaren Begriffs', *Zeitschrift für Soziologie* 20, 1991.

Hornung, Klaus, *Der Jungdeutsche Orden* (Düsseldorf: Droste, 1958).

Ishida, Yuji, *Jungkonservative in der Weimarer Republik. Der Ring-Kreis 1928–1933* (Frankfurt: Lang, 1988).

Jaeger, Hans, 'Generation in der Geschichte. Überlegungen zu einem umstrittenen Konzept', *Geschichte und Gesellschaft* 3, 1977.

Jaide, Walter, *Generation eines Jahrhunderts. Wechsel der Jugendgenerationen im Jahrhunderttrend. Zur Sozialgeschichte der Jugend in Deutschland, 1871–1985* (Opladen: Leske und Budrich, 1988).

Jansen, Christian, *Professoren und Politik. Politisches Denken und Handeln der Heidelberger Hochschullehrer 1914–1935* (Göttingen: Vandenhoeck und Ruprecht, 1992).

Jarauch, Konrad, *Deutsche Studenten 1800–1970* (Frankfurt: Suhrkamp, 1984).

Jochmann, Werner, *Gesellschaftskrise und Judenfeindschaft in Deutschland 1870–1945* (Hamburg: Christians Verlag, 1988).

—'Die Ausbreitung des Antisemitismus in Deutschland 1914–1923', in Werner E. Mosse and Arnold Paucker (eds.), *Deutsches Judentum in Krieg und Revolution 1916–1923* (Tübingen: Mohr, 1974).

Kahlenberg, Friedrich, 'Großhessenpläne und Separatismus. Das Problem der Zukunftorientierung des Rhein–Main Gebietes nach dem Ersten Weltkrieg (1918–1923)', in J. Barmann et al. (eds.), *Festschrift Ludwig Petry*, vol. 2, (Wiesbaden: Steiner, 1969).

Kaiser, Joseph H., 'Europäisches Großraumdenken. Die Steigerung geschichtlicher Größen als Rechtsproblem', in Hans Barion (ed.), *Epirrhosis. Festgabe für Carl Schmitt* (Berlin: Duncker und Humblot, 1968).

Kampe, Norbert, *Studenten und 'Judenfrage' im deutschen Kaiserreich. Die Entstehung einer akademischen Trägerschicht des Antisemitismus* (Göttingen: Vandenhoeck und Ruprecht, 1987).

Kater, Michael, *Studentenschaft und Rechtsradikalismus in Deutschland, 1918–1933. Eine sozialgeschichtliche Studie zur Bildungskrise in der Weimarer Republik* (Hamburg: Hoffman und Campe, 1969).

Keßler, Alexander, *Der Jungdeutsche Orden in den Jahren der Entscheidung 1928–1930*, 2 vols. (Munich: Lohmüller, 1975–6).

Klemperer, Klemens, *Konservative Bewegungen zwischen Kaiserreich und Nationalsozialismus* (Munich: Oldenbourg, 1962).

Klingemann, Carsten, 'Die deutsche Sozialwissenschaften zwischen den beiden Weltkriegen. Mythos und Realität von Kontinuitätbrüchen', in Gerhard Göhler and Bodo Zeuner (eds.), *Kontinuitäten und Brüche in der deutschen Politikwissenschaft* (Baden-Baden: Nomos, 1991).

Kluke, Paul, *Dir Stiftungsuniversität Frankfurt am Main, 1918–1932* (Frankfurt: Kramer, 1972).

Knöpp, Friedrich, 'Der Volksstadt Hessen, 1918–1933', in Uwe Schultz (ed.), *Die Geschichte Hessens* (Stuttgart: Theiss, 1983).

Kolb, Eberhard, *Die Weimarer Republik* (Munich: Oldenbourg, 2000).

Krabbe, Wolfgang R. (ed.), *Politische Jugend in der Weimarer Republik* (Bochum: Brockmeyer, 1993).

Krause, Eckart, et al. (eds.), *Hochschulalltag im 'Dritten Reich'. Die Hamburger Universität 1933–1945*, 3 vols. (Berlin; Hamburg: Reimer Verlag, 1991).

Kreutzberger, Wolfgang, *Studenten und Politik 1918–1933. Der Fall Freiburg im Breisgau* (Göttingen: Vandenhoeck und Ruprecht, 1972).

Krüger, Sabine, 'Das Kaiser-Wilhelm-Institut für deutsche Geschichte [Berlin] von 1917 bis 1945', *Berichte und Mitteilungen der Max-Planck Gesellschaft* 6, 1980.

Kruse, Wolfgang, *Eine Welt von Feinden. Der große Krieg 1914–1918* (Frankfurt: Fischer, 1997).

Kruz, Lothar (ed.), *200 Jahre zwischen Schloß und Dom. Ein Lesebuch zur Vergangenheit und Gegenwart der Westfälischen Wilhelms-Universität Münster* (Münster: published at author's expense, 1980).

Laqueur, Walter, *Die deutsche Jugendbewegung. Eine historische Studie* (Cologne: Wissenschaft und Politik, 1962).

Lehten, Helmut, *Verhaltenslehren der Kälte. Lebensversuche zwischen den Kriegen* (Frankfurt: Suhrkamp, 1994).

Leisen, Adolf, *Die Ausbreitung des völkischen Gedankens in den Studentenschaft der Weimarer Republik*, typewritten thesis (Heidelberg, 1964).

Lenk, Kurt, *Deutscher Konservatismus* (New York: Campus, 1989).

Lohalm, Uwe, *Völkischer Radikalismus. Die Geschichte des deutschvölkischen Schutz- und Trutzbundes 1919–1923* (Hamburg: Leibnitz Verlag, 1970).

Mauch, Hans-Joachim, *Nationalsozialistische Wehrorganisationen in der Weimarer Republik. Zur Entwicklung und Ideologie des 'Paramilitarismus'* (Frankfurt: Lang, 1982).

McDougall, Walter A., *France's Rhineland Diplomacy, 1914–1924* (Princeton, N.J.: Princeton University Press, 1978).

Michalsky, Gabrielle, *Der Antisemitismus im deutschen akademischen Leben in der Zeit nach dem Ersten Weltkrieg* (Frankfurt: Lang, 1980).

Miethke, Jürgen, *Geschichte in Heidelberg. 100 Jahre historisches Seminar. 50 Jahre Institut für fränkisch–pfälzische Geschichte und Landeskunde* (Berlin: Springer Verlag, 1992).

Mommsen, Hans, *Die verspielte Freiheit. Der Weg der Republik von Weimar in den Untergang 1918–1933* (Berlin: Propyläen, 1989).

— 'Generationskonflikt und Jugendrevolt in der Weimarer Republik', in Thomas Kœbner (ed.), *'Mit uns zieht die neue Zeit'. Der Mythos Jugend* (Frankfurt: Suhrkamp, 1985).

Morsey, Rudolf, 'Die Rheinlande, Preußen und das Reich 1914–1945', *Rheinische Vierteljahresblätter* 30, 1965.

Mosse, George L., *De la Grande Guerre au totalitarisme. La brutalisation des sociétés européennes* (Paris: Hachette, 1999).

Nipperdey, Thomas, 'Die deutsche Studentenschaft in den ersten Jahren der Weimarer Republik', in Adolf Grimme (ed.), *Kulturverwaltung der zwanziger Jahren* (Stuttgart: Kohlhammer, 1961).

Petry, Ludwig, 'Zur Rolle der Universität Breslau in der Zeit des Nationalsozialismus. Aus Erinnerungen, Aufzeichnungen und Korrespondenzen eines Habilitanden und Dozenten der philosophischen Fakultät', in Lothar Bossle et al. (eds.), *Nationalsozialismus und Widerstand in Schlesien* (Sigmaringen: Thorbecke, 1989).

Petzold, Joachim, 'Juni-Klub', in Dieter Fricke (ed.), *Lexikon zur Parteiengeschichte* (Cologne: Pahl-Rutgenstein, 1983–6).

Petzold, Joachim, *Wegbereiter des deutschen Faschismus. Der jungkonservatismus in der Weimarer Republik* (Cologne: Pahl-Rutgenstein, 1983).

Peukert, Detlev, *Die Weimarer Republik. Krisenjahre der klassischen Moderne* (Frankfurt: Suhrkamp, 1983).

Philipp, Werner, 'Nationalsozialismus und Ostwissenschaften', in Wolfgang Abendroth (ed.), *Nationalsozialismus und die deutsche Universität* (Berlin: Gruyter, 1966).

Pieper, Helmut, *Die Minderheitenfrage und das deutsche Reich 1919–1933/34* (Hamburg: Metzner, 1974).

Pingel, Henner, *100 Jahre TH Darmstadt. Wissenschaft und Technik für wenn? Ein Beitrag zur Entwicklung von Hochschule und Studentenschaft* (Darmstadt: published at author's expense, 1977).

Pohl, Karl Heinrich, 'Der "Rheinlandkommissar" und die besetzten deutschen Gebiete. Regionale Einflüsse bei den innenpolitischen Auseinandersetzungen um die "Rückwirkung" von Locarno', *Jahrbuch für westdeutsche Landesgeschichte* 5, 1979.

Pommerin, Rainer, *Sterilisierung der 'Rheinlandbastarde'. Das Schicksal einer deutschen farbigen Minderheit, 1918–1937* (Düsseldorf: Droste, 1979).

Pöppinghege, Rainer, *Absage an die Republik. Das politische Verhalten der Studentenschaft der Westfälischen Universität Münster 1918–1945* (Münster: Agenda Verlag, 1994).

Rammstedt, Otthein, *Die deutsche Soziologie 1933–1945. Die Normalität einer Anpassung. Mit einer Bibliographie soziologischer Titel 1933–1945* (Frankfurt: Suhrkamp, 1986).

—'Theorie und Empirie des Volksfeindes. Zur Entwicklung einer "deutschen Soziologie"', in Peter Lundgreen (ed.), *Wissenschaft im Dritten Reich* (Frankfurt: Suhrkamp, 1985).

Reimer, Klaus, *Rheinlandfrage und Rheinlandbewegung, 1918–1933. Ein Beitrag zur Geschichte der regionalistischen Bestrebung in Deutschland* (Frankfurt: Lang, 1979).

Remes, Friedrich W., *Die Sorbenfrage 1918–1919. Untersuchung einer gescheiterten Autonomie bewegung* (Bautzen: Domowina Verlag, 1993).

Ringer, Frederic, *The Decline of German Mandarins. The German Academic Community, 1890–1930* (Cambridge, Mass.: Harvard University Press, 1969).

Roessling, Udo, 'Ernst Jünger und der "Standarte"-Kreis als Vertreter des sogenannten "Neuen Nationalismus" in der Weimarer Republik', *Jenaer Beiträge zur Parteiengeschichte* 48, 1986.

Rürup, Reinhard (ed.), *Wissenschaft und Gesellschaft. Beiträge zur Geschichte der TH/TU Berlin, 1879–1979*, vol. 1 (Berlin: Springer Verlag, 1979).

Salewski, Michael, *Die Gleichschaltung der Christian-Albrechts-Universität im April 1933* (Kiel: Informations- und Pressestelle der Universität Kiel, 1983).

Schmidt, Manfred (ed.), ' . . . *Treu und fest hinten dem Führer. Die Anfänge des Nationalsozialismus an der Universität Tübingen 1926–1934'. Begleitheft zu einer Ausstellung des Universitätsarchivs Tübingen* (Tübingen: Werkschriften des Universitätsarchivs, 1983).

Schmidt, Siegfried, et al., *Alma Mater Jenensis. Geschichte der Universität Jena* (Weimar: Böhlau, 1983).

Schneider, Ulrich, 'Widerstand und Verfolgung an der Marburger Universität, 1933–1945', in D. Kramer and C. Vanja (eds.), *Universität und demokratische*

Bewegung. Ein Lesebuch zur 450–Jahrfeier der Philipps-Universität Marburg (Marburg: Arbeiterbewegung und Gesellschaftwissenschaft, 1977).

Schöttler, Peter (ed.), *Geschichtsschreibung als Legitimationswissenschaft 1918–1945* (Frankfurt: Suhrkamp, 1997).

Schreiner, Klaus, 'Politischer Messianismus, Führergedanke und Führererwartung in der Weimarer Republik', in Manfred Hettling (ed.), *Was ist Gesellschaftsgeschichte? Positionen, Themen, Analysen. Hans-Ulrich Wehler zum 60. Geburtstag* (Munich: C. H. Beck, 1991).

Schultz, Gerhard, 'Der "nationale Klub von 1919" zu Berlin. Zum politischen Zerfall einer Gesellschaft', *Jahrbuch für die Geschichte Mittel- und Ostdeutschlands* 11, 1962.

—*Aufstieg des Nationalsozialismus. Krise und Revolution in Deutschland* (Berlin; Vienna: Propyläen, 1975).

Schwabe, Klaus, *Dir Ruhrkrise 1923* (Paderborn: Schöningh, 1984).

Schwartz, Jürgen, *Studenten in der Weimarer Republik. Die deutsche Studentenschaft in der Zeit von 1918–1923 und ihre Stellung zur Politik* (Berlin: Duncker und Humblot, 1971).

Seidel, Rita, et al. (eds.), *Universität Hannover 1831–1981. Festschrift für 150-jähriges Bestehen der Universität Hannover*, 2 vols. (Hanover, 1981).

Seier, Helmut, 'Radikalisierung und Reform als Problem der Universität Marburg 1918–1933', *Academia Marburgensis* 1, 1977.

Spitznagel, Peter, *Studentenschaft und Nationalsozialismus in Würzburg*, thesis (Würzburg, 1974).

Spitznagel, Peter and Geoffrey J. Giles, *Studentenschaft und Nationalsozialismus in Würzburg, 1927–1933. Der NSD-Studentbund und der Geist der studentischen Korporationen*, colloquium, 4–5 October 1975 (Würzburg: Deutsche Gesellschaft für Hochschulkunde, 1974).

Stambolis, Barbara, *Der Mythos der jungen Generationen. Ein Beitrag zur politischen Kultur der Weimarer Republik*, typewritten thesis (Bochum, 1984).

Steinberg, Michael, *Sabers and Brown Shirts. The German Students' Path to National Socialism 1918–1945* (Chicago: Chicago University Press, 1977).

Steinmetz, Max, *Geschichte der Universität Jena 1548/58–1958. Festgabe zur Universitätsjubiläum* (Jena: Fischer, 1958).

Stern, Fritz, *The Politics of Cultural Despair: A Study in the Rise of the Germanic Ideology* (Berkeley: University of California Press, 1961).

Stolze, Elke, *Die Martin-Luther-Universität Halle-Wittenberg während der Herrschaft des Faschismus*, typewritten thesis (Halle, 1982).

Stoy, Manfred and Walter Leitsch, *Das Seminar für osteuropäische Geschichte der Universität Wien, 1907–1948* (Vienna: Böhlau, 1983).

Strauss, Herbert and Norbert Kampe (eds.), *Antisemitismus. Von der Judenfeindschaft zum Holocaust* (Frankfurt: Campus, 1985).

Ströle-Bühler, Heike, *Studentischer Antisemitismus in der Weimarer Republik. Eine Analyse der Burschenschaftlichen Blätter 1918–1933* (Frankfurt: Suhrkamp, 1991).

Stuchlik, Gerda, *Goethe im Braunhemd. Universität Frankfurt 1933–1945* (Frankfurt: Röderberg Verlag, 1984).

Süss, Martin, *Rheinhessen unter französischer Besatzung. Vom Waffenstillstand im*

November 1918 bis zum Ende der Separatismusunruhen im Februar 1924 (Stuttgart: Steiner, 1988).

Theweleit, Klaus, *Männerphantasien*, 2 vols. (Frankfurt: Roter Stern, 1977–8).

Thieme, Frank, *Rassentheorie zwischen Mythos und Tabu. Der Beitrag der Sozialwissenschaft zur Entstehung und Wirkung der Rassenideologie in Deutschland* (Frankfurt: Lang, 1988).

Thimme, Annelise, *Flucht in den Mythos. Die deutschnationale Volkspartei und die Niederlage von 1918* (Göttingen: Vandenhoeck und Ruprecht, 1969).

Verhey, Jeffrey, *The Spirit of 1914. Militarism, Myth and Mobilization in Germany* (Cambridge: Cambridge University Press, 2000).

Voigt, Gerd, *Rußland in der deutschen Geschichtsschreibung 1843–1945* (Berlin: Akademie Verlag, 1994).

Volkov, Shulamit, 'Kontinuität und Diskontinuität im deustchen Antisemitismus, 1878–1945', *VfZ* 33, 1985.

Voss, Ingrid and Jürgen Voss, 'Die *Revue Rhénane* als Instrument der französischen Kulturpolitik am Rhein, 1920–1930', *Archiv für Kulturgeschichte* 64, 1982.

Wein, Franziska, *Deutschlands Strom – Frankreichs Grenze. Geschichte und Propaganda am Rhein, 1919–1930* (Essen: Klartext, 1992).

Weindling, Paul, *L'Hygiène de la race*, vol. 1: *Hygiène raciale et eugénisme médical en Allemagne, 1870–1933*, pref. Benoît Massin (Paris: La Découverte, 1998).

Weingand, Hans-Peter, *Die technische Hochschule Graz. Vorgeschichte, Geschichte und Nachgeschichte des Nationalsozialismus an einer Institution* (Graz: Hochschülerschaft der TU Graz, 1988).

Weisbrod, Bernd, 'Violence et culture politique en Allemagne entre les deux guerres', *XXe Siècle – Revue d'histoire* 34, 1992.

Wentzcke, Paul, et al. (eds.), *Darstellungen und Quellen zur Geschichte der deutschen Einheitsbewegung im neunzehnten und zwanzigsten Jahrhundert*, 15 vols. (Heidelberg: Winter, 1957–92).

Wolgast, Eike, 'Geschichte der Universität Heidelberg im Dritten Reich', in *Die Geschichte der Universität Heidelberg. Vorträge im Wintersemester 1985–86* (Heidelberg: Heidelberger Verlagsanstalt, 1986).

Zimmerman, Ludwig, *Frankreichs Ruhrpolitik. Von Versailles bis zum Dawesplan* (Göttingen: Musterschmidt, 1971).

Zuckmayer, Carl, 'Franzosenzeit (1918–1930)', *Blätter der Carl Zuckmayer Gesellschaft* 4/1, 1978.

The Third Reich

Adam, Uwe Dietrich, *Judenpolitik im Dritten Reich* (Düsseldorf: Droste, 1972).

Anderson, Dennis L., *The Academy for German Law*, PhD thesis (Ann Arbor, 1982).

Ayçoberry, Pierre, *La Société allemande sous le Troisième Reich* (Paris: Le Seuil, 1998).

Baird, Jay W., *The Mythical World of Nazi War Propaganda, 1939–1945* (Minneapolis: University of Minnesota Press, 1974).

Baum, Reiner C., *The Holocaust and the German Elite. Genocide and National Suicide in Germany, 1871–1945* (London: Totowa, 1981).

Bédarida, François, 'Kérygme nazi et religion séculière', *Esprit* 218, 1996.

—(ed.), *La Politique nazie d'extermination* (Paris: IHTP-Albin Michel, 1989).

Behrenbeck, Sabine, *Der Kult um die toten Helden. Nationalsozialistische Mythen, Riten und Symbole, 1923–1945* (Cologne: SH Verlag, 1996).

Bendersky, Joseph W., *Carl Schmitt, Theorist for the Reich* (Princeton, N.J.: Princeton University Press, 1983).

Benz, Wolfgang, *Die Dimension des Völkermords. Die Zahl der jüdischen Opfer des Nationalsozialismus* (Munich: DVA, 1991).

Bock, Gisela, *Zwangssterilisation im Dritten Reich* (Opladen: Westdeutscher Verlag, 1986).

Bouretz, Pierre, 'Penser au XXe siècle. La place de l'énigme totalitaire', *Esprit* 218, 1996.

Bracher, Karl Dietrich, *The German Dictatorship: The Origins, Structure, and Effects of National Socialism*, tr. Jean Steinberg (London: Weidenfeld and Nicolson, 1971).

—*Zeitgeschichtliche Kontroverse. Um Faschismus, Totalitarismus und Demokratie* (Munich: Piper, 1976).

Brandes, Detlef, *Die Tschechen unter deutschem Protektorat* (Munich: Oldenbourg, 1975).

Breitling, Rupert, *Die nationalsozialistische Rassenlehre. Entstehung, Ausbreitung, Nützen und Schaden einer politischen Ideologie* (Meisenheim: Hain Verlag, 1971).

Broszat, Martin, *The Hitler State: The Foundation and Development of the Internal Structure of the Third Reich*, tr. John W. Hiden (London: Longman, 1981).

—'Die völkische Ideologie und der Nationalsozialismus', *Deutsche Rundschau* 84, 1958.

Burleigh, Michael and Wolfgang Wippermann, *The Racial State: Germany 1933–1945* (Cambridge: Cambridge University Press, 1991).

Burrin, Philippe, *Hitler and the Jews: The Genesis of the Holocaust*, tr. Patsy Southgate (London: Arnold, 1994).

Cabannes, Bruno, 'Du baroque au nazisme: une histoire religieuse de la politique' (interview with George Mosse), *Revue européenne d'histoire – European Review of History* 1/2, 1994.

Cabannes, Bruno, Édouard Husson and Christian Ingrao, 'Le nazisme: millénarisme ou domination charismatique?' (interview with Ian Kershaw), *Revue européenne d'histoire – European Review of History* 3/2, 1996.

Childers, Thomas and Jane Caplan (eds.), *Reevaluating the Third Reich. Interpretations and Debates* (New York: Holmes and Meier, 1993).

Conte, Édouard and Cornelia Essner, *La Quête de la race. Une anthropologie du nazisme* (Paris: Hachette, 1995).

—'*Völkerkunde* et nazisme, ou l'Ethnologie sous l'empire des raciologues', *L'Homme* 129, 1994.

Dahrendorf, Ralf, *Society and Democracy in Germany* (London: Weidenfeld and Nicolson, 1968).

Diner, Dan, 'Rassistisches Völkerrecht. Elemente einer nationalsozialistischen Weltordnung', *VfZ* 37, 1989.

Ehlich, Konrad (ed.), *Sprache im Faschismus* (Frankfurt: Suhrkamp, 1989).

Fahlbusch, Michael, et al., *Geographie und Nationalsozialismus. Drei Fallstudien* _zur Institution Geographie im Deutschen Reich und in der Schweiz_ (Kassel: Gesamthochschule, 1989).

Feest, David, 'Abgrenzung oder Assimilation: Überlegung zum Wandel der deutschbaltischen Ideologien 1918–1939 anhand _Baltischen Monatschrifts_', _Zeitschrift für Ostmitteleuropa-Forschung_ 45, 1996.

Fischer, Hans, _Völkerkunde im Nationalsozialismus. Aspekte der Anpassung. Affinität und Behauptung einer wissenschaftlichen Disziplin_ (Berlin; Hamburg: Reimer, 1990).

Frei, Norbert, _National Socialist Rule in Germany: The Führer State, 1939–1945_, tr. Simon B. Steyne (Oxford: Blackwell, 1993).

—(ed.), _Medizin und Gesundheitspolitik in der NS-Zeit_ (Munich: Oldenbourg, 1991).

Friedländer, Saul, _Nazi Germany and the Jews_, vol. 1: _The Years of Persecution, 1933–1939_ (London: Weidenfeld and Nicolson, 1997).

Gamm, Hans Jochen, _Der braune Kult. Das Dritte Reich und seine Ersatzreligion_ (Hamburg: Rütten und Löning Verlag, 1962).

Ganssmüller, Christian, _Die Erbgesundheitspolitik des Dritten Reiches. Planung, Durchführung and Durchsetzung_ (Cologne; Vienna: Böhlau, 1987).

Giles, Geoffrey, 'The rise of the National Socialist Students' Association and the failure of political education in the Third Reich', in Peter Stachura (ed.), _The Shaping of Nazi States_ (London: Croom Helm, 1978).

Giman, Sander L., 'Seuche in Deutschland 1939–1989: Kulturelle Vorstellungen von Rasse, Raum und Krankheit', _1999. Zeitschrift zur Geschichte des 20. und 21 Jahrhunderts_ 6/4, 1991.

Goldhagen, Erich, 'Weltanschauung und Erlösung. Zum Antisemitismus der nationalsozialistischen Führungsschicht', _VfZ_ 24, 1976.

Gruchmann, Lothar, '"Blutschutzgesetz" und Justiz', _Aus Politik und Zeitgeschichte_ 48, 1985.

Hagemann, Ernst, _Nachtrag zu Hitler. Drittes Reich – Weltanschauung und Endkampf im Nationalsozialismus_ (Frankfurt: Fischer, 1990).

Haiger, Ernst, 'Politikwissenschaft und Auslandswissenschaft im Dritten Reich. Deutsche Hochschule für Politik und auslandswissenschaftliche Fakultät der Berliner Universität', in Gerhard Göhler and Bodo Zeuner (eds.), _Kontinuitäten und Bruche in der deutschen Politikwissenschaft_ (Baden-Baden: Nomos, 1991).

Hartmann, Frank, _Denker denken Geschichte. Erkundungen zu Philosophie und Nationalsozialismus_ (Vienna: Passagen Verlag, 1994).

Hauner, Milan, 'A German racial revolution?', _Journal of Contemporary History_ 19, 1984.

Hauschild, Thomas (ed.), _Lebenslust und Fremdenfurcht. Ethnologie im Dritten Reich_ (Frankfurt: Suhrkamp, 1995).

Heiber, Helmut, _Universität unterm Hakenkreuz_, 2 vols. (Munich: Saur, 1991–2).

—_Walter Frank und sein Reichsinstitut für Geschichte des neuen Deutschlands_ (Stuttgart: DVA, 1966).

Hellmer, Joachim, _Der Gewohnheitsverbrecher und die Sicherungsverwahrung 1934–1945_ (Berlin: Duncker und Humblot, 1961).

Herbert, Ulrich, _Arbeit, Volkstum, Weltanschauung. Über Fremde und Deutsche im 20. Jahrhundert_ (Frankfurt: Fischer, 1995).

—'Arbeit und Vernichtung. Ökonomisches Interesse und Primat der "Weltanschauung" im Nationalsozialismus', in Ulrich Herbert (ed.), *Europa und der Reichseinsatz. Ausländische Zivilarbeiter, Kriegsgefangene und KZ-Häftlinge in Deutschland 1933–1945* (Essen: Klartext, 1991).

—'Rassismus und rationales Kalkül. Zum Stellenwert utilitaristischer verbrämter Legitimationsstrategien in der nationalsozialistischen Weltanschauung', in Wolfgang Schneider (ed.), *'Vernichtungspolitik'. Eine Debatte über den Zusammenhang von Sozialpolitik und Genozid im nationalsozialistischen Deutschland* (Hamburg: Junius, 1991).

Herbst, Ludolf, *Das nationalsozialistische Deutschland 1933–1945. Die Entfesselung der Gewalt: Rassismus und Krieg* (Frankfurt: Suhrkamp, 1996).

Hillgruber, Andreas, 'Die "Endlösung" und das deutsche Ostimperium als Kernstück des rassenideologischen Programms des Nationalsozialismus', *VfZ* 20, 1972.

Hirsch, Martin, Dietmund Majer and Jürgen Meinck, *Recht, Verwaltung und Justiz im Nationalsozialismus* (Cologne: Bund Verlag, 1984).

Hirschfeld, Gerhard and Lothar Kettenacker (eds.), *The Führer State, Myth and Reality: Studies on the Structure and Politics of the Third Reich* (Stuttgart: Klett-Cotta, 1981).

Höhne, Heinz, *Canaris*, tr. J. Maxwell Brownjohn (London: Secker and Warburg, 1979).

Institut für Zeitgeschichte (collective), *NS-Recht in historischer Perspektive*, texts from the colloquium of the IfZ (Munich: Oldenbourg, 1981).

Jäckel, Eberhard, *Hitlers Herrschaft. Vollzug einer Weltanschauung* (Stuttgart: DVA, 1985).

—*Hitlers Weltanschauung. Entwurf einer Herrschaft* (Stuttgart: DVA, 1981).

Kater, Michael, 'Generationskonflikt als Entwicklungsfaktor in der NS-Bewegung vor 1933', *Geschichte und Gesellschaft* 11, 1985.

—'Bürgerliche Jugendbewegung und Hitlerjugend in Deutschland, 1926–1939', *Archiv für Soziologie* 17, 1977.

—'Die NS-Studentenbund von 1926–1928. Randgruppe zwischen Hitler und Strasser', *VfZ* 22, 1974.

Kershaw, Ian, *Popular Opinion and Political Dissent in the Third Reich: Bavaria 1933–1945*, new edn (Oxford: Clarendon Press, 2002).

—*Hitler* (Harlow: Longman, 1991).

Kershaw, Ian and Moshé Lewin (eds.), *Stalinism and Nazism: Dictatorships in Comparison* (Cambridge: Cambridge University Press, 1997).

Ketelsen, Uwe-Karsten, *Von heroischen Sein und völkischen Tod. Zur Dramatik des Dritten Reichs* (Bonn: Bouvier, 1970).

Klemperer, Victor: *The Language of the Third Reich: LTI, Lingua Tertii Imperii: A Philologist's Notebook*, tr. Martin Brady (London: Continuum, 2006).

Kleßmann, Christoph, 'Osteuropaforschung und Lebensraumpolitik im Dritten Reich', *Aus Politik und Zeitgeschichte* B7/84, 1984.

Klingemann, Carsten, 'Les sociologues nazis et Max Weber, 1933–1945', *Genèses* 21, 1995.

Kruger, Peter, 'Hitlers Europapolitik', in Wolfgang Benz, Hans Bucheim and Hans

Mommsen (eds.), *Der Nationalsozialismus. Studien zur Ideologie und Herrschaft* (Frankfurt: Fischer, 1993).

Kruse, Christina, *Die Volkswirtschaftslehre im Nationalsozialismus* (Freiburg: Haufe, 1988).

Larsen, Stein Ugelvik, Bernt Hagtvet and Jan Petter Myklebust (eds.) *Who Were the Fascists? Social Roots of European Fascism* (Bergen: Universitetsforlaget, 1980).

Lerner, Daniel, *The Nazi Elite* (Stanford: Stanford University Press, 1951).

Loewenberg, Peter, 'The psychohistorical origins of the Nazi youth cohort', *American Historical Review* 76, 1971.

Lübbe, Hermann, 'Rationalität und Irrationalität des Völkermords', in Hanno Loewy (ed.), *Holocaust. Die Grenzen des Verstehens. Eine Debatte über die Besetzung der Geschichte* (Reinbeck: Rowohlt, 1992).

Ludwig, Esther, 'Adolf Helbok und die "Gleichschaltung" des Seminars für Landesgeschichte und Siedlungskunde an der Leipziger Universität (1935–1941)', *Wissenschaftliche Zeitschrift der Humboldt-Universität zu Berlin. Gesellschafts- und sprachwissenschaftliche Reihe* 11, 1991.

Lutzhöft, Hans-Jürgen, *Der nordische Gedanke in Deutschland 1920–1940* (Stuttgart: Klett-Cotta, 1971).

Majer, Diemut, 'Die Perversion des Völkerrechts unter dem Nationalsozialismus', *Jahrbuch des Instituts für deutsche Geschichte* 14, 1985.

—*Grundlagen des nationalsozialistischen Rechtssytems: Führerprinzip, Sonderrecht, Einheitspartei* (Stuttgart: Kohlhammer, 1987).

—*'Fremdvölkische' im Dritten Reich. Ein Beitrag zur nationalsozialistischen Rechtssetzung und Rechtspraxis in Verwaltung und Justiz* (Boppard: Boldt, 1981).

Massin, Benoît, 'Anthropologie raciale et national-socialisme: heurs et malheurs du paradigme de la "race"', in Jeanne Olff-Nathan (ed.), *La Science sous le Troisième Reich* (Paris: Le Seuil, 1993).

Mehring, Reinhard, 'Vom Umgang mit Carl Schmitt. Zur neueren Literatur', *Geschichte und Gesellschaft* 19, 1983.

Merkl, Peter, *Political Violence under the Swastika. 581 Earlier Nazis* (Princeton, N.J.: Princeton University Press, 1975).

Messerschmidt, Manfred, 'Revision, Neue Ordnung, Krieg. Akzente der Völkerrechtswissenschaft in Deutschland 1933–1945', *Militärgeschichtliche Mitteilungen* 1, 1971.

Mommsen, Hans, *Der Nationalsozialismus und die deutsche Gesellschaft. Ausgewählte Aufsätze*, ed. Lutz Niethammer and Bernd Weisbrod (Reinbeck: Rowohlt, 1991).

—'Nationalsozialismus als vorgetäuschte Modernisierung', in Walther Pehle (ed.), *Der historische Ort des Nationalsozialismus* (Frankfurt: Fischer, 1990).

—'Die Funktion des Antisemitismus im Dritten Reich. Das Beispiel des November-Pogroms', in Günter Brakelman and Martin Rosowski (eds.), *Antisemitismus. Von religiöser Judenfeindschaft zur Rassenideologie* (Göttingen: Vandenhoeck und Ruprecht, 1989).

—'Nationalsozialismus', in C. D. Kernig (ed.), *Sowjetsystem und demokratische Gesellschaft*, vol. 4 (Freiburg: Herder, 1971).

—*Beamtentum im Dritten Reich* (Stuttgart: Klett-Cotta, 1966).

Mommsen, Hans and Suzan Willems (eds.), *Herrschaftsalltag im Dritten Reich. Studien und Texte* (Düsseldorf: Schwann in Patmos Verlag, 1988).

Mosse, George, *Toward a General Theory of Fascism. International Fascism: New Thoughts and New Approaches* (London: Sage, 1979).

— *Nazi Culture* (New York: Grosset and Dunlap, 1966).

— *The Crisis of German Ideology: Intellectual Origins of the Third Reich* (New York: Grosset and Dunlap, 1964).

Nagel, Brigitte, *Die Welteislehre. Ihre Geschichte und ihre Rolle im Dritten Reich* (Stuttgart: Verlag für Geschichte der Naturwissenschaften und der Technik, 1991).

Nasarski, Gerlind, *Osteuropa. Vorstellungen in der konservativ-revolutionären Publizistik. Analyse der Zeitschrift 'Deutsches Volkstum' 1917–1941* (Frankfurt: Lang, 1974).

Neuberger, Helmut, *Freimaurerei und Nationalsozialismus. Die Verfolgung der deutschen Freimaurerei durch völkische Bewegungen und Nationalsozialismus 1918–1945* (Hamburg: Bauhütten, 1980).

Nolte, Ernst, 'Slawen, Juden und Bolschewiki in der Ideologie des Nationalsozialismus', in Ernst Nolte, *Lehrstück oder Tragödie? Beiträge zur Interpretation der Geschichte des 20. Jahrhunderts* (Cologne: Böhlau, 1991).

Patzöld, Kurt, 'Antikommunismus und Antibolschewismus als Instrumente der Kriegsvorbereitung und Kriegspolitik', in Norbert Frei and Hermann Kling (eds. with the collaboration of Margrit Brandt), *Der nationalsozialistische Krieg* (Frankfurt; New York: Campus, 1990).

Pauley, Bruce F., *Hitler and the Forgotten Nazis. A History of Austrian National Socialism* (London: Macmillan, 1981).

Peukert, Detlev, *Volksgenosse und Gemeinschaftsfremde* (Cologne: Bund Verlag, 1982).

Pohlmann, Friedrich, *Ideologie und Terror im Nationalsozialismus* (Pfaffenweiler: Centaurus Verlagsgesellschaft, 1992).

Pois, Robert A., *National Socialism and the Religion of Nature* (London: Croom Helm, 1986).

Proctor, Robert, *Racial Hygiene. Medicine under the Nazis* (Cambridge, Mass.: Harvard University Press, 1988).

Rebentisch, Dieter, *Führerstaat und Verwaltung im Zweiten Weltkrieg. Verfassungsentwicklung und Verwaltungspolitik 1939–1945* (Stuttgart: Steiner-Verlag-Wiesbaden, 1989).

— 'Nationalsozialistische Revolution, Parteiherrschaft und totaler Krieg in Hessen 1933–1945', in Uwe Schultz (ed.), *Die Geschichte Hessens* (Stuttgart: Theiss, 1983).

Rhodes, James, *The Hitler Movement: A Modern Millenarian Revolution* (Stanford: Stanford University Press, 1980).

Rössler, Mechtild, *Wissenschaft und Lebensraum. Geographische Ostforschung im Nationalsozialismus. Ein Beitrag zur Disziplingeschichte der Geographie* (Berlin; Hamburg: Reimer, 1990).

Saller, Karl, *Die Rassenlehre des Nationalsozialismus in Wissenschaft und Propaganda* (Darmstadt: Progress-Gesellschaft, 1966).

Schmuhl, Hans-Walter, 'Rassismus unter den Bedingungen charismatischer

Herrschaft. Zum Übergang von der Verfolgung zur Vernichtung gesellschaft-licher Minderheiten im Dritten Reich', in Karl Dietrich Bracher, Manfred Funke and Hans-Adolf Jacobsen (eds.), *Deutschland 1933–1945. Neue Studien zur nation-alsozialistischen Herrschaft* (Düsseldorf: Bundeszentrale für politische Bildung, 1992).

— *Rassenhygiene, Nationalsozialismus, Euthanasie. Von der Verhütung zur Vernichtung 'lebensunwerten Lebens' 1890–1945* (Göttingen: Vandenhoeck und Ruprecht, 1987).

Schöttler, Peter, 'Le nazisme et les savants', *Genèses* 21 (special issue), 1995.

Sofsky, Wolfgang, *The Order of Terror: The Concentration Camp*, tr. William Templer (Princeton, N.J.: University of Princeton Press, 1997).

Steinert, Marlis, 'Fascisme et national-socialisme. Cas singulier, cas spécifique, phénomène générique?', in S. Friedländer, H. Kapur and A. Reszler (eds), *L'Historien et les relations internationales. Recueil d'études en hommage à Jacques Freymond* (Geneva: IUHEI, 1981).

— *Capitulation, 1945: The Story of the Dönitz Regime*, tr. Richard Barry (London: Constable, 1969).

Stern, J. P., *Hitler: The Führer and the People*, rev. edn (London: Fontana, 1990).

Struve, Walter, *Elites against Democracy. Leadership Ideals in Bourgeois Political Thought in Germany 1890–1933* (Princeton, N.J.: Princeton University Press, 1973).

Thamer, Hans Ulrich, *Die Deutschen und ihre Nation*, vol. 5: *Verführung und Gewalt. Deutschland 1933–1945* (Berlin: Siedler, 1986).

Vondung, Klaus, *The Apocalypse in Germany*, tr. Stephen D. Ricks (Columbia, Mo.; London: University of Missouri Press, 2000).

— *Magie und Manipulation. Ideologischer Kult und politische Religion des Nationalsozialismus* (Göttingen: Vandenhoeck und Ruprecht, 1971).

Wegner, Bernd (ed.), *From Peace to War: Germany, Soviet Russia and the World, 1939–1941* (Providence, R.I.; Oxford: Berghahn Books, 1997).

Weindling, Paul, *Health, Race and German Politics between National Unification and Nazism, 1870–1945* (Cambridge: Cambridge University Press, 1993).

— '"Mustergau" Thüringen. Rassenhygiene zwischen Ideologie und Machtpolitik', in Norbert Frei (ed.), *Medizin und Gesundheitspolitik in der NS-Zeit* (Munich: Oldenbourg, 1991).

Weingart, Peter, 'Eugenische Utopie. Entwürfe für die Rationalisierung der menschlichen Entwicklung', in Harald Welzer (ed.), *Nationalsozialismus und Moderne* (Tübingen: Diskord Verlag, 1993).

— 'Eugenik: eine angewandte Wissenschaft', in Peter Lundgreen (ed.) *Wissenschaft im Dritten Reich* (Frankfurt: Suhrkamp, 1985).

Weingart, Peter, et al. (eds.), *Rasse, Blut und Gene. Geschichte der Eugenik und Rassenhygiene in Deutschland* (Frankfurt: Suhrkamp, 1992).

Welzer, Harald (ed.), *Nationalsozialismus und Moderne* (Tübingen: Diskord Verlag, 1993).

Willing, Georg Franz, *'Bin ich schuldig?' Leben und Wirken des Reichsstudentenführers und Gauleiters Dr. Gustav Adolf Scheel 1907–1979. Eine Biographie* (Leoni: Druffel Verlag, 1987). (This is an apologia.)

Wippermann, Wolfgang, *Faschismustheorien: zum Stand der gegenwärtigen Diskussionen* (Darmstadt: Wissenschaftliche Buchgesellschaft, 1980).

Zimmerman, Michael, *Verfolgt, vertrieben, vernichtet. Die nationalsozialistische Vernichtungspolitik gegen Sinti und Roma* (Essen: Klartext, 1989).

Specialized works on the SS, the SD, the RSHA and their elites

Ackerman, Josef, *Heinrich Himmler als Ideologe* (Göttingen: Musterschmidt, 1970).

Aronson, Shlomo, *Heydrich und die Frühgeschichte von Gestapo und des SD 1931–1945* (Berlin: Ernst Reuter Gesellschaft, 1967).

Aronson, Shlomo and Richard Breitman, 'Eine unbekannte Himmler-Rede von Januar 1943', *VfZ* 38, 1990.

Banach, Jens, *Heydrichs Elite. Das Führerkorps der Sicherheitspolizei und des SD 1936–1945* (Paderborn: Schöningh, 1998).

Behringer, Wolfgang, 'Von Krieg zu Krieg. Neue Perspektiven auf das Buch von Günther Franz', in Benigna von Krusenstjern and Hans Medick (eds.), *Zwischen Alltag und Katastrophe. Der Dreißigjährige Krieg aus der Nähe* (Göttingen: Vandenhoeck und Ruprecht, 1999).

Birn, Ruth Bettina, *Die höheren SS- und Polizeiführer, Himmlers Vertreter im Reich und in den besetzten Gebieten* (Düsseldorf: Droste, 1986).

Black, Peter, *Kaltenbrunner: Ideological Soldier of the Third Reich* (Princeton, N.J.: Princeton University Press, 1984).

Boehnert, Gunnar, *A Sociography of the SS Officer Corps, 1925–1939*, PhD thesis (London, 1977).

Botsch, Gideon, '"Geheime Ostforschung" im SD. Zur Entstehungsgeschichte und Tätigkeit des "Wannsee-Instituts" 1935–1945', *ZfG* 6, 2000.

Breitmann, Richard, *The Architect of Genocide. Heinrich Himmler and the Final Solution* (Zurich: Pendo Verlag, 2000).

Browder, George C., *Hitler's Enforcers. The Gestapo and the SS Security Service in the Nazi Revolution* (Oxford; New York: Oxford University Press, 1996).

—*Foundations of the Nazi Police State. The Formation of SIPO and SD* (Lexington: University Press of Kentucky, 1990).

—'Die Anfänge des SD. Dokumente aus der Organisationsgeschichte', *VfZ* 27, 1979.

—'The SD: Significance of Organization and Image', in George Mosse (ed.), *Police Forces in History* (London: Sage, 1975).

—*SIPO and SD, 1931–1940: Formation of an Instrument of Power*, PhD thesis (Madison: University of Wisconsin, 1968).

Buchheim, Hans, 'Die SS in der Verfassung des Dritten Reichs', *VfZ* 3, 1955.

Buchheim, Hans, Martin Broszat, Helmut Krausnick and Hans Adolf Jacobsen (eds.), *Anatomy of the SS State*, tr. Richard Barry et al. (London: Collins, 1968).

Combs, William L., *The Voice of the SS. A History of the SS Journal 'Das Schwarze Korps'* (New York: Lang, 1986).

Deschner, Günther, *Heydrich: The Pursuit of Total Power*, tr. Sandra Bance, Brenda Woods and David Ball (London: Orbis, 1981).

Dicks, Henry V., *Licensed Mass Murder: A Socio-Psychological Study of Some SS*

Killers (London: Chatto; Heinemann Educational for Sussex University Press, 1972).

Eidenbenz, Mathias, *'Blut und Boden'. Zur Funktion und Genesis der Metaphern des Agrarismus und Biologismus in der nationalsozialistischen Bauernpropaganda R. W. Darrés* (Berne: Lang, 1993).

Fraenkel, Heinrich and Roger Manvell, *Heinrich Himmler* (London: Heinemann, 1965).

Gellately, Robert, 'Gestapo und Terror. Perspektiven auf die Sozialgeschichte des nationalsozialistischen Herrschaftssystems', in Alf Lüdke (ed.), *'Sicherheit' und 'Wolhfahrt'. Polizei, Gesellschaft und Herrschaft im 19. und 20. Jahrhundert* (Frankfurt: Suhrkamp, 1992).

—*The Gestapo and German society: Enforcing Racial Policy 1933–1945* (Oxford: Clarendon Press, 1990).

Georg, Enno, *Die wirtschaftliche Unternehmungen der SS* (Munich: DVA, 1963).

Graber, George, *The Life and Times of Reinhard Heydrich* (New York: McKay, 1980).

Graf, Christoph, 'The genesis of the Gestapo', *Journal of Contemporary History* 22, 1987.

—*Politische Polizei zwischen Demokratie und Diktatur* (East Berlin: Colloquium Verlag, 1983).

Haar, Ingo, 'Deutsche "Ostforschung" und Antisemitismus', *ZfG* 6, 2000.

Hachmeister, Lutz, *Der Gegnerforscher. Zur Karriere des SS-Führers Franz Alfred Six* (Munich: C. H. Beck, 1998).

Hagen, Walter, *Die geheime Front. Organisationen, Personen und Aktionen des deutschen Geheimdienstes* (Stuttgart: Nibelungen Verlag, 1950).

Hartung, Ulrike, *Raubzüge in der Sowjetunion. Das Sonderkommando Künsberg 1941–1943* (Bremen: Temmen, 1997).

Herbert, Ulrich, *Best: Biographische Studien über Radikalismus, Weltanschauung und Vernunft 1903–1989* (Bonn: Dietz, 1996).

Höhne, Heinz, *The Order of the Death's Head: The Story of Hitler's SS*, tr. Richard Barry (London: Penguin, 2000).

Infield, Glen B., *Skorzeny: Hitler's Commando* (New York: St. Martin's Press, 1981).

Kater, Michael, *Das 'Ahnenerbe' der SS 1935–1945. Ein Beitrag zur Kulturpolitik des Dritten Reichs* (Stuttgart: DVA, 1974).

Koehl, Robert L., *The Black Corps: The Structure and Power Struggles of the Nazi SS* (Madison: University of Wisconsin Press, 1983).

—*RKFDV: German Resettlement and Population Policy, 1939–1945. A History of the Reich Commission for the Strengthening of Germandom* (Cambridge: Cambridge University Press, 1957).

Kohlhaas, Elisabeth, 'Die Mitarbeiter der Gestapo – quantitative und qualitative Befunde', *Archiv für Polizeigeschichte* 6, vols. 1–2, 1995.

Krausnick, Helmut and Hans-Heinrich Wilhelm, *Die Truppe des Weltanschauungskrieges: Die Einsatzgruppen der Sicherheitspolizei und des SD 1938–1942*, 2 vols. (Stuttgart: DVA, 1981).

Lichtenstein, Heiner, *Himmlers grüne Helfer. Die Schutz- und Ordnungspolizei im 'Dritten Reich'* (Cologne: Bund Verlag, 1990).

Loewenberg, Peter, 'The unsuccessful adolescence of Heinrich Himmler', in

Peter Loewenberg, *Decoding the Past. The Psychohistorical Approach* (Berkeley: University of California Press, 1985).

Lozowick, Yaacov, '*Rollbahn Mord*: the early activities of the *Einsatzgruppe C*', *Holocaust and Genocide Studies* 2, 1987.

Lumans, Valdis O., *Himmler's Auxiliaries. The Volksdeutsche Mittelstelle and the German National Minorities of Europe 1933–1945* (Chapel Hill: University of North Carolina Press, 1993).

Mallmann, Michael and Gerhard Paul, *Die Gestapo. Mythos und Realität* (Darmstadt: Wissenschaftliche Buchgesellschaft, 1995).

Matthäus, Jürgen, '"Weltanschauliche Forschung und Auswertung". Aus den Akten des Amtes VII im Reichssicherheitshauptamt', *Jahrbuch für Antisemitismusforschung* 5, 1996.

Nippert, Erwin, *Prinz Albrecht-Straße 8* (Berlin [GDR]: Brandenburgisches Verlagshaus, 1988).

Paetel, Karl O., 'Die SS. Ein Beitrag zur Soziologie des Nationalsozialismus', *VfZ* 2, 1954.

Pingel, Falk, *Häftlinge unter SS-Herrschaft. Widerstand, Selbstbehauptung und Vernichtung im Konzentrationslager* (Hamburg: Hoffmann und Campe, 1978).

Plum, Günter, 'Staatspolizei und innere Verwaltung 1934–1936', *VfZ* 13, 1965.

Prinz, Arthur, 'The role of the Gestapo in obstructing and promoting Jewish emigration', *Yad Vashem Studies* 2, 1958.

Ramme, Alwin, *Der Sicherheitsdienst der SS. Zu seiner Funktion im faschistischen Machtapparat und im Besatzungsregime des sogennanten Generalgouvernements Polen* (Berlin: Deutscher Militärverlag, 1970).

Rebentisch, Dieter, 'Wilhelm Stuckart, 1902–1953', in Kurt Jeserich and Helmut Neuhaus (eds.), *Persönlichkeiten der Verwaltung. Biographien zur deutschen Verwaltungsgeschichte 1648–1975* (Stuttgart: Kohlkammer, 1991).

— 'Persönlichkeitsprofil und Karriereverlauf der nationalsozialistischen Führungskader in Hessen 1928–1945', *Hessisches Jahrbuch für Landesgeschichte* 33, 1983.

Ritter, Ernst, *Das Deutsche Ausland-Institut in Stuttgart 1917–1945. Ein Beispiel deutscher Volkstumarbeit zwischen den Weltkriegen* (Wiesbaden: Steiner, 1976).

Roth, Karl-Heinz, 'Heydrichs Professor: Historiographie des "Volkstums" und der Massenvernichtungen. Der Fall Hans Joachim Beyer', in Peter Schöttler (ed.), *Geschichtsschreibung als Legitimationswissenschaft 1918–1945* (Frankfurt: Suhrkamp, 1997).

— 'Ärzte als Vernichtungspläner: Hans Ehlich, die Amtsgruppe III B des Reichssicherheitshauptamtes und der nationalsozialistische Genozid 1939–1945', in M. Hubenstorf et al. (eds.), *Medizingeschichte und Gesellschaftskritik. Festschrift für Gerhard Baader* (Husum: Matthiesen, 1997).

— '"Generalplan Ost" und der Mord an den Juden: der "Fernplan um der Umsiedlung in den Ostprovinzen" aus dem Reichssicherheitshauptamt vom November 1939', *1999* 2, 1997.

Rürup, Reinhard, *Topographie des Terrors: Gestapo, SD und RSHA auf der Prinz-Albrecht-Gelände. Eine Dokumentation* (Berlin: Topographie des Terrors Stiftung, 1987).

Safrian, Hans, *Eichmann und seine Gehilfen* (Frankfurt: Fischer, 1995).

Schattenfroh, Reinhold and Johannes Tuchel, *Zentrale des Terrors. Prinz-Albrecht-Straße 8. Hauptquartier der Gestapo* (Berlin: Siedler, 1987).

Scheffler, Wolfgang, 'Zur Praxis der SS- und Polizeigerichtsbarkeit im Dritten Reich', in Ernst Fraenkel, Günther Doeker and Winfried Steffani (eds.), *Klassenjustiz und Pluralismus. Festschrift für Ernst Fraenkel zum 75. Geburtstag* (Hamburg: Hoffman und Campe, 1973).

Schneider, Jost W. and Stuart Russell, *Heinrich Himmlers Burg. Bildchronik der SS-Schule Haus Wewelsburg, 1934–1945 Das weltanschauliche Zentrum der SS.* (Essen: Heitz und Höffkes, 1989).

Seckendorf, Martin, 'Kulturelle Deutschtumspflege im Übergang von Weimar zu Hitler am Beispiel des deutschen Ausland-Institut (DAI). Eine Fallstudie', in Wolfgang Jacobeit et al., *Völkische Wissenschaft. Gestalten und Tendenzen der deutschen und österreichischen Volkskunde in der ersten Hälfte des 20. Jahrhunderts. Helmut Paul Fielhauer gewidmet* (Vienna: Böhlau, 1994).

Sellmann, Michael, '*Propaganda und SD. Meldungen aus dem Reich' im Kriegsjahr 1944* (Stuttgart: Klett-Cotta, 1995).

Simon, Gerd, *Germanistik in dem Planspiel des Sicherheitsdienstes der SS*, vol. 1 (Tübingen: Gift Verlag, 1998).

Smith, Bradley F., *Heinrich Himmler: A Nazi in the Making, 1900–1926* (Stanford: Hoover Institution Press, 1971).

Steiner, John M., *Power Politics and Social Change in National Socialist Germany. A Process of Escalation into Mass Destruction* (Paris; The Hague: Mouton, 1976).

—'Über das Glaubensbekenntnis der SS', in Joachim Hütter et al. (eds.), *Tradition und Neubeginn. Internationale Forschungen zur deutschen Geschichte im 20. Jahrhundert* (Cologne: Heymann, 1975).

Steuer, Claudia, *Theodor Dannecker. Ein Funktionär der Endlösung* (Essen: Klartext, 1995).

Stokes, Lawrence D., 'Otto Ohlendorf, the *Sicherheitsdienst* and public opinion in Nazi Germany', in George Mosse (ed.), *Police Forces in History* (London: Sage, 1975).

—*The Sicherheitsdienst (SD) of the Reichsführer SS and German Public Opinion, September 1939–June 1941*, PhD thesis (Baltimore: Johns Hopkins University, 1972).

Von Hentig, Hans W., 'Beiträge zu einer Sozialgeschichte des Dritten Reichs', *VfZ* 16, 1968.

Wagner, Patrick, *Volksgemeinschaft ohne Verbrecher. Konzeption und Praxis der Kriminalpolizei in der Zeit der Weimarer Republik und des Nationalsozialismus* (Hamburg: Christians Verlag, 1996).

Wegner, Bernd, *Hitlers politische Soldaten: die Waffen-SS 1933–1945* (Paderborn: Schöningh, 1982).

Wildt, Michael, 'Das Führungskorps des Reichssicherheitshauptamtes. Eine Kollektivbiographie' (Freiburg im Breisgau, paper given at the seminar of Prof. Herbert, 1996).

—'Der Hamburger Gestapochef Bruno Streckenbach. Eine nationalsozialistische Karriere' in Franck Bajohr and Joachim Szodrynski (eds.), *Hamburg in der NS-Zeit. Ergebnisse neuerer Forschungen* (Hamburg: Ergebnisse Verlag, 1995).

—'Avant la "Solution finale". La politique juive du service de sécurité de la SS, 1935–1938', *Genèses* 21, 1995.

— *Die Judenpolitik des SD, 1935–1938. Eine Dokumentation* (Munich: Oldenbourg, 1995).

Wilhelm, Hans-Heinrich, 'Der SD und die Kirchen in den besetzten Ostgebieten', *Militärgeschichtlichen Mitteilungen* 29, 1981.

Ziegler, Herbert F., *Nazi Germany's New Aristocracy: The SS Leadership, 1925–1939* (Princeton, N.J.: Princeton University Press, 1989).

Zipfel, Friedrich, 'Gestapo and SD: a sociographic profile of the organizers of the terror', in Stein Ugelvik Larsen et al. (eds.), *Who Were the Fascists? Social Roots of European Fascism* (Bergen: Universitetsforlaget, 1980).

Works on the Nazi policy of creating elites

Arntz, Hans-Dieter, *Ordensburg Vogelsang, 1934–1945: Erziehung zur politischen Führung im Dritten Reich* (Euskirchen: Kümpel, 1986).

Eilers, Rolf, *Die nationalsozialistische Schulungspolitik. Eine Studie zur Fonktion der Erziehung im totalitären Staat* (Cologne: Westdeutscher Verlag, 1963).

Flessau, Kurt-Ingo (ed.), *Erziehung im Nationalsozialismus* (Cologne: Böhlau, 1987).

Heinemann, Manfred, *Erziehung und Schulung im Dritten Reich*, 4 vols. (Stuttgart: Klett-Cotta, 1980).

Hüser, Karl, *Wewelsburg 1933–1945. Kult- und Terrorstätte der SS. Eine Dokumentation* (Paderborn: Bonifatius Druckerei, 1982).

Kanz, Heinrich (ed.), *Der Nationalsozialismus als Erziehungsproblem. Die Erziehungsgeschichte 1933–1945* (Frankfurt: Lang, 1984).

Keim, Helmut, *Volksbildung in Deutschland* (Braunschweig: Westermann, 1976).

Kuppfer, Heinrich, *Der Faschismus und das Menschenbild der deutschen Pädagogik* (Frankfurt: Fischer, 1984).

Meyer, Harald, *Wewelsburg. SS-Burg und Konzentrationslager* (Paderborn: Meter, 1982).

Rempel, Gerhard, *Hitler's Children. The Hitler Youth and the SS* (Chapel Hill: University of North Carolina Press, 1989).

Scholtz, Harald, *Erziehung und Unterricht unterm Hakenkreuz* (Göttingen: Vandenhoeck und Ruprecht, 1985).

—'Die "NS-Ordensburger"', *VfZ* 15, 1960.

Schulze-Kossens, Richard, *Militärischer Führernachwuchs der Waffen-SS. Die Junkerschulen* (Osnabrück: Munin Verlag, 1982).

Werner, Karl-Ferdinand, *Das NS-Geschichtsbild und die deutsche Geschichtswissenschaft* (Stuttgart: Klett-Cotta, 1967).

Nazism and the 1939–1945 war: war, occupied territories, extermination

Aly, Götz, *Final Solution: Nazi Population Policy and the Murder of the European Jews*, tr. Belinda Cooper and Allison Brown (London: Arnold, 1999).

Aly, Götz and Susanne Heim, _Vordenker der Vernichtung. Auschwitz und die deutschen Pläne für eine neue europäische Ordnung_ (Frankfurt: Fischer, 1991).

Aschenauer, Rudolf, _Krieg ohne Grenzen. Der Partisanenkampf gegen Deutschland 1939–1945_ (Leoni: Druffel Verlag, 1982). (This is a work of apologia, produced by the man who defended the war criminals at Nuremberg.)

Bartov, Omer, _Hitler's Army. Soldiers, Nazis, and War in the Third Reich_ (Oxford: Oxford University Press, 1994).

— _The Eastern Front, 1941–1945. German Troops and the Barbarization of Warfare_, 2nd edn (Basingstoke: Palgrave in association with St Antony's College, Oxford, 2001).

Beer, Matthias, 'Die Entwicklung der Gaswagen beim Mord an den europäischen Juden', _VfZ_ 35, 1987.

Behrenbeck, Sabine, 'Heldenkult und Opfermythos. Mechanismen der Kriegsbegeisterung 1918–1945', in Marel van der Linden and Gottfried Mergner (eds.), _Kriegsbegeisterung und mentale Kriegsvorbereitung. Interdisziplinäre Studien_ (Berlin: Duncker und Humblot, 1991).

Benz, Wolfgang, 'Der Generalplan Ost. Germanizierungspolitik in den besetzten Ostgebieten', in Wolfgang Benz (ed.), _Herrschaft und Gesellschaft im nationalsozialistischen Staat_ (Frankfurt: Suhrkamp, 1990).

Boberach, Heinz, 'Die Stimmung in Deutschland im letzten Kriegsjahr 1944–1945', _Studien und Forschungen des Instituts für Niederösterreichische Landesgeschichte_ 20/1, 1995.

Braumandl, Wolfgang, _Die Wirtschafts- und Sozialpolitik des deutschen Reiches im Sudetenland 1938–1945_ (Nuremberg: Preussler, 1998).

Breitman, Richard, _Official Secrets: What the Nazis Planned, What the British and Americans Knew_ (London: Allen Lane, 1999).

Broszat, Martin, _Nationalsozialistische Polenpolitik, 1939–1945_ (Stuttgart: DVA, 1961).

Browning, Christopher, _Ordinary Men: Reserve Police Battalion 101 and the Final Solution in Poland_ (London: Penguin, 2001).

— _The Path to Genocide. Essays on Launching the Final Solution_ (Cambridge: Cambridge University Press, 1992).

— 'Wehrmacht reprisal policy and the mass murder of Jews in Serbia', _Militärgeschichtliche Mitteilungen_ 31, 1983.

Burleigh, Michael, _Germany Turns Eastwards. A Study of 'Ostforschung' in the Third Reich_ (Cambridge: Cambridge University Press, 1991).

— 'Albert Brackmann (1871–1952) _Ostforscher_. The years of retirement', _Journal of Contemporary History_ 23, 1988.

Bytwerk, Randall L., 'The rhetoric of defeat. Nazi propaganda in 1945', _Central States Speech Journal_ 29, 1978.

Caregorodcev, Genadij I. and Natalia Decker, 'Zu den Folgen der faschistischen Politik für das Gesundheitswesen und den Gesundheitszustand der Bevölkerung in den zeitweilig okkupierten Gebieten der Sowjetunion', in Achim Thom and Genadij I. Caregorodcev (eds.), _Medizin unterm Hakenkreuz_ (Berlin [GDR]: VEB Verlag, 1989).

Chiari, Bernhard, _Alltag hinter der Front. Besatzung, Kollaboration und Widerstand in Weißrußland 1941–1944_ (Düsseldorf: Droste, 1998).

—'Deutsche Zivilverwaltung in Weißrußland 1941–1944. Die lokale Perspektive der Besatzungsgeschichte', *Militärgeschichtliche Mitteilungen* 52, 1993.

Cooper, Matthew, *The Phantom War. The German Struggle against Soviet Partisans, 1941–1944* (London: Macdonald and Jane's, 1979).

Dean, Martin, *Collaboration in the Holocaust. Crimes of the Local Police in Bielorussia and Ukraine, 1941–1944* (New York: St. Martin's Press, 2000).

Fahlbusch, Michael, *Wissenschaft im Dienst der nationalsozialistischen Politik? Die 'volksdeutschen Forschungsgemeinschaften' von 1931–1945* (Baden-Baden: Nomos, 1999).

Fox, John P., 'Der Fall Katyn und die Propaganda des NS-Regimes', *VfZ* 30, 1982.

Fröhlich, Elke, 'Katyn in neuem Licht? Goebbels und der Mord an den polnischen Offizieren im 2. Weltkrieg', *Geschichte in Wissenschaft und Unterrichte* 37, 1986.

Gebel, Ralf, *'Heim ins Reich'. Konrad Heinlein und der Reichsgau Sudetenland (1938–1945)* (Munich: Oldenbourg, 1999).

Gerlach, Christian, *Kalkulierte Morde. Die deutsche Wirtschafts- und Vernichtungspolitik in Weißrußland* (Hamburg: Hamburger Edition, 1999).

—'Die Wannsee-Konferenz, das Schicksal der deutschen Juden und Hitlers politische Grundsatzentscheidung, alle Juden Europas zu ermorden', *Werkstattgeschichte* 18, 1998.

—*Krieg, Ernährung, Völkermord. Forschungen zur deutschen Vernichtungspolitik* (Hamburg: Hamburger Edition, 1998).

Goldhagen, Daniel, *Hitler's Willing Executioners: Ordinary Germans and the Holocaust* (London: Little, Brown, 1996).

Grassman, Gerhard Otto, 'Die deutsche Besatzungsgesetzgebung während des zweiten Weltkrieges', *Studien des Instituts für Besatzungsfrage in Tübingen* 14, 1958.

Gröning, Gert, et al., *Der Drang nach Osten. Zur Entwicklung der Landespflege im Nationalsozialismus und während des Zweiten Weltkrieges in den 'eingegliederten Ostgebieten'* (Munich: Oldenbourg, 1987).

Hedegaard, Ole A., 'SS-Division "Handschar" – en militær og etnik tragedie', *Militært Tidsskrift* 124/3, 1995.

Heer, Hannes and Klaus Naumann (eds.), *Vernichtungskrieg. Verbrechen der Wehrmacht 1941–1944* (Hamburg: Hamburger Edition, 1995).

Heiber, Helmut, 'Der *Generalplan Ost*', *VfZ* 6, 1958.

Heinemann, Ulrich, 'Krieg und Frieden an der "inneren Front". Normalität und Zustimmung, Terror und Opposition im Dritten Reich', in Christoph Kleßmann (ed.), *Nicht nur Hitlers Krieg. Der Zweite Weltkrieg und die Deutschen* (Düsseldorf: Droste, 1989).

Herbert, Ulrich, 'Die Planung der wirtschaftlichen Ausbeutung der UdSSR', in Lutz Niethammer et al., *Bürgerliche Gesellschaft in Deutschland. Fragen, Perspektiven* (Frankfurt: Fischer, 1990).

—(ed.) *Nationalsozialistische Vernichtungspolitik 1939–1945. Neue Forschungen und Kontroversen* (Frankfurt: Fischer, 1998).

Herzstein, Robert Edwin, *When Nazi Dreams Come True. The Third Reich's Internal Struggle over the Future of Europe after a German Victory. A Look at the Nazi Mentality* (London: Abacus, 1982).

Hilberg, Raul, *Sources of Holocaust Research. An Analysis* (Chicago: I. R. Dee, 2001).
— *The Destruction of the European Jews* (New York: Holmes and Meier, 1985).
— *Perpetrators, Victims, Bystanders: The Jewish Catastrophe 1933–1945* (London: Secker and Warburg, 1995).
Hory, Ladislaus and Martin Broszat, *Der kroatische Ustascha-Staat 1941–1945* (Stuttgart: DVA, 1964).
Jacobsen, Hans-Adolf, 'Krieg in Weltanschauung und Praxis des Nationalsozialismus (1919–1945)', in Karl Dietrich Bracher et al. (eds.), *Nationalsozialistische Diktatur 1933–1945. Eine Bilanz* (Bonn: Bundeszentrale für politische Bildung, 1983).
Jansen, Christian and Arno Weckbecker, *Der 'volksdeutsche Selbstschutz' in Polen 1939/40* (Munich: Oldenbourg, 1992).
Karner, Stefan, 'Die Aussiedlung der Slowenen in der Untersteiermark. Ein Beispiel nationalsozialistischer Volkstumpolitik', *Österreichisches Ostheft* 22, 1978.
Kettenacker, Lothar, *Nationalsozialistische Volkstumpolitik in Elsaß* (Stuttgart: DVA, 1973).
Klein, Peter and Andrej Angvick (ed.), *Die Einsatzgruppen in der besetzten Sowjetunion 1941/42. Die Tätigkeits- und Lageberichte des Chefs der Sicherheitspolizei und des SD* (Berlin: Edition Hentrich, 1997).
Kühnrich, Heinz, *Der Partisanenkrieg in Europa 1939–1945* (Berlin: Dietz, 1968).
Latzel, Klaus, *Deutsche Soldaten – nationalsozialistischer Krieg? Kriegserlebnis – Kriegserfahrung 1939–1945* (Paderborn: Schöningh, 1998).
Longerich, Peter, *Holocaust. The Nazi Persecution and Murder of the Jews* (Oxford: Oxford University Press, 2010).
Loock, Hans-Dietrich, 'Zur "Großgermanischen" Politik des Dritten Reiches', *VfZ* 8, 1960.
Madajczyk, Czesław (ed.), *Vom Generalplan Ost zum Generalsiedlungsplan* (Munich: Saur, 1994).
— *Die Okkupationspolitik Nazideutschlands in Polen 1939–1945* (Berlin [GDR]: Akademie Verlag, 1987).
Manoschek, Walter, *'Serbien ist judenfrei'. Militärische Besatzungspolitik und Judenvernichtung in Serbien 1941–1942* (Munich: Oldenbourg, 1993).
— (ed.), *Die Wehrmacht im Rassenkrieg. Der Vernichtungskrieg hinter der Front* (Vienna: Picus Verlag, 1996).
Mayer, Arno J., *Der Krieg als Kreuzzug. Das deutsche Reich, Hitlers Wehrmacht und die 'Endlösung'* (Reinbeck: Rowohlt, 1989).
Messerschmidt, Manfred, 'Rassistische Motivation bei der Bekämpfung des Widerstandes in Serbien?', in Werner Röhr et al. (eds.), *Faschismus und Rassismus. Kontroversen um Ideologie und Opfer* (Berlin: Akademie Verlag, 1992).
Meyer, Ahlrich, 'Großraumpolitik und Kollaboration im Westen', in Horst Kars et al. (eds.), *Modelle für ein deutsches Europa. Ökonomie und Herrschaft im Großwirtschaftsraum. Beiträge zur nationalsozialistischen Gesundheits- und Sozialpolitik* 10, 1992.
Mommsen, Hans, 'Umvolkspläne des Nationalsozialismus und der Holocaust', in Helge Grabitz, Klaus Bläistein and Johannes Tuchel (eds.), *Die Normalität des*

Verbrechens. Festschrift für Wolfgang Scheffler zum 65. Geburtstag (Berlin: Edition Hentrich, 1994).

—'Die Realisierung der Utopie. Die "Endlösung der Judenfrage" im Dritten Reich', *Geschichte und Gesellschaft* 9, 1983.

Müller, Rolf-Dieter, *Hitlers Ostkrieg und die deutsche Siedlungspolitik. Die Zusammenarbeit von Wehrmacht, Wirtschaft und SS* (Frankfurt: Fischer,1991).

Musial, Bogdan, *'Konterrevolutionäre Elemente sind zu erschiessen'. Die Brutalisierung des deutsch-sowjetischen Kriegs im Sommer 1941* (Berlin: Propyläen, 2000).

Myllyniemi, Seppo, *Die Neuordnung der baltischen Länder 1941–1944. Zum national-sozialistischen Inhalt der deutschen Besatzungspolitik*, typewritten thesis (Helsinki, 1973).

Neubauer, Wolfgang, 'Das Kaiser-Wilhelm-Institut für deutsche Geschichte im Zeitalter der Weltkriege', *Historisches Jahrbuch* 113, 1993.

Ogorreck, Ralf, *Die Einsatzgruppen und die 'Genesis der Endlösung'* (Berlin: Metropol, 1996).

Paris, Edmond, *Genocide in Satellite Croatia 1941–1945. A Record of Racial and Religious Persecutions and Massacres*, tr. Lois Perkins (Chicago: American Institute for Balkan Affairs, 1962).

Peukert, Detlev, 'Die Genesis der "Endlösung" aus dem Geist der Wissenschaft', in Detlev Peukert (ed.), *Max Webers Diagnose der Moderne* (Göttingen: Vandenhoeck und Ruprecht, 1989).

Pohl, Dieter, *Nationalsozialistische Judenverfolgung in Ostgalizien 1941–1944. Organisation und Durchführung eines staatlichen Massenverbrechens* (Munich: Oldenbourg, 1996).

—'Großraumplanung und NS-Völkermord', *Historisches Jahrbuch* 114/1, 1994.

—*Von der 'Judenpolitik' zum Judenmord. Der Distrikt Lublin des Generalgouvernements 1939–1944* (Frankfurt: Lang, 1993).

Popielski, Bolesław, 'Die Tragödie der polnischen Universitätsprofessoren in Lemberg', in Burchard Brentjes (ed.), *Wissenschaft unter dem NS-Regime* (Berlin; New York: Lang, 1992).

Presse, Bernhard, *Judenmord in Lettland, 1941–1945* (Berlin: Metropol, 1988).

Röhr, Werner, 'Die faschistische Okkupationspolitik in Polen 1939 bis 1945 und die Stellung dieses Landes in den Plänen für eine "Neuordnung" Europas', *1999* 7/3, 1992).

Rössler, Mechtild and Sabine Schleiermacher (eds.), *Der 'Generalplan Ost'. Hauptlinien der nationalsozialistischen Planungs- und Vernichtungspolitik* (Berlin: Akademie Verlag, 1993).

Roth, Karl-Heinz, 'Bevölkerungspolitik und Zwangsarbeit im "Generalplan Ost"', *Mitteilungen der Dokumentationsstelle für NS-Sozialpolitik* 1/3, 1985.

Rürup, Reinhard and Peter Jahn (eds.), *Erobern und Vernichten. Der Krieg gegen die Sowjetunion 1941–1945. Essays* (Berlin: Metropol, 1992).

Salewsky, Michael, 'Europa. Idee und Wirklichkeit in der nationalsozialistischen Weltanschauung und politischen Praxis', in Franz Otmar (ed.), *Europas Mitte* (Göttingen; Zürich: Muster-Schmidt, 1987).

Sandkühler, Thomas, *'Endlösung' in Galizien. Der Judenmord in Ostpolen und die Rettungsinitiativen von Berthold Beitz 1941–1944* (Bonn: Dietz, 1996).

Schneider, Wolfgang, '*Vernichtungspolitik*'. *Eine Debatte über den Zusammenhang von Sozialpolitik und Genozid im nationalsozialistischen Deutschland* (Hamburg: Junius, 1991).

Schulte, Theo, *The German Army and Nazi Politics in Occupied Russia* (Oxford: Oxford University Press, 1989).

Spector, Shmuel, 'Aktion 1005 – effacing the murder of millions', *Holocaust and Genocide Studies* 5, 1990.

Steinert, Marlis, *Hitler's War and the Germans: Public Mood and Attitude during the Second World War*, ed. and tr. Thomas E. de Witt (Athens, Ohio: Ohio University Press, 1977).

Streit, Christian, 'Ostkrieg, Antibolschewismus und "Endlösung"', *Geschichte und Gesellschaft* 17, 1991.

Sundhaussen, Holm, *Wirtschaftsgeschichte Kroatiens im nationalsozialistischen Großraum 1941–1945. Das Scheitern einer Ausbeutungsstrategie* (Stuttgart: DVA, 1983).

Ueberschär, Gerd R. and Wolfram Wette (eds.), '*Unternehmen Barbarossa*': *der deutsche Überfall auf die Sowjetunion 1941. Berichte, Analysen, Dokumente* (Frankfurt: Fischer, 1997).

Vogel, Detlev (ed.), *Andere Helme – andere Menschen? Heimaterfahrung und Frontalltag im Zweiten Weltkrieg. Ein internationaler Vergleich* (Essen: Klartext, 1995).

Voigt, Gerd and Johannes Kalisch, '"Reichsuniversität Posen". Zur Rolle der faschistischen deutschen Ostforschung im Zweiten Weltkrieg', in Alfred Anderle and Werner Basler (eds.), *Juni 1941. Beiträge zur Geschichte des hitlerfaschistischen Überfalls auf die Sowjetunion* (Berlin [GDR]: Rütten und Loening, 1961).

Volkmann, Hans-Erich (ed.), *Das Rußlandbild im Dritten Reich* (Cologne: Böhlau, 1994).

Wasser, Bruno, *Himmlers Raumplanung im Osten. 'Generalplan Ost' in Polen 1940– 1944* (Basle: Birkhäuser, 1993).

—*Die Neugestaltung des Ostens. Ostkolonisation in Polen während der deutschen Besatzung 1939–1944 unter besonderer Berücksichtigung der Zamojszczyna im Distrikt Lublin*, typewritten thesis (Berlin, 1991).

Weber, Wolfram, *Die innere Sicherheit im besetzten Belgien und Nordfrankreich 1940–1944* (Düsseldorf: Droste, 1978).

Wilhelm, Hans-Heinrich, *Rassenpolitik und Kriegsführung. Sicherheitspolizei und Wehrmacht in Polen und der Sowjetunion* (Passau: R. Rothe, 1991).

Witte, Peter, et al. (eds.), *Der Dienstkalender Heinrich Himmlers 1941/42* (Hamburg: Hamburger Edition, 1999).

Wobbe, Theresa, *Nach Osten. Verdeckte Spuren nationalsozialistischer Verbrechen* (Frankfurt: Verlag Neue Kritik, 1992).

Wolfganger, Dieter, *Die nationalsozialistische Politik in Lotharingen, 1940–1945*, typewritten thesis (Saarbrücken, 1977).

Wróblewska, Teresa, 'Die Rolle und Aufgaben einer nationalsozialistischen Universität in den sogenannten östlichen Gebieten am Beispiel der Reichsuniversität Posen 1941–1945', *Information zur Erziehungs- und Bildungshistorischen Forschung* 14, 1980.

Zeidler, Manfred, *Kriegsende im Osten: Die Rote Armee und die Besetzung Deutschlands östlich von Oder und Neiße 1944–45* (Munich: Oldenbourg, 1996).

Zorn, Gerda, *Nach Ostland geht unser Ritt. Deutsche Eroberungspolitik zwischen Germanisierung und Völkermord* (Berlin; Bonn: Dietz, 1980).

ZStL (ed.), *NS-Verbrechen anläßlich des Partisanenkampfes in der UdSSR, 1941–1944* (Ludwigsburg: ZStL Edition, 1969).

After Nazism: trials and de-Nazification

Bayle, François, *Psychologie et éthique du national-socialisme. Étude anthropologique des dirigeants SS* (Paris: PUF, 1953).

Bower, Tom, *Blind Eye to Murder. Britain, America and the Purging of Nazi Germany – A Pledge Betrayed*, new edn (London: Warner, 1997).

Broszat, Martin, 'Siegerjustiz oder strafrechtliche "Selbstreinigung". Aspekte der Vergangenheitsbewältigung der deutschen Justiz während der Besatzungszeit 1945–1949', *VfZ* 29, 1981.

Bude, Heinz, *Bilanz der Nachfolge. Die Bundesrepublik und der Nationalsozialismus* (Frankfurt: Suhrkamp, 1992).

Buscher, Frank M., *The U.S. War Crimes Trial Program in Germany, 1946–1955* (New York; London: Greenwood, 1989).

Frei, Norbert, *Adenauer's Germany and the Nazi Past. The Politics of Amnesty and Integration*, tr. Joel Golb (New York: Columbia University Press, 2002).

Friedrich, Jörg, *Die kalte Amnestie. NS-Täter in der Bundesrepublik* (Frankfurt: Fischer, 1985).

Füstenau, Justus, *Entnazifierung. Ein Kapitel deutscher Nachkriegspolitik* (Berlin: Neuwied, 1969).

Henke, Klaus-Dietmar (ed.), *Die politische Säuberung in Europa. Die Abrechnung mit Faschismus und Kollaboration nach dem Zweiten Weltkrieg* (Munich: DTV, 1991).

Hoffmann, Christa, *Stunden Null? Vergangenheitsbewältigung in Deutschland 1945 und 1989* (Berlin; Bonn: Bouvier, 1992).

Kielmansegg, Peter, *Lange Schatten. Vom Umgang der Deutschen mit der nationalsozialistischen Vergangenheit* (Berlin: Siedler, 1989).

Kittel, Manfred, *Die Legende von der 'zweiten Schuld'. Vergangenheitsbewältigung in der Ära Adenauer* (Frankfurt; Berlin: Ullstein, 1986).

Oppitz, Ulrich-Dieter, *Strafverfolgung und Strafvollstreckung bei NS-Gewaltverbrechen. Dargestellt anhand von 542 rechtskräftigen Urteilen deutscher Gerichte aus der Zeit von 1946–1975* (Ulm: Braunland, 1979).

Schörken, Rolf, *Jugend 1945. Politisches Denken und Lebensgeschichte* (Opladen: Leske und Budrich, 1990).

Schornstheimer, Michael, *Bombenstimmung und Katzenjammer. Vergangenheitsbewältigung. Quick und Stern in den fünfziger Jahren* (Cologne: Pahl-Rugenstein, 1989).

Schwartz, Thomas A., 'Die Begnadigung deutscher Kriegsverbrecher. John McCloy und die Häftlinge von Landsberg', *VfZ* 38, 1990.

—*America's Germany. John J. McCloy and the Federal Republic of Germany* (Cambridge, Mass.; London: Harvard University Press, 1991).

Sigel, Robert, *Im Interesse der Gerechtigkeit. Die Dachauer Kriegsverbrecherprozesse 1945–1948* (Frankfurt: Campus, 1992).

Smith, Bradley F., *Reaching Judgment at Nuremberg* (New York: Basic Books, 1977).

Steinbach, Peter, *Nationalsozialistische Gewaltverbrechen. Die Diskussion in der deutschen Öffentlichkeit nach 1945* (Berlin: Colloquium Verlag, 1981).

Wember, Heiner, *Umerziehung im Lager. Internierung und Bestrafung von Nationalsozialisten in der britischen Besatzungszone Deutschlands 1948–1953* (Essen: Klartext, 1988).

Zeidler, Manfred, *Stalinjustiz kontra NS-Verbrechen: die Kriegsverbrecherprozesse gegen deutsche Kriegsgefangene in der UdSSR in den Jahren 1943–1952. Kenntnisstand und Forschungsprobleme. Berichte und Studien* 9 (Dresden: Hannah-Arendt-Institut für Totalitarismusforschung, 1996).

Index